YOWAMUSHI PEDAL

WATARU WATANABE

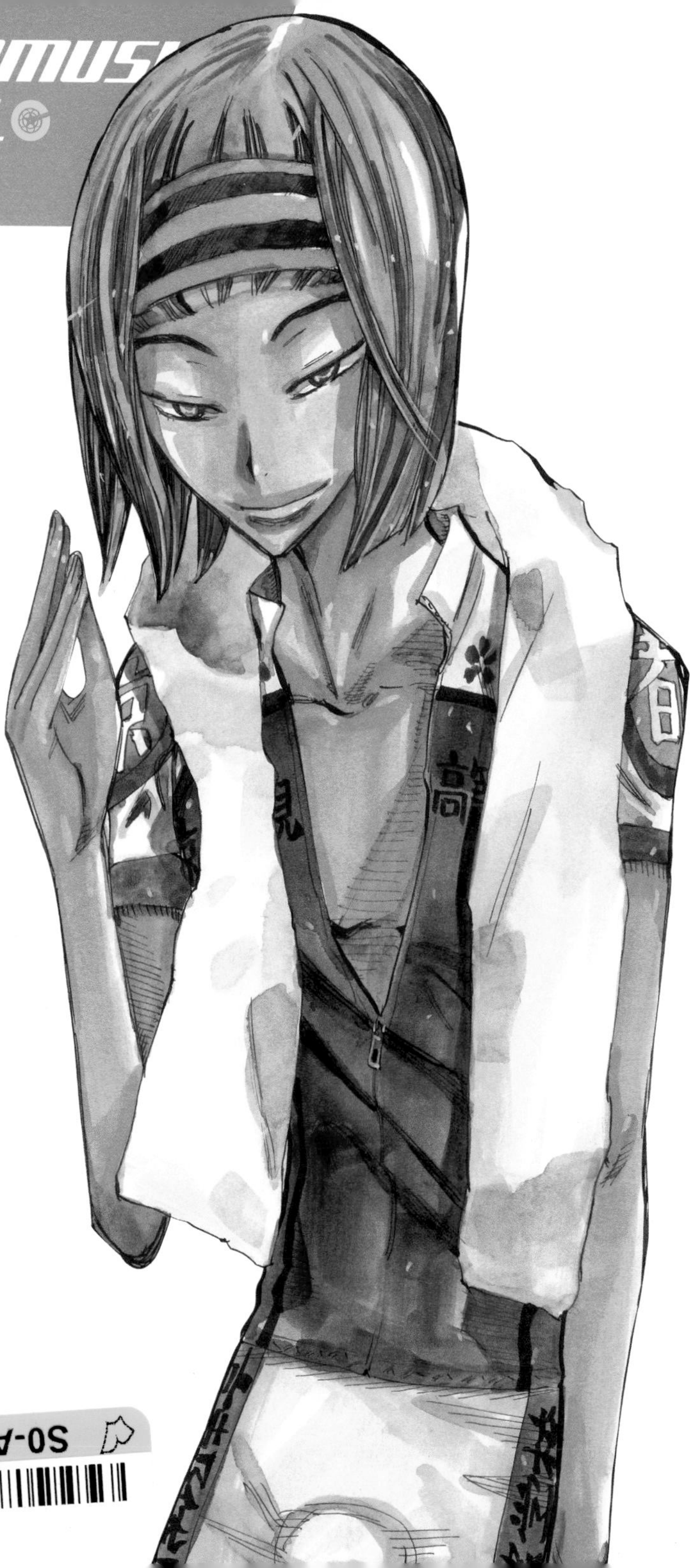

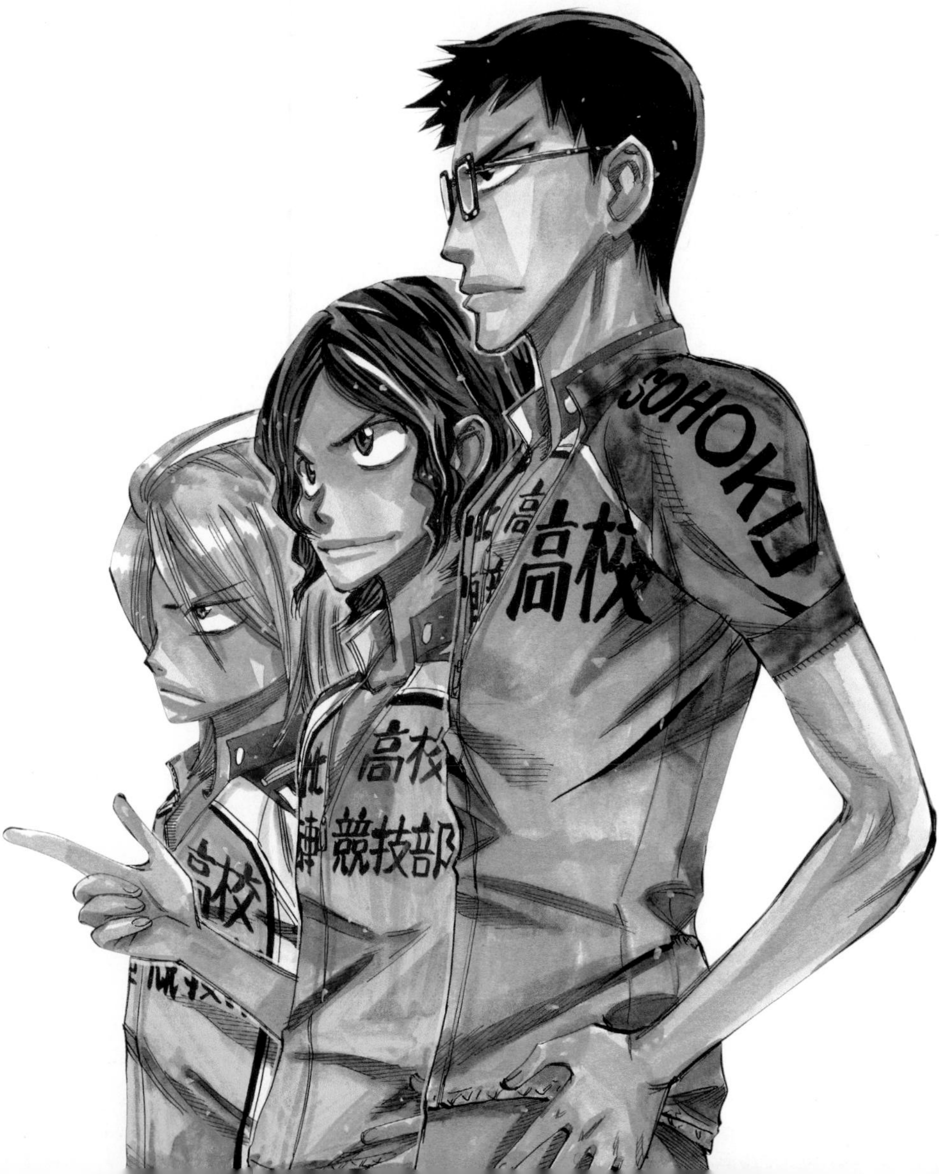
SOHOKU
高校
高校
競技部
高校

YOWAMUSHI PEDAL

WATARU WATANABE

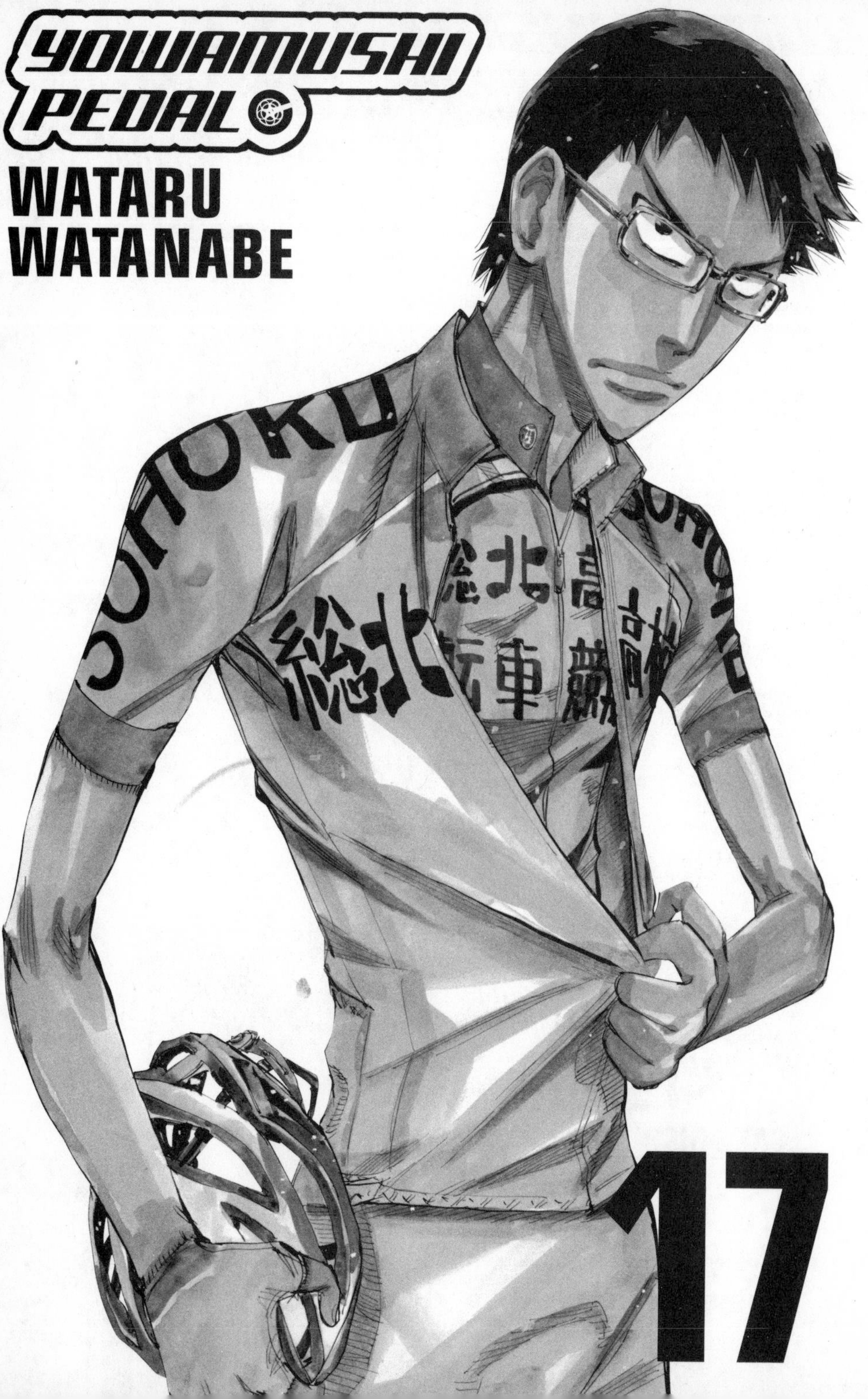
SOHOKU
総北

17

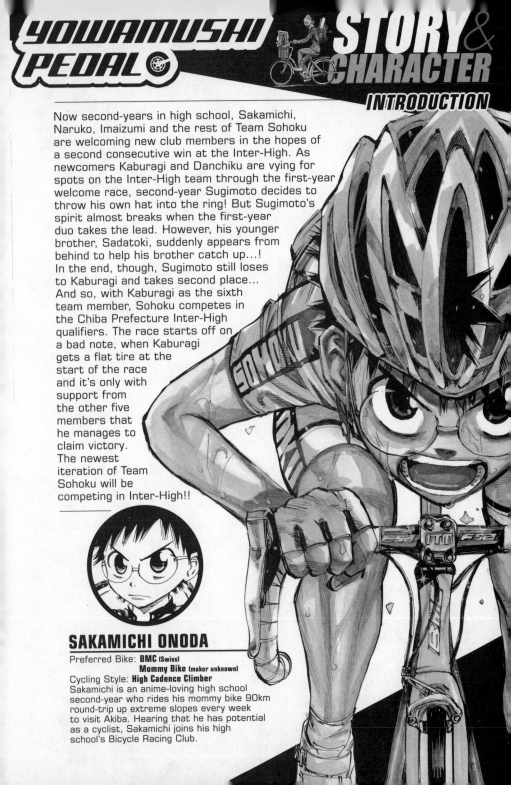

YOWAMUSHI PEDAL

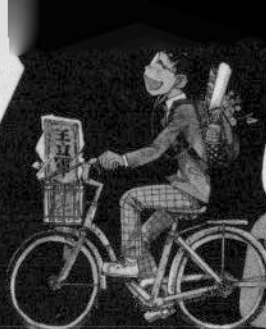

千葉

STORY & CHARACTER

INTRODUCTION

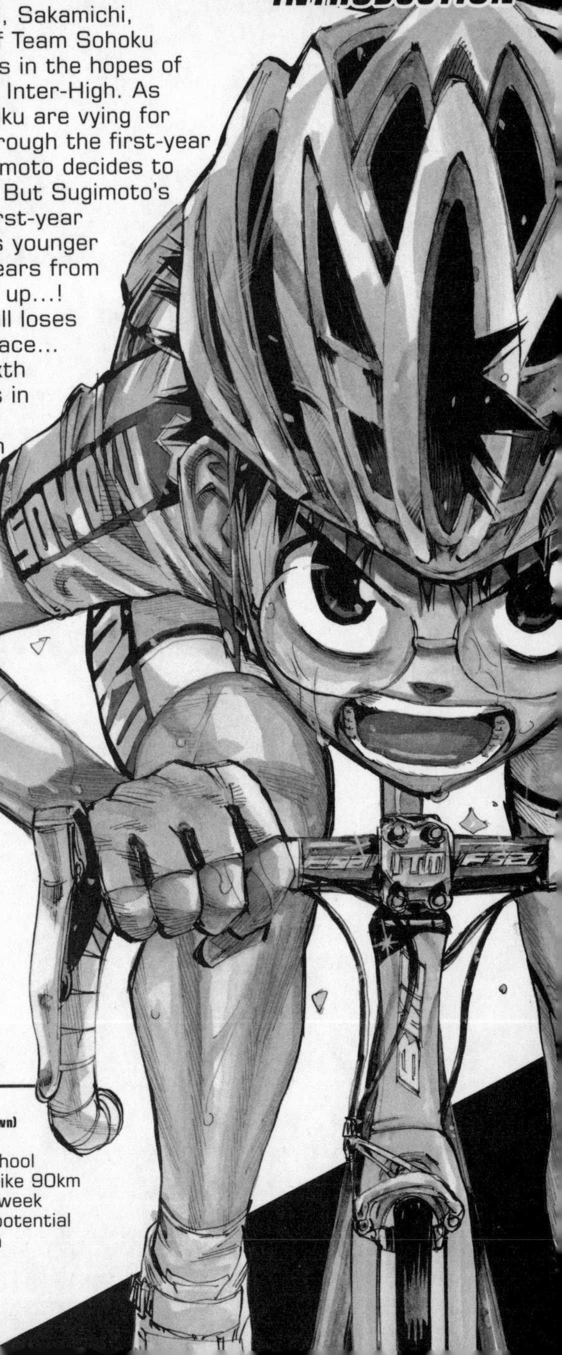

SOHOKU

Now second-years in high school, Sakamichi, Naruko, Imaizumi and the rest of Team Sohoku are welcoming new club members in the hopes of a second consecutive win at the Inter-High. As newcomers Kaburagi and Danchiku are vying for spots on the Inter-High team through the first-year welcome race, second-year Sugimoto decides to throw his own hat into the ring! But Sugimoto's spirit almost breaks when the first-year duo takes the lead. However, his younger brother, Sadatoki, suddenly appears from behind to help his brother catch up...! In the end, though, Sugimoto still loses to Kaburagi and takes second place... And so, with Kaburagi as the sixth team member, Sohoku competes in the Chiba Prefecture Inter-High qualifiers. The race starts off on a bad note, when Kaburagi gets a flat tire at the start of the race and it's only with support from the other five members that he manages to claim victory. The newest iteration of Team Sohoku will be competing in Inter-High!!

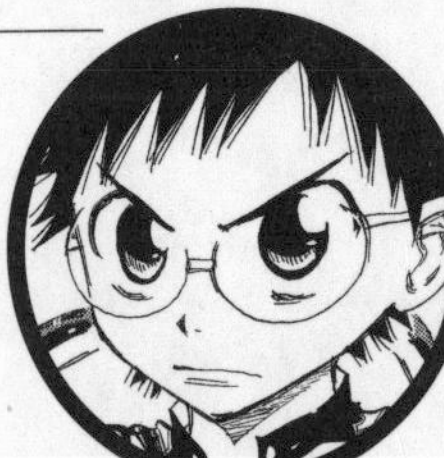

SAKAMICHI ONODA

Preferred Bike: **BMC (Swiss)**
Mommy Bike (maker unknown)
Cycling Style: **High Cadence Climber**
Sakamichi is an anime-loving high school second-year who rides his mommy bike 90km round-trip up extreme slopes every week to visit Akiba. Hearing that he has potential as a cyclist, Sakamichi joins his high school's Bicycle Racing Club.

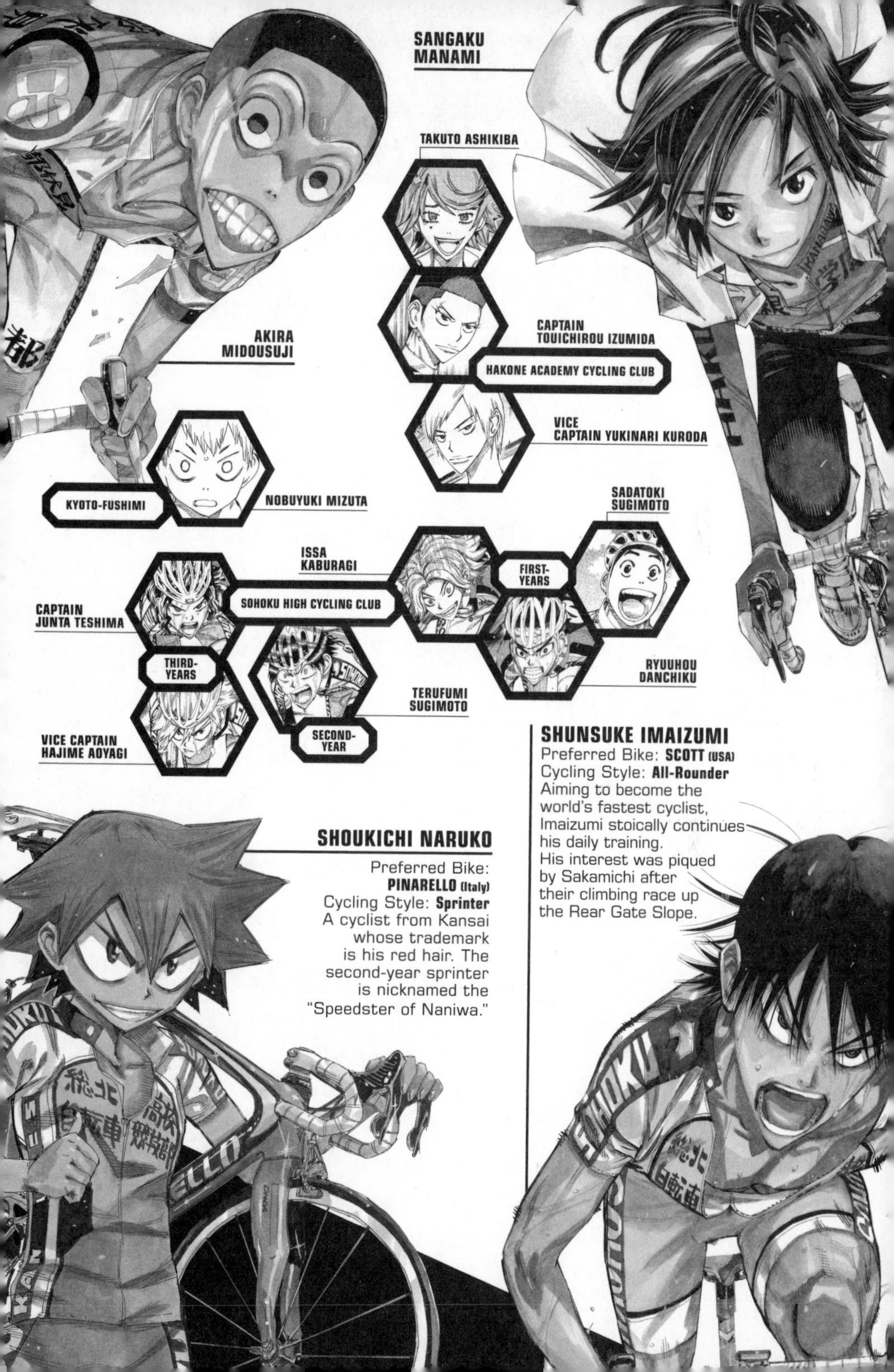

SANGAKU MANAMI
TAKUTO ASHIKIBA
CAPTAIN TOUICHIROU IZUMIDA
HAKONE ACADEMY CYCLING CLUB
VICE CAPTAIN YUKINARI KURODA
AKIRA MIDOUSUJI
KYOTO-FUSHIMI
NOBUYUKI MIZUTA
SADATOKI SUGIMOTO
ISSA KABURAGI
FIRST-YEARS
SOHOKU HIGH CYCLING CLUB
CAPTAIN JUNTA TESHIMA
RYUUHOU DANCHIKU
THIRD-YEARS
TERUFUMI SUGIMOTO
SECOND-YEAR
VICE CAPTAIN HAJIME AOYAGI
SHUNSUKE IMAIZUMI
Preferred Bike: SCOTT (USA)
Cycling Style: All-Rounder
Aiming to become the world's fastest cyclist, Imaizumi stoically continues his daily training. His interest was piqued by Sakamichi after their climbing race up the Rear Gate Slope.
SHOUKICHI NARUKO
Preferred Bike: PINARELLO (Italy)
Cycling Style: Sprinter
A cyclist from Kansai whose trademark is his red hair. The second-year sprinter is nicknamed the "Speedster of Naniwa."

VOL.17 YOWAMUSHI PEDAL CONTENTS

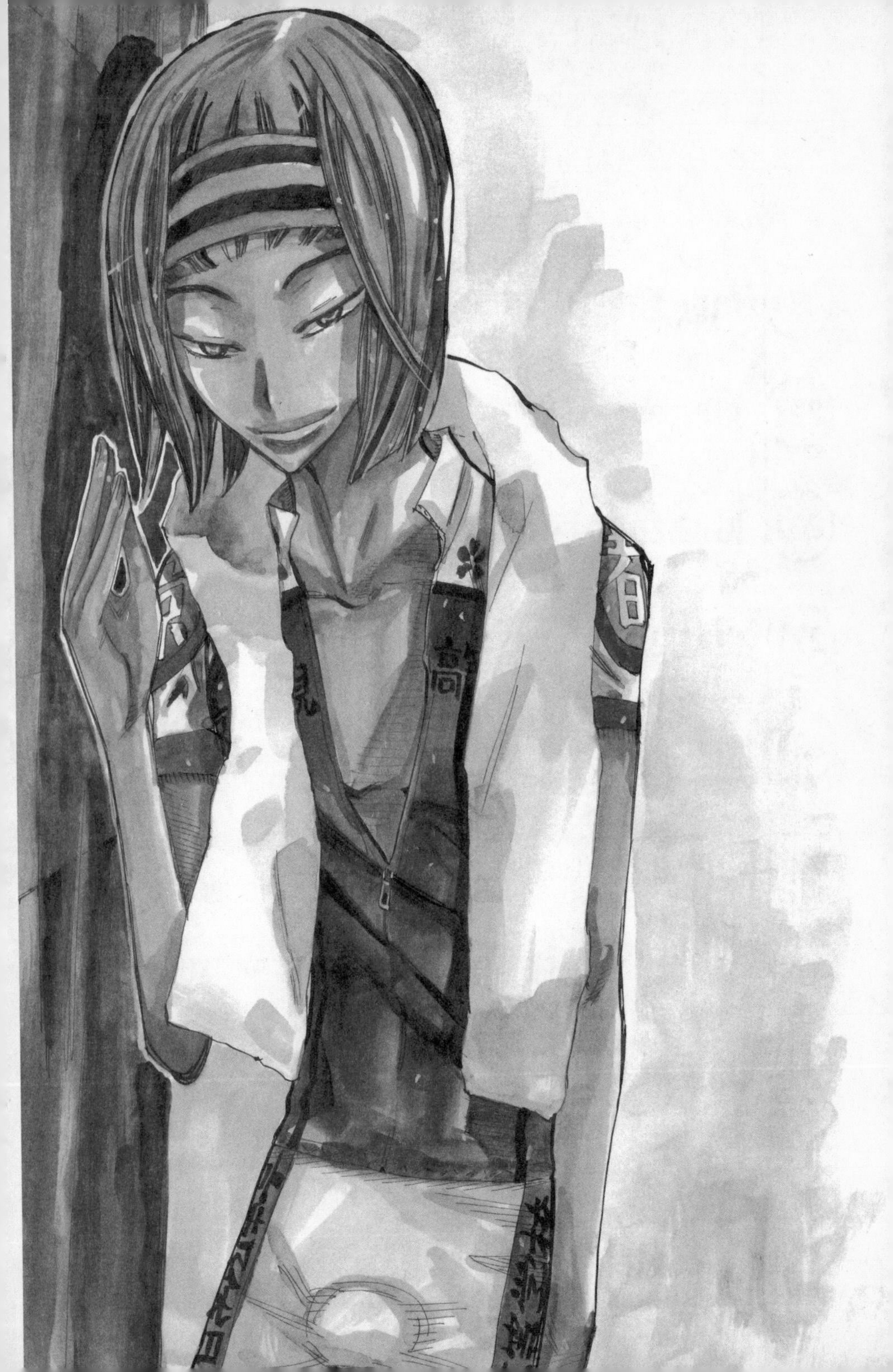

RIDE.279 PHONE CALL

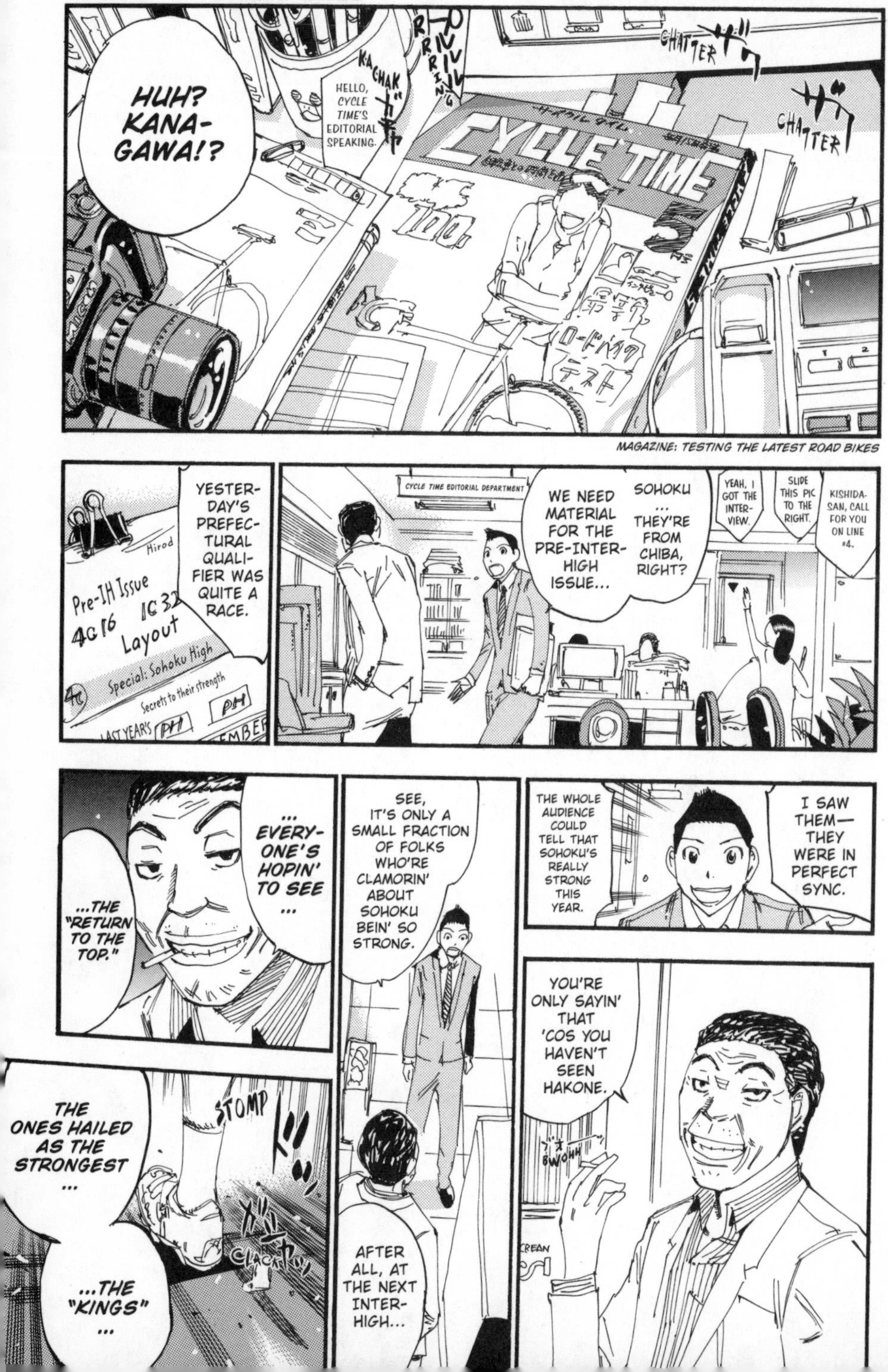
CHATTER
CHATTER
RRRING
KACHAK
HELLO, CYCLE TIME'S EDITORIAL SPEAKING.
HUH? KANAGAWA!?
CYCLE TIME
MAGAZINE: TESTING THE LATEST ROAD BIKES
KISHIDA-SAN, CALL FOR YOU ON LINE #4.
SLIDE THIS PIC TO THE RIGHT.
YEAH, I GOT THE INTERVIEW.
SOHOKU... THEY'RE FROM CHIBA, RIGHT?
WE NEED MATERIAL FOR THE PRE-INTER-HIGH ISSUE...
CYCLE TIME EDITORIAL DEPARTMENT
YESTERDAY'S PREFECTURAL QUALIFIER WAS QUITE A RACE.
Pre-IH Issue
4C16 1C32
Layout
Special: Sohoku High
Secrets to their strength
LAST YEAR'S
I SAW THEM—THEY WERE IN PERFECT SYNC.
THE WHOLE AUDIENCE COULD TELL THAT SOHOKU'S REALLY STRONG THIS YEAR.
YOU'RE ONLY SAYIN' THAT 'COS YOU HAVEN'T SEEN HAKONE.
BWOHH
CREAN
SEE, IT'S ONLY A SMALL FRACTION OF FOLKS WHO'RE CLAMORIN' ABOUT SOHOKU BEIN' SO STRONG.
AFTER ALL, AT THE NEXT INTER-HIGH...
...EVERYONE'S HOPIN' TO SEE...
...THE "RETURN TO THE TOP."
STOMP
CLACK
THE ONES HAILED AS THE STRONGEST...
...THE "KINGS"...

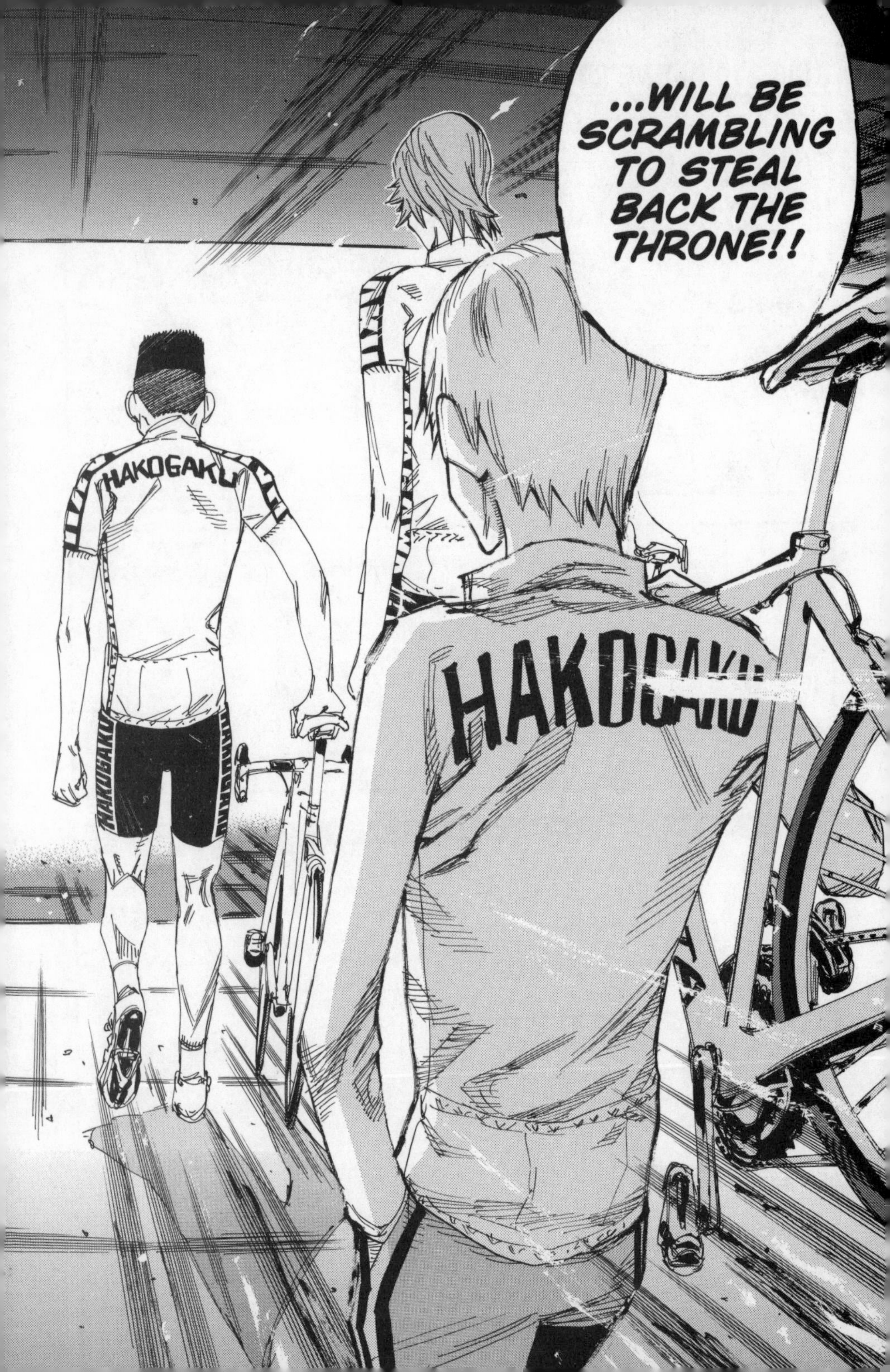
...WILL BE SCRAMBLING TO STEAL BACK THE THRONE!!
HAKOGAKU
HAKOGAKU

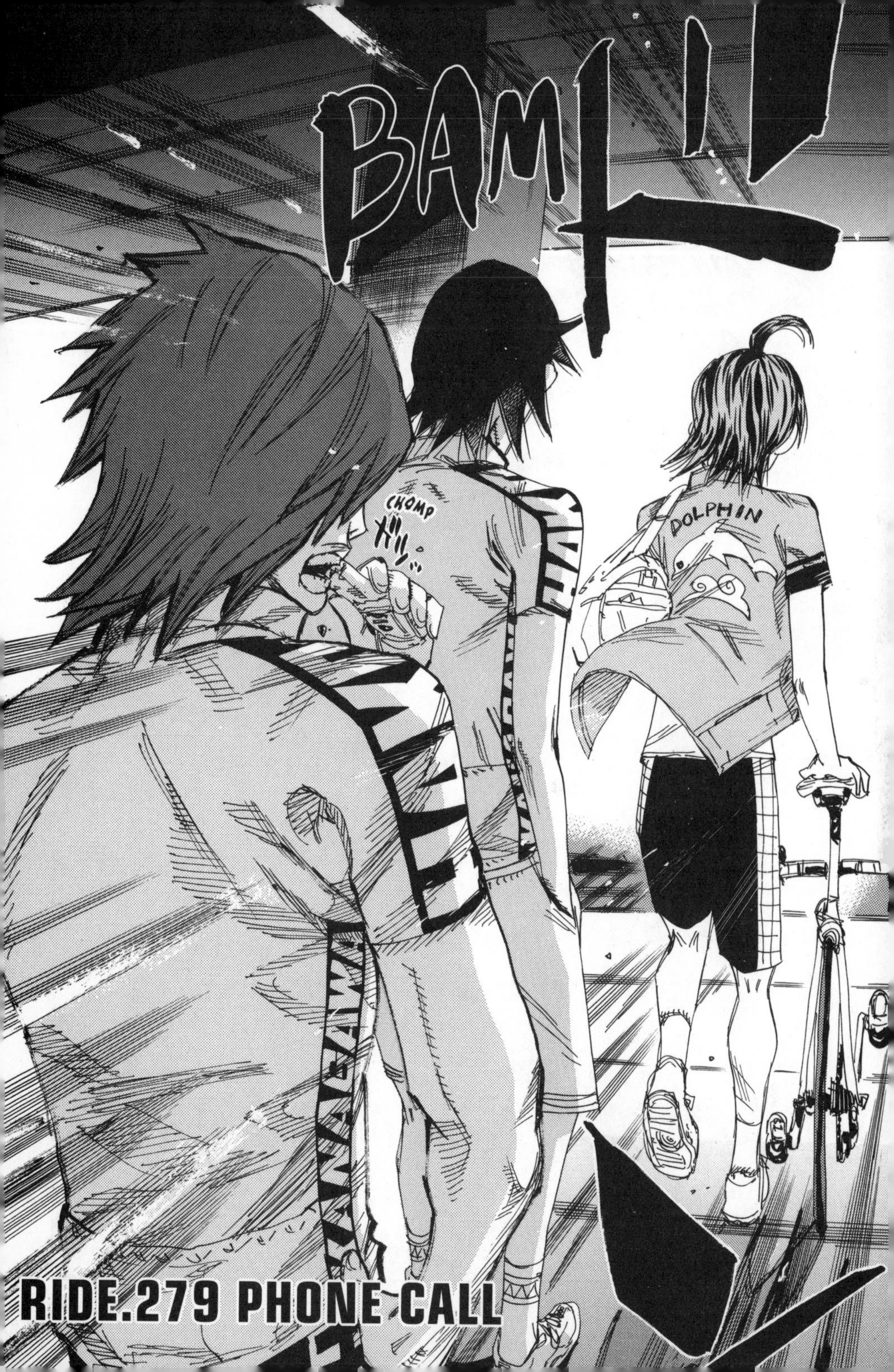
BAM!!
CHOMP
DOLPHIN

RIDE.279 PHONE CALL

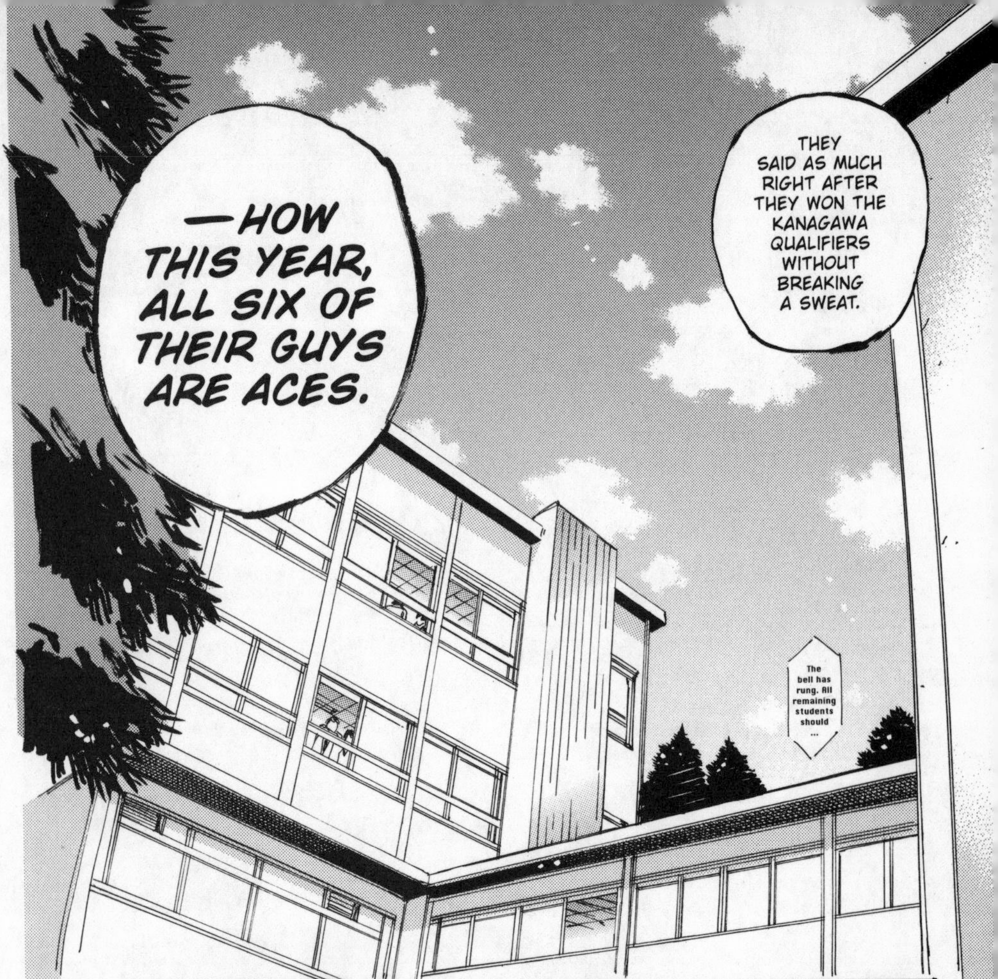
THEY SAID AS MUCH RIGHT AFTER THEY WON THE KANAGAWA QUALIFIERS WITHOUT BREAKING A SWEAT.
—HOW THIS YEAR, ALL SIX OF THEIR GUYS ARE ACES.
The bell has rung. All remaining students should ...

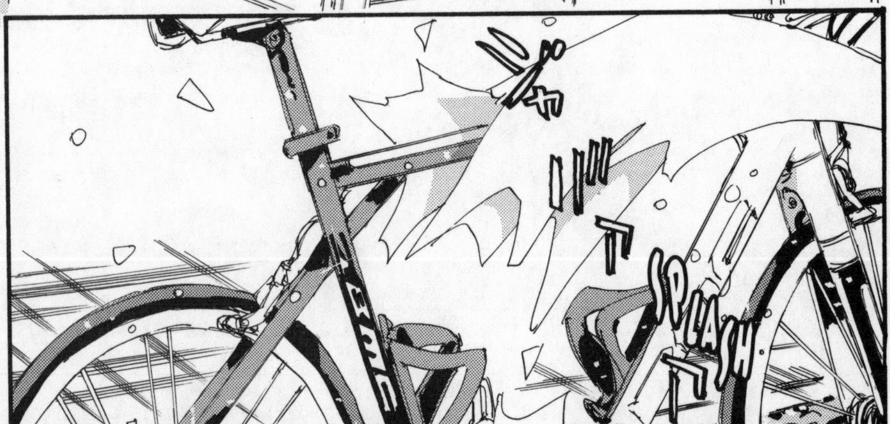
SPLASH

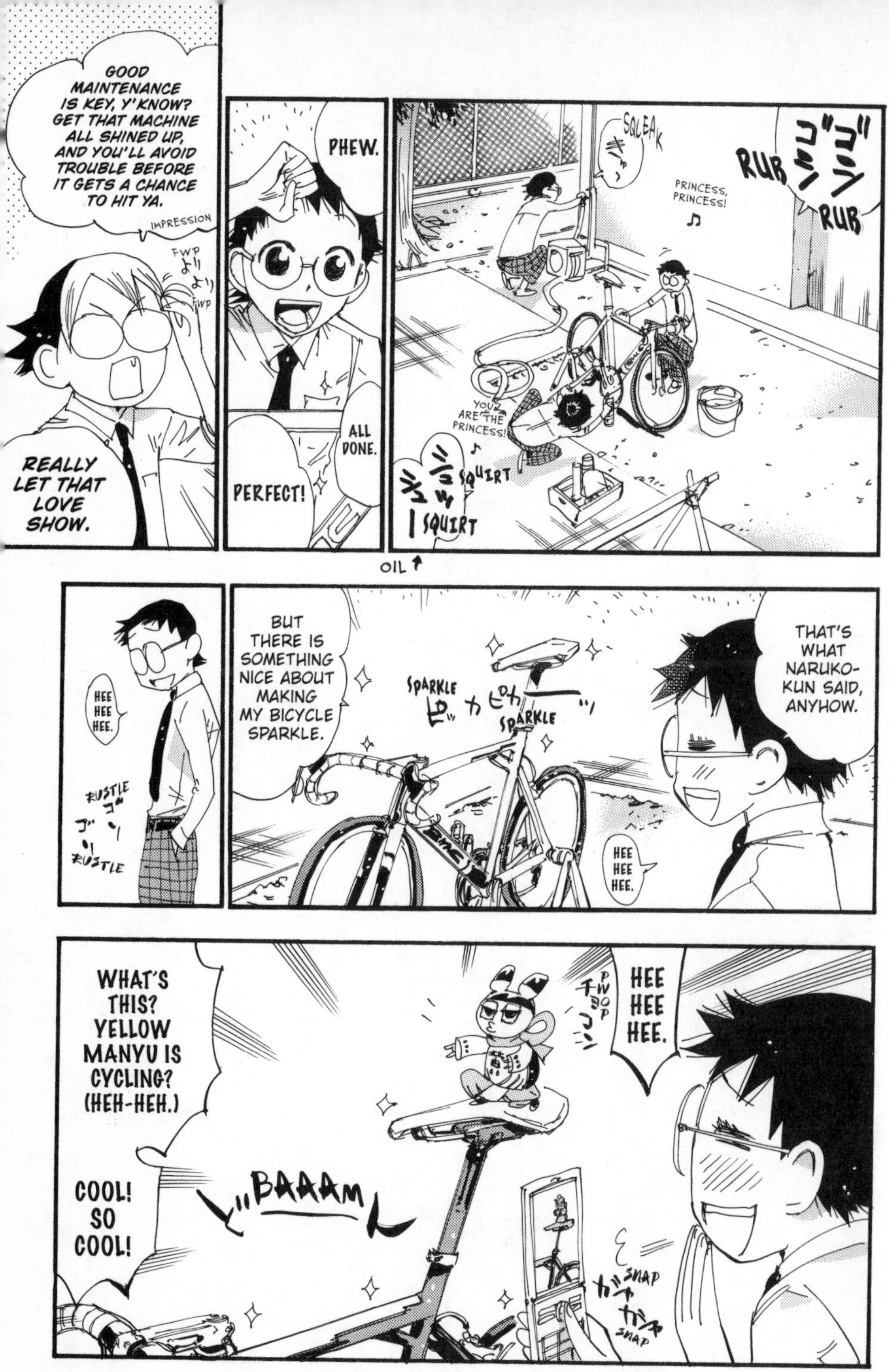

RUB RUB
SQUEAK
PRINCESS, PRINCESS! ♪
YOU ARE THE PRINCESS! ♪
SQUIRT SQUIRT
OIL
PHEW.
ALL DONE.
PERFECT!
GOOD MAINTENANCE IS KEY, Y'KNOW? GET THAT MACHINE ALL SHINED UP, AND YOU'LL AVOID TROUBLE BEFORE IT GETS A CHANCE TO HIT YA.
IMPRESSION
FWP FWP
REALLY LET THAT LOVE SHOW.
THAT'S WHAT NARUKO-KUN SAID, ANYHOW.
HEE HEE HEE.
BUT THERE IS SOMETHING NICE ABOUT MAKING MY BICYCLE SPARKLE.
SPARKLE SPARKLE
HEE HEE HEE.
RUSTLE RUSTLE
HEE HEE HEE.
PWOP
WHAT'S THIS? YELLOW MANYU IS CYCLING? (HEH-HEH.)
COOL! SO COOL!
BAAAM
SNAP SNAP

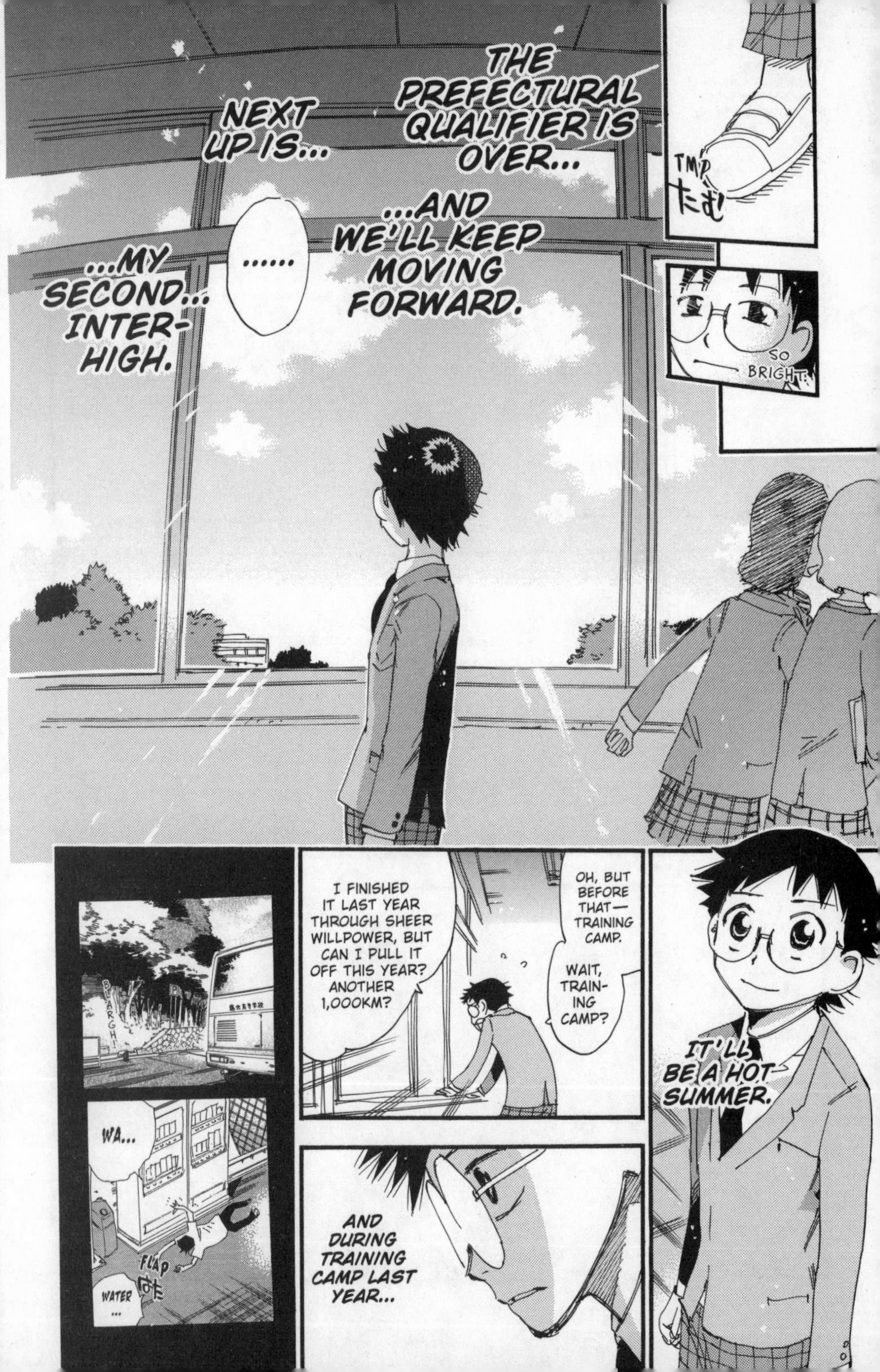
TMP
たむ
SO BRIGHT
THE PREFECTURAL QUALIFIER IS OVER...
...AND WE'LL KEEP MOVING FORWARD.
NEXT UP IS...
......
...MY SECOND... INTER-HIGH.
IT'LL BE A HOT SUMMER.
OH, BUT BEFORE THAT— TRAINING CAMP.
WAIT, TRAINING CAMP?
I FINISHED IT LAST YEAR THROUGH SHEER WILLPOWER, BUT CAN I PULL IT OFF THIS YEAR? ANOTHER 1,000KM?
AND DURING TRAINING CAMP LAST YEAR...
BLARGH!
WA...
FLAP
ぱた
WATER ...

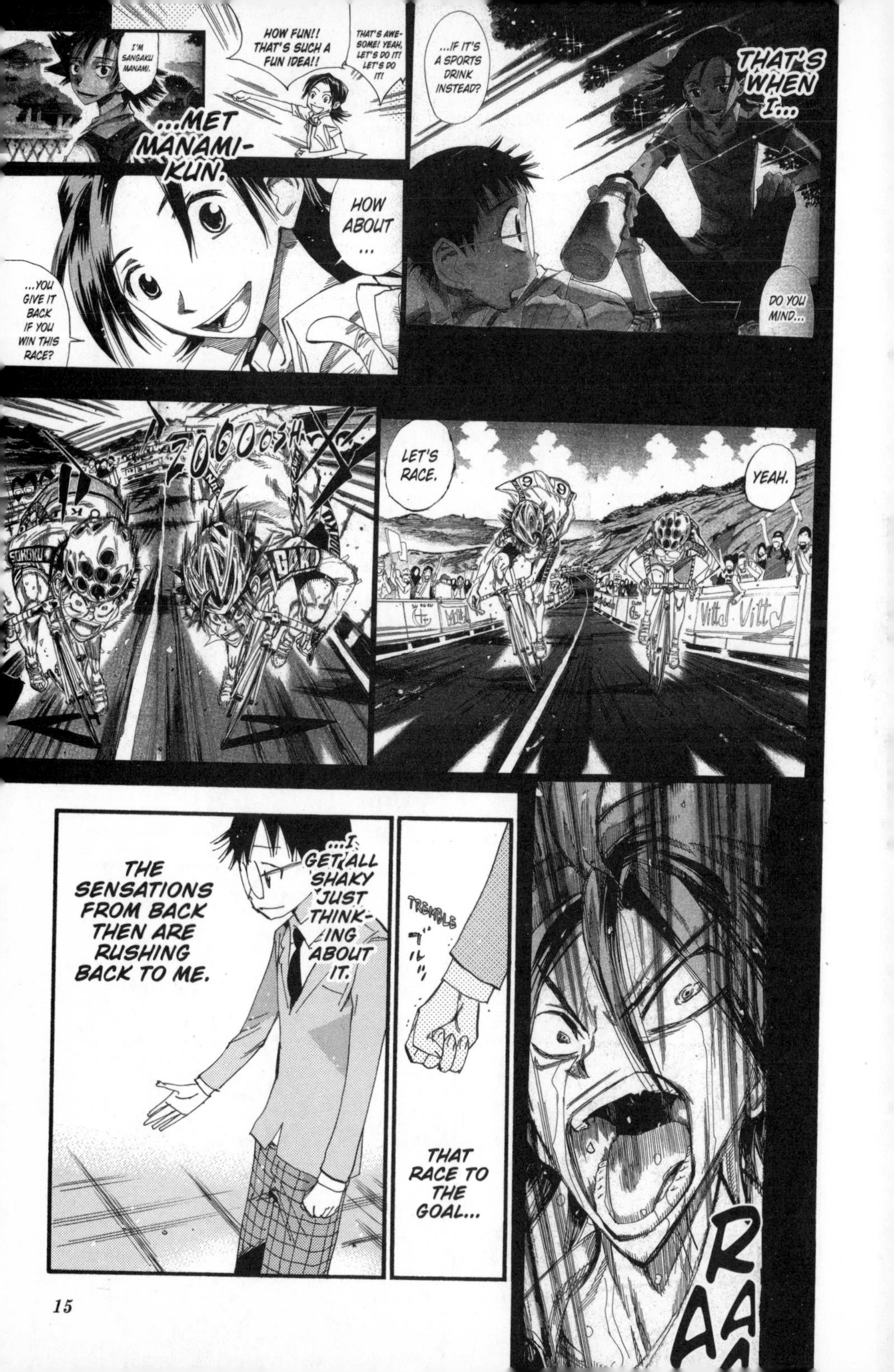

THAT'S WHEN I...
DO YOU MIND...
...IF IT'S A SPORTS DRINK INSTEAD?
HOW FUN!! THAT'S SUCH A FUN IDEA!!
THAT'S AWESOME! YEAH, LET'S DO IT! LET'S DO IT!
I'M SANGAKU MANAMI.
...MET MANAMI-KUN.
HOW ABOUT...
...YOU GIVE IT BACK IF YOU WIN THIS RACE?
LET'S RACE.
YEAH.
ZOOOOSH
RAA
TREMBLE
THAT RACE TO THE GOAL...
THE SENSATIONS FROM BACK THEN ARE RUSHING BACK TO ME.
...I GET ALL SHAKY JUST THINKING ABOUT IT.

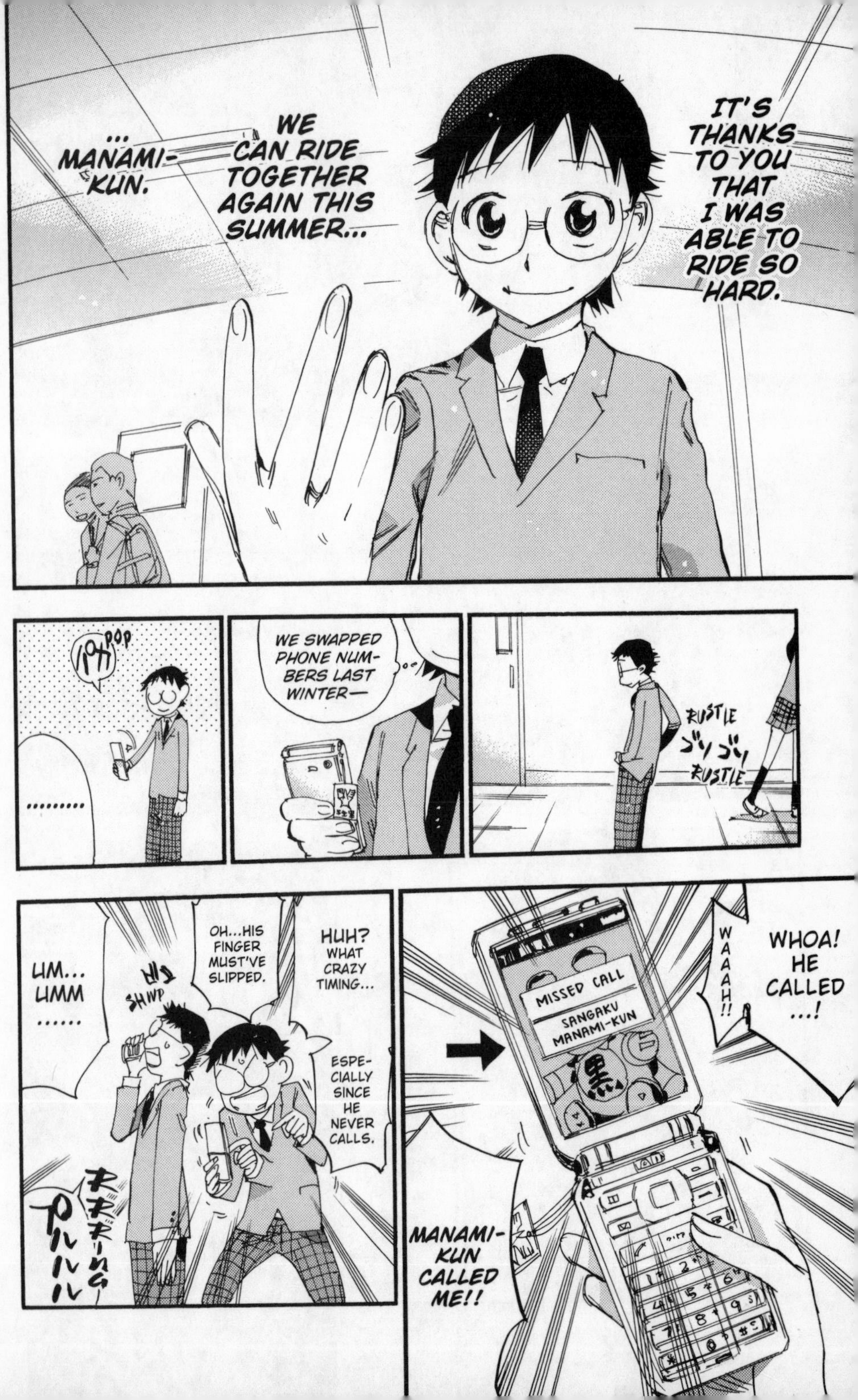
IT'S THANKS TO YOU THAT I WAS ABLE TO RIDE SO HARD.
WE CAN RIDE TOGETHER AGAIN THIS SUMMER...
...MANAMI-KUN.
RUSTLE
RUSTLE
WE SWAPPED PHONE NUMBERS LAST WINTER—
POP
....
WHOA! HE CALLED ...!
WAAAAH!!
MISSED CALL
SANGAKU MANAMI-KUN
MANAMI-KUN CALLED ME!!
HUH? WHAT CRAZY TIMING...
OH...HIS FINGER MUST'VE SLIPPED.
ESPECIALLY SINCE HE NEVER CALLS.
UM... UMM ......
SHWP
RRRING

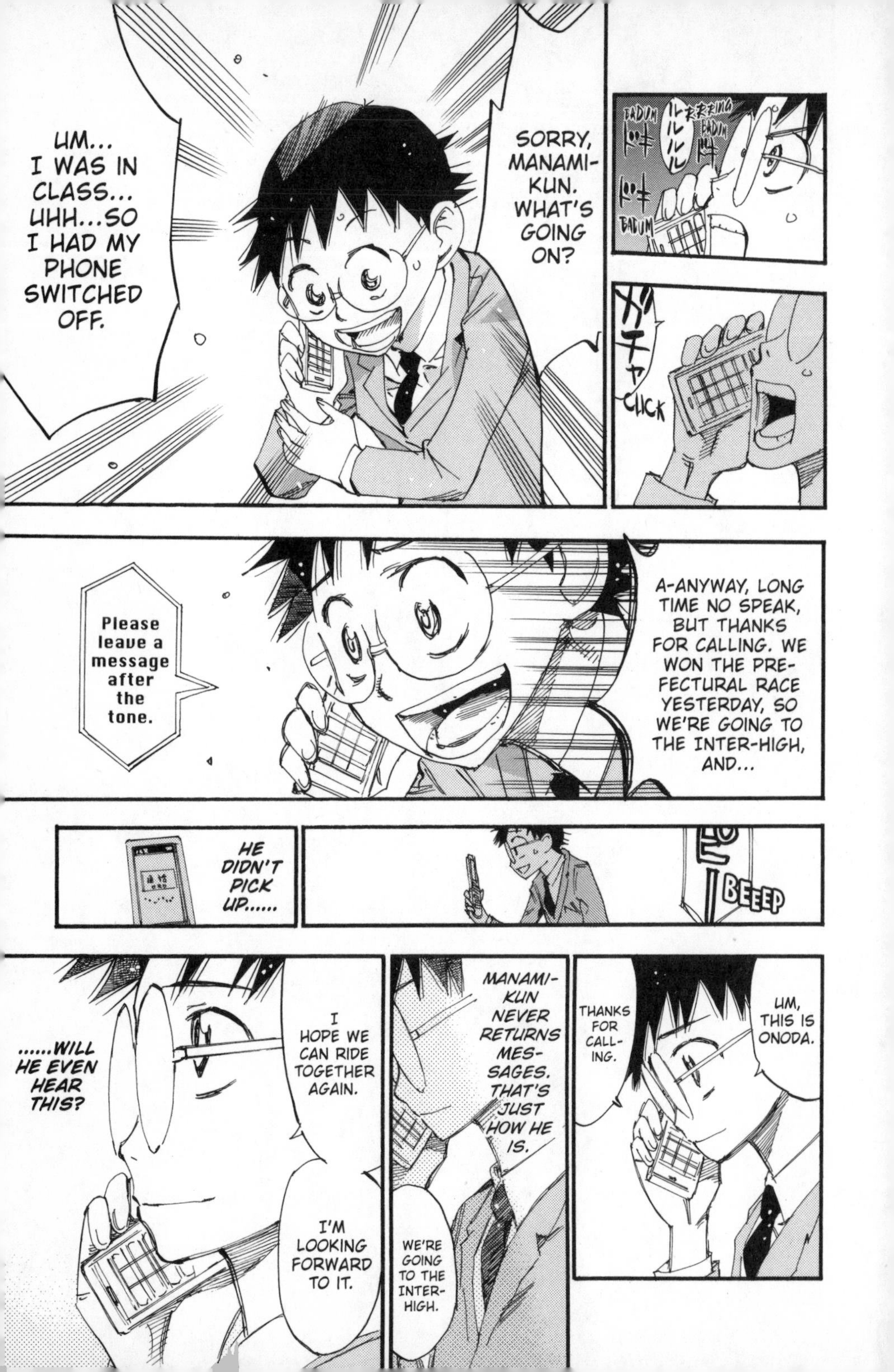

BADUM
ドキ
ルルルル
RRRRING
BADUM
ドキ
ドキ
BADUM
ガチャ
CLICK
SORRY, MANAMI-KUN. WHAT'S GOING ON?
UM... I WAS IN CLASS... UHH...SO I HAD MY PHONE SWITCHED OFF.
A-ANYWAY, LONG TIME NO SPEAK, BUT THANKS FOR CALLING. WE WON THE PRE-FECTURAL RACE YESTERDAY, SO WE'RE GOING TO THE INTER-HIGH, AND...
Please leave a message after the tone.
BEEEP
HE DIDN'T PICK UP......
UM, THIS IS ONODA.
THANKS FOR CALL-ING.
MANAMI-KUN NEVER RETURNS MES-SAGES. THAT'S JUST HOW HE IS.
WE'RE GOING TO THE INTER-HIGH.
I HOPE WE CAN RIDE TOGETHER AGAIN.
......WILL HE EVEN HEAR THIS?
I'M LOOKING FORWARD TO IT.

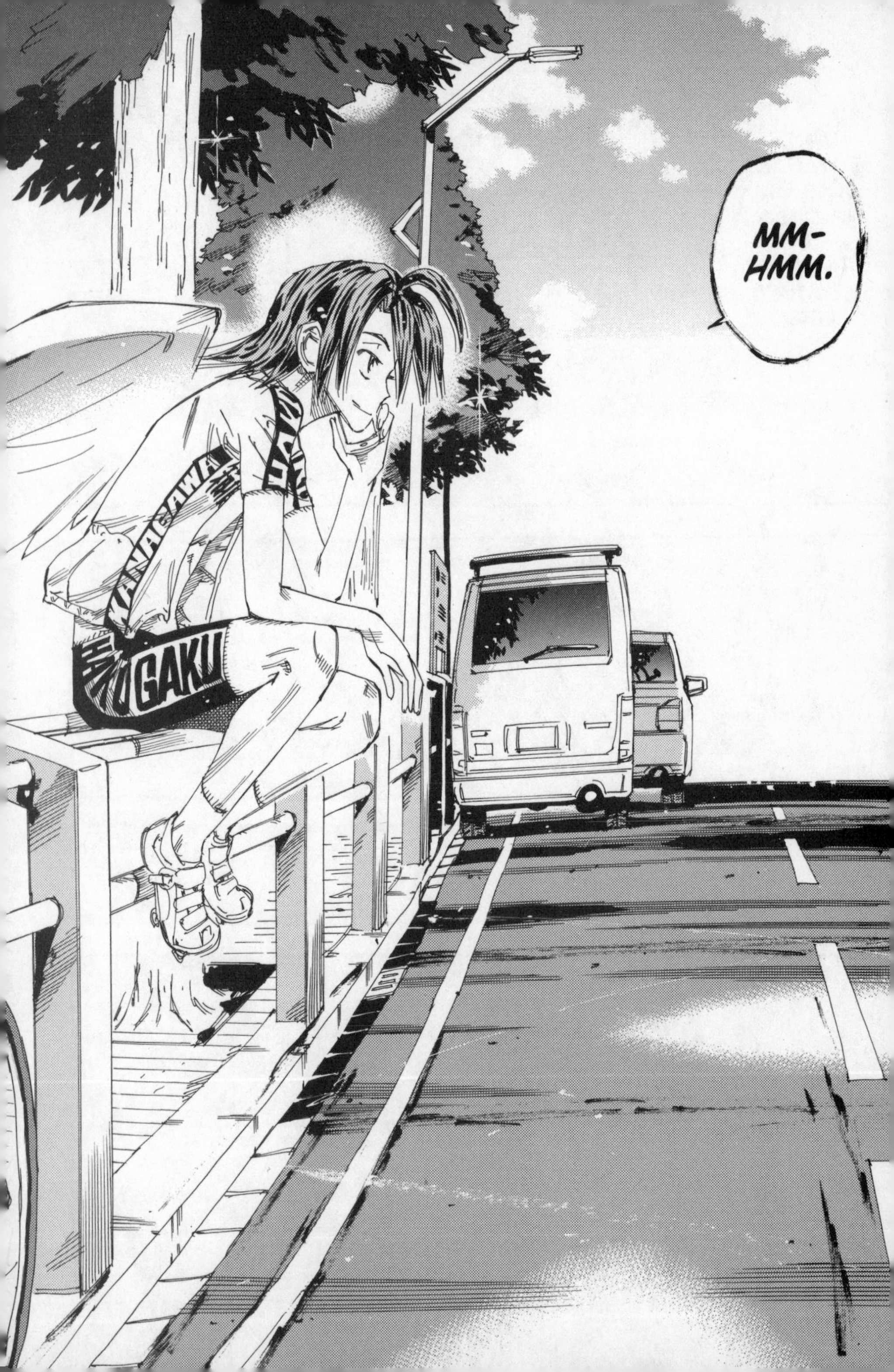
MM-
HMM.
HAKOGAKU
KANAGAWA

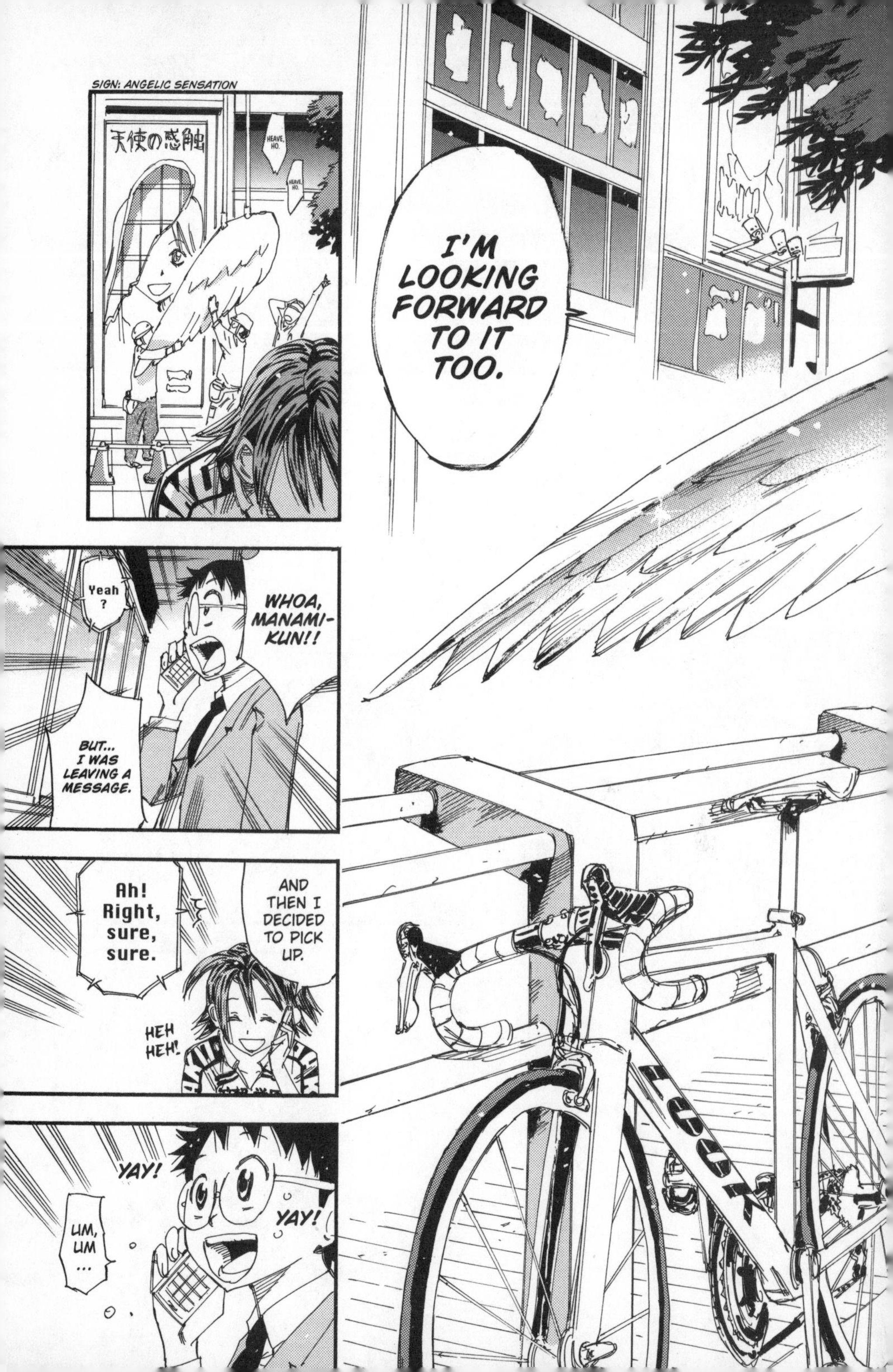
I'M LOOKING FORWARD TO IT TOO.
SIGN: ANGELIC SENSATION
天使の感触
HEAVE, HO.
HEAVE, HO.
WHOA, MANAMI-KUN!!
Yeah?
BUT... I WAS LEAVING A MESSAGE.
AND THEN I DECIDED TO PICK UP.
Ah! Right, sure, sure.
HEH HEH!
YAY!
YAY!
UM, UM ...

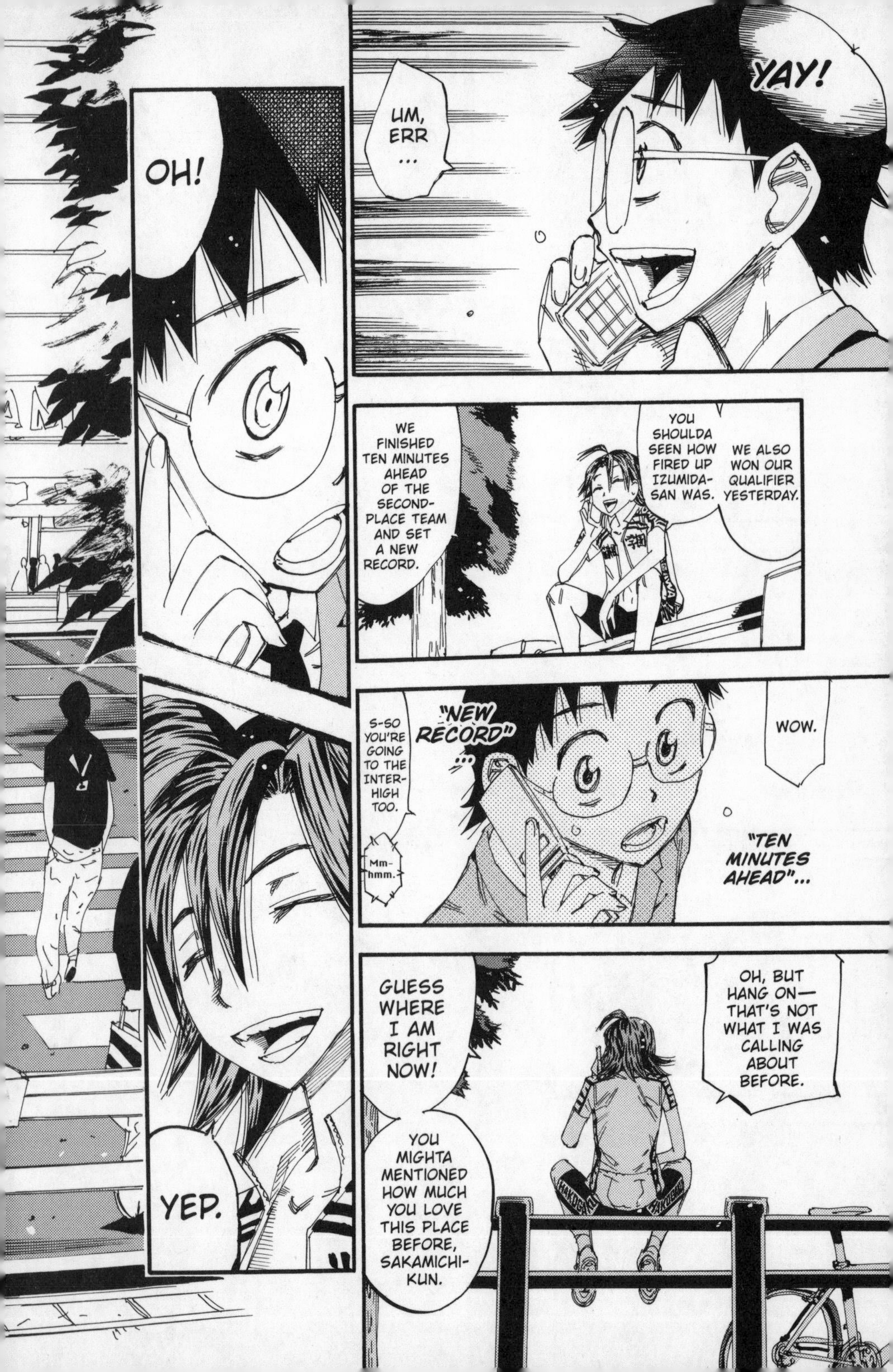

YAY!
UM, ERR ...
WE ALSO WON OUR QUALIFIER YESTERDAY.
YOU SHOULDA SEEN HOW FIRED UP IZUMIDA-SAN WAS.
WE FINISHED TEN MINUTES AHEAD OF THE SECOND-PLACE TEAM AND SET A NEW RECORD.
OH!
WOW.
"TEN MINUTES AHEAD"...
"NEW RECORD"...
S-SO YOU'RE GOING TO THE INTER-HIGH TOO.
Mm-hmm.
OH, BUT HANG ON—THAT'S NOT WHAT I WAS CALLING ABOUT BEFORE.
GUESS WHERE I AM RIGHT NOW!
YOU MIGHTA MENTIONED HOW MUCH YOU LOVE THIS PLACE BEFORE, SAKAMICHI-KUN.
YEP.

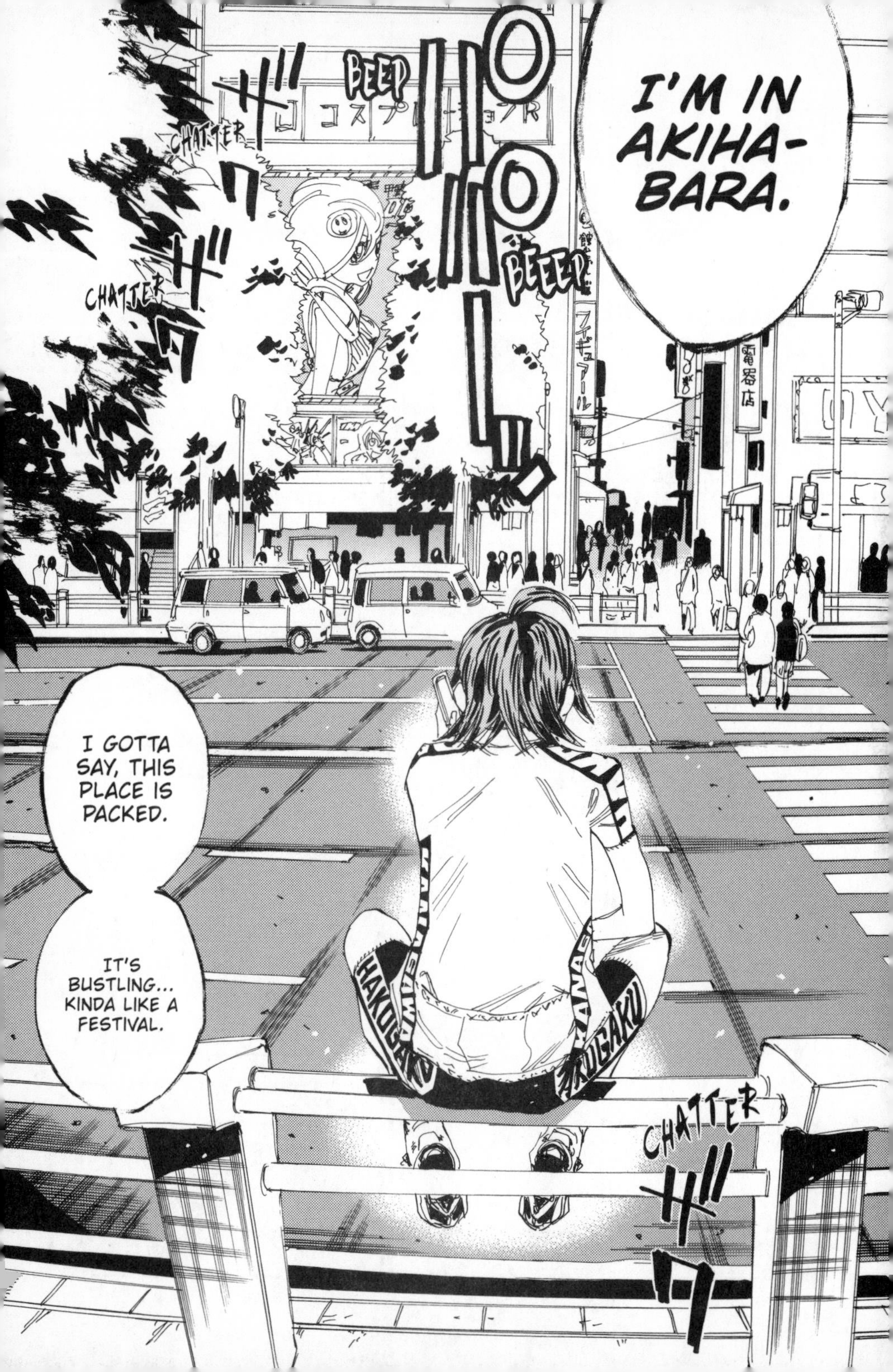
I'M IN AKIHA-BARA.
BEEEP
BEEP
CHATTER
CHATTER
I GOTTA SAY, THIS PLACE IS PACKED.
IT'S BUSTLING... KINDA LIKE A FESTIVAL.
CHATTER
HAKOGAKU
HAKOGAKU

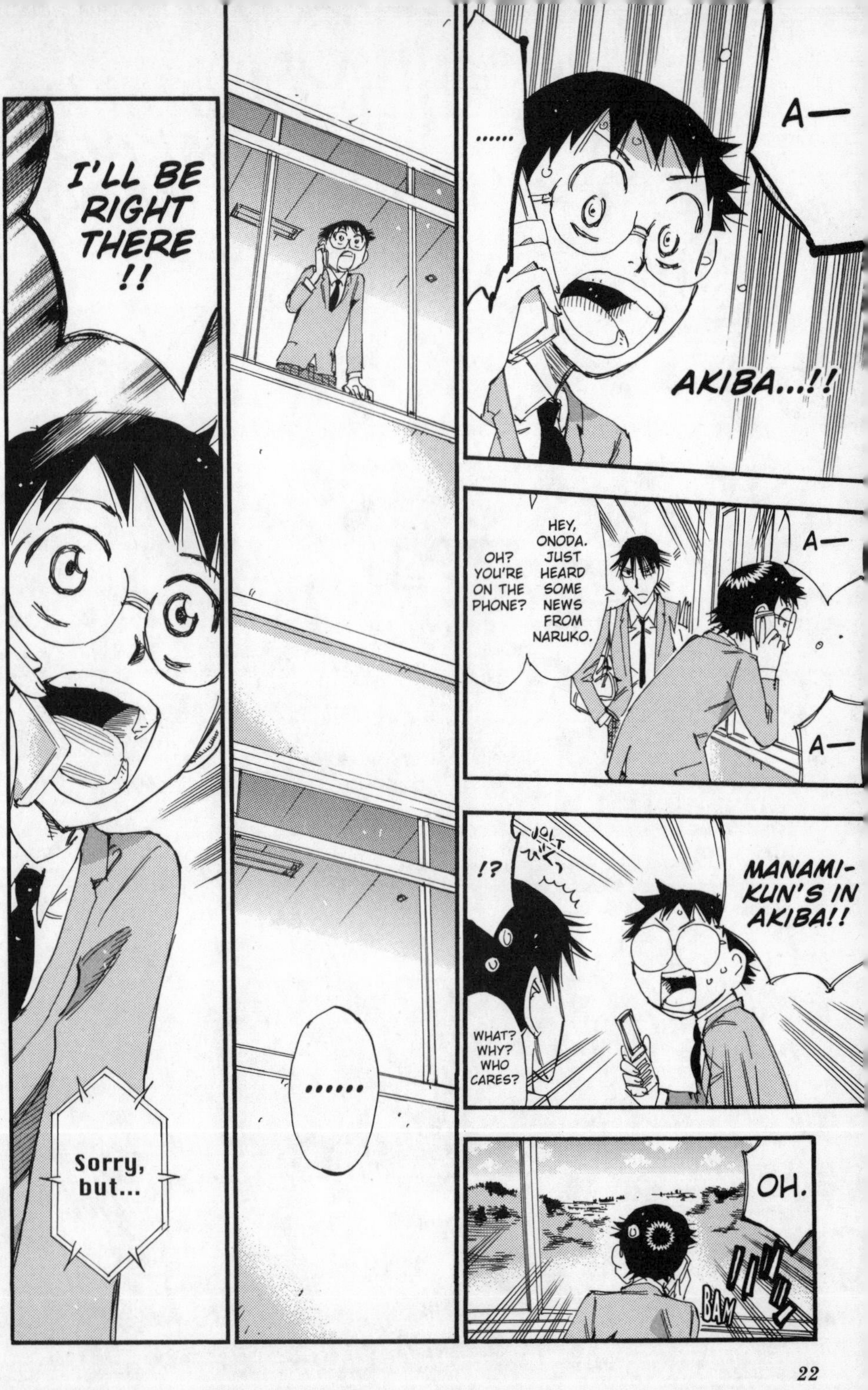

A—
......
AKIBA...!!
A—
HEY, ONODA. JUST HEARD SOME NEWS FROM NARUKO.
OH? YOU'RE ON THE PHONE?
A—
MANAMI-KUN'S IN AKIBA!!
JOLT
!?
WHAT? WHY? WHO CARES?
OH.
BAM
......
I'LL BE RIGHT THERE!!
Sorry, but...

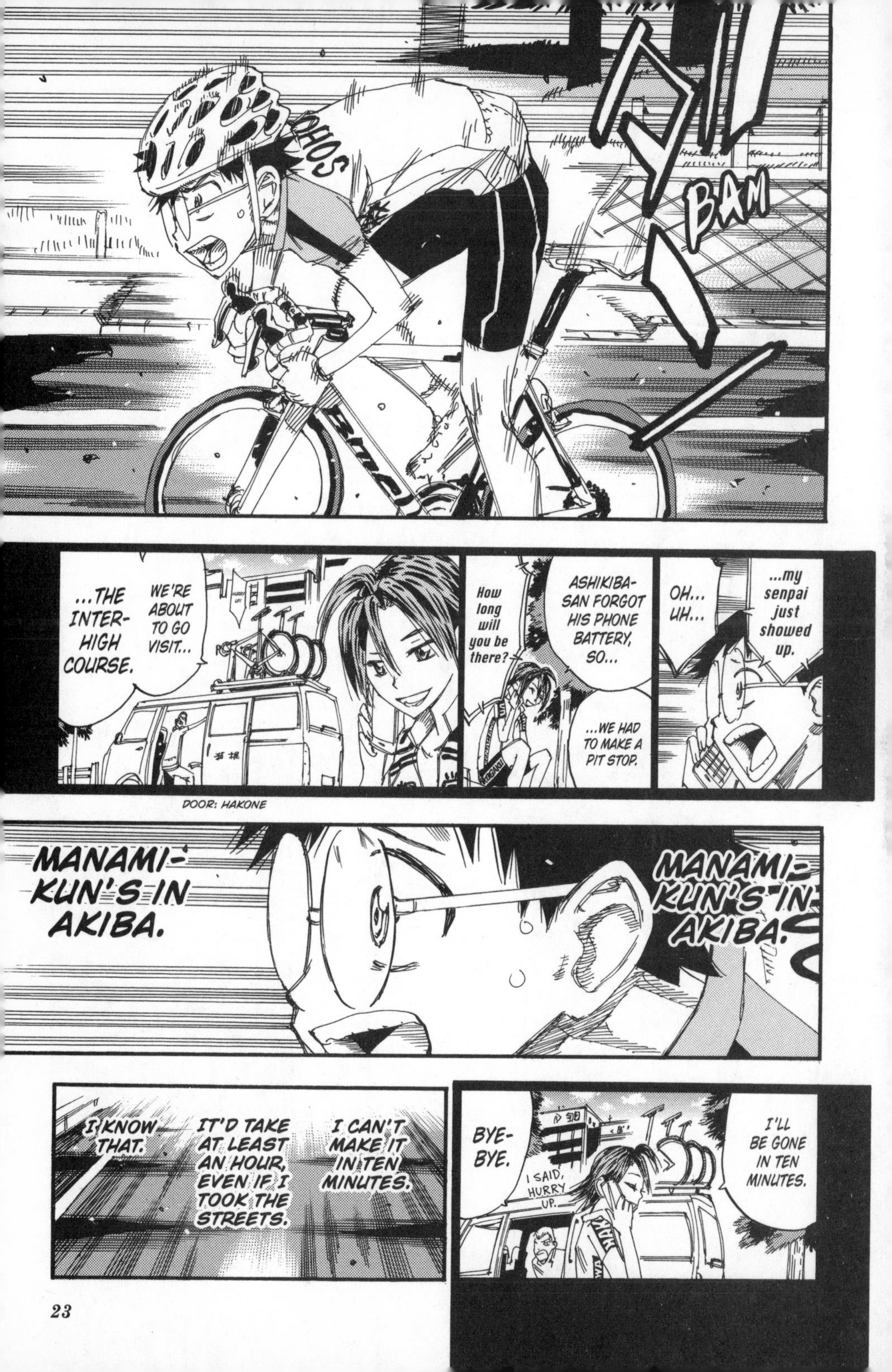
BAM
...my senpai just showed up.
OH... UH...
ASHIKIBA-SAN FORGOT HIS PHONE BATTERY, SO...
...WE HAD TO MAKE A PIT STOP.
How long will you be there?
WE'RE ABOUT TO GO VISIT...
HURRY UP!
...THE INTER-HIGH COURSE.
DOOR: HAKONE
MANAMI-KUN'S IN AKIBA.
MANAMI-KUN'S IN AKIBA.
I'LL BE GONE IN TEN MINUTES.
BYE-BYE.
I SAID, HURRY UP.
I CAN'T MAKE IT IN TEN MINUTES.
IT'D TAKE AT LEAST AN HOUR, EVEN IF I TOOK THE STREETS.
I KNOW THAT.

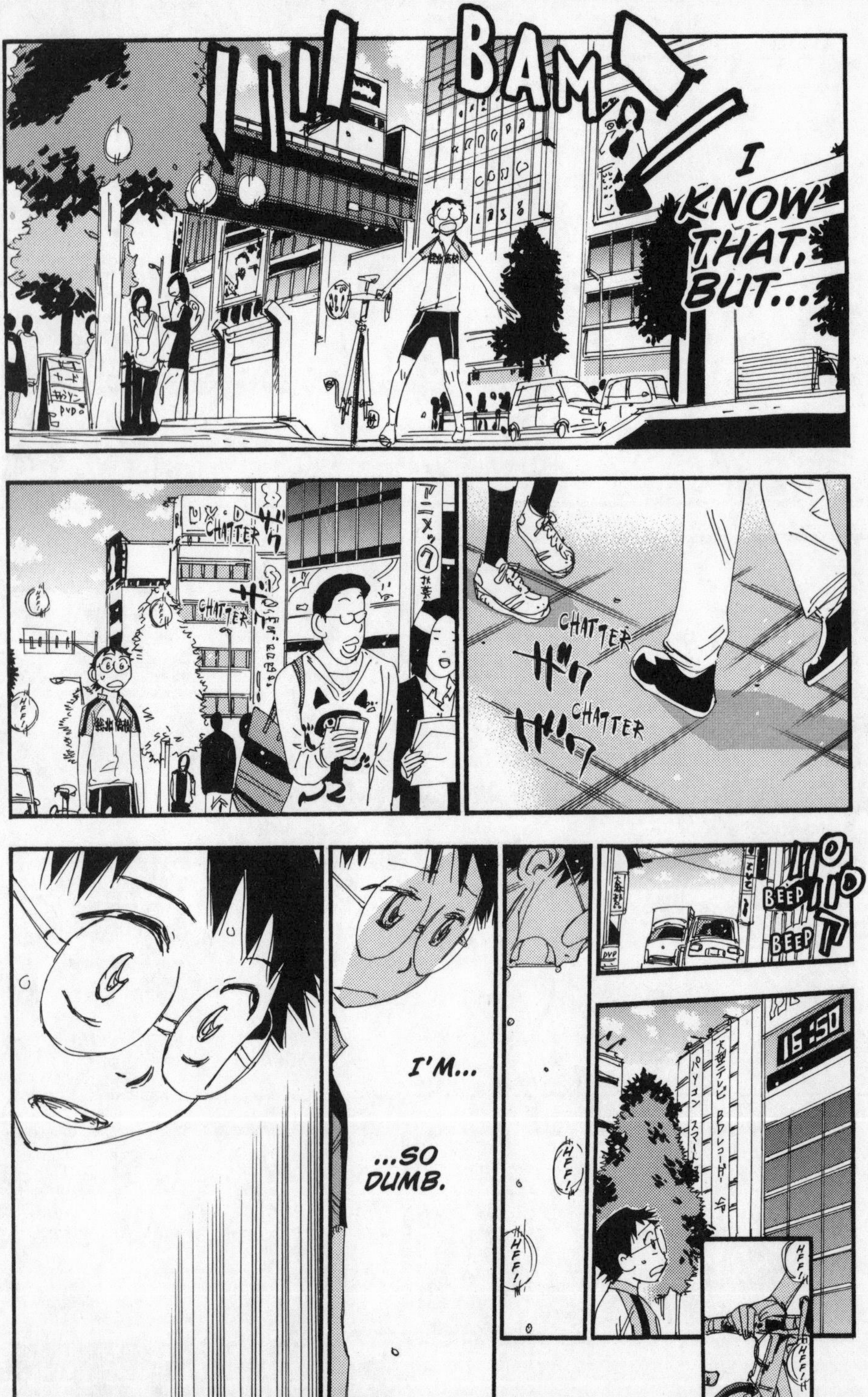
BAM
I KNOW THAT, BUT...
CHATTER
CHATTER
CHATTER
CHATTER
BEEP
BEEP
16:50
HFF!
HFF!
HFF!
HFF!
I'M...
...SO DUMB.

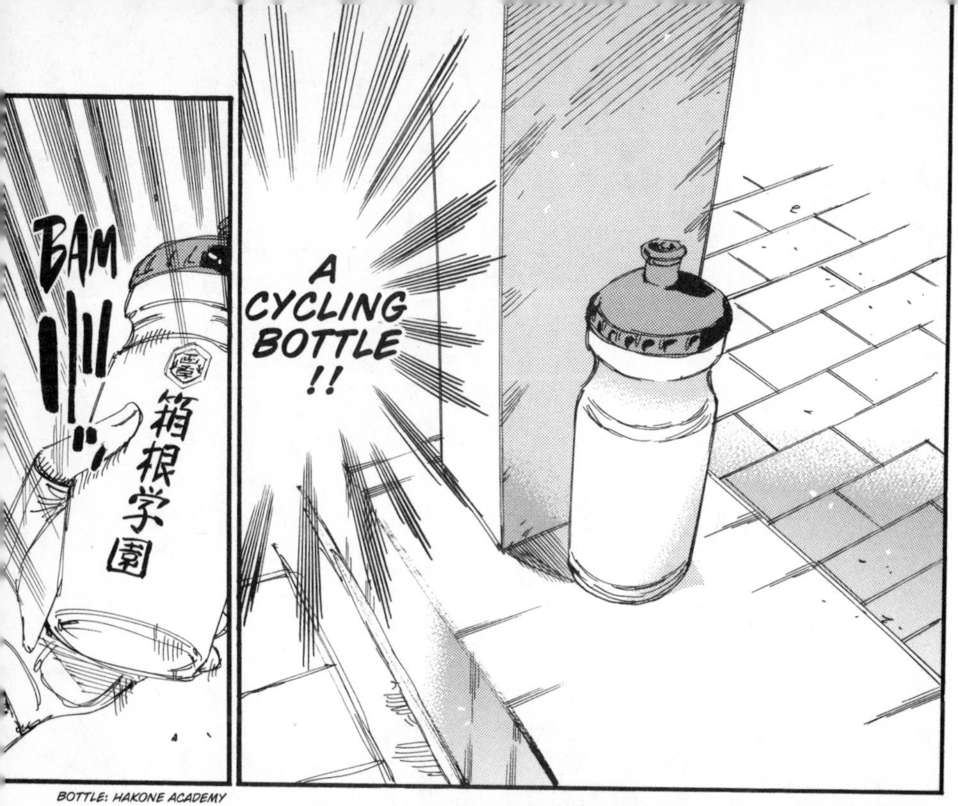
A CYCLING BOTTLE!!
BAM!!!
箱根学園

BOTTLE: HAKONE ACADEMY

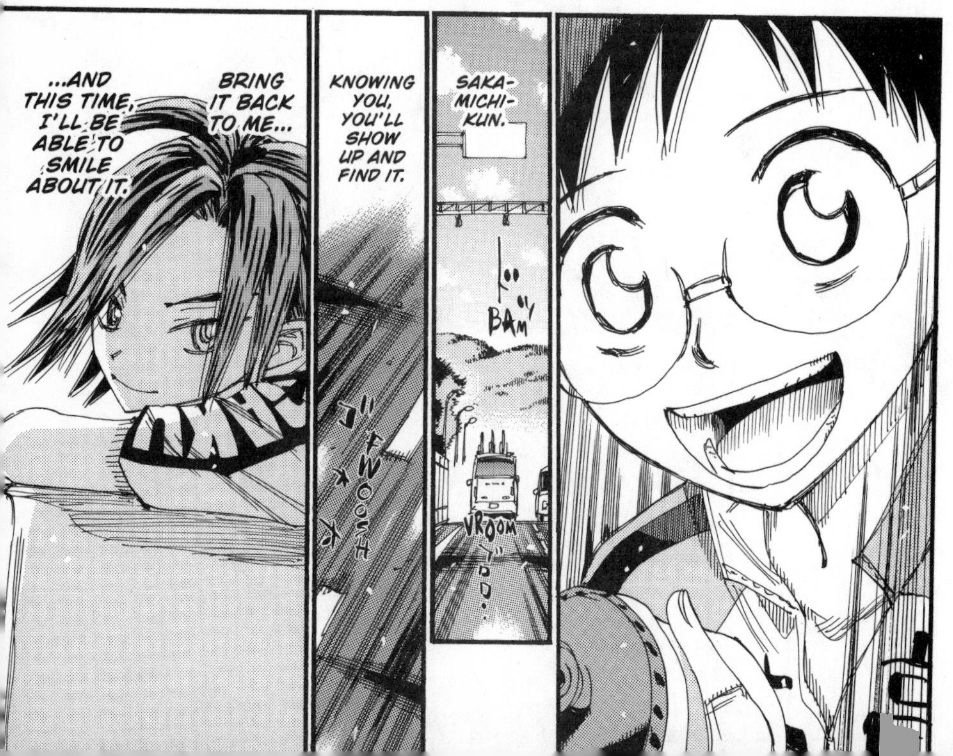
SAKA-MICHI-KUN.
BAM
VROOM
KNOWING YOU, YOU'LL SHOW UP AND FIND IT.
FWOOSH
BRING IT BACK TO ME...
...AND THIS TIME, I'LL BE ABLE TO SMILE ABOUT IT.

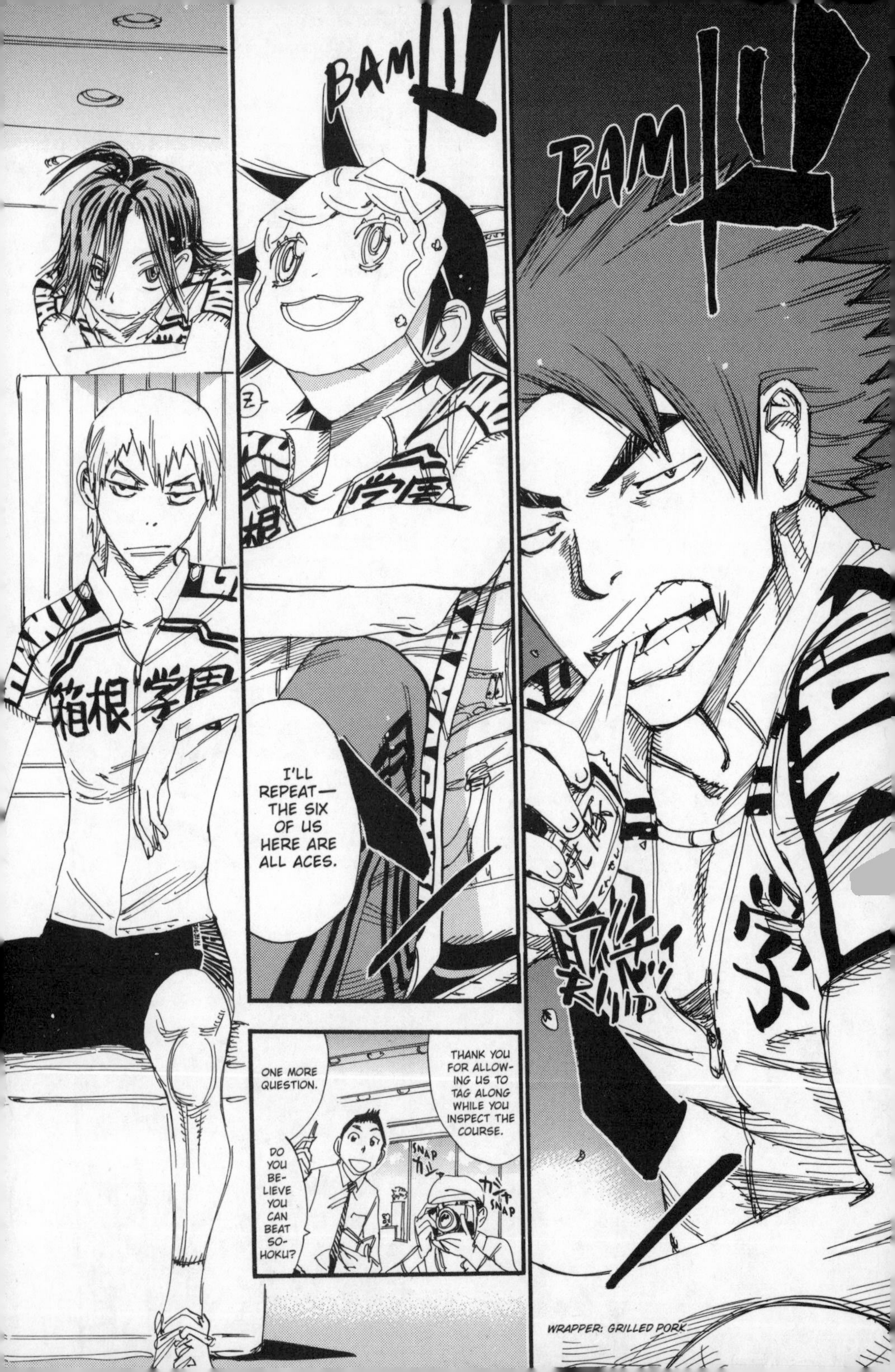
BAM!!
RIIIP
WRAPPER: GRILLED PORK
BAM!!
I'LL REPEAT—THE SIX OF US HERE ARE ALL ACES.
THANK YOU FOR ALLOWING US TO TAG ALONG WHILE YOU INSPECT THE COURSE.
ONE MORE QUESTION.
DO YOU BELIEVE YOU CAN BEAT SOHOKU?
SNAP
SNAP

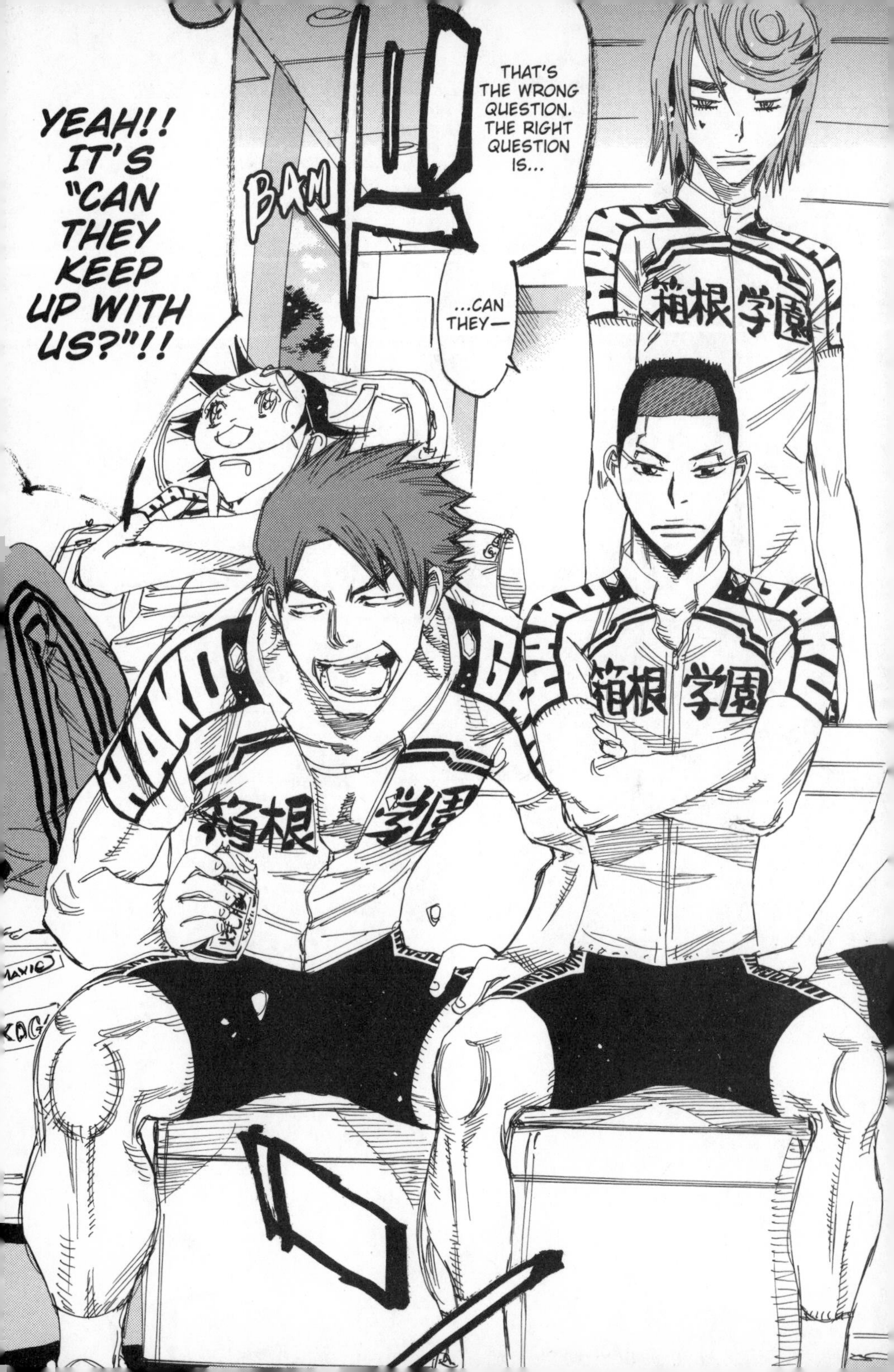
THAT'S THE WRONG QUESTION. THE RIGHT QUESTION IS...
...CAN THEY—
BAM
YEAH!! IT'S "CAN THEY KEEP UP WITH US?"!!
箱根学園

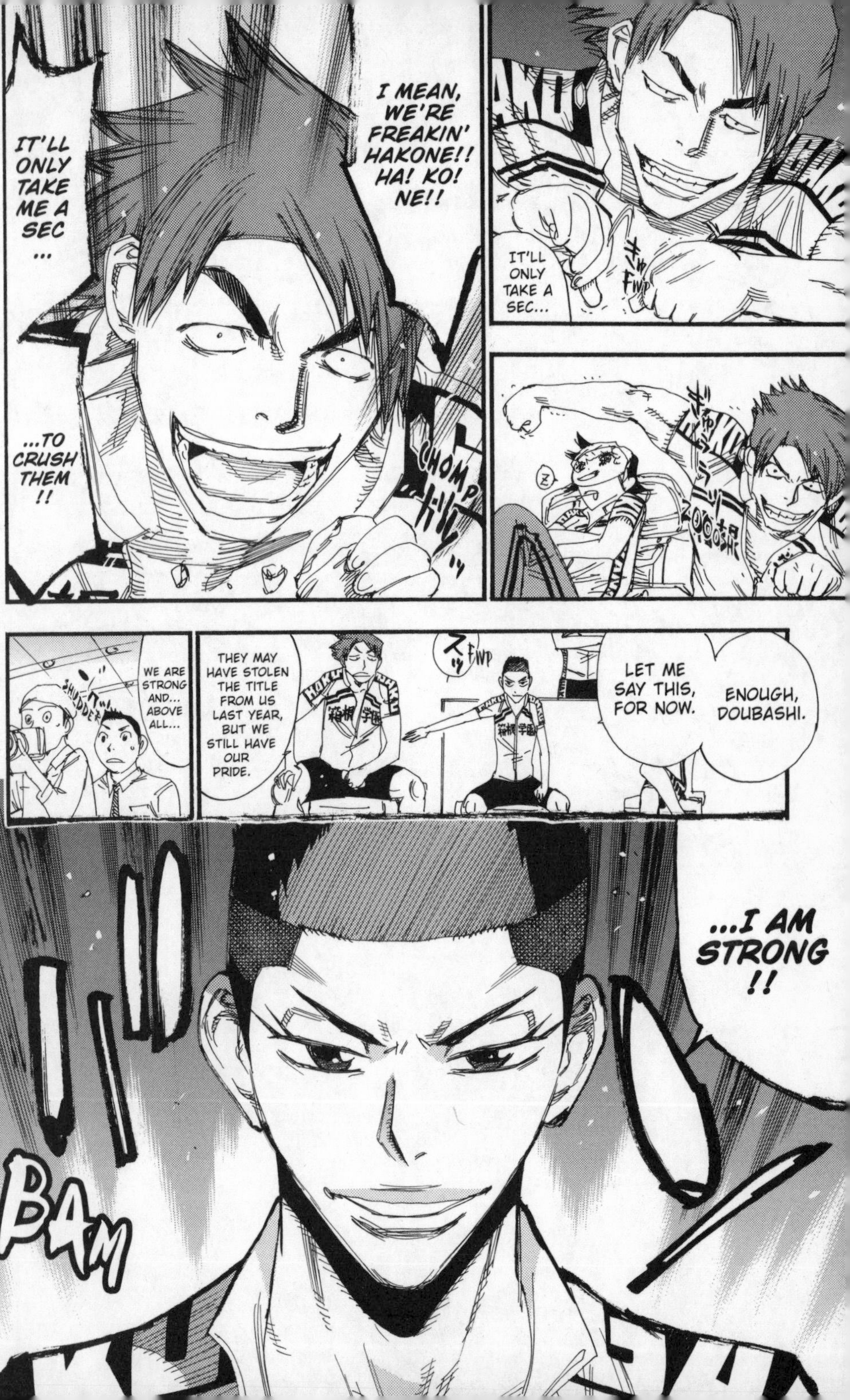
IT'LL ONLY TAKE A SEC...
FWP
ZOOOSH
I MEAN, WE'RE FREAKIN' HAKONE!! HA! KO! NE!!
IT'LL ONLY TAKE ME A SEC...
...TO CRUSH THEM!!
CHOMP
ENOUGH, DOUBASHI.
LET ME SAY THIS, FOR NOW.
FWP
THEY MAY HAVE STOLEN THE TITLE FROM US LAST YEAR, BUT WE STILL HAVE OUR PRIDE.
WE ARE STRONG AND... ABOVE ALL...
SHUDDER
...I AM STRONG!!
BAM

RIDE.280 1,000KM, ONCE MORE

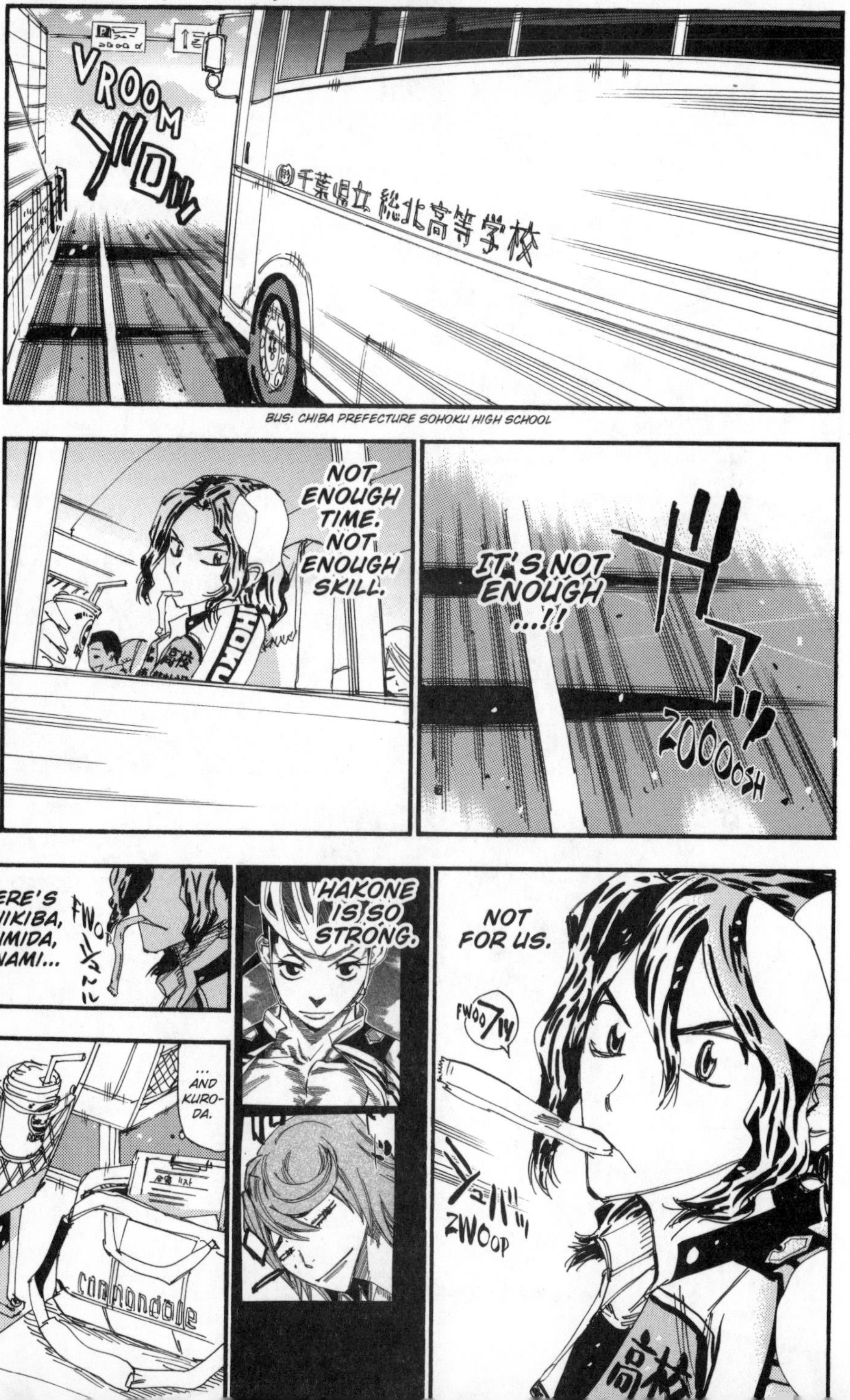
VROOM
千葉県立 総北高等学校
BUS: CHIBA PREFECTURE SOHOKU HIGH SCHOOL
IT'S NOT ENOUGH ...!!
ZOOOOSH
NOT ENOUGH TIME. NOT ENOUGH SKILL.
NOT FOR US.
FWOOP
ZWOOP
HAKONE IS SO STRONG.
THERE'S ASHIKIBA, IZUMIDA, MANAMI...
FWOOP
... AND KURODA.

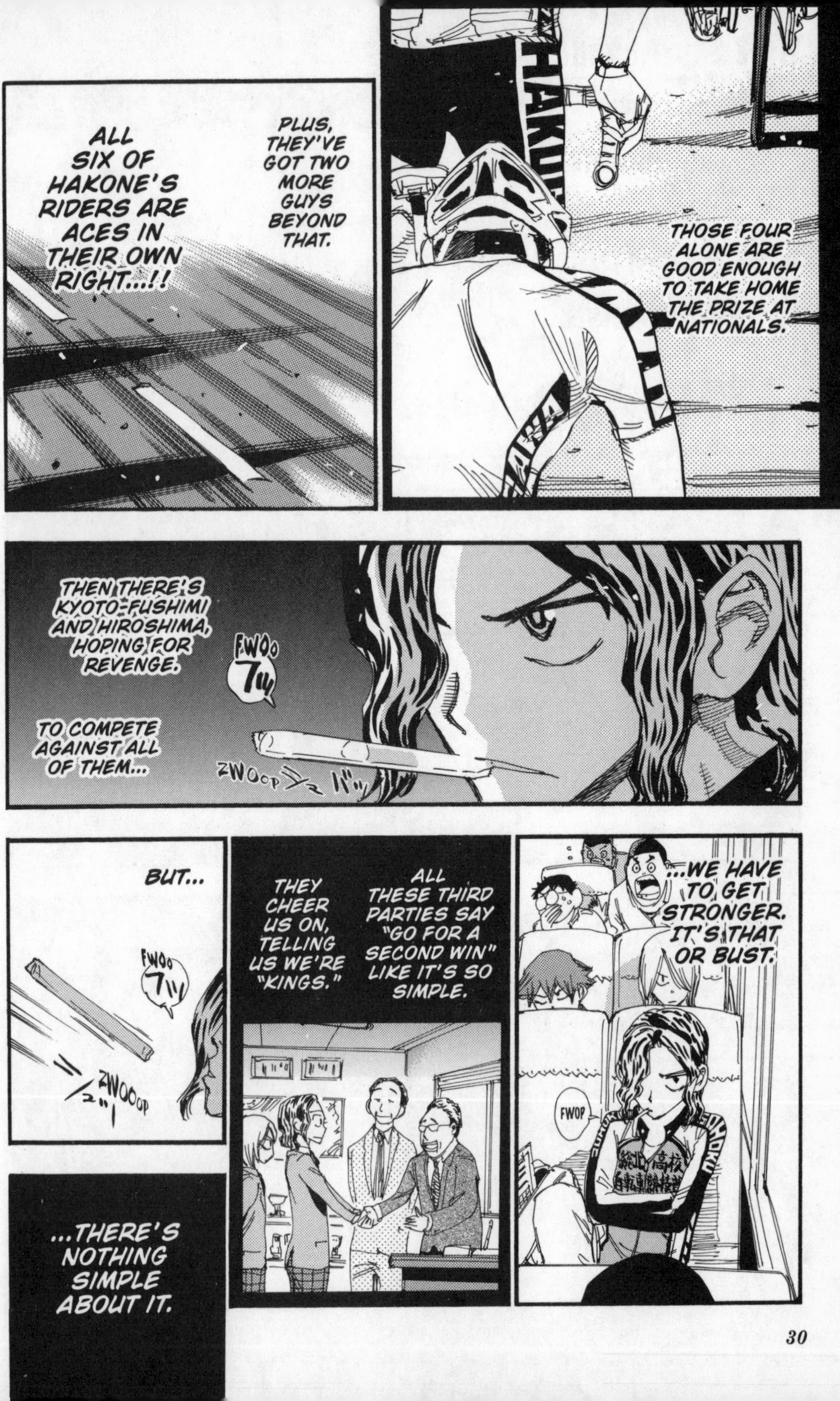
THOSE FOUR ALONE ARE GOOD ENOUGH TO TAKE HOME THE PRIZE AT NATIONALS.
PLUS, THEY'VE GOT TWO MORE GUYS BEYOND THAT.
ALL SIX OF HAKONE'S RIDERS ARE ACES IN THEIR OWN RIGHT...!!
THEN THERE'S KYOTO-FUSHIMI AND HIROSHIMA, HOPING FOR REVENGE.
FWOOP
TO COMPETE AGAINST ALL OF THEM...
ZWOOP
...WE HAVE TO GET STRONGER. IT'S THAT OR BUST.
FWOP
ALL THESE THIRD PARTIES SAY "GO FOR A SECOND WIN" LIKE IT'S SO SIMPLE.
THEY CHEER US ON, TELLING US WE'RE "KINGS."
BUT...
FWOOP
ZWOOOP
...THERE'S NOTHING SIMPLE ABOUT IT.

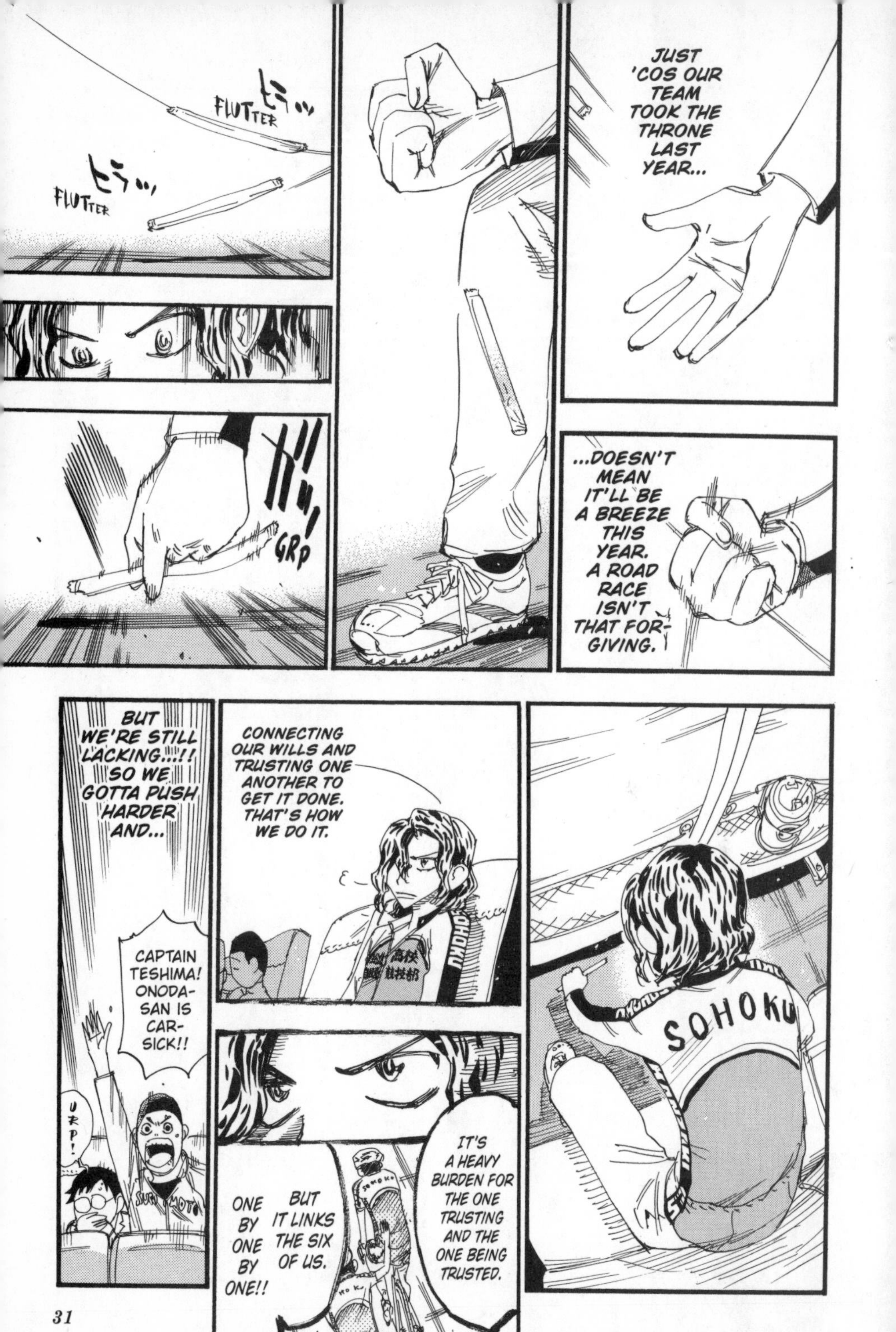
JUST 'COS OUR TEAM TOOK THE THRONE LAST YEAR...
...DOESN'T MEAN IT'LL BE A BREEZE THIS YEAR. A ROAD RACE ISN'T THAT FORGIVING.
ヒラッ
FLUTTER
ヒラッ
FLUTTER
GRp
CONNECTING OUR WILLS AND TRUSTING ONE ANOTHER TO GET IT DONE. THAT'S HOW WE DO IT.
IT'S A HEAVY BURDEN FOR THE ONE TRUSTING AND THE ONE BEING TRUSTED.
BUT IT LINKS THE SIX OF US.
ONE BY ONE BY ONE!!
BUT WE'RE STILL LACKING...!! SO WE GOTTA PUSH HARDER AND...
CAPTAIN TESHIMA! ONODA-SAN IS CARSICK!!
URP!
SOHOKU

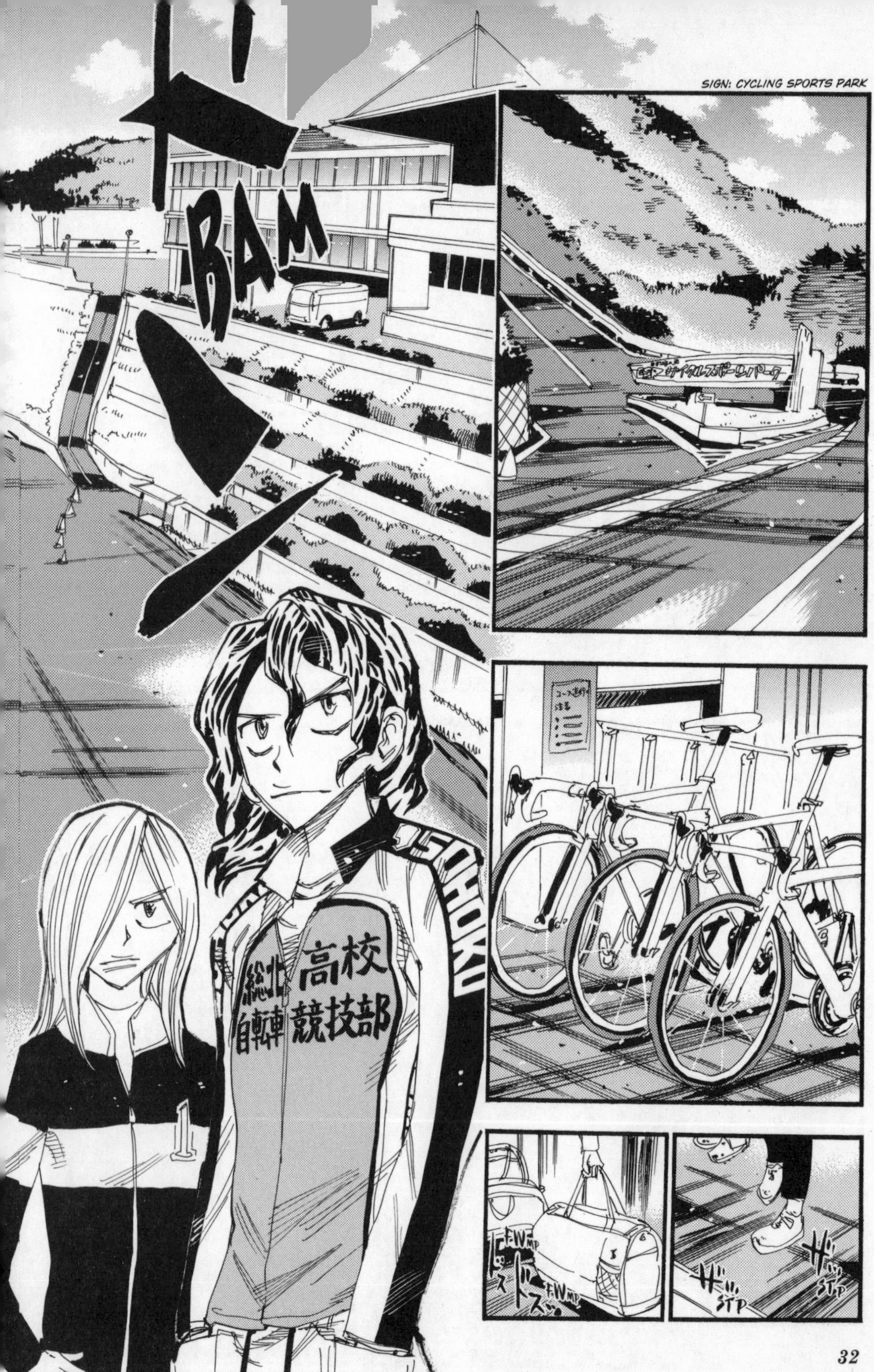
SIGN: CYCLING SPORTS PARK
BAM
総北高校
自転車競技部
SOHOKU
STP
STP
FWMP
FWMP

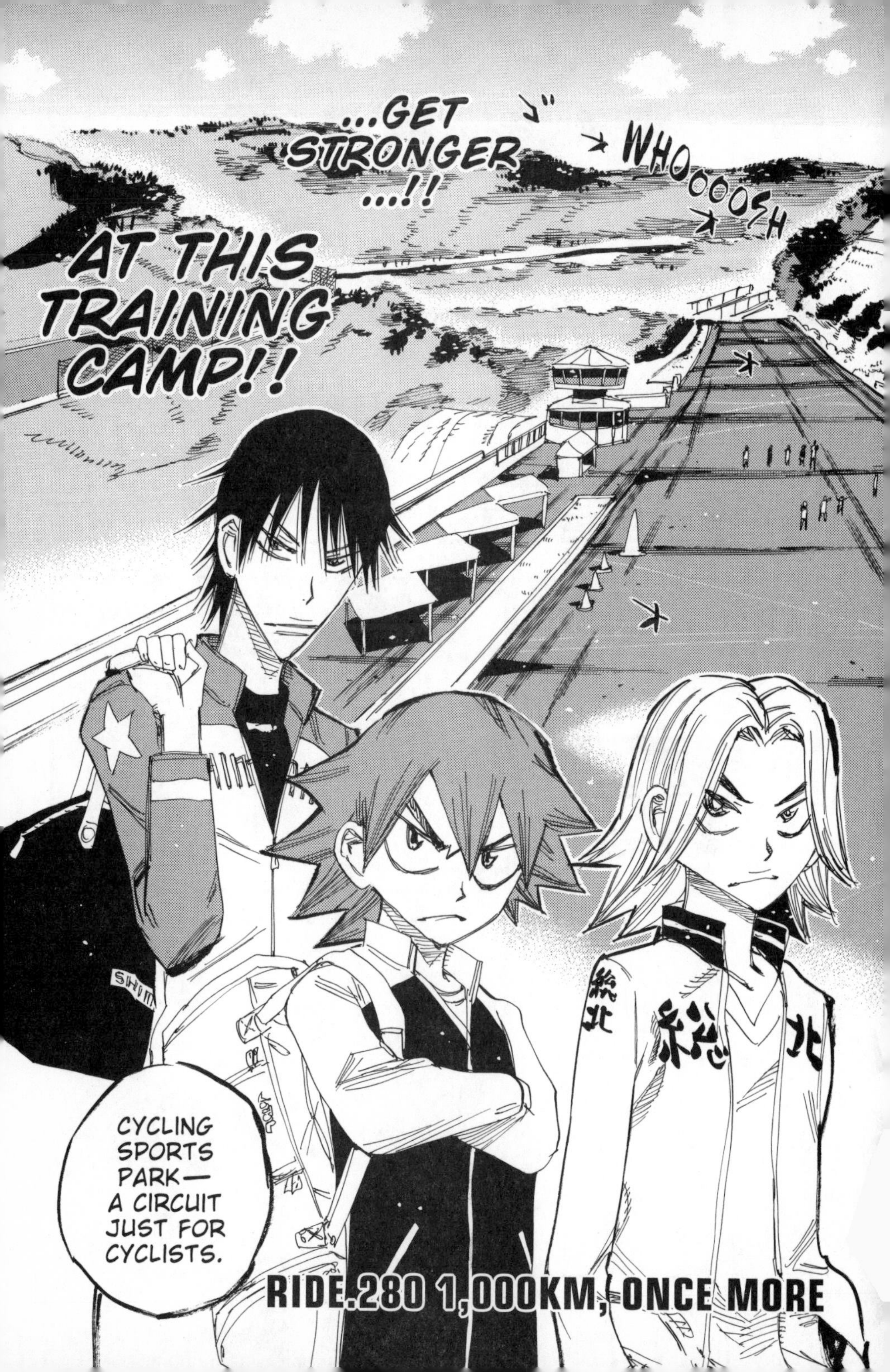
WHOOOOSH
...GET STRONGER...!!
AT THIS TRAINING CAMP!!
CYCLING SPORTS PARK—A CIRCUIT JUST FOR CYCLISTS.
RIDE.280 1,000KM, ONCE MORE

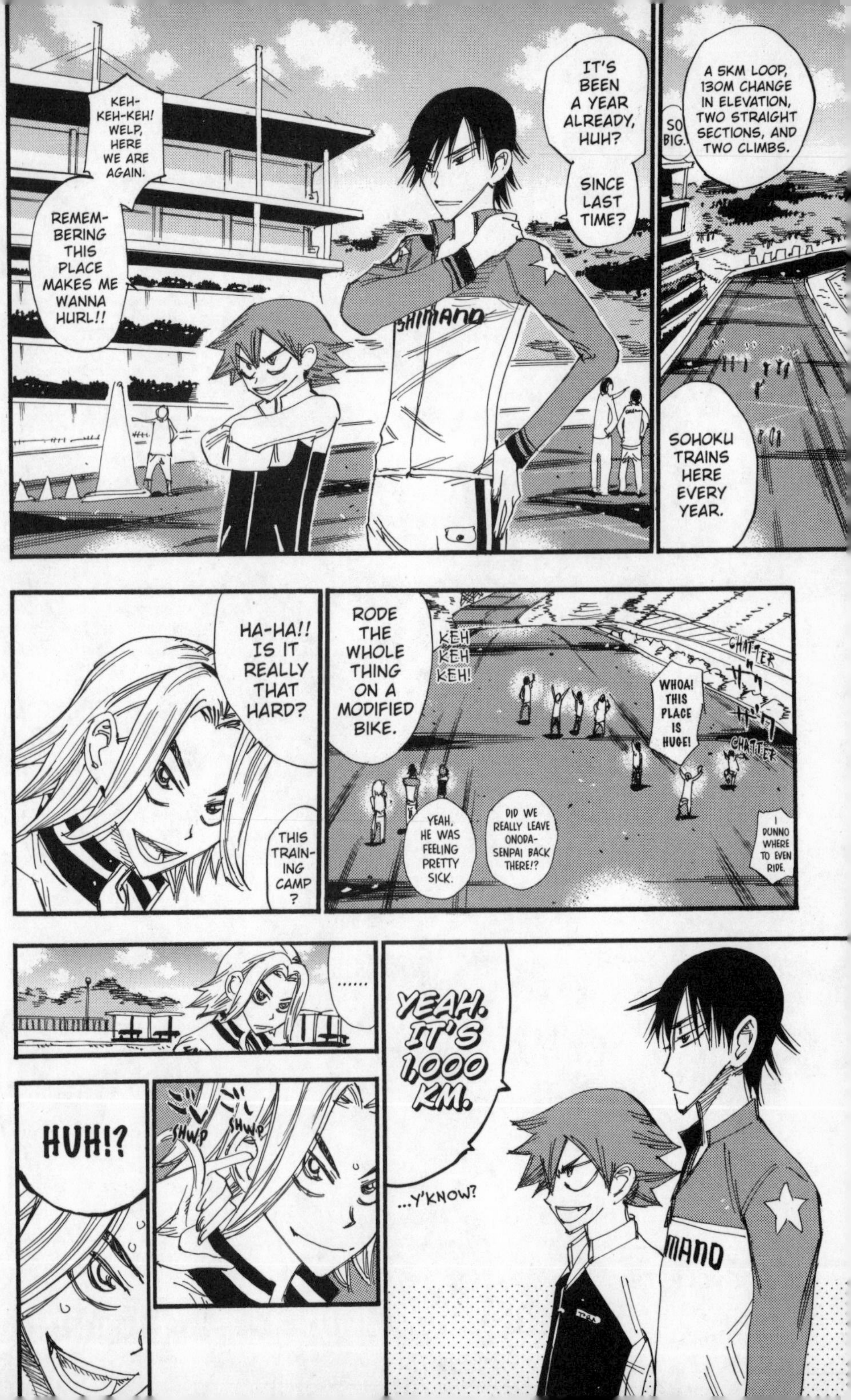
A 5KM LOOP, 130M CHANGE IN ELEVATION, TWO STRAIGHT SECTIONS, AND TWO CLIMBS.
SO BIG.
SOHOKU TRAINS HERE EVERY YEAR.
IT'S BEEN A YEAR ALREADY, HUH?
SINCE LAST TIME?
KEH-KEH-KEH! WELP, HERE WE ARE AGAIN.
REMEMBERING THIS PLACE MAKES ME WANNA HURL!!
CHATTER
WHOA! THIS PLACE IS HUGE!
CHATTER
KEH KEH KEH!
RODE THE WHOLE THING ON A MODIFIED BIKE.
I DUNNO WHERE TO EVEN RIDE.
DID WE REALLY LEAVE ONODA-SENPAI BACK THERE!?
YEAH, HE WAS FEELING PRETTY SICK.
HA-HA!! IS IT REALLY THAT HARD?
THIS TRAINING CAMP?
YEAH. IT'S 1,000 KM.
...Y'KNOW?
......
SHWP SHWP
HUH!?

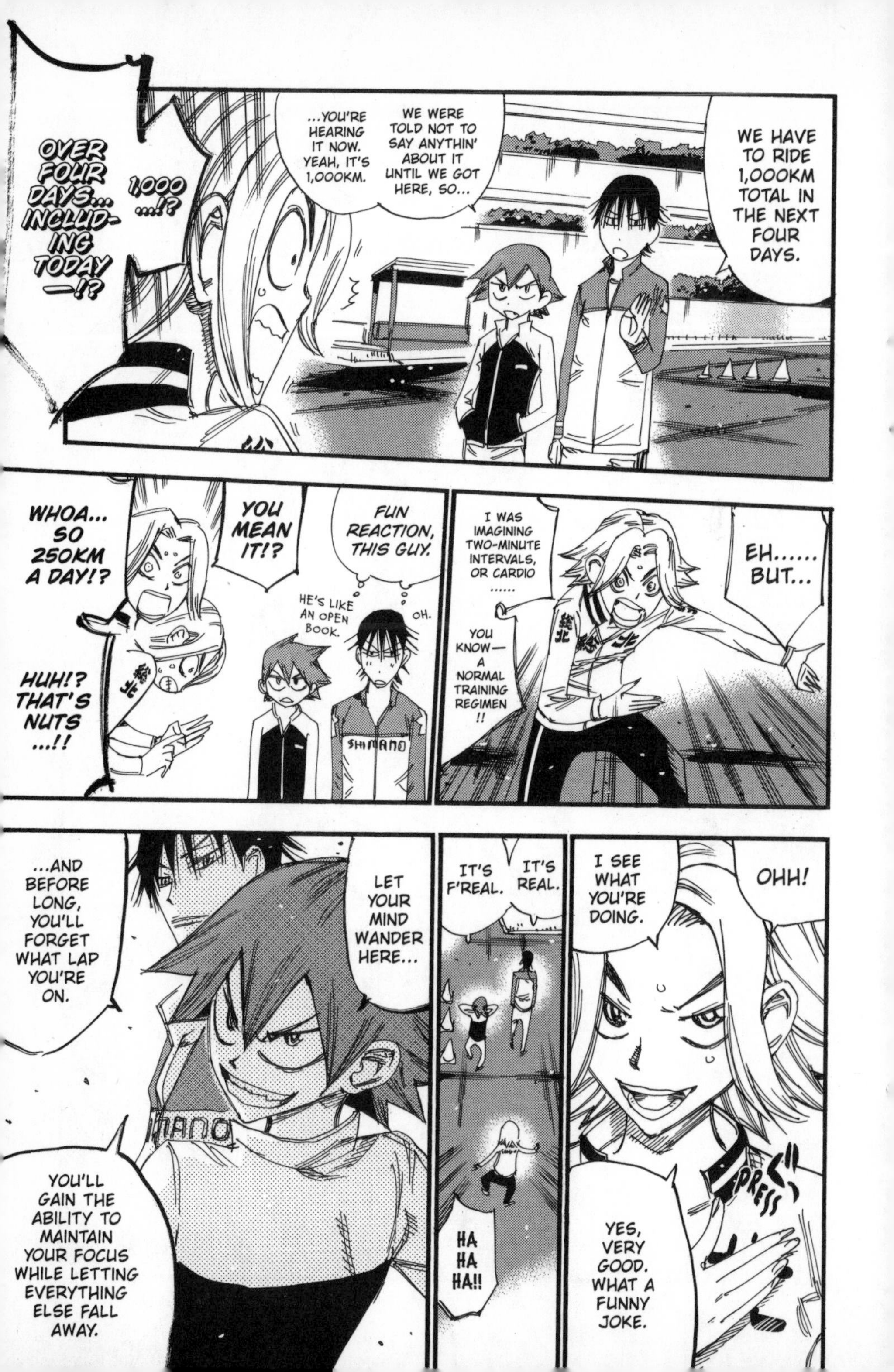
WE HAVE TO RIDE 1,000KM TOTAL IN THE NEXT FOUR DAYS.
WE WERE TOLD NOT TO SAY ANYTHIN' ABOUT IT UNTIL WE GOT HERE, SO...
...YOU'RE HEARING IT NOW. YEAH, IT'S 1,000KM.
1,000 ...!?
OVER FOUR DAYS... INCLUDING TODAY—!?
EH...... BUT...
I WAS IMAGINING TWO-MINUTE INTERVALS, OR CARDIO ......
YOU KNOW—A NORMAL TRAINING REGIMEN !!
FUN REACTION, THIS GUY.
OH.
HE'S LIKE AN OPEN BOOK.
YOU MEAN IT!?
WHOA... SO 250KM A DAY!?
HUH!? THAT'S NUTS ...!!
OHH!
I SEE WHAT YOU'RE DOING.
PRESS
YES, VERY GOOD. WHAT A FUNNY JOKE.
IT'S REAL.
IT'S F'REAL.
HA HA HA!!
LET YOUR MIND WANDER HERE...
...AND BEFORE LONG, YOU'LL FORGET WHAT LAP YOU'RE ON.
YOU'LL GAIN THE ABILITY TO MAINTAIN YOUR FOCUS WHILE LETTING EVERYTHING ELSE FALL AWAY.

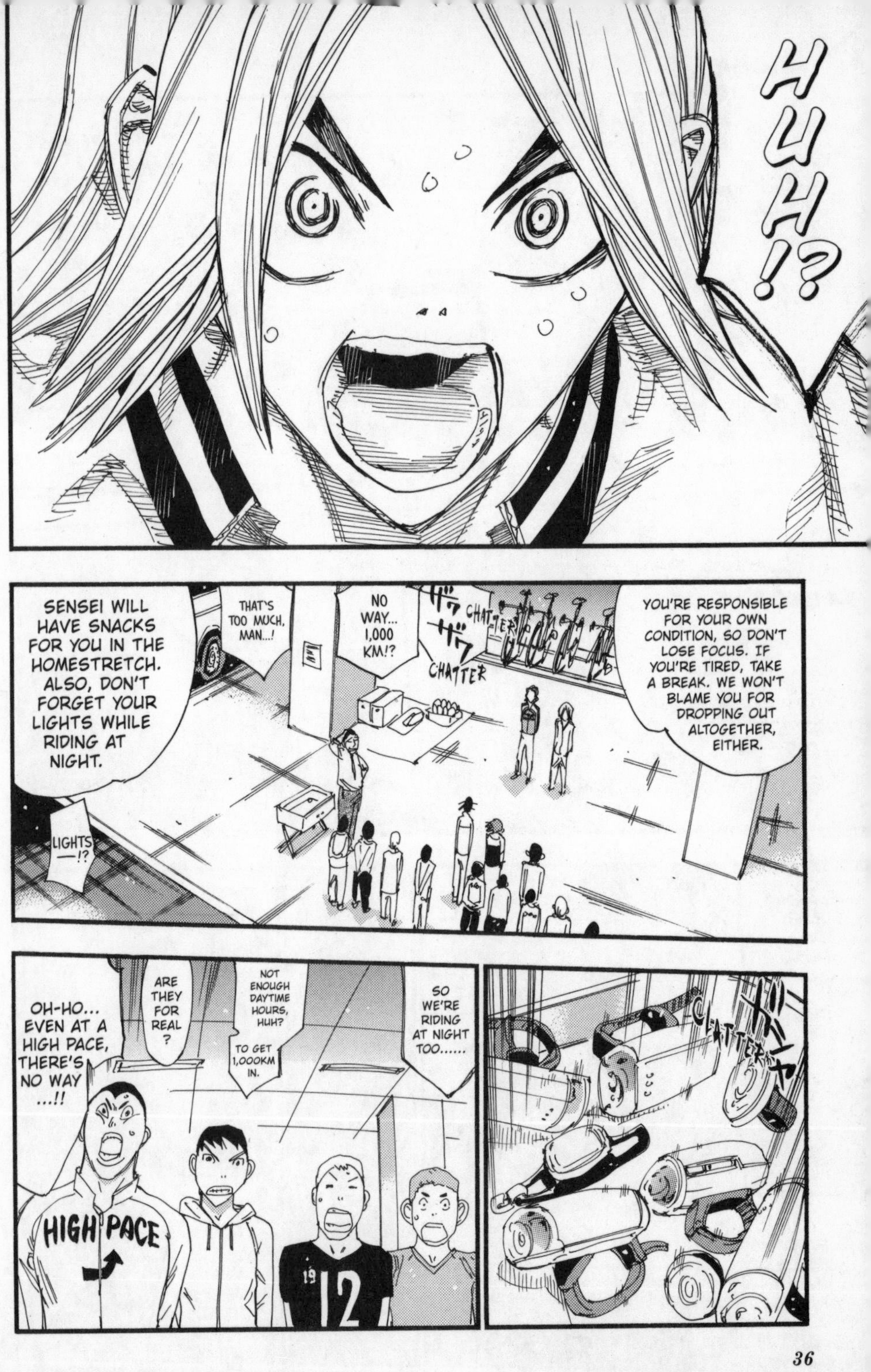
HUH!?
YOU'RE RESPONSIBLE FOR YOUR OWN CONDITION, SO DON'T LOSE FOCUS. IF YOU'RE TIRED, TAKE A BREAK. WE WON'T BLAME YOU FOR DROPPING OUT ALTOGETHER, EITHER.
CHATTER
CHATTER
NO WAY... 1,000 KM!?
THAT'S TOO MUCH, MAN...!
SENSEI WILL HAVE SNACKS FOR YOU IN THE HOMESTRETCH. ALSO, DON'T FORGET YOUR LIGHTS WHILE RIDING AT NIGHT.
LIGHTS —!?
CLATTER
SO WE'RE RIDING AT NIGHT TOO......
NOT ENOUGH DAYTIME HOURS, HUH?
TO GET 1,000KM IN.
ARE THEY FOR REAL?
OH-HO... EVEN AT A HIGH PACE, THERE'S NO WAY ...!!
HIGH PACE
19
12

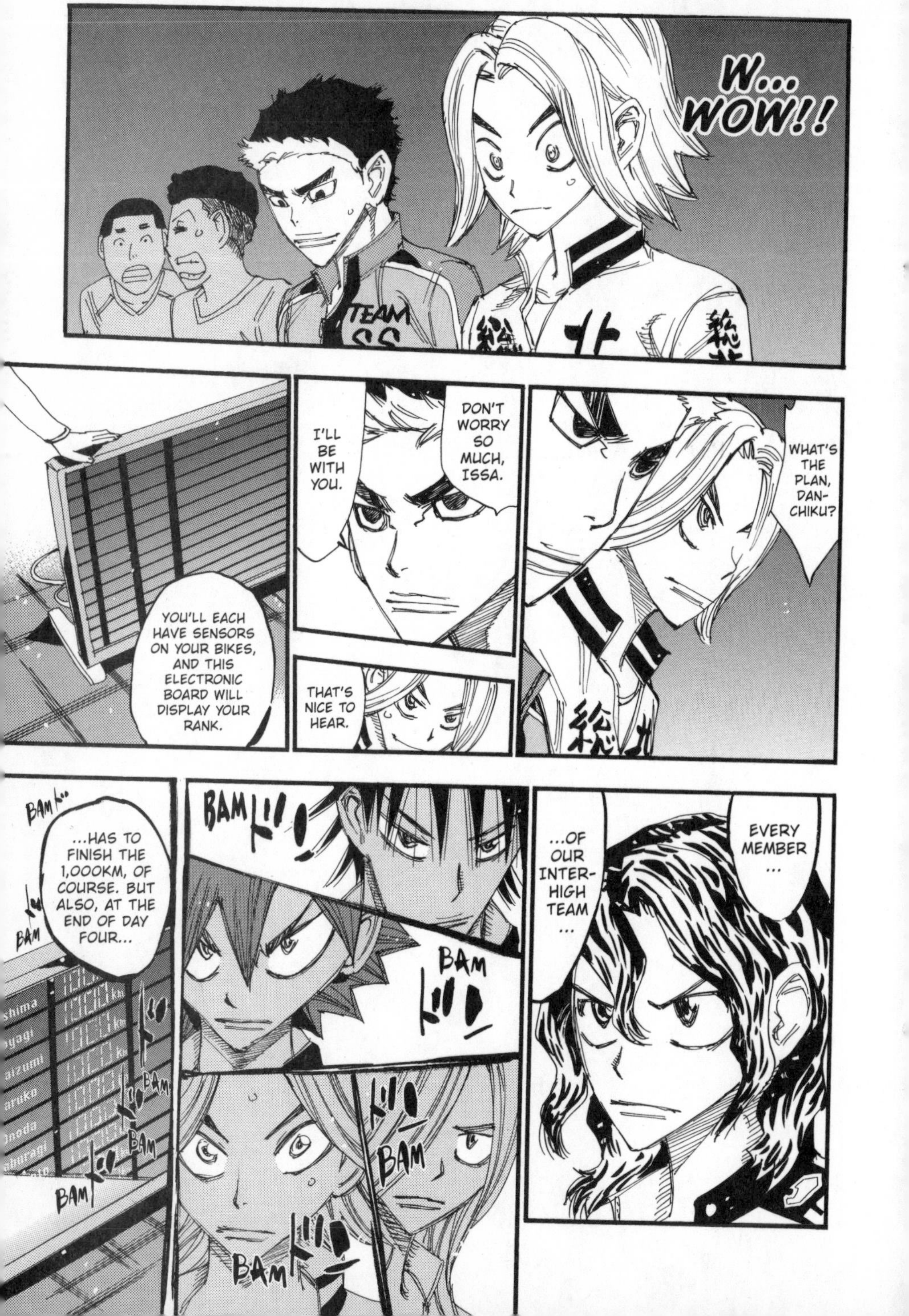
W... WOW!!
WHAT'S THE PLAN, DAN-CHIKU?
DON'T WORRY SO MUCH, ISSA.
I'LL BE WITH YOU.
THAT'S NICE TO HEAR.
YOU'LL EACH HAVE SENSORS ON YOUR BIKES, AND THIS ELECTRONIC BOARD WILL DISPLAY YOUR RANK.
EVERY MEMBER ...
...OF OUR INTER-HIGH TEAM ...
BAM
BAM
BAM
BAM
...HAS TO FINISH THE 1,000KM, OF COURSE. BUT ALSO, AT THE END OF DAY FOUR...
BAM
BAM
BAM
BAM
BAM

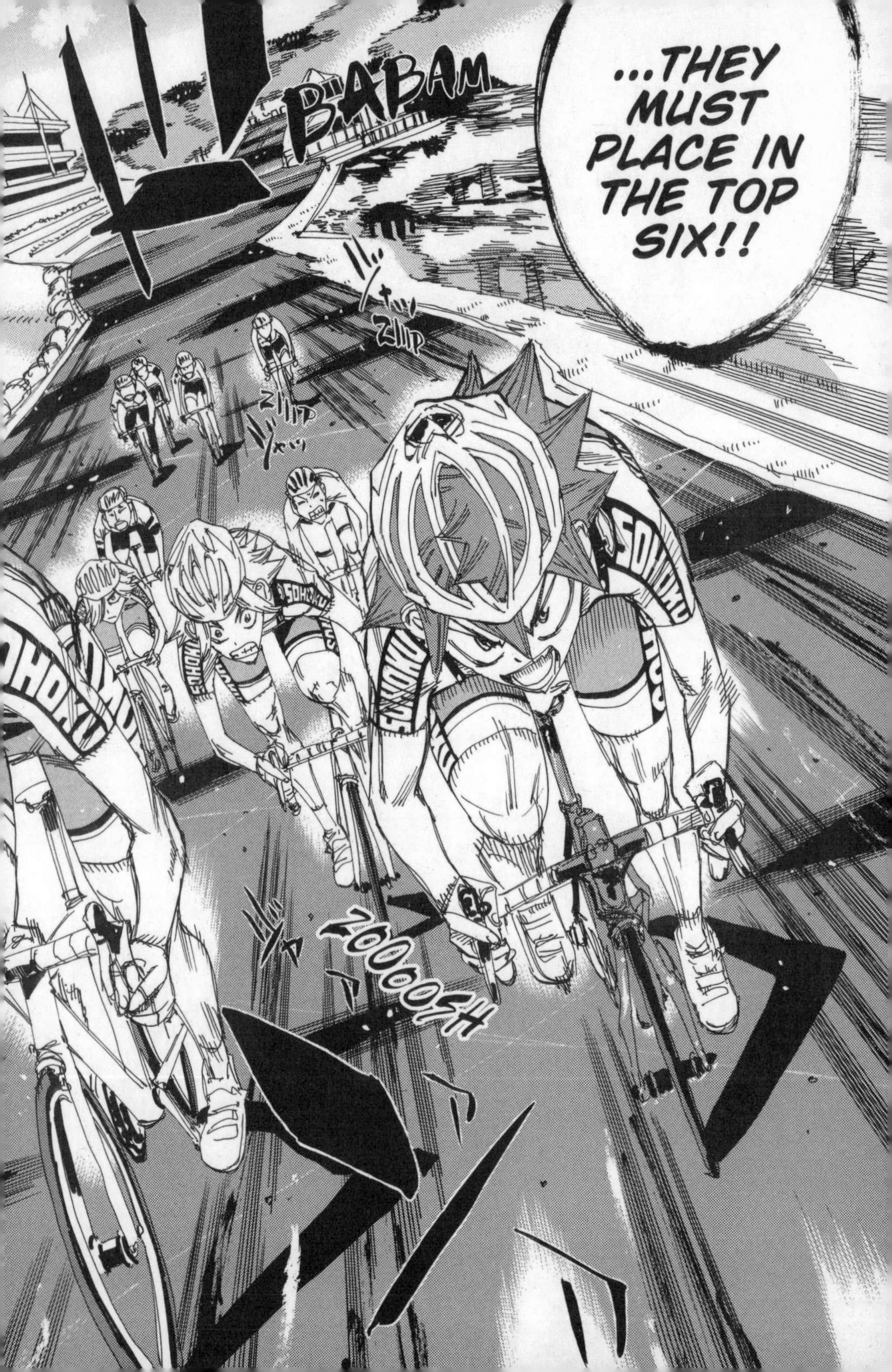
...THEY MUST PLACE IN THE TOP SIX!!
BABAM
ZIIIP
ZIIIP
ZOOOOSH

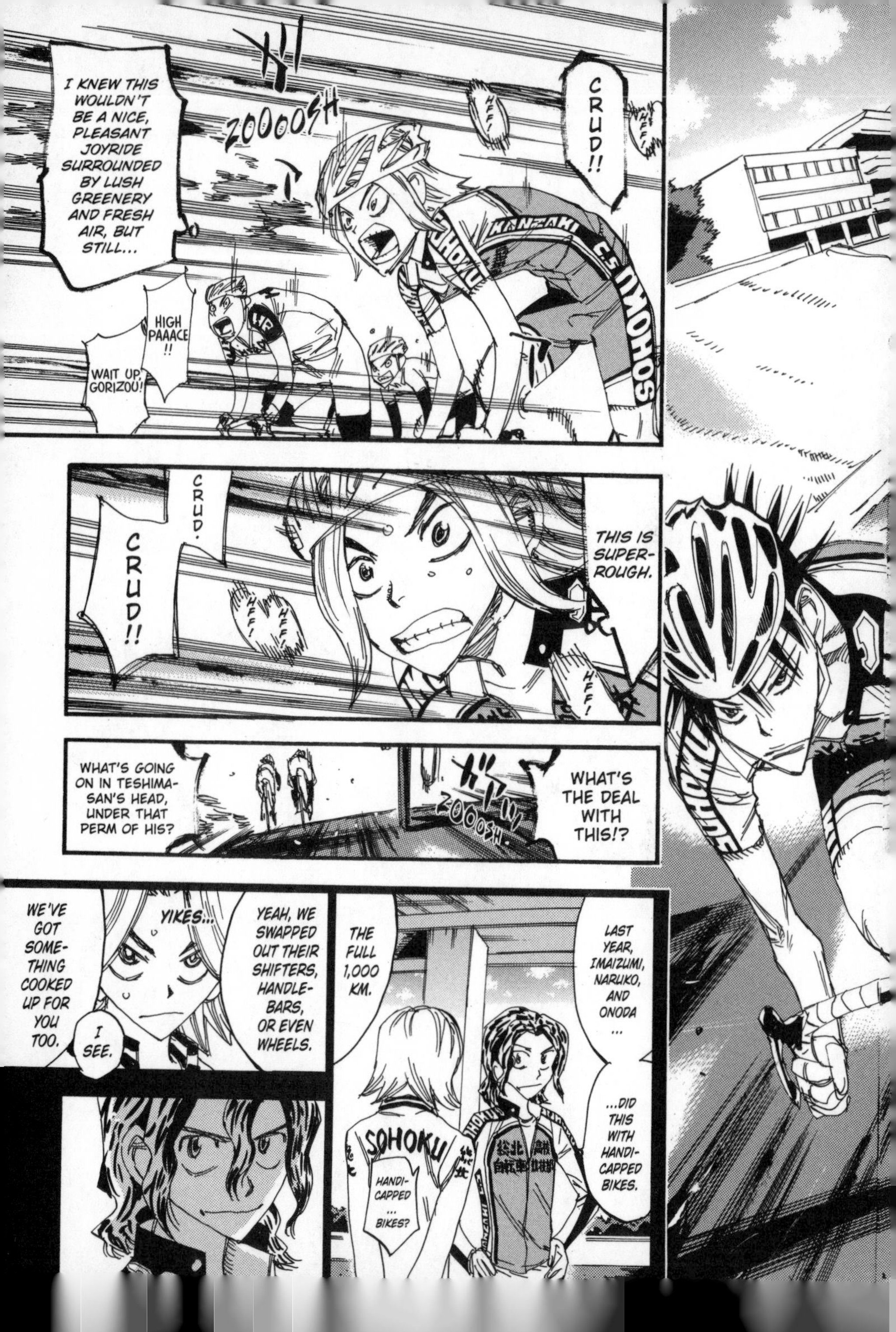
HFF! HFF!
CRUD!!
HFF!
ZOOOOSH
I KNEW THIS WOULDN'T BE A NICE, PLEASANT JOYRIDE SURROUNDED BY LUSH GREENERY AND FRESH AIR, BUT STILL...
HIGH PAAACE!!
WAIT UP, GORIZOU!
THIS IS SUPER-ROUGH.
HFF!
HFF! HFF!
CRUD.
CRUD!!
WHAT'S THE DEAL WITH THIS!?
ZOOOSH
WHAT'S GOING ON IN TESHIMA-SAN'S HEAD, UNDER THAT PERM OF HIS?
LAST YEAR, IMAIZUMI, NARUKO, AND ONODA ...
...DID THIS WITH HANDI-CAPPED BIKES.
THE FULL 1,000 KM.
SOHOKU
HANDI-CAPPED ... BIKES?
YEAH, WE SWAPPED OUT THEIR SHIFTERS, HANDLE-BARS, OR EVEN WHEELS.
YIKES...
WE'VE GOT SOME-THING COOKED UP FOR YOU TOO.
I SEE.

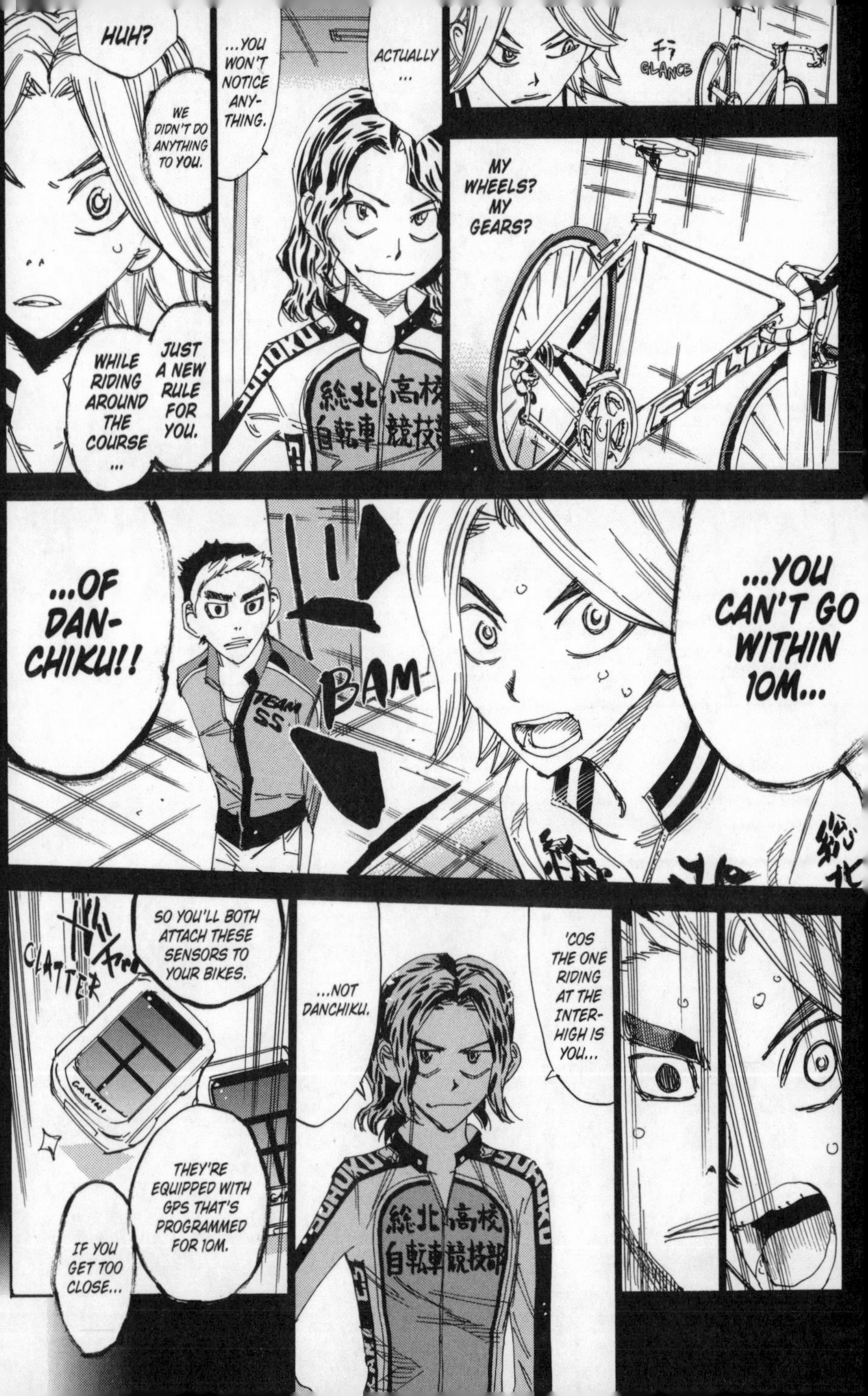

チラ
GLANCE
MY WHEELS? MY GEARS?
ACTUALLY...
...YOU WON'T NOTICE ANY-THING.
HUH?
WE DIDN'T DO ANYTHING TO YOU.
JUST A NEW RULE FOR YOU.
WHILE RIDING AROUND THE COURSE...
...YOU CAN'T GO WITHIN 10M...
BAM
...OF DAN-CHIKU!!
'COS THE ONE RIDING AT THE INTER-HIGH IS YOU...
...NOT DANCHIKU.
総北高校
自転車競技部
SO YOU'LL BOTH ATTACH THESE SENSORS TO YOUR BIKES.
CLATTER
THEY'RE EQUIPPED WITH GPS THAT'S PROGRAMMED FOR 10M.
IF YOU GET TOO CLOSE...

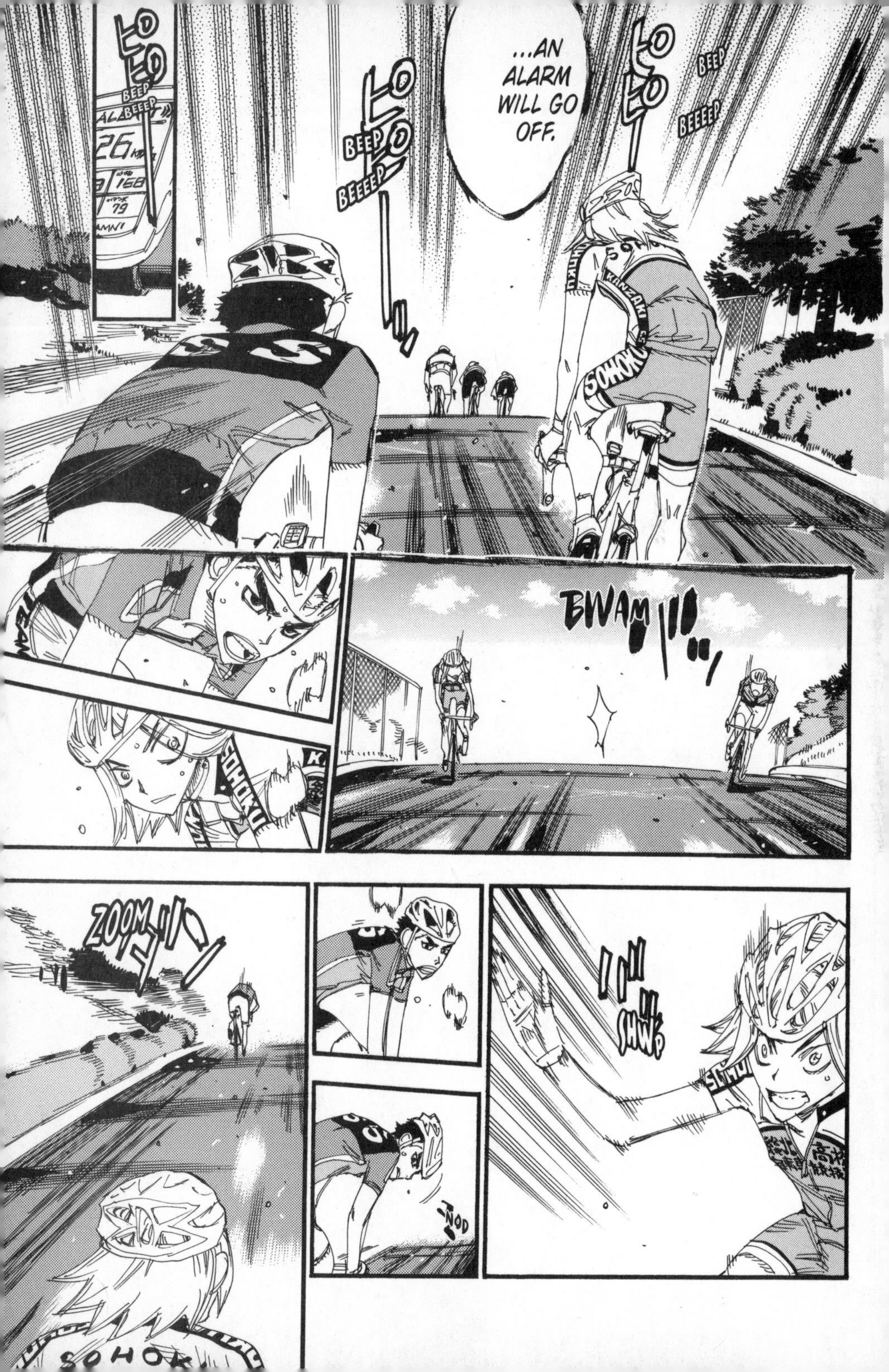
BEEP
BEEEEP
...AN ALARM WILL GO OFF.
BEEP
BEEEEP
BEEP
BEEEEP
BWAM
SHWP
NOD
ZOOM

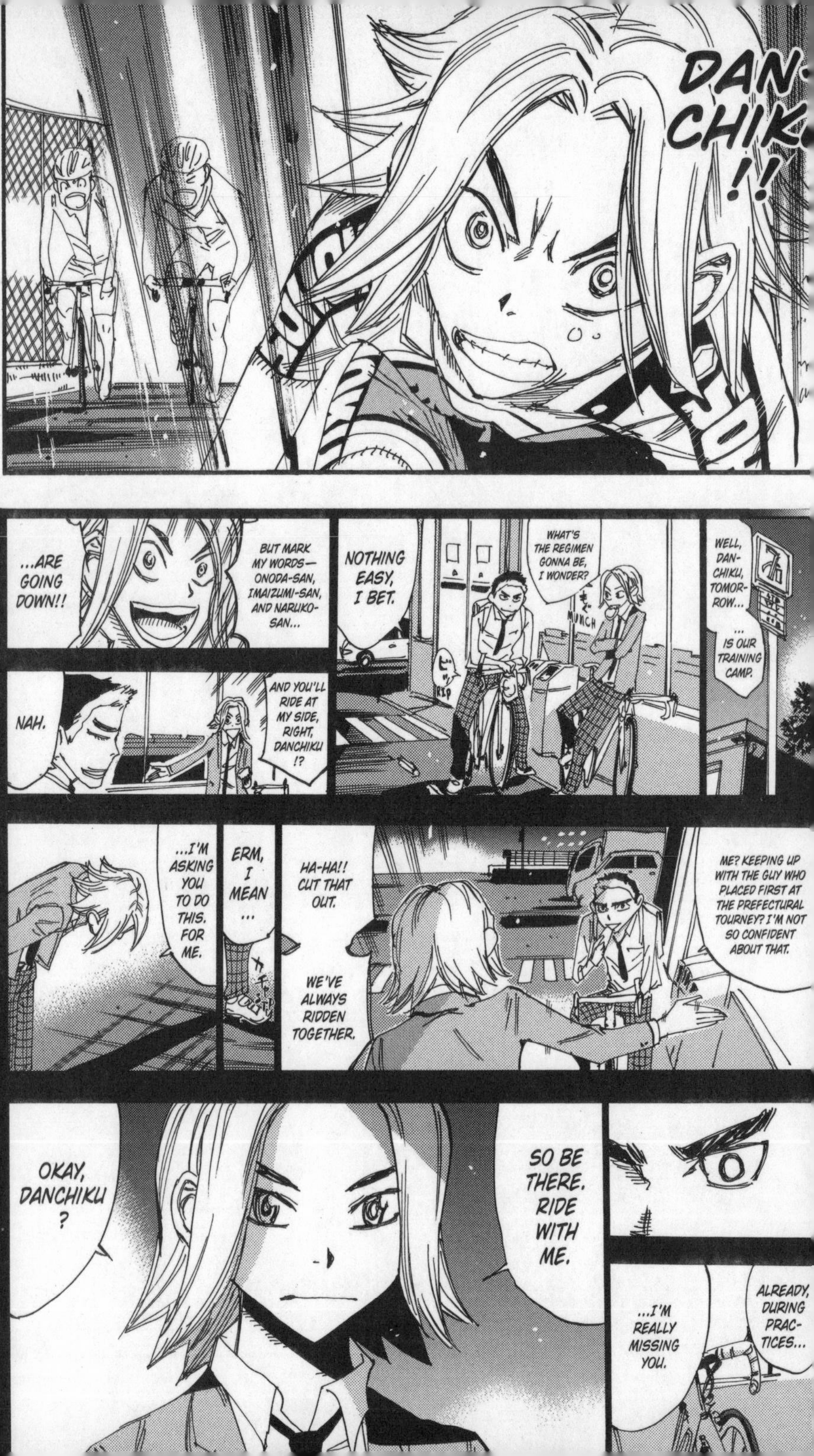
DAN-CHIKU!!
WELL, DANCHIKU, TOMORROW...
...IS OUR TRAINING CAMP.
WHAT'S THE REGIMEN GONNA BE, I WONDER?
MUNCH
NOTHING EASY, I BET.
BUT MARK MY WORDS—ONODA-SAN, IMAIZUMI-SAN, AND NARUKO-SAN...
...ARE GOING DOWN!!
AND YOU'LL RIDE AT MY SIDE, RIGHT, DANCHIKU!?
NAH.
ME? KEEPING UP WITH THE GUY WHO PLACED FIRST AT THE PREFECTURAL TOURNEY? I'M NOT SO CONFIDENT ABOUT THAT.
HA-HA!! CUT THAT OUT.
WE'VE ALWAYS RIDDEN TOGETHER.
ERM, I MEAN...
...I'M ASKING YOU TO DO THIS. FOR ME.
ALREADY, DURING PRACTICES...
...I'M REALLY MISSING YOU.
SO BE THERE. RIDE WITH ME.
OKAY, DANCHIKU?

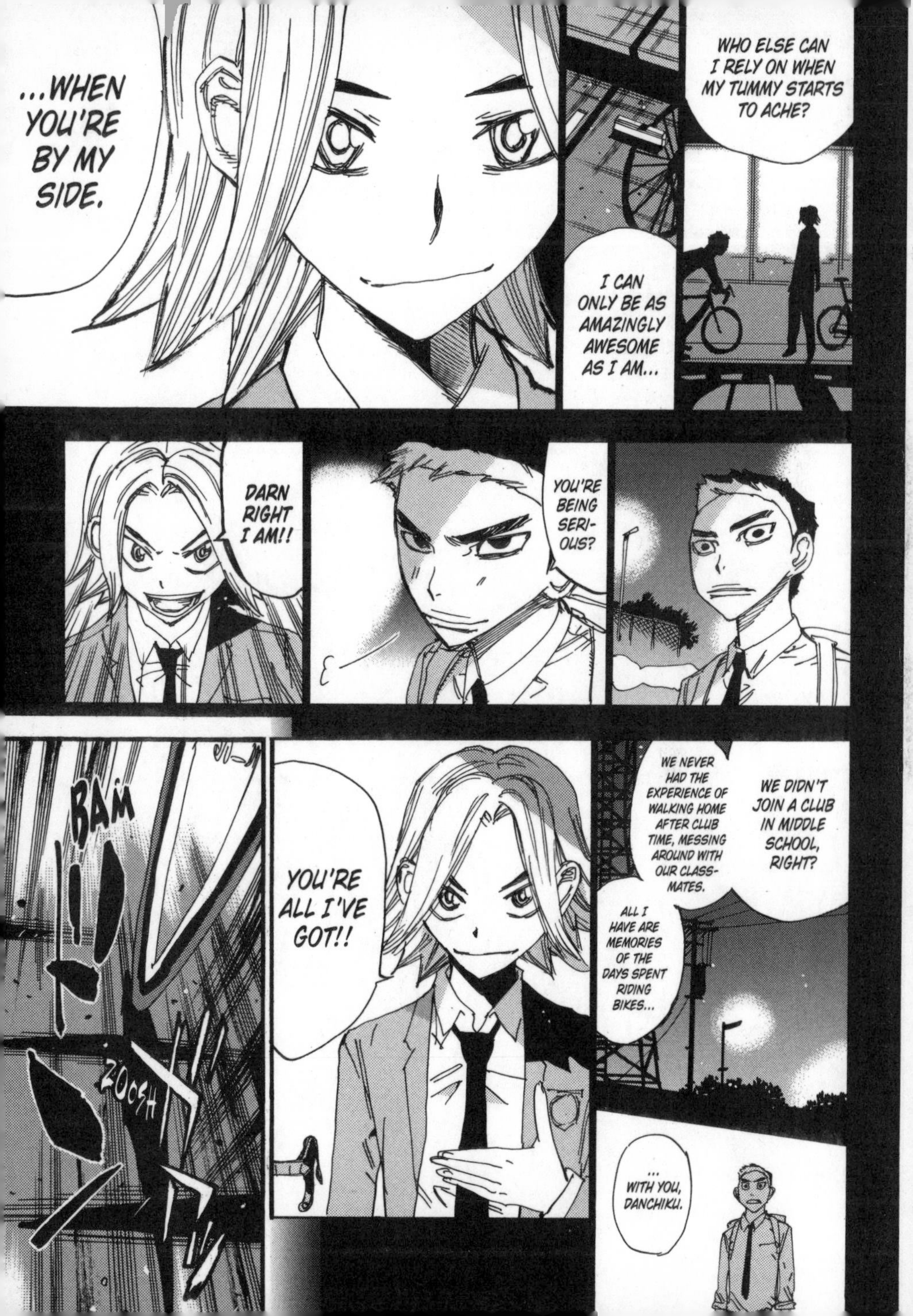
WHO ELSE CAN I RELY ON WHEN MY TUMMY STARTS TO ACHE?
I CAN ONLY BE AS AMAZINGLY AWESOME AS I AM...
...WHEN YOU'RE BY MY SIDE.
YOU'RE BEING SERI-OUS?
DARN RIGHT I AM!!
WE DIDN'T JOIN A CLUB IN MIDDLE SCHOOL, RIGHT?
WE NEVER HAD THE EXPERIENCE OF WALKING HOME AFTER CLUB TIME, MESSING AROUND WITH OUR CLASS-MATES.
ALL I HAVE ARE MEMORIES OF THE DAYS SPENT RIDING BIKES...
...WITH YOU, DANCHIKU.
YOU'RE ALL I'VE GOT!!
BAM
ZOOSH

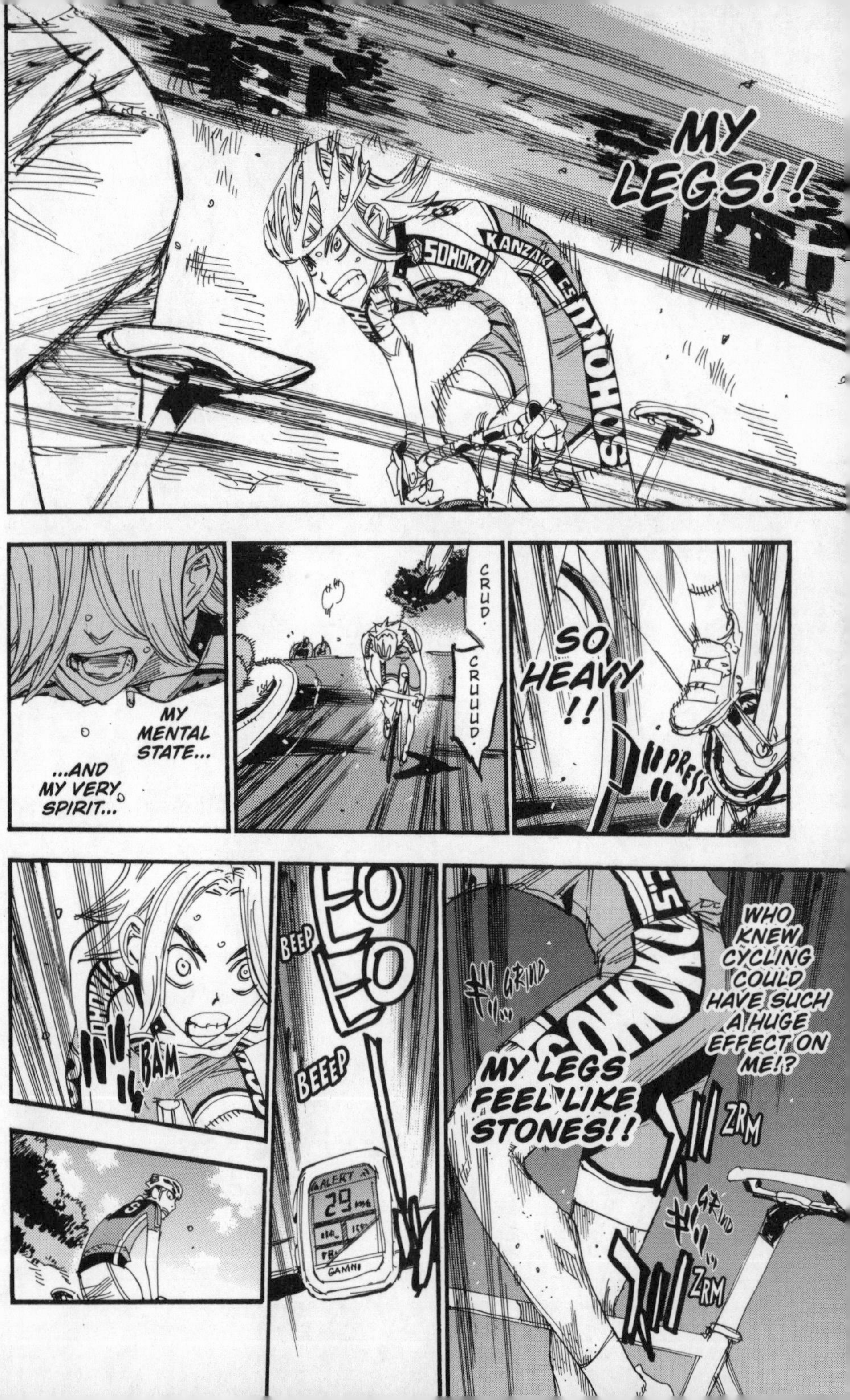
MY LEGS!!
SO HEAVY!!
PRESS
CRUD.
CRUUUD.
MY MENTAL STATE...
...AND MY VERY SPIRIT...
WHO KNEW CYCLING COULD HAVE SUCH A HUGE EFFECT ON ME!?
GRIND
MY LEGS FEEL LIKE STONES!!
ZRM
GRIND
ZRM
BEEP
BEEEP
ALERT
29
BAM

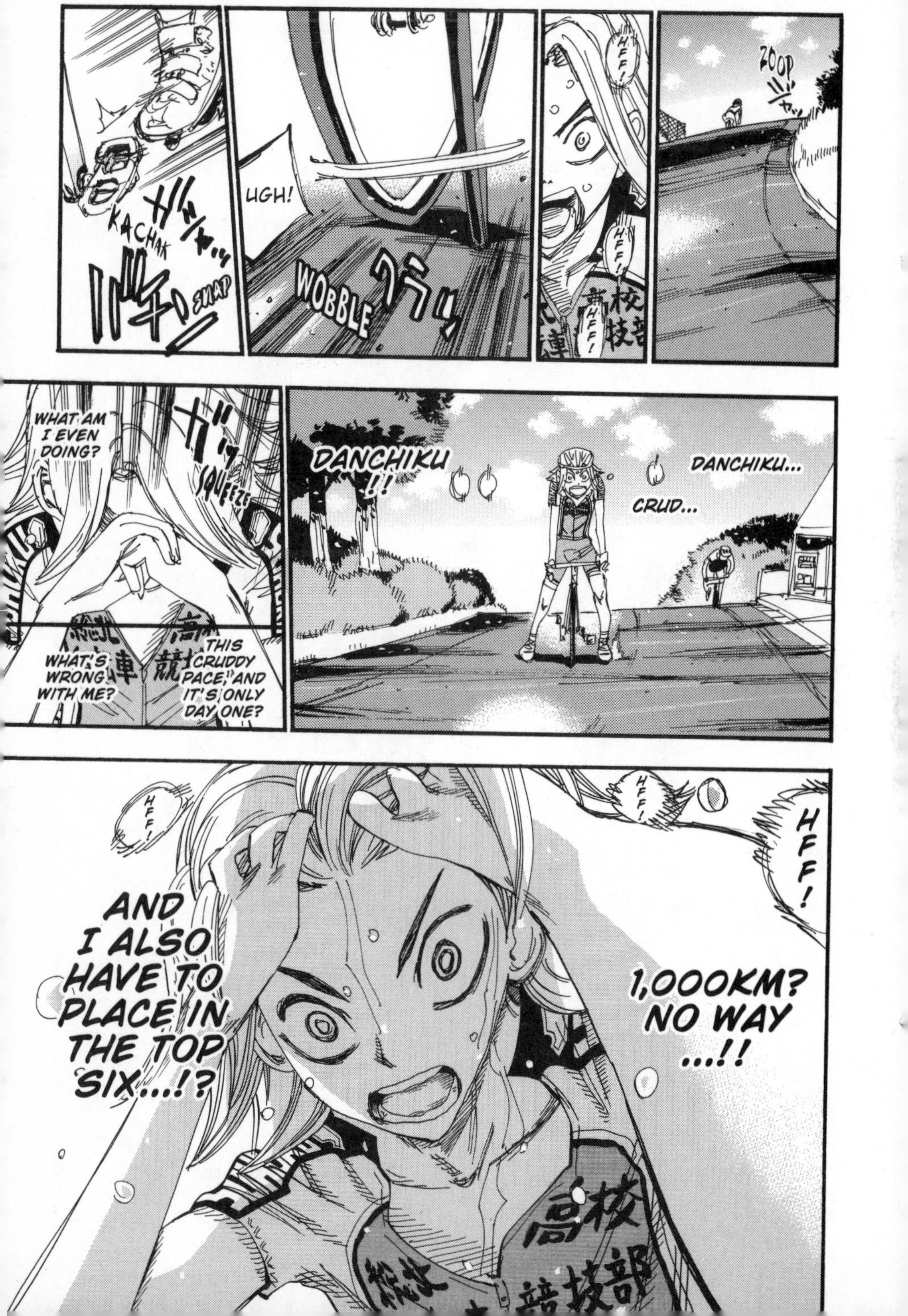
ZOOP
HFF!
HFF!
HFF!
UGH!
WOBBLE
KACHAK
SNAP
DANCHIKU...
CRUD...
DANCHIKU!!
WHAT AM I EVEN DOING?
SQUEEZE
THIS CRUDDY PACE, AND IT'S ONLY DAY ONE?
WHAT'S WRONG WITH ME?
HFF!
HFF!
1,000KM? NO WAY ...!!
AND I ALSO HAVE TO PLACE IN THE TOP SIX...!?
HFF!

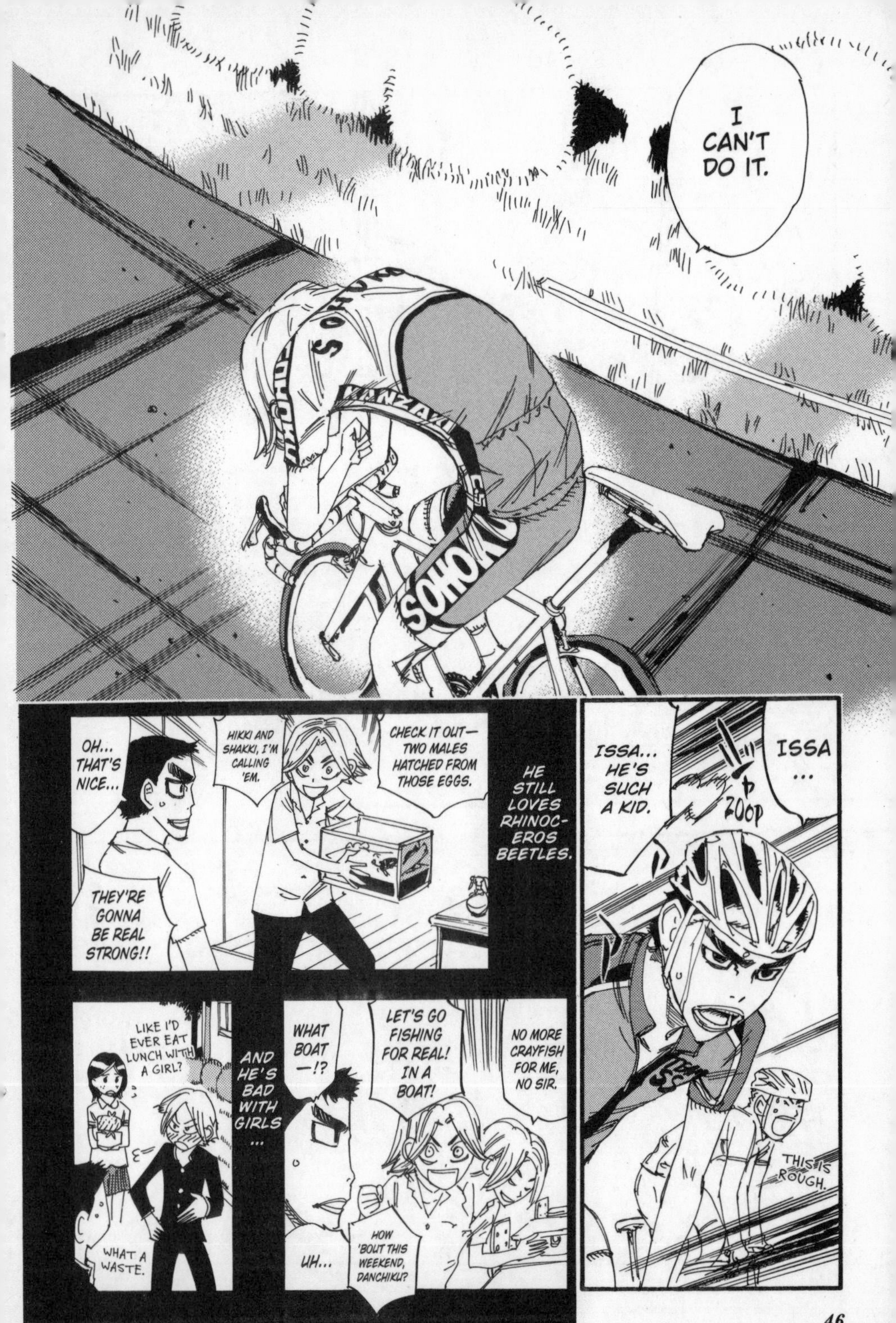
I CAN'T DO IT.
ISSA...
ISSA... HE'S SUCH A KID.
ZOOP
THIS IS ROUGH.
HE STILL LOVES RHINOCEROS BEETLES.
CHECK IT OUT— TWO MALES HATCHED FROM THOSE EGGS.
HIKKI AND SHAKKI, I'M CALLING 'EM.
OH... THAT'S NICE...
THEY'RE GONNA BE REAL STRONG!!
NO MORE CRAYFISH FOR ME, NO SIR.
LET'S GO FISHING FOR REAL! IN A BOAT!
WHAT BOAT —!?
HOW 'BOUT THIS WEEKEND, DANCHIKU?
UH...
AND HE'S BAD WITH GIRLS...
LIKE I'D EVER EAT LUNCH WITH A GIRL?
WHAT A WASTE.

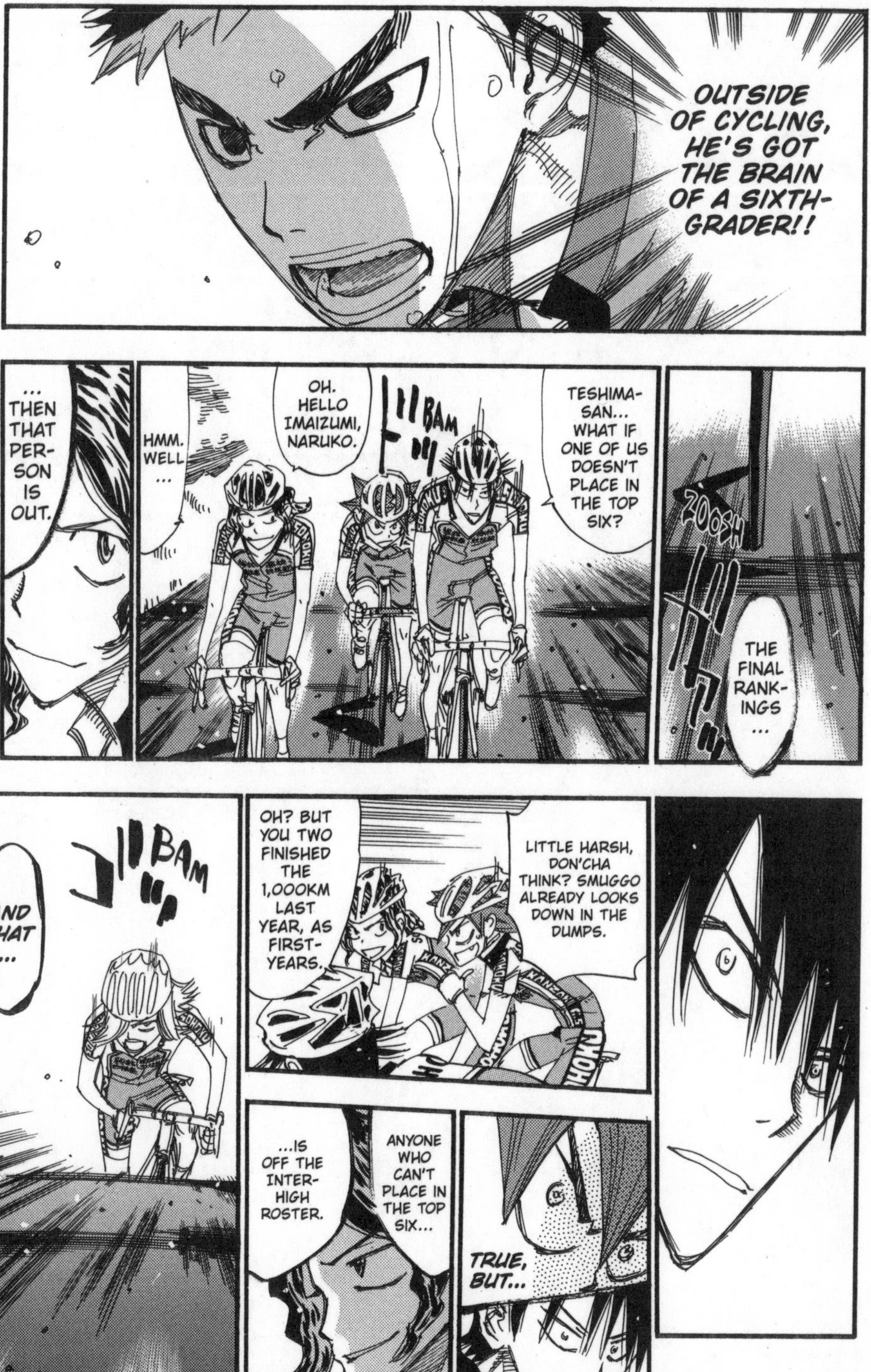
OUTSIDE OF CYCLING, HE'S GOT THE BRAIN OF A SIXTH-GRADER!!
ZOOSH
THE FINAL RANKINGS...
TESHIMA-SAN... WHAT IF ONE OF US DOESN'T PLACE IN THE TOP SIX?
BAM
OH. HELLO IMAIZUMI, NARUKO.
HMM. WELL...
...THEN THAT PERSON IS OUT.
LITTLE HARSH, DON'CHA THINK? SMUGGO ALREADY LOOKS DOWN IN THE DUMPS.
OH? BUT YOU TWO FINISHED THE 1,000KM LAST YEAR, AS FIRST-YEARS.
TRUE, BUT...
ANYONE WHO CAN'T PLACE IN THE TOP SIX...
...IS OFF THE INTER-HIGH ROSTER.
BAM
AND THAT...

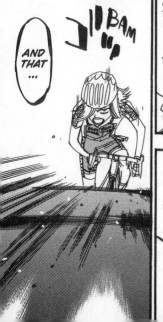

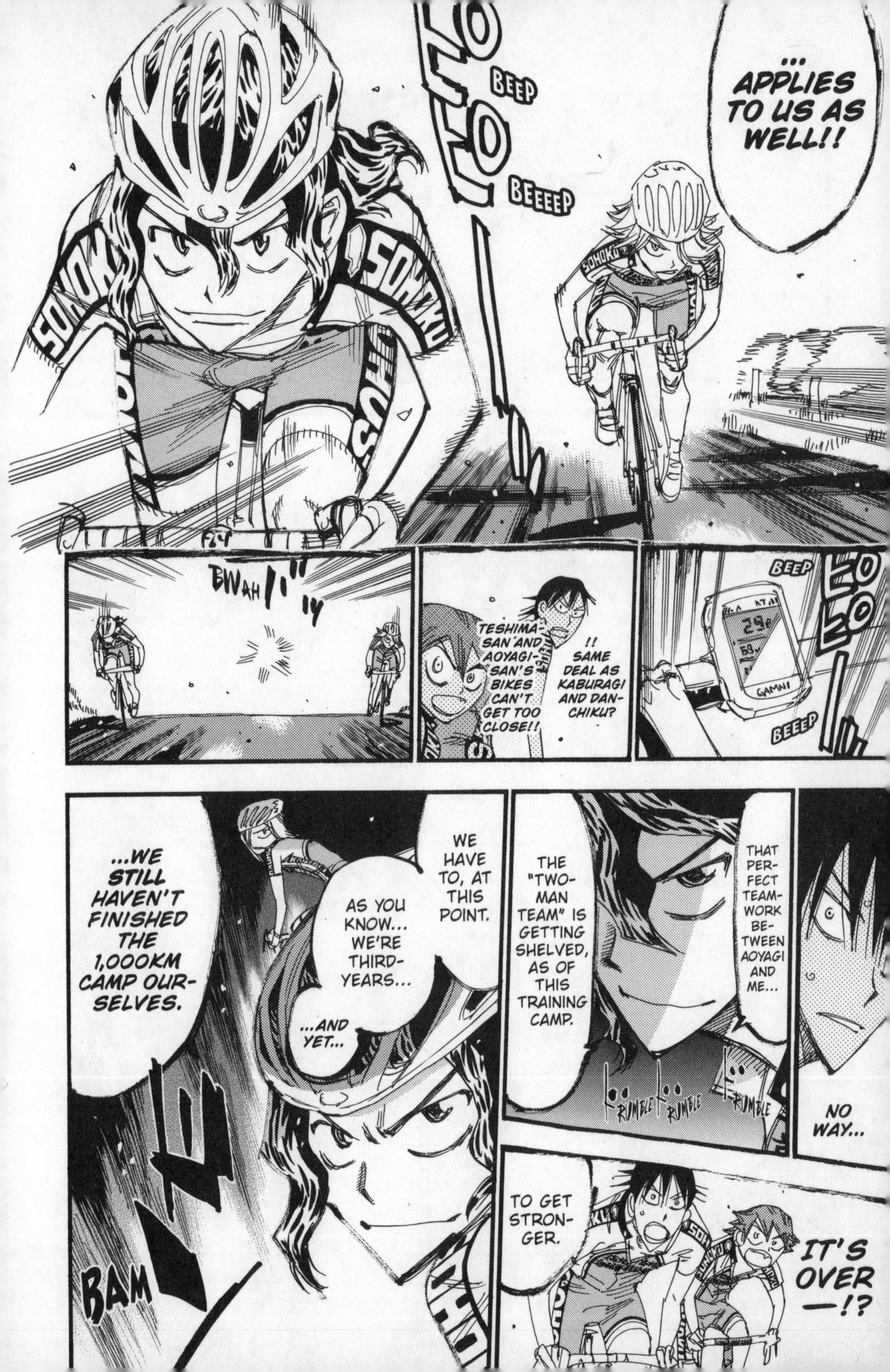
... APPLIES TO US AS WELL!!
BEEP
BEEEEP
BEEP
BEEEP
!! SAME DEAL AS KABURAGI AND DANCHIKU?
TESHIMA-SAN AND AOYAGI-SAN'S BIKES CAN'T GET TOO CLOSE!!
BWAH
THAT PERFECT TEAMWORK BETWEEN AOYAGI AND ME...
NO WAY...
THE "TWO-MAN TEAM" IS GETTING SHELVED, AS OF THIS TRAINING CAMP.
RUMBLE RUMBLE RUMBLE
IT'S OVER—!?
TO GET STRONGER.
WE HAVE TO, AT THIS POINT.
AS YOU KNOW... WE'RE THIRD-YEARS...
...AND YET...
...WE STILL HAVEN'T FINISHED THE 1,000KM CAMP OURSELVES.
BAM

RIDE.281 KABURAGI, ALL ALONE

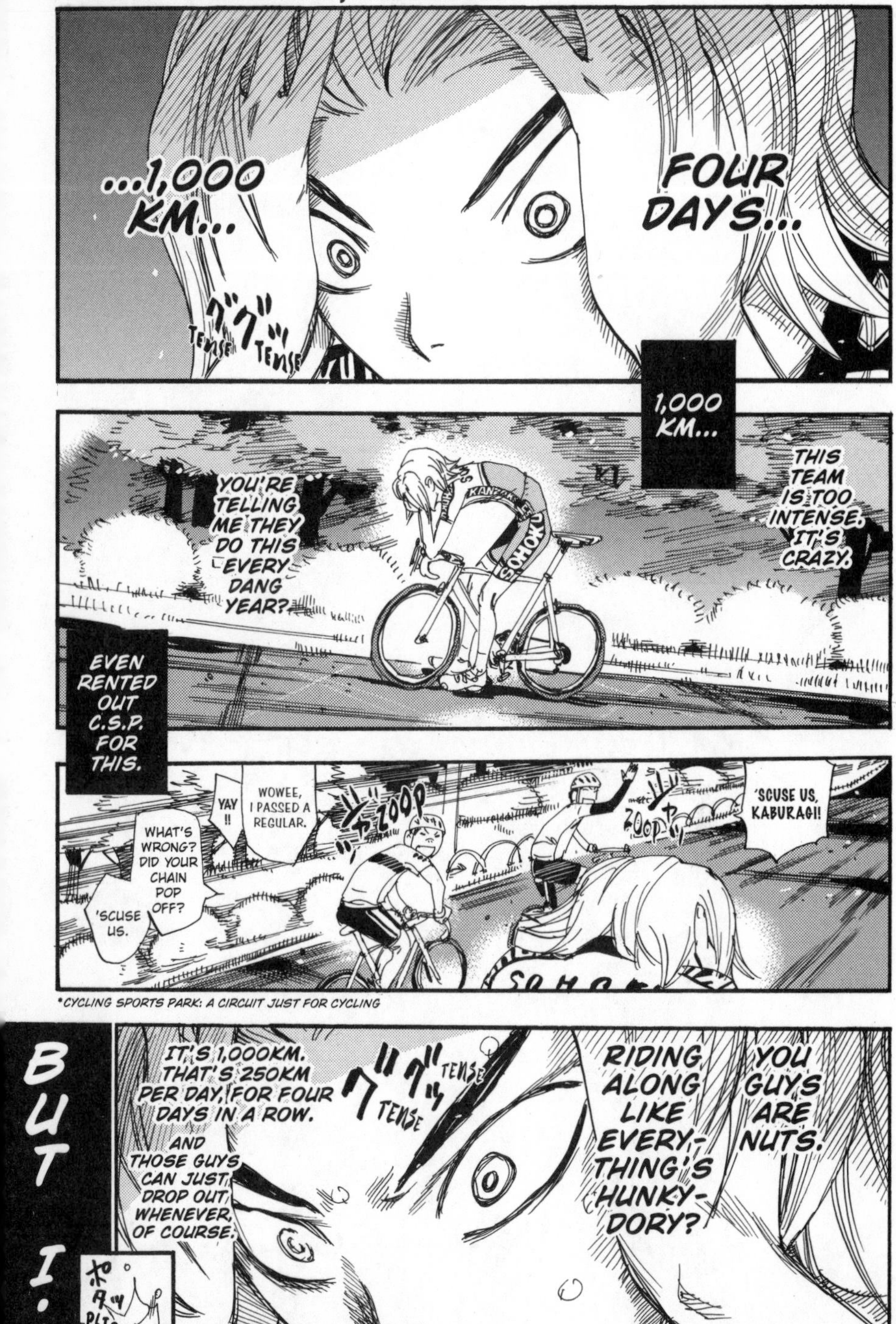
FOUR DAYS...
...1,000 KM...
TENSE TENSE
1,000 KM...
THIS TEAM IS TOO INTENSE. IT'S CRAZY.
YOU'RE TELLING ME THEY DO THIS EVERY DANG YEAR?
EVEN RENTED OUT C.S.P. FOR THIS.
'SCUSE US, KABURAGI!
ZOOP
WOWEE, I PASSED A REGULAR.
YAY!!
ZOOP
WHAT'S WRONG? DID YOUR CHAIN POP OFF?
'SCUSE US.
YOU GUYS ARE NUTS.
RIDING ALONG LIKE EVERYTHING'S HUNKY-DORY?
TENSE TENSE
IT'S 1,000KM. THAT'S 250KM PER DAY, FOR FOUR DAYS IN A ROW.
AND THOSE GUYS CAN JUST DROP OUT WHENEVER, OF COURSE.
BUT I...
PLIP

*CYCLING SPORTS PARK: A CIRCUIT JUST FOR CYCLING

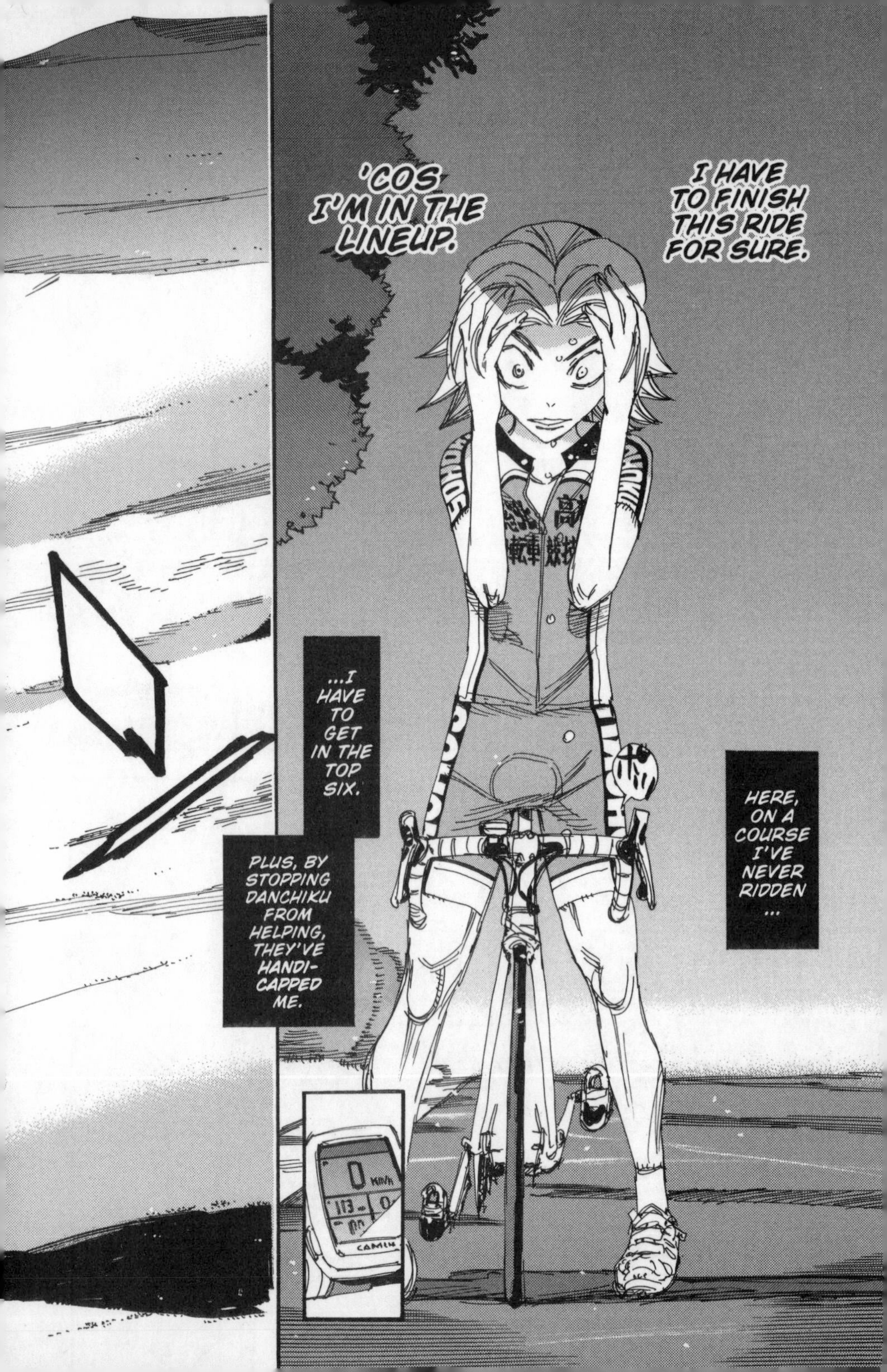
I HAVE TO FINISH THIS RIDE FOR SURE.
'COS I'M IN THE LINEUP.
HERE, ON A COURSE I'VE NEVER RIDDEN...
...I HAVE TO GET IN THE TOP SIX.
PLUS, BY STOPPING DANCHIKU FROM HELPING, THEY'VE HANDI-CAPPED ME.

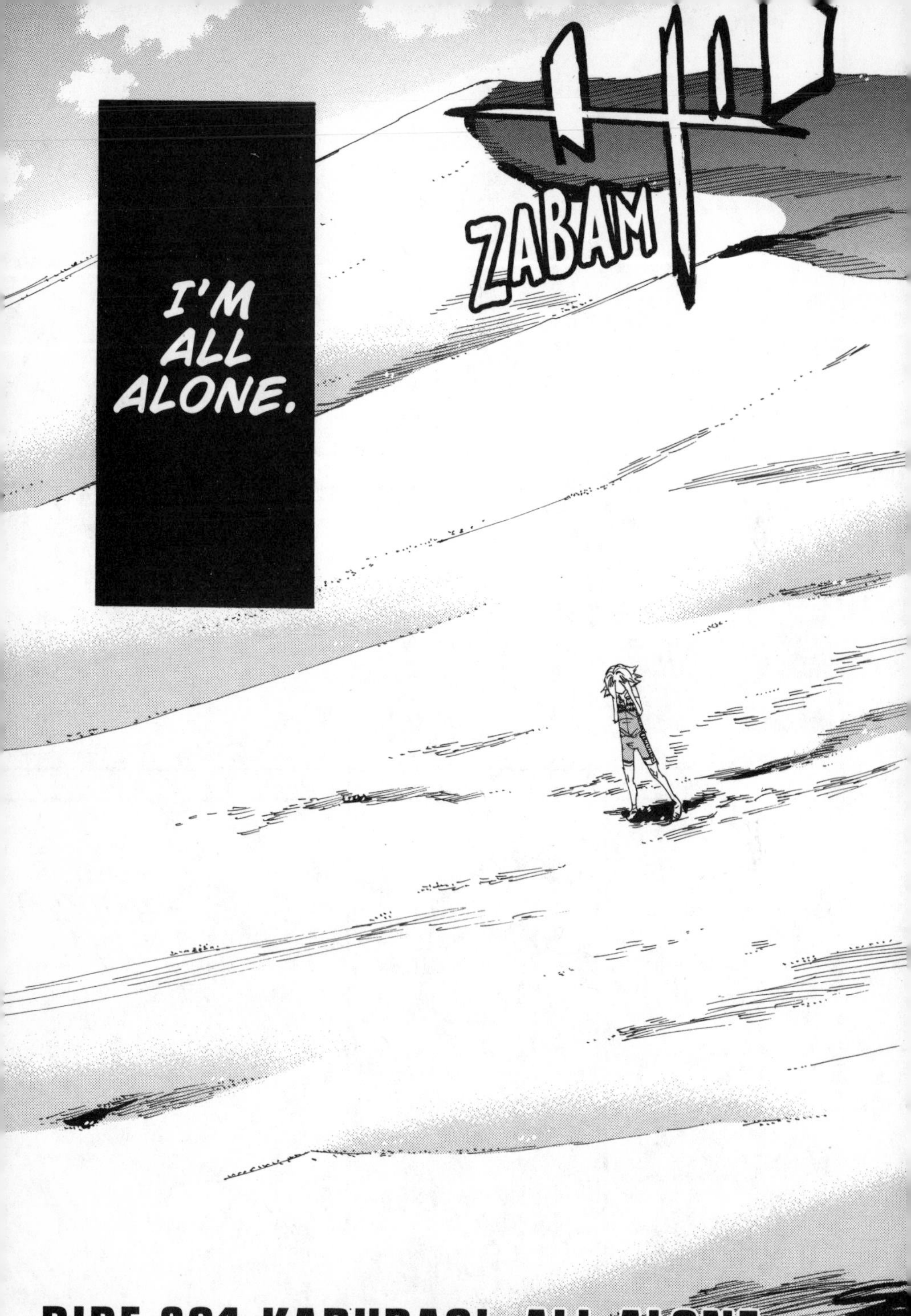
I'M ALL ALONE.
ZABAM

RIDE.281 KABURAGI, ALL ALONE

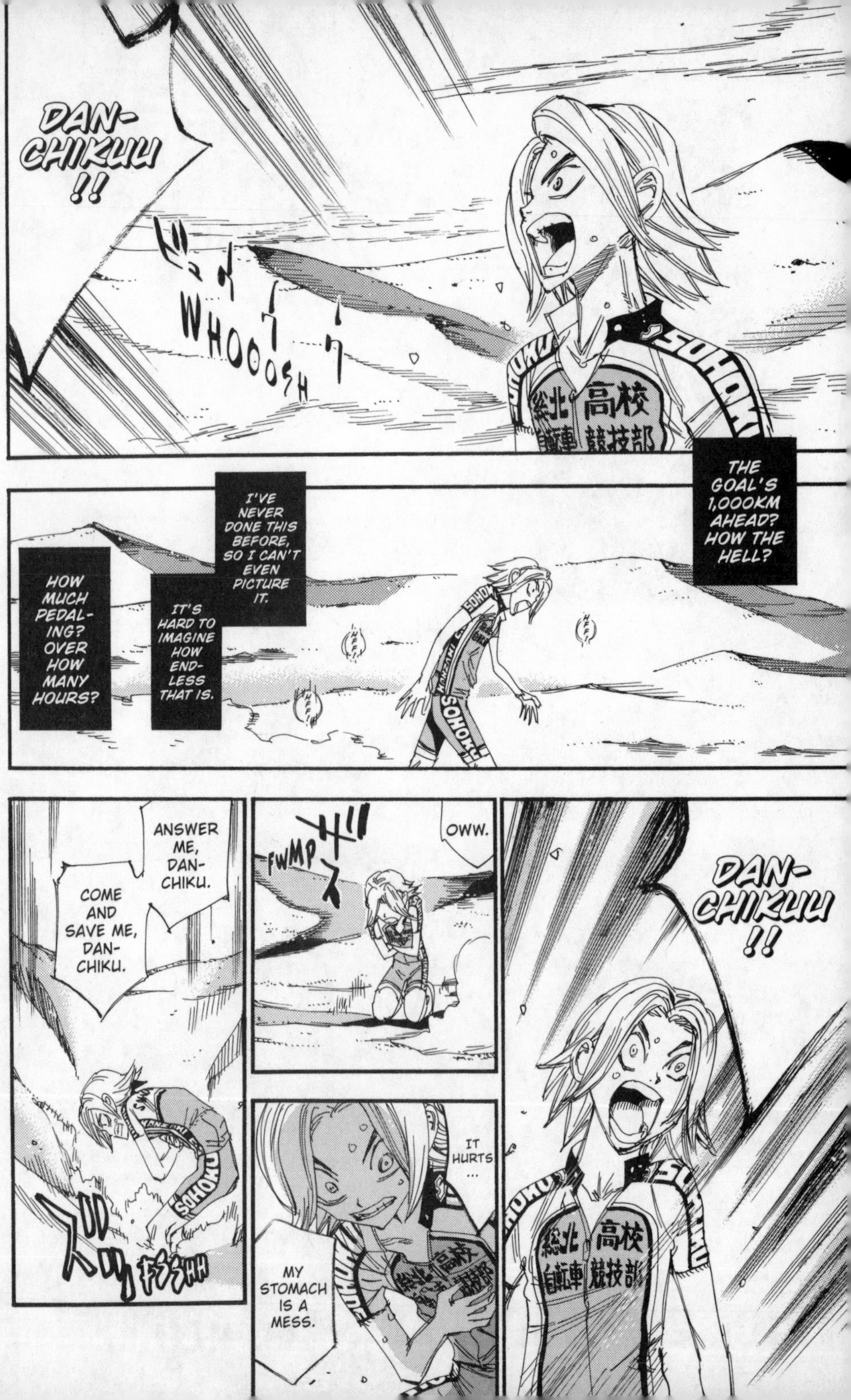
DAN-CHIKUU!!
WHOOOSH
THE GOAL'S 1,000KM AHEAD? HOW THE HELL?
I'VE NEVER DONE THIS BEFORE, SO I CAN'T EVEN PICTURE IT.
IT'S HARD TO IMAGINE HOW END-LESS THAT IS.
HOW MUCH PEDAL-ING? OVER HOW MANY HOURS?
DAN-CHIKUU!!
OWW.
FWMP
IT HURTS...
MY STOMACH IS A MESS.
ANSWER ME, DAN-CHIKU.
COME AND SAVE ME, DAN-CHIKU.
FSSHH

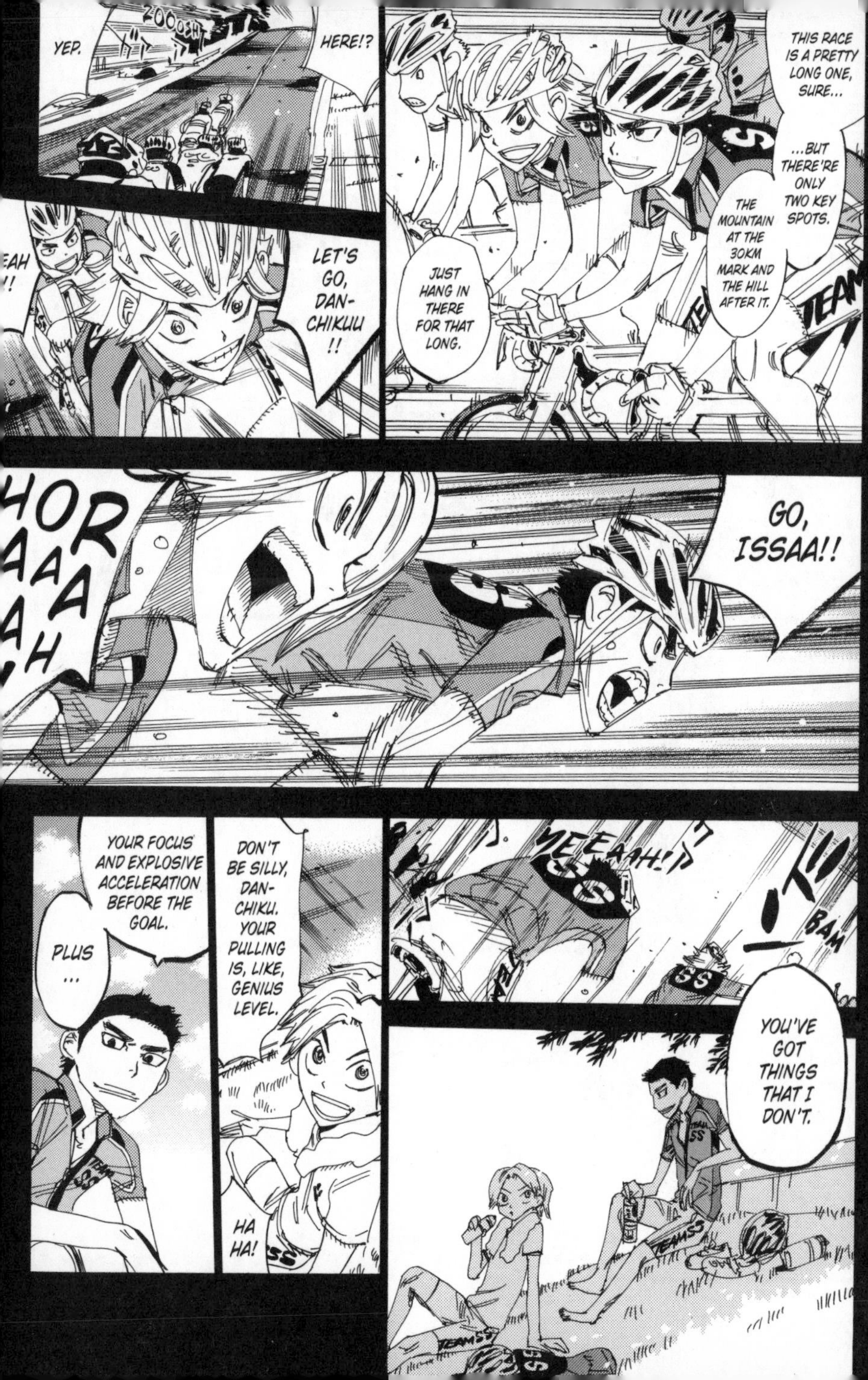

THIS RACE IS A PRETTY LONG ONE, SURE...
...BUT THERE'RE ONLY TWO KEY SPOTS.
THE MOUNTAIN AT THE 30KM MARK AND THE HILL AFTER IT.
JUST HANG IN THERE FOR THAT LONG.
ZOOOSH
HERE!?
YEP.
LET'S GO, DAN-CHIKUU!!
GO, ISSAA!!
YEEAAH!!
BAM
YOU'VE GOT THINGS THAT I DON'T.
DON'T BE SILLY, DAN-CHIKU. YOUR PULLING IS, LIKE, GENIUS LEVEL.
HA HA!
YOUR FOCUS AND EXPLOSIVE ACCELERATION BEFORE THE GOAL.
PLUS ...

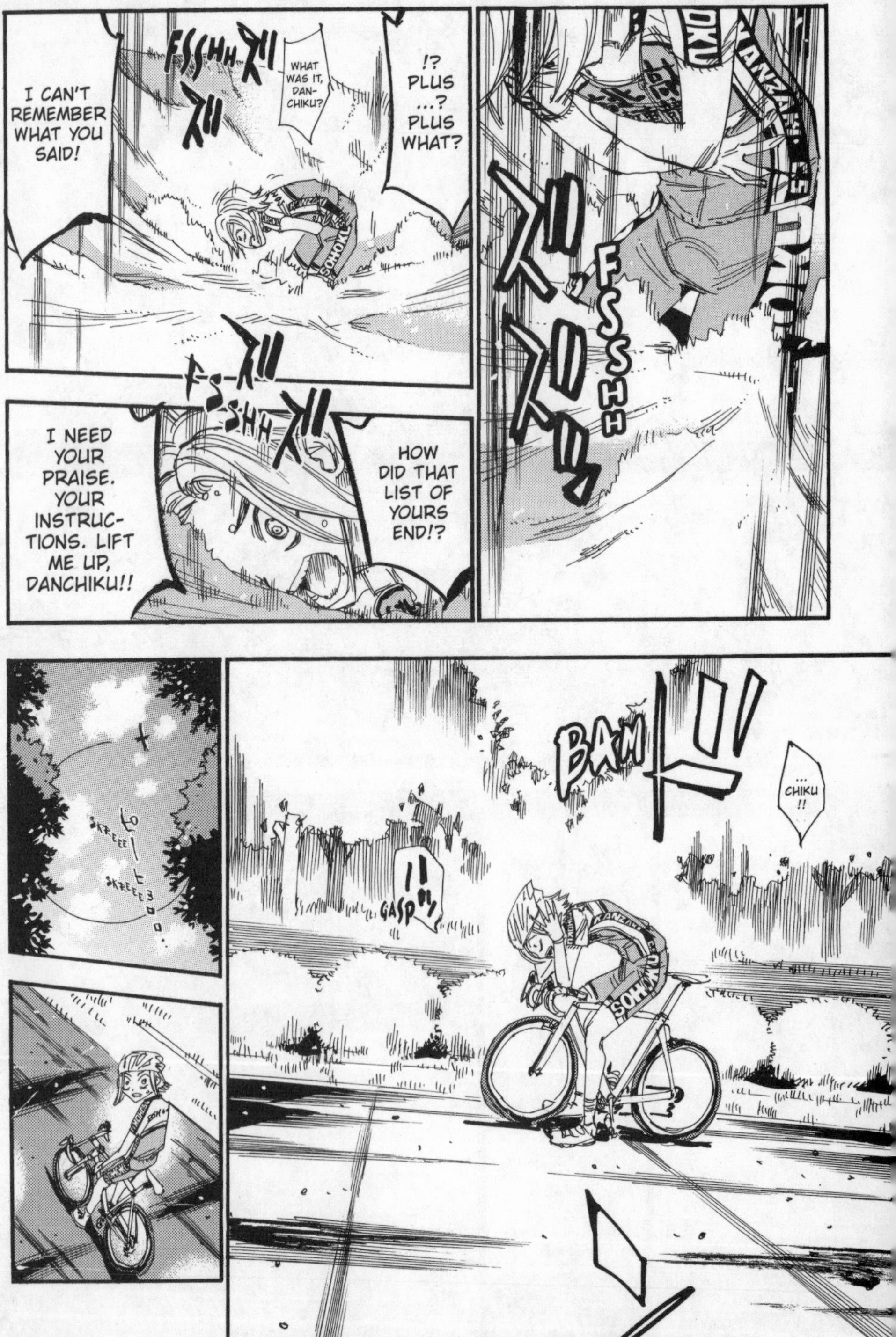
FSSHH
!? PLUS ...? PLUS WHAT?
WHAT WAS IT, DAN-CHIKU?
FSSHH
I CAN'T REMEMBER WHAT YOU SAID!
HOW DID THAT LIST OF YOURS END!?
F-S-SHH
I NEED YOUR PRAISE. YOUR INSTRUC-TIONS. LIFT ME UP, DANCHIKU!!
BAM!!
...CHIKU!!
GASP
SKREEE
SKREEE

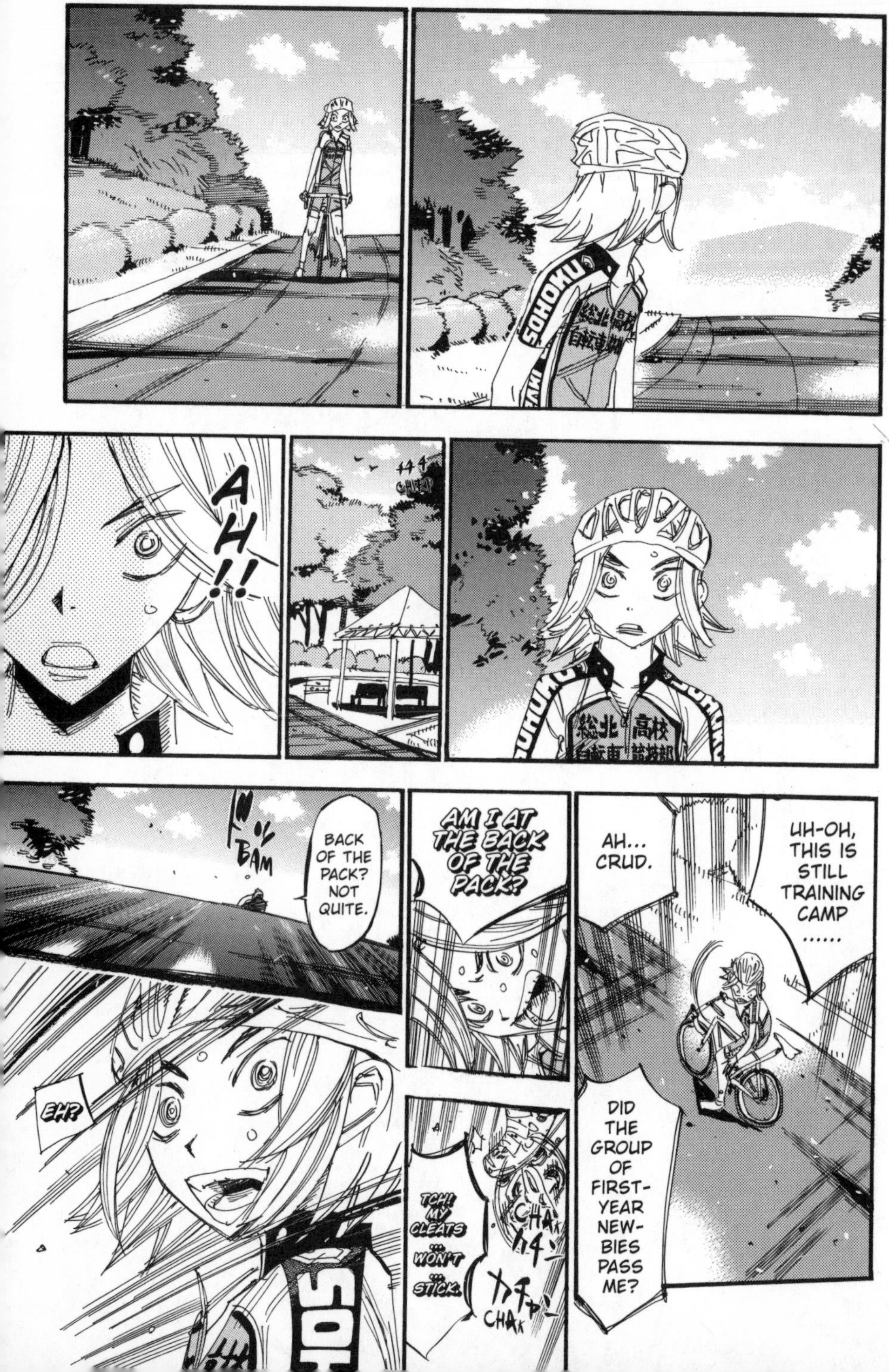
CHIRP
AH!!
UH-OH, THIS IS STILL TRAINING CAMP ......
AH... CRUD.
DID THE GROUP OF FIRST-YEAR NEW-BIES PASS ME?
AM I AT THE BACK OF THE PACK?
CHAK
TCH! MY CLEATS ... WON'T ... STICK.
CHAK
BAM
BACK OF THE PACK? NOT QUITE.
EH?

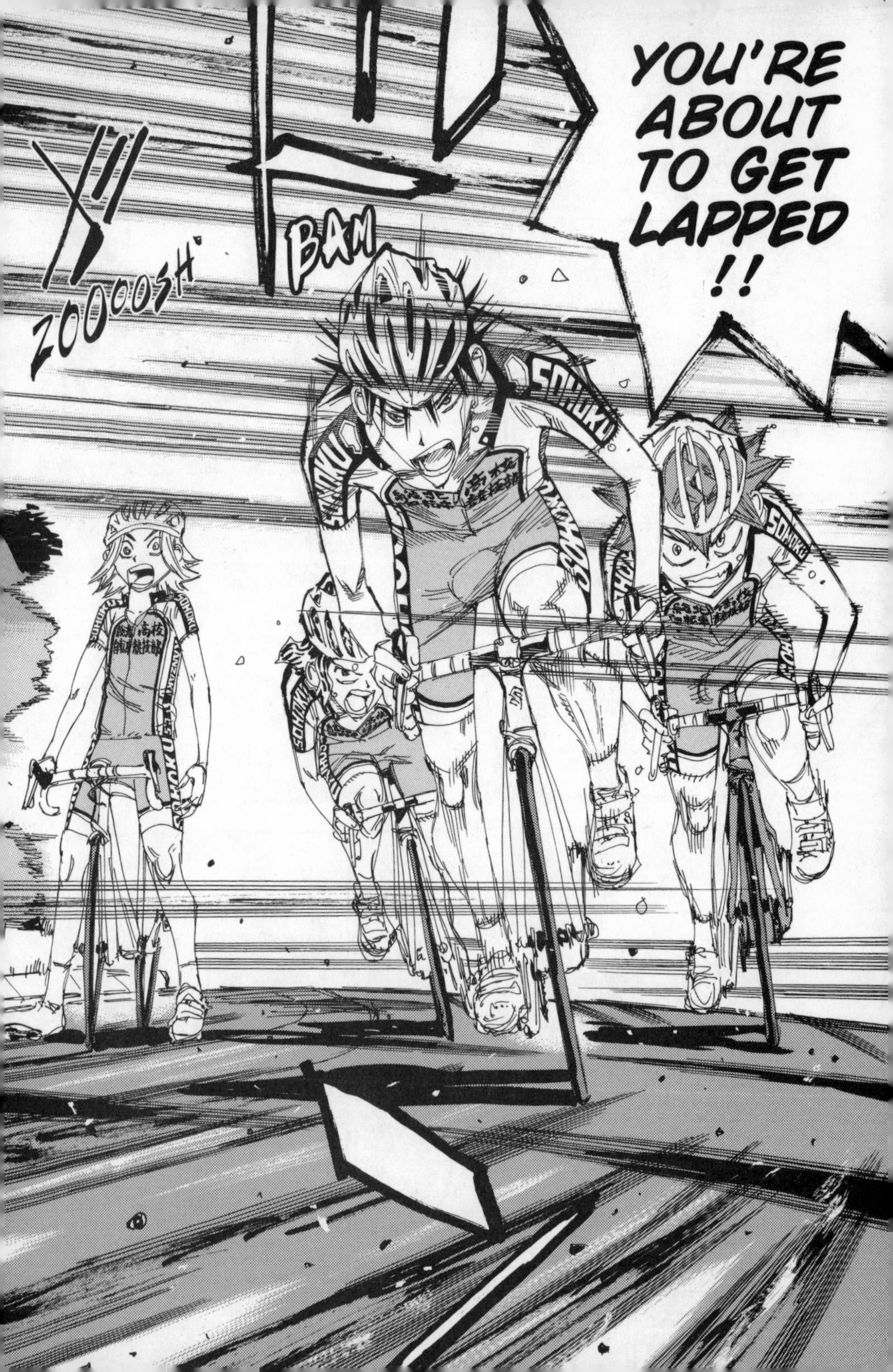
YOU'RE ABOUT TO GET LAPPED !!
BAM
ZOOOOSH

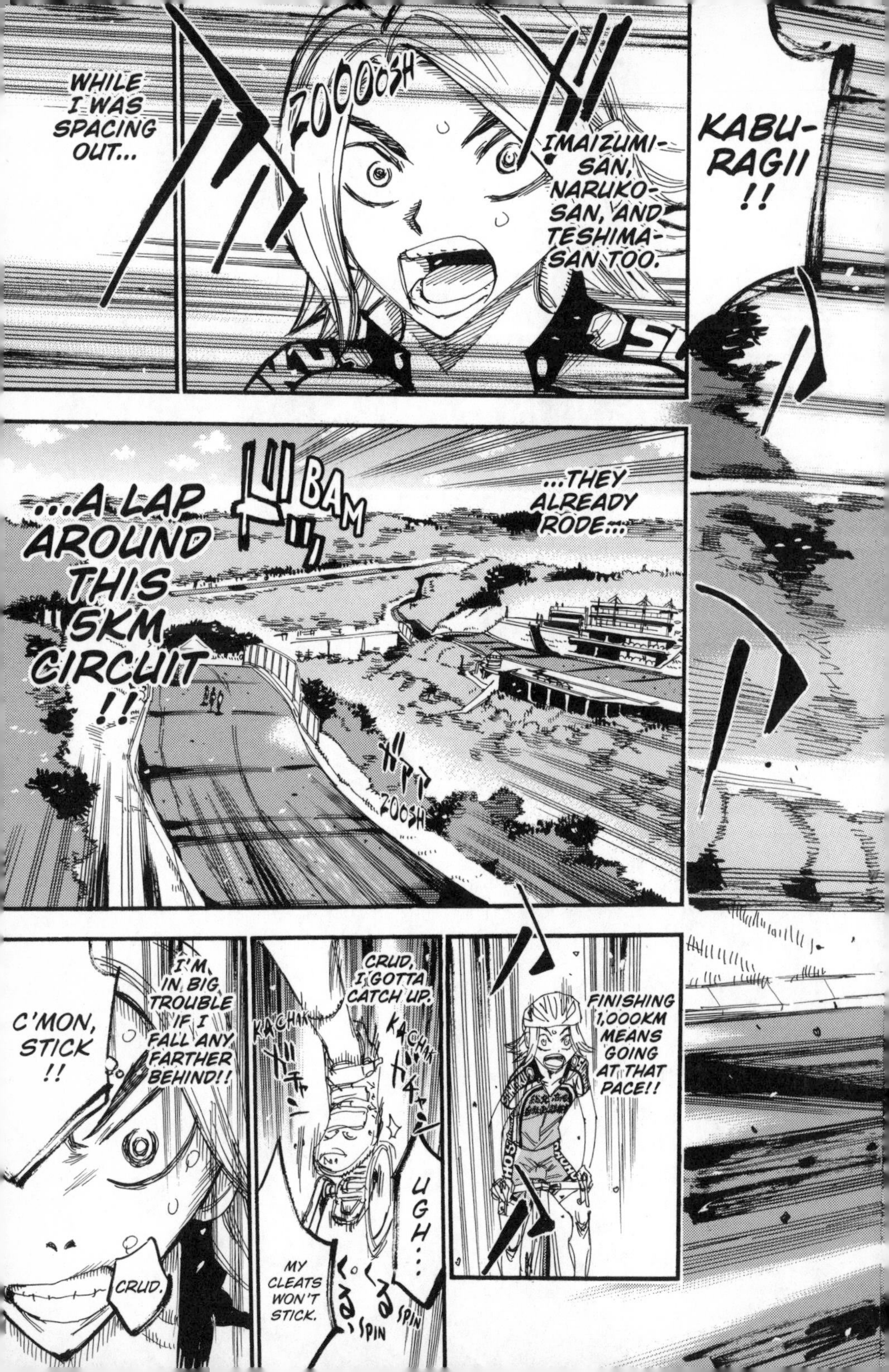
KABURAGI!!
ZOOOOSH
IMAIZUMI-SAN, NARUKO-SAN, AND TESHIMA-SAN TOO.
WHILE I WAS SPACING OUT...
BAM
...THEY ALREADY RODE...
...A LAP AROUND THIS 5KM CIRCUIT!!
ZOOSH
FINISHING 1,000KM MEANS GOING AT THAT PACE!!
CRUD, I GOTTA CATCH UP.
KACHAK
KACHAK
UGH...
MY CLEATS WON'T STICK.
SPIN
SPIN
I'M IN BIG TROUBLE IF I FALL ANY FARTHER BEHIND!!
C'MON, STICK!!
CRUD.

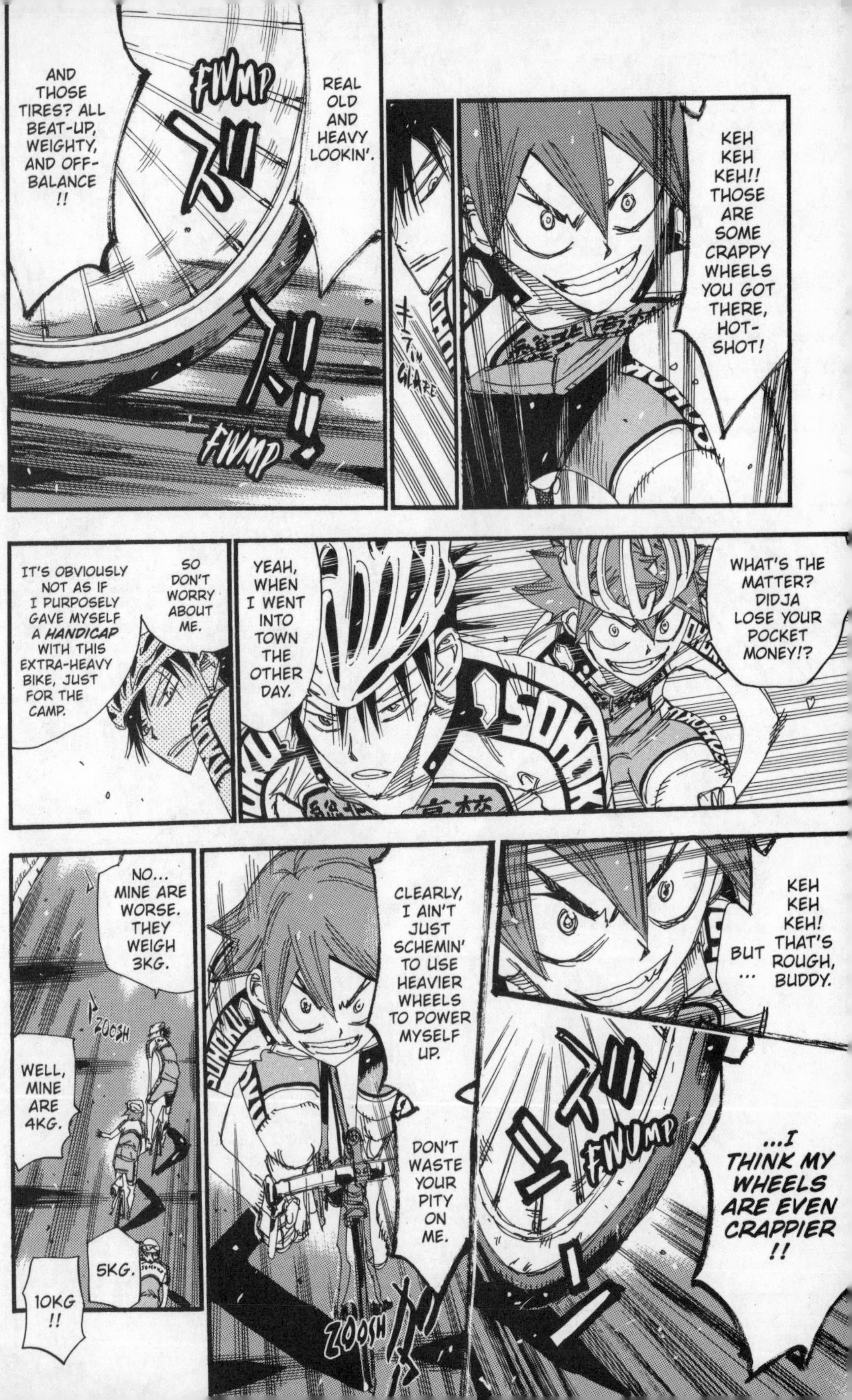
KEH KEH KEH!! THOSE ARE SOME CRAPPY WHEELS YOU GOT THERE, HOT-SHOT!
GLARE
REAL OLD AND HEAVY LOOKIN'.
AND THOSE TIRES? ALL BEAT-UP, WEIGHTY, AND OFF-BALANCE!!
FWMP
FWMP
WHAT'S THE MATTER? DIDJA LOSE YOUR POCKET MONEY!?
YEAH, WHEN I WENT INTO TOWN THE OTHER DAY.
SO DON'T WORRY ABOUT ME.
IT'S OBVIOUSLY NOT AS IF I PURPOSELY GAVE MYSELF A *HANDICAP* WITH THIS EXTRA-HEAVY BIKE, JUST FOR THE CAMP.
KEH KEH KEH! THAT'S ROUGH, BUDDY.
BUT...
...I THINK MY WHEELS ARE EVEN CRAPPIER!!
FWUMP
CLEARLY, I AIN'T JUST SCHEMIN' TO USE HEAVIER WHEELS TO POWER MYSELF UP.
DON'T WASTE YOUR PITY ON ME.
ZOOSH
NO... MINE ARE WORSE. THEY WEIGH 3KG.
ZOOSH
WELL, MINE ARE 4KG.
5KG.
10KG!!

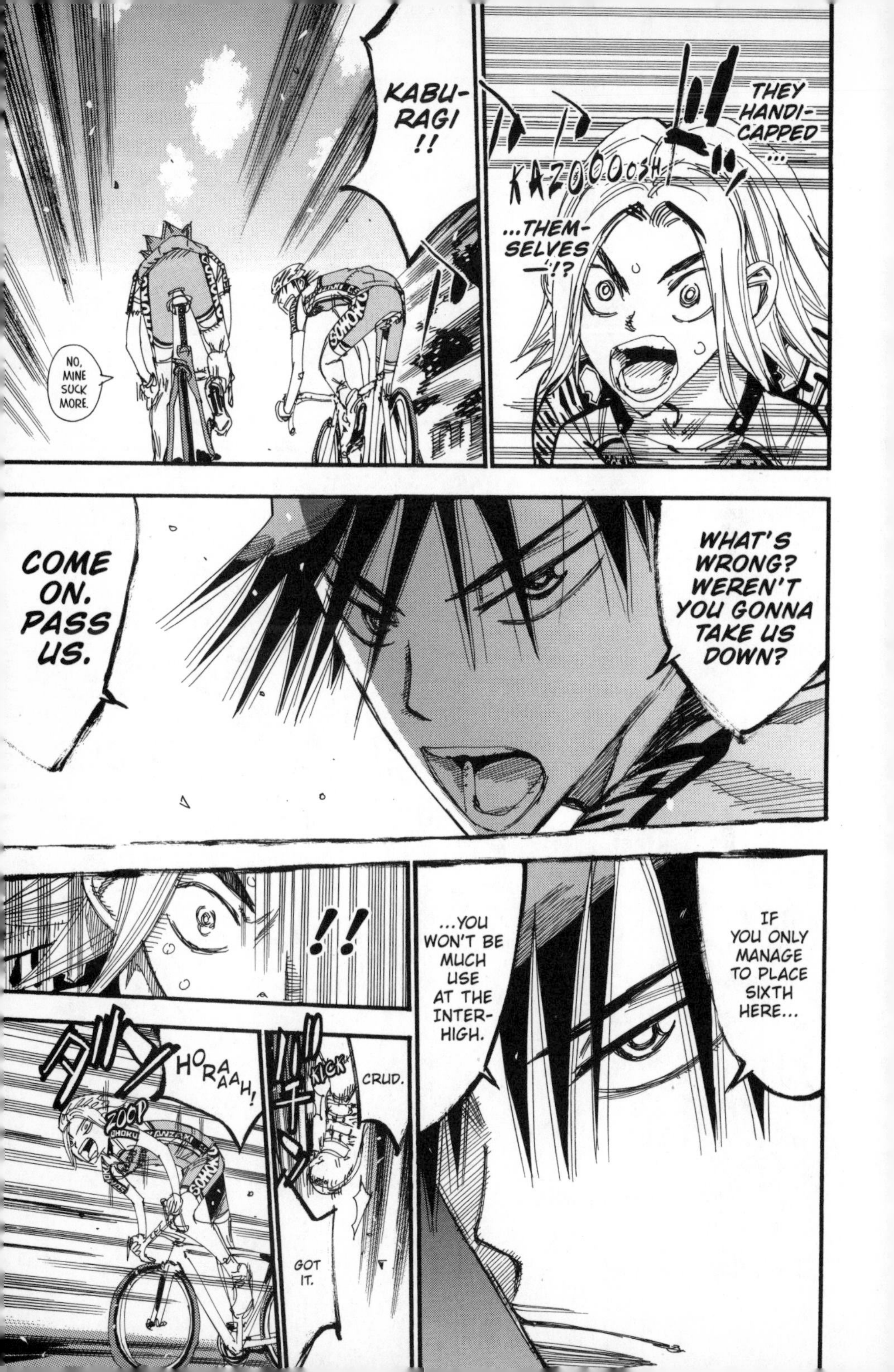
THEY HANDI-CAPPED...
KAZOOOOOSH
...THEM-SELVES—!?
KABU-RAGI!!
NO, MINE SUCK MORE.
WHAT'S WRONG? WEREN'T YOU GONNA TAKE US DOWN?
COME ON. PASS US.
IF YOU ONLY MANAGE TO PLACE SIXTH HERE...
...YOU WON'T BE MUCH USE AT THE INTER-HIGH.
!!
KICK
CRUD.
GOT IT.
HORAAAH!
ZOOP

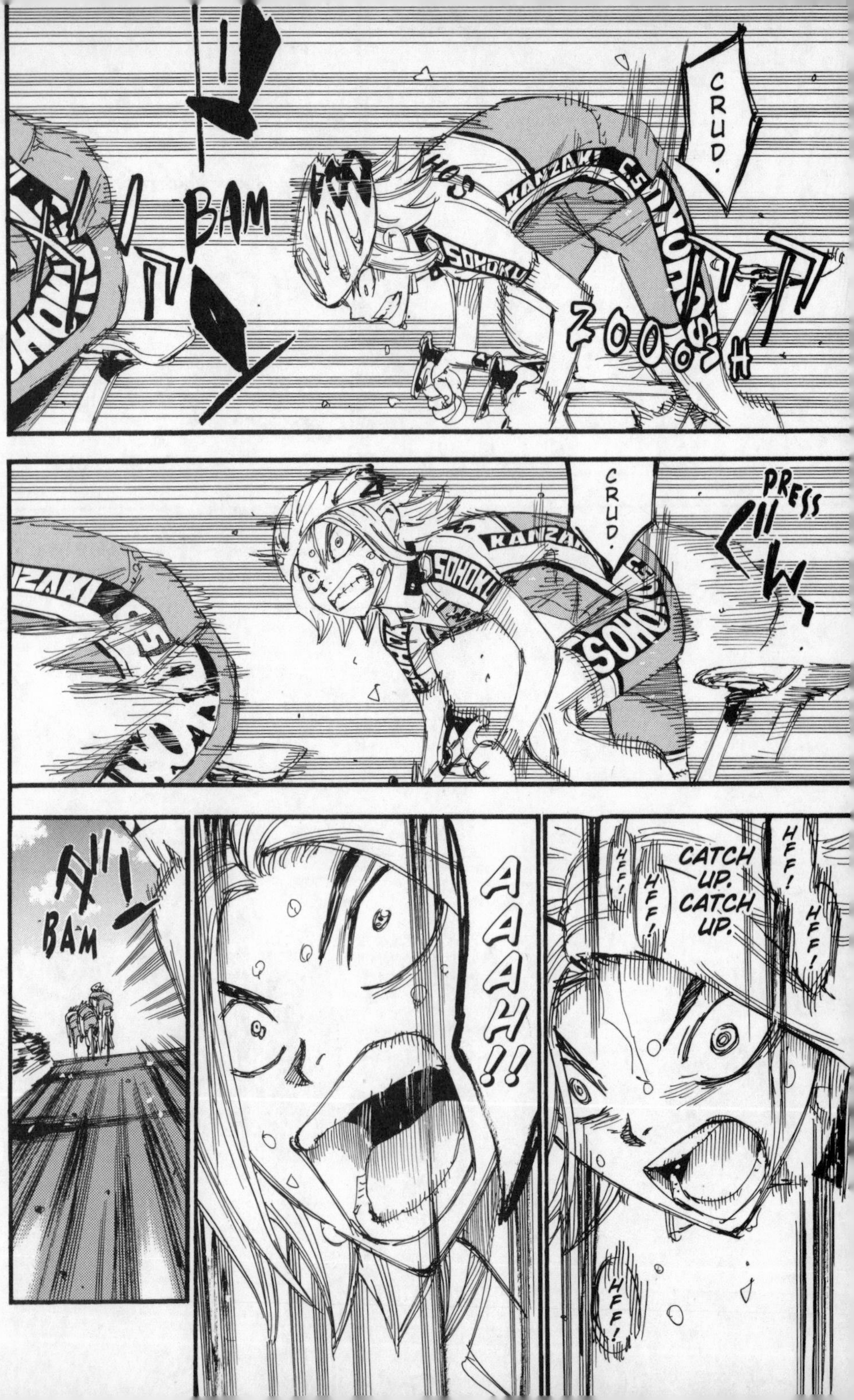
CRUD.
ZOOOSH
BAM
PRESS
CRUD.
HFF! HFF!
HFF! HFF!
CATCH UP. CATCH UP.
HFF!
AAAAH!!
BAM

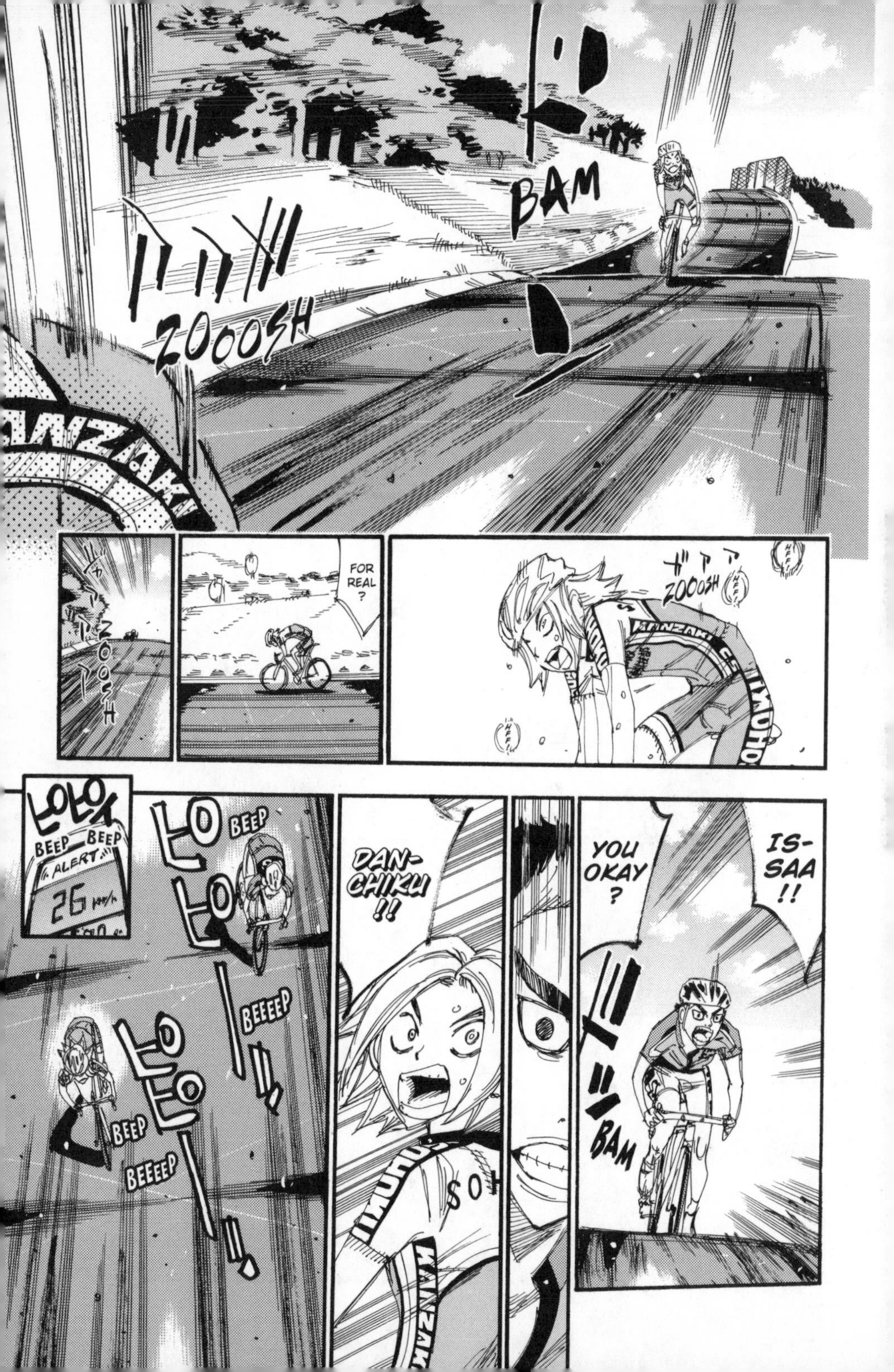
BAM
ZOOOSH
HEF!
ZOOOSH
HEF!
HEF!
FOR REAL?
ZOOOSH
IS-SAA!!
YOU OKAY?
BAM
DAN-CHIKU!!
BEEP BEEP
ALERT
26 km/h
BEEP
BEEEEP
BEEP
BEEEEP

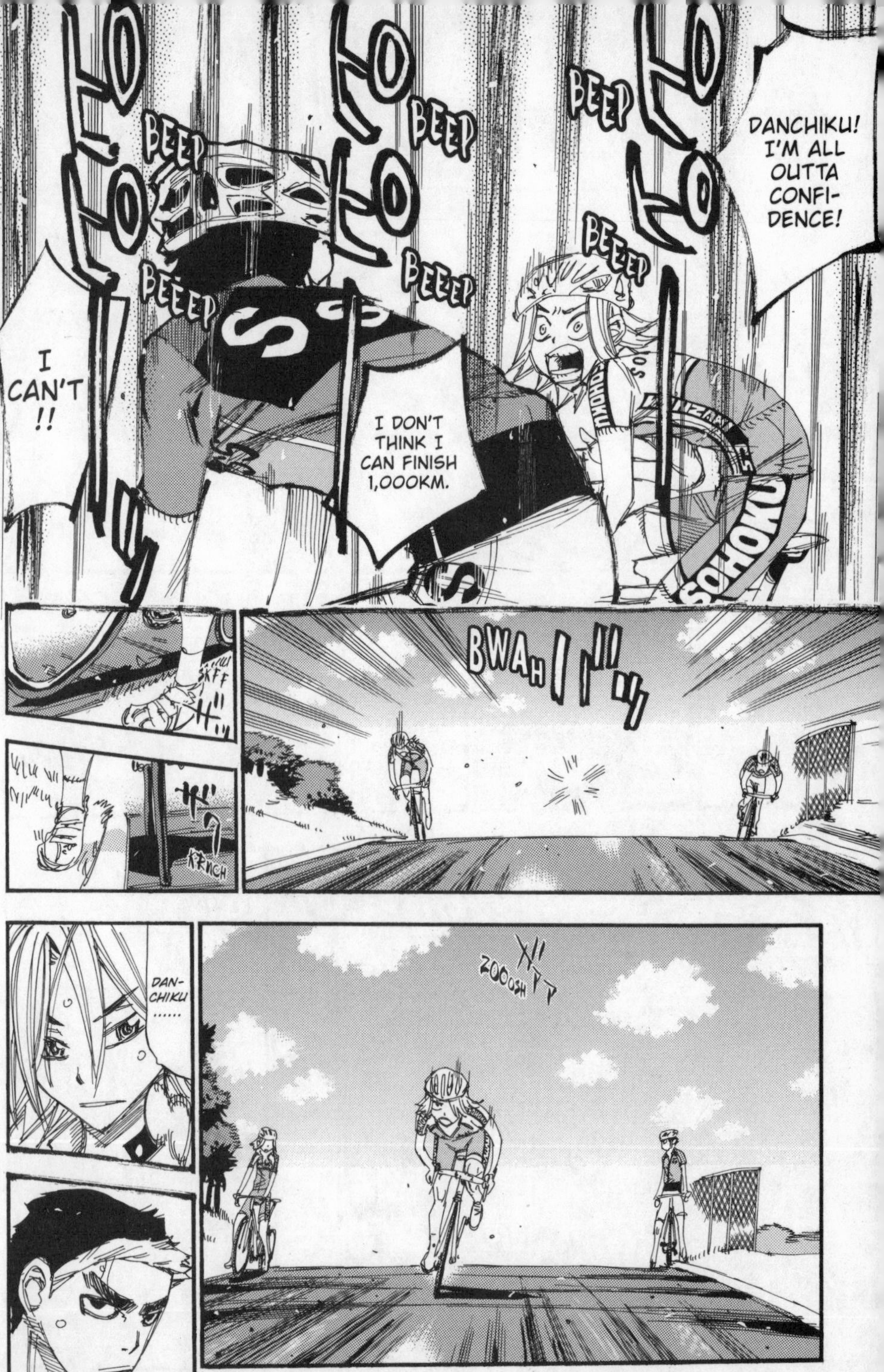

BEEP
BEEEP
DANCHIKU! I'M ALL OUTTA CONFIDENCE!
BEEP
BEEEP
BEEP
BEEEP
I DON'T THINK I CAN FINISH 1,000KM.
I CAN'T!!
BWAH
SKFF
KRNCH
ZOOOSH
DAN-CHIKU......

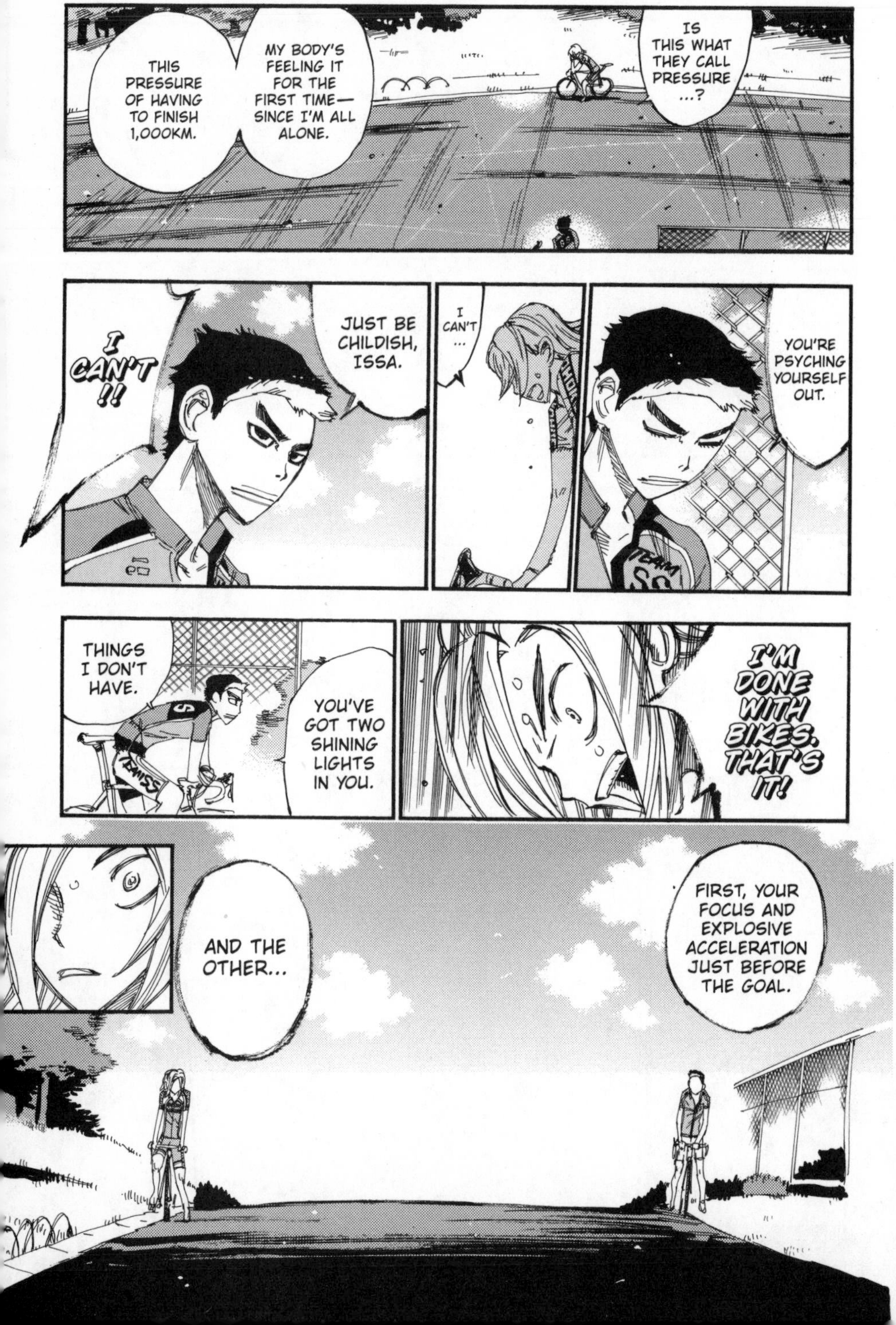
IS THIS WHAT THEY CALL PRESSURE ...?
MY BODY'S FEELING IT FOR THE FIRST TIME— SINCE I'M ALL ALONE.
THIS PRESSURE OF HAVING TO FINISH 1,000KM.
YOU'RE PSYCHING YOURSELF OUT.
I CAN'T ...
JUST BE CHILDISH, ISSA.
I CAN'T!!
I'M DONE WITH BIKES. THAT'S IT!
YOU'VE GOT TWO SHINING LIGHTS IN YOU.
THINGS I DON'T HAVE.
FIRST, YOUR FOCUS AND EXPLOSIVE ACCELERATION JUST BEFORE THE GOAL.
AND THE OTHER...

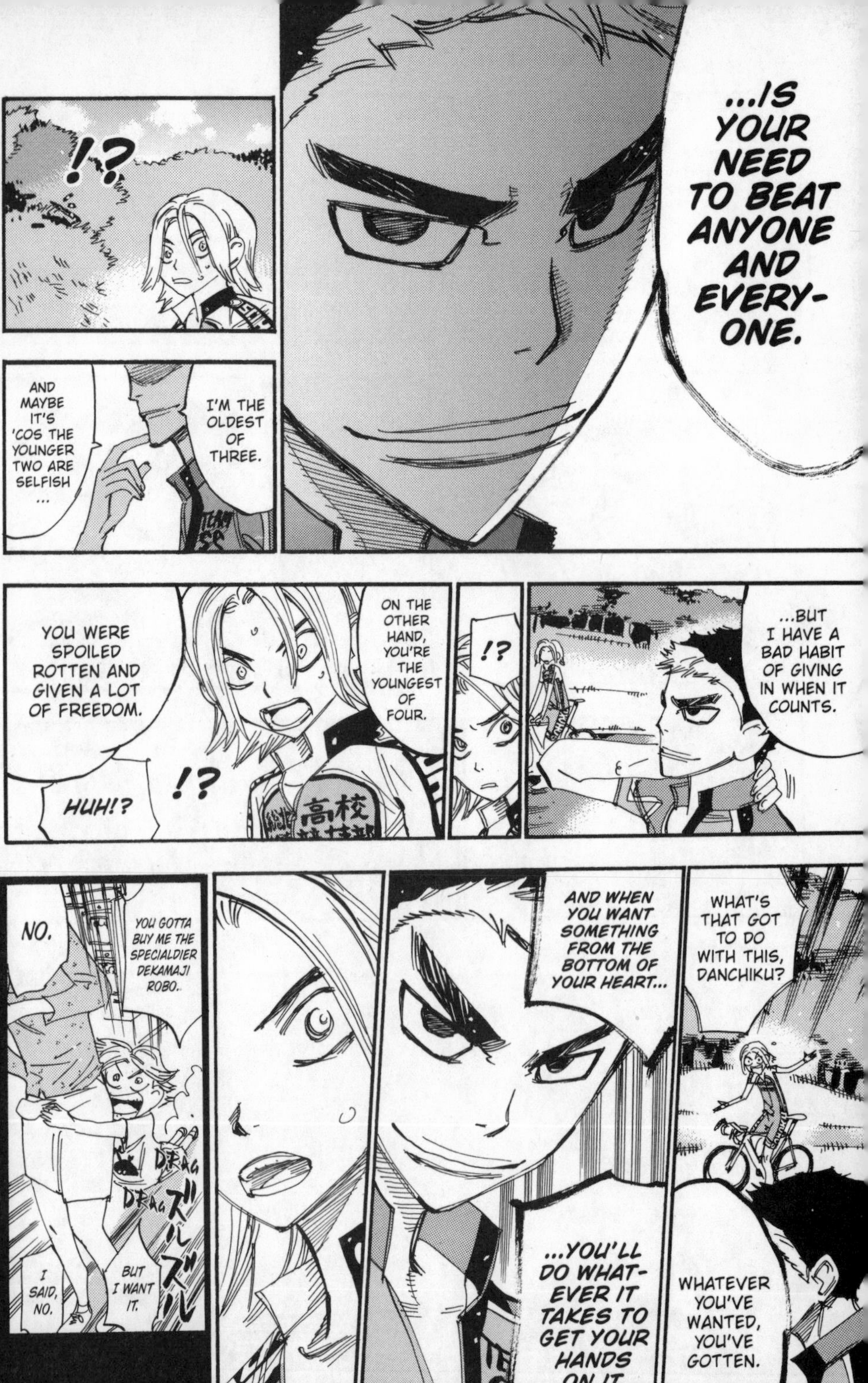
...IS YOUR NEED TO BEAT ANYONE AND EVERY-ONE.
!?
I'M THE OLDEST OF THREE.
AND MAYBE IT'S 'COS THE YOUNGER TWO ARE SELFISH ...
...BUT I HAVE A BAD HABIT OF GIVING IN WHEN IT COUNTS.
!?
ON THE OTHER HAND, YOU'RE THE YOUNGEST OF FOUR.
YOU WERE SPOILED ROTTEN AND GIVEN A LOT OF FREEDOM.
!?
HUH!?
WHAT'S THAT GOT TO DO WITH THIS, DANCHIKU?
WHATEVER YOU'VE WANTED, YOU'VE GOTTEN.
AND WHEN YOU WANT SOMETHING FROM THE BOTTOM OF YOUR HEART...
...YOU'LL DO WHATEVER IT TAKES TO GET YOUR HANDS ON IT.
YOU GOTTA BUY ME THE SPECIALDIER DEKAMAJI ROBO..
NO.
BUT I WANT IT.
I SAID, NO.
DRAG DRAG
ズルズル

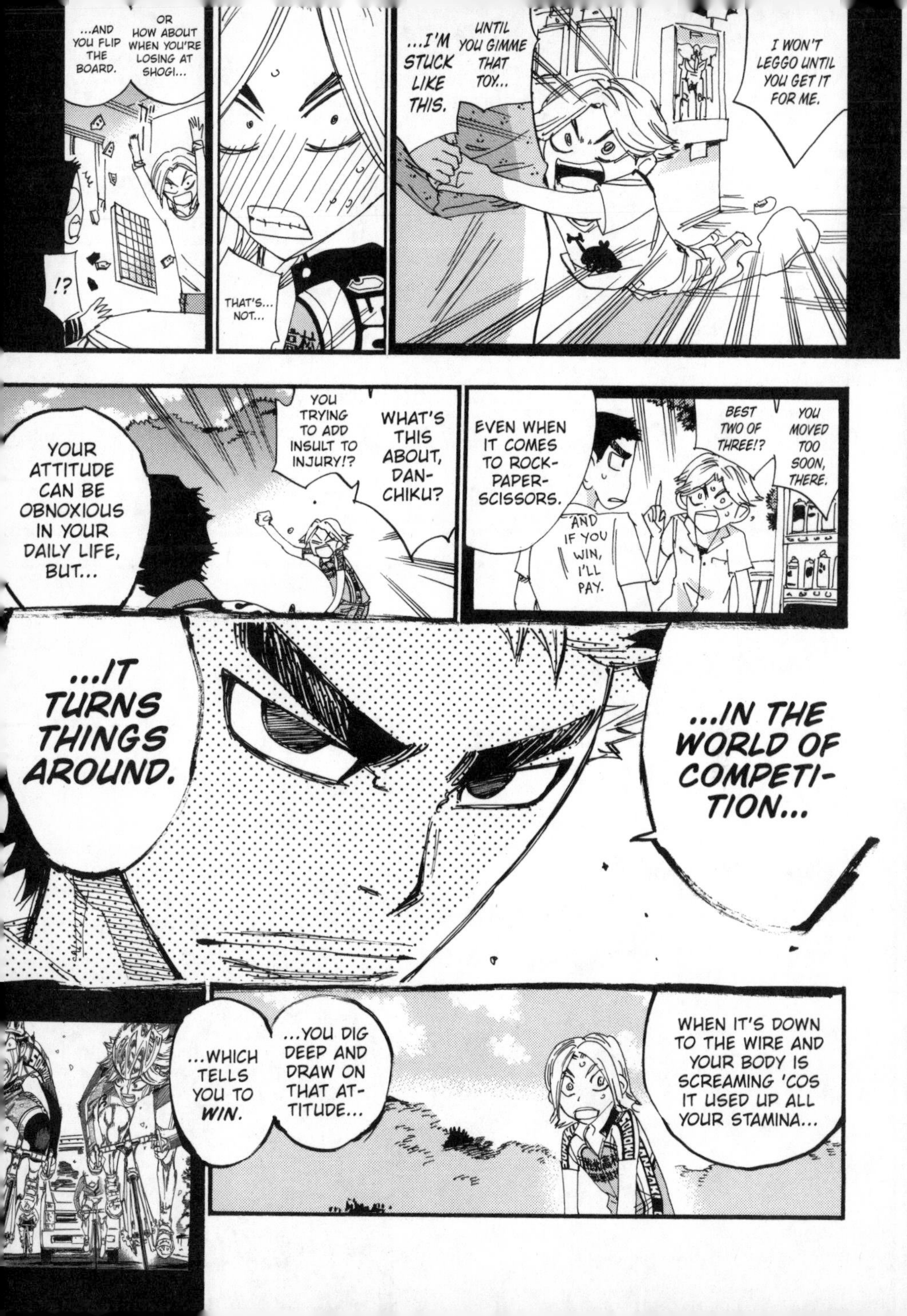
I WON'T LEGGO UNTIL YOU GET IT FOR ME.
UNTIL YOU GIMME THAT TOY...
...I'M STUCK LIKE THIS.
THAT'S... NOT...
OR HOW ABOUT WHEN YOU'RE LOSING AT SHOGI...
...AND YOU FLIP THE BOARD.
!?
YOU MOVED TOO SOON, THERE.
BEST TWO OF THREE!?
EVEN WHEN IT COMES TO ROCK-PAPER-SCISSORS.
AND IF YOU WIN, I'LL PAY.
WHAT'S THIS ABOUT, DAN-CHIKU?
YOU TRYING TO ADD INSULT TO INJURY!?
YOUR ATTITUDE CAN BE OBNOXIOUS IN YOUR DAILY LIFE, BUT...
...IN THE WORLD OF COMPETITION...
...IT TURNS THINGS AROUND.
WHEN IT'S DOWN TO THE WIRE AND YOUR BODY IS SCREAMING 'COS IT USED UP ALL YOUR STAMINA...
...YOU DIG DEEP AND DRAW ON THAT ATTITUDE...
...WHICH TELLS YOU TO WIN.

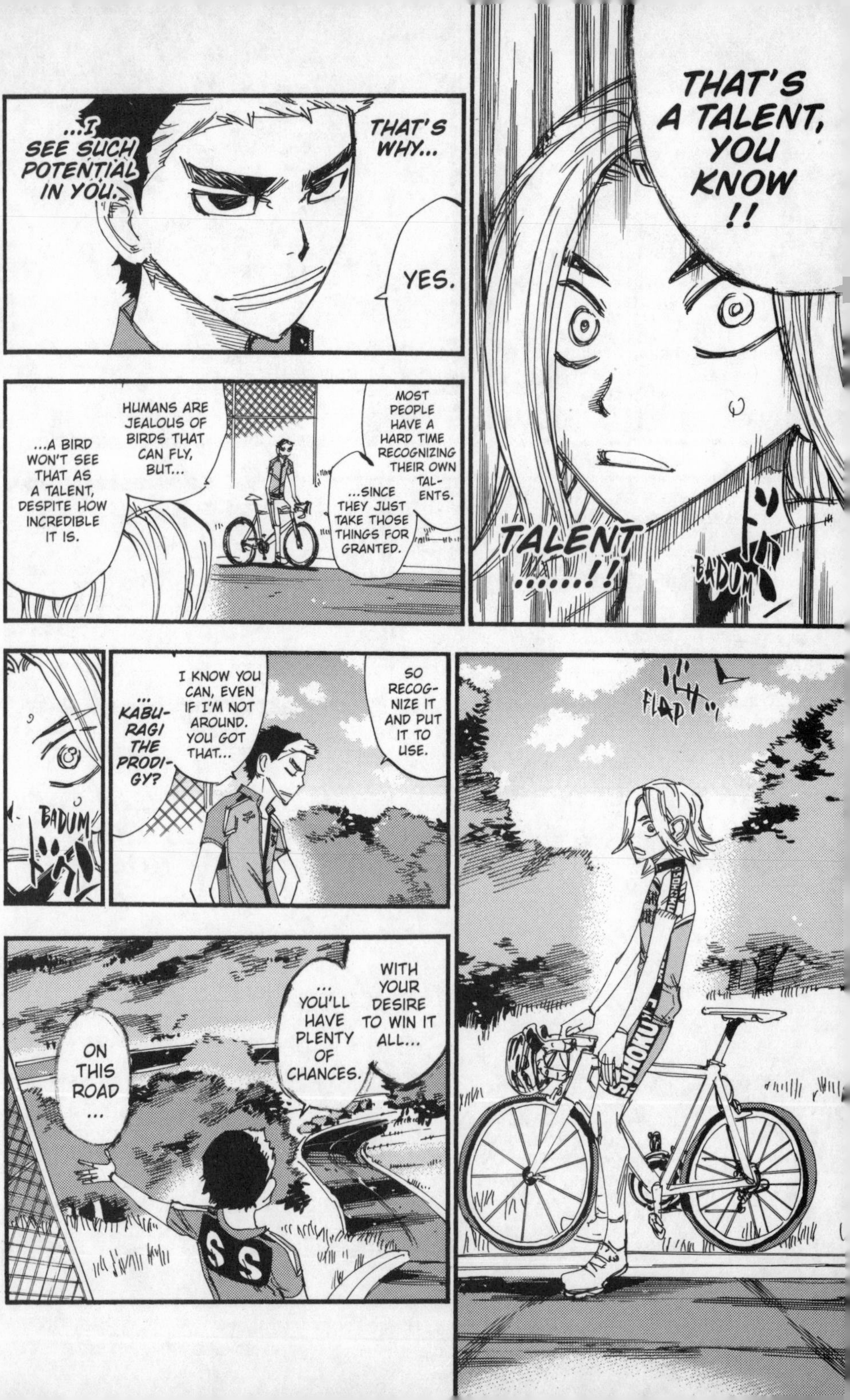
THAT'S A TALENT, YOU KNOW!!
TALENT......!!
BADUM
THAT'S WHY...
...I SEE SUCH POTENTIAL IN YOU.
YES.
MOST PEOPLE HAVE A HARD TIME RECOGNIZING THEIR OWN TALENTS.
...SINCE THEY JUST TAKE THOSE THINGS FOR GRANTED.
HUMANS ARE JEALOUS OF BIRDS THAT CAN FLY, BUT...
...A BIRD WON'T SEE THAT AS A TALENT, DESPITE HOW INCREDIBLE IT IS.
FLAP
SO RECOGNIZE IT AND PUT IT TO USE.
I KNOW YOU CAN, EVEN IF I'M NOT AROUND. YOU GOT THAT...
...KABURAGI THE PRODIGY?
BADUM
WITH YOUR DESIRE TO WIN IT ALL...
...YOU'LL HAVE PLENTY OF CHANCES.
ON THIS ROAD...

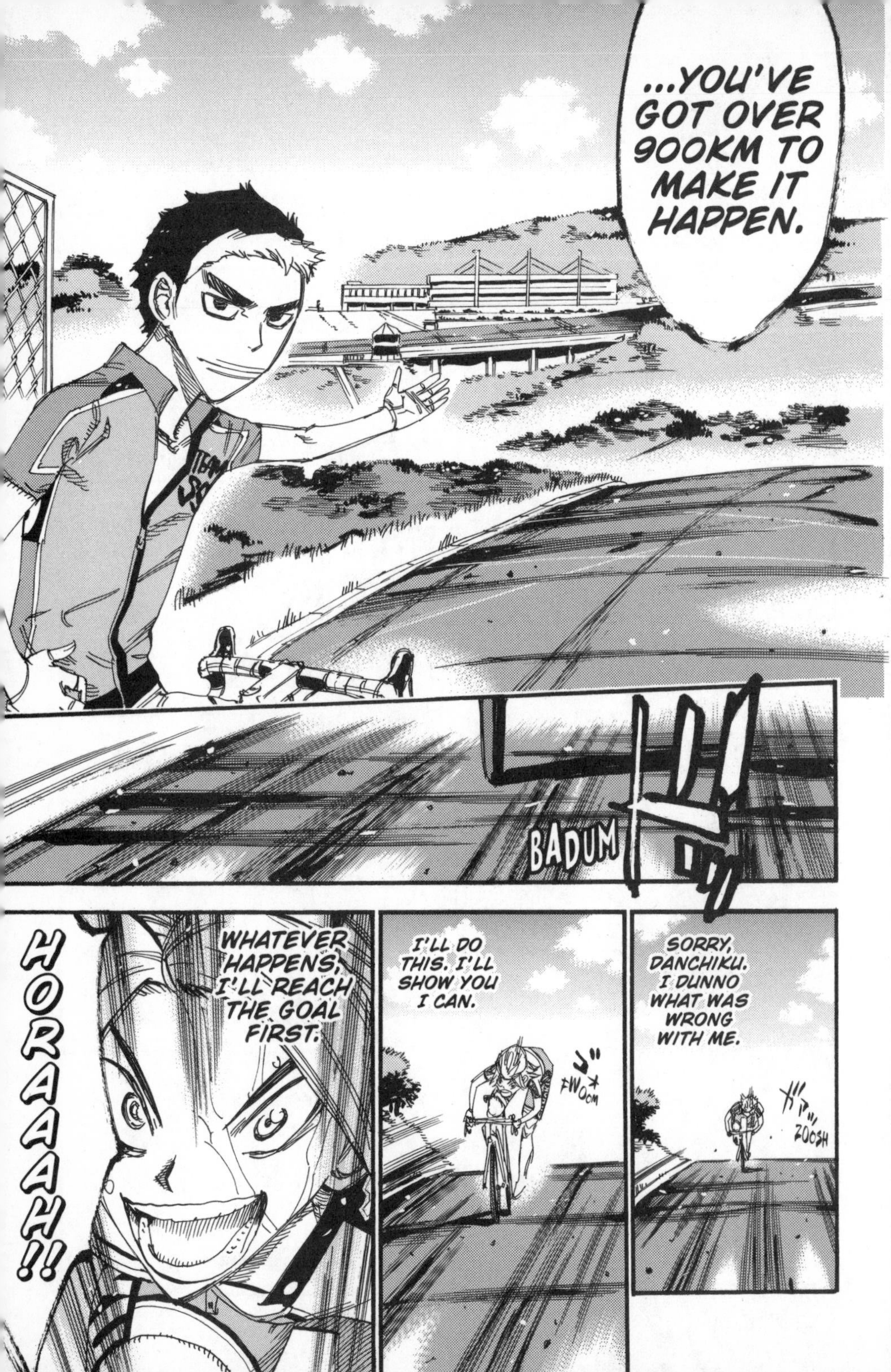
...YOU'VE GOT OVER 900KM TO MAKE IT HAPPEN.
BADUM
SORRY, DANCHIKU. I DUNNO WHAT WAS WRONG WITH ME.
ZOOSH
I'LL DO THIS. I'LL SHOW YOU I CAN.
FWOOM
WHATEVER HAPPENS, I'LL REACH THE GOAL FIRST.
HORAAAAH!!

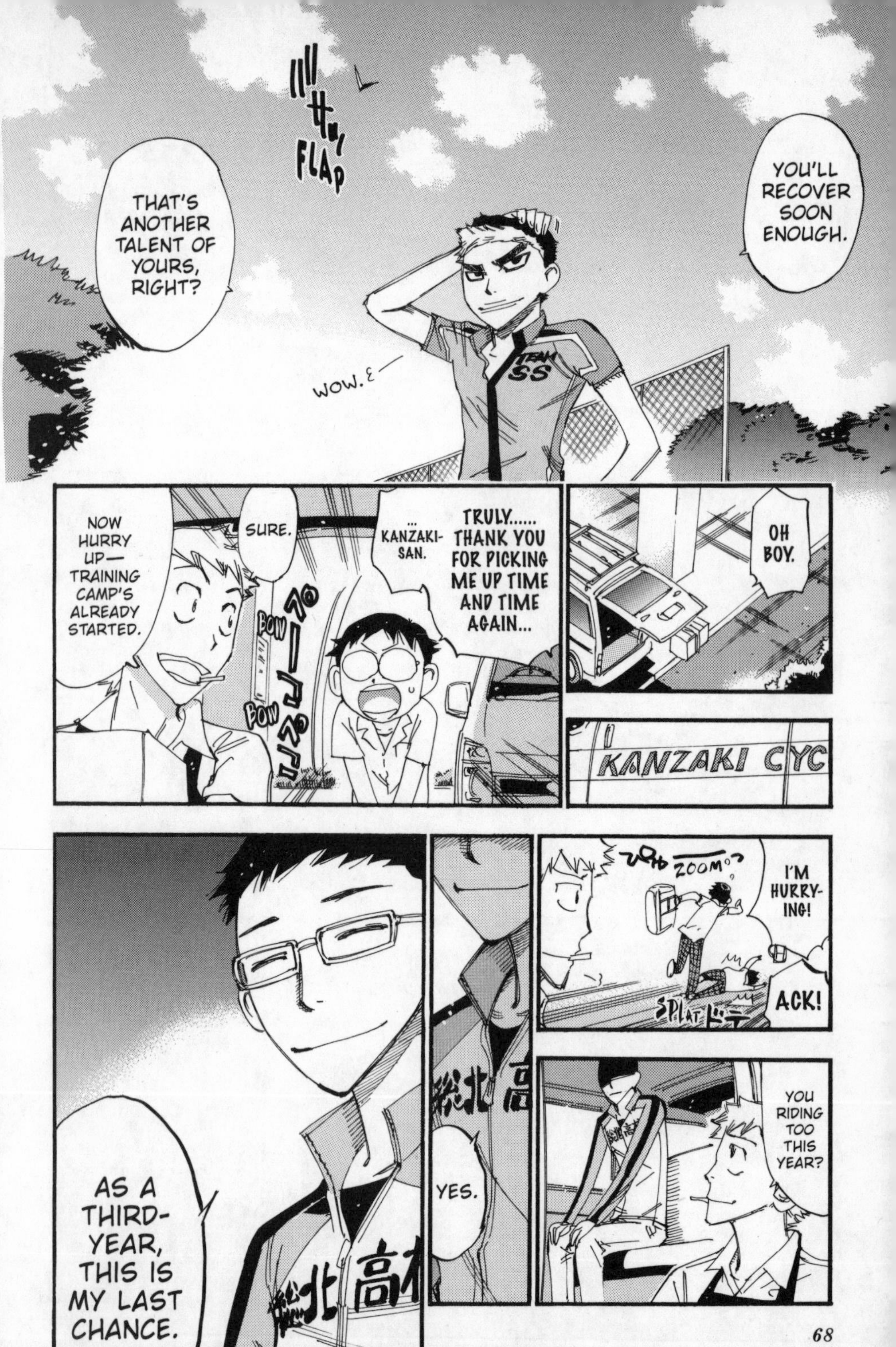
YOU'LL RECOVER SOON ENOUGH.
FLAP
THAT'S ANOTHER TALENT OF YOURS, RIGHT?
WOW.
OH BOY.
KANZAKI CYC
TRULY...... THANK YOU FOR PICKING ME UP TIME AND TIME AGAIN...
... KANZAKI-SAN.
BOW BOW
SURE.
NOW HURRY UP— TRAINING CAMP'S ALREADY STARTED.
I'M HURRY-ING!
ZOOM
ACK!
SPLAT
YOU RIDING TOO THIS YEAR?
YES.
AS A THIRD-YEAR, THIS IS MY LAST CHANCE.

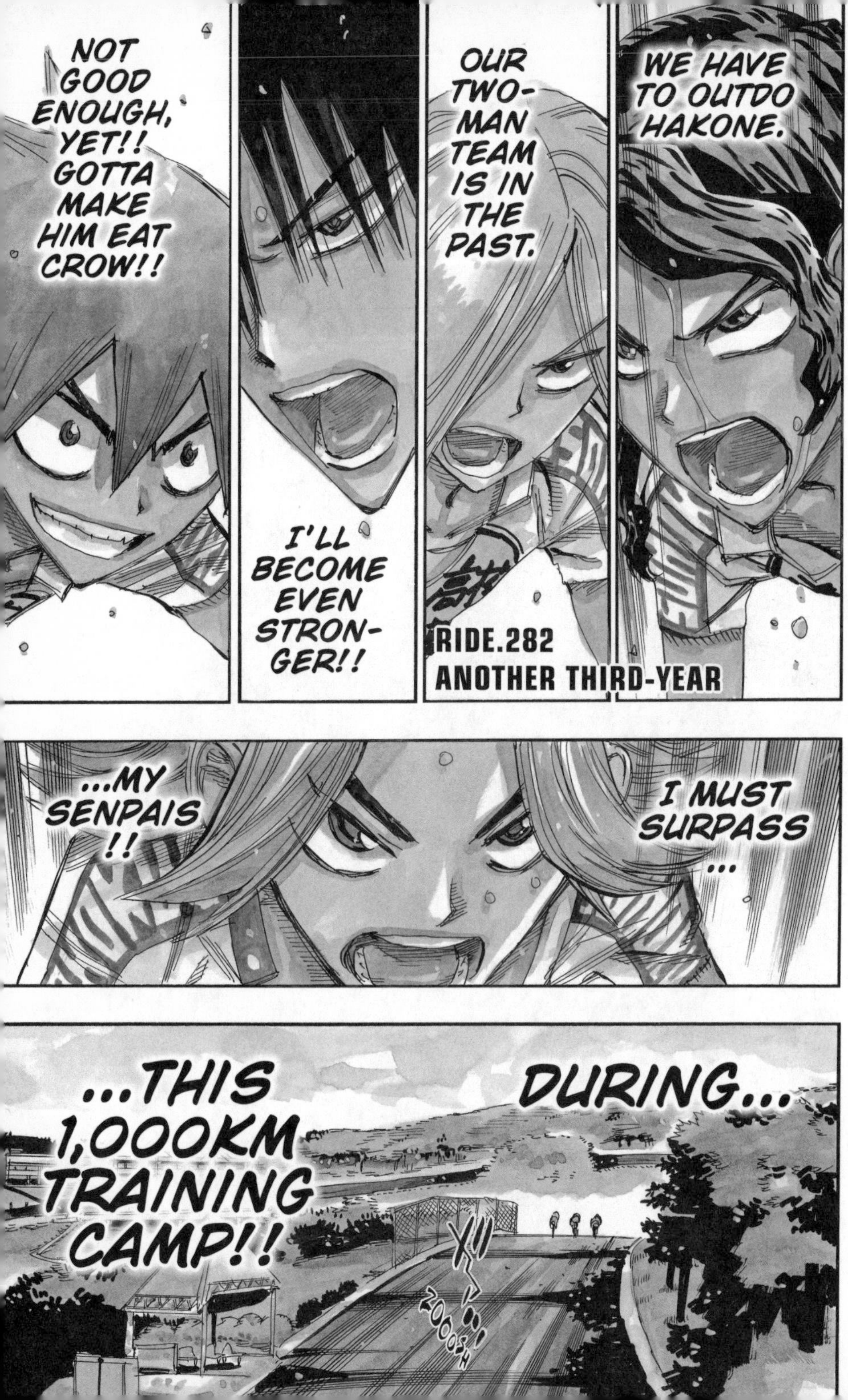
WE HAVE TO OUTDO HAKONE.
OUR TWO-MAN TEAM IS IN THE PAST.
RIDE.282
ANOTHER THIRD-YEAR
I'LL BECOME EVEN STRONGER!!
NOT GOOD ENOUGH, YET!! GOTTA MAKE HIM EAT CROW!!
I MUST SURPASS...
...MY SENPAIS!!
DURING...
...THIS 1,000KM TRAINING CAMP!!
ZOOOSH

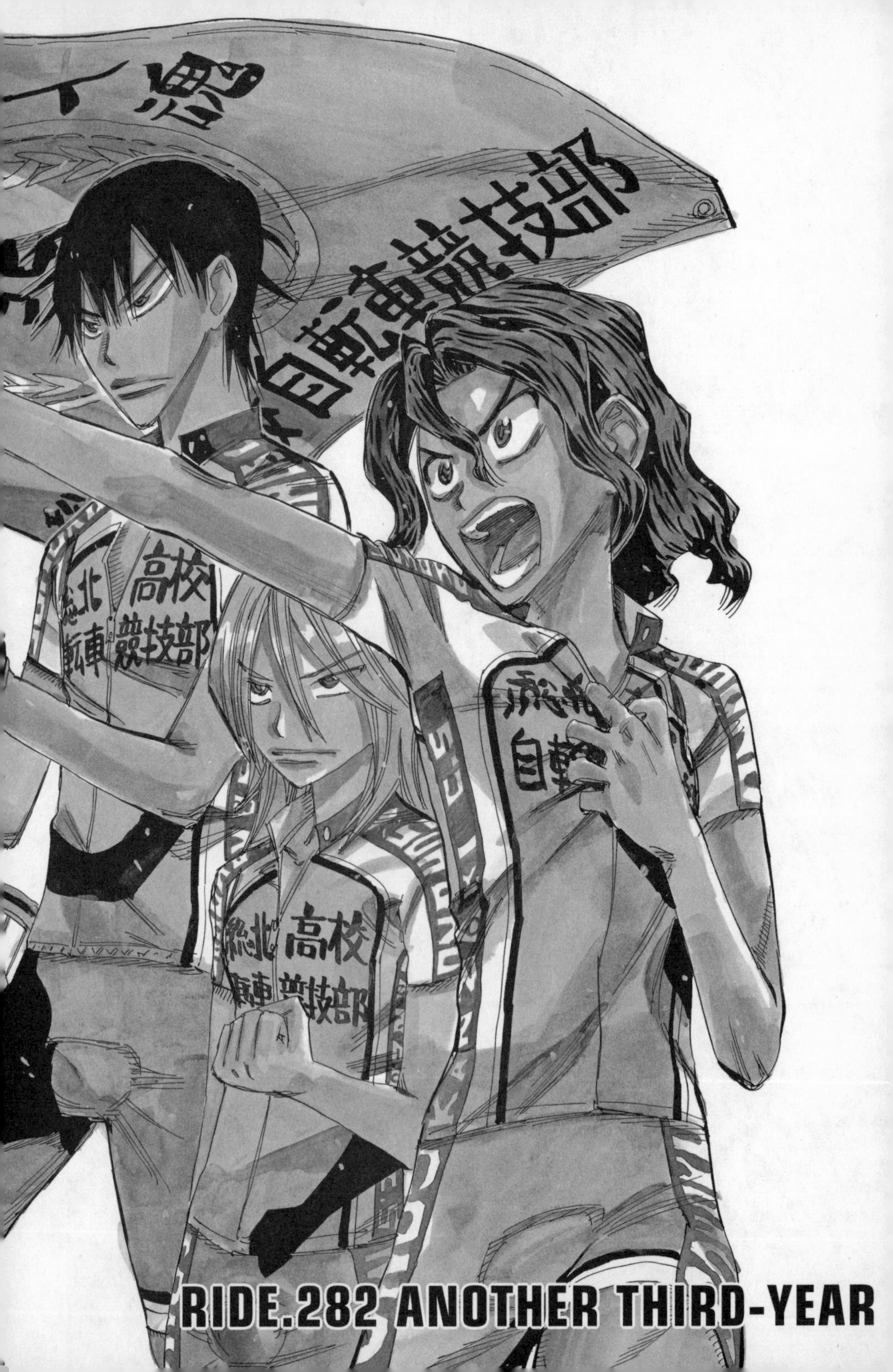
自転車競技部
総北 高校
自転車 競技部

RIDE.282 ANOTHER THIRD-YEAR

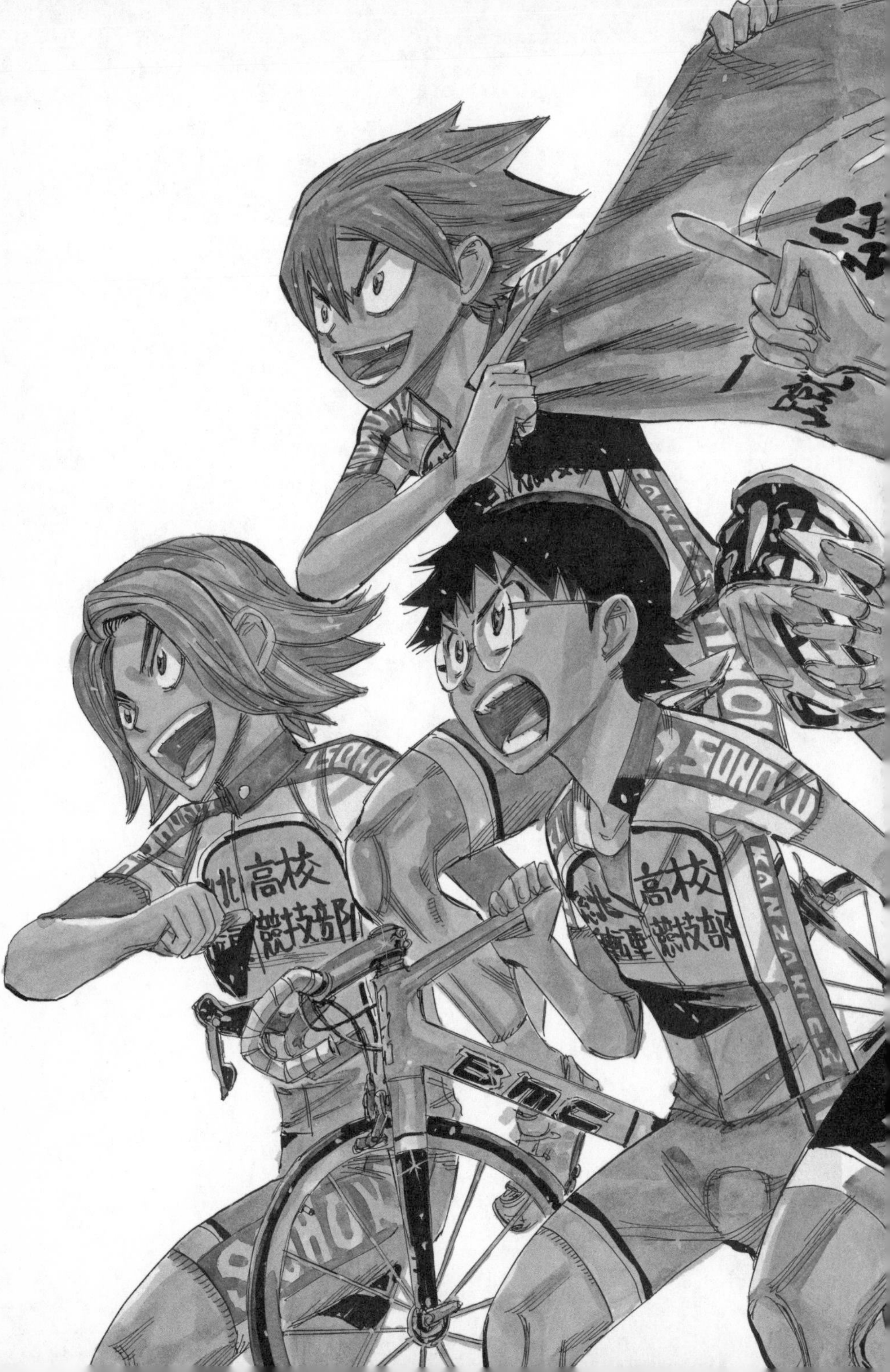
高校
競技部
BMC

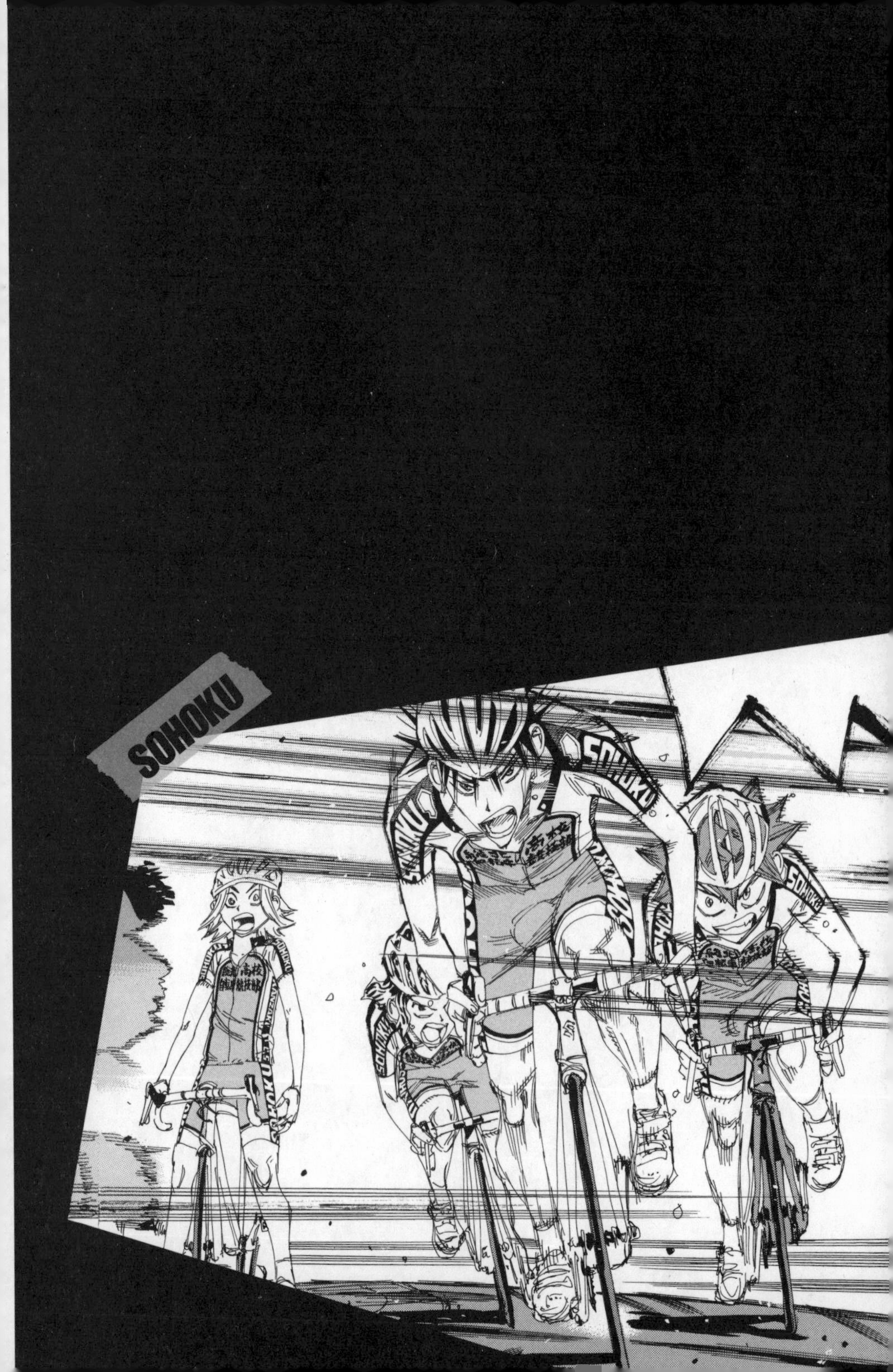
SOHOKU

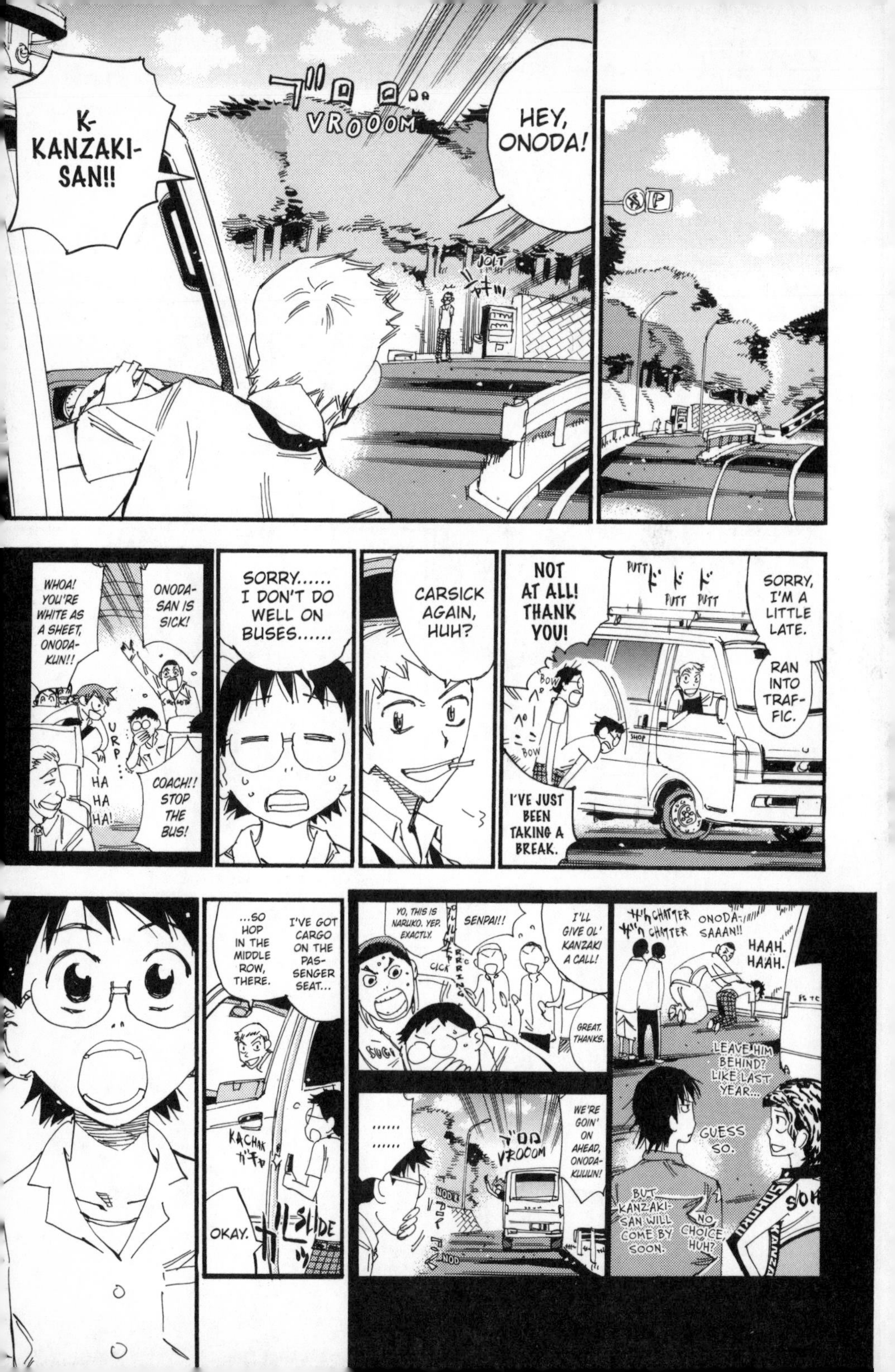

HEY, ONODA!
VROOOM
K-KANZAKI-SAN!!
JOLT
SORRY, I'M A LITTLE LATE.
RAN INTO TRAFFIC.
PUTT PUTT PUTT
NOT AT ALL! THANK YOU!
BOW
BOW
I'VE JUST BEEN TAKING A BREAK.
CARSICK AGAIN, HUH?
SORRY...... I DON'T DO WELL ON BUSES......
ONODA-SAN IS SICK!
WHOA! YOU'RE WHITE AS A SHEET, ONODA-KUN!!
URP...
HA HA HA!
COACH!! STOP THE BUS!
ONODA-SAAAN!!
HAAH. HAAH.
CHATTER CHATTER
LEAVE HIM BEHIND? LIKE LAST YEAR...
GUESS SO.
NO CHOICE, HUH?
BUT KANZAKI-SAN WILL COME BY SOON.
I'LL GIVE OL' KANZAKI A CALL!
SENPAI!!
YO, THIS IS NARUKO. YEP. EXACTLY.
RRRING
GREAT. THANKS.
WE'RE GOIN' ON AHEAD, ONODA-KUUUN!
VROOOM
......
......
NOD
NOD
I'VE GOT CARGO ON THE PASSENGER SEAT...
...SO HOP IN THE MIDDLE ROW, THERE.
KACHAK
SLIDE
OKAY.

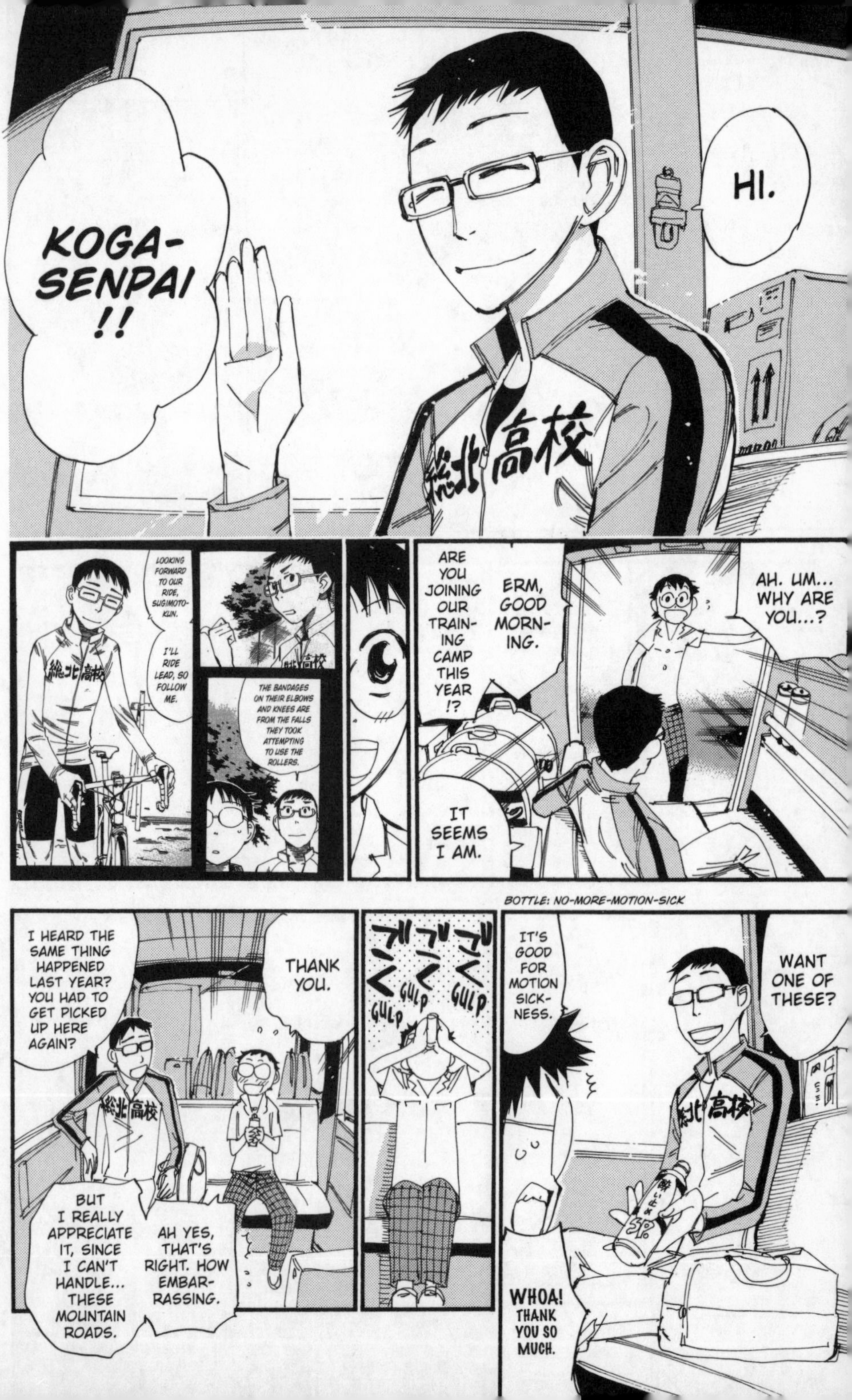
HI.
KOGA-SENPAI!!
AH. UM... WHY ARE YOU...?
ERM, GOOD MORNING.
ARE YOU JOINING OUR TRAINING CAMP THIS YEAR!?
IT SEEMS I AM.
THE BANDAGES ON THEIR ELBOWS AND KNEES ARE FROM THE FALLS THEY TOOK ATTEMPTING TO USE THE ROLLERS.
LOOKING FORWARD TO OUR RIDE, SUGIMOTO-KUN.
I'LL RIDE LEAD, SO FOLLOW ME.
BOTTLE: NO-MORE-MOTION-SICK
WANT ONE OF THESE?
IT'S GOOD FOR MOTION SICK-NESS.
WHOA! THANK YOU SO MUCH.
GULP GULP GULP
THANK YOU.
I HEARD THE SAME THING HAPPENED LAST YEAR? YOU HAD TO GET PICKED UP HERE AGAIN?
AH YES, THAT'S RIGHT. HOW EMBAR-RASSING.
BUT I REALLY APPRECIATE IT, SINCE I CAN'T HANDLE... THESE MOUNTAIN ROADS.

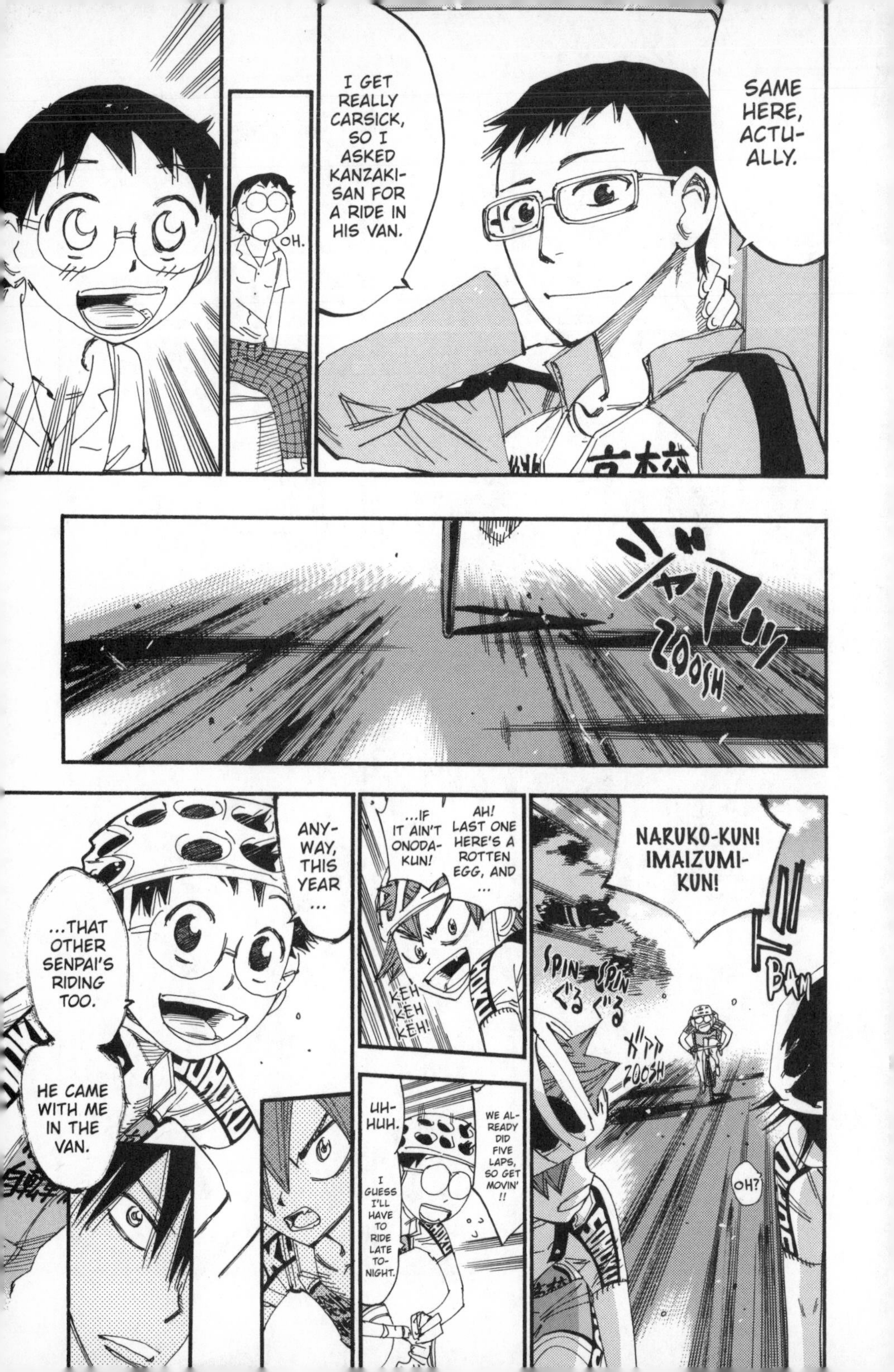
SAME HERE, ACTUALLY.
I GET REALLY CARSICK, SO I ASKED KANZAKI-SAN FOR A RIDE IN HIS VAN.
OH.
ZOOSH
NARUKO-KUN! IMAIZUMI-KUN!
BAM
SPIN SPIN
ZOOSH
OH?
AH! LAST ONE HERE'S A ROTTEN EGG, AND ...
...IF IT AIN'T ONODA-KUN!
KEH KEH KEH!
WE ALREADY DID FIVE LAPS, SO GET MOVIN'!!
UH-HUH.
I GUESS I'LL HAVE TO RIDE LATE TONIGHT.
ANYWAY, THIS YEAR...
...THAT OTHER SENPAI'S RIDING TOO.
HE CAME WITH ME IN THE VAN.

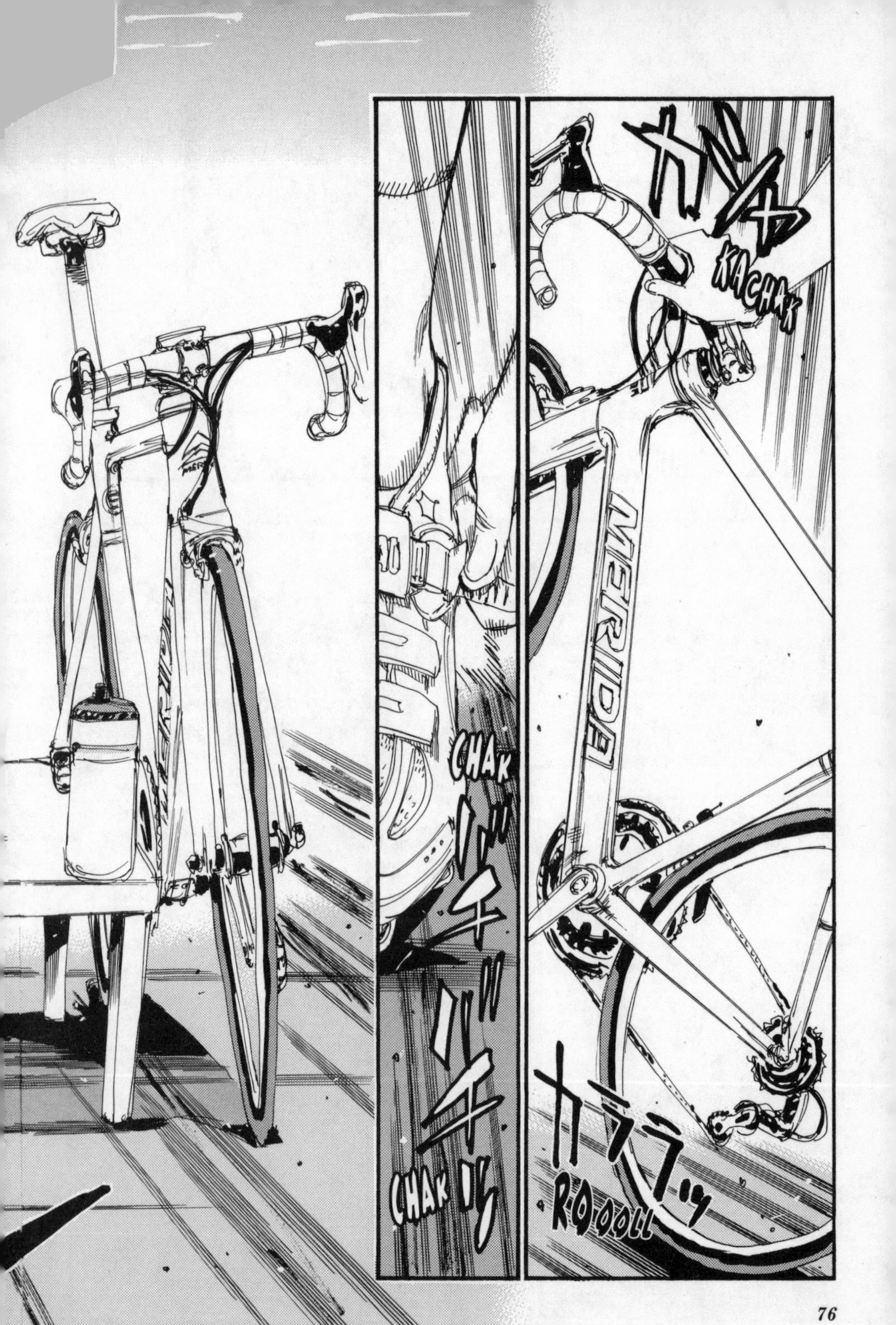
ガシャ
KACHAK
カララッ
ROOOLL
CHAK
CHAK!!

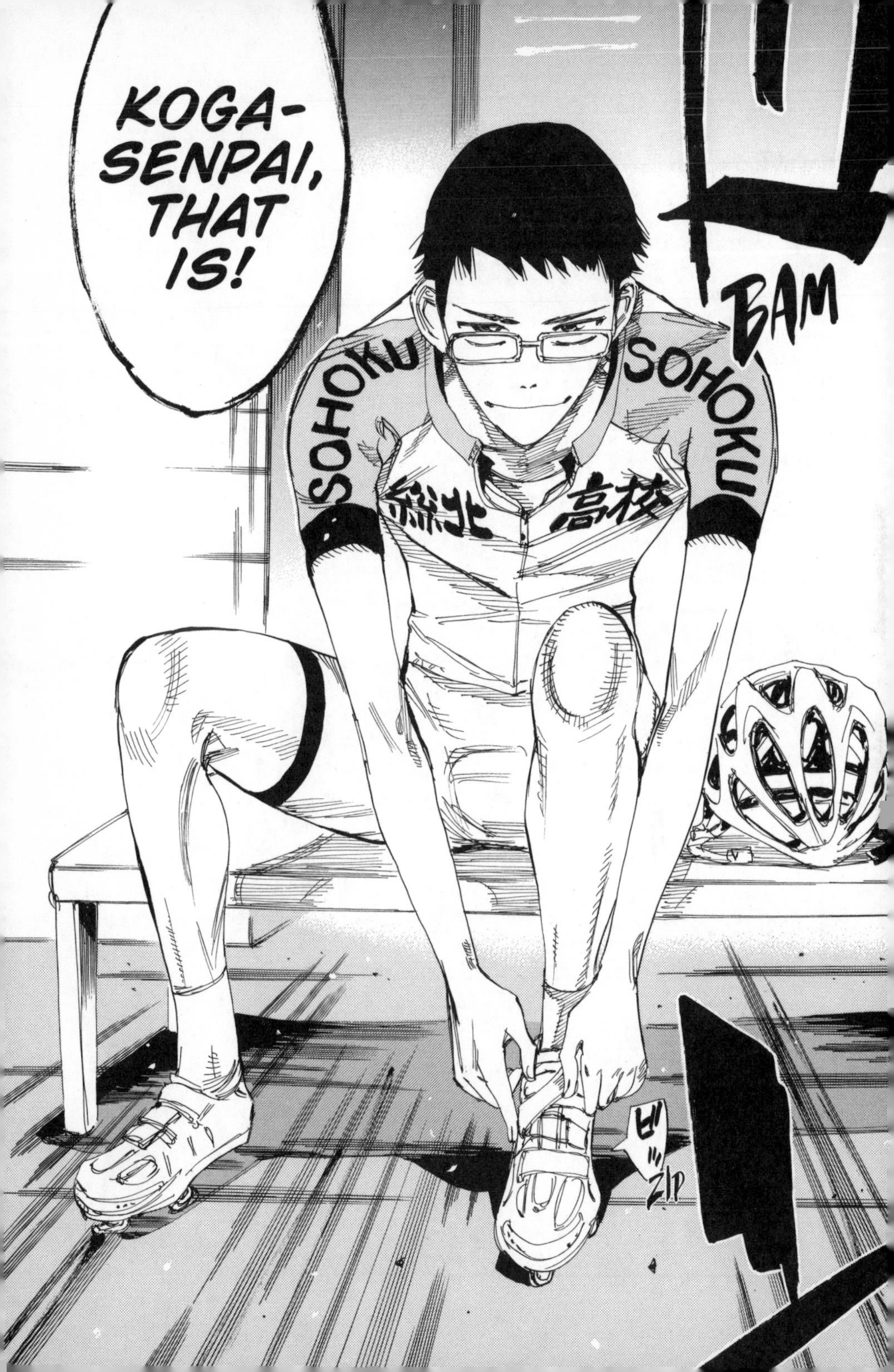
KOGA-SENPAI, THAT IS!
BAM
ZIP

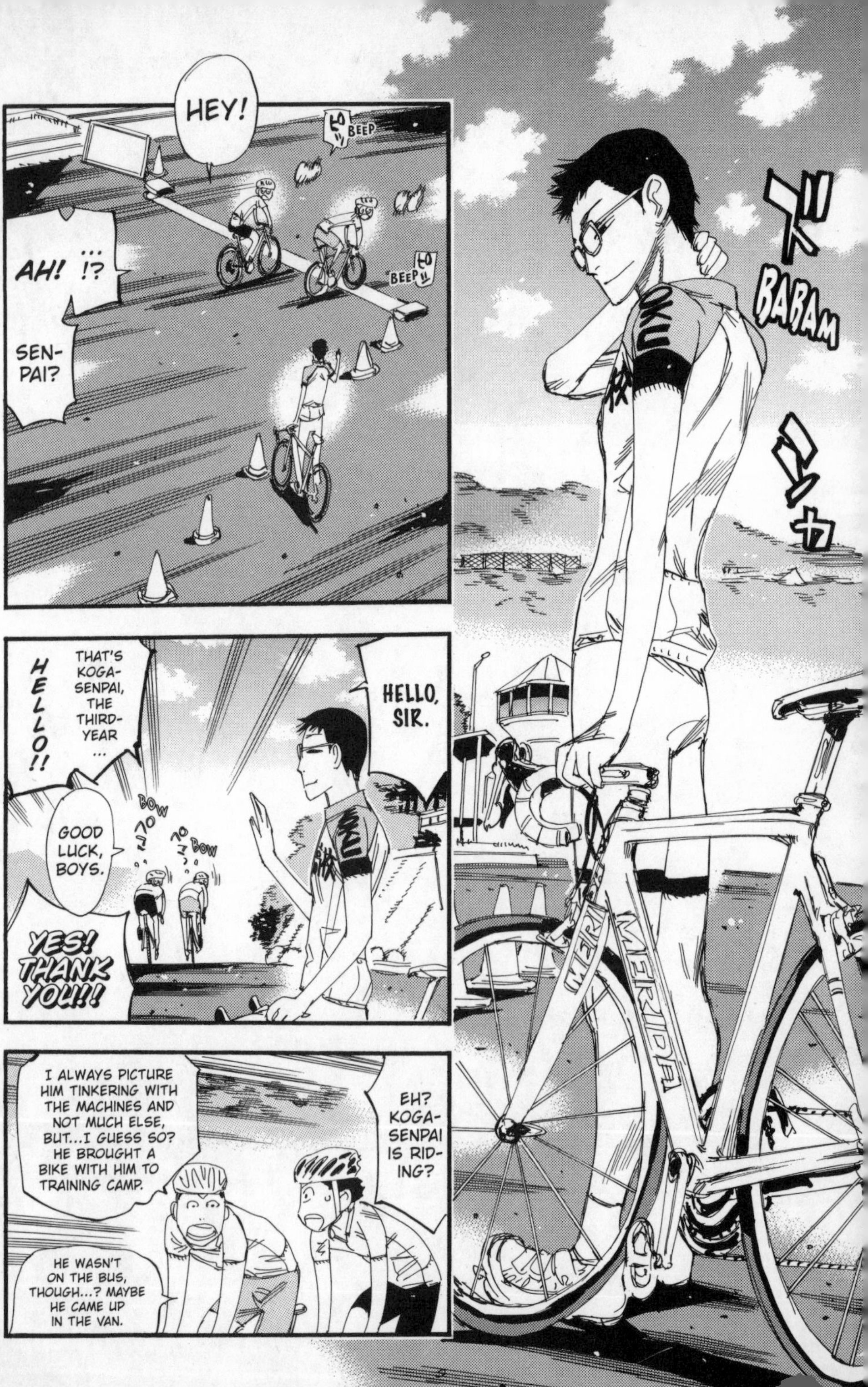
BARAM
HEY!
BEEP
...!?
BEEP
AH!
SEN-PAI?
HELLO, SIR.
THAT'S KOGA-SENPAI, THE THIRD-YEAR...
HELLO!!
BOW
BOW
GOOD LUCK, BOYS.
YES! THANK YOU!!
EH? KOGA-SENPAI IS RIDING?
I ALWAYS PICTURE HIM TINKERING WITH THE MACHINES AND NOT MUCH ELSE, BUT...I GUESS SO? HE BROUGHT A BIKE WITH HIM TO TRAINING CAMP.
HE WASN'T ON THE BUS, THOUGH...? MAYBE HE CAME UP IN THE VAN.

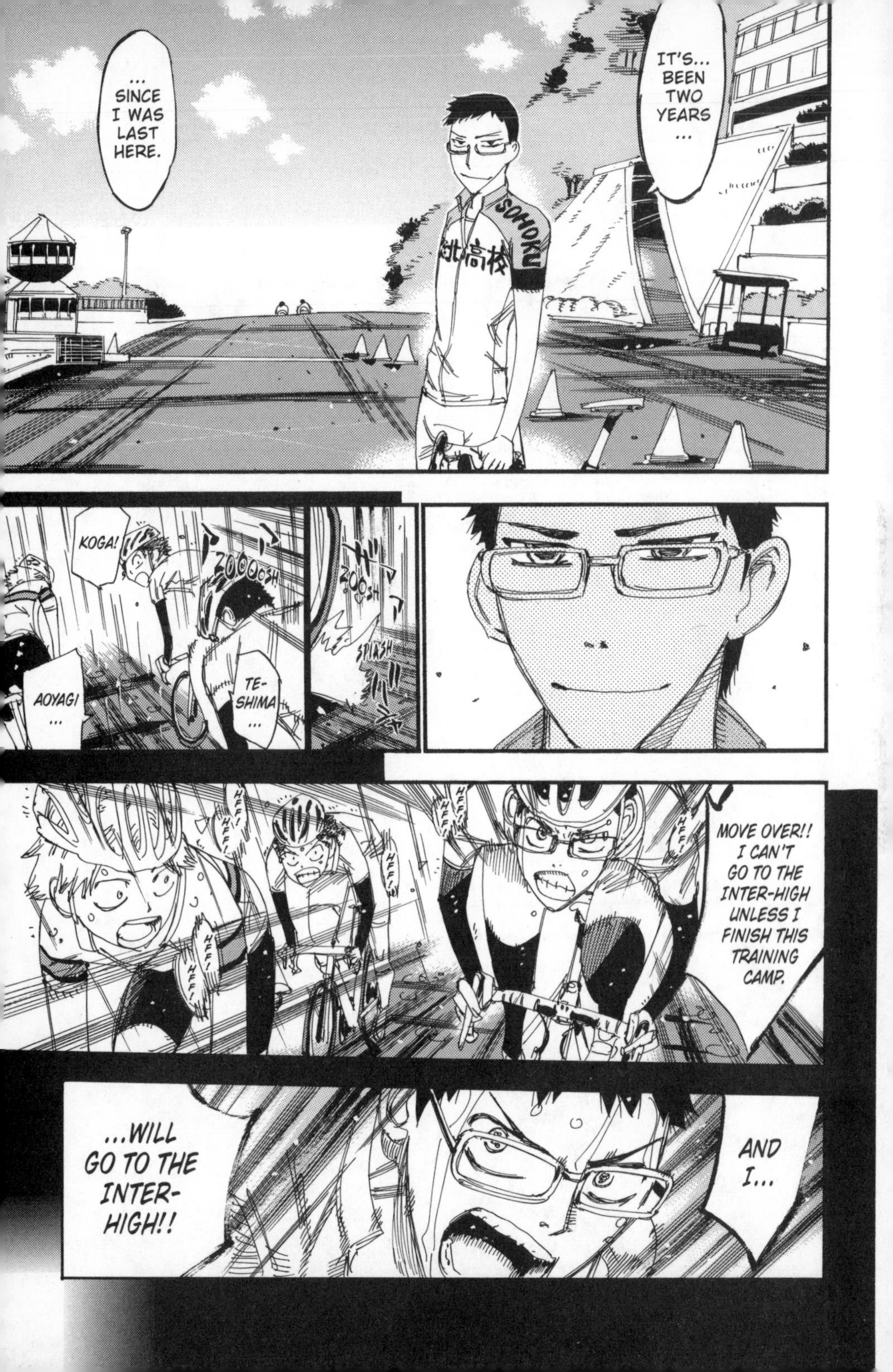
IT'S... BEEN TWO YEARS...
...SINCE I WAS LAST HERE.
ZOOSH
SPLASH
ZOOOOOSH!
KOGA!
TE-SHIMA...
AOYAGI...
MOVE OVER!! I CAN'T GO TO THE INTER-HIGH UNLESS I FINISH THIS TRAINING CAMP.
HFF! HFF!
HFF! HFF!
HFF! HFF!
AND I...
...WILL GO TO THE INTER-HIGH!!

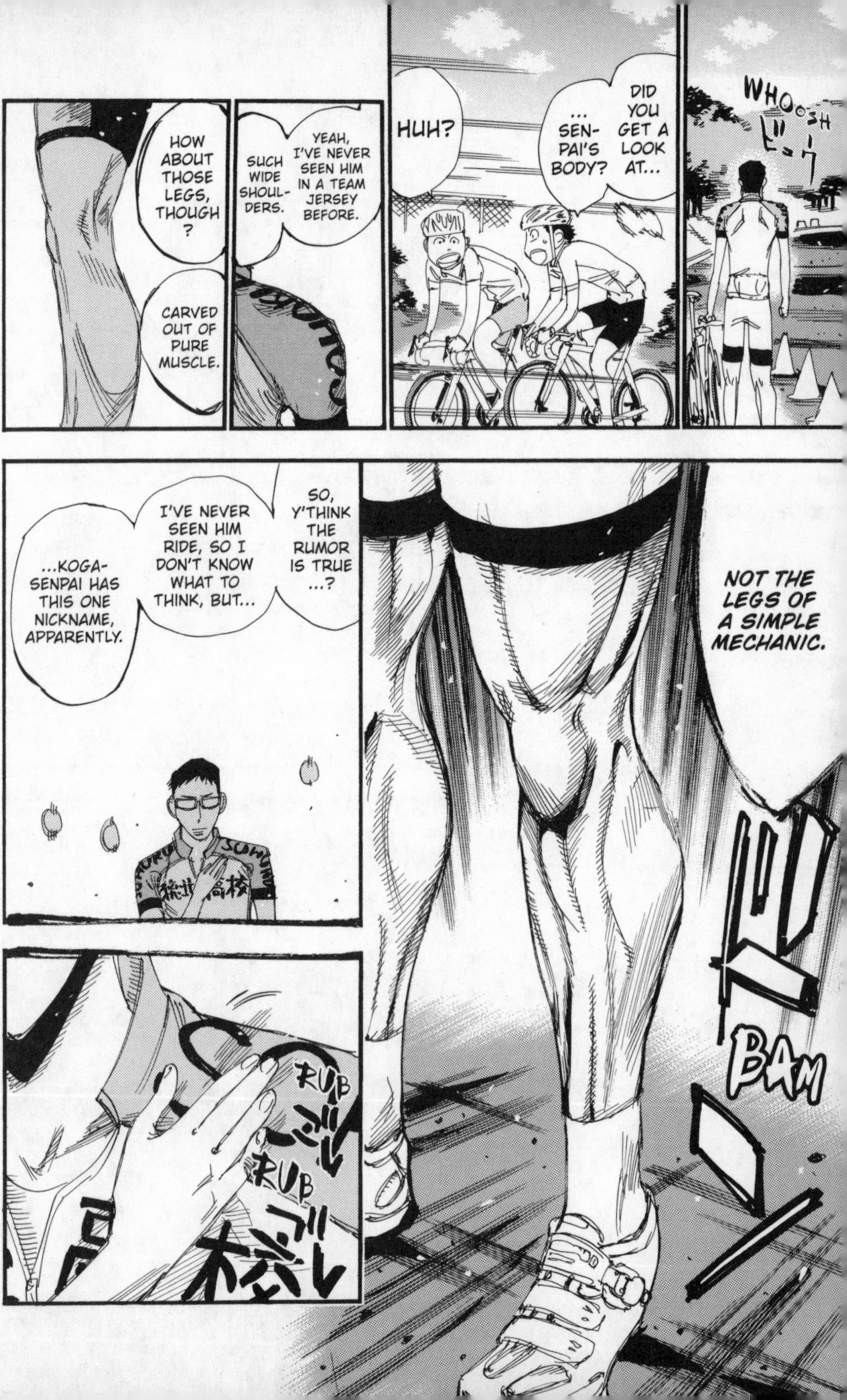
WHOOSH
DID YOU GET A LOOK AT... ...SENPAI'S BODY?
HUH?
YEAH, I'VE NEVER SEEN HIM IN A TEAM JERSEY BEFORE.
SUCH WIDE SHOULDERS.
HOW ABOUT THOSE LEGS, THOUGH?
CARVED OUT OF PURE MUSCLE.
NOT THE LEGS OF A SIMPLE MECHANIC.
BAM
SO, Y'THINK THE RUMOR IS TRUE...?
I'VE NEVER SEEN HIM RIDE, SO I DON'T KNOW WHAT TO THINK, BUT...
...KOGA-SENPAI HAS THIS ONE NICKNAME, APPARENTLY.
RUB
RUB

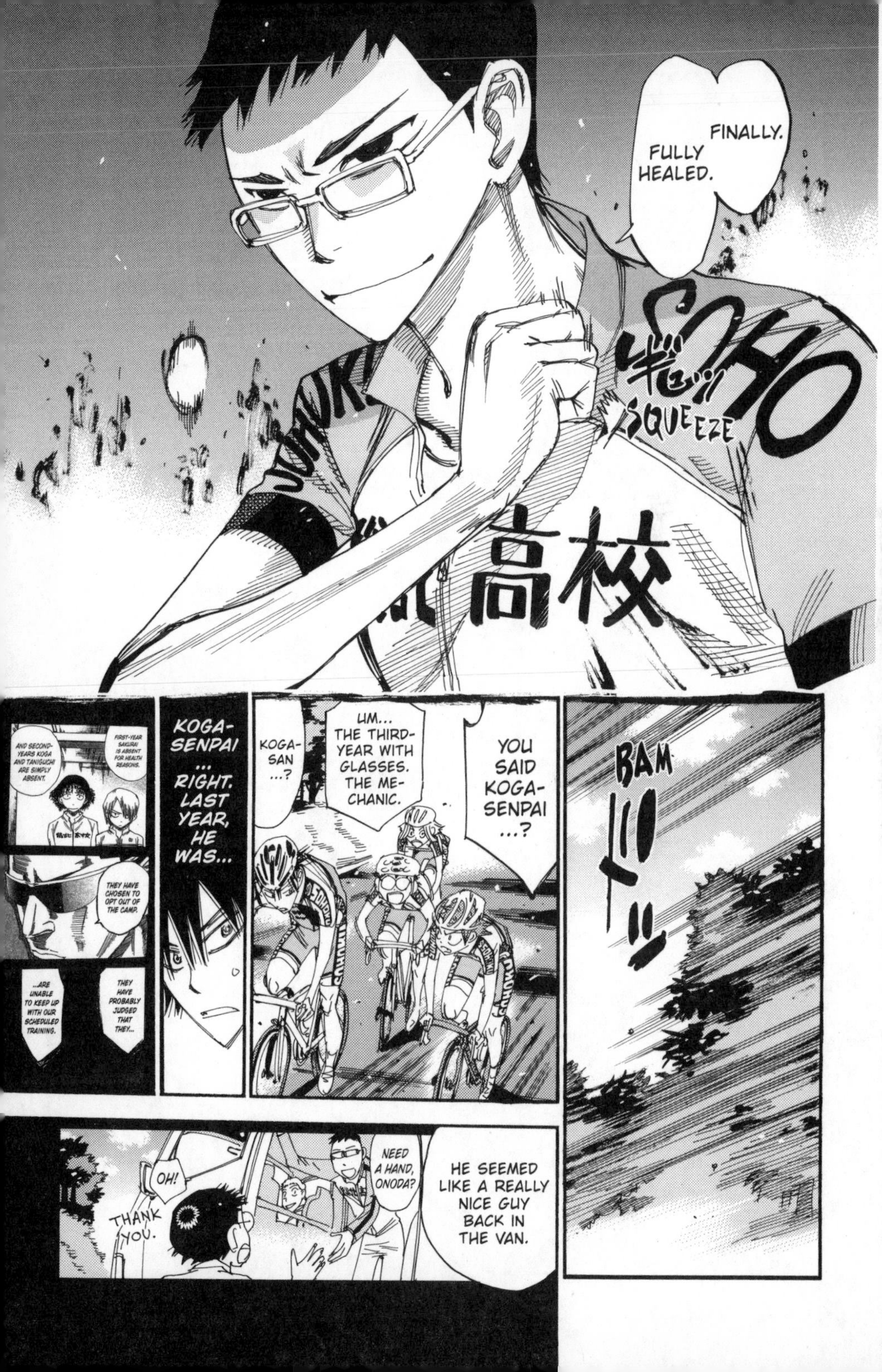
FINALLY. FULLY HEALED.
SQUEEZE
BAM
YOU SAID KOGA-SENPAI...?
UM... THE THIRD-YEAR WITH GLASSES. THE MECHANIC.
KOGA-SAN...?
KOGA-SENPAI... RIGHT. LAST YEAR, HE WAS...
FIRST-YEAR SAKURAI IS ABSENT FOR HEALTH REASONS.
AND SECOND-YEARS KOGA AND TANIGUCHI ARE SIMPLY ABSENT.
THEY HAVE CHOSEN TO OPT OUT OF THE CAMP.
THEY HAVE PROBABLY JUDGED THAT THEY...
...ARE UNABLE TO KEEP UP WITH OUR SCHEDULED TRAINING.
HE SEEMED LIKE A REALLY NICE GUY BACK IN THE VAN.
NEED A HAND, ONODA?
OH!
THANK YOU.

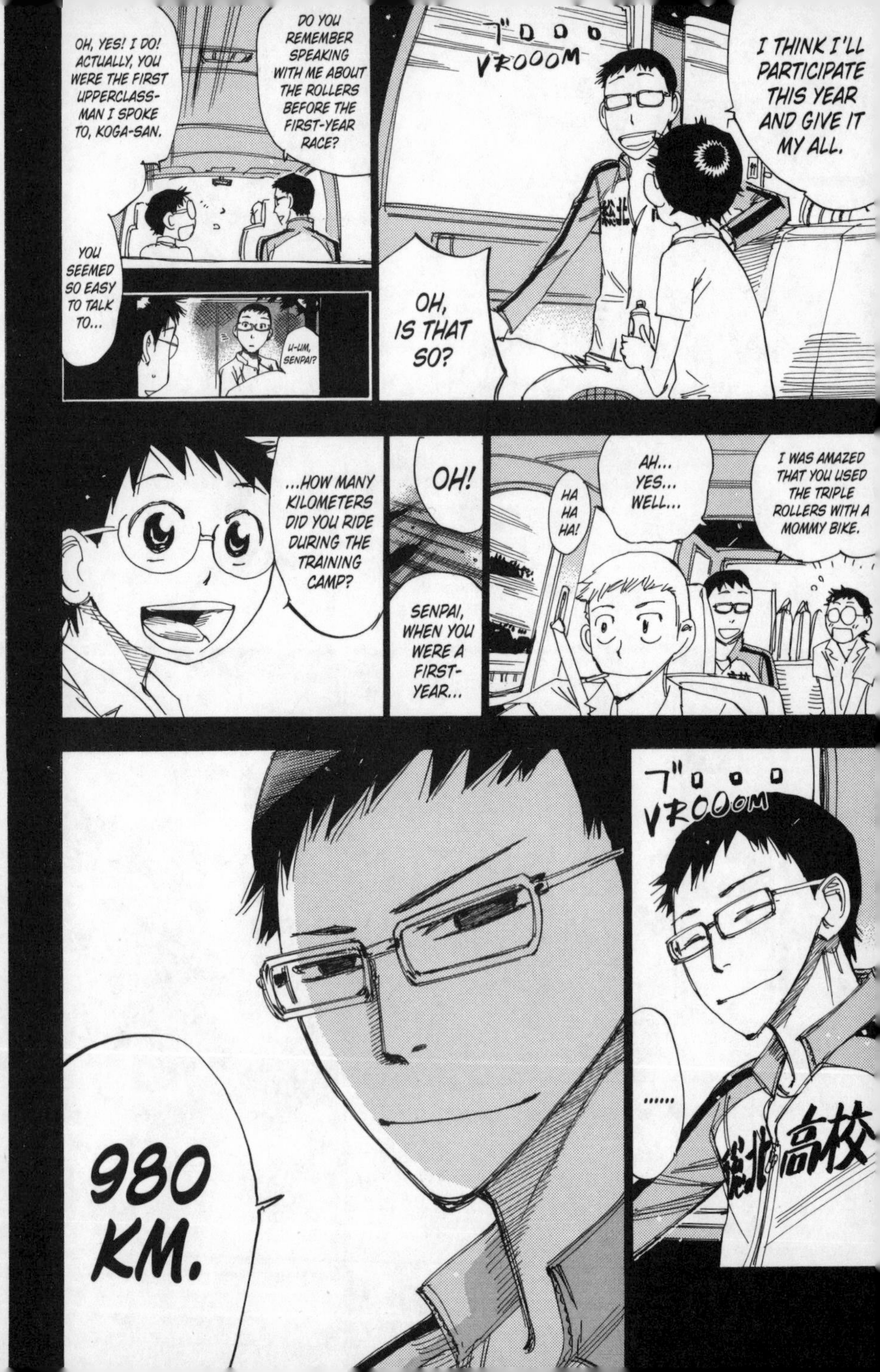
VROOOM
I THINK I'LL PARTICIPATE THIS YEAR AND GIVE IT MY ALL.
OH, IS THAT SO?
DO YOU REMEMBER SPEAKING WITH ME ABOUT THE ROLLERS BEFORE THE FIRST-YEAR RACE?
OH, YES! I DO! ACTUALLY, YOU WERE THE FIRST UPPERCLASSMAN I SPOKE TO, KOGA-SAN.
YOU SEEMED SO EASY TO TALK TO...
U-UM, SENPAI?
I WAS AMAZED THAT YOU USED THE TRIPLE ROLLERS WITH A MOMMY BIKE.
AH... YES... WELL...
HA HA HA!
OH!
SENPAI, WHEN YOU WERE A FIRST-YEAR...
...HOW MANY KILOMETERS DID YOU RIDE DURING THE TRAINING CAMP?
VROOOM
......
980 KM.

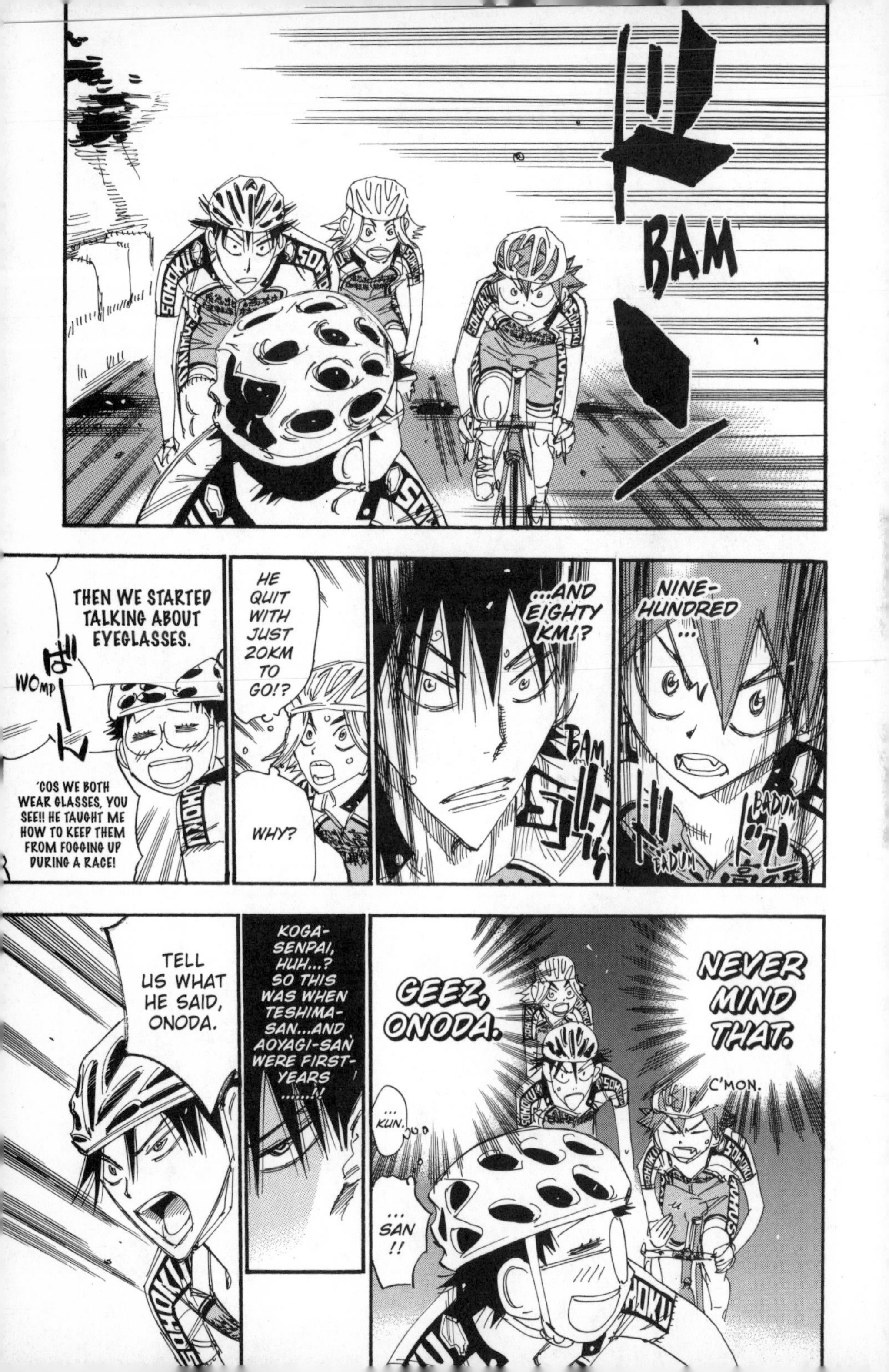

BAM
NINE-HUNDRED...
BADUM
BADUM
...AND EIGHTY KM!?
BAM
HE QUIT WITH JUST 20KM TO GO!?
WHY?
THEN WE STARTED TALKING ABOUT EYEGLASSES.
WOMP
'COS WE BOTH WEAR GLASSES, YOU SEE!! HE TAUGHT ME HOW TO KEEP THEM FROM FOGGING UP DURING A RACE!
NEVER MIND THAT.
GEEZ, ONODA.
C'MON.
...KUN.
...SAN!!
KOGA-SENPAI, HUH...? SO THIS WAS WHEN TESHIMA-SAN...AND AOYAGI-SAN WERE FIRST-YEARS......!!
TELL US WHAT HE SAID, ONODA.

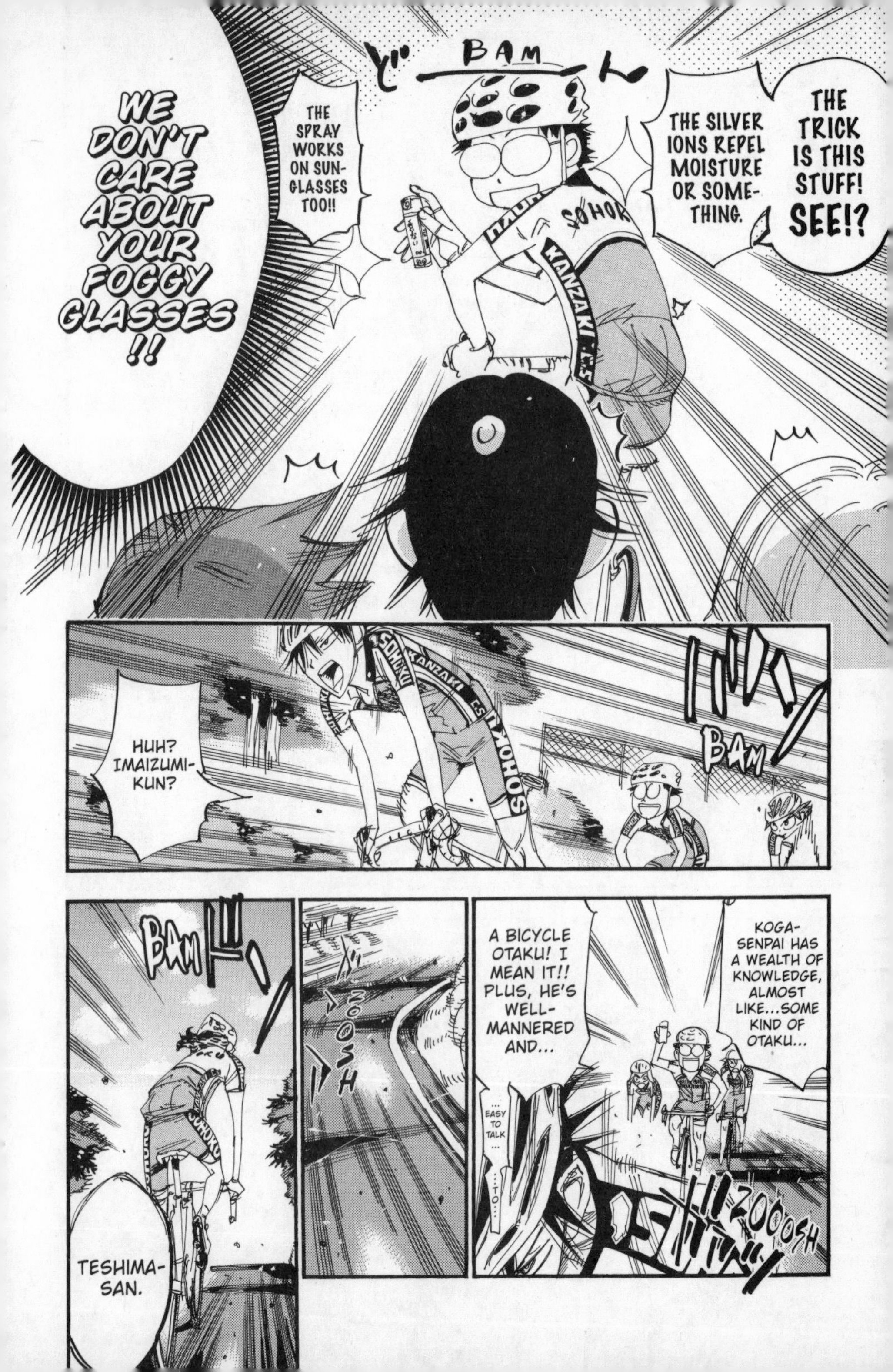

THE TRICK IS THIS STUFF! SEE!?
THE SILVER IONS REPEL MOISTURE OR SOME-THING.
BAM
THE SPRAY WORKS ON SUN-GLASSES TOO!!
WE DON'T CARE ABOUT YOUR FOGGY GLASSES!!
BAM
HUH? IMAIZUMI-KUN?
KOGA-SENPAI HAS A WEALTH OF KNOWLEDGE, ALMOST LIKE...SOME KIND OF OTAKU...
A BICYCLE OTAKU! I MEAN IT!! PLUS, HE'S WELL-MANNERED AND...
ZOOOSH
EASY TO TALK... ...TO...
WHOOSH
BAM
TESHIMA-SAN.

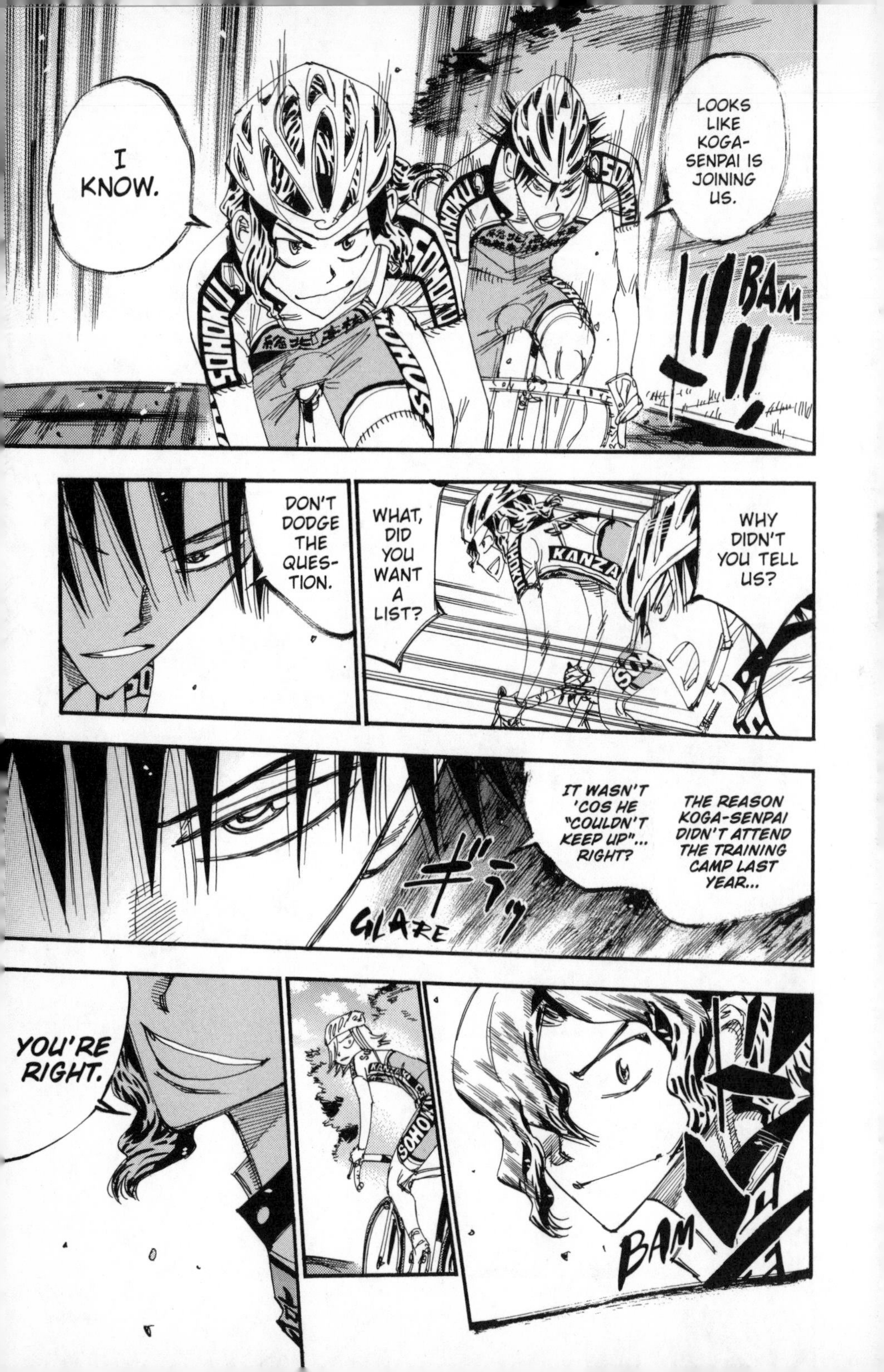
LOOKS LIKE KOGA-SENPAI IS JOINING US.
BAM
I KNOW.
WHY DIDN'T YOU TELL US?
WHAT, DID YOU WANT A LIST?
DON'T DODGE THE QUESTION.
THE REASON KOGA-SENPAI DIDN'T ATTEND THE TRAINING CAMP LAST YEAR...
IT WASN'T 'COS HE "COULDN'T KEEP UP"... RIGHT?
GLARE
BAM
YOU'RE RIGHT.

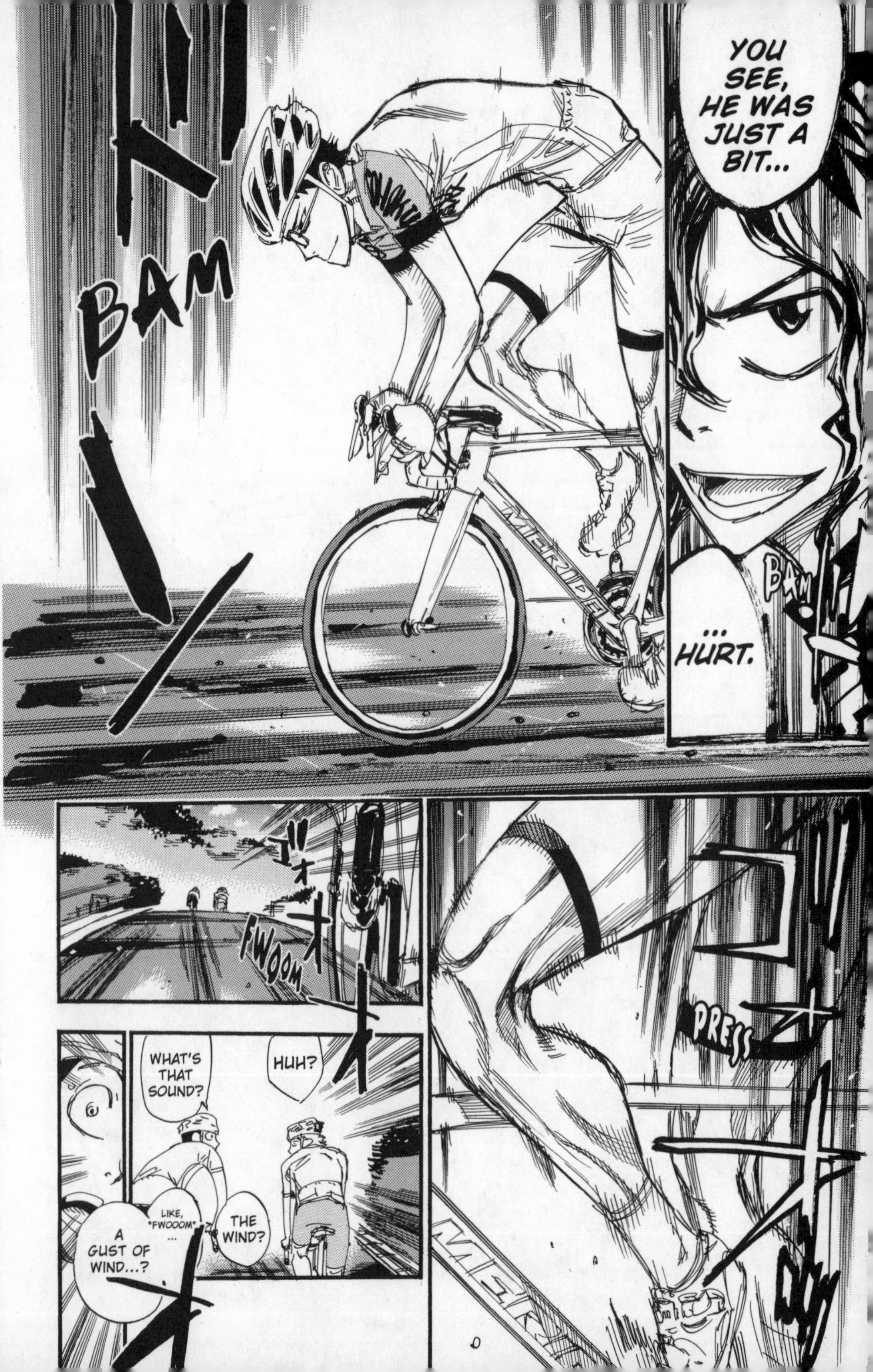
YOU SEE, HE WAS JUST A BIT...
BAM
...HÜRT.
BAM
PRESS
FWOOM
HUH?
WHAT'S THAT SOUND?
THE WIND?
LIKE, "FWOOOM"...
A GUST OF WIND...?

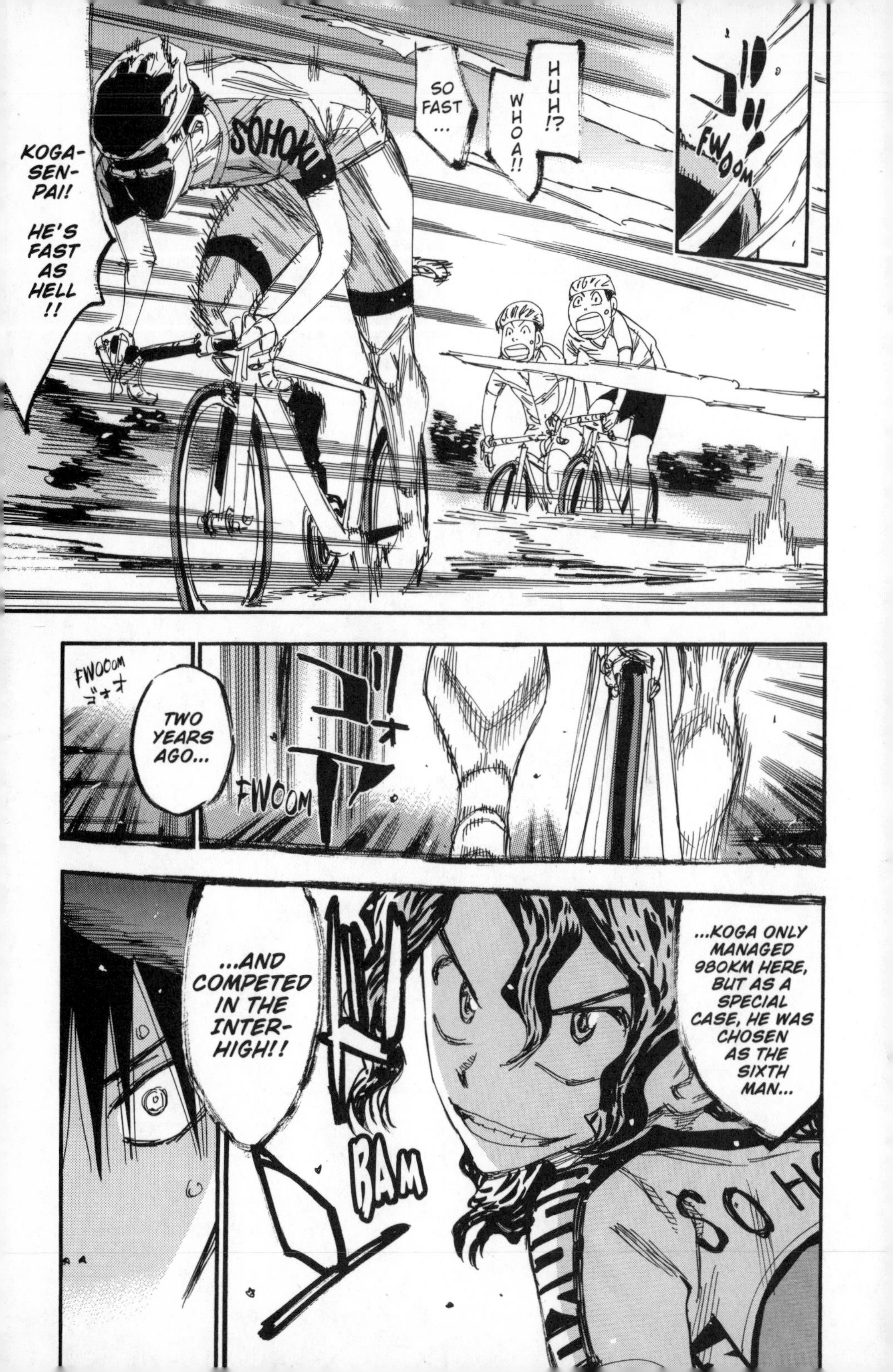
FWOOM
HUH!? WHOA!!
SO FAST...
KOGA-SEN-PAI! HE'S FAST AS HELL!!
TWO YEARS AGO...
FWOOM
FWOOOM ゴォオ
...KOGA ONLY MANAGED 980KM HERE, BUT AS A SPECIAL CASE, HE WAS CHOSEN AS THE SIXTH MAN...
...AND COMPETED IN THE INTER-HIGH!!
BAM

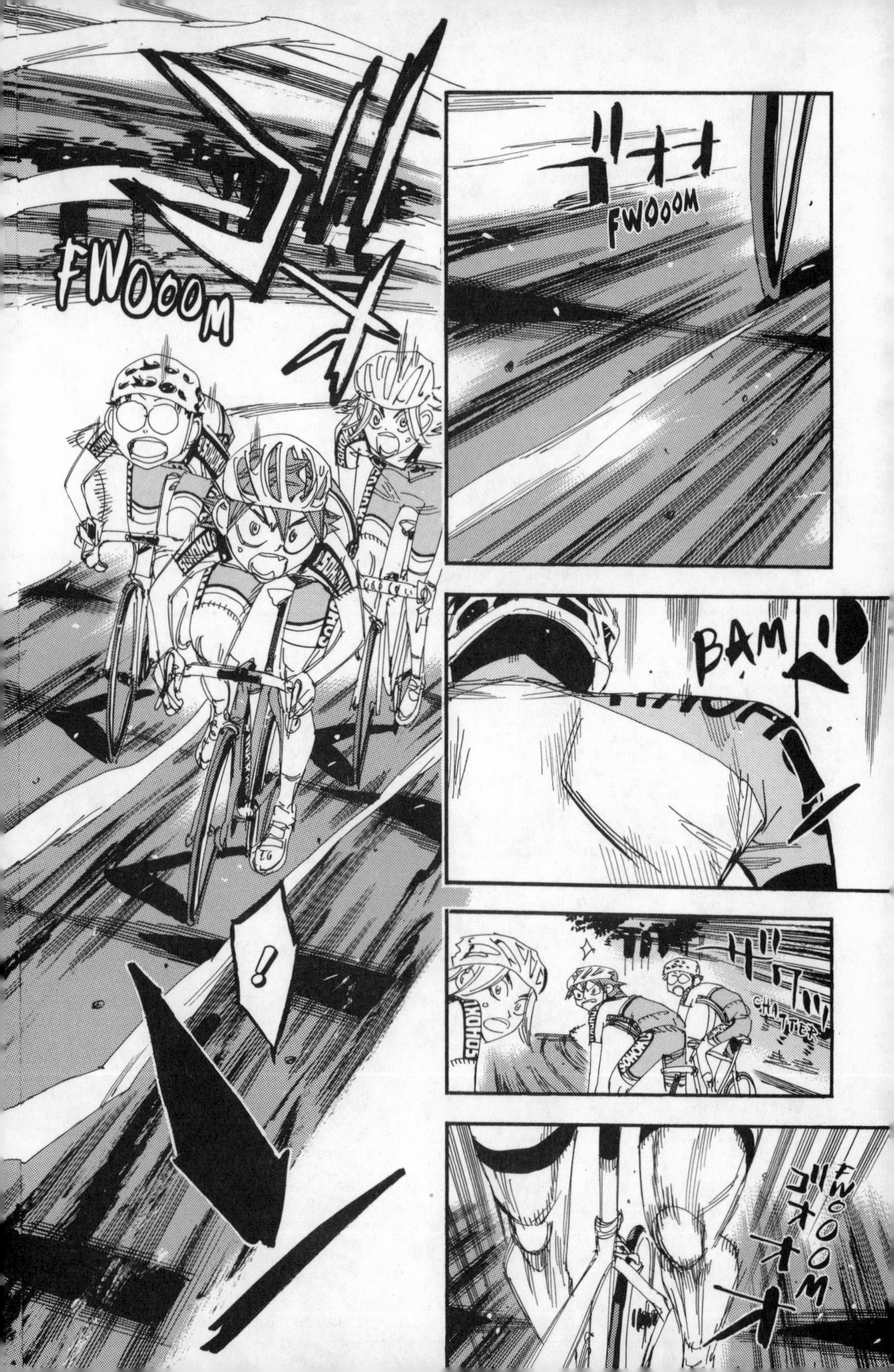
ゴオオ
FWOOOM
BAM
ザワ
CHATTER
ゴオオオ
FWOOOOM
FWOOOM
!

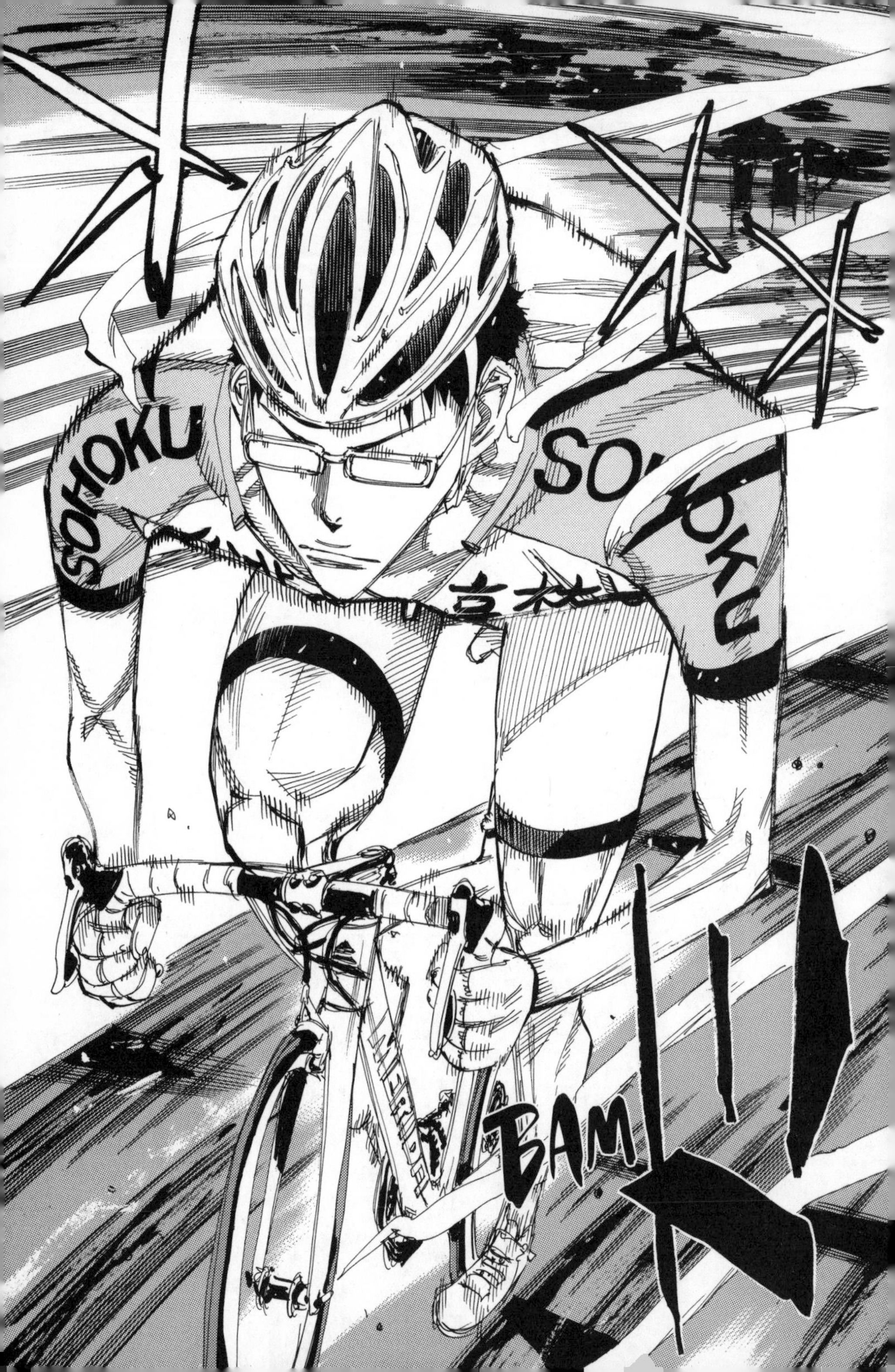
BAM

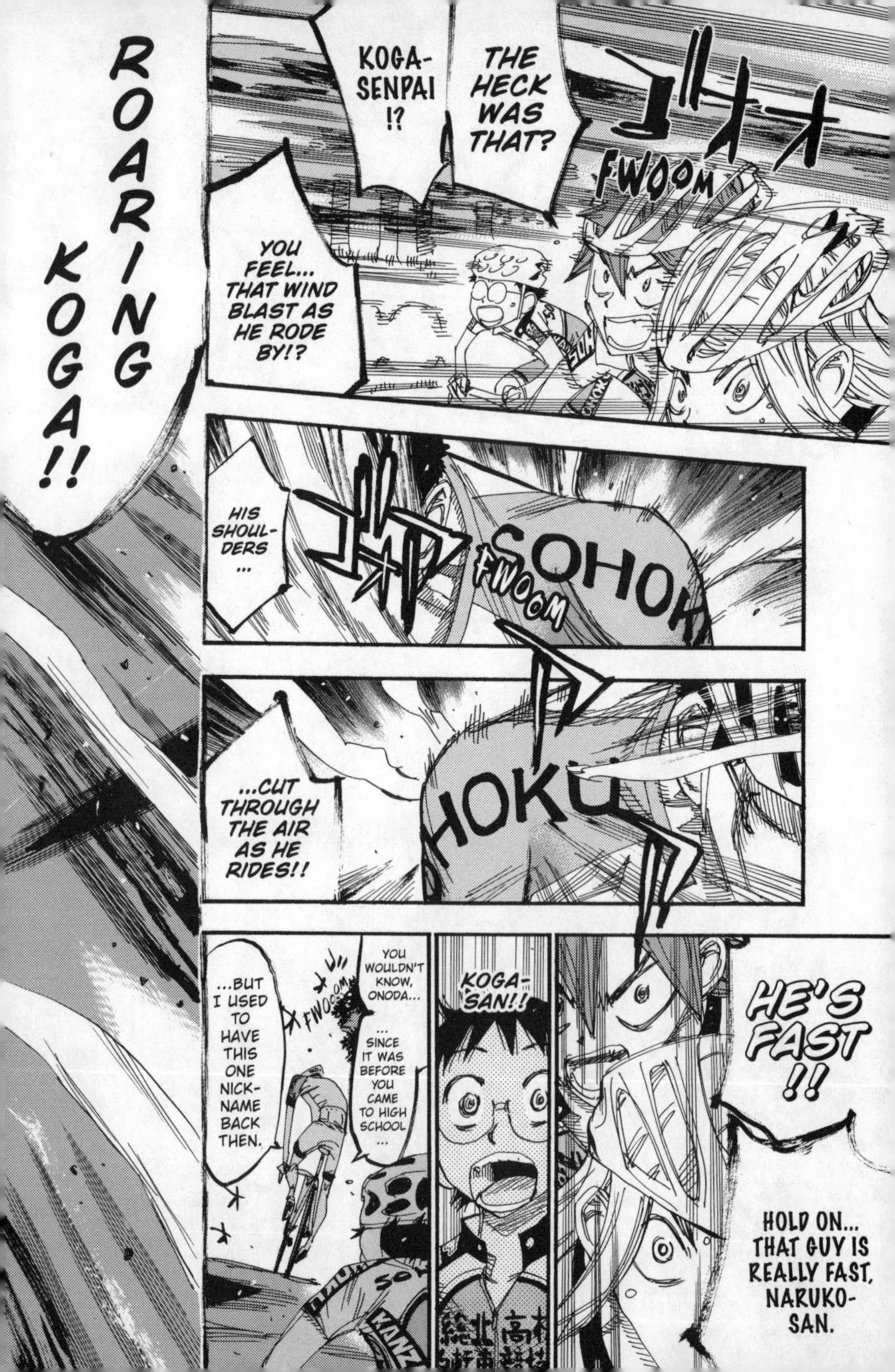
FWOOM
THE HECK WAS THAT?
KOGA-SENPAI!?
YOU FEEL... THAT WIND BLAST AS HE RODE BY!?
HIS SHOULDERS...
FWOOM
...CUT THROUGH THE AIR AS HE RIDES!!
HE'S FAST!!
HOLD ON... THAT GUY IS REALLY FAST, NARUKO-SAN.
KOGA-SAN!!
YOU WOULDN'T KNOW, ONODA...
...SINCE IT WAS BEFORE YOU CAME TO HIGH SCHOOL...
...BUT I USED TO HAVE THIS ONE NICKNAME BACK THEN.
FWOOOM
ROARING KOGA!!

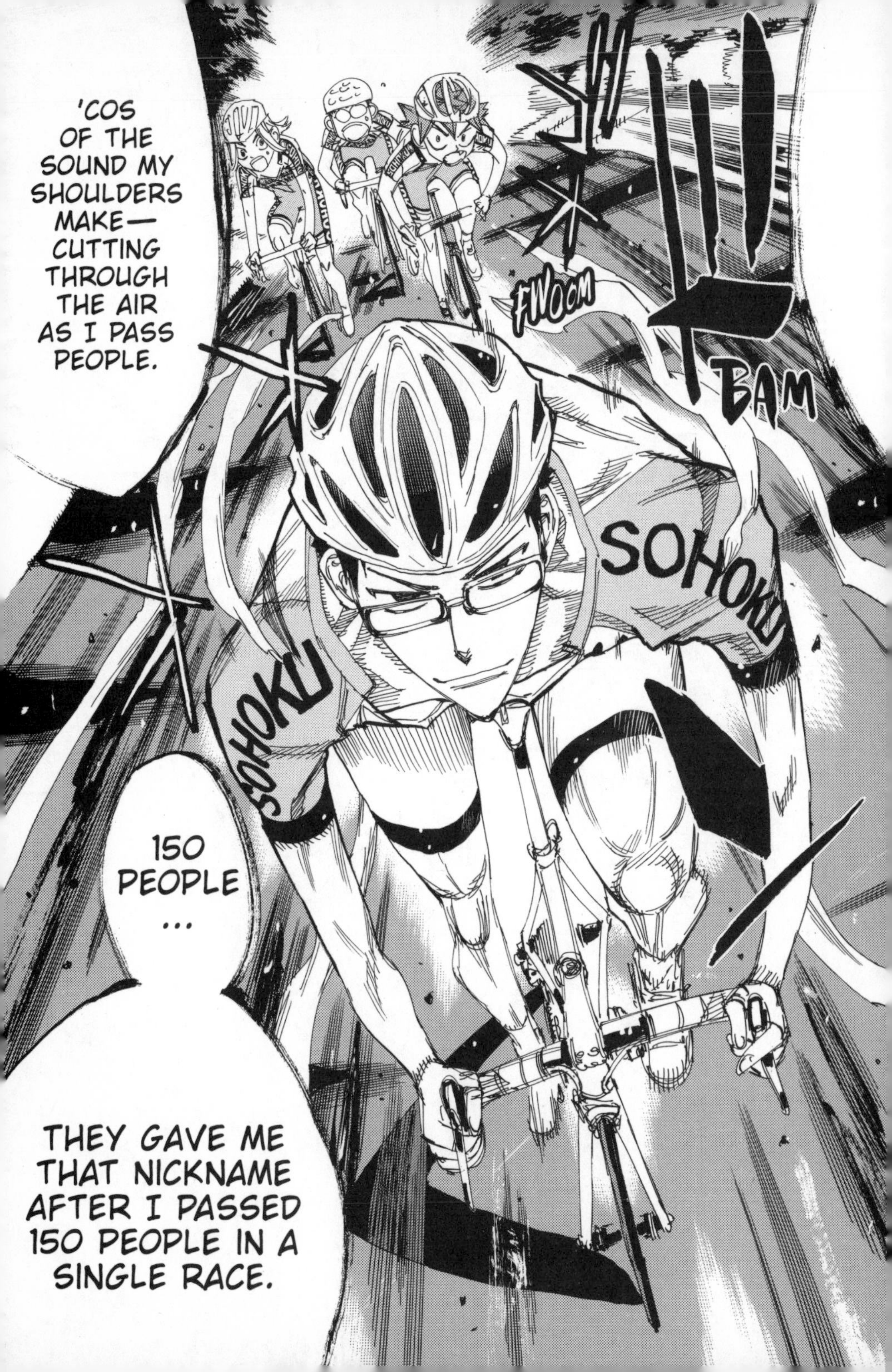
'COS OF THE SOUND MY SHOULDERS MAKE—CUTTING THROUGH THE AIR AS I PASS PEOPLE.
FWOOM
BAM
SOHOKU
SOHOKU
150 PEOPLE ...
THEY GAVE ME THAT NICKNAME AFTER I PASSED 150 PEOPLE IN A SINGLE RACE.

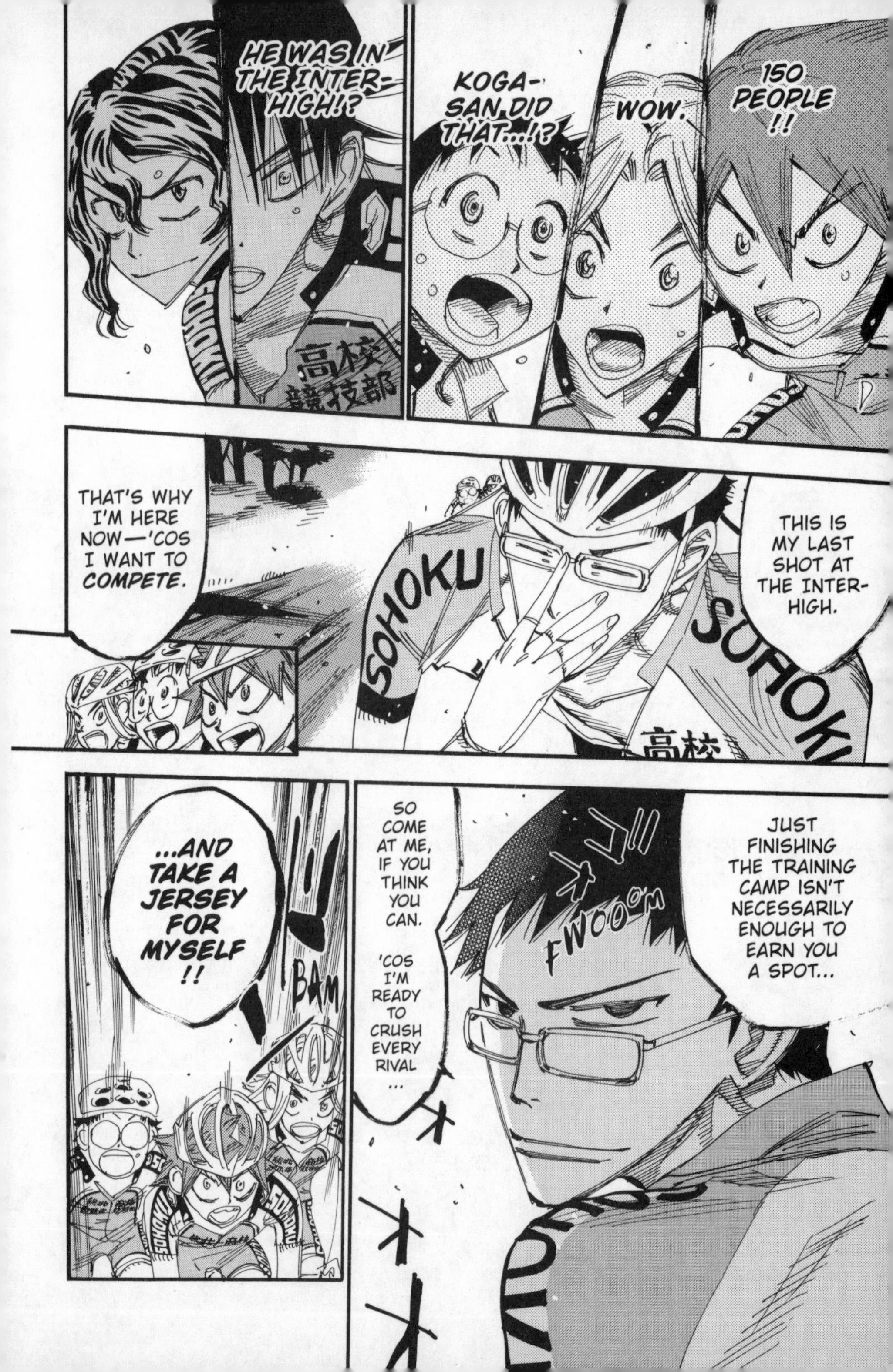
150 PEOPLE !!
WOW.
KOGA-SAN DID THAT...!?
HE WAS IN THE INTER-HIGH!?
THIS IS MY LAST SHOT AT THE INTER-HIGH.
THAT'S WHY I'M HERE NOW—'COS I WANT TO COMPETE.
JUST FINISHING THE TRAINING CAMP ISN'T NECESSARILY ENOUGH TO EARN YOU A SPOT...
FWOOOM
SO COME AT ME, IF YOU THINK YOU CAN.
'COS I'M READY TO CRUSH EVERY RIVAL ...
...AND TAKE A JERSEY FOR MYSELF !!
BAM

RIDE.283 ROARING KOGA

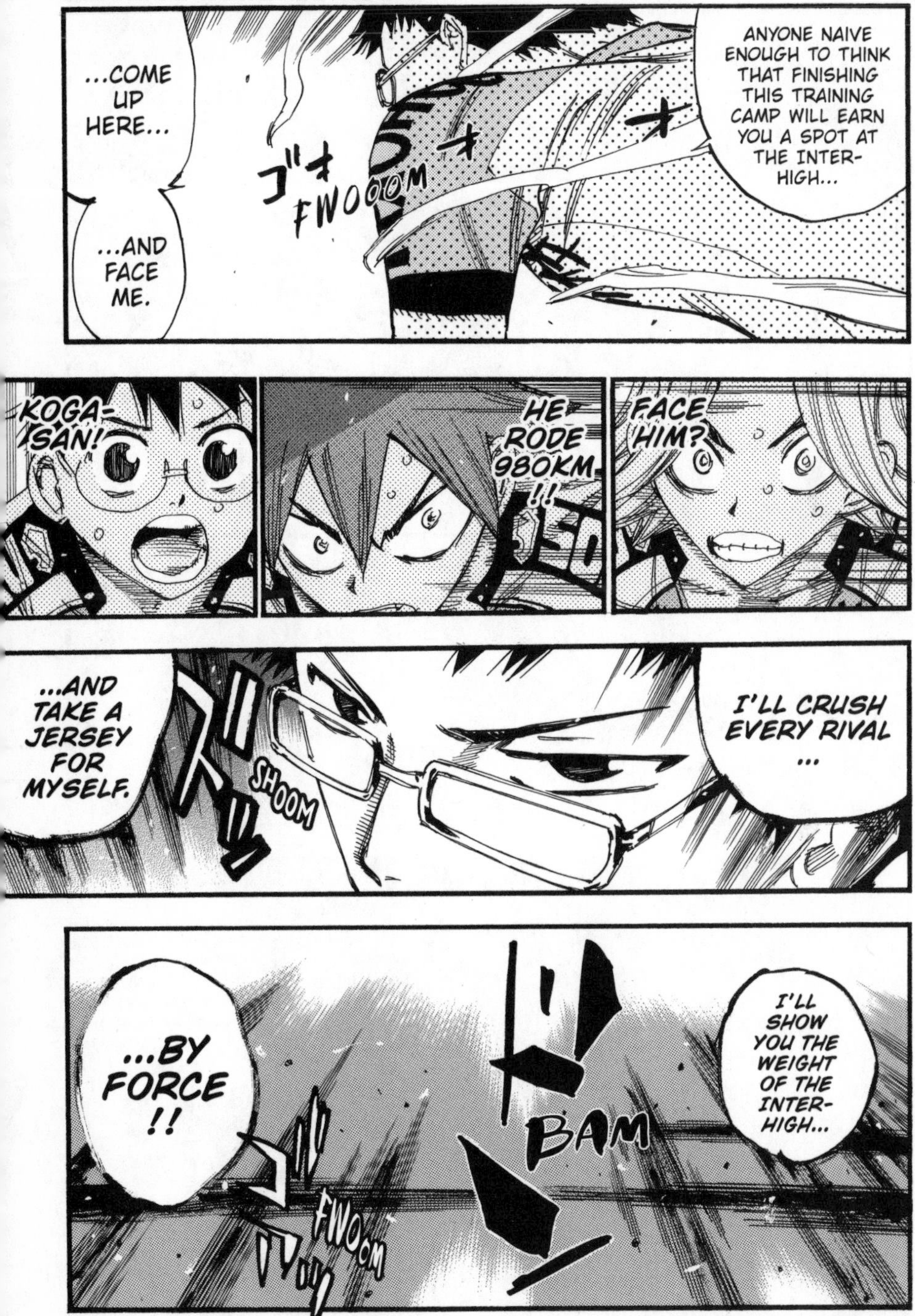
ANYONE NAIVE ENOUGH TO THINK THAT FINISHING THIS TRAINING CAMP WILL EARN YOU A SPOT AT THE INTER-HIGH...
FWOOOM
...COME UP HERE...
...AND FACE ME.
FACE HIM?
HE RODE 980KM!!
KOGA-SAN!
I'LL CRUSH EVERY RIVAL...
SHOOM
...AND TAKE A JERSEY FOR MYSELF.
I'LL SHOW YOU THE WEIGHT OF THE INTER-HIGH...
BAM
FWOOM
...BY FORCE!!

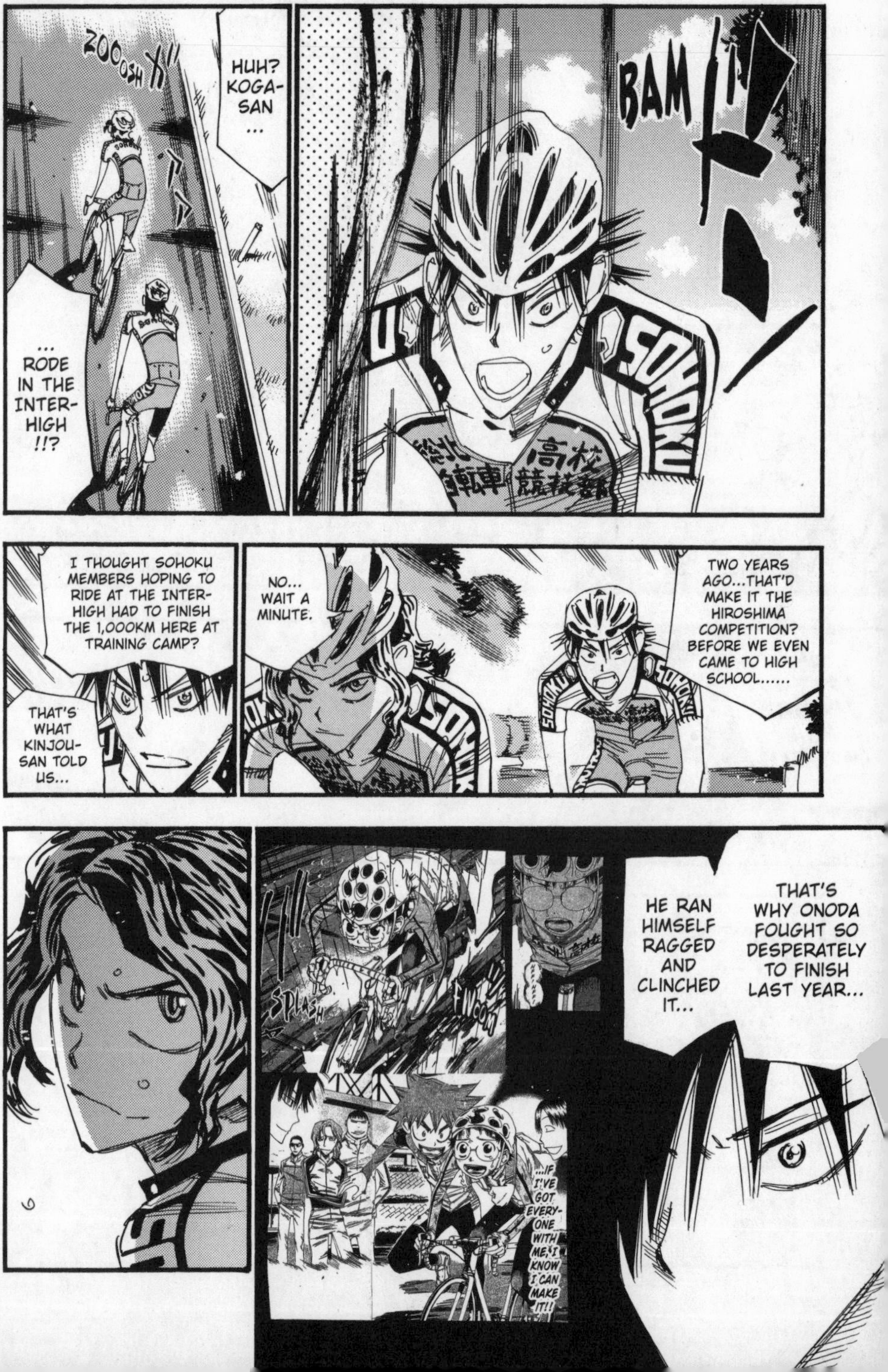
BAM
HUH? KOGA-SAN ...
ZOOOSH
... RODE IN THE INTER-HIGH !!?
TWO YEARS AGO...THAT'D MAKE IT THE HIROSHIMA COMPETITION? BEFORE WE EVEN CAME TO HIGH SCHOOL......
NO... WAIT A MINUTE.
I THOUGHT SOHOKU MEMBERS HOPING TO RIDE AT THE INTER-HIGH HAD TO FINISH THE 1,000KM HERE AT TRAINING CAMP?
THAT'S WHAT KINJOU-SAN TOLD US...
THAT'S WHY ONODA FOUGHT SO DESPERATELY TO FINISH LAST YEAR...
HE RAN HIMSELF RAGGED AND CLINCHED IT...
SPLASH
FWOOM
...IF I'VE GOT EVERYONE WITH ME, I KNOW I CAN MAKE IT!!

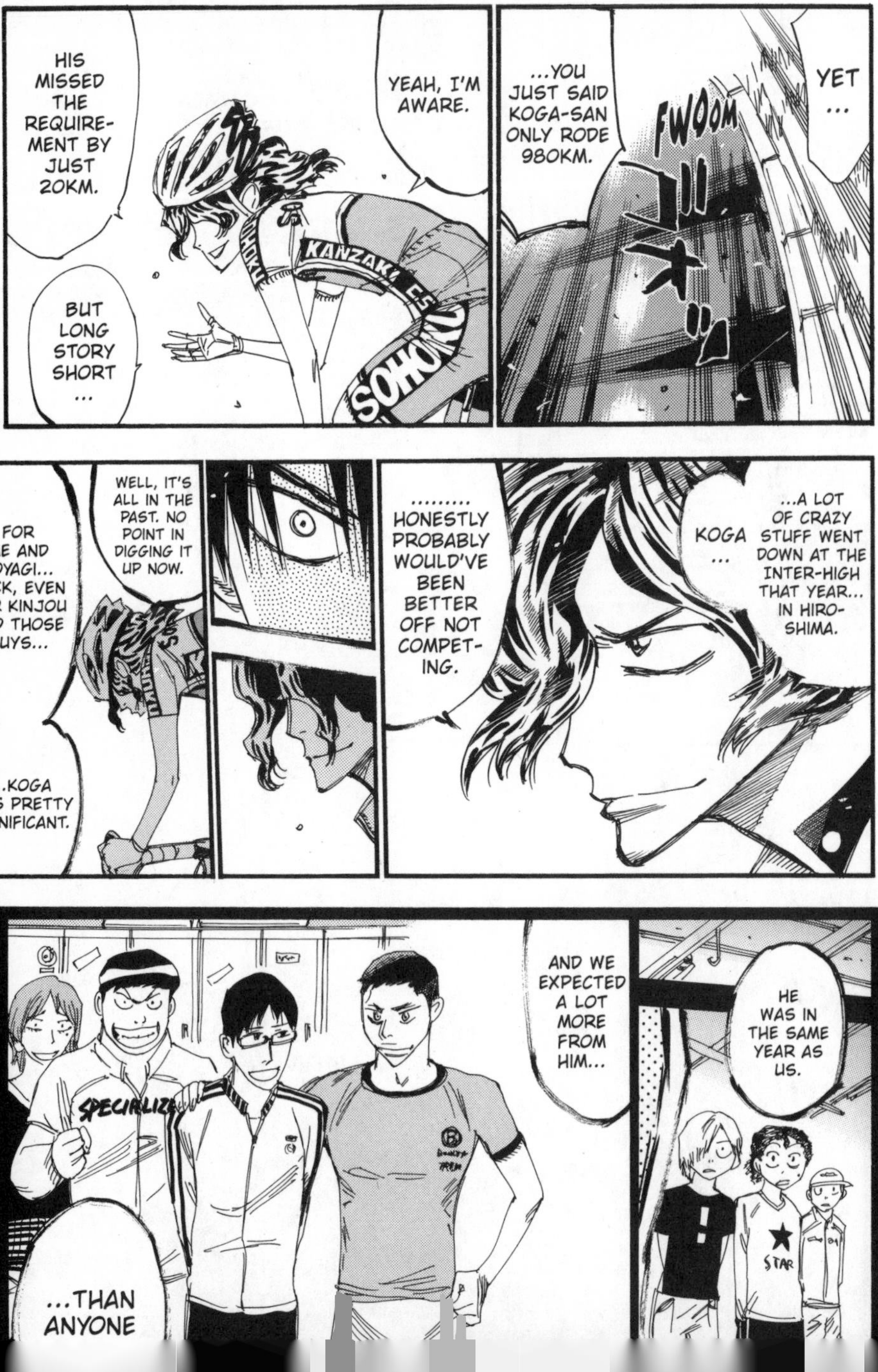
YET ...
...YOU JUST SAID KOGA-SAN ONLY RODE 980KM.
FWOOM
YEAH, I'M AWARE.
HIS MISSED THE REQUIRE-MENT BY JUST 20KM.
BUT LONG STORY SHORT ...
...A LOT OF CRAZY STUFF WENT DOWN AT THE INTER-HIGH THAT YEAR... IN HIRO-SHIMA.
KOGA ...
.... HONESTLY PROBABLY WOULD'VE BEEN BETTER OFF NOT COMPET-ING.
WELL, IT'S ALL IN THE PAST. NO POINT IN DIGGING IT UP NOW.
FOR ME AND AOYAGI... HECK, EVEN FOR KINJOU AND THOSE GUYS...
...KOGA WAS PRETTY SIGNIFICANT.
HE WAS IN THE SAME YEAR AS US.
AND WE EXPECTED A LOT MORE FROM HIM...
...THAN ANYONE

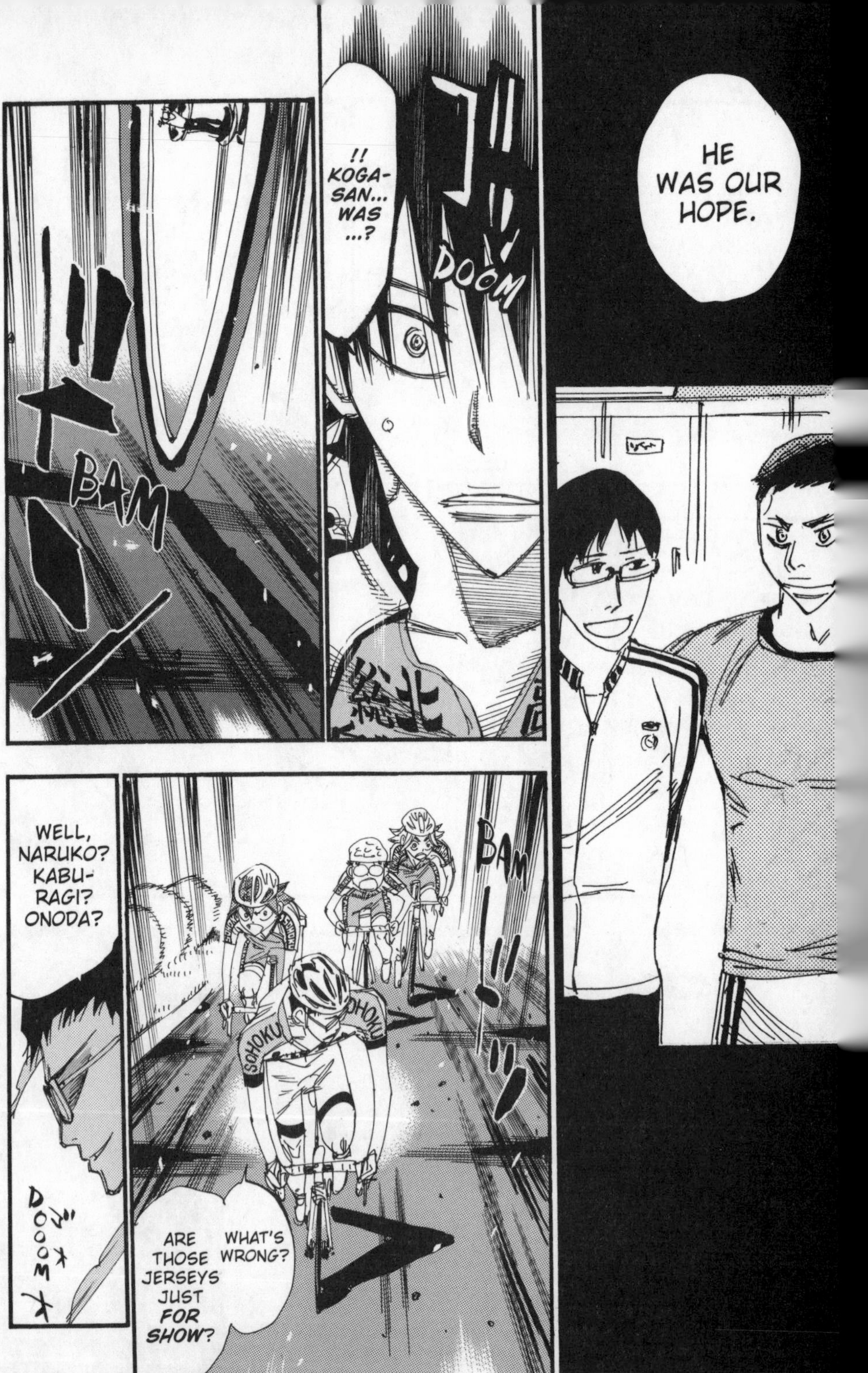
HE WAS OUR HOPE.
!! KOGA-SAN... WAS ...?
DOOM
BAM
BAM
WHAT'S WRONG?
ARE THOSE JERSEYS JUST *FOR SHOW?*
WELL, NARUKO? KABURAGI? ONODA?
DOOOOM

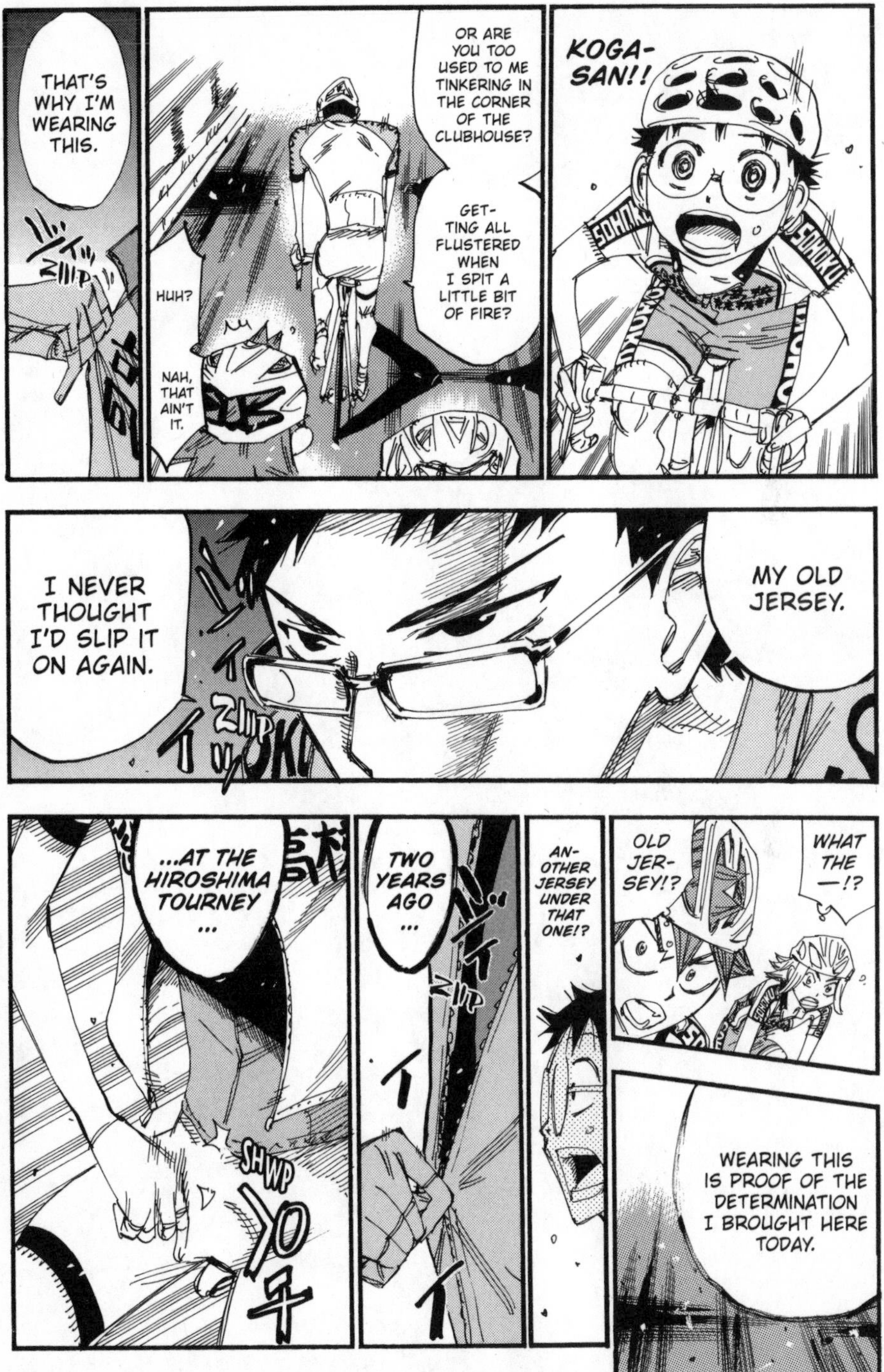

KOGA-SAN!!
OR ARE YOU TOO USED TO ME TINKERING IN THE CORNER OF THE CLUBHOUSE?
GET-TING ALL FLUSTERED WHEN I SPIT A LITTLE BIT OF FIRE?
HUH?
NAH, THAT AIN'T IT.
THAT'S WHY I'M WEARING THIS.
ZIIIP
MY OLD JERSEY.
I NEVER THOUGHT I'D SLIP IT ON AGAIN.
ZIIIP
WHAT THE —!?
OLD JER-SEY!?
WEARING THIS IS PROOF OF THE DETERMINATION I BROUGHT HERE TODAY.
AN-OTHER JERSEY UNDER THAT ONE!?
TWO YEARS AGO ...
ZIIIP
...AT THE HIROSHIMA TOURNEY ...
SHWP

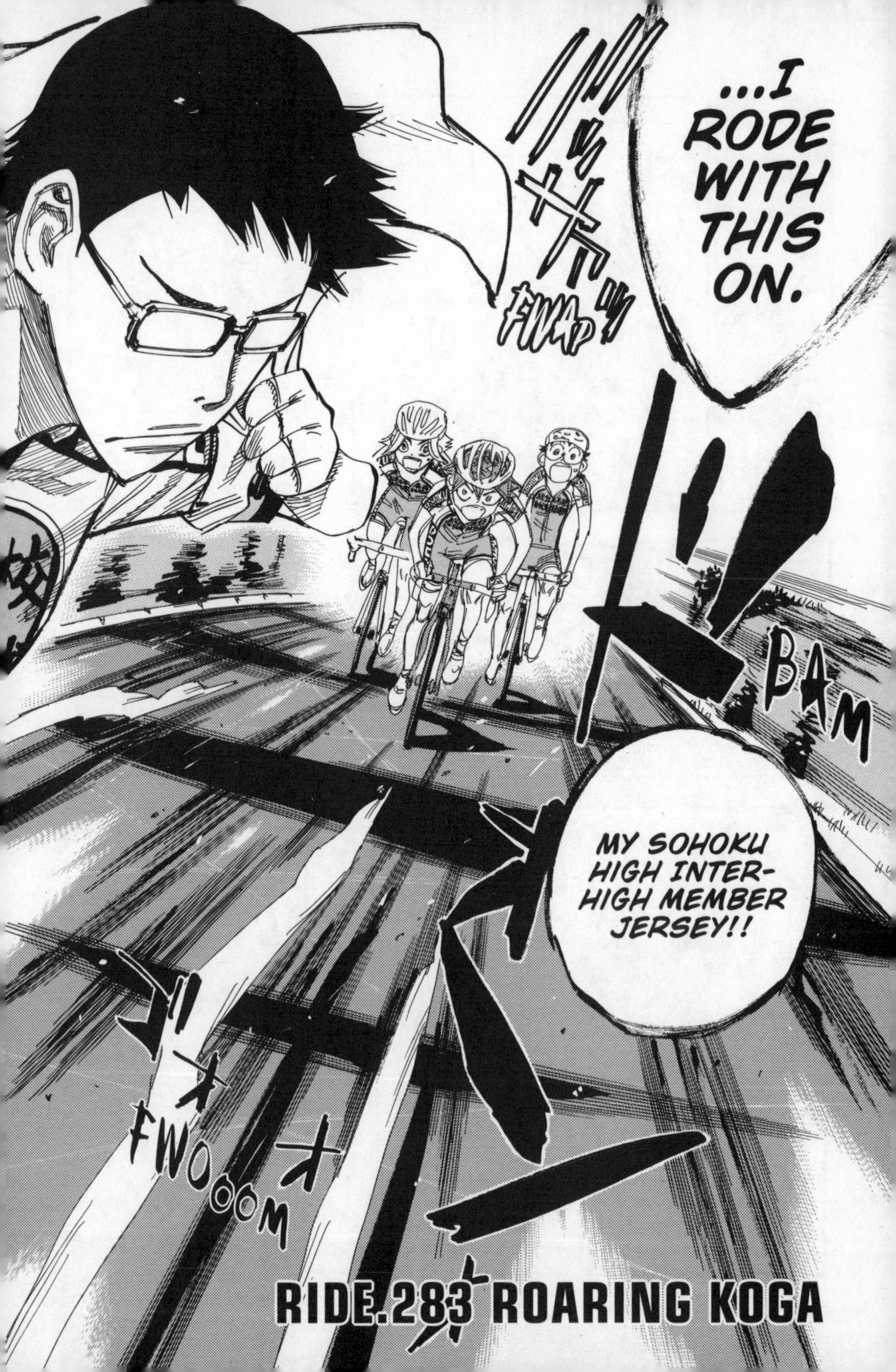
...I RODE WITH THIS ON.
FWAP
BAM
MY SOHOKU HIGH INTER-HIGH MEMBER JERSEY!!
FWOOOM
RIDE.283 ROARING KOGA

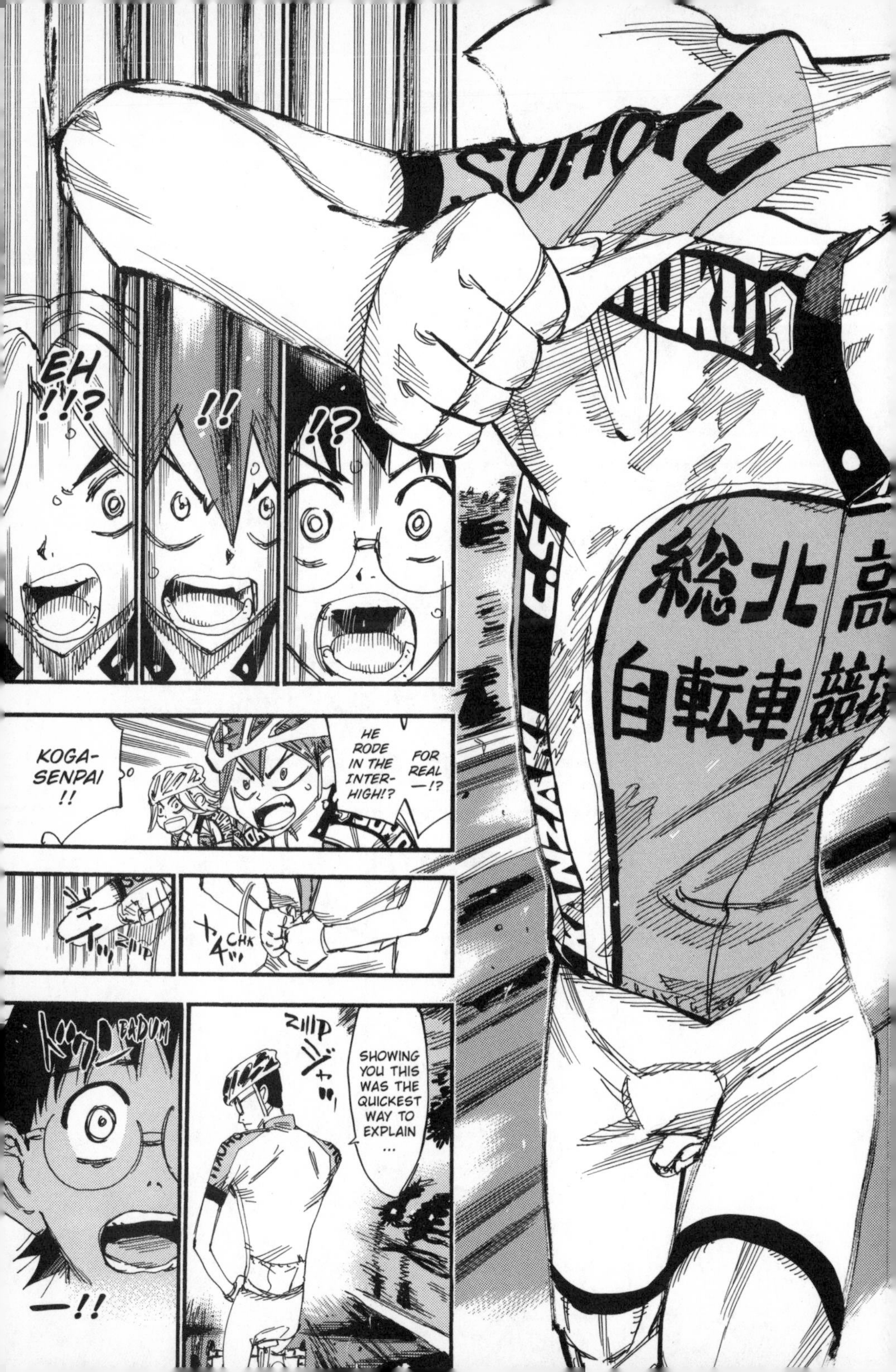
総北高
自転車
!?
!!
EH!!?
FOR REAL—!?
HE RODE IN THE INTER-HIGH!?
KOGA-SENPAI!!
CHK
ZIIP
ZIIP
SHOWING YOU THIS WAS THE QUICKEST WAY TO EXPLAIN...
BADUM
—!!

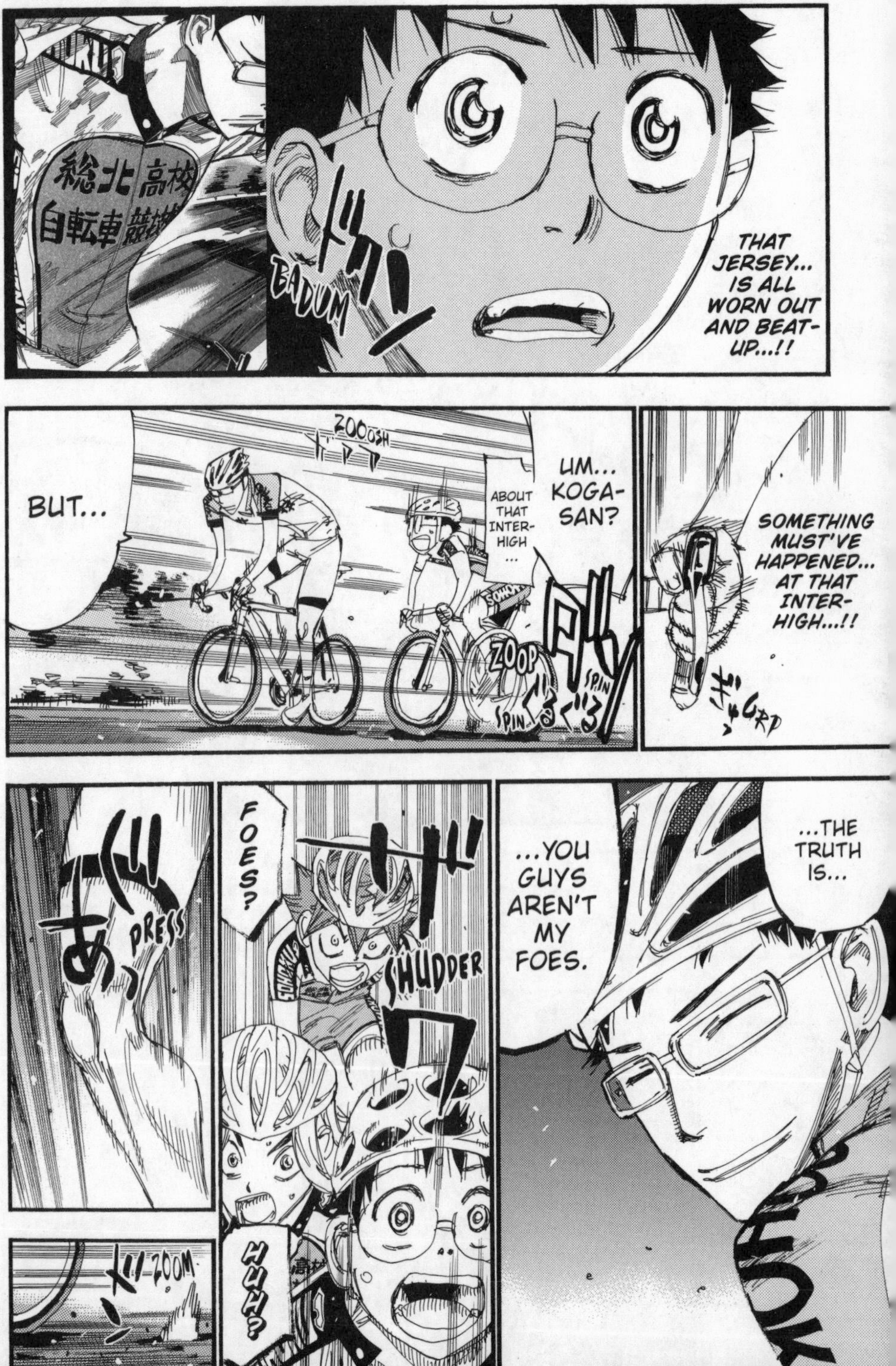
ドクン
BADUM
THAT JERSEY... IS ALL WORN OUT AND BEAT-UP...!!
総北高校
自転車競技
SOMETHING MUST'VE HAPPENED... AT THAT INTER-HIGH...!!
ぎゅ GRP
UM... KOGA-SAN?
ABOUT THAT INTER-HIGH...
ZOOOSH
BUT...
ZOOP
SPIN SPIN ぐるぐる
...THE TRUTH IS...
...YOU GUYS AREN'T MY FOES.
SHOK
FOES?
ザワ SHUDDER
HUH?
くぃっ PRESS
ZOOM

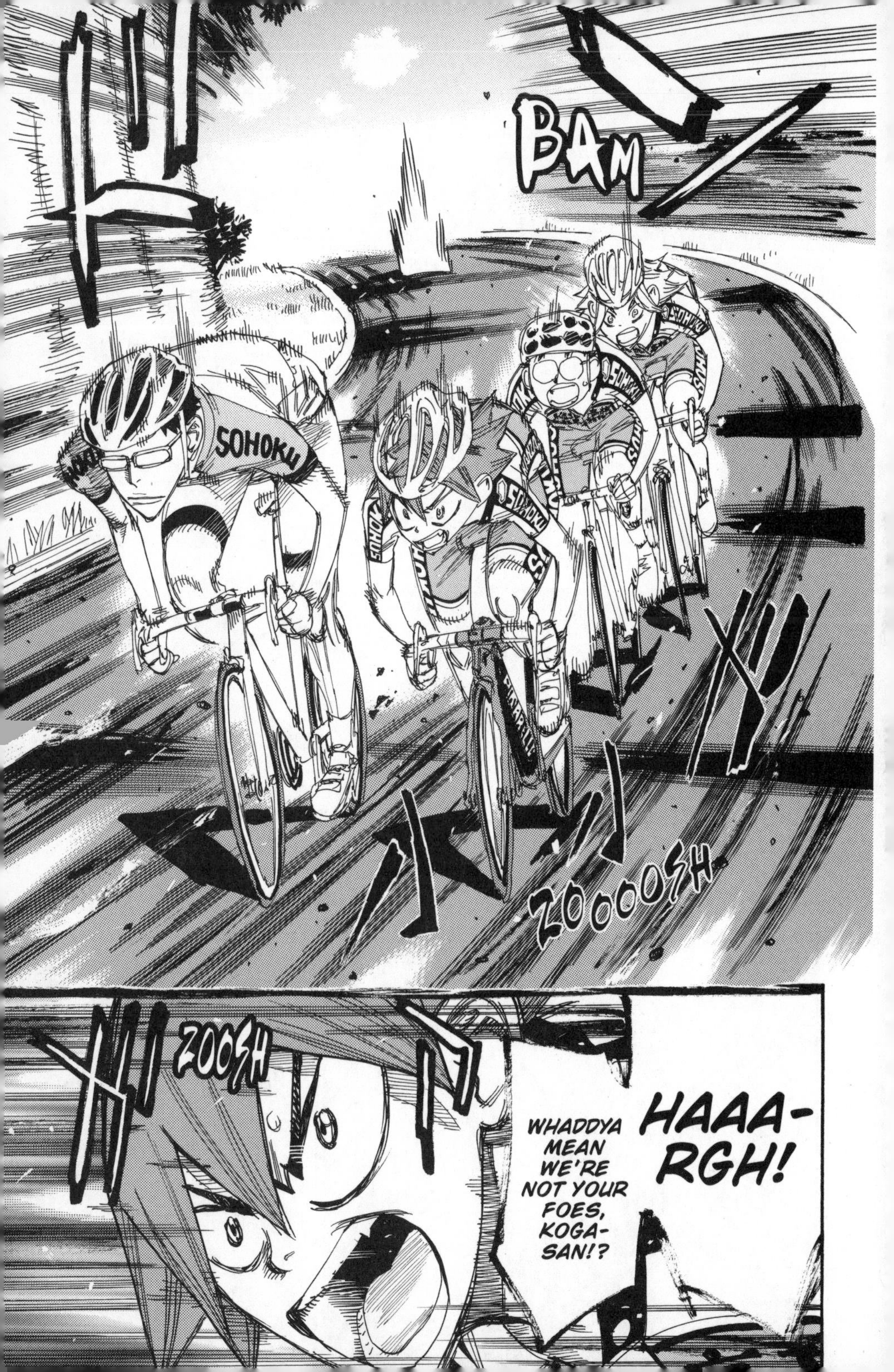
BAM
SOHOKU
ZOOOOOSH
ZOOSH
HAAA-
RGH!
WHADDYA MEAN WE'RE NOT YOUR FOES, KOGA-SAN!?

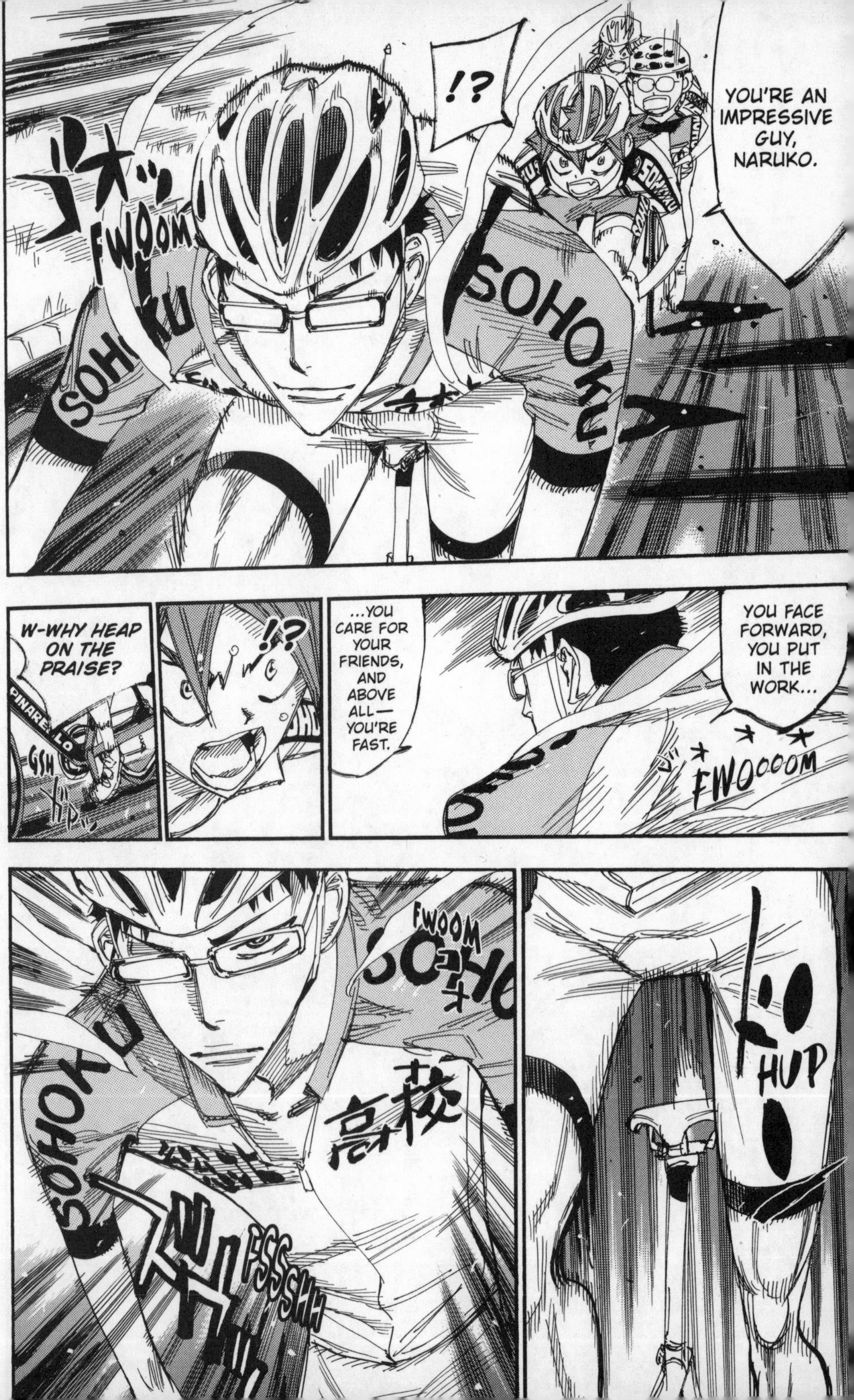
YOU'RE AN IMPRESSIVE GUY, NARUKO.
!?
FWOOM
YOU FACE FORWARD, YOU PUT IN THE WORK...
FWOOOOM
...YOU CARE FOR YOUR FRIENDS, AND ABOVE ALL— YOU'RE FAST.
!?
W-WHY HEAP ON THE PRAISE?
GSH
HUP
FWOOM
FSSSHH

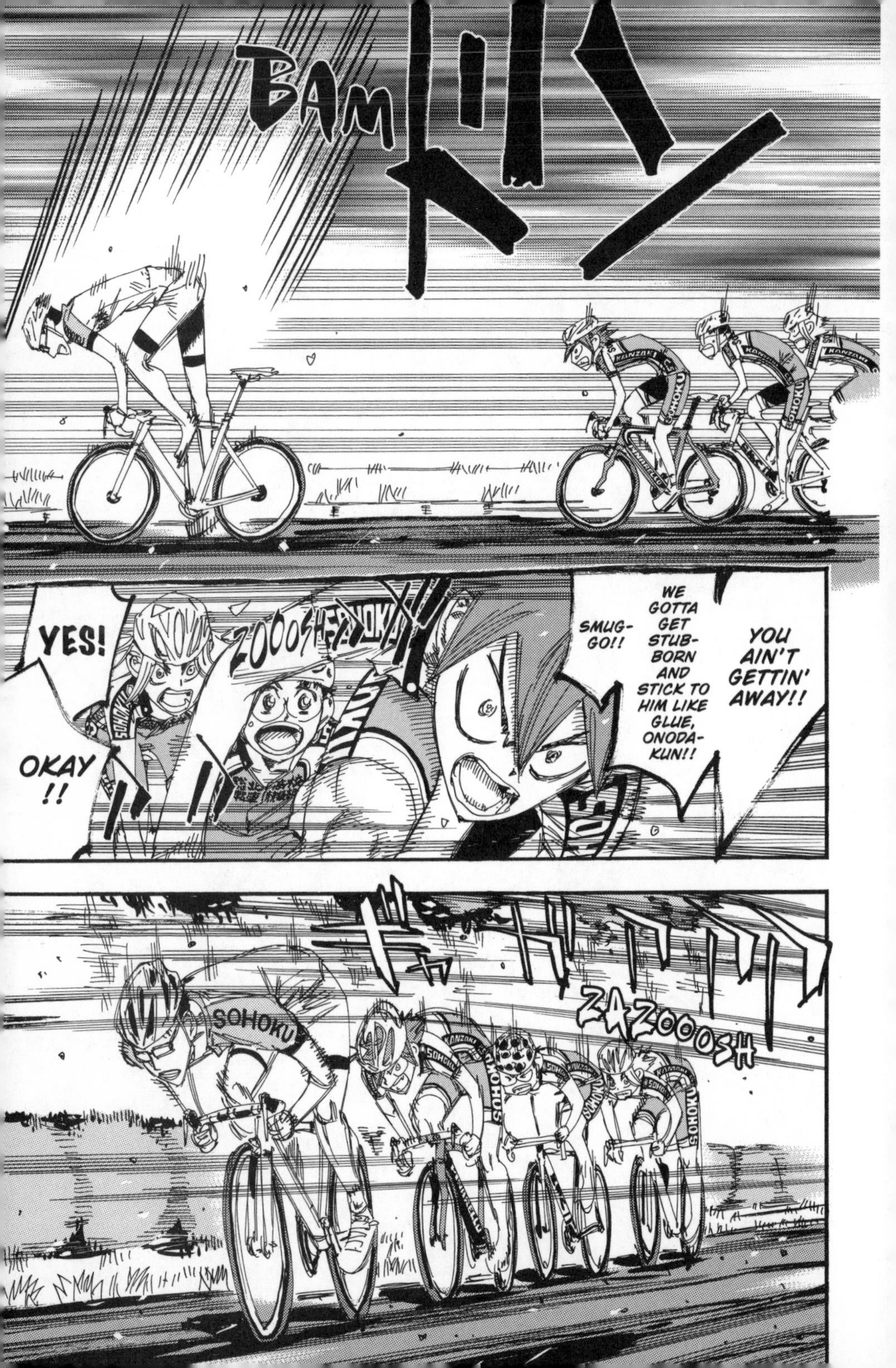
BAM
ドーン
YOU AIN'T GETTIN' AWAY!!
WE GOTTA GET STUB-BORN AND STICK TO HIM LIKE GLUE, ONODA-KUN!!
SMUG-GO!!
ZOOOSH
YES!
OKAY!!
ZAZOOOOSH

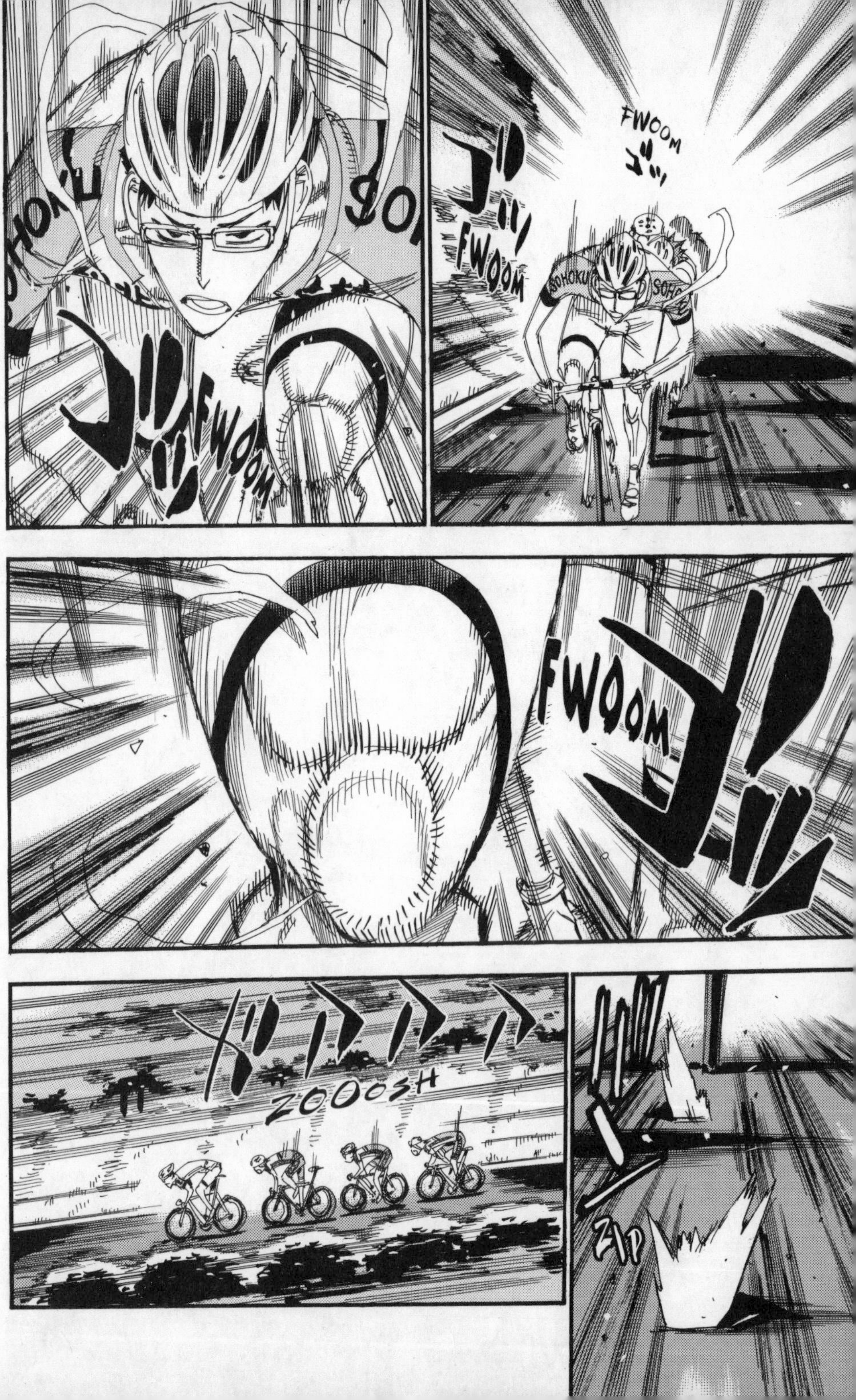
FWOOM
SOHOKU
SOHOKU
FWOOM
SOHOKU
SOHOKU
FWOOM
FWOOM
ZIP
ZOOOSH

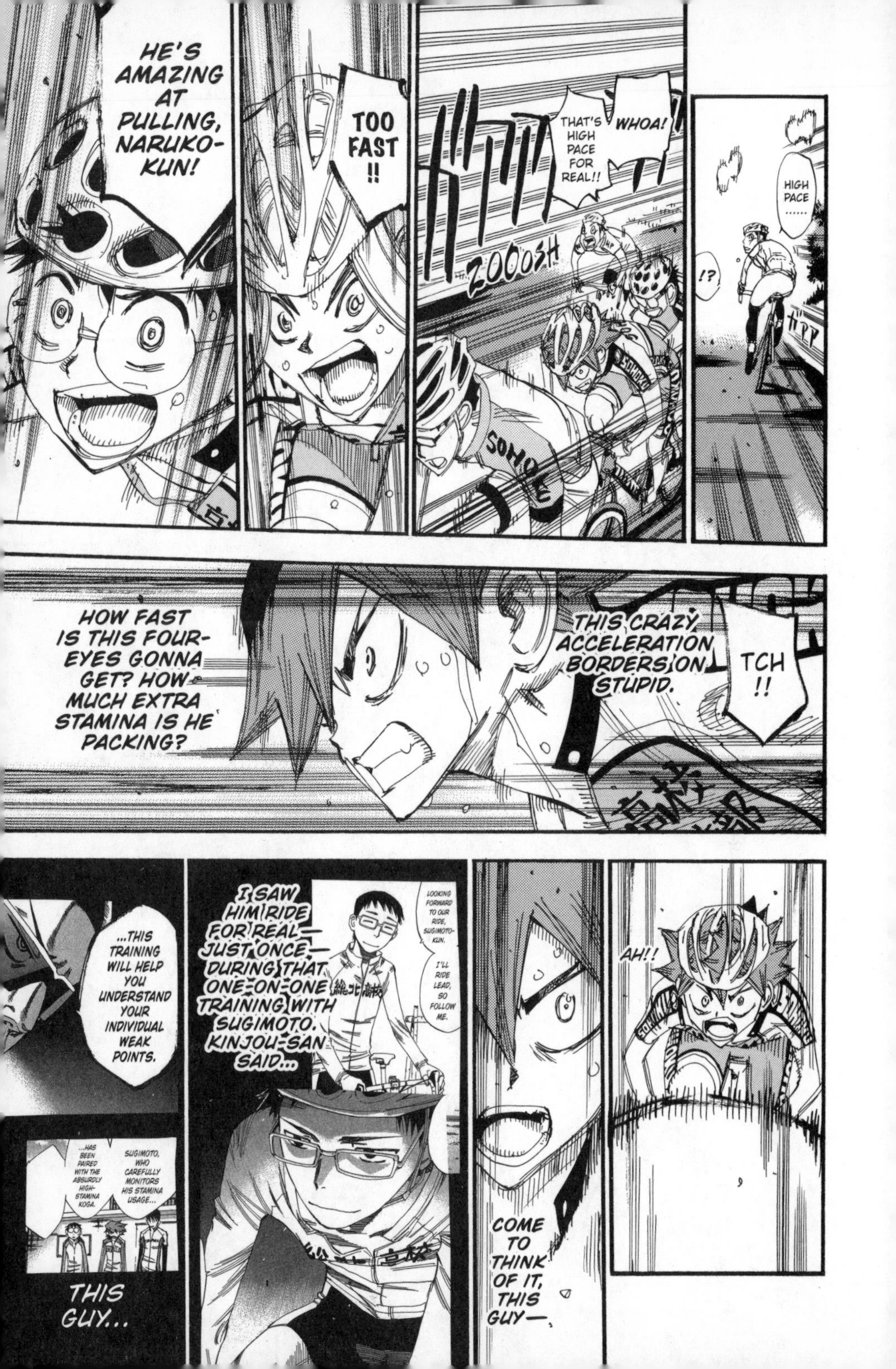

HIGH PACE ......
!?
WHOA!
THAT'S HIGH PACE FOR REAL!!
ZOOOSH
TOO FAST !!
HE'S AMAZING AT PULLING, NARUKO-KUN!
TCH !!
THIS CRAZY ACCELERATION BORDERS ON STUPID.
HOW FAST IS THIS FOUR-EYES GONNA GET? HOW MUCH EXTRA STAMINA IS HE PACKING?
AH!!
COME TO THINK OF IT, THIS GUY—
LOOKING FORWARD TO OUR RIDE, SUGIMOTO-KUN.
I'LL RIDE LEAD, SO FOLLOW ME.
I SAW HIM RIDE FOR REAL—JUST ONCE—DURING THAT ONE-ON-ONE TRAINING WITH SUGIMOTO. KINJOU-SAN SAID...
...THIS TRAINING WILL HELP YOU UNDERSTAND YOUR INDIVIDUAL WEAK POINTS.
SUGIMOTO, WHO CAREFULLY MONITORS HIS STAMINA USAGE...
...HAS BEEN PAIRED WITH THE ABSURDLY HIGH-STAMINA KOGA.
THIS GUY...

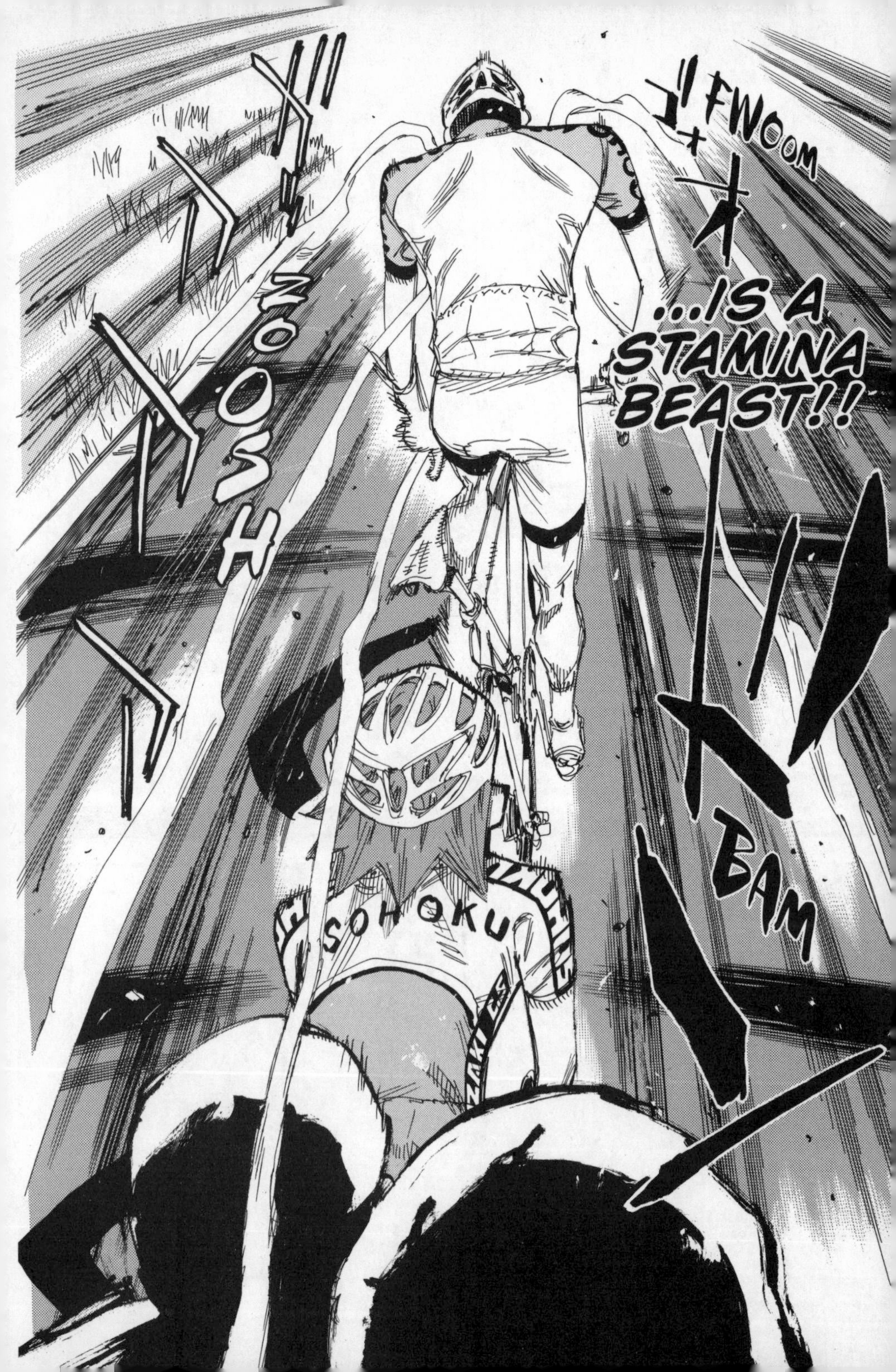
FWOOM
...IS A STAMINA BEAST!!
BAM
ZOOOSH
SOHOKU

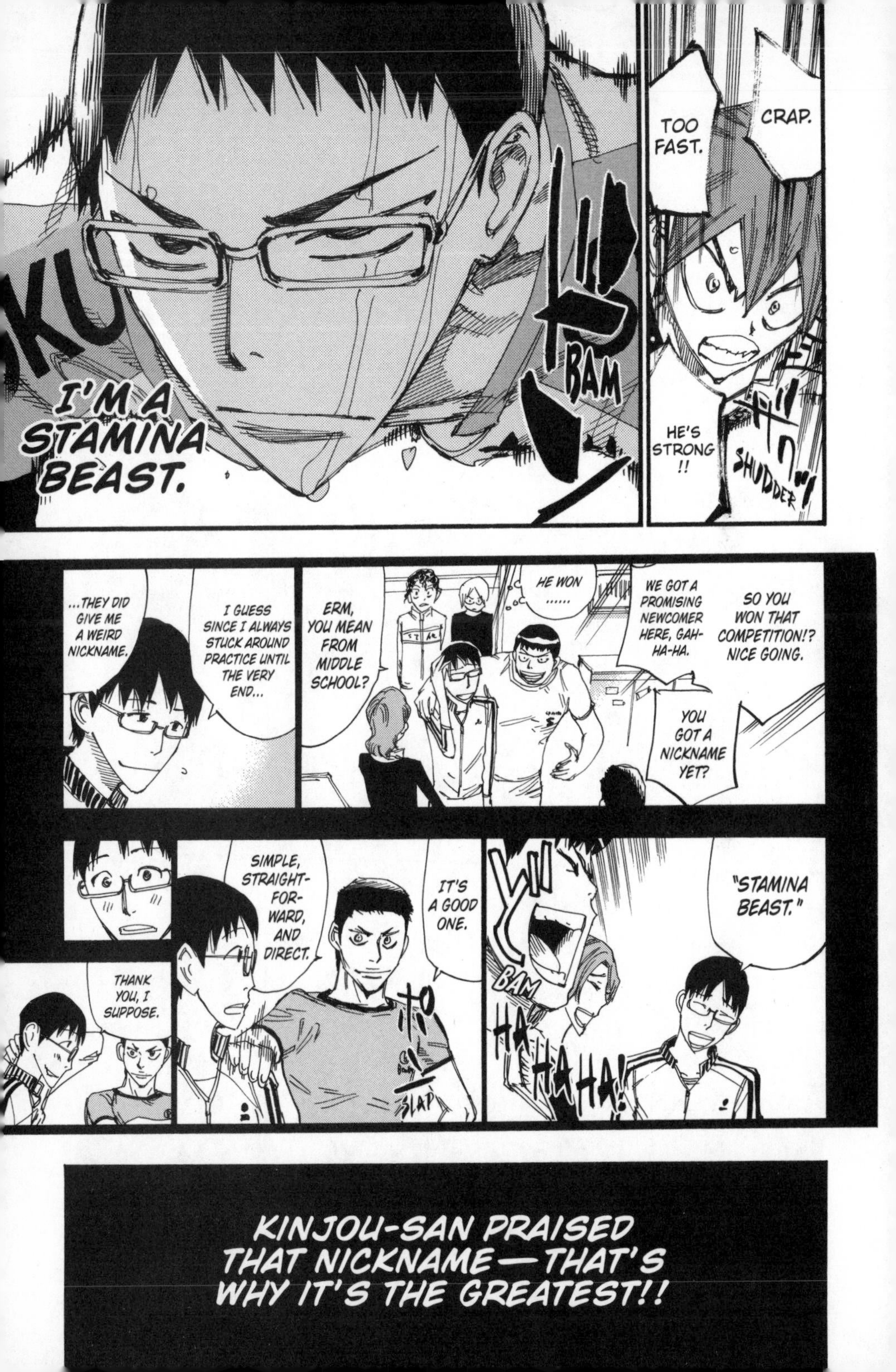
CRAP.
TOO FAST.
HE'S STRONG !!
SHUDDER
BAM
I'M A STAMINA BEAST.
SO YOU WON THAT COMPETITION!? NICE GOING.
WE GOT A PROMISING NEWCOMER HERE, GAH-HA-HA.
HE WON ......
YOU GOT A NICKNAME YET?
ERM, YOU MEAN FROM MIDDLE SCHOOL?
I GUESS SINCE I ALWAYS STUCK AROUND PRACTICE UNTIL THE VERY END...
...THEY DID GIVE ME A WEIRD NICKNAME.
"STAMINA BEAST."
BAM
HAHAHA!
IT'S A GOOD ONE.
SIMPLE, STRAIGHT-FOR-WARD, AND DIRECT.
SLAP
THANK YOU, I SUPPOSE.
KINJOU-SAN PRAISED THAT NICKNAME—THAT'S WHY IT'S THE GREATEST!!

ZOOOSH

BAM

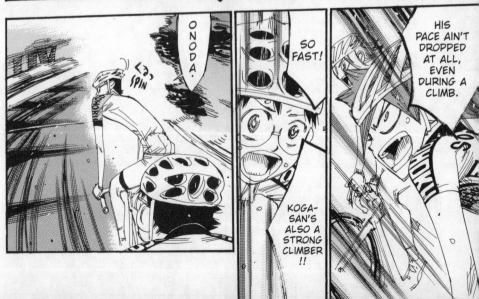

ONODA.

[う] SPIN

SO FAST!

HIS PACE AIN'T DROPPED AT ALL, EVEN DURING A CLIMB.

KOGA-SAN'S ALSO A STRONG CLIMBER!!

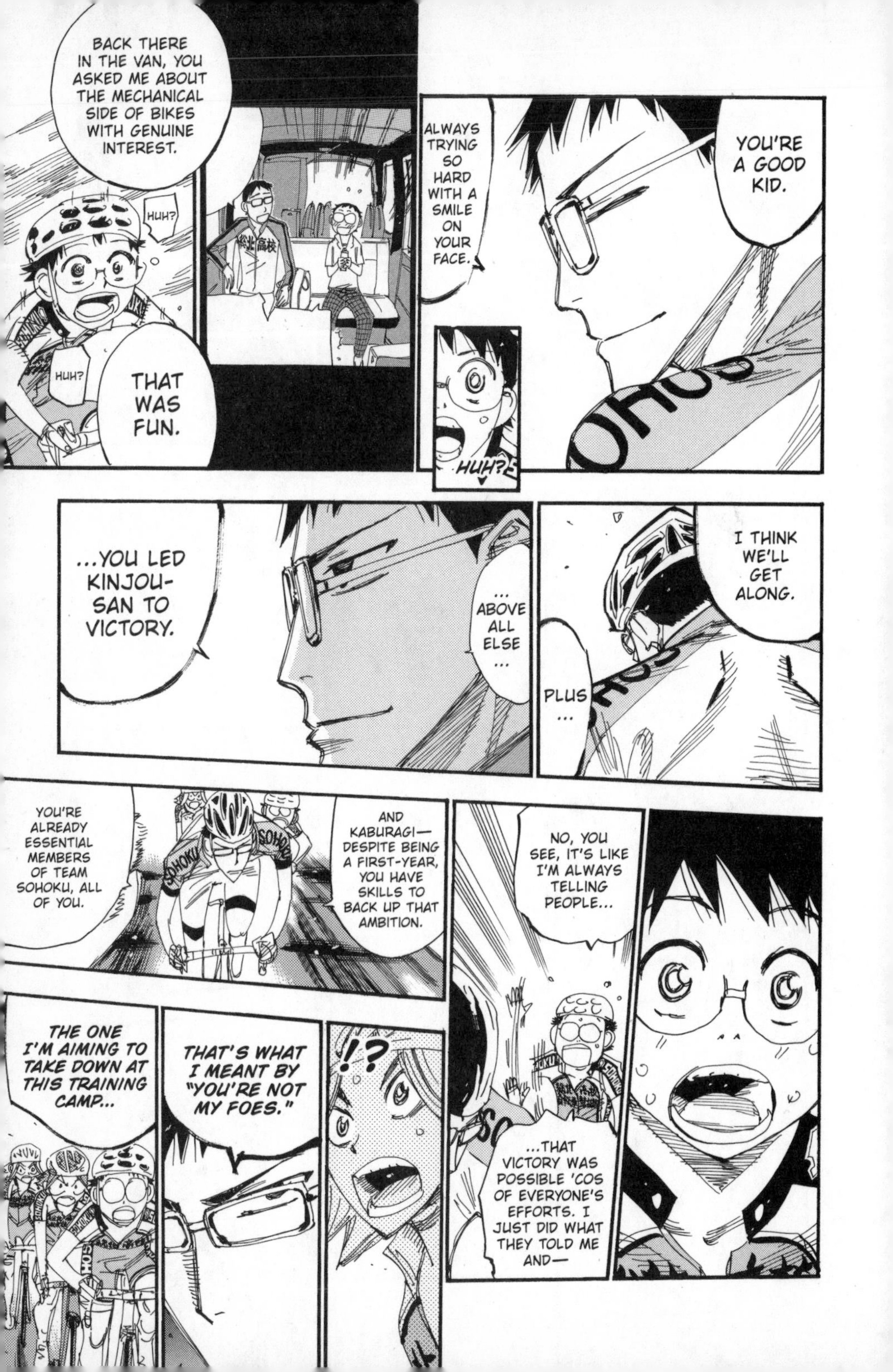
YOU'RE A GOOD KID.
ALWAYS TRYING SO HARD WITH A SMILE ON YOUR FACE.
HUH?!
BACK THERE IN THE VAN, YOU ASKED ME ABOUT THE MECHANICAL SIDE OF BIKES WITH GENUINE INTEREST.
HUH?
HUH?
THAT WAS FUN.
I THINK WE'LL GET ALONG.
PLUS...
...ABOVE ALL ELSE...
...YOU LED KINJOU-SAN TO VICTORY.
NO, YOU SEE, IT'S LIKE I'M ALWAYS TELLING PEOPLE...
...THAT VICTORY WAS POSSIBLE 'COS OF EVERYONE'S EFFORTS. I JUST DID WHAT THEY TOLD ME AND—
AND KABURAGI—DESPITE BEING A FIRST-YEAR, YOU HAVE SKILLS TO BACK UP THAT AMBITION.
YOU'RE ALREADY ESSENTIAL MEMBERS OF TEAM SOHOKU, ALL OF YOU.
!?
THAT'S WHAT I MEANT BY "YOU'RE NOT MY FOES."
THE ONE I'M AIMING TO TAKE DOWN AT THIS TRAINING CAMP...

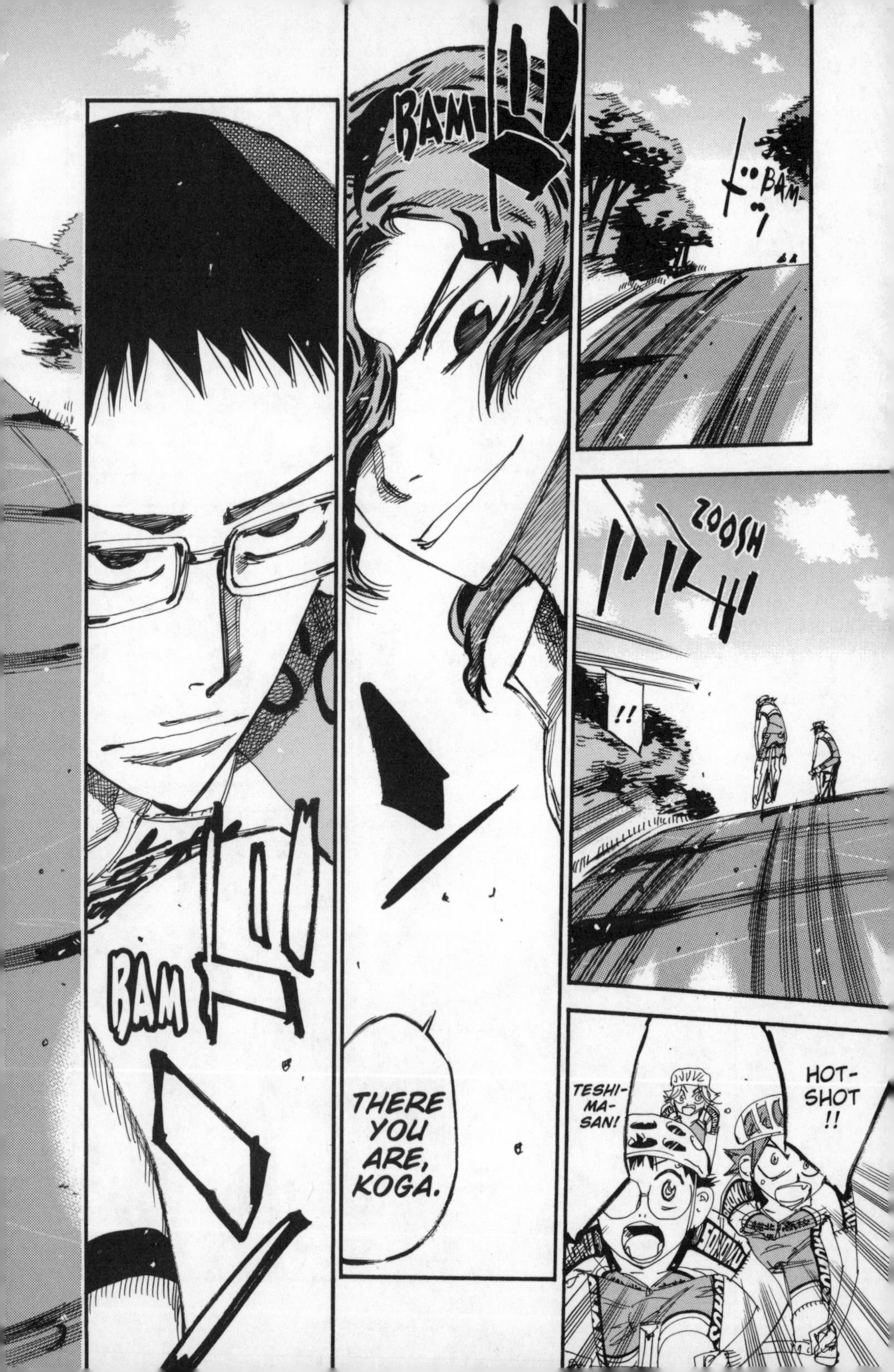
BAM
ZOOSH
!!
HOT-SHOT!!
TESHIMA-SAN!
BAM
THERE YOU ARE, KOGA.
BAM

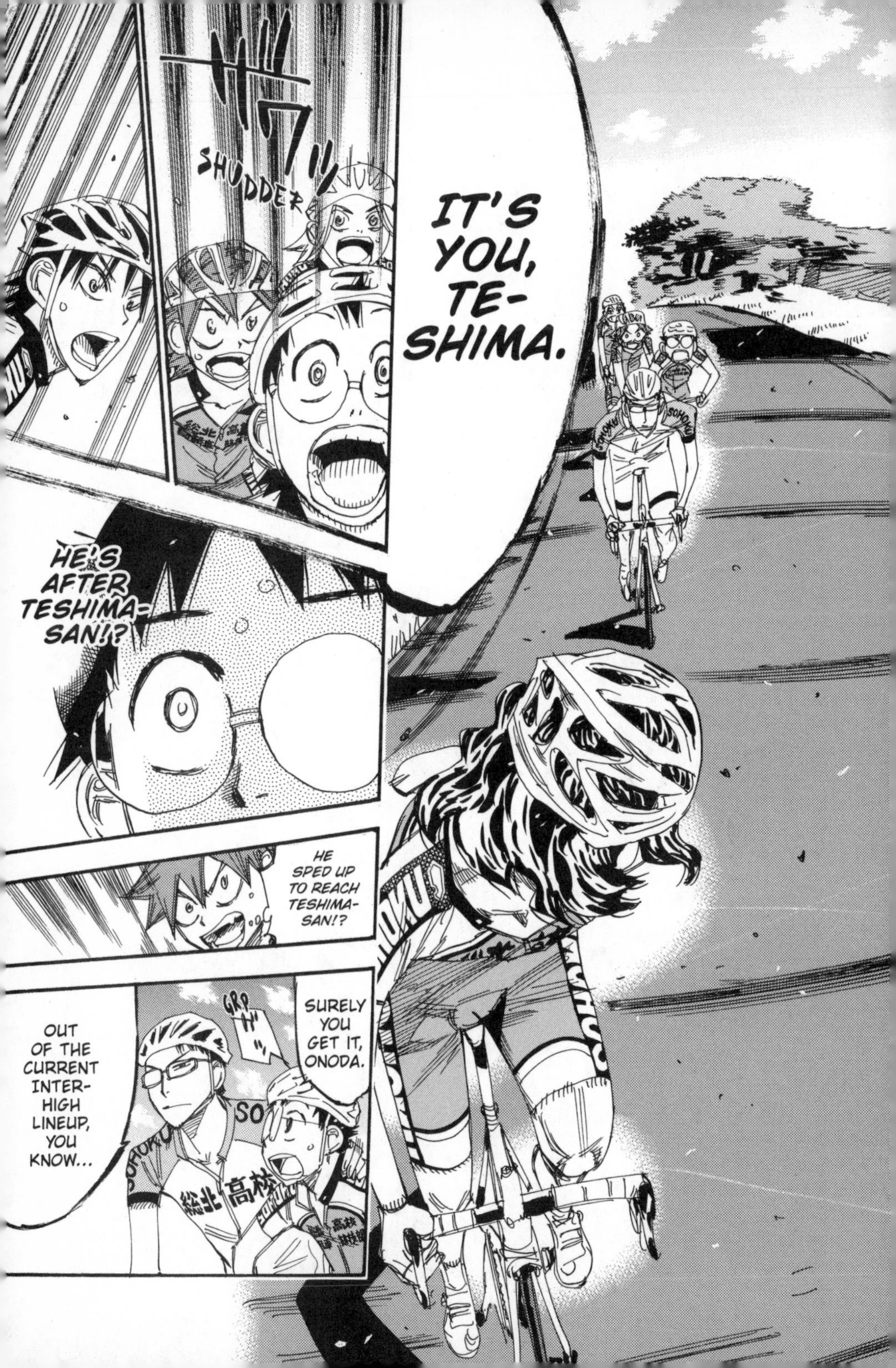
IT'S YOU, TESHIMA.
SHUDDER
HE'S AFTER TESHIMA-SAN!?
HE SPED UP TO REACH TESHIMA-SAN!?
SURELY YOU GET IT, ONODA.
GRP
OUT OF THE CURRENT INTER-HIGH LINEUP, YOU KNOW...

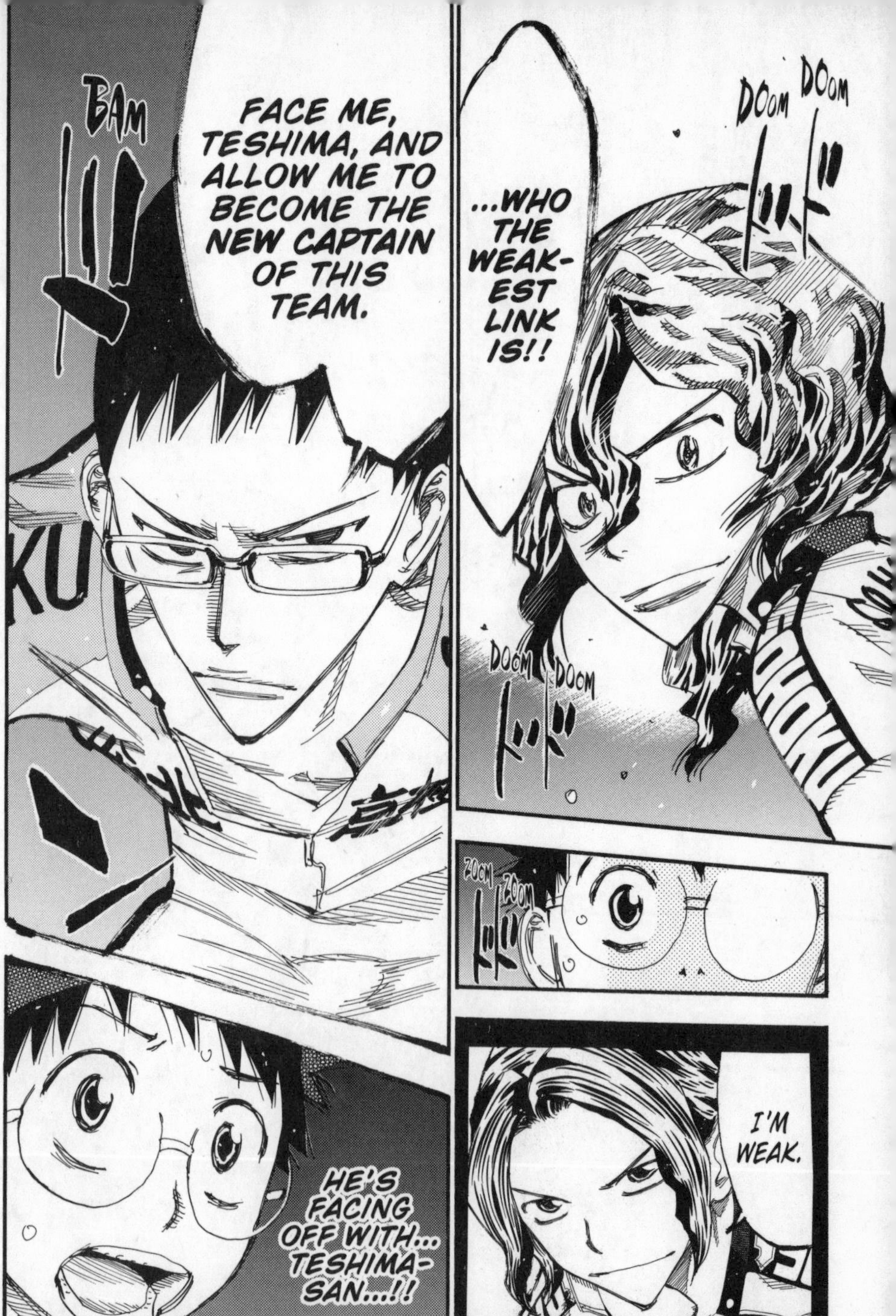
DOOM DOOM
...WHO THE WEAK-EST LINK IS!!
DOOM DOOM
BAM
FACE ME, TESHIMA, AND ALLOW ME TO BECOME THE NEW CAPTAIN OF THIS TEAM.
ZOOM ZOOM
HE'S FACING OFF WITH... TESHIMA-SAN...!!
I'M WEAK.

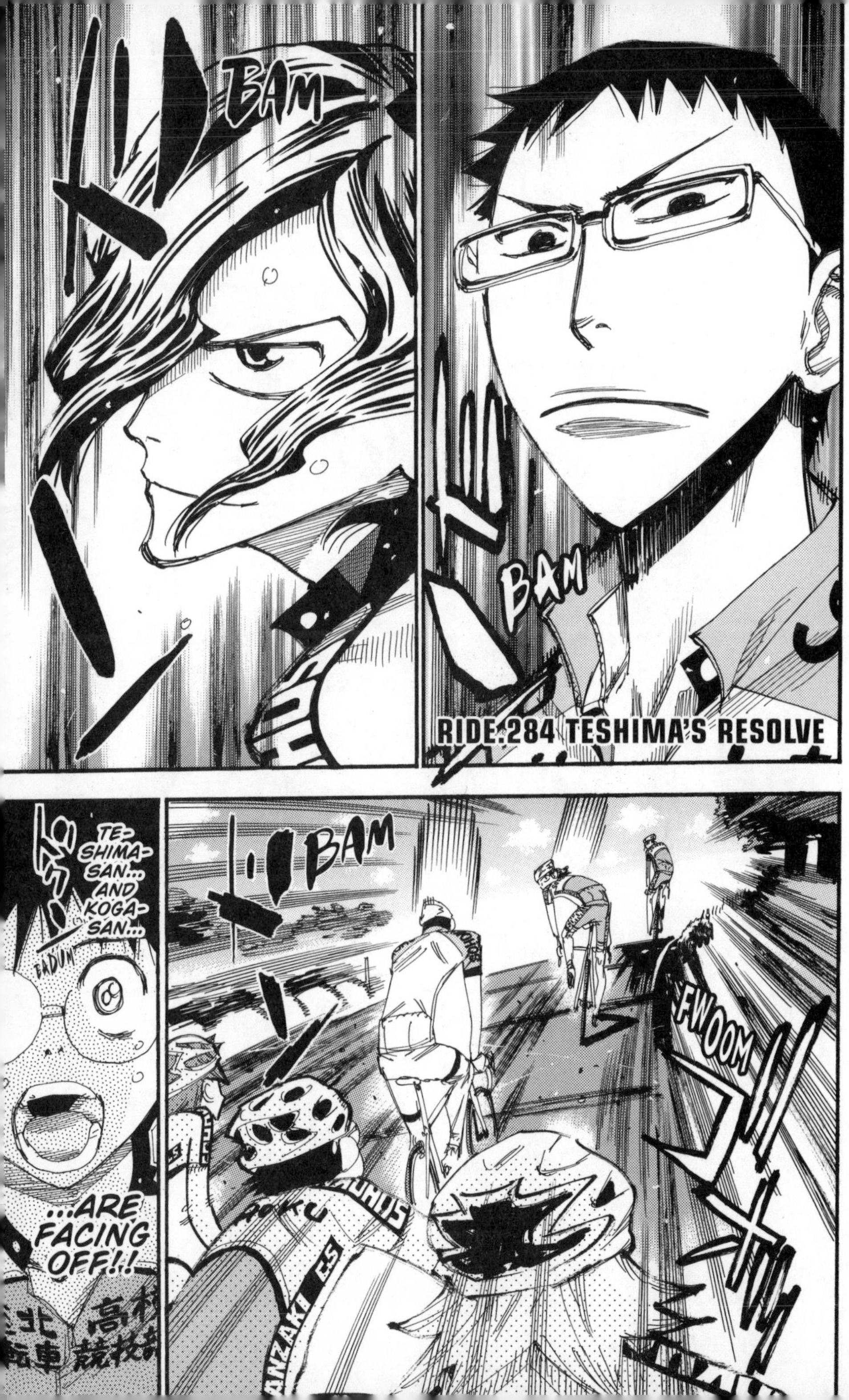
BAM
RIDE.284 TESHIMA'S RESOLVE
BAM
BAM
FWOOM
TE-SHIMA-SAN... AND KOGA-SAN...
BADUM
...ARE FACING OFF!!

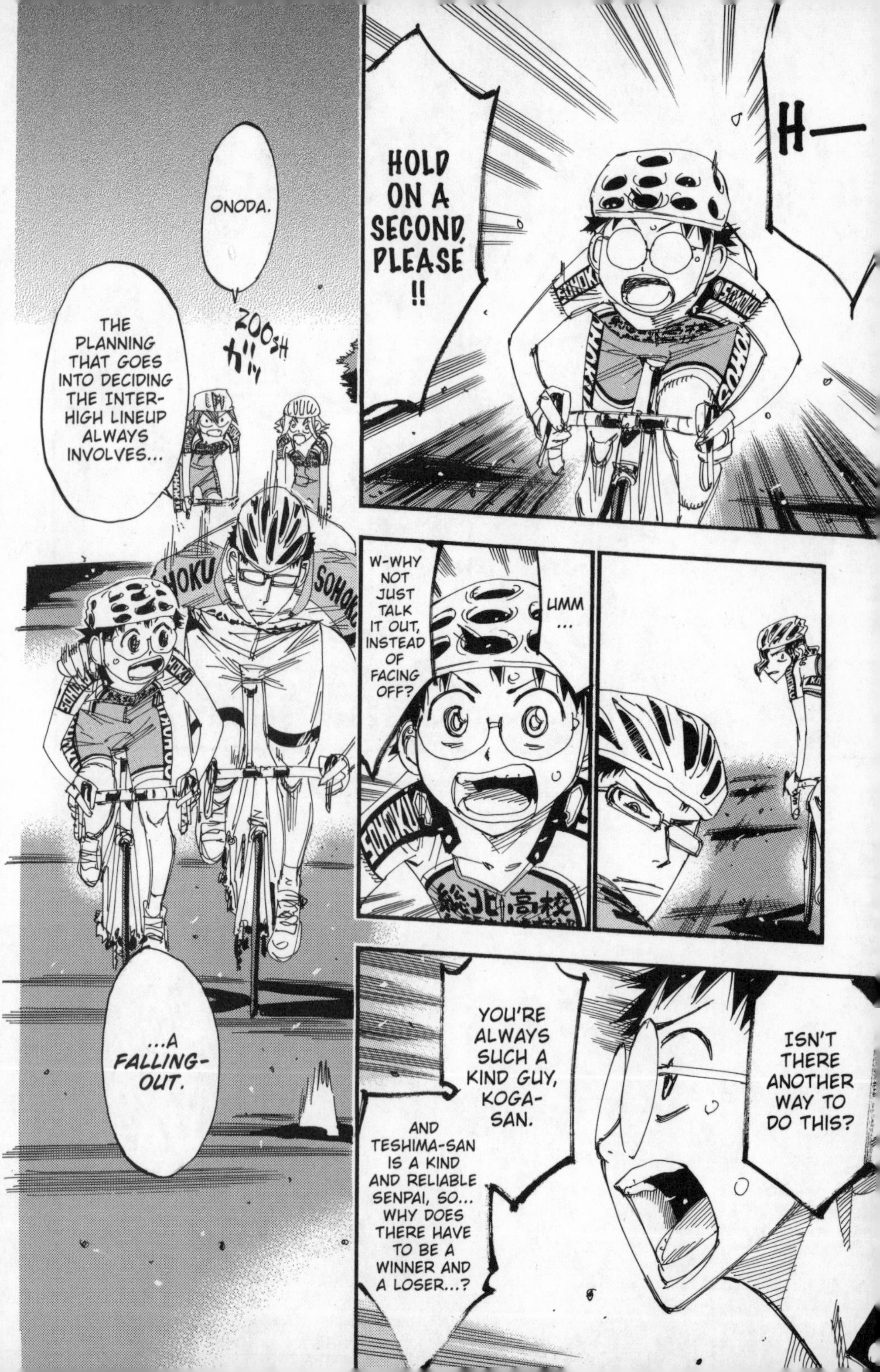
H—
HOLD ON A SECOND, PLEASE!!
UMM...
W-WHY NOT JUST TALK IT OUT, INSTEAD OF FACING OFF?
ISN'T THERE ANOTHER WAY TO DO THIS?
YOU'RE ALWAYS SUCH A KIND GUY, KOGA-SAN.
AND TESHIMA-SAN IS A KIND AND RELIABLE SENPAI, SO... WHY DOES THERE HAVE TO BE A WINNER AND A LOSER...?
ONODA.
ZOOSH ガッ
THE PLANNING THAT GOES INTO DECIDING THE INTER-HIGH LINEUP ALWAYS INVOLVES...
...A *FALLING-OUT.*

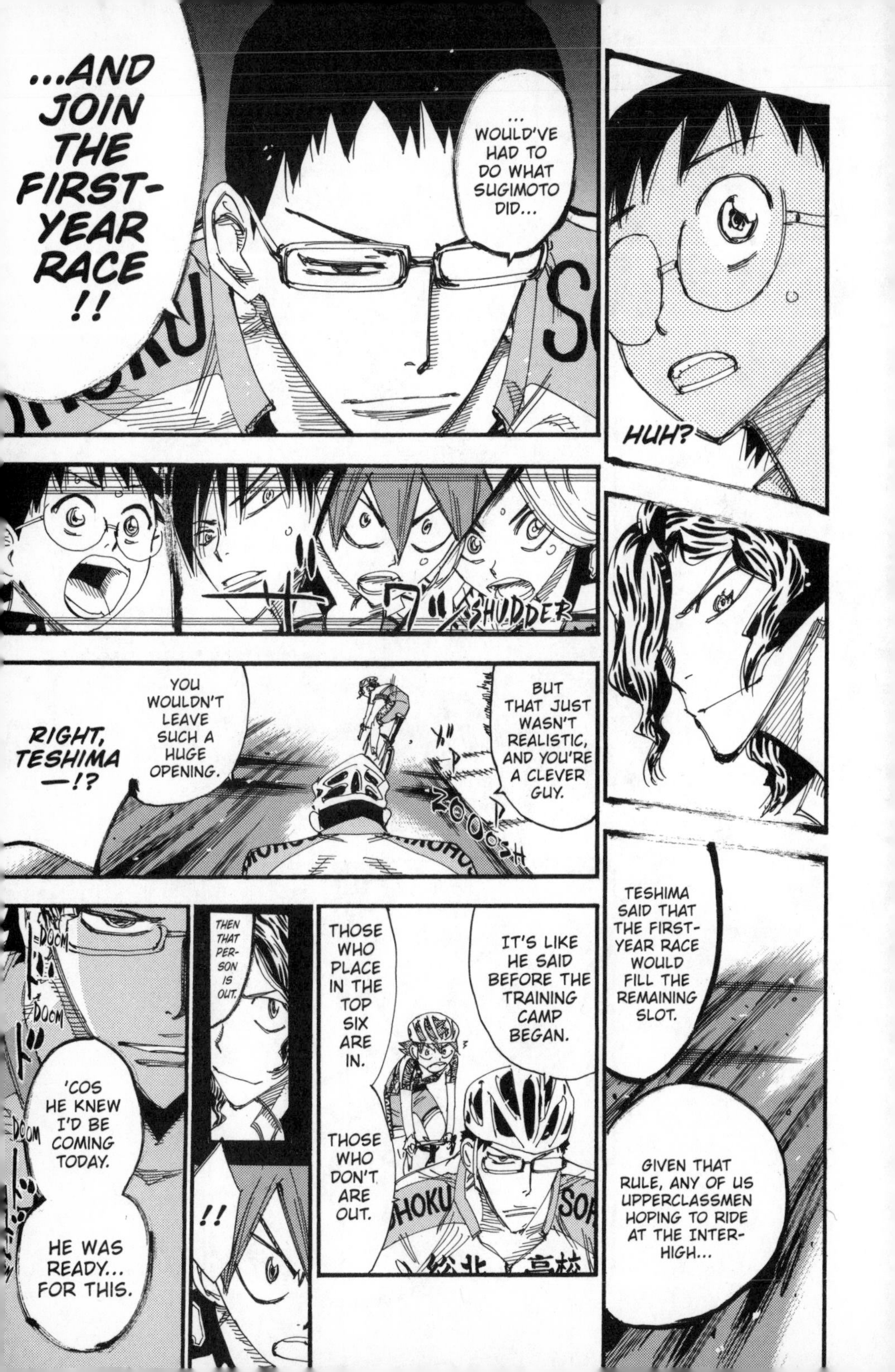
HUH?
...WOULD'VE HAD TO DO WHAT SUGIMOTO DID...
...AND JOIN THE FIRST-YEAR RACE!!
SHUDDER
BUT THAT JUST WASN'T REALISTIC, AND YOU'RE A CLEVER GUY.
YOU WOULDN'T LEAVE SUCH A HUGE OPENING.
RIGHT, TESHIMA—!?
ZOOOSH
TESHIMA SAID THAT THE FIRST-YEAR RACE WOULD FILL THE REMAINING SLOT.
GIVEN THAT RULE, ANY OF US UPPERCLASSMEN HOPING TO RIDE AT THE INTER-HIGH...
IT'S LIKE HE SAID BEFORE THE TRAINING CAMP BEGAN.
THOSE WHO PLACE IN THE TOP SIX ARE IN.
THOSE WHO DON'T ARE OUT.
THEN THAT PERSON IS OUT.
!!
DOOM
DOOM
DOOM
'COS HE KNEW I'D BE COMING TODAY.
HE WAS READY... FOR THIS.

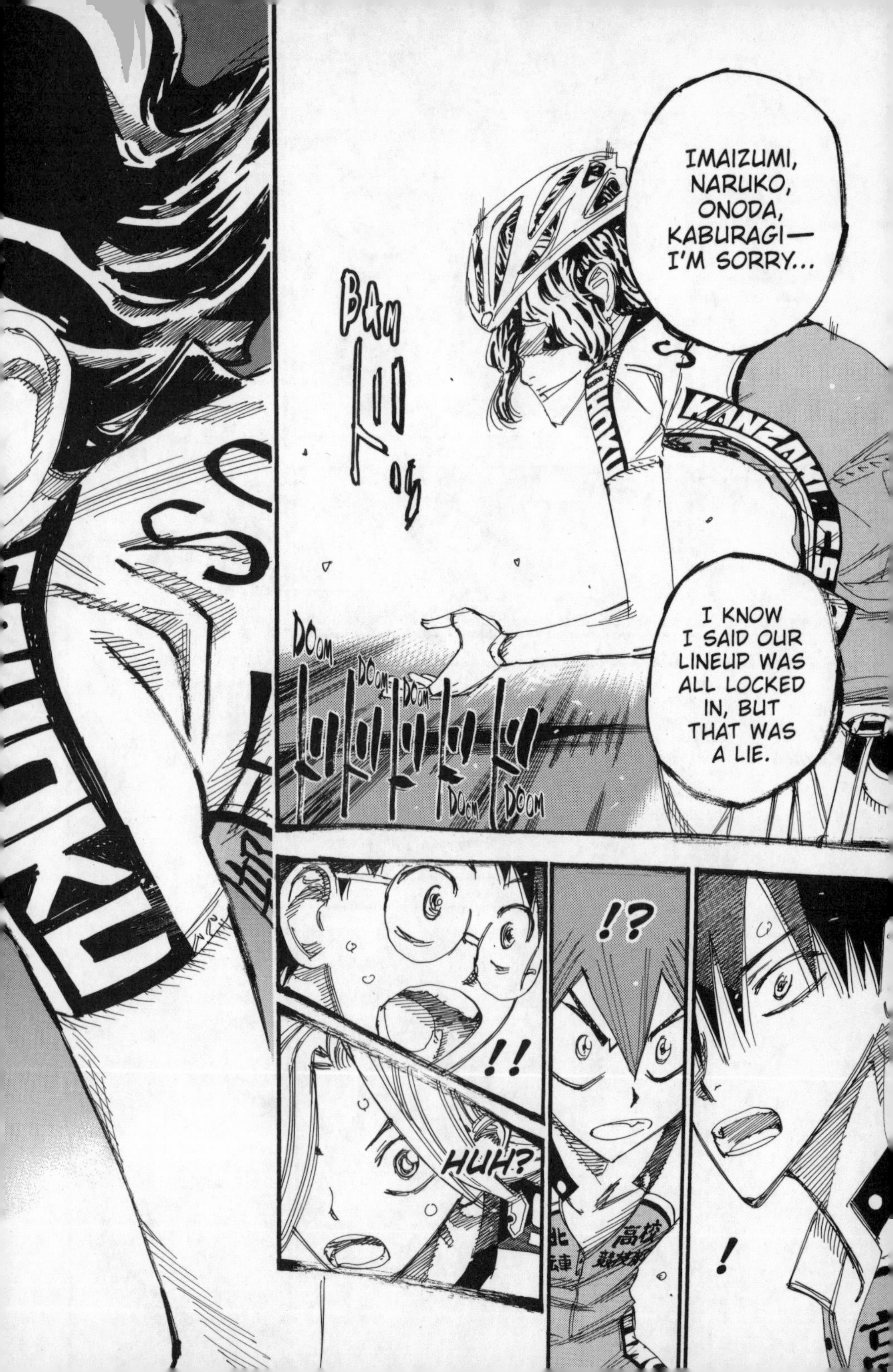
IMAIZUMI, NARUKO, ONODA, KABURAGI— I'M SORRY...
I KNOW I SAID OUR LINEUP WAS ALL LOCKED IN, BUT THAT WAS A LIE.
BAM
DOOM
DOOM
DOOM
DOOM
DOOM
!
!?
!!
HUH?

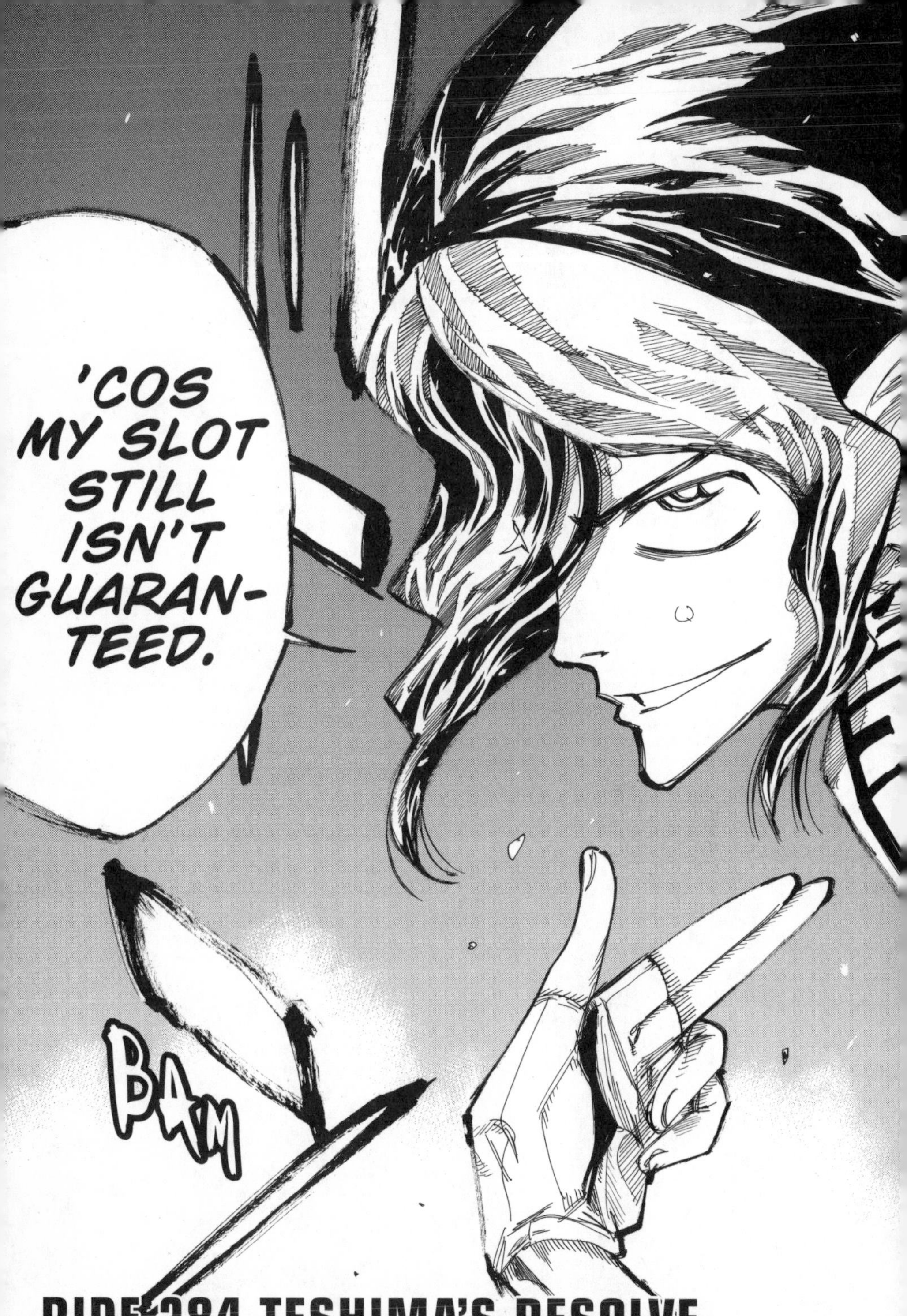
'COS MY SLOT STILL ISN'T GUARAN-TEED.
BAM

RIDE.284 TESHIMA'S RESOLVE

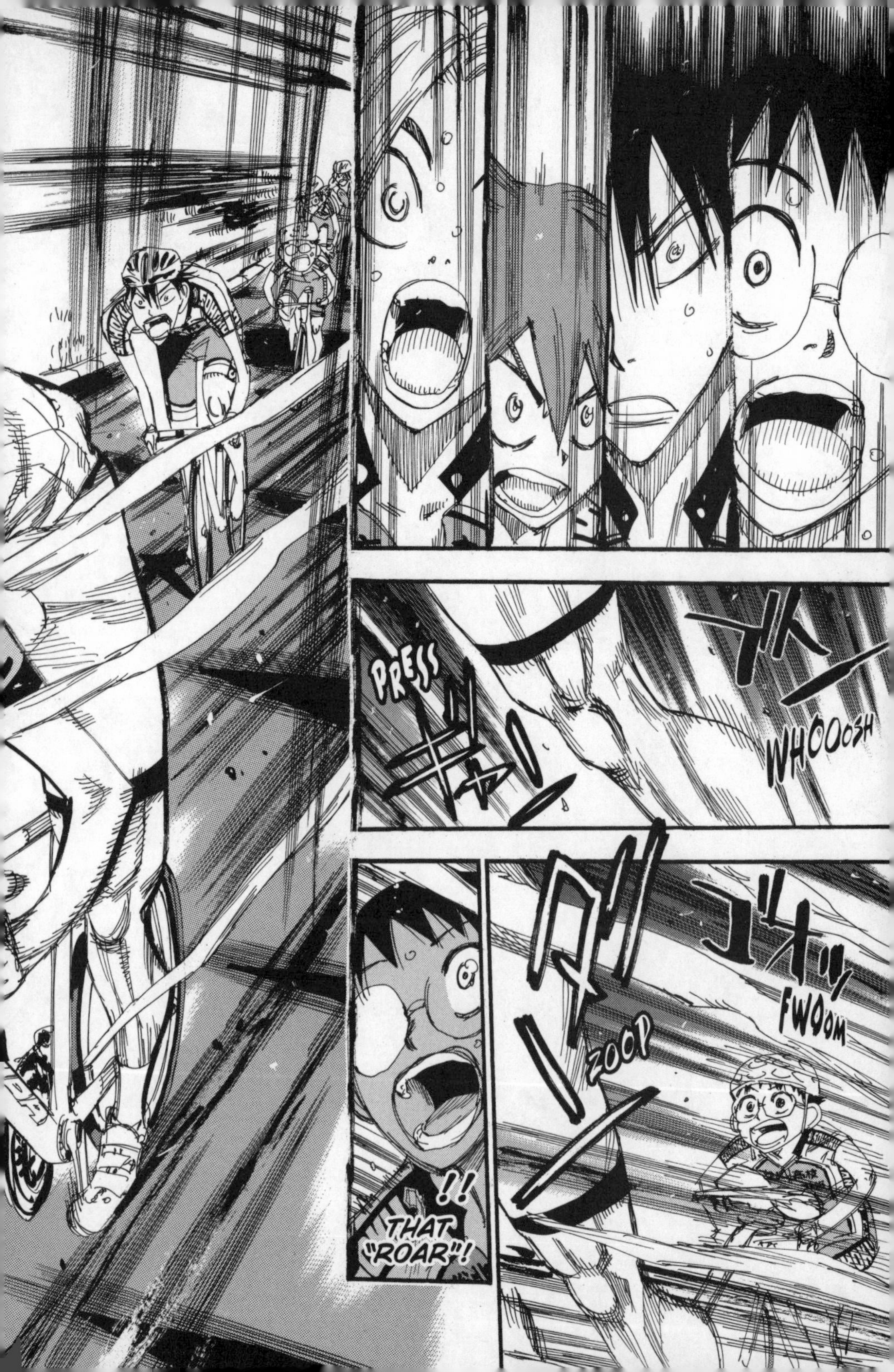
WHOOOSH
PRESS
FWOOM
ZOOP
!!
THAT "ROAR"!

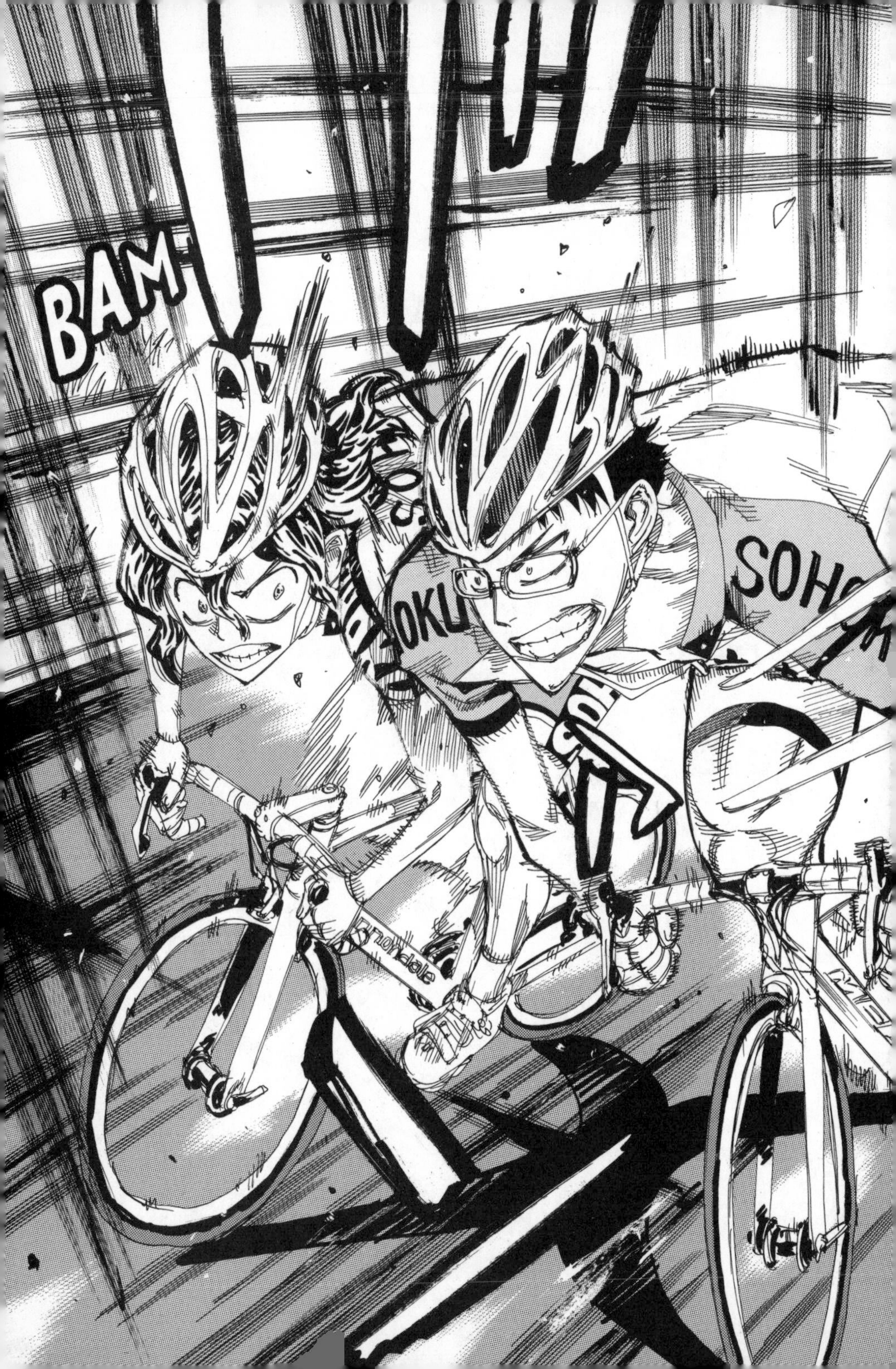
BAM
SOHO
OKU

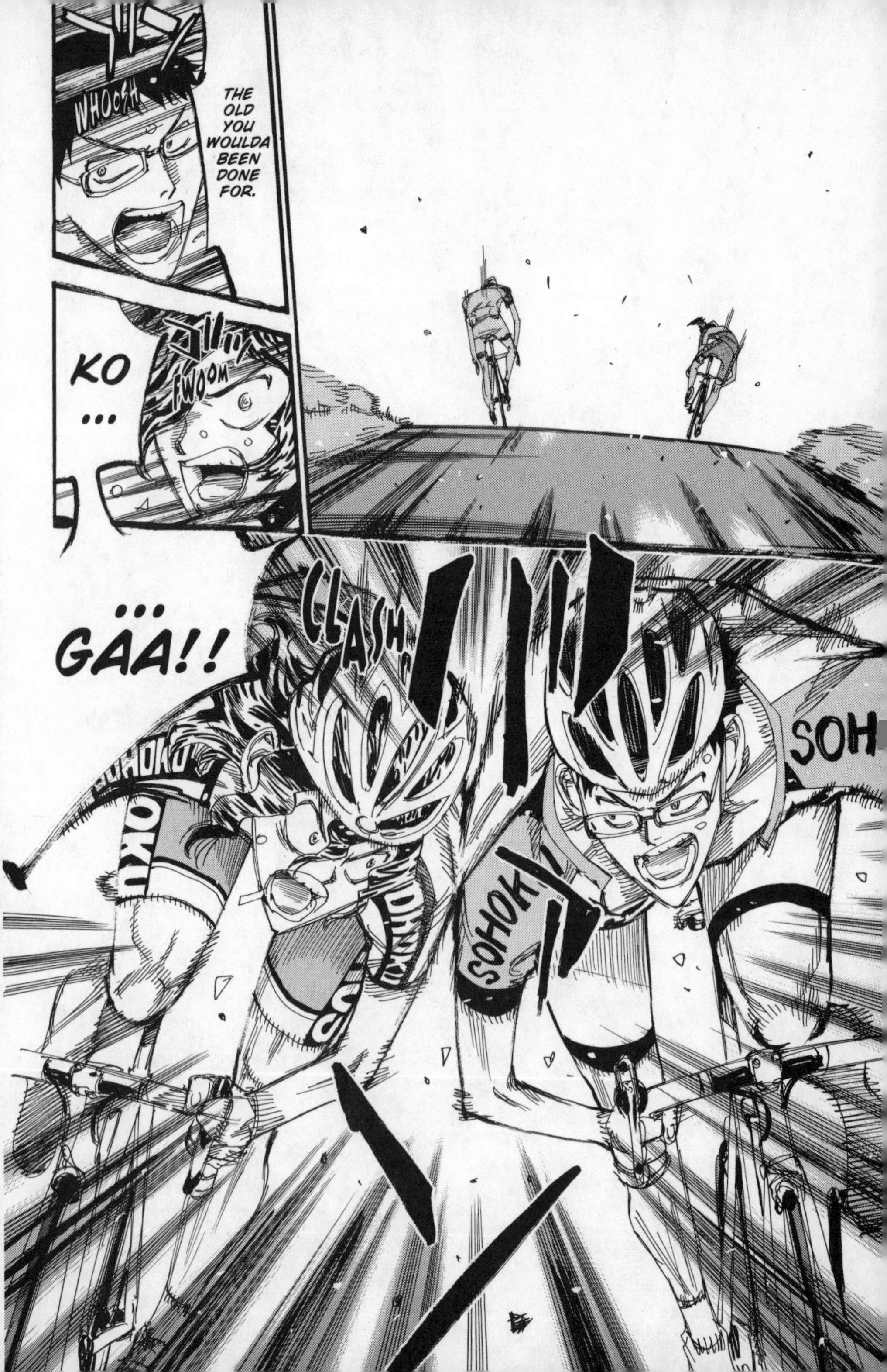

WHOOSH
THE OLD YOU WOULDA BEEN DONE FOR.
FWOOM
KO...
...GAA!!
CLASH

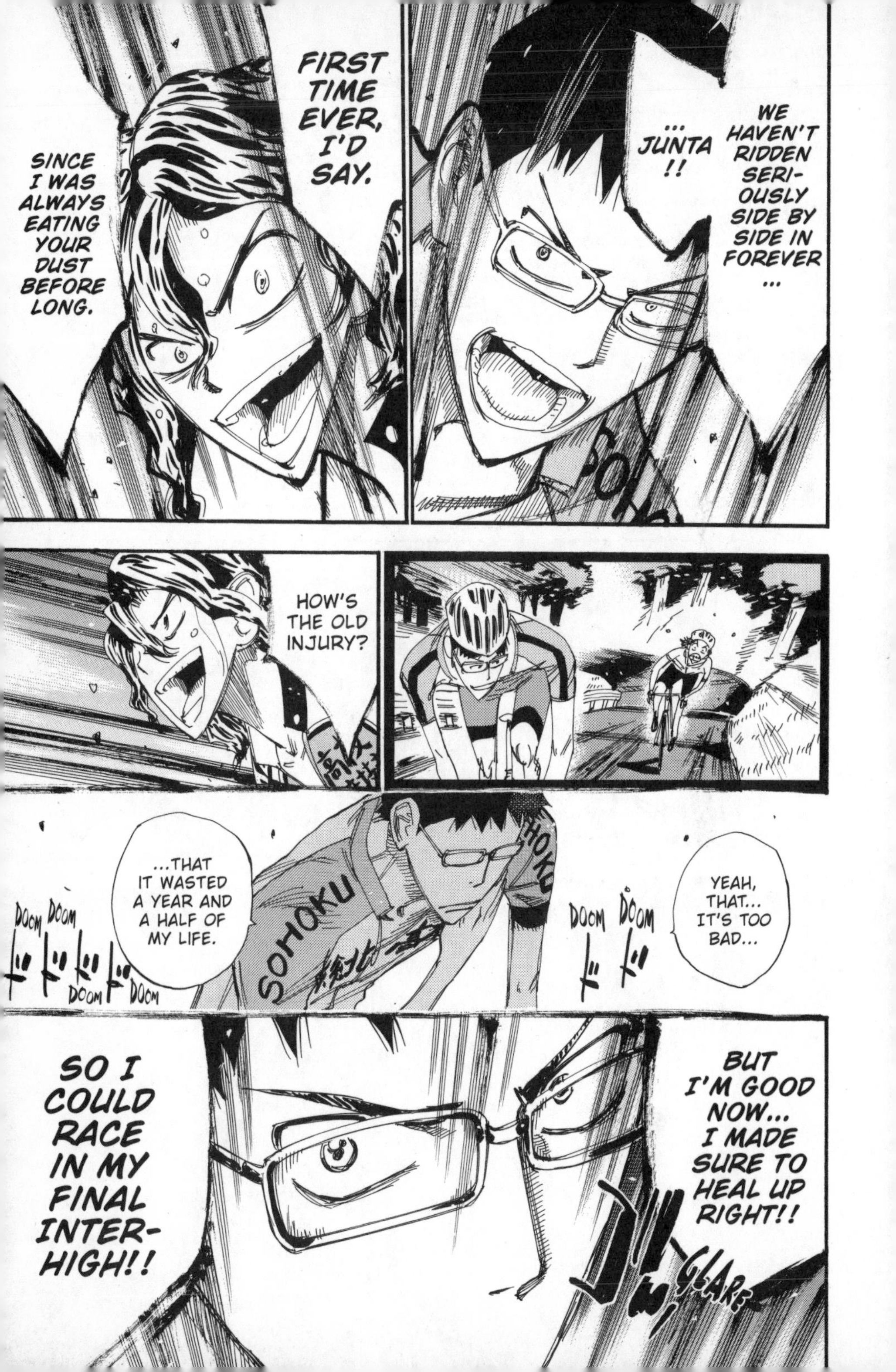
WE HAVEN'T RIDDEN SERIOUSLY SIDE BY SIDE IN FOREVER...
...JŪNTA!!
FIRST TIME EVER, I'D SAY.
SINCE I WAS ALWAYS EATING YOUR DUST BEFORE LONG.
HOW'S THE OLD INJURY?
YEAH, THAT... IT'S TOO BAD...
DOOM DOOM
...THAT IT WASTED A YEAR AND A HALF OF MY LIFE.
DOOM DOOM DOOM DOOM
BUT I'M GOOD NOW... I MADE SURE TO HEAL UP RIGHT!!
GLARE
SO I COULD RACE IN MY FINAL INTER-HIGH!!

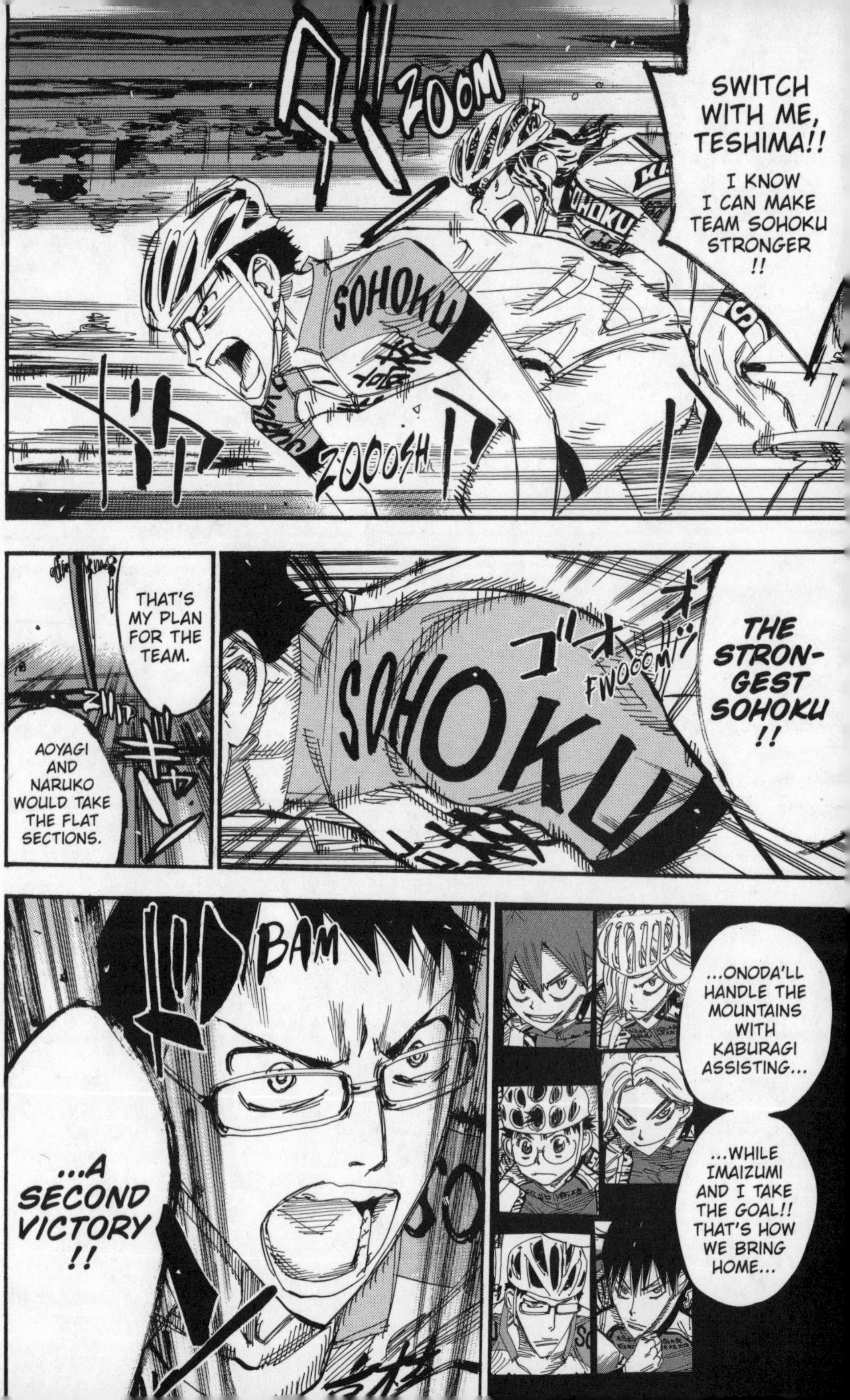
ZOOM
SWITCH WITH ME, TESHIMA!!
I KNOW I CAN MAKE TEAM SOHOKU STRONGER!!
ZOOOSH
THE STRONG-EST SOHOKU!!
FWOOOM
THAT'S MY PLAN FOR THE TEAM.
AOYAGI AND NARUKO WOULD TAKE THE FLAT SECTIONS.
...ONODA'LL HANDLE THE MOUNTAINS WITH KABURAGI ASSISTING...
...WHILE IMAIZUMI AND I TAKE THE GOAL!! THAT'S HOW WE BRING HOME...
BAM
...A SECOND VICTORY!!

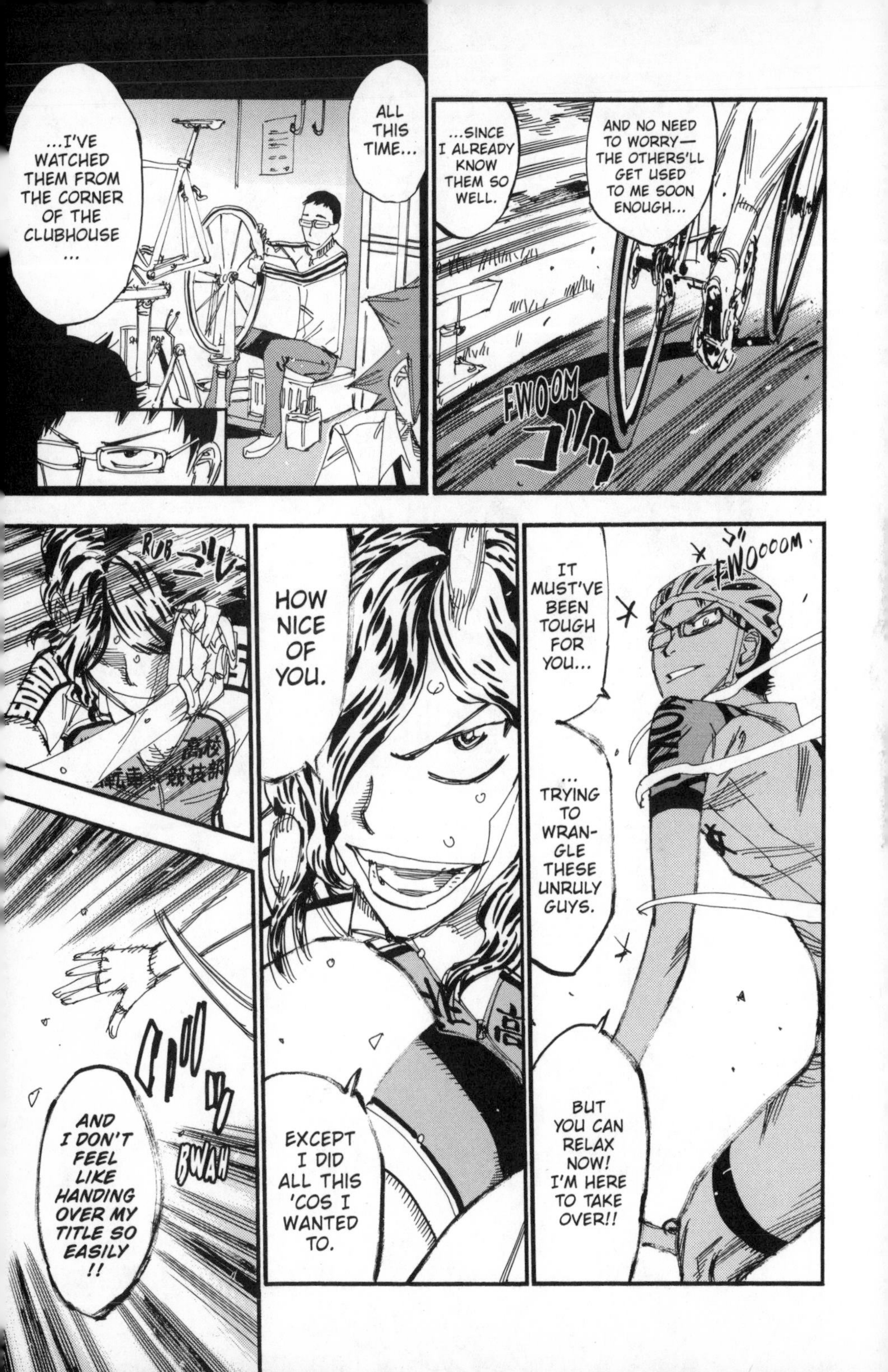
AND NO NEED TO WORRY— THE OTHERS'LL GET USED TO ME SOON ENOUGH...
...SINCE I ALREADY KNOW THEM SO WELL.
FWOOM
ALL THIS TIME...
...I'VE WATCHED THEM FROM THE CORNER OF THE CLUBHOUSE...
FWOOOOM
IT MUST'VE BEEN TOUGH FOR YOU...
...TRYING TO WRANGLE THESE UNRULY GUYS.
BUT YOU CAN RELAX NOW! I'M HERE TO TAKE OVER!!
HOW NICE OF YOU.
EXCEPT I DID ALL THIS 'COS I WANTED TO.
RUB
BWAH
AND I DON'T FEEL LIKE HANDING OVER MY TITLE SO EASILY!!

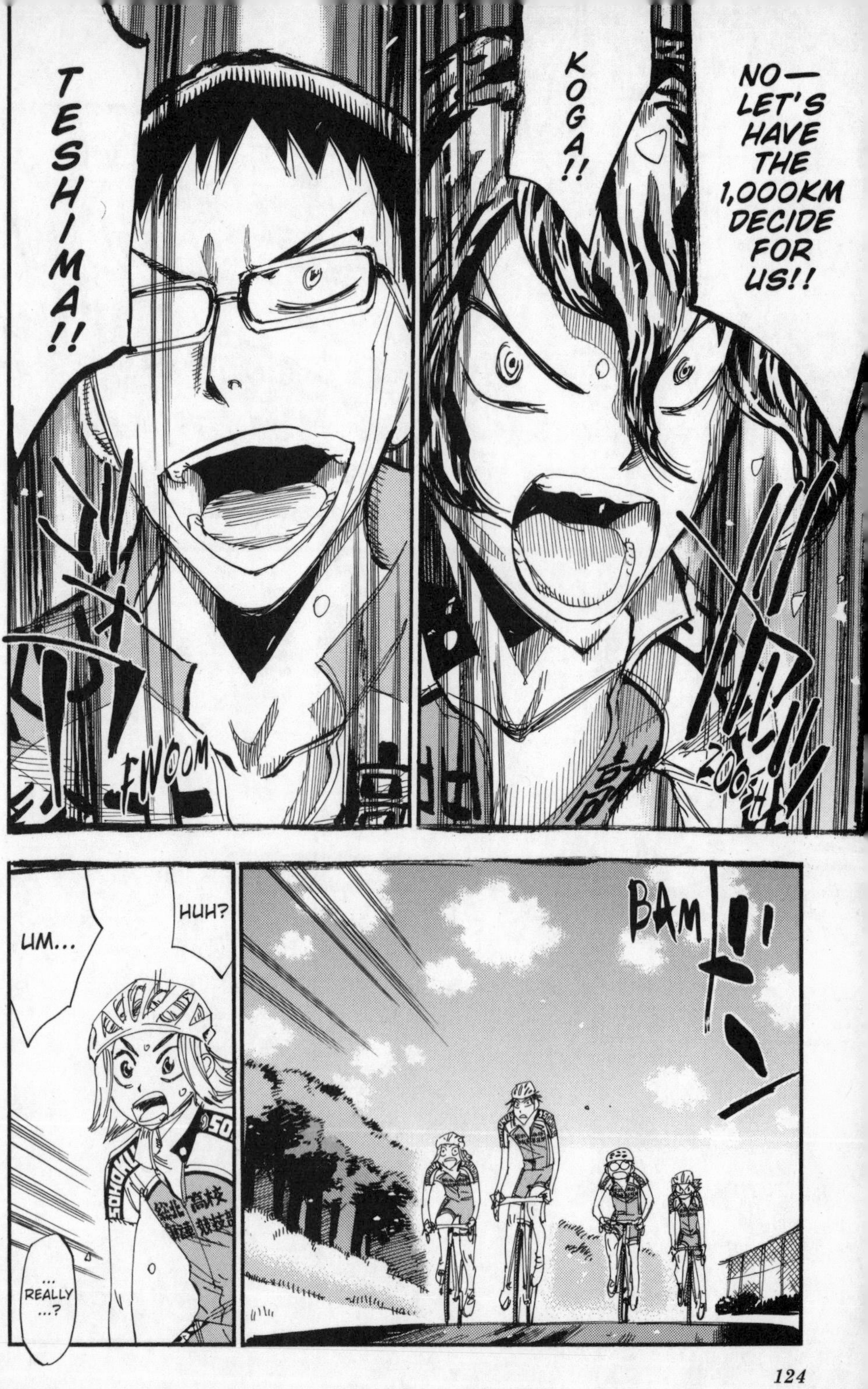
NO— LET'S HAVE THE 1,000KM DECIDE FOR US!!
KOGA!!
ZOOSH
TESHIMA!!
FWOOM
BAM!!
HUH?
UM...
...REALLY...?

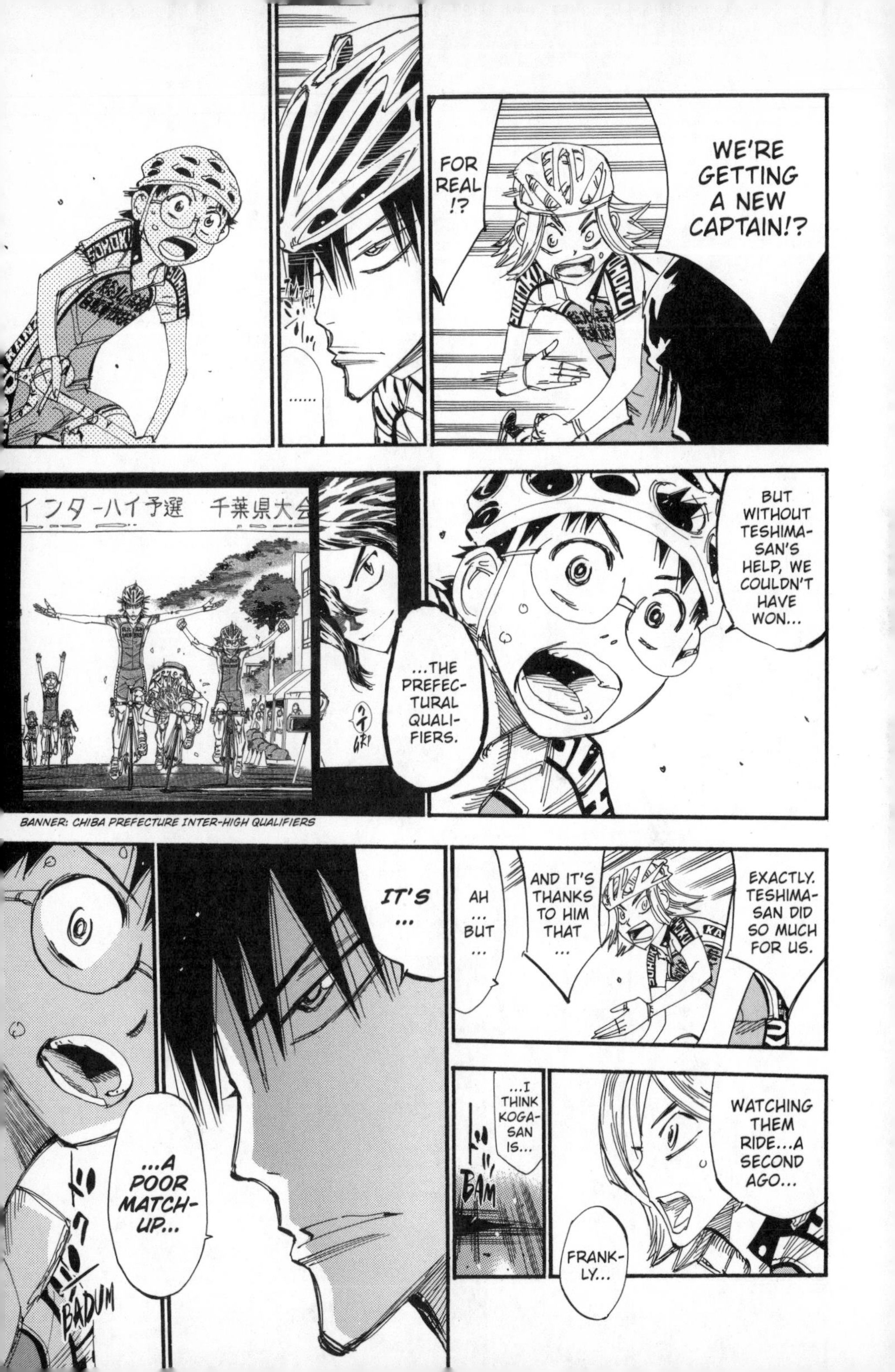
WE'RE GETTING A NEW CAPTAIN!?
FOR REAL !?
TWITCH
......
BUT WITHOUT TESHIMA-SAN'S HELP, WE COULDN'T HAVE WON...
...THE PREFECTURAL QUALIFIERS.
GRIP
インターハイ予選 千葉県大会
BANNER: CHIBA PREFECTURE INTER-HIGH QUALIFIERS
EXACTLY. TESHIMA-SAN DID SO MUCH FOR US.
AND IT'S THANKS TO HIM THAT ...
AH ... BUT ...
WATCHING THEM RIDE...A SECOND AGO...
FRANKLY...
...I THINK KOGA-SAN IS...
BAM
IT'S ...
...A POOR MATCH-UP...
BADUM

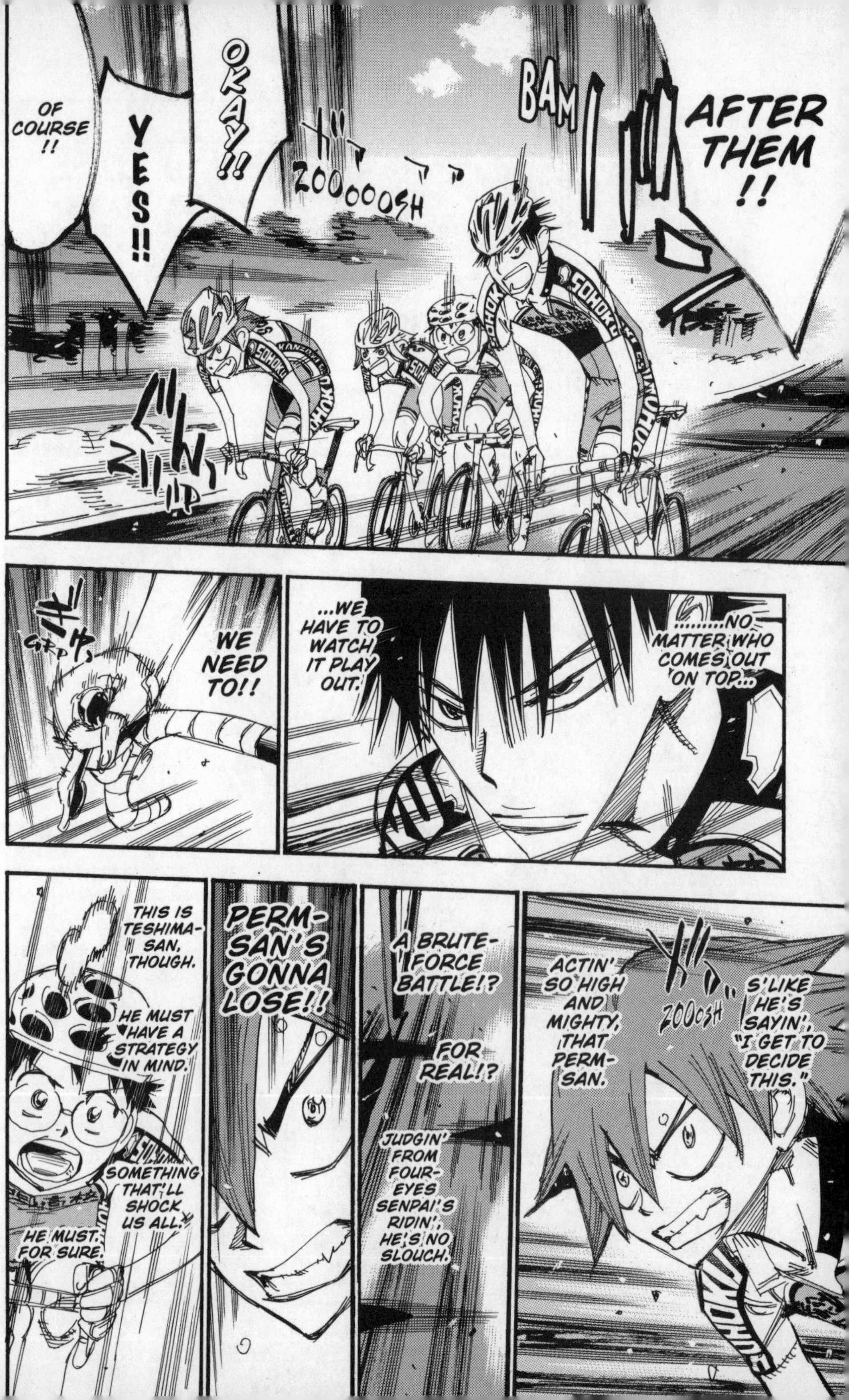
AFTER THEM!!
BAM
ZOOOOOOSH
OKAY!!
YES!!
OF COURSE!!
ZIIIP
..........NO MATTER WHO COMES OUT ON TOP...
...WE HAVE TO WATCH IT PLAY OUT.
WE NEED TO!!
GRIP
S'LIKE HE'S SAYIN', "I GET TO DECIDE THIS."
ZOOOSH
ACTIN' SO HIGH AND MIGHTY, THAT PERM-SAN.
A BRUTE-FORCE BATTLE!?
FOR REAL!?
JUDGIN' FROM FOUR-EYES SENPAI'S RIDIN', HE'S NO SLOUCH.
PERM-SAN'S GONNA LOSE!!
THIS IS TESHIMA-SAN, THOUGH.
HE MUST HAVE A STRATEGY IN MIND.
SOMETHING THAT'LL SHOCK US ALL.
HE MUST. FOR SURE.

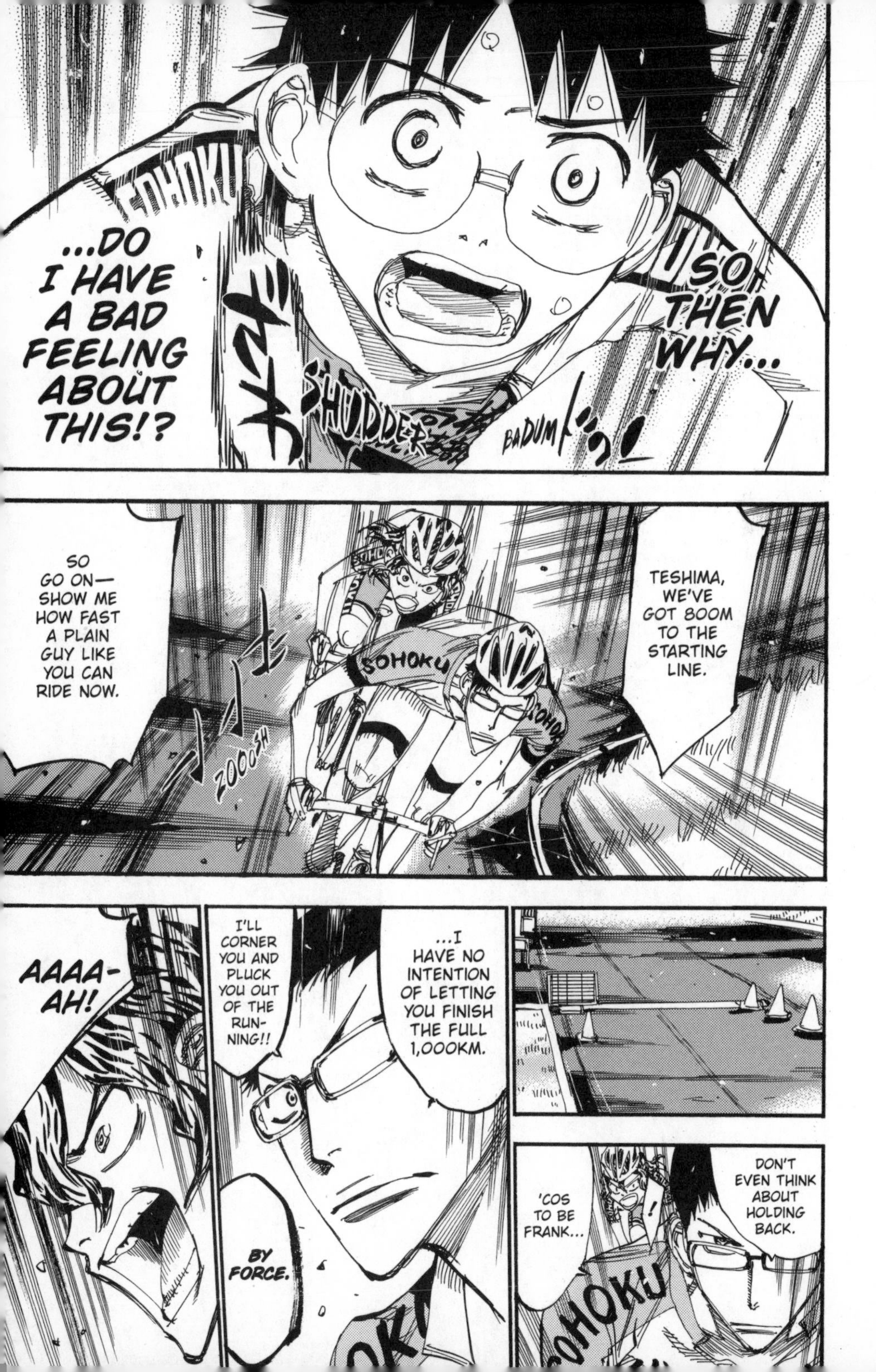
SO THEN WHY...
...DO I HAVE A BAD FEELING ABOUT THIS!?
SHUDDER
BADUM
TESHIMA, WE'VE GOT 800M TO THE STARTING LINE.
SO GO ON— SHOW ME HOW FAST A PLAIN GUY LIKE YOU CAN RIDE NOW.
ZOOOSH
DON'T EVEN THINK ABOUT HOLDING BACK.
'COS TO BE FRANK...
...I HAVE NO INTENTION OF LETTING YOU FINISH THE FULL 1,000KM.
I'LL CORNER YOU AND PLUCK YOU OUT OF THE RUN-NING!!
BY FORCE.
AAAA-AH!

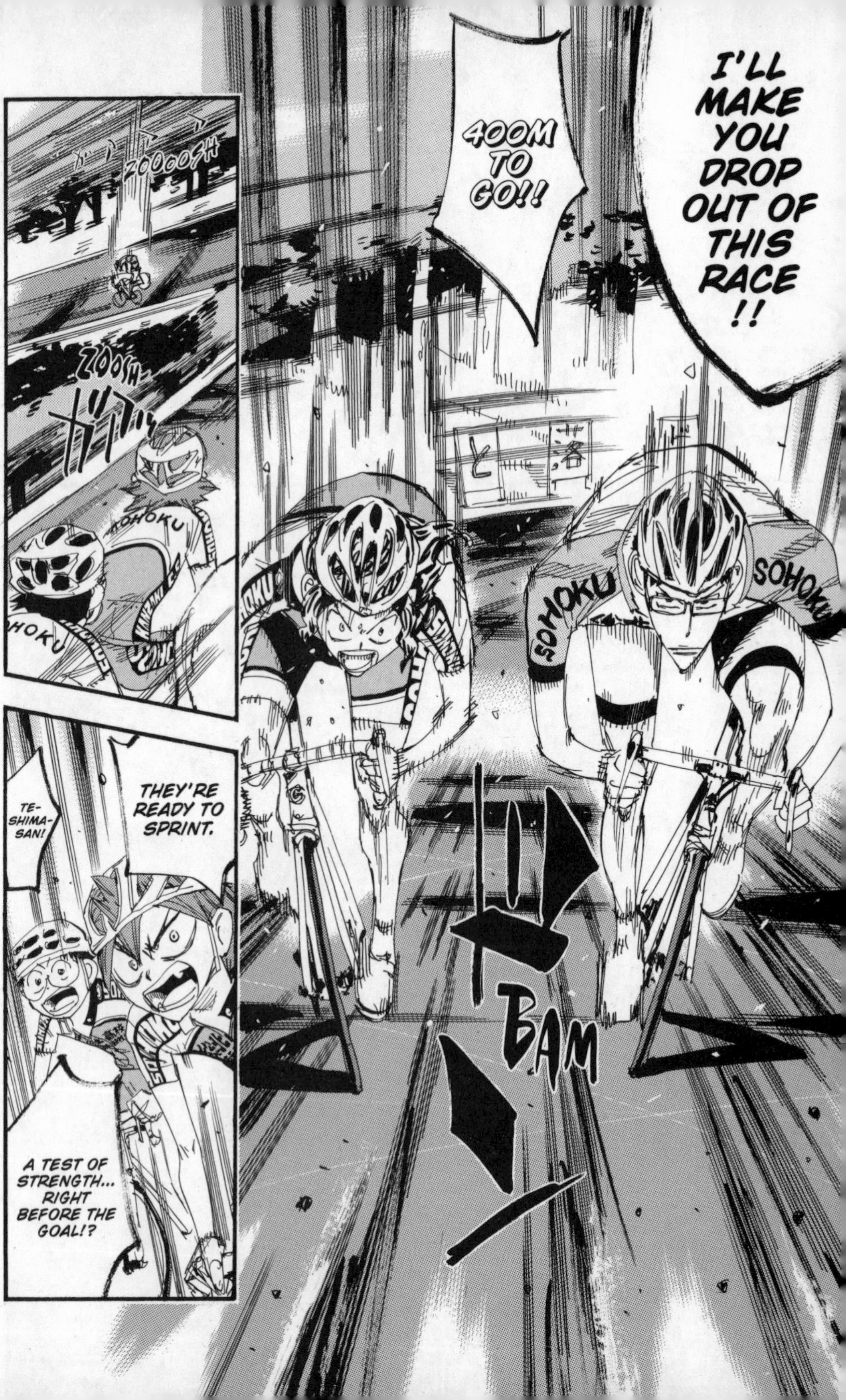
I'LL MAKE YOU DROP OUT OF THIS RACE!!
400M TO GO!!
BAM
ZOOOOSH
ZOOSH
THEY'RE READY TO SPRINT.
TE-SHIMA-SAN!
A TEST OF STRENGTH... RIGHT BEFORE THE GOAL!?

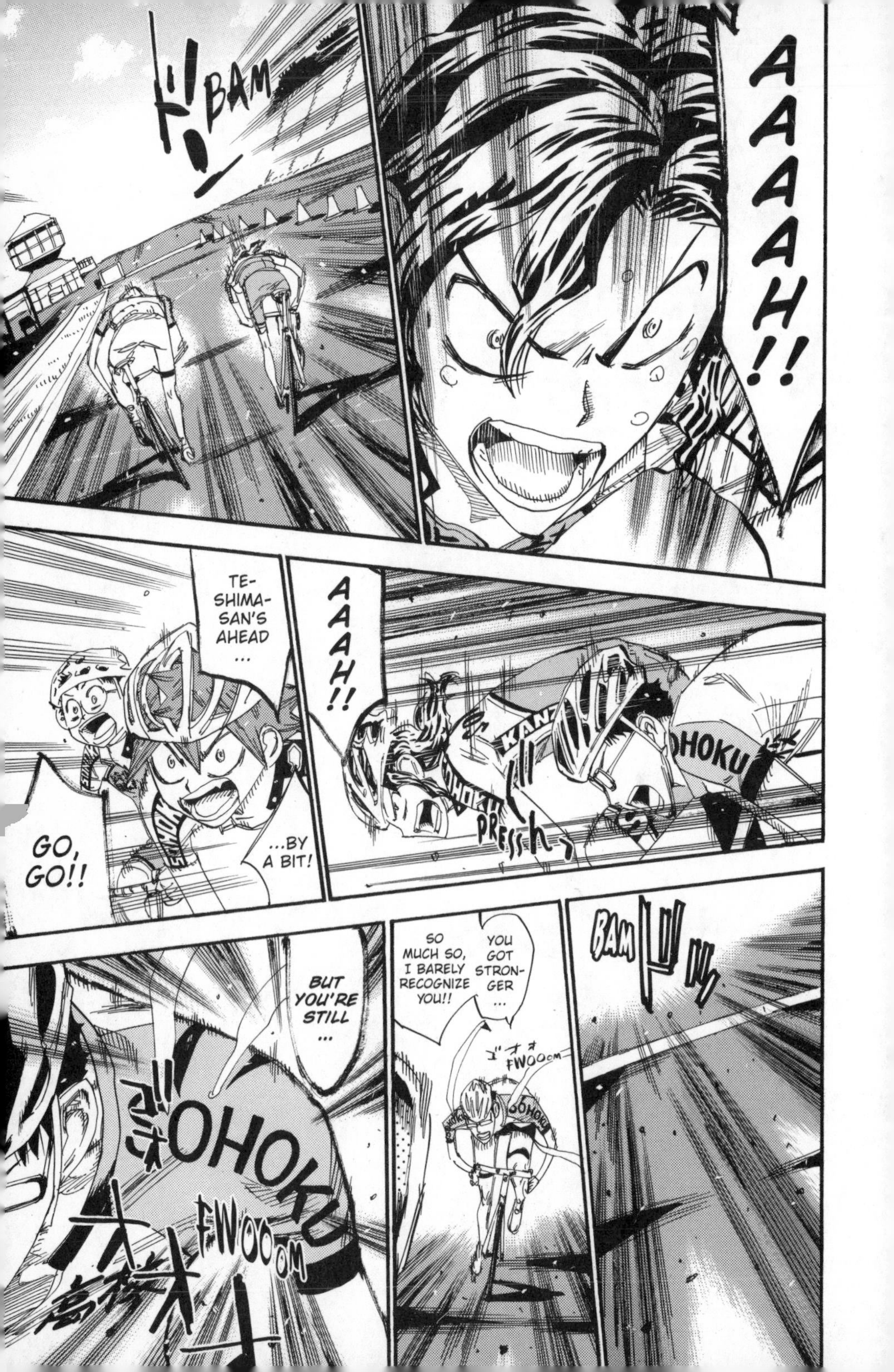
AAAAAH!!
BAM
AAAH!!
PRESSh
TE-SHIMA-SAN'S AHEAD ...
...BY A BIT!
GO, GO!!
BAM
YOU GOT STRONGER ...
SO MUCH SO, I BARELY RECOGNIZE YOU!!
FWOOom
BUT YOU'RE STILL ...
FWOOOm

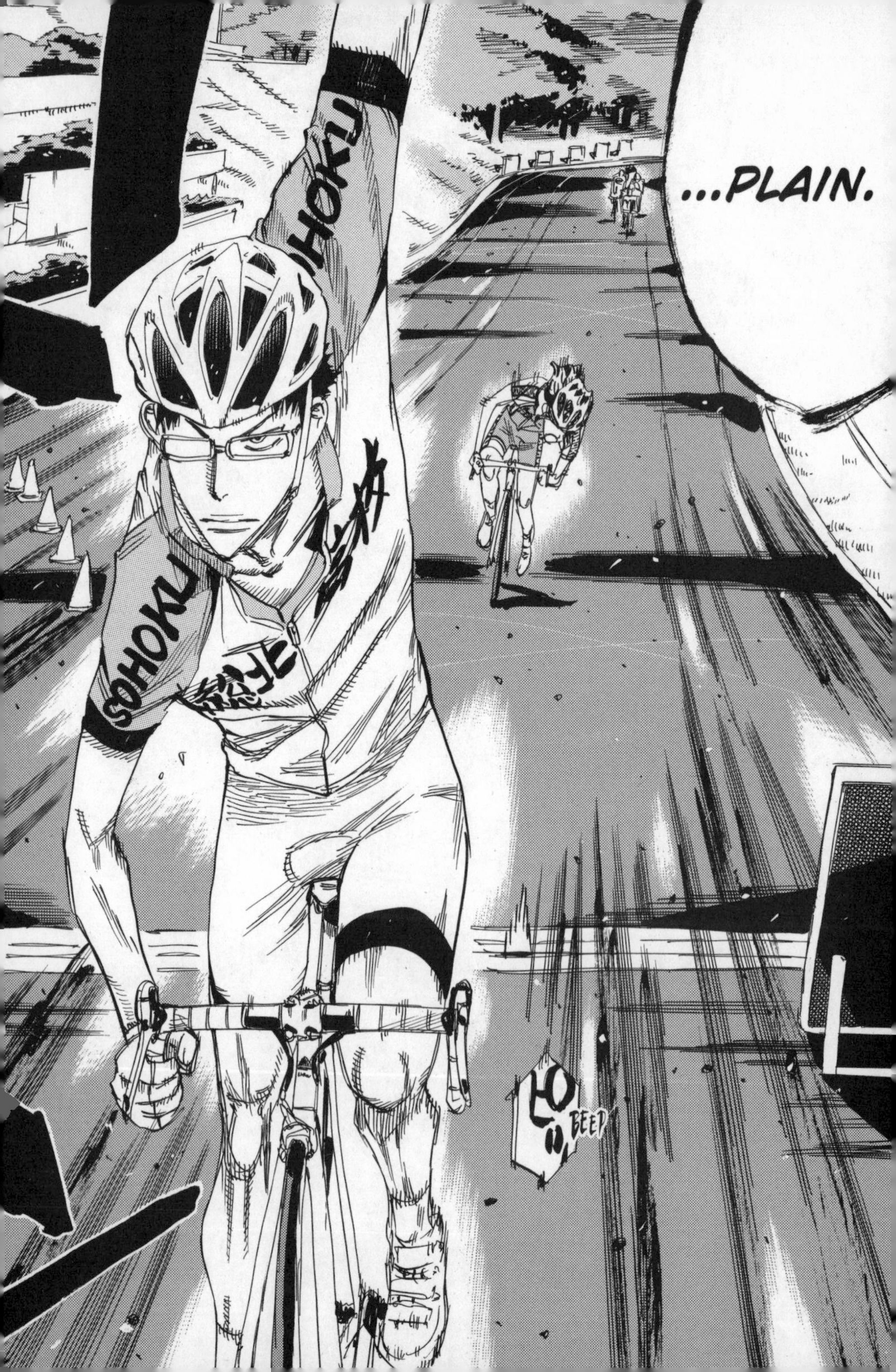
...PLAIN.
SOHOKU
SOHOKU
BEEP

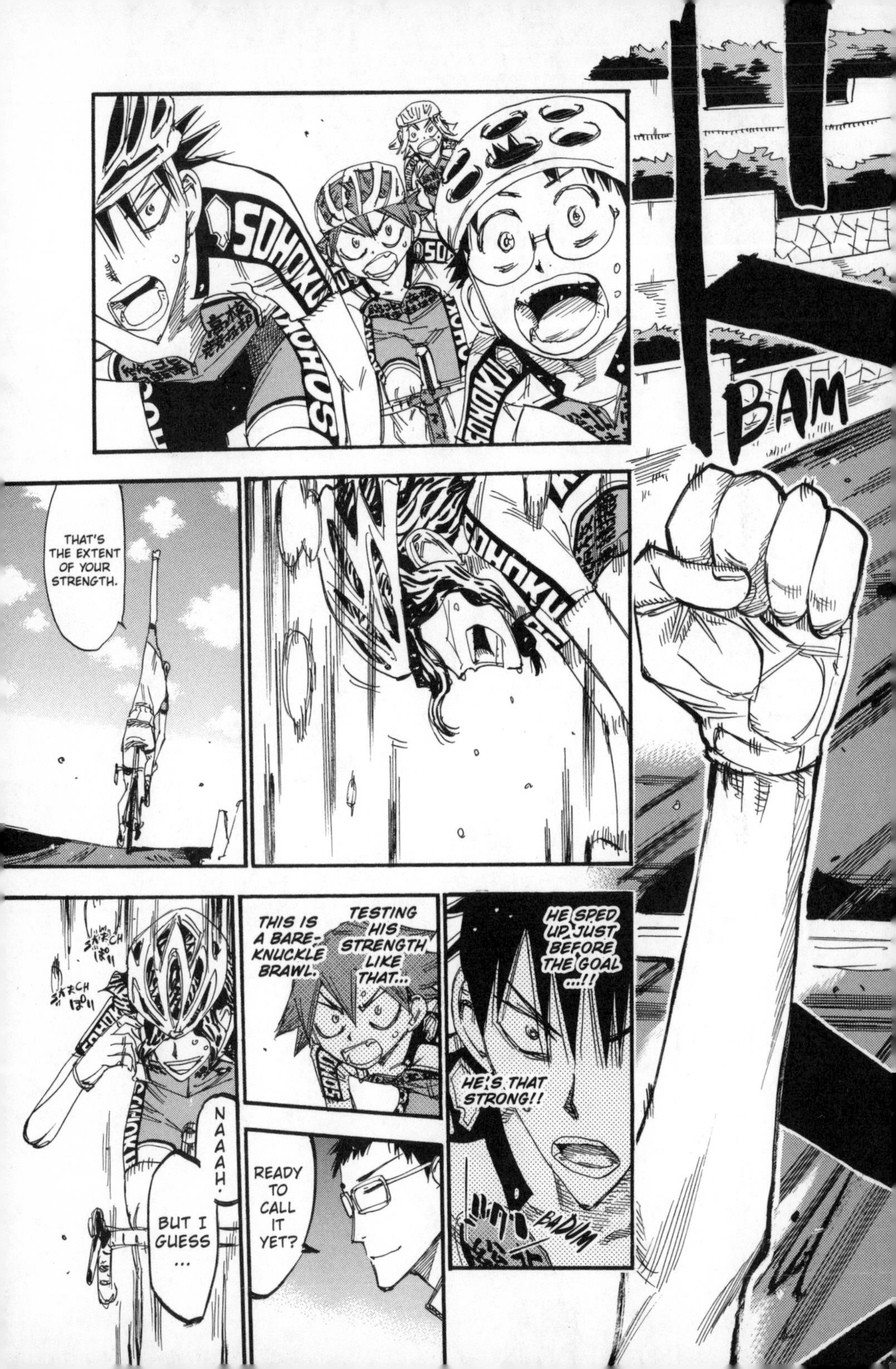
BAM
THAT'S THE EXTENT OF YOUR STRENGTH.
HE SPED UP JUST BEFORE THE GOAL ...!!
HE'S THAT STRONG!!
BADUM
TESTING HIS STRENGTH LIKE THAT...
THIS IS A BARE-KNUCKLE BRAWL.
READY TO CALL IT YET?
SKRCH
SKRCH
NAAAAH.
BUT I GUESS ...

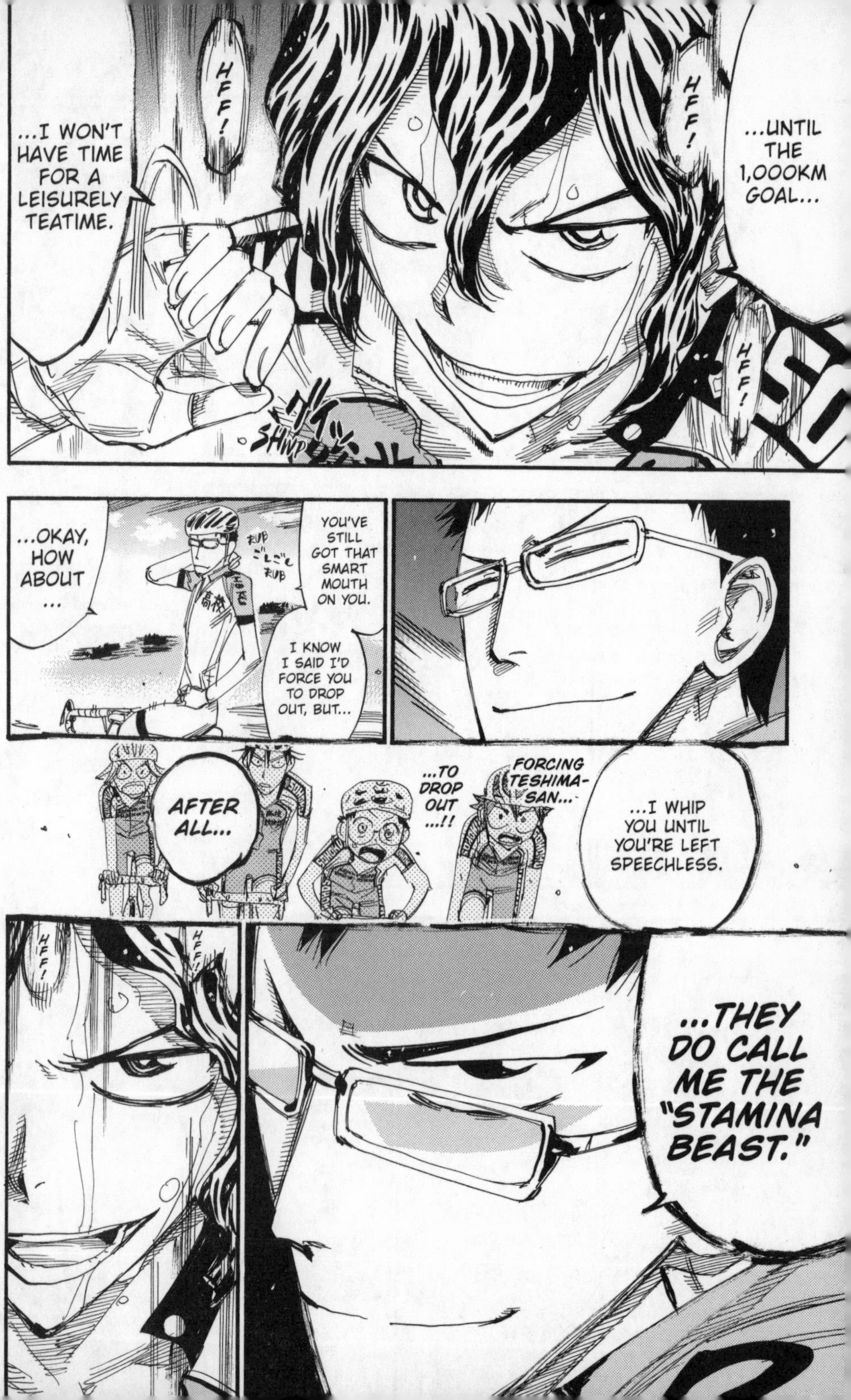
...UNTIL THE 1,000KM GOAL...
HFF!
HFF!
HFF!
...I WON'T HAVE TIME FOR A LEISURELY TEATIME.
SHWP
YOU'VE STILL GOT THAT SMART MOUTH ON YOU.
RUB RUB
I KNOW I SAID I'D FORCE YOU TO DROP OUT, BUT...
...OKAY, HOW ABOUT ...
...I WHIP YOU UNTIL YOU'RE LEFT SPEECHLESS.
FORCING TESHIMA-SAN...
...TO DROP OUT ...!!
AFTER ALL...
...THEY DO CALL ME THE "STAMINA BEAST."
HFF!
HFF!

RIDE.285 TESHIMA VS. KOGA

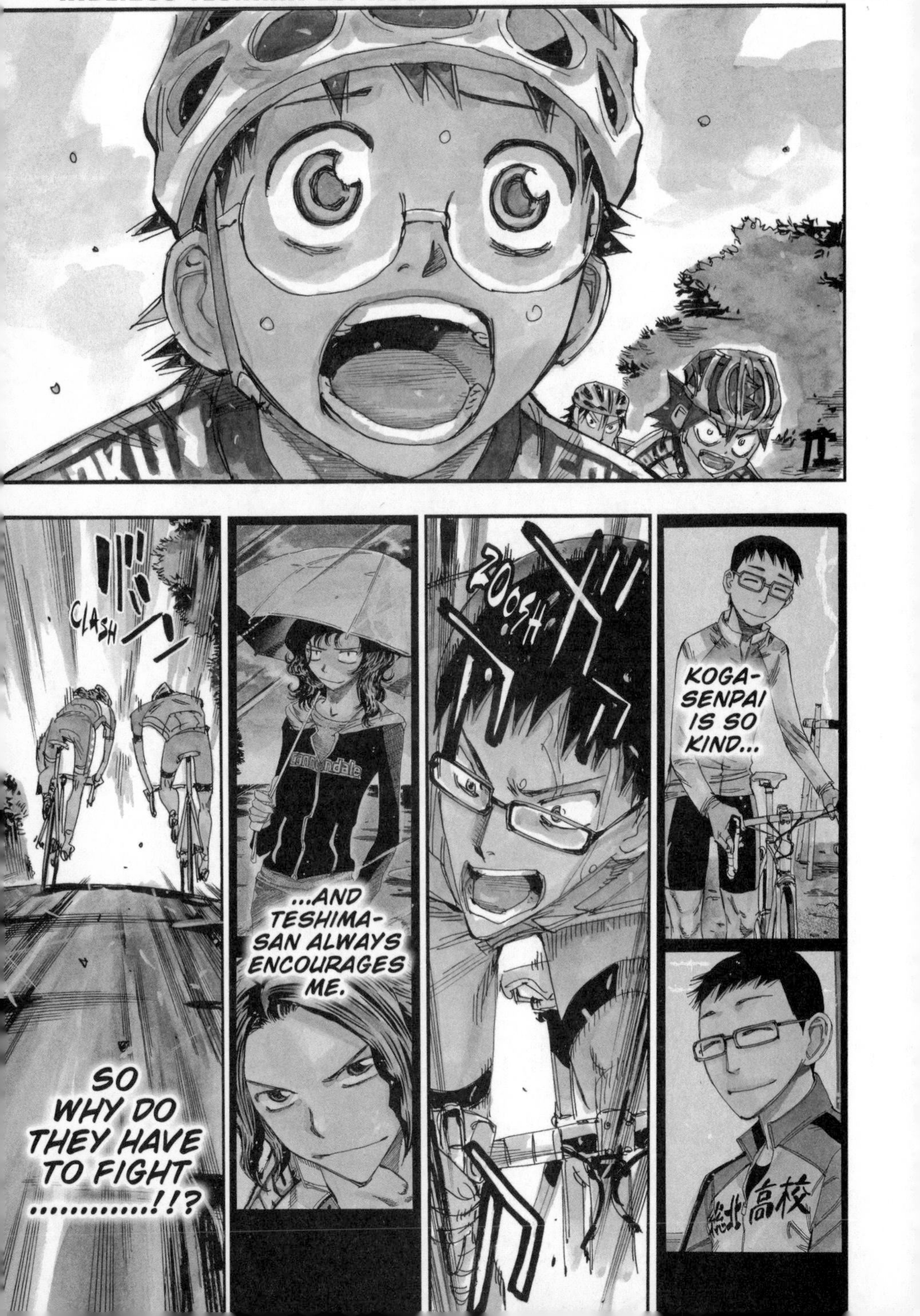
KOGA-SENPAI IS SO KIND...
ZOOSH
...AND TESHIMA-SAN ALWAYS ENCOURAGES ME.
CLASH
SO WHY DO THEY HAVE TO FIGHT ....!!?

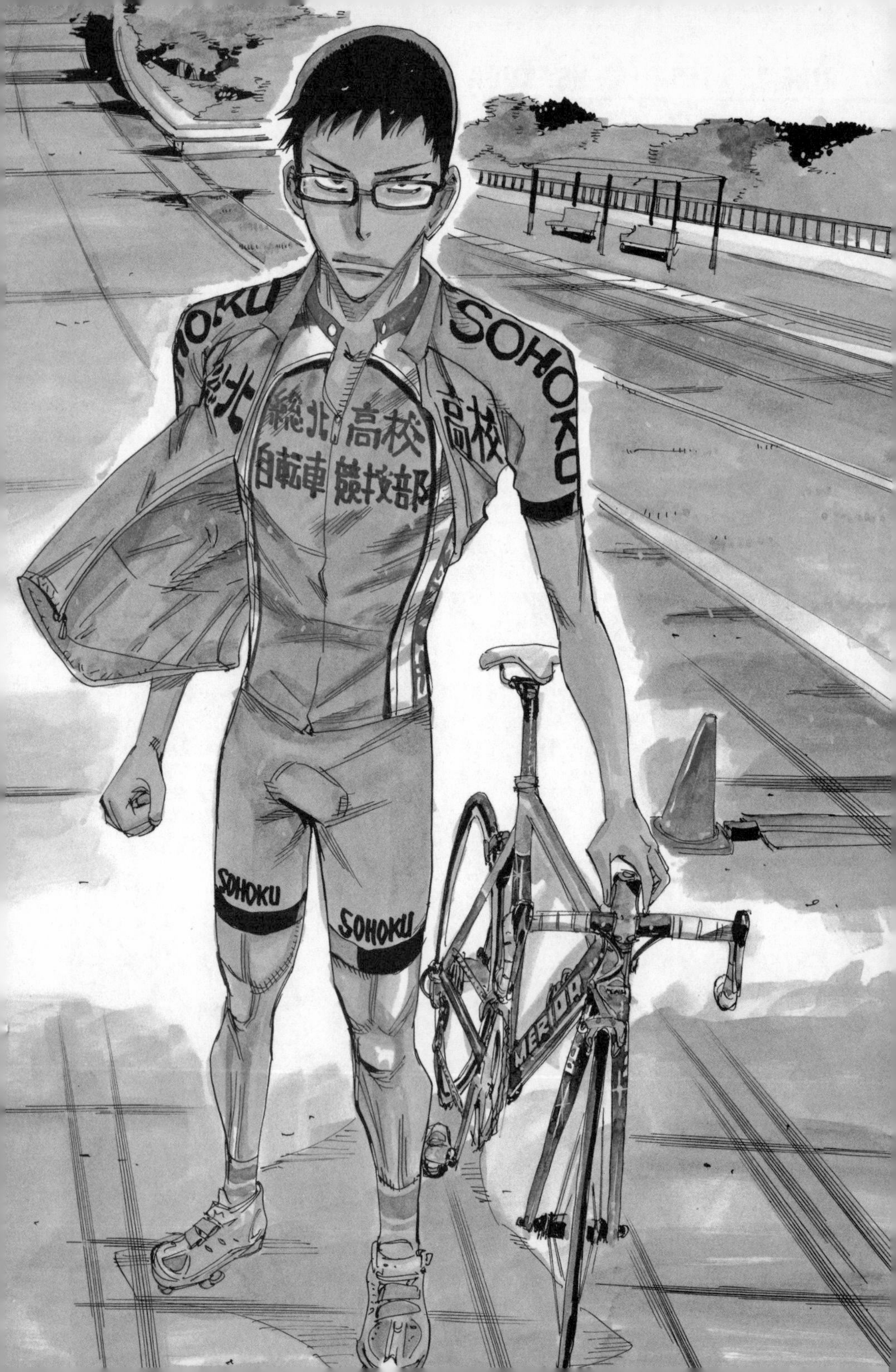
SOHOKU
總北高校
自転車競技部
高校
SOHOKU
SOHOKU

RIDE.285 TESHIMA VS. KOGA

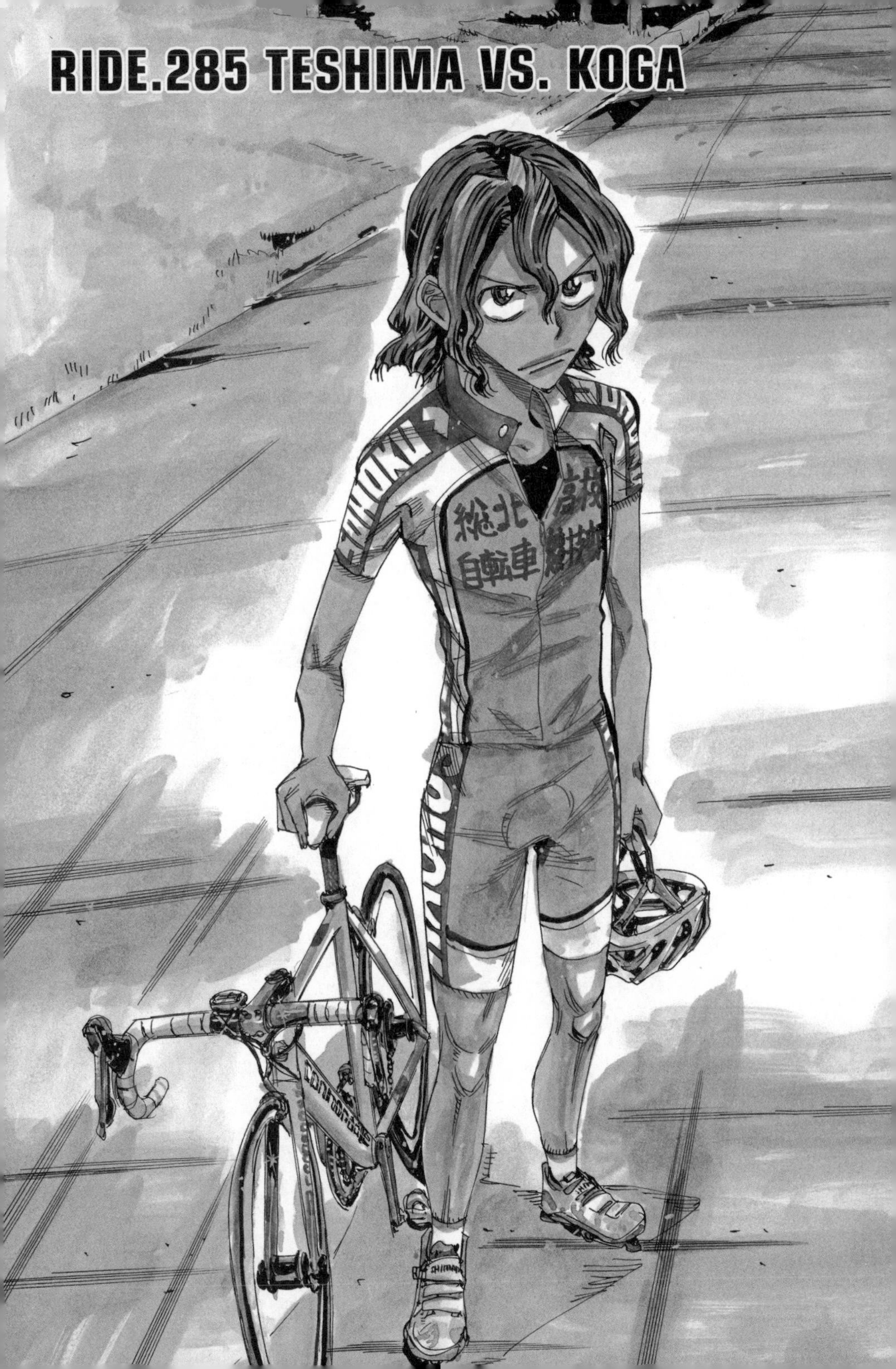

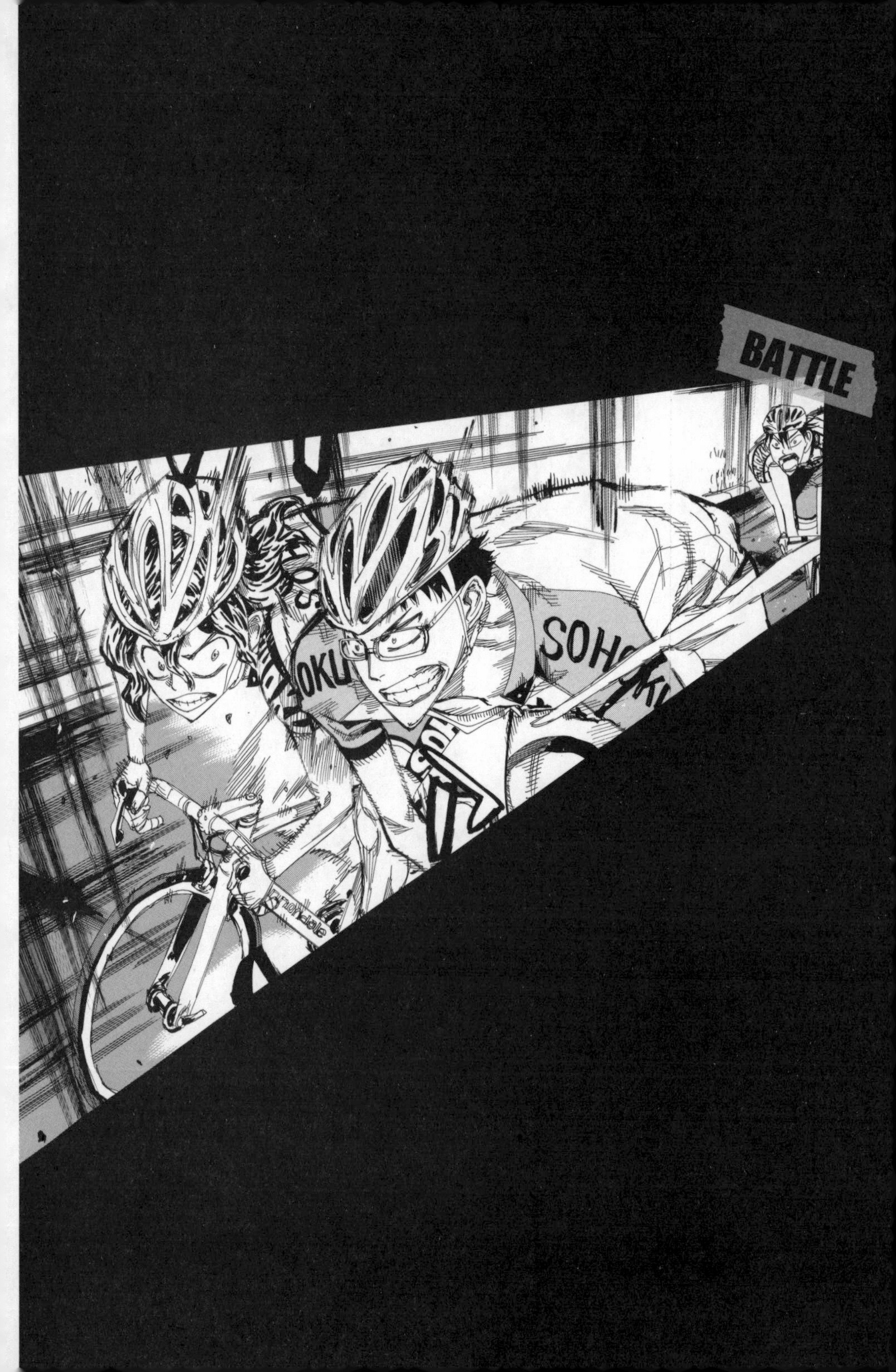
BATTLE

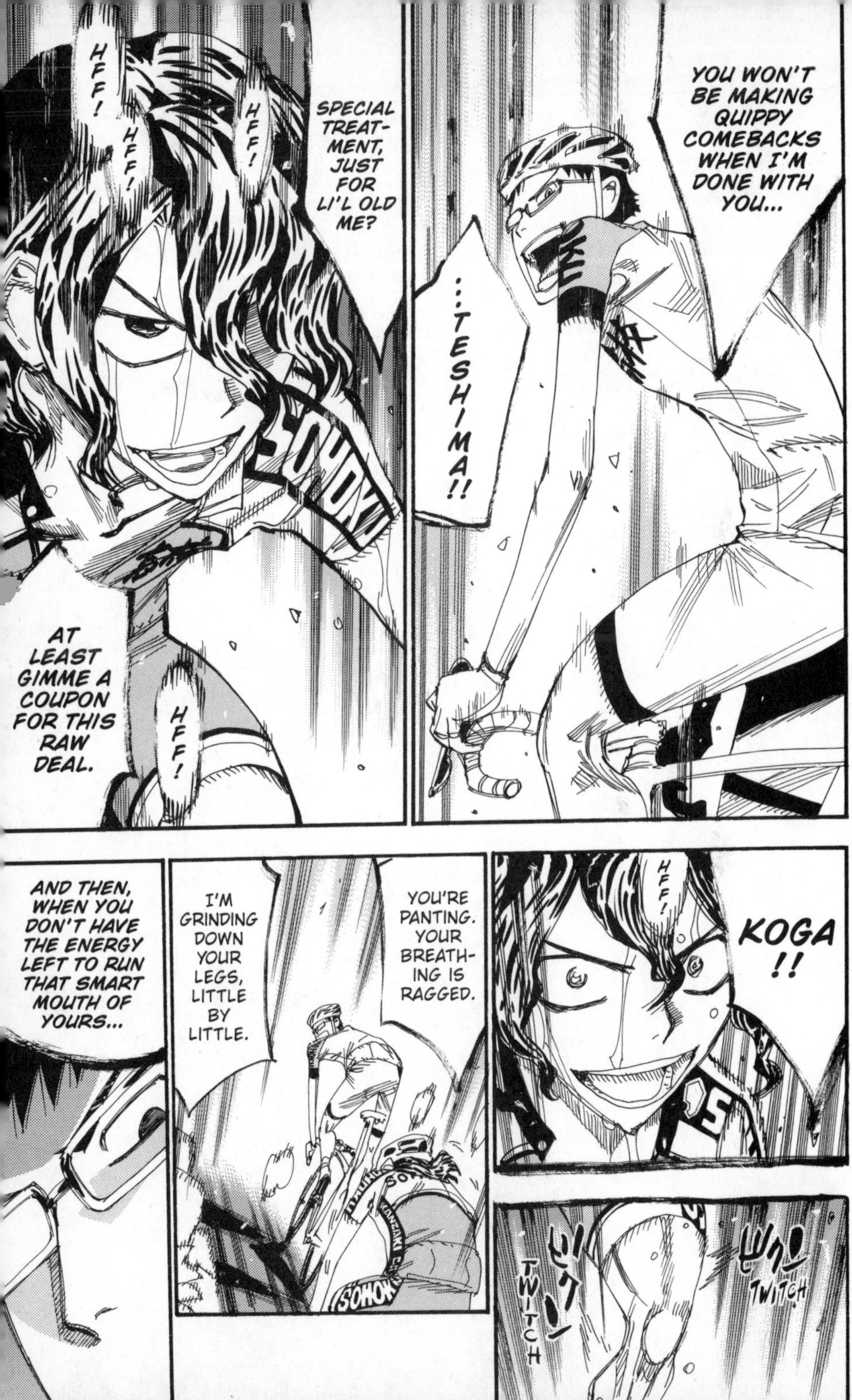

YOU WON'T BE MAKING QUIPPY COMEBACKS WHEN I'M DONE WITH YOU...
...TESHIMA!!
HFF! HFF! HFF!
SPECIAL TREATMENT, JUST FOR LI'L OLD ME?
AT LEAST GIMME A COUPON FOR THIS RAW DEAL.
HFF!
HFF!
KOGA!!
TWITCH
TWITCH
YOU'RE PANTING. YOUR BREATHING IS RAGGED.
I'M GRINDING DOWN YOUR LEGS, LITTLE BY LITTLE.
AND THEN, WHEN YOU DON'T HAVE THE ENERGY LEFT TO RUN THAT SMART MOUTH OF YOURS...

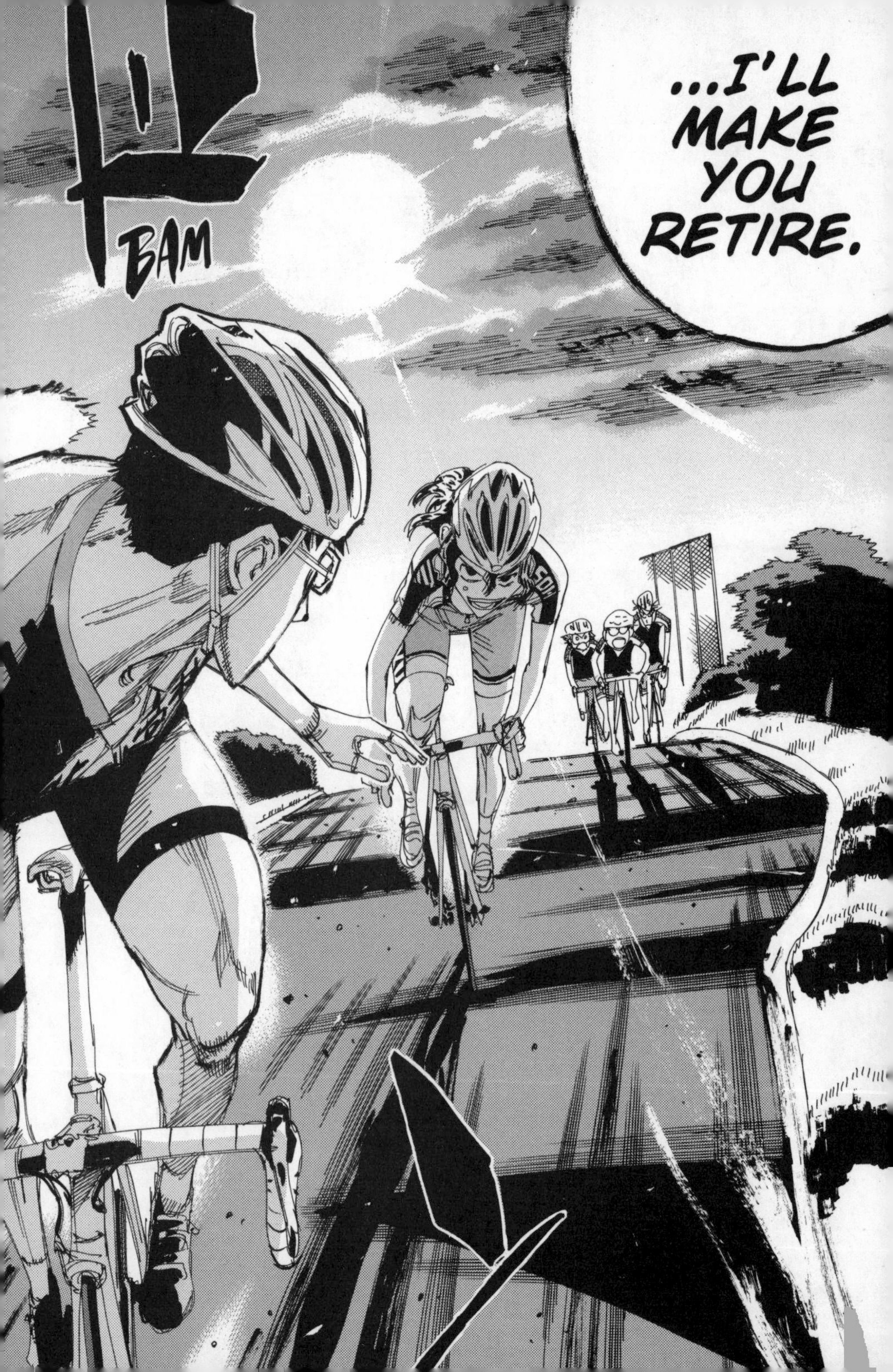
...I'LL MAKE YOU RETIRE.
BAM

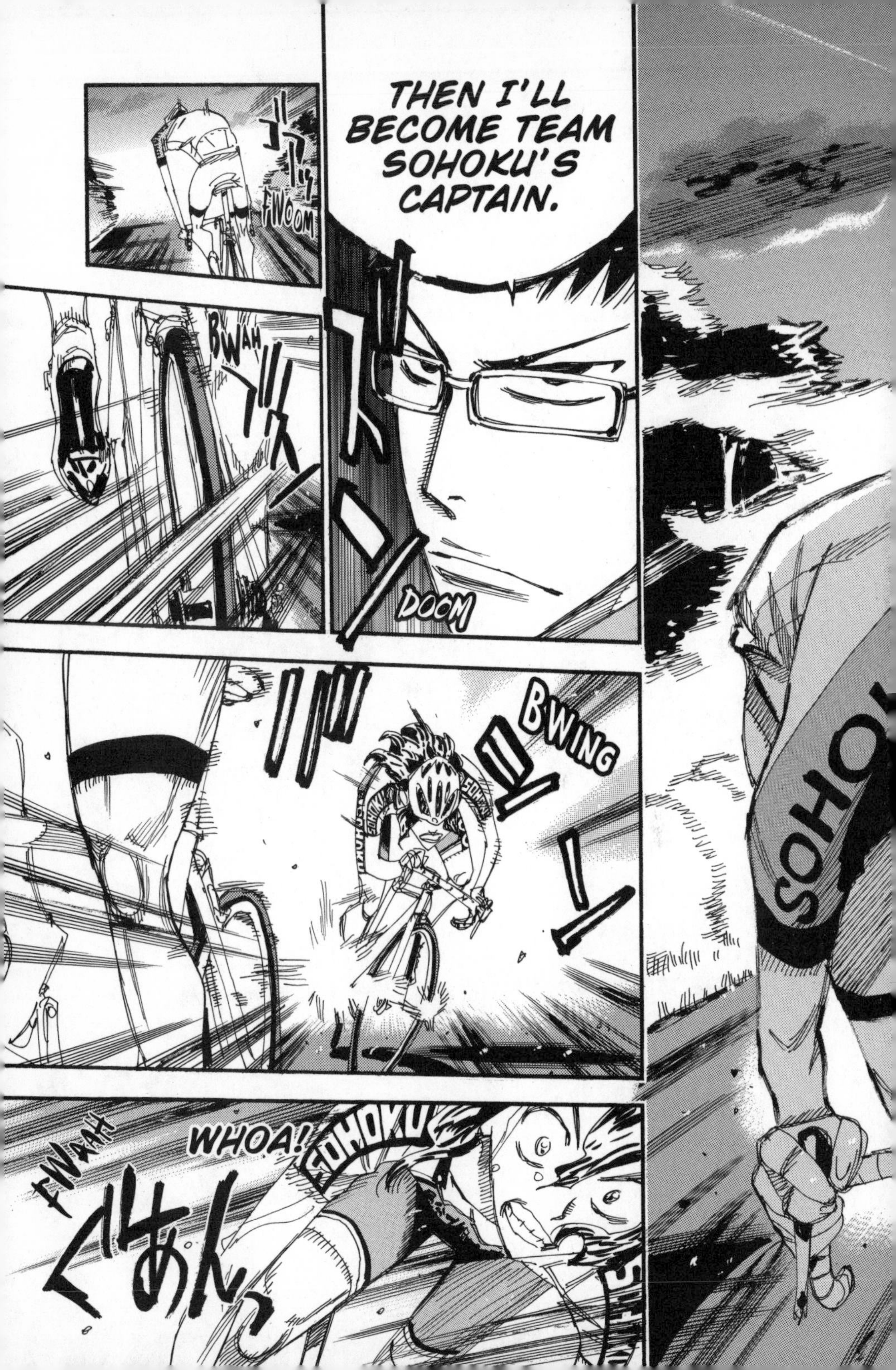
THEN I'LL BECOME TEAM SOHOKU'S CAPTAIN.
DOOM
FWOOM
BWAH
BWING
WHOA!
FWAAH

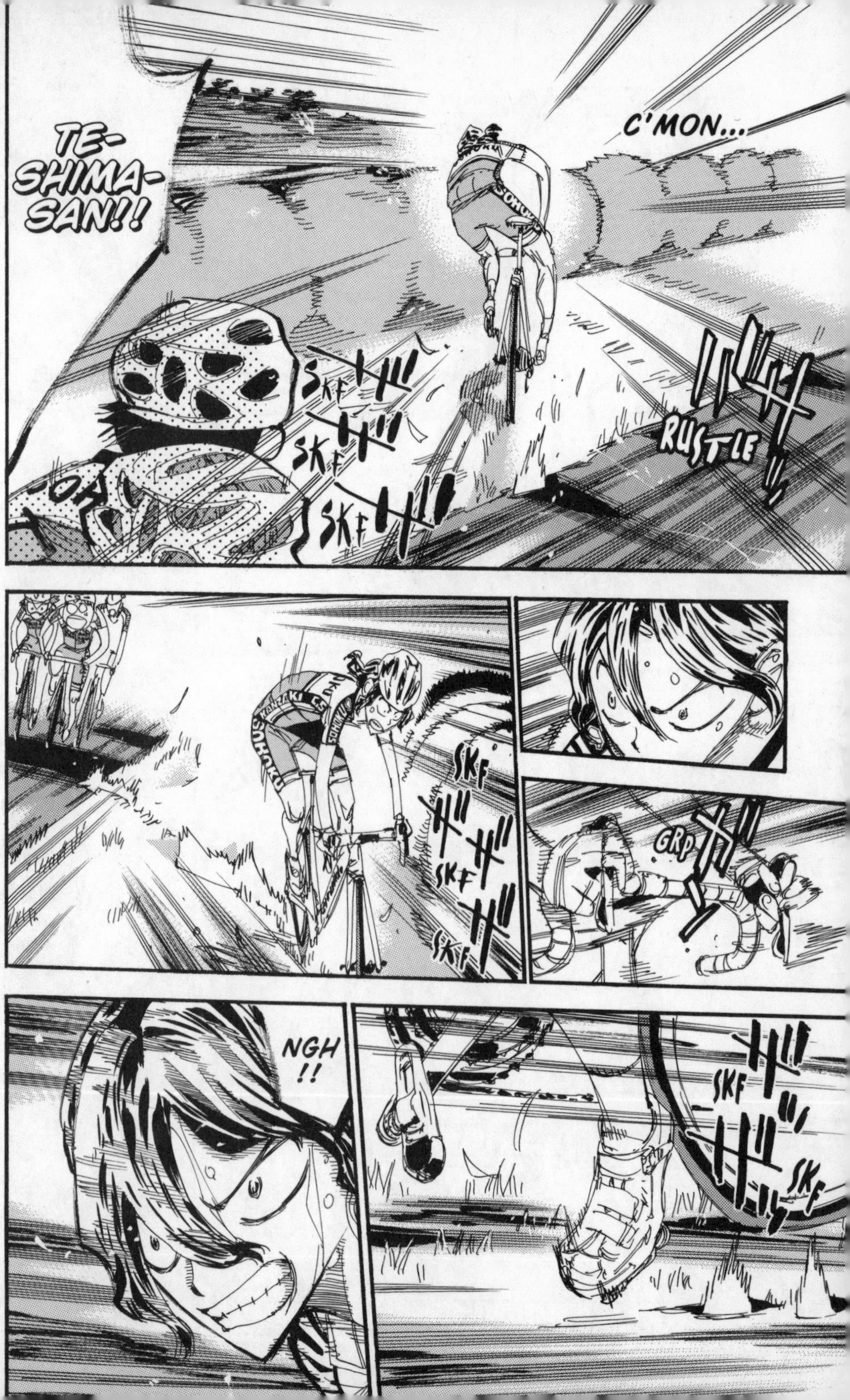
C'MON...
TE-SHIMA-SAN!!
RUSTLE
SKF
SKF
SKF
GRP
SKF
SKF
SKF
SKF
SKF
NGH!!

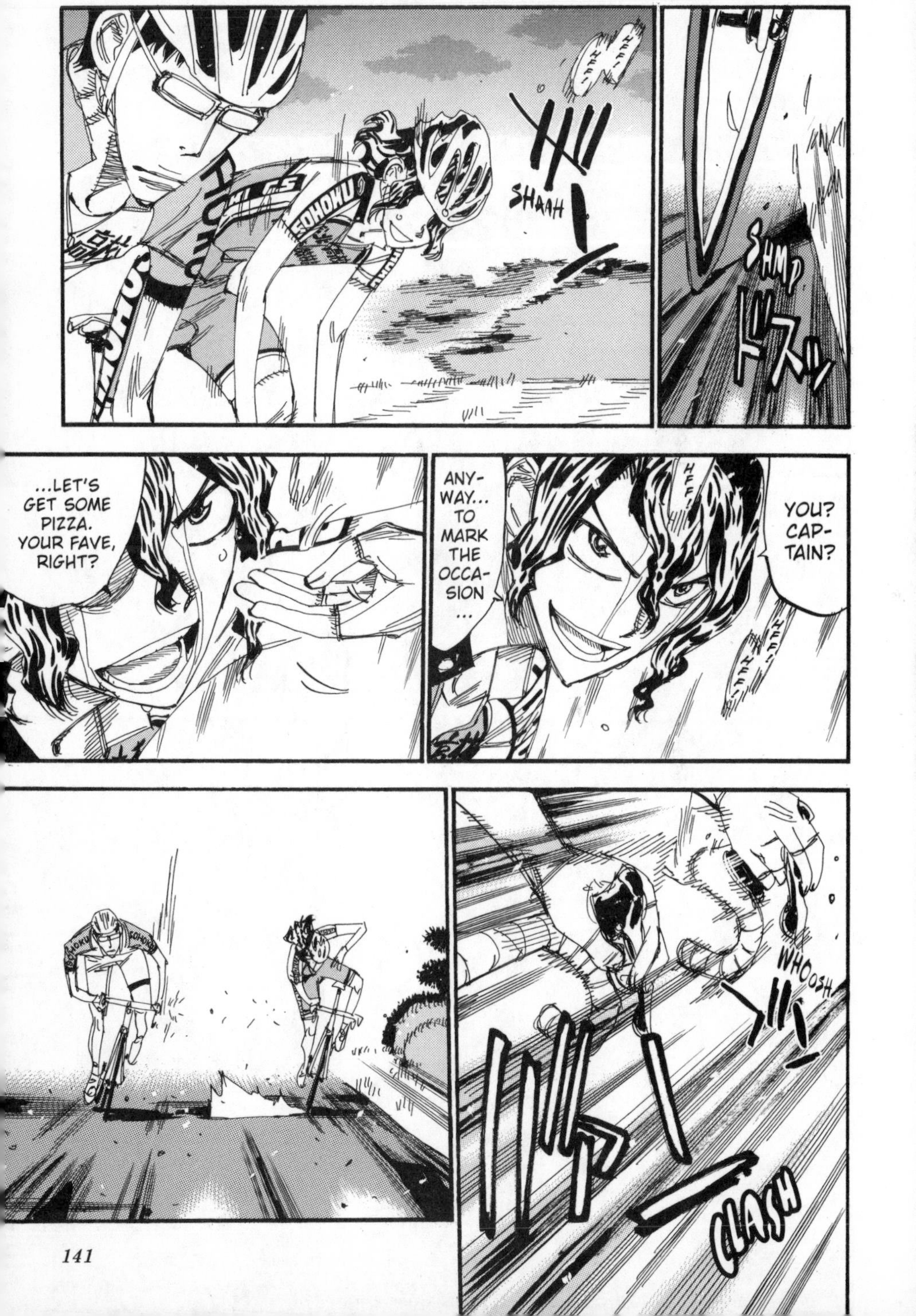
SHMP
ドスッ
HFF! HFF!
SHAAH
YOU? CAPTAIN?
HFF!
ANYWAY... TO MARK THE OCCASION...
HFF! HFF!
...LET'S GET SOME PIZZA. YOUR FAVE, RIGHT?
WHOOSH
CLASH

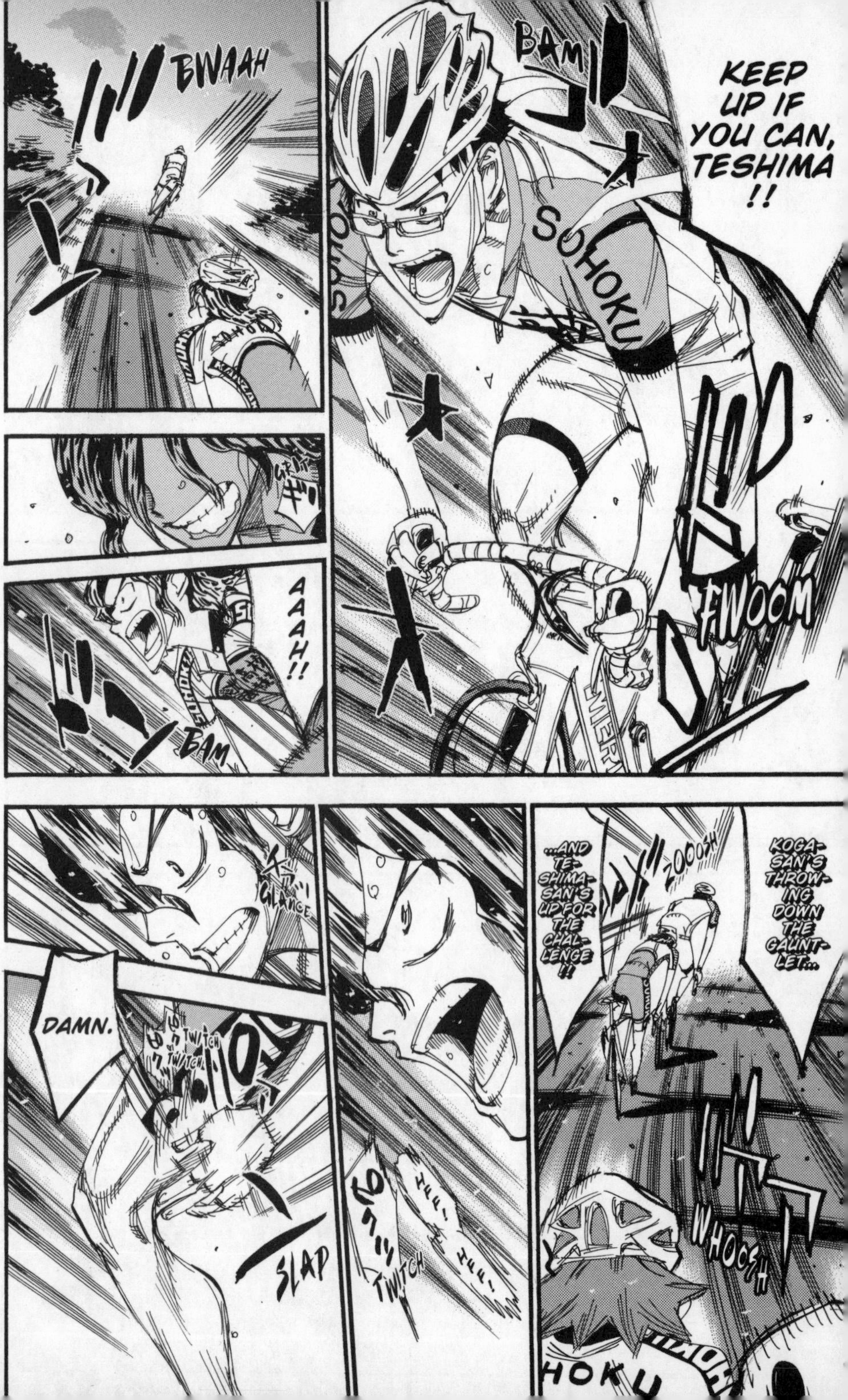
BAM
KEEP UP IF YOU CAN, TESHIMA!!
FWOOM
BWAAH
GRIT
AAAAH!!
BAM
KOGA-SAN'S THROWING DOWN THE GAUNTLET...
...AND TESHIMA-SAN'S UP FOR THE CHALLENGE!!
ZOOOSH
WHOOSH
HUU! HUU! HUU!
TWITCH
GLANCE
DAMN.
TWITCH TWITCH
SLAP

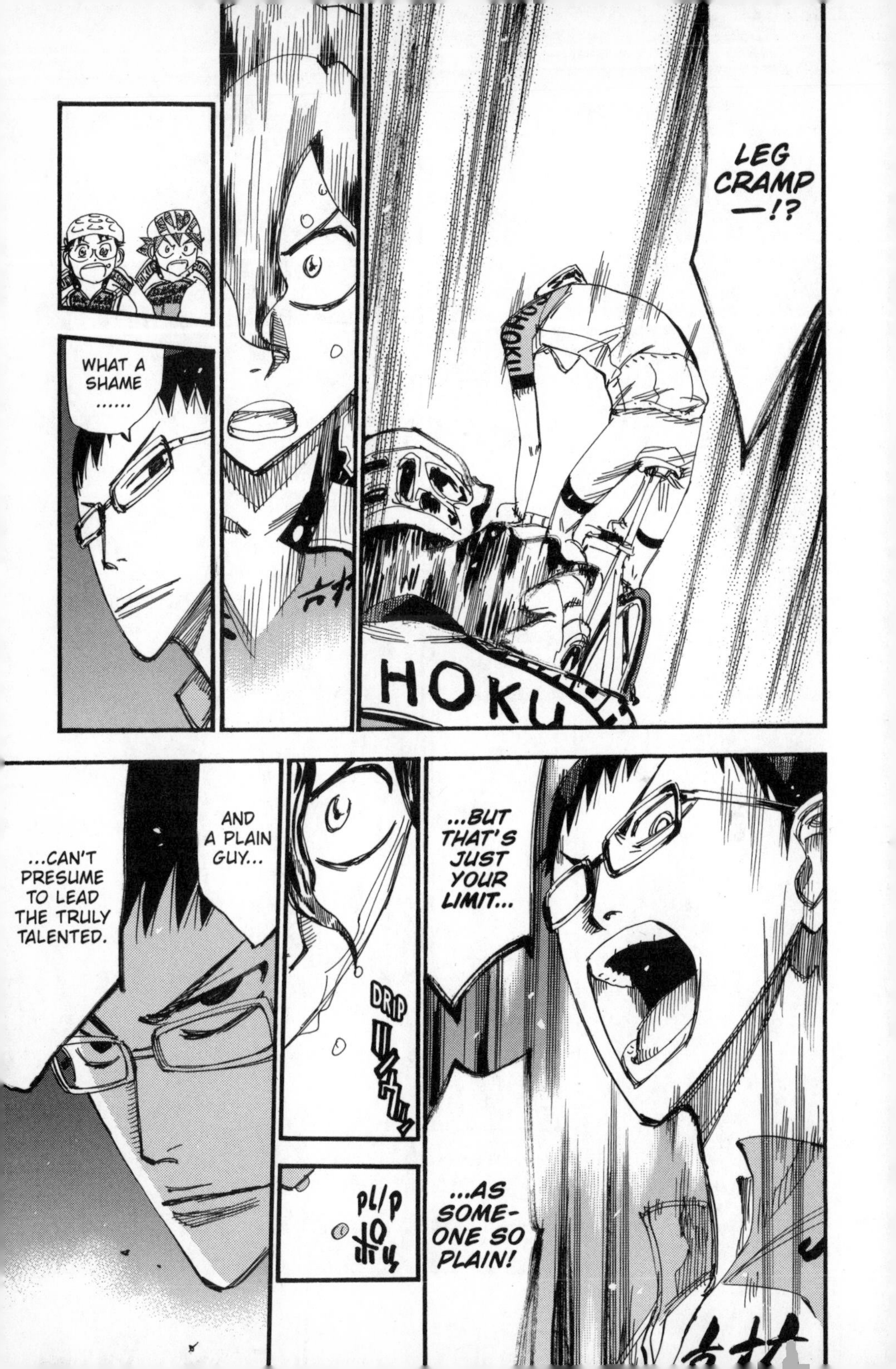

LEG CRAMP—!?
WHAT A SHAME ......
...BUT THAT'S JUST YOUR LIMIT...
...AS SOME-ONE SO PLAIN!
AND A PLAIN GUY...
DRIP
plip
...CAN'T PRESUME TO LEAD THE TRULY TALENTED.

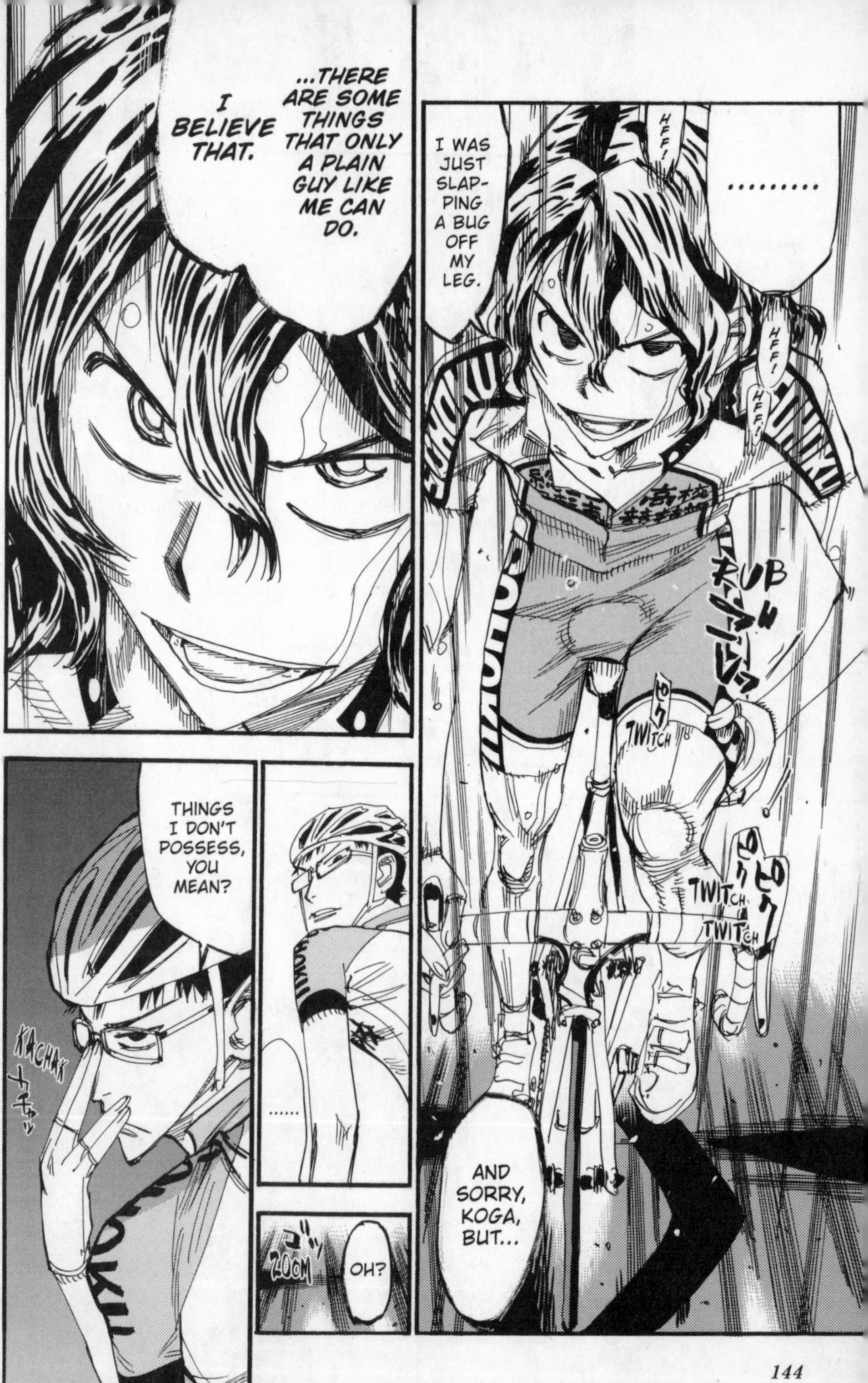

HFF!
I WAS JUST SLAPPING A BUG OFF MY LEG.
....
HFF!
HFF!
RUB
TWITCH
TWITCH
TWITCH
AND SORRY, KOGA, BUT...
...THERE ARE SOME THINGS THAT ONLY A PLAIN GUY LIKE ME CAN DO.
I BELIEVE THAT.
......
ZOOM
OH?
THINGS I DON'T POSSESS, YOU MEAN?
KACHAK

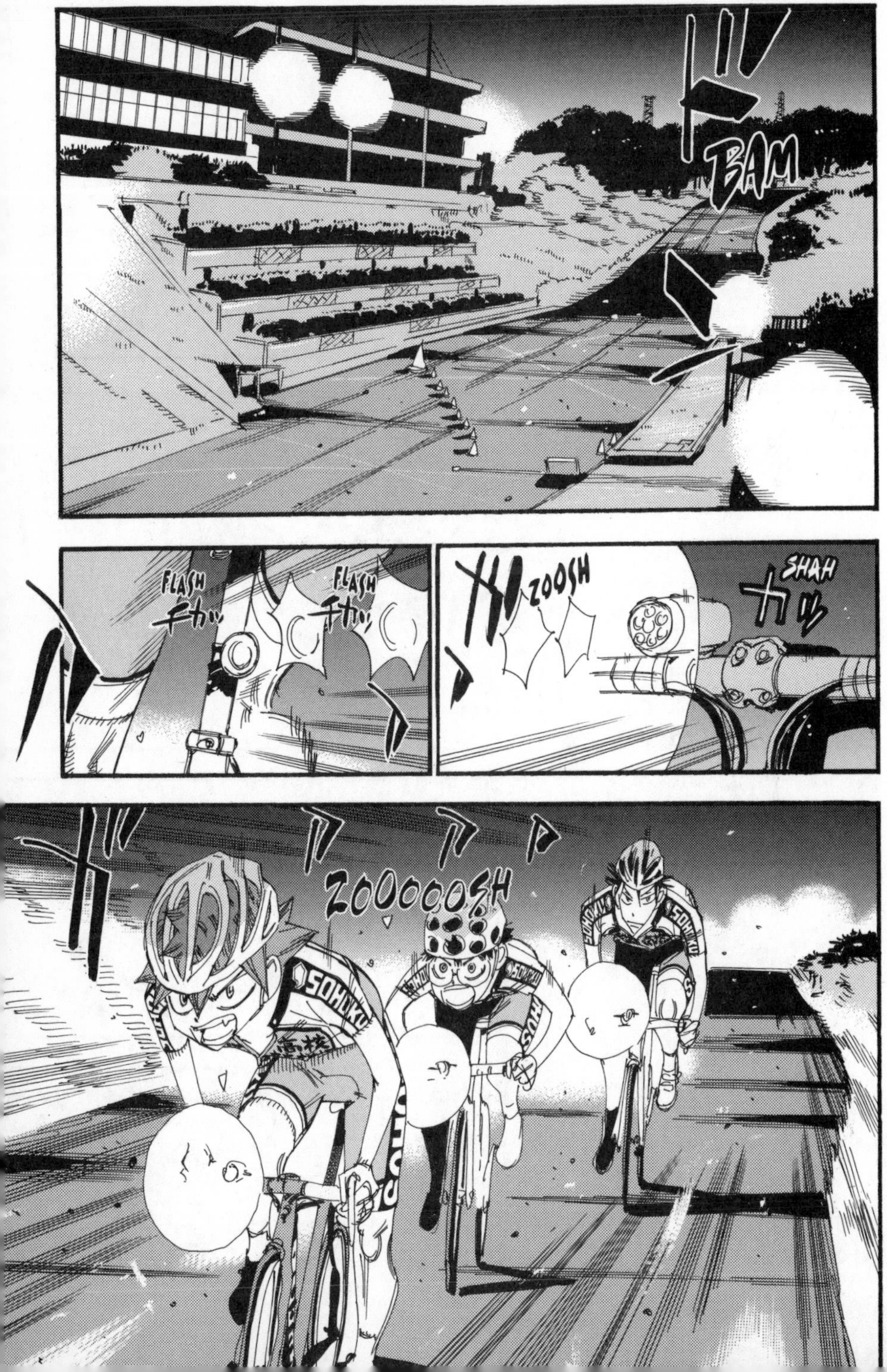
BAM
ZOOSH
SHAH
FLASH
チカッ
FLASH
チカッ
ZOOOOOSH

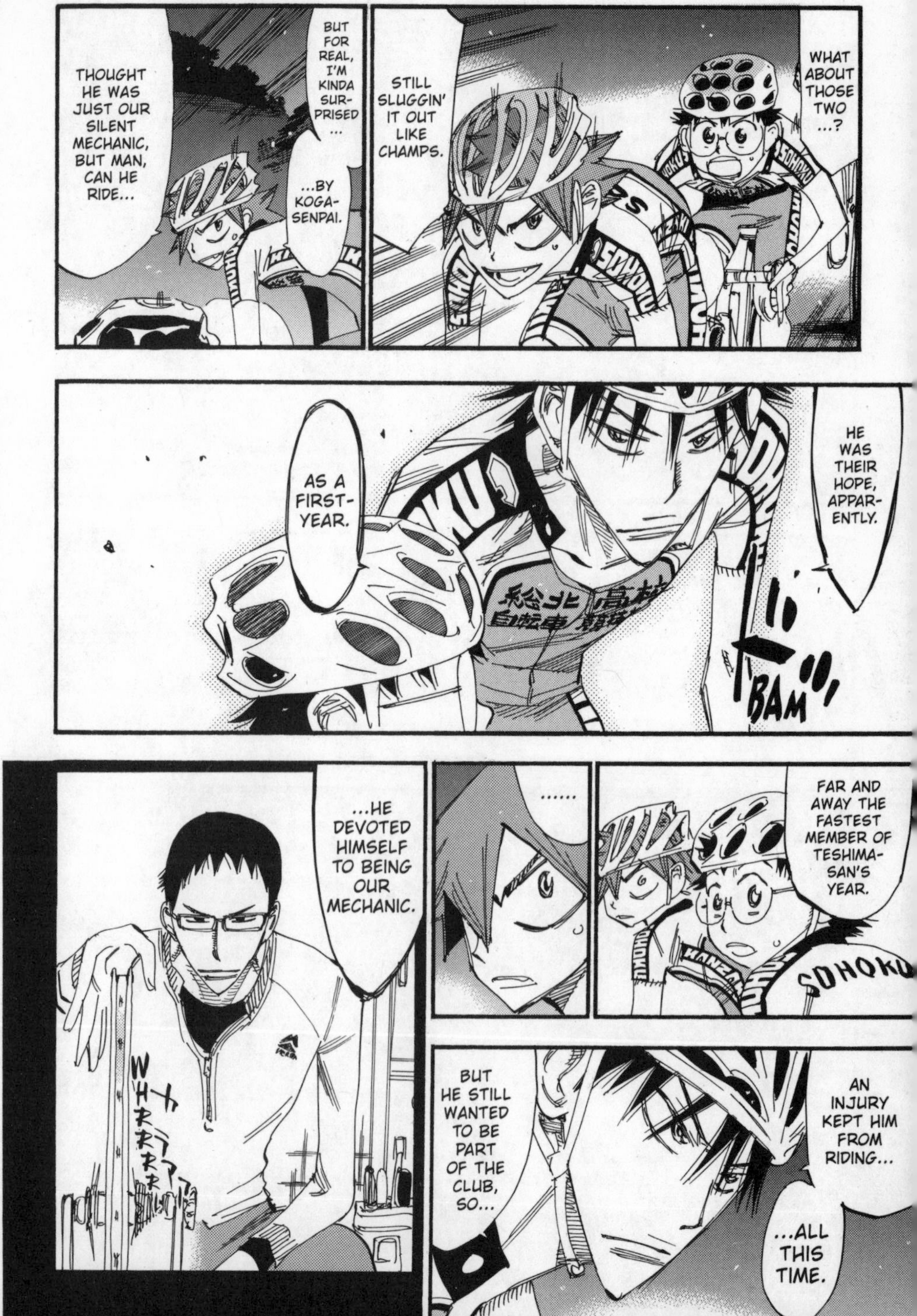
WHAT ABOUT THOSE TWO ...?
STILL SLUGGIN' IT OUT LIKE CHAMPS.
BUT FOR REAL, I'M KINDA SUR-PRISED ...
...BY KOGA-SENPAI.
THOUGHT HE WAS JUST OUR SILENT MECHANIC, BUT MAN, CAN HE RIDE...
HE WAS THEIR HOPE, APPAR-ENTLY.
AS A FIRST-YEAR.
BAM
FAR AND AWAY THE FASTEST MEMBER OF TESHIMA-SAN'S YEAR.
......
AN INJURY KEPT HIM FROM RIDING...
...ALL THIS TIME.
BUT HE STILL WANTED TO BE PART OF THE CLUB, SO...
...HE DEVOTED HIMSELF TO BEING OUR MECHANIC.

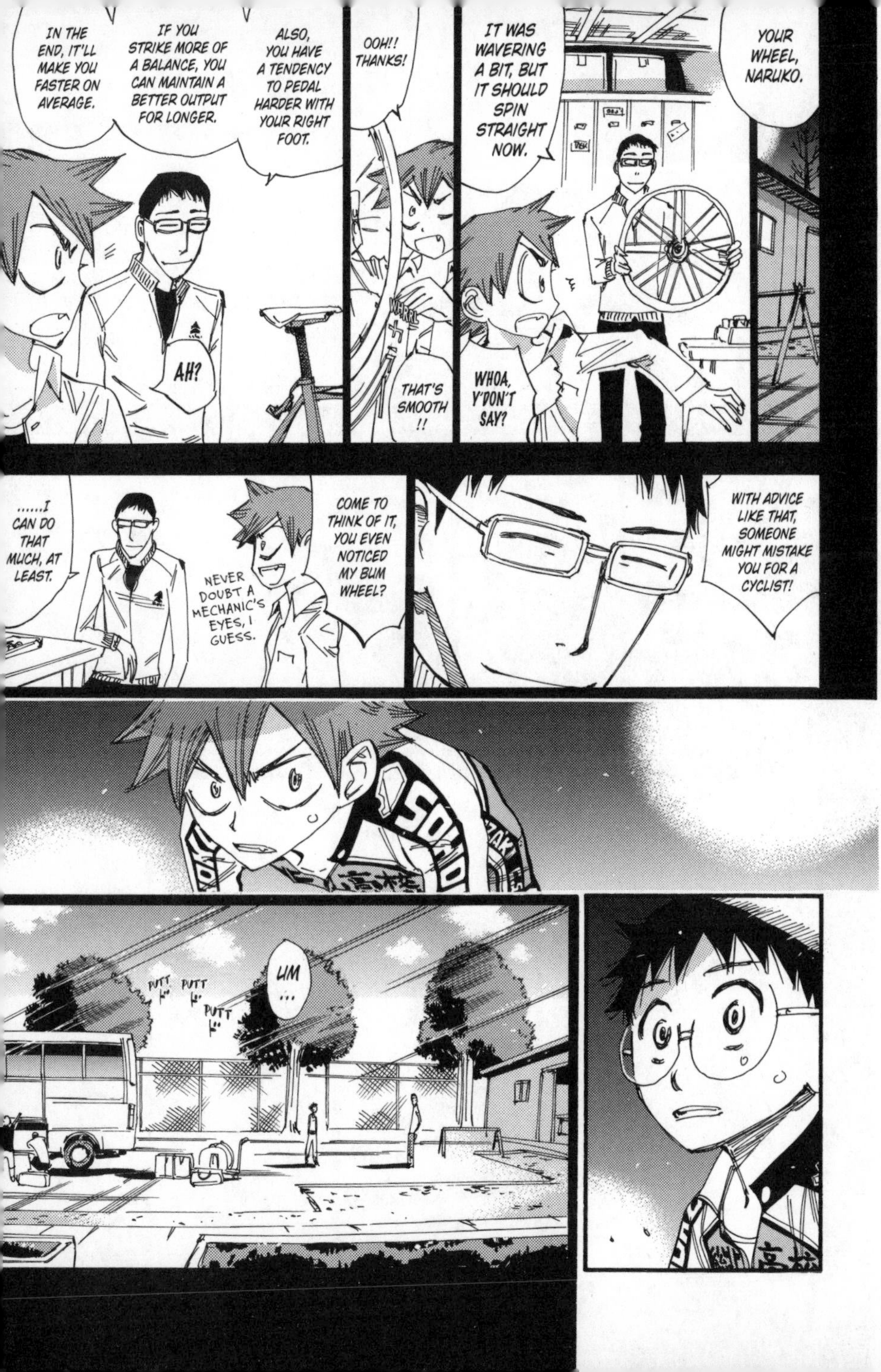
YOUR WHEEL, NARUKO.
IT WAS WAVERING A BIT, BUT IT SHOULD SPIN STRAIGHT NOW.
WHOA, Y'DON'T SAY?
OOH!! THANKS!
WHRRL
THAT'S SMOOTH !!
ALSO, YOU HAVE A TENDENCY TO PEDAL HARDER WITH YOUR RIGHT FOOT.
IF YOU STRIKE MORE OF A BALANCE, YOU CAN MAINTAIN A BETTER OUTPUT FOR LONGER.
IN THE END, IT'LL MAKE YOU FASTER ON AVERAGE.
AH?
WITH ADVICE LIKE THAT, SOMEONE MIGHT MISTAKE YOU FOR A CYCLIST!
COME TO THINK OF IT, YOU EVEN NOTICED MY BUM WHEEL?
NEVER DOUBT A MECHANIC'S EYES, I GUESS.
......I CAN DO THAT MUCH, AT LEAST.
UM ...
PUTT PUTT PUTT

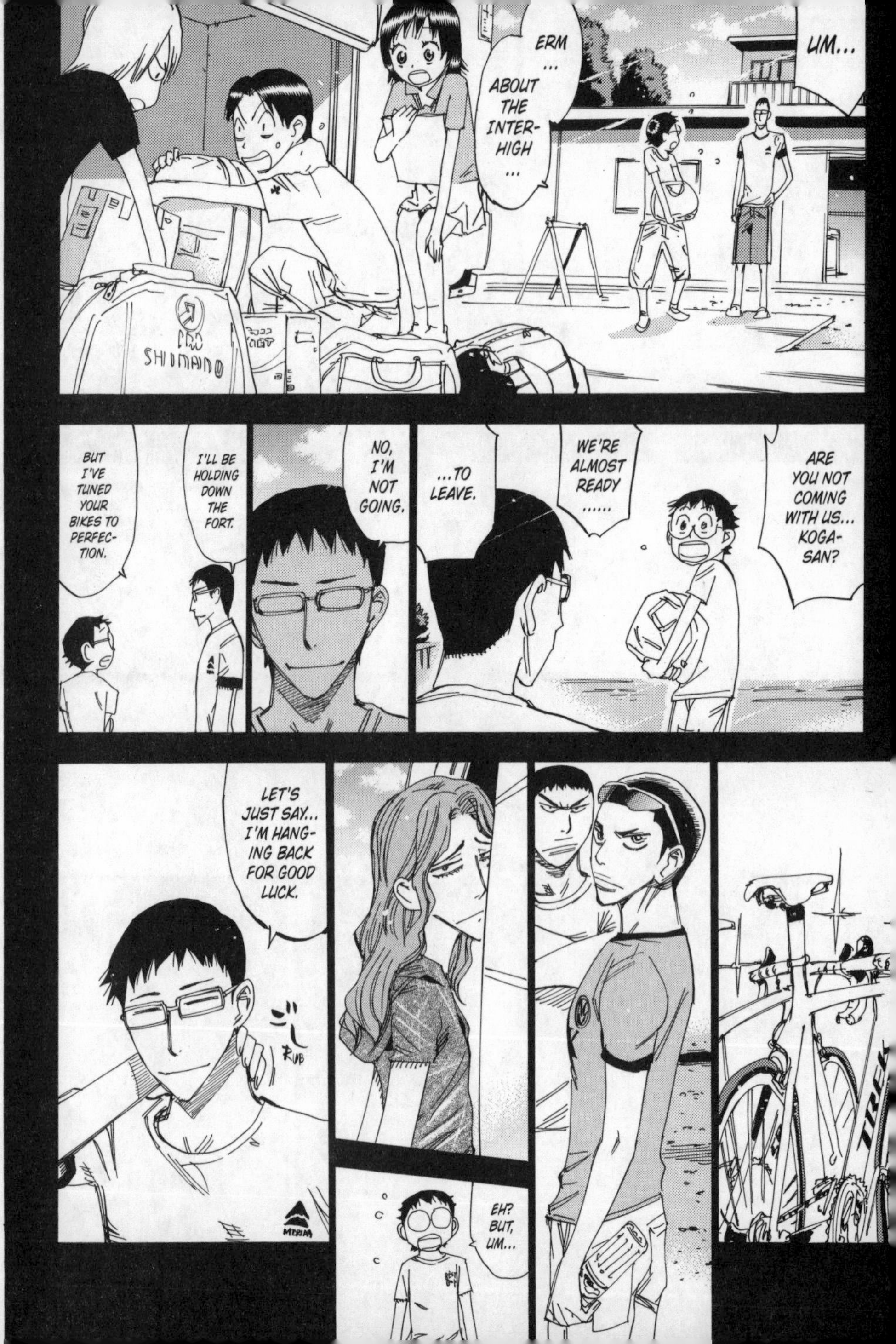
UM...
ERM ... ABOUT THE INTER-HIGH ...
ARE YOU NOT COMING WITH US... KOGA-SAN?
WE'RE ALMOST READY ......
...TO LEAVE.
NO, I'M NOT GOING.
I'LL BE HOLDING DOWN THE FORT.
BUT I'VE TUNED YOUR BIKES TO PERFECTION.
EH? BUT, UM...
LET'S JUST SAY... I'M HANGING BACK FOR GOOD LUCK.
RUB

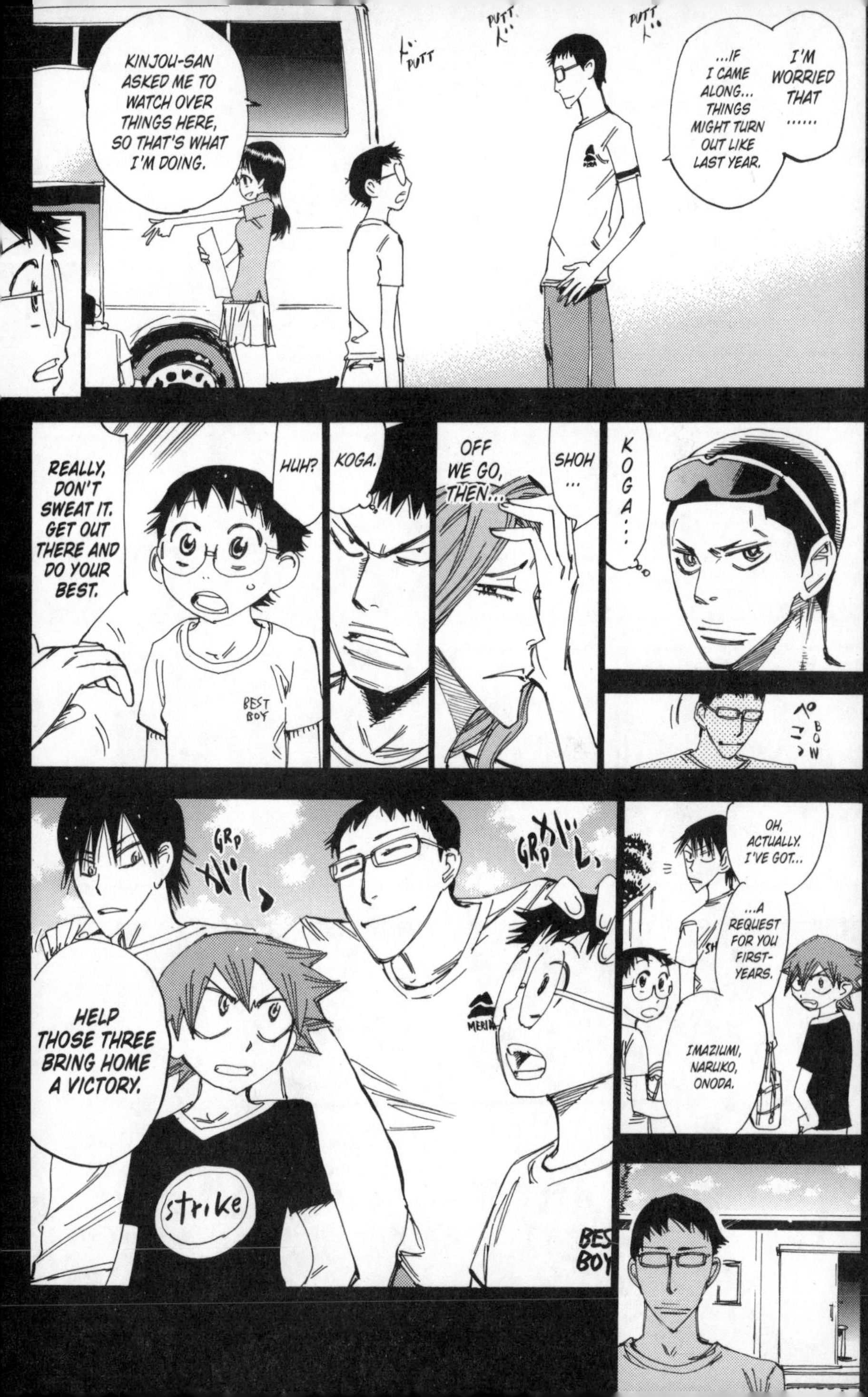

I'M WORRIED THAT ......
...IF I CAME ALONG... THINGS MIGHT TURN OUT LIKE LAST YEAR.
PUTT
PUTT
PUTT
KINJOU-SAN ASKED ME TO WATCH OVER THINGS HERE, SO THAT'S WHAT I'M DOING.
KOGA...
BOW
SHOH...
OFF WE GO, THEN...
KOGA.
HUH?
REALLY, DON'T SWEAT IT. GET OUT THERE AND DO YOUR BEST.
OH, ACTUALLY. I'VE GOT...
...A REQUEST FOR YOU FIRST-YEARS.
IMAZIUMI, NARUKO, ONODA.
GRP
GRP
HELP THOSE THREE BRING HOME A VICTORY.

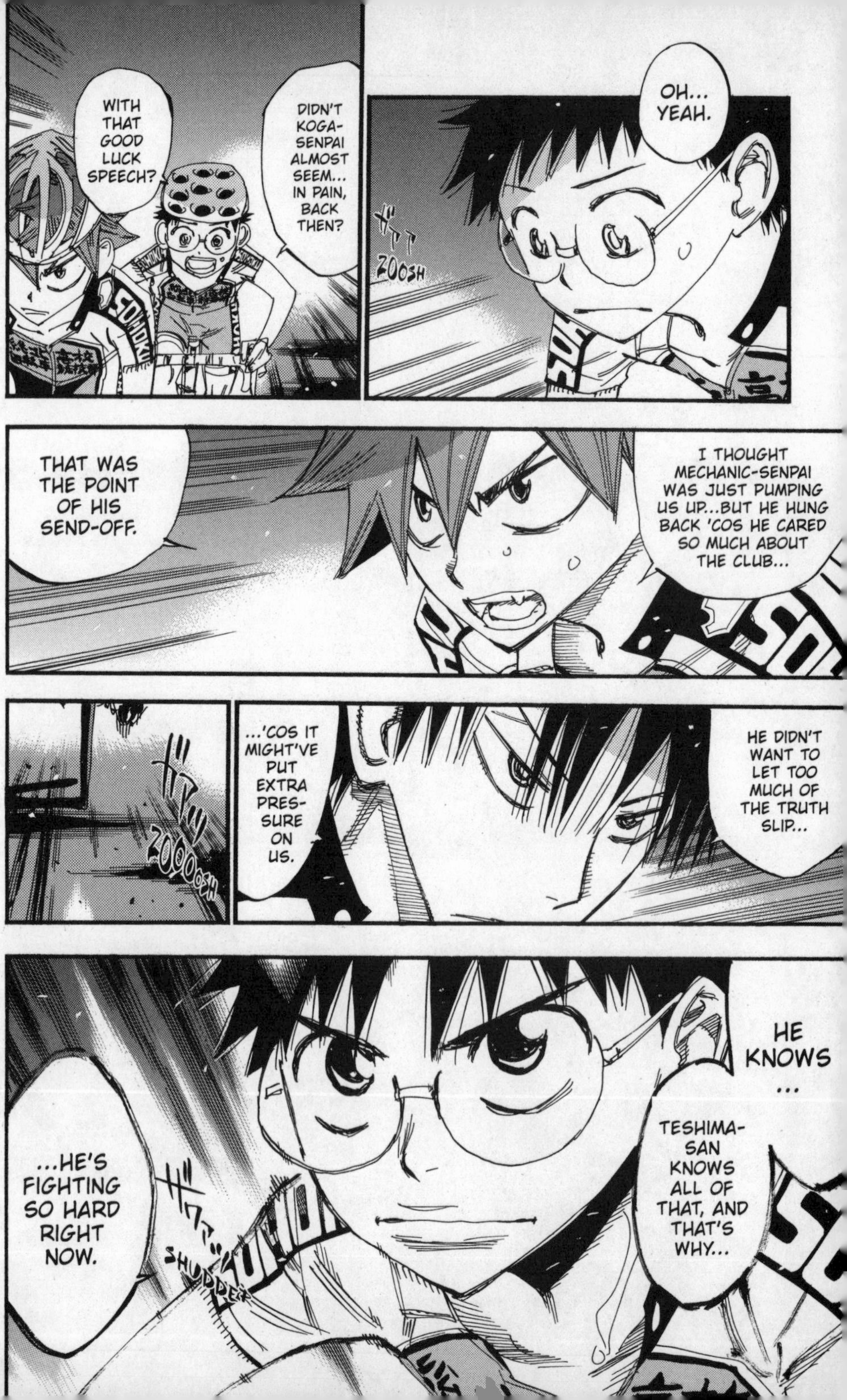
OH... YEAH.
ZOOSH
DIDN'T KOGA-SENPAI ALMOST SEEM... IN PAIN, BACK THEN?
WITH THAT GOOD LUCK SPEECH?
I THOUGHT MECHANIC-SENPAI WAS JUST PUMPING US UP...BUT HE HUNG BACK 'COS HE CARED SO MUCH ABOUT THE CLUB...
THAT WAS THE POINT OF HIS SEND-OFF.
HE DIDN'T WANT TO LET TOO MUCH OF THE TRUTH SLIP...
...'COS IT MIGHT'VE PUT EXTRA PRES-SURE ON US.
ZOOOOSH
HE KNOWS...
TESHIMA-SAN KNOWS ALL OF THAT, AND THAT'S WHY...
SHUDDER
...HE'S FIGHTING SO HARD RIGHT NOW.

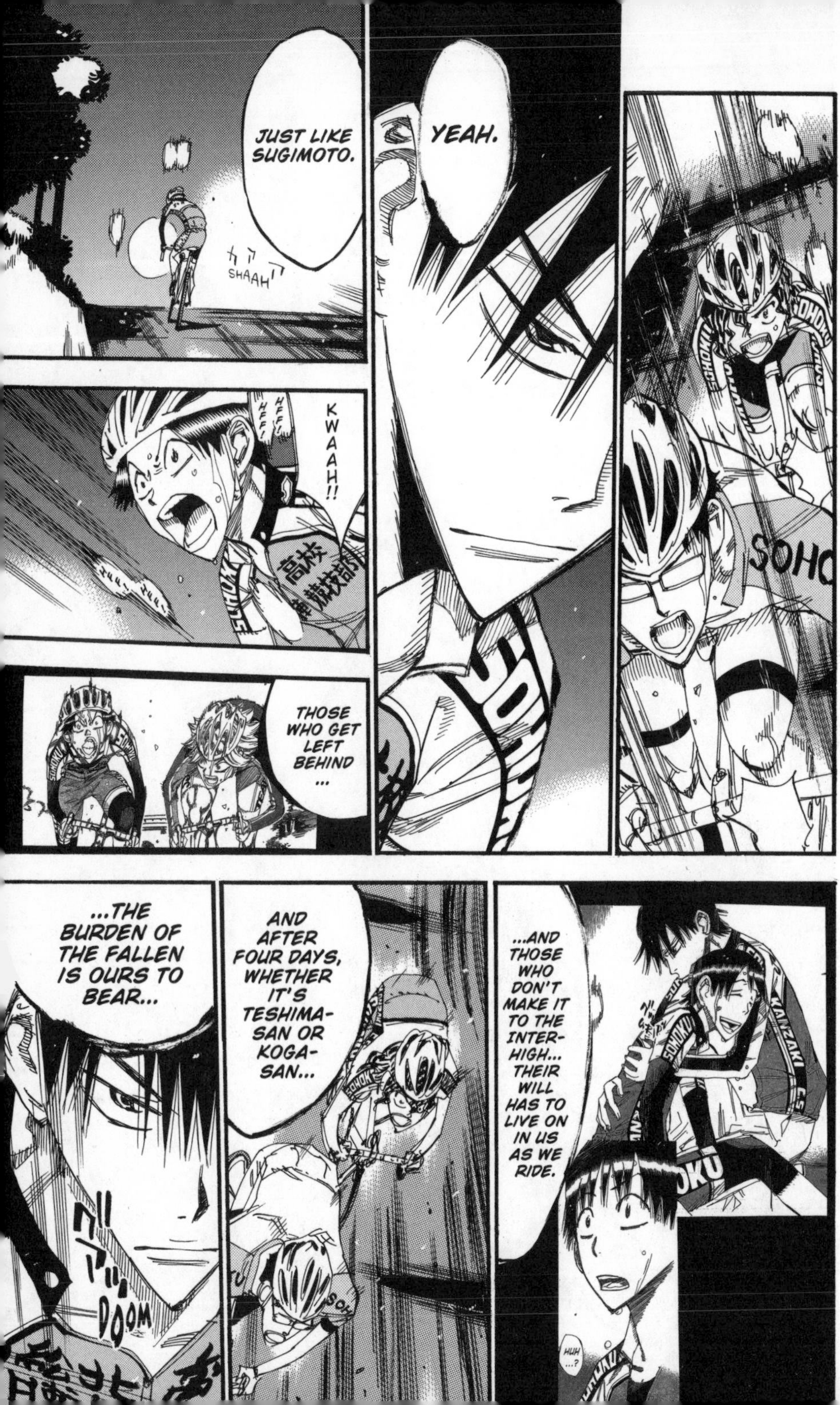
YEAH.
JUST LIKE SUGIMOTO.
SHAAH
HFF! HFF!
KWAAAH!!
THOSE WHO GET LEFT BEHIND ...
...AND THOSE WHO DON'T MAKE IT TO THE INTER-HIGH... THEIR WILL HAS TO LIVE ON IN US AS WE RIDE.
HUH ...?
AND AFTER FOUR DAYS, WHETHER IT'S TESHIMA-SAN OR KOGA-SAN...
...THE BURDEN OF THE FALLEN IS OURS TO BEAR...
DOOM

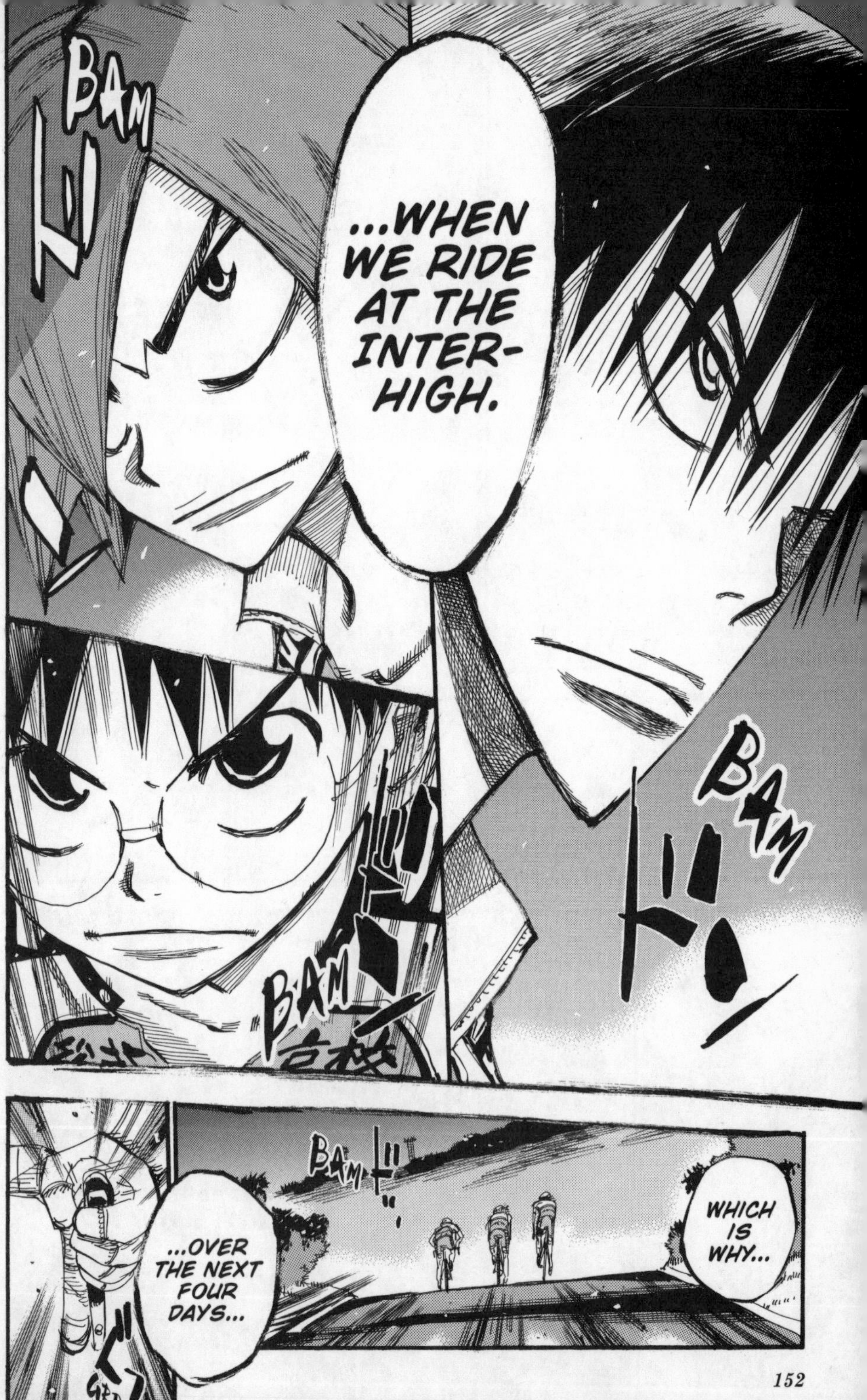
...WHEN WE RIDE AT THE INTER-HIGH.
BAM
BAM
BAM
WHICH IS WHY...
BAM
...OVER THE NEXT FOUR DAYS...
GRP

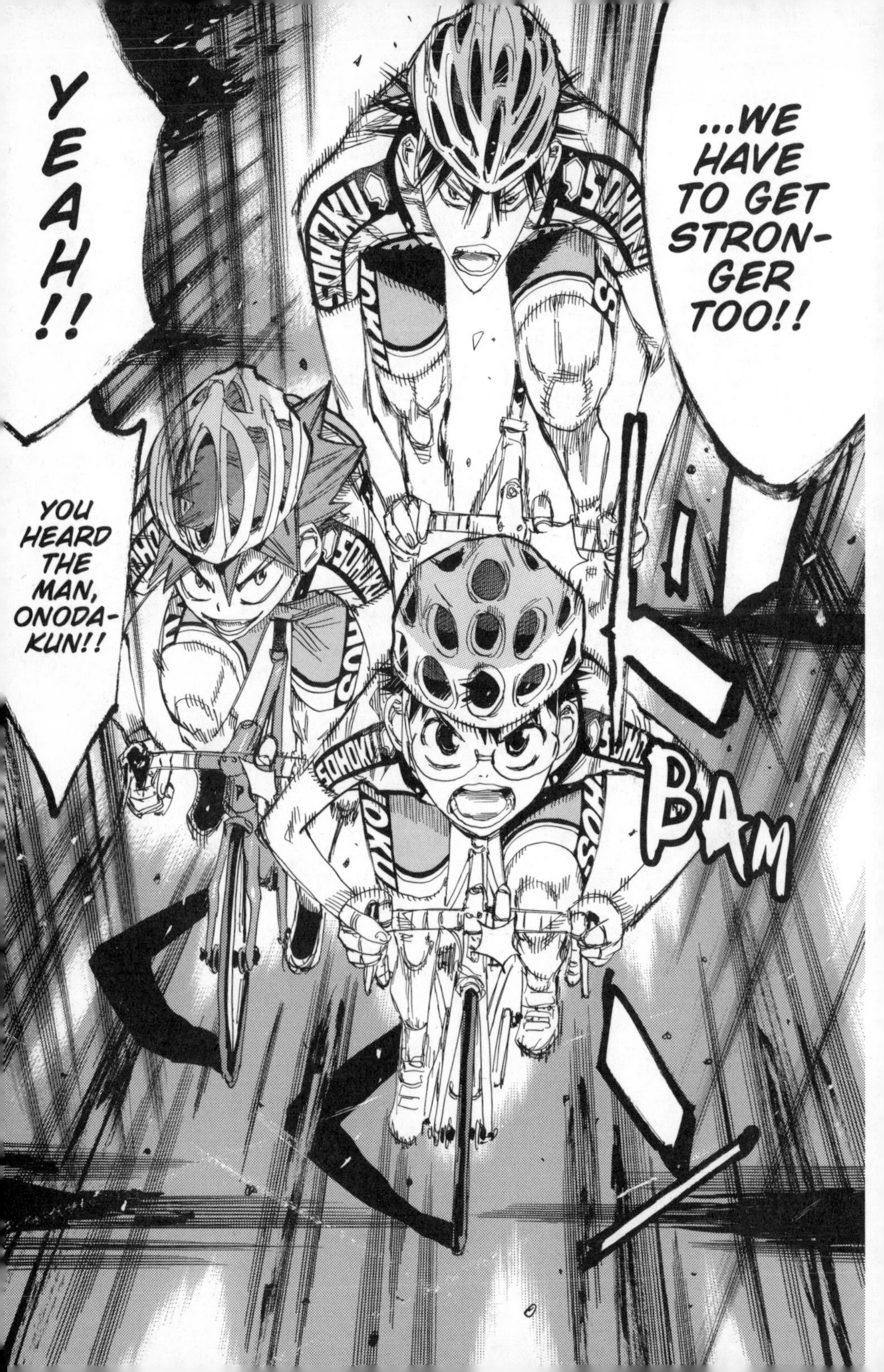
...WE HAVE TO GET STRONGER TOO!!
YEAH!!
YOU HEARD THE MAN, ONODA-KUN!!
BAM

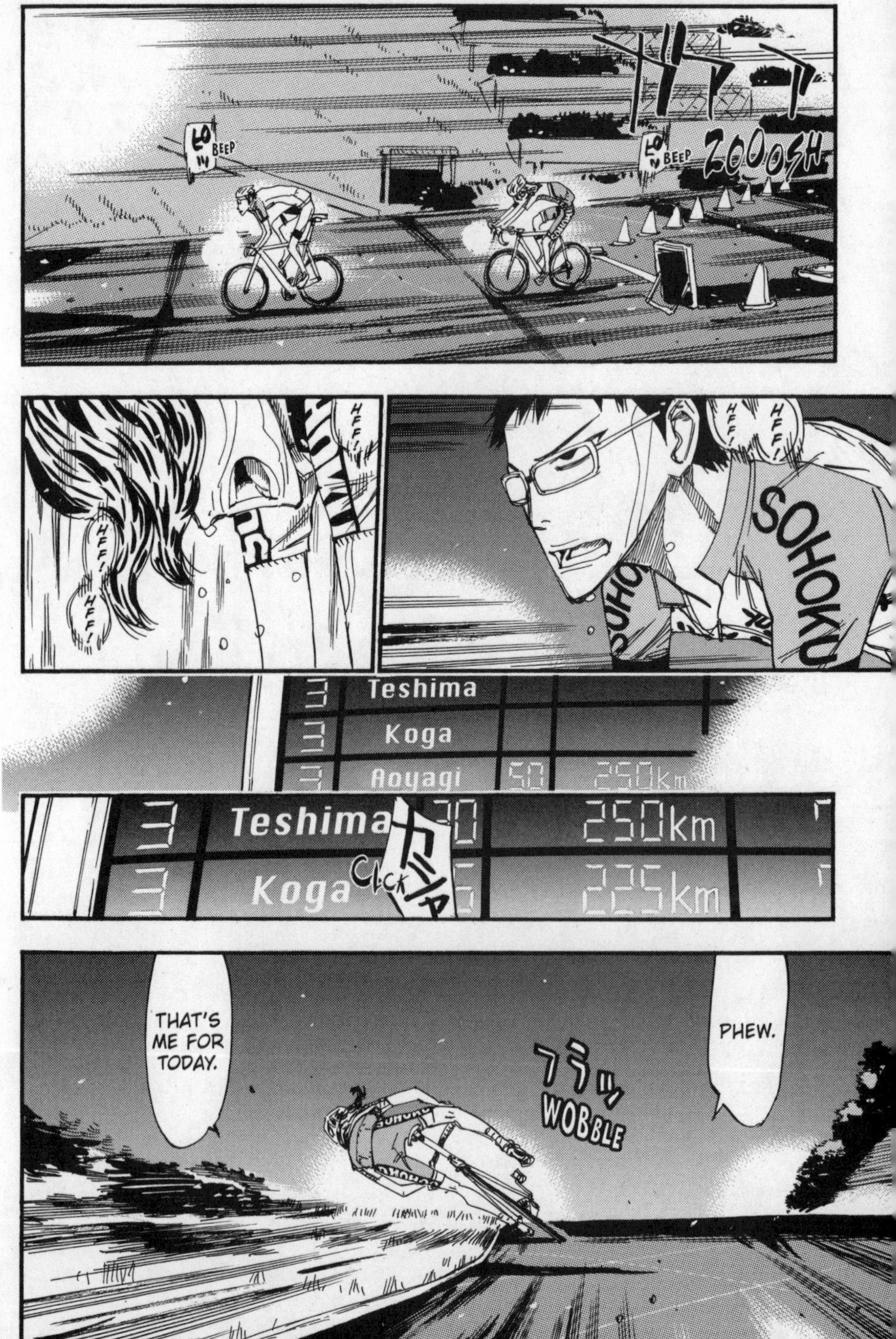
BEEP
ZOOOSH
BEEP
HFF!
HFF!
SOHOKU
HFF!
HFF!
Teshima
Koga
Aoyagi 50 250km
Teshima 250km
CLICK
Koga 225km
PHEW.
WOBBLE
THAT'S ME FOR TODAY.

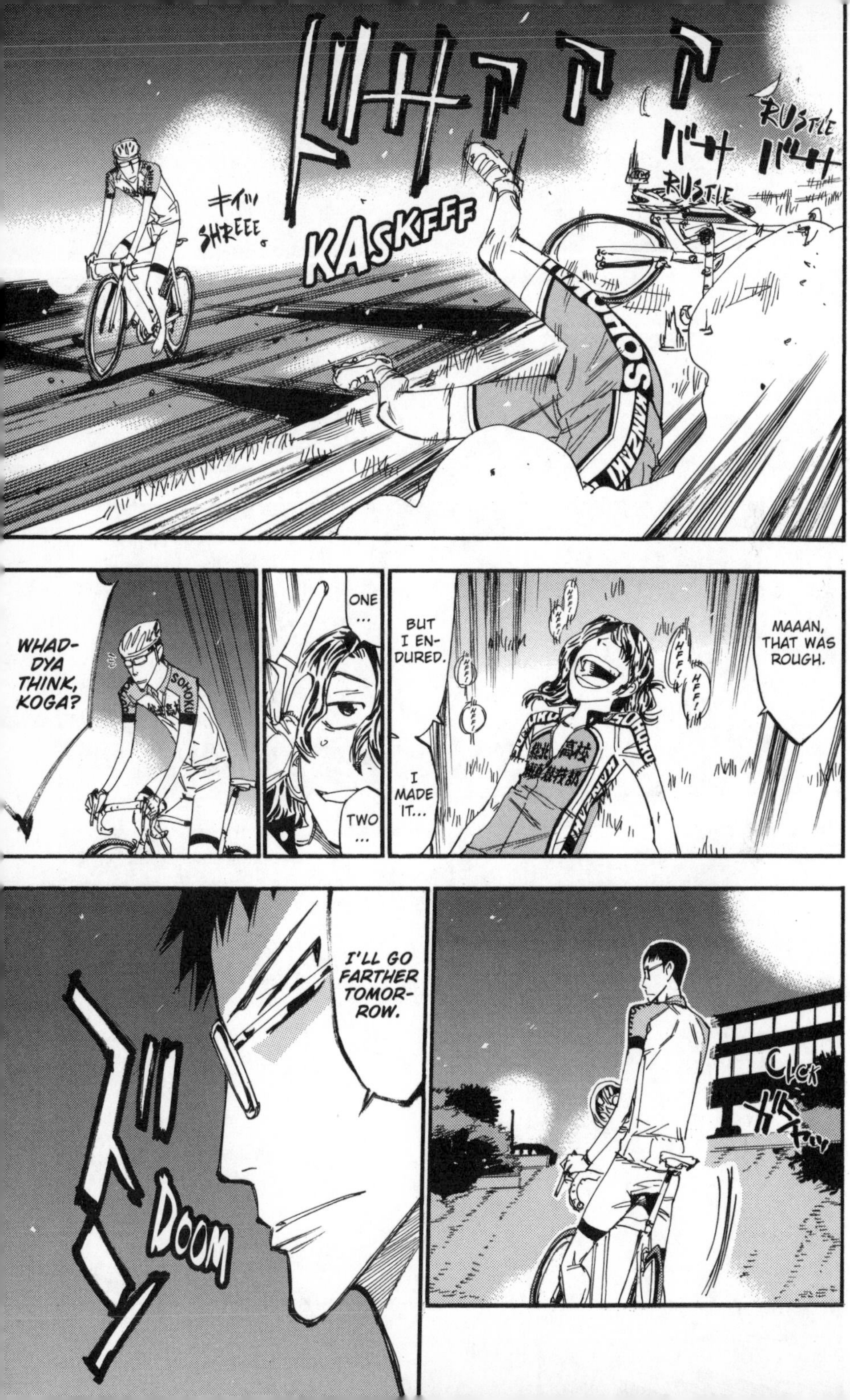

RUSTLE
バサ
バサ
RUSTLE
KASKFFF
キイッ
SHREEE
MAAAN, THAT WAS ROUGH.
HFF!
HFF!
HFF!
HFF!
HFF!
HFF!
BUT I EN-DURED.
I MADE IT...
ONE...
TWO...
WHAD-DYA THINK, KOGA?
CLICK
I'LL GO FARTHER TOMOR-ROW.
DOOM

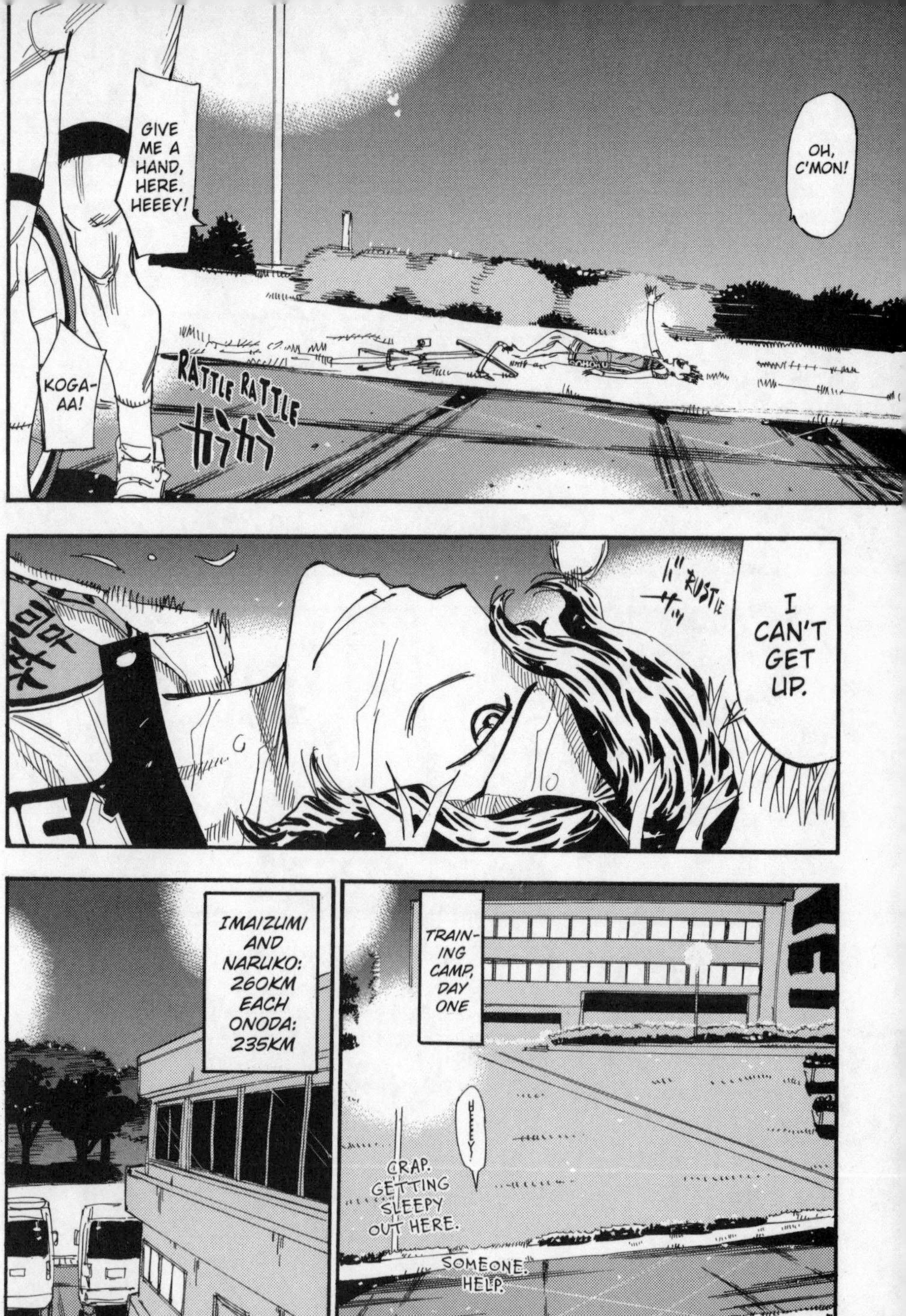
OH, C'MON!
GIVE ME A HAND, HERE. HEEEY!
KOGA-AA!
RATTLE RATTLE
I CAN'T GET UP.
RUSTLE
TRAIN-ING CAMP, DAY ONE
HEEEY!
CRAP. GETTING SLEEPY OUT HERE.
SOMEONE. HELP.
I'M YOUR CAPTAIN.
IMAIZUMI AND NARUKO: 260KM EACH ONODA: 235KM

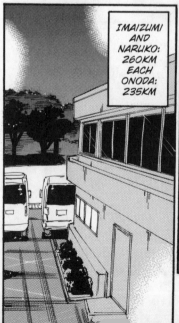

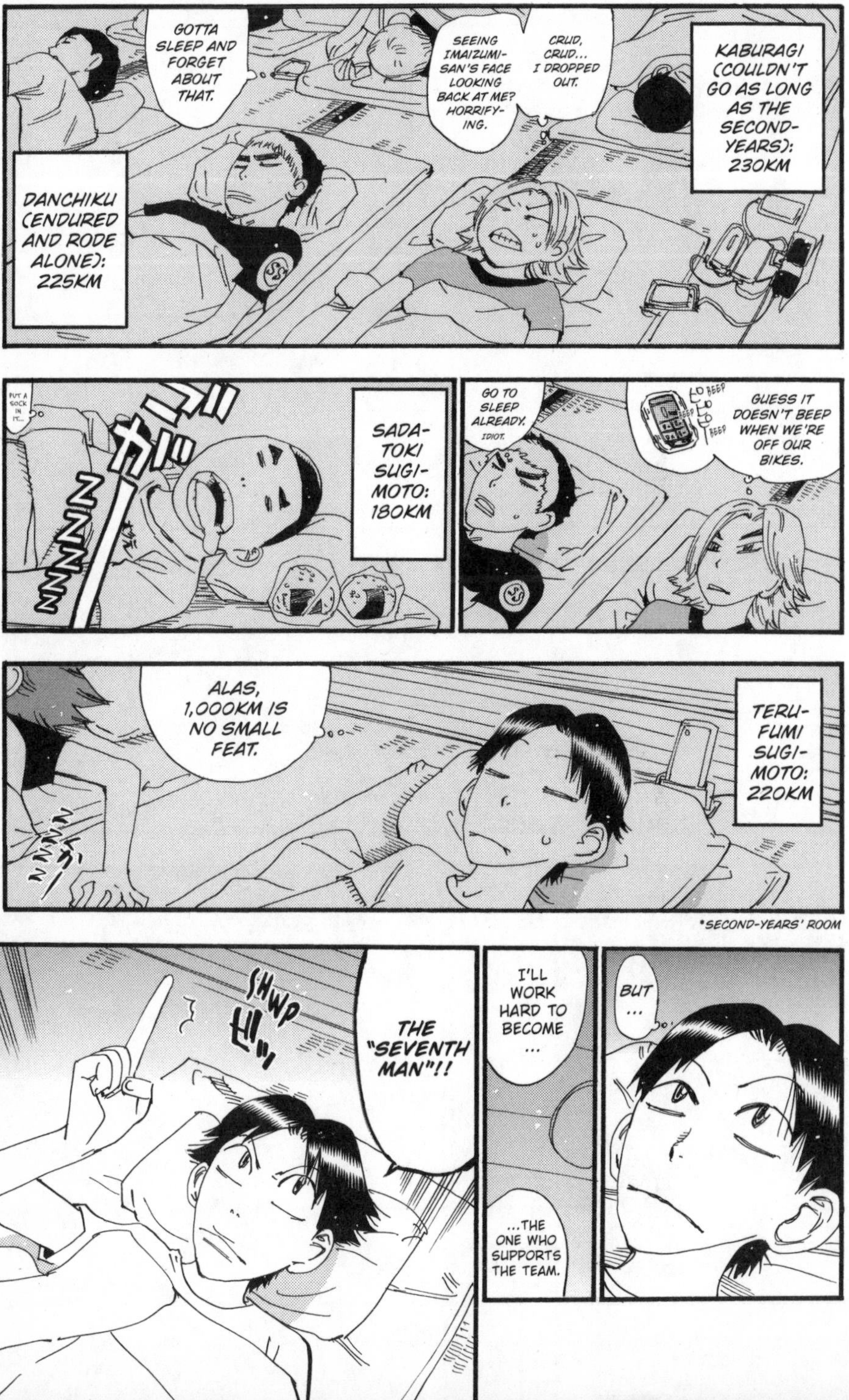
KABURAGI (COULDN'T GO AS LONG AS THE SECOND-YEARS): 230KM
CRUD, CRUD... I DROPPED OUT.
SEEING IMAIZUMI-SAN'S FACE LOOKING BACK AT ME? HORRIFYING.
GOTTA SLEEP AND FORGET ABOUT THAT.
DANCHIKU (ENDURED AND RODE ALONE): 225KM
BEEP BEEP BEEP
GUESS IT DOESN'T BEEP WHEN WE'RE OFF OUR BIKES.
GO TO SLEEP ALREADY. IDIOT.
SADATOKI SUGIMOTO: 180KM
PUT A SOCK IN IT...
ZZZZZ
TERUFUMI SUGIMOTO: 220KM
ALAS, 1,000KM IS NO SMALL FEAT.
*SECOND-YEARS' ROOM
BUT...
I'LL WORK HARD TO BECOME...
...THE ONE WHO SUPPORTS THE TEAM.
THE "SEVENTH MAN"!!
SHWP

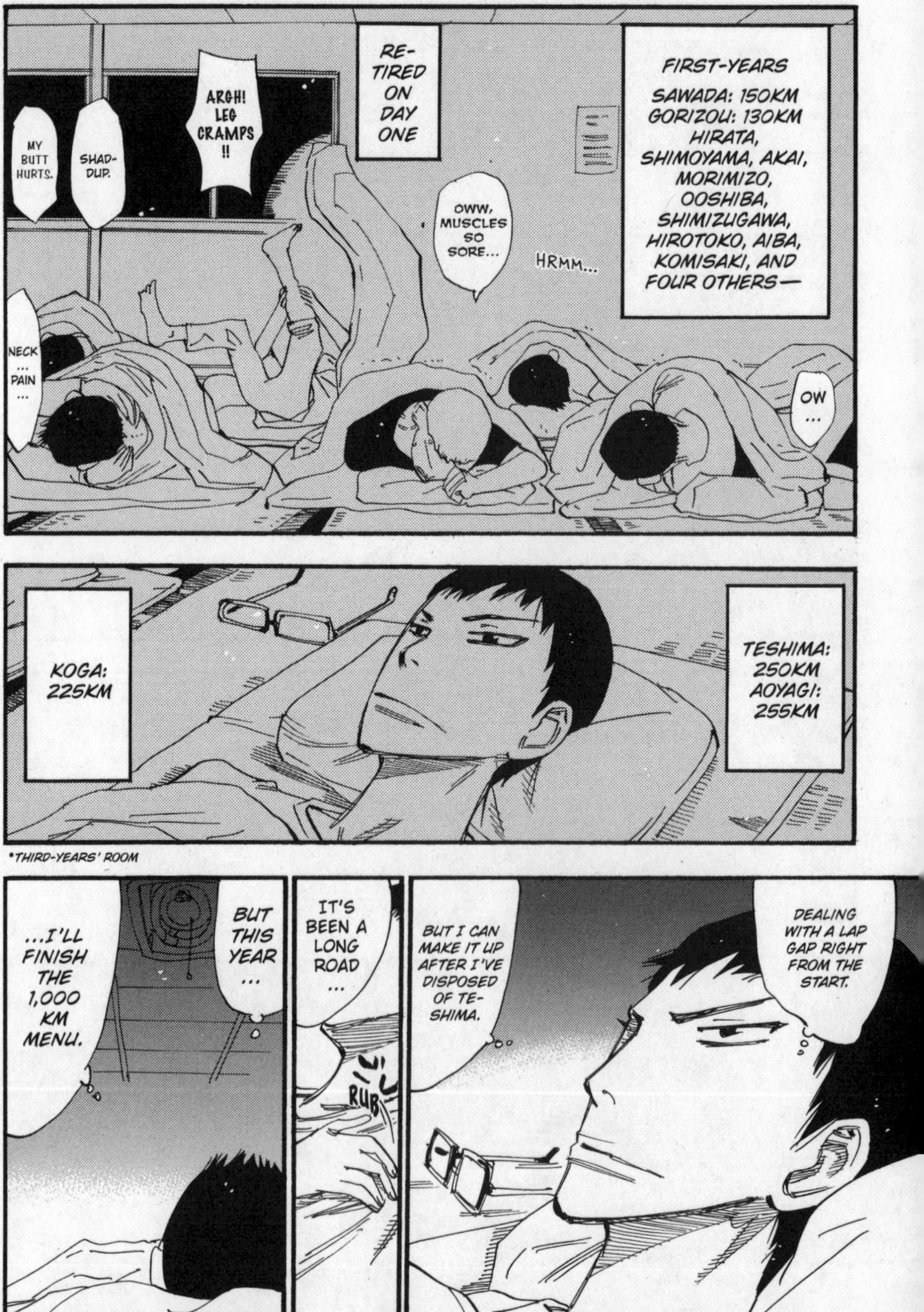
FIRST-YEARS
SAWADA: 150KM
GORIZOU: 130KM
HIRATA, SHIMOYAMA, AKAI, MORIMIZO, OOSHIBA, SHIMIZUGAWA, HIROTOKO, AIBA, KOMISAKI, AND FOUR OTHERS—
RE-TIRED ON DAY ONE
OW ...
HRMM...
OWW, MUSCLES SO SORE...
ARGH! LEG CRAMPS !!
SHAD-DUP.
MY BUTT HURTS.
NECK ... PAIN ...
TESHIMA: 250KM
AOYAGI: 255KM
KOGA: 225KM
*THIRD-YEARS' ROOM
DEALING WITH A LAP GAP RIGHT FROM THE START.
BUT I CAN MAKE IT UP AFTER I'VE DISPOSED OF TE-SHIMA.
IT'S BEEN A LONG ROAD ...
RUB
BUT THIS YEAR ...
...I'LL FINISH THE 1,000 KM MENU.

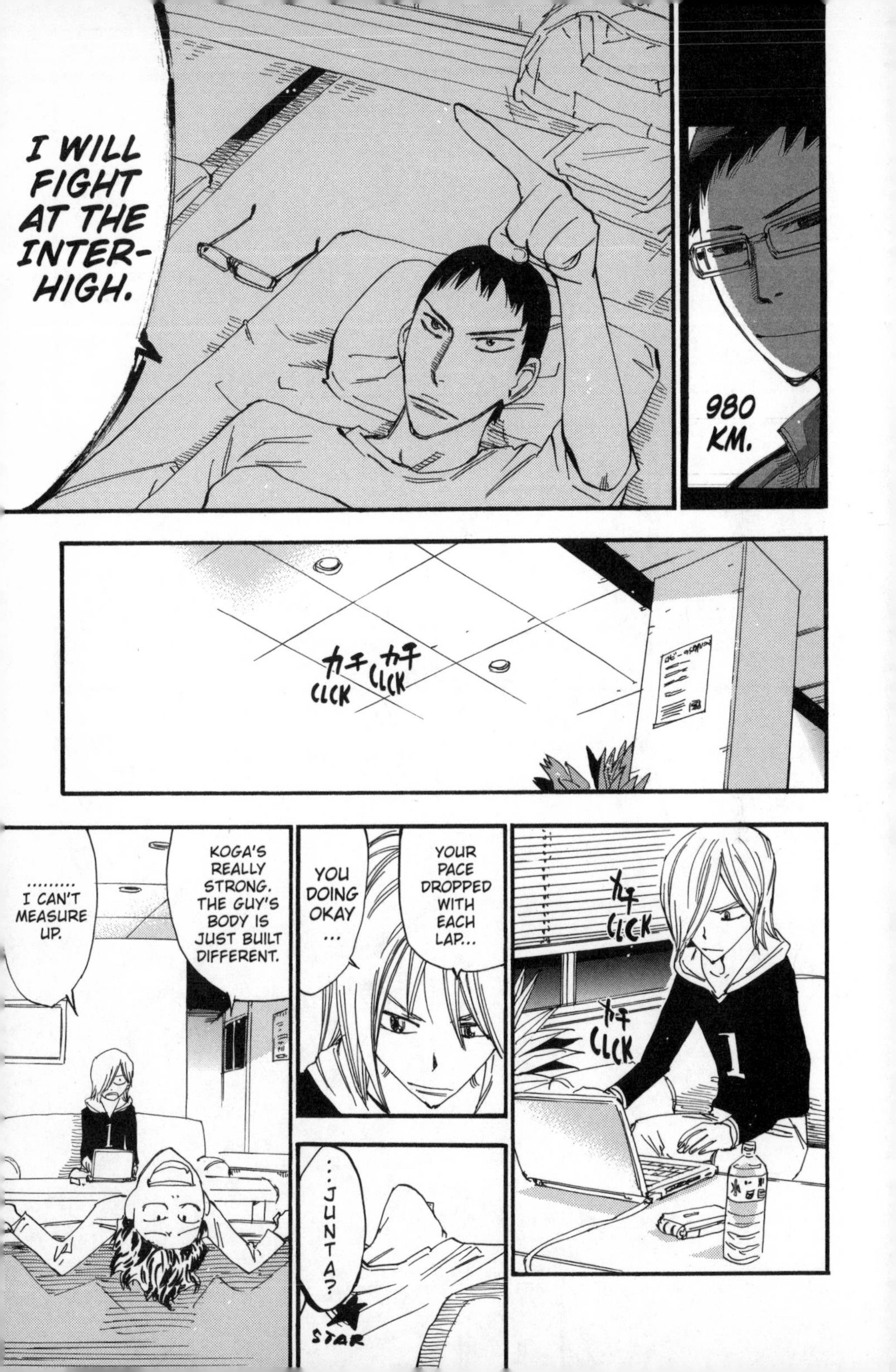
980 KM.
I WILL FIGHT AT THE INTER-HIGH.
カチ CLCK
カチ CLCK
カチ CLCK
カチ CLCK
YOUR PACE DROPPED WITH EACH LAP...
YOU DOING OKAY...
...JUNTA?
STAR
KOGA'S REALLY STRONG. THE GUY'S BODY IS JUST BUILT DIFFERENT.
.... I CAN'T MEASURE UP.

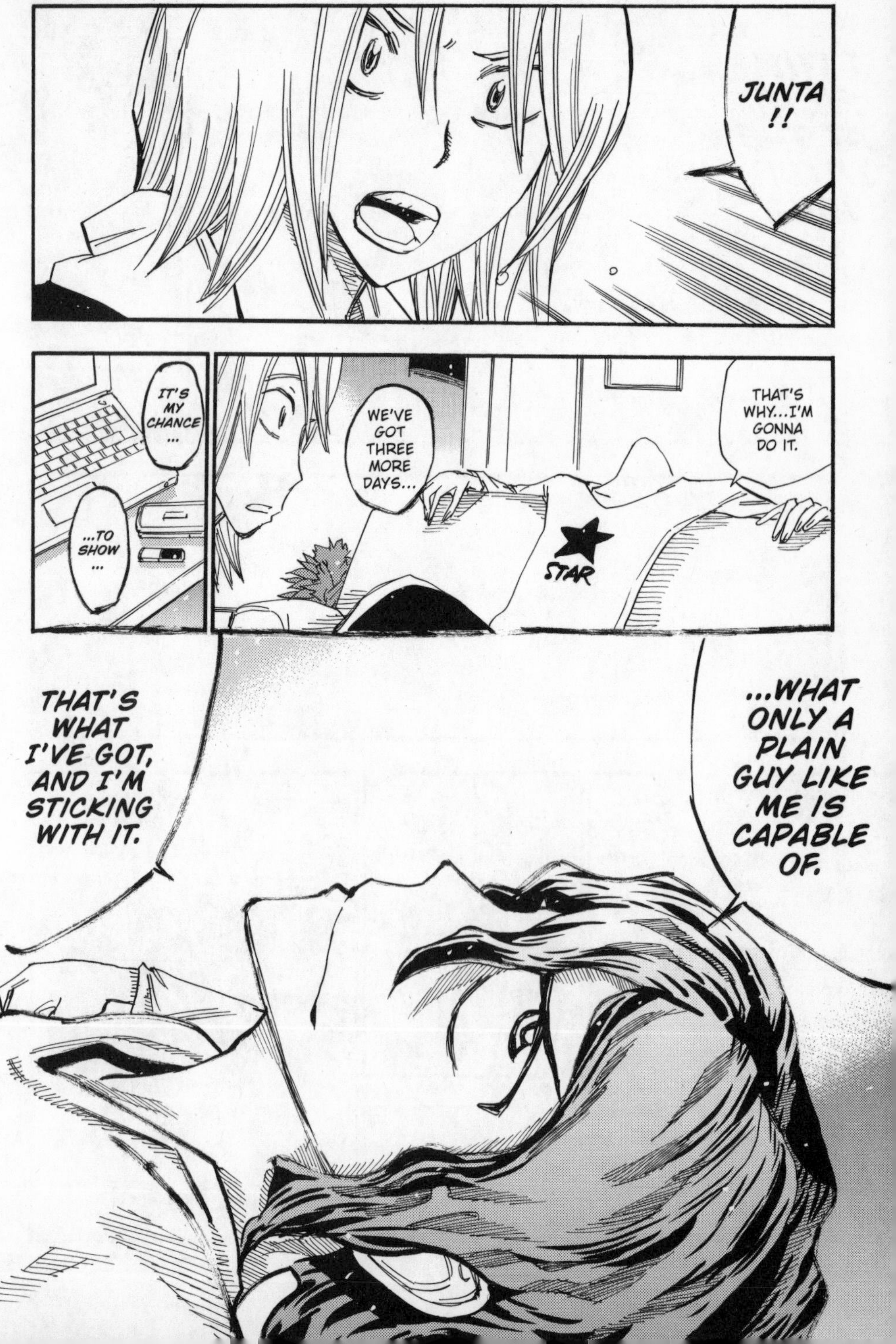
JUNTA!!
THAT'S WHY...I'M GONNA DO IT.
WE'VE GOT THREE MORE DAYS...
STAR
IT'S MY CHANCE...
...TO SHOW...
...WHAT ONLY A PLAIN GUY LIKE ME IS CAPABLE OF.
THAT'S WHAT I'VE GOT, AND I'M STICKING WITH IT.

RIDE.286 TRAINING CAMP, DAY TWO: START!!

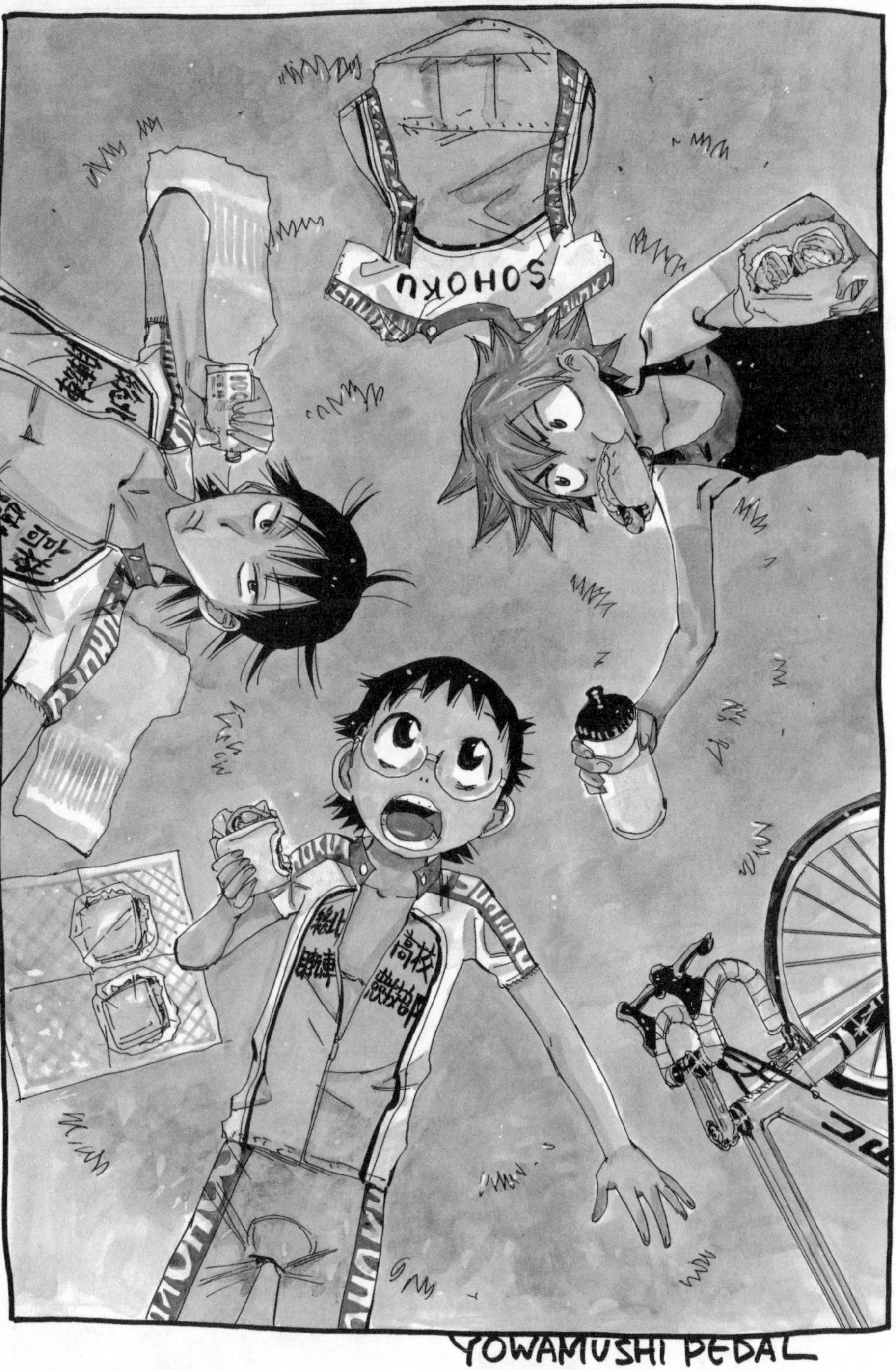
SOHOKU

YOWAMUSHI PEDAL

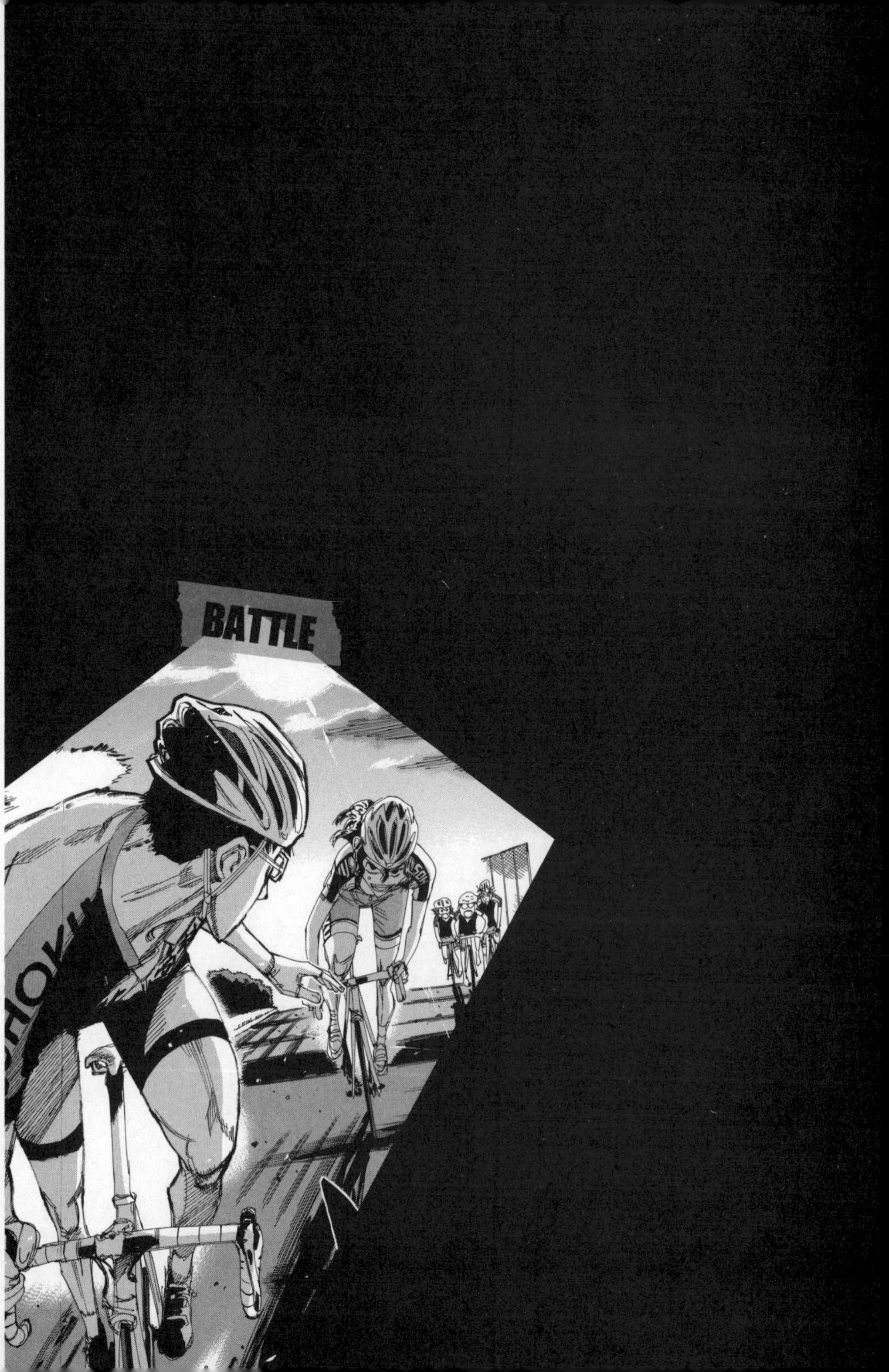
BATTLE

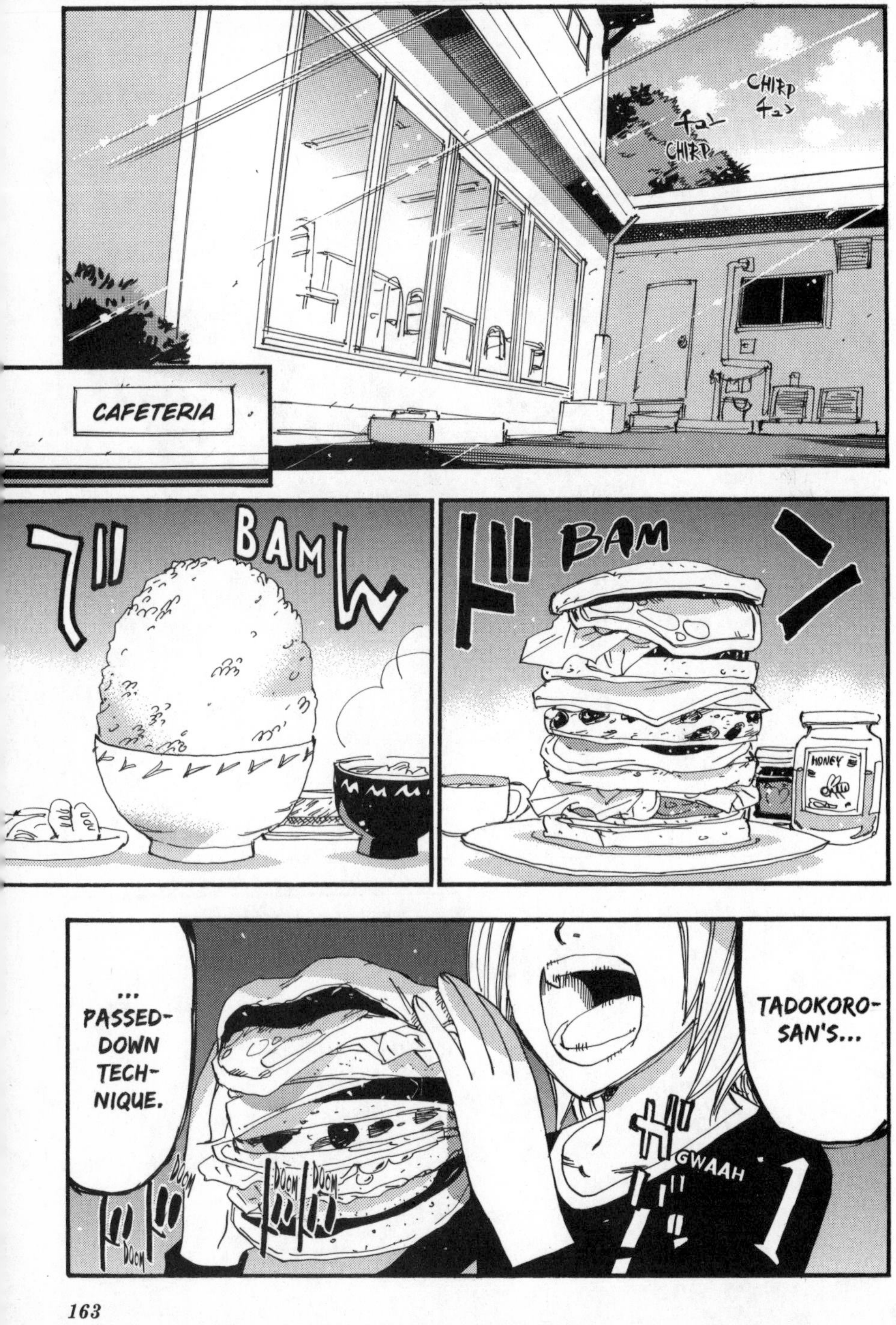
CHIRP
チュン
チュン
CHIRP
CAFETERIA
ドン
BAM
BAM
TADOKORO-SAN'S...
GWAAH
...PASSED-DOWN TECHNIQUE.
DOOM
DOOM
DOOM
DOOM

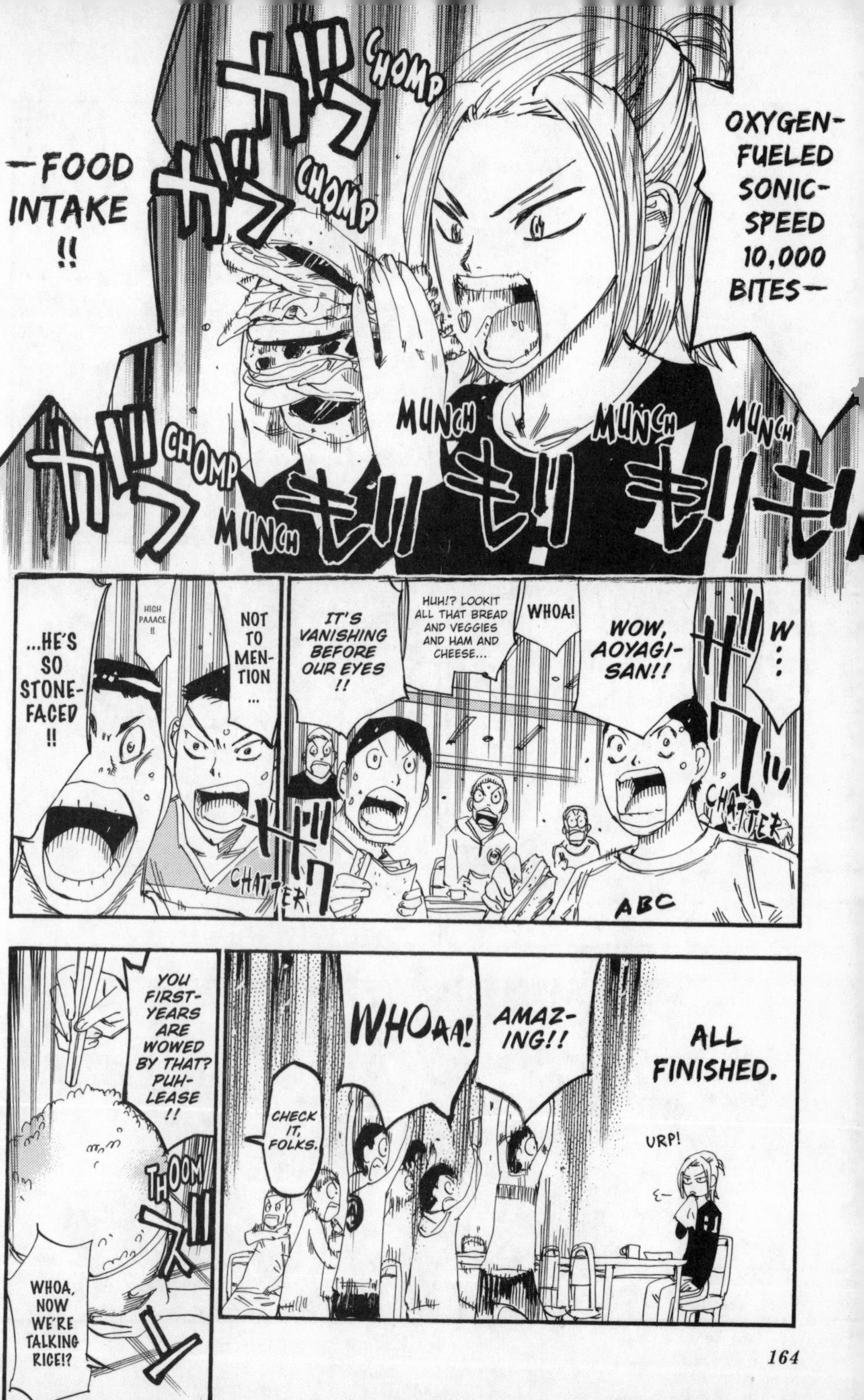
OXYGEN-FUELED SONIC-SPEED 10,000 BITES—
CHOMP
CHOMP
—FOOD INTAKE !!
MUNCH
MUNCH
MUNCH
CHOMP
MUNCH
W...
WOW, AOYAGI-SAN!!
CHATTER
ABC
WHOA!
HUH!? LOOKIT ALL THAT BREAD AND VEGGIES AND HAM AND CHEESE...
IT'S VANISHING BEFORE OUR EYES !!
CHATTER
NOT TO MEN-TION ...
HIGH PAAACE !!
...HE'S SO STONE-FACED !!
ALL FINISHED.
URP!
AMAZ-ING!!
WHOAA!
CHECK IT, FOLKS.
YOU FIRST-YEARS ARE WOWED BY THAT? PUH-LEASE !!
THOOM
WHOA, NOW WE'RE TALKING RICE!?

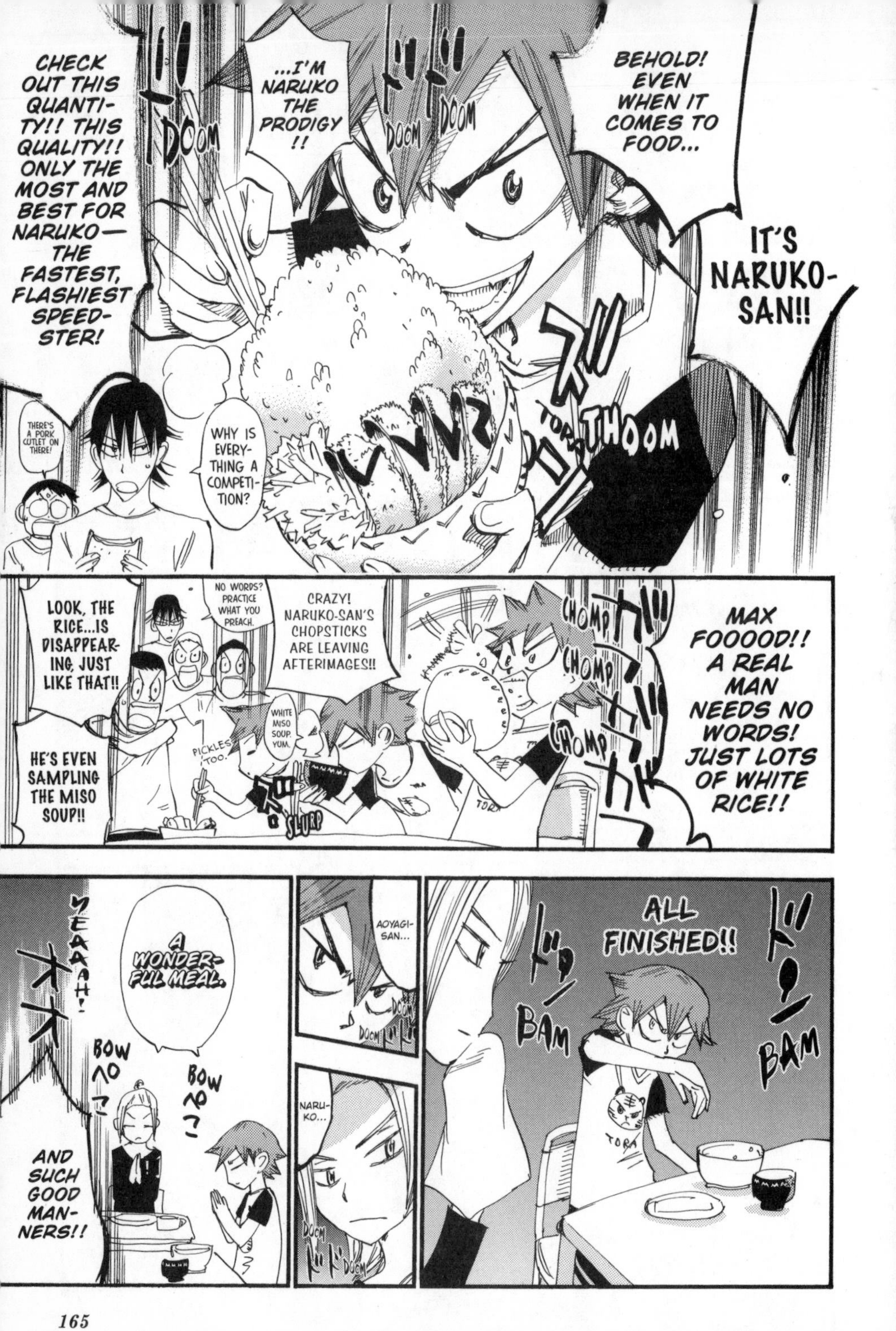
BEHOLD! EVEN WHEN IT COMES TO FOOD...
...I'M NARUKO THE PRODIGY!!
DOOM DOOM
CHECK OUT THIS QUANTITY!! THIS QUALITY!! ONLY THE MOST AND BEST FOR NARUKO—THE FASTEST, FLASHIEST SPEEDSTER!
DOOM
IT'S NARUKO-SAN!!
THOOM
TORA
WHY IS EVERYTHING A COMPETITION?
THERE'S A PORK CUTLET ON THERE!
MAX FOOOOD!! A REAL MAN NEEDS NO WORDS! JUST LOTS OF WHITE RICE!!
CHOMP CHOMP CHOMP
CRAZY! NARUKO-SAN'S CHOPSTICKS ARE LEAVING AFTERIMAGES!!
NO WORDS? PRACTICE WHAT YOU PREACH.
WHITE MISO SOUP. YUM.
PICKLES TOO.
LOOK, THE RICE...IS DISAPPEARING, JUST LIKE THAT!!
HE'S EVEN SAMPLING THE MISO SOUP!!
SLURP
ALL FINISHED!!
BAM
BAM
AOYAGI-SAN...
DOOM DOOM
NARUKO...
DOOM DOOM
A WONDERFUL MEAL.
YEAAAAH!
BOW
BOW
AND SUCH GOOD MANNERS!!

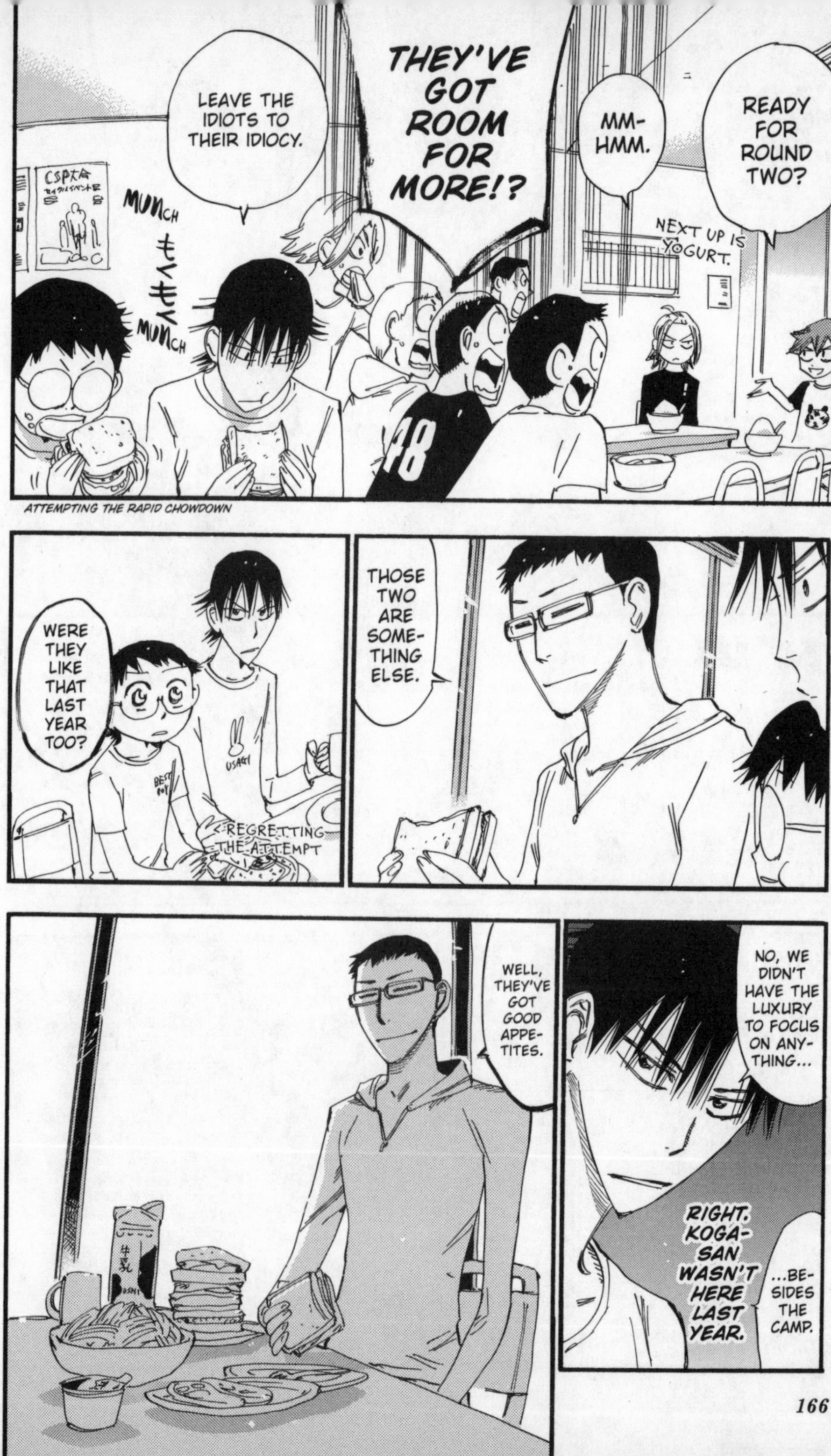
READY FOR ROUND TWO?
NEXT UP IS YOGURT.
MM-HMM.
THEY'VE GOT ROOM FOR MORE!?
LEAVE THE IDIOTS TO THEIR IDIOCY.
MUNCH
もくもく
MUNCH
ATTEMPTING THE RAPID CHOWDOWN
THOSE TWO ARE SOMETHING ELSE.
WERE THEY LIKE THAT LAST YEAR TOO?
REGRETTING THE ATTEMPT
NO, WE DIDN'T HAVE THE LUXURY TO FOCUS ON ANYTHING...
...BESIDES THE CAMP.
RIGHT. KOGA-SAN WASN'T HERE LAST YEAR.
WELL, THEY'VE GOT GOOD APPETITES.

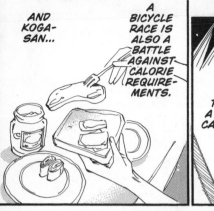

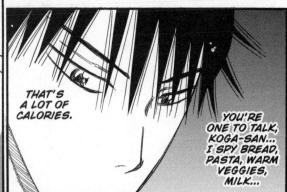

THAT'S A LOT OF CALORIES.
YOU'RE ONE TO TALK, KOGA-SAN... I SPY BREAD, PASTA, WARM VEGGIES, MILK...
A BICYCLE RACE IS ALSO A BATTLE AGAINST CALORIE REQUIREMENTS.
AND KOGA-SAN...
...ISN'T HOLDING BACK ....!!
IT'S A REAL BATTLE ...
...AGAINST TESHIMA-SAN!!
GRIN
......
WEATHER CLEARED UP.
THAT MORNING FOG WAS INTENSE, WASN'T IT, ONODA?
UM, YES.
YOU SEE, THE TWO OF US GOT UP EARLY TO DO SOME RIDING, SINCE WE ARRIVED LATE YESTERDAY.

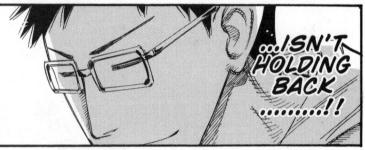

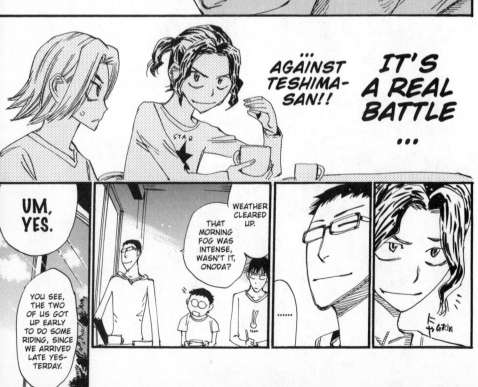

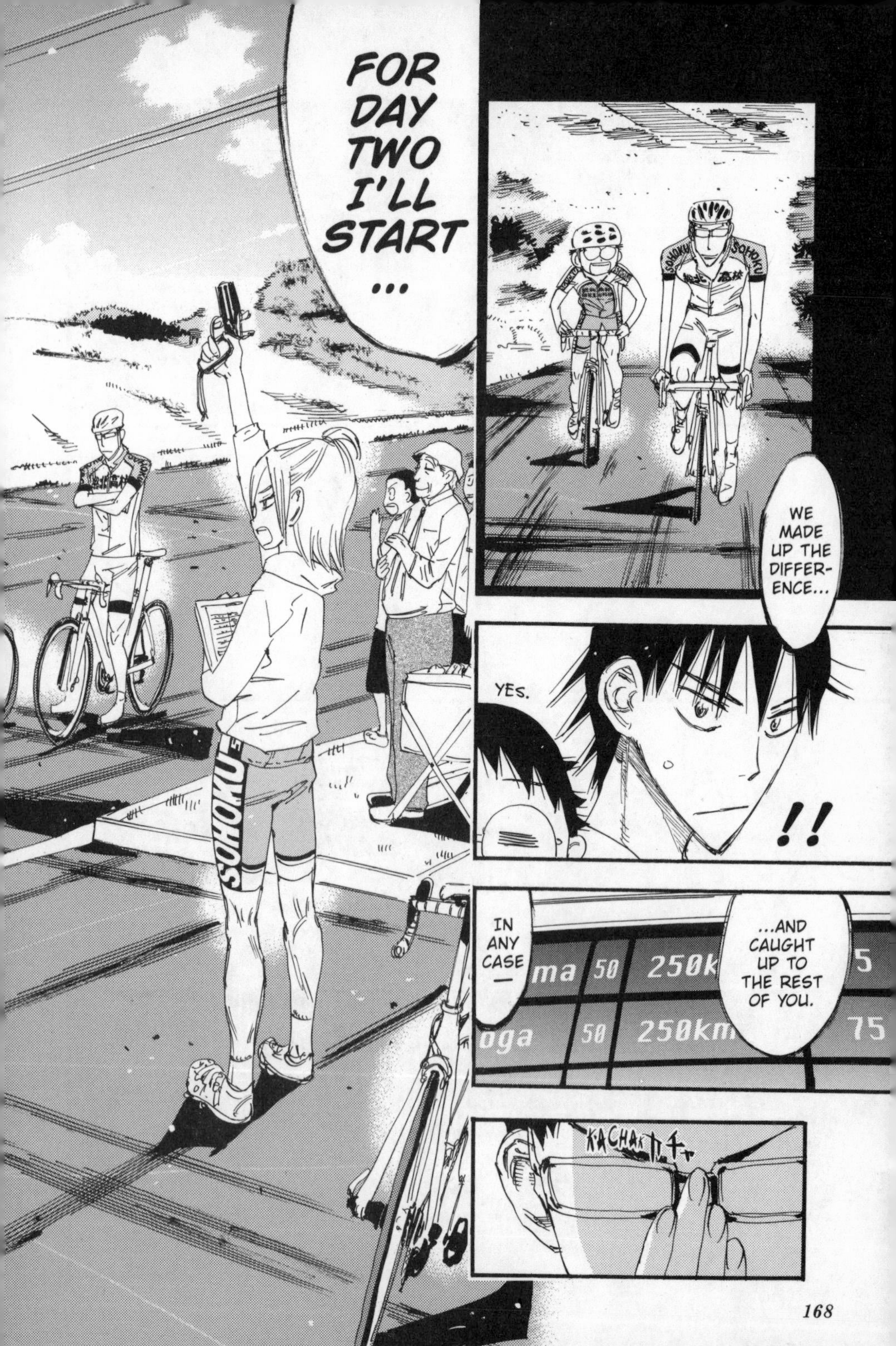
WE MADE UP THE DIFFER-ENCE...
YES.
!!
...AND CAUGHT UP TO THE REST OF YOU.
IN ANY CASE—
ma 50 250k 5
oga 50 250km 75
KACHA カチャ
FOR DAY TWO I'LL START...

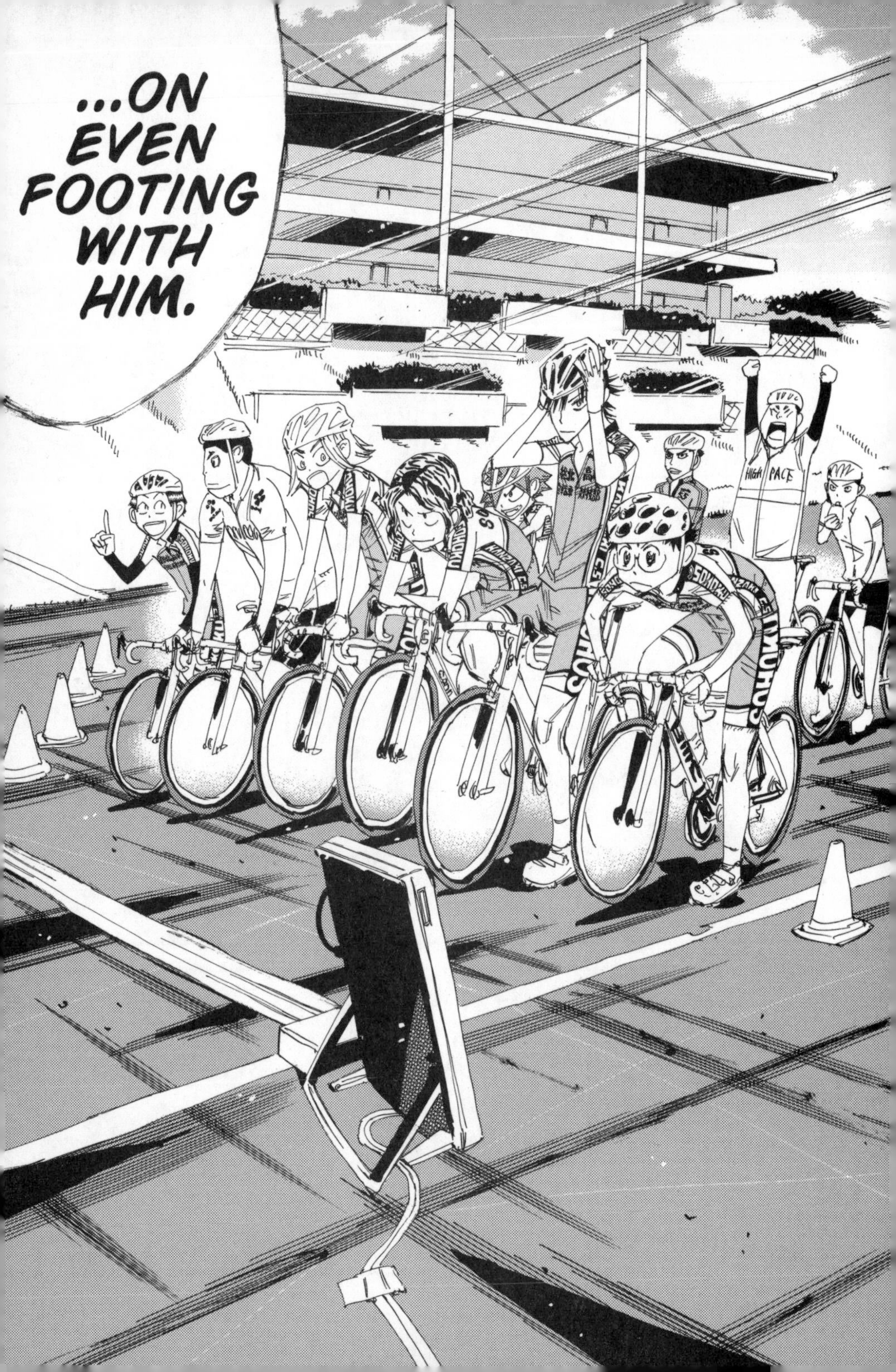
...ON EVEN FOOTING WITH HIM.

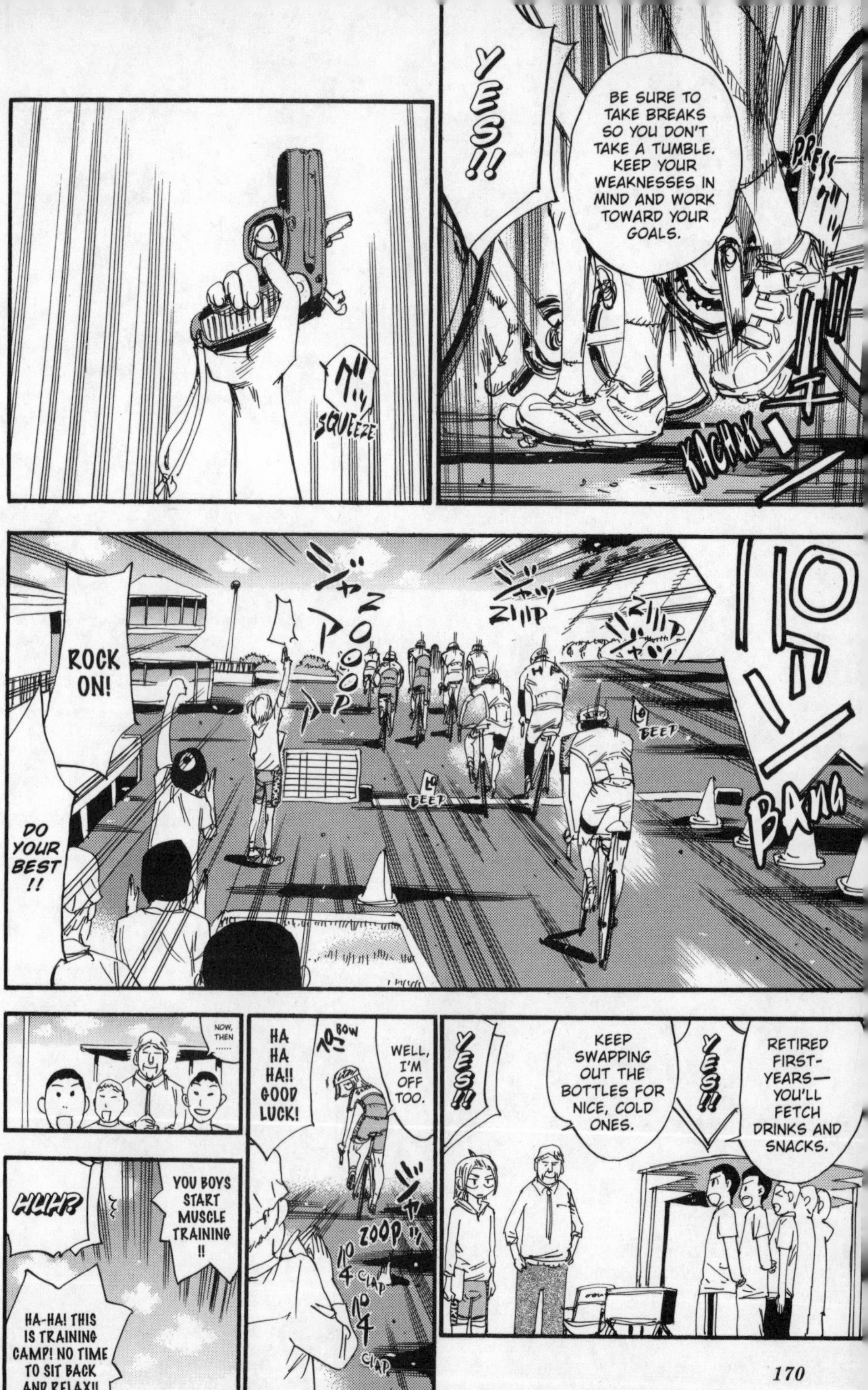
BE SURE TO TAKE BREAKS SO YOU DON'T TAKE A TUMBLE. KEEP YOUR WEAKNESSES IN MIND AND WORK TOWARD YOUR GOALS.
YES!!
PRESS
KACHAK
SQUEEZE
BANG
ZIIIP
ZIIIP
ZOOOOOP
BEEP
BEEP
ROCK ON!
DO YOUR BEST!!
RETIRED FIRST-YEARS—YOU'LL FETCH DRINKS AND SNACKS.
YES!!
KEEP SWAPPING OUT THE BOTTLES FOR NICE, COLD ONES.
YES!!
WELL, I'M OFF TOO.
BOW
HA HA HA!! GOOD LUCK!
ZOOP
CLAP
CLAP
NOW, THEN ......
YOU BOYS START MUSCLE TRAINING!!
HUH?
HA-HA! THIS IS TRAINING CAMP! NO TIME TO SIT BACK AND RELAX!!

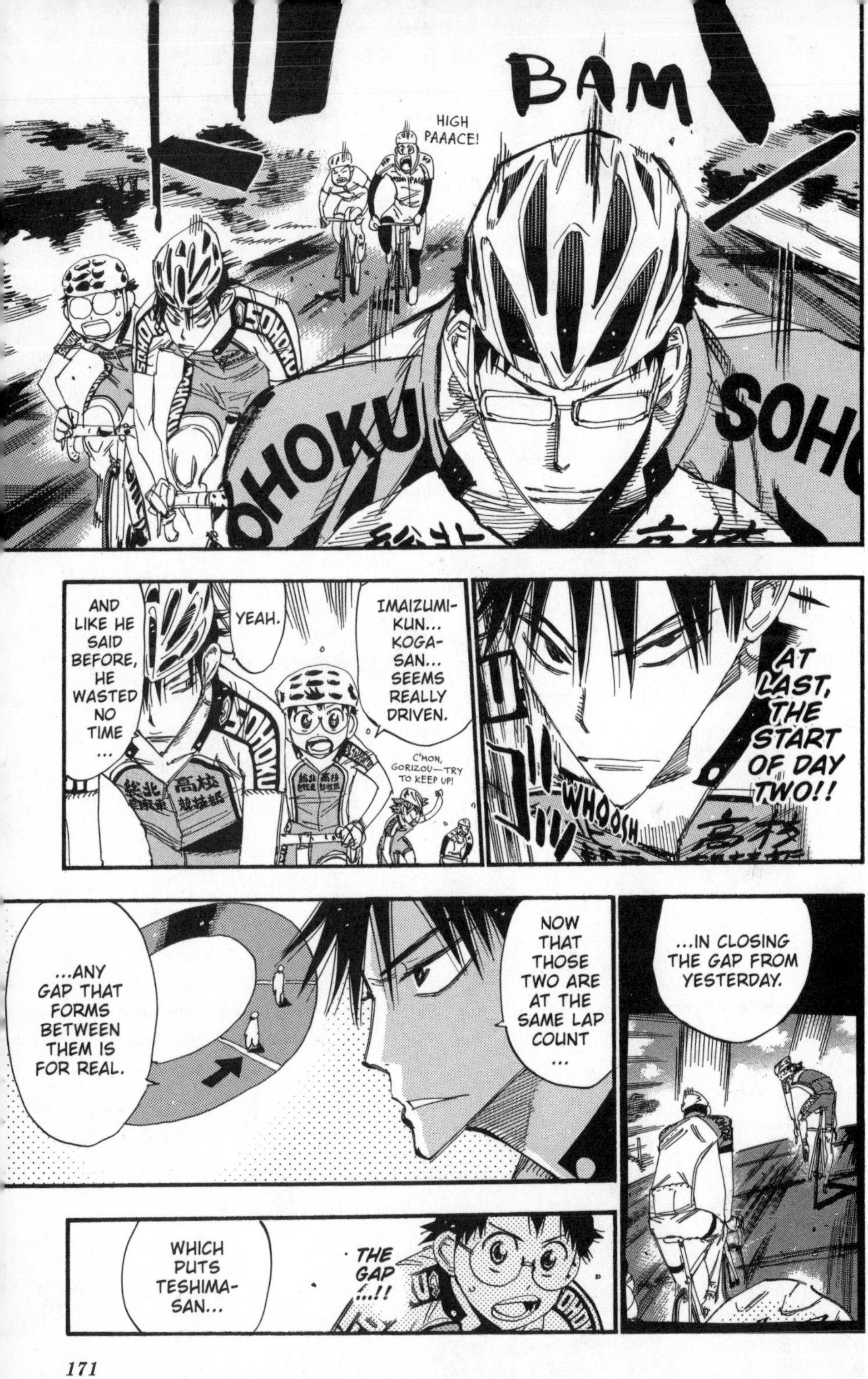
BAM
HIGH PAAACE!
AT LAST, THE START OF DAY TWO!!
WHOOSH
IMAIZUMI-KUN... KOGA-SAN... SEEMS REALLY DRIVEN.
YEAH.
AND LIKE HE SAID BEFORE, HE WASTED NO TIME...
C'MON, GORIZOU—TRY TO KEEP UP!
NOW THAT THOSE TWO ARE AT THE SAME LAP COUNT...
...ANY GAP THAT FORMS BETWEEN THEM IS FOR REAL.
THE GAP...!!
WHICH PUTS TESHIMA-SAN...
...IN CLOSING THE GAP FROM YESTERDAY.

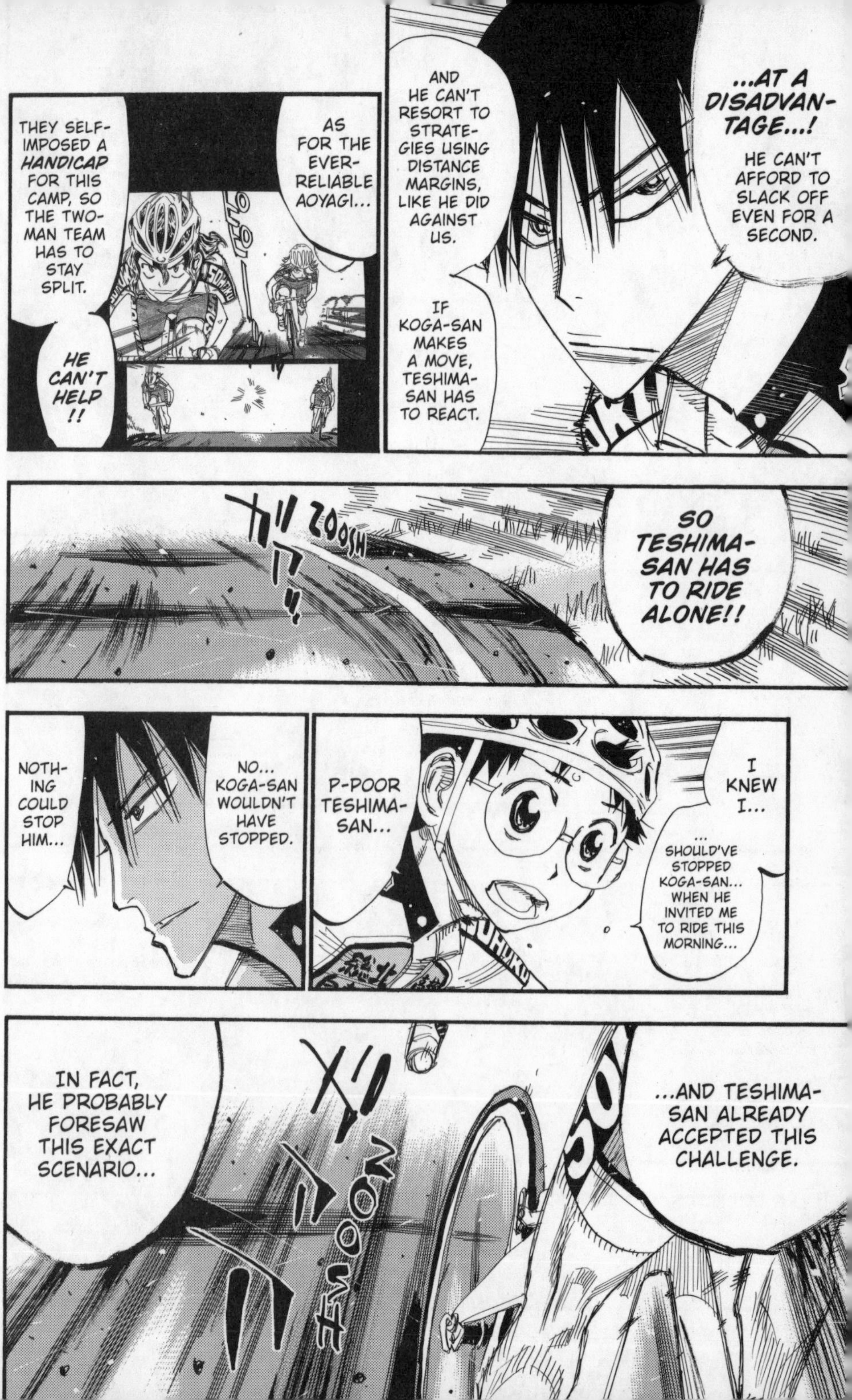

...AT A DISADVANTAGE...!
HE CAN'T AFFORD TO SLACK OFF EVEN FOR A SECOND.
AND HE CAN'T RESORT TO STRATEGIES USING DISTANCE MARGINS, LIKE HE DID AGAINST US.
IF KOGA-SAN MAKES A MOVE, TESHIMA-SAN HAS TO REACT.
AS FOR THE EVER-RELIABLE AOYAGI...
THEY SELF-IMPOSED A HANDICAP FOR THIS CAMP, SO THE TWO-MAN TEAM HAS TO STAY SPLIT.
HE CAN'T HELP!!
ZOOSH
SO TESHIMA-SAN HAS TO RIDE ALONE!!
I KNEW I...
...SHOULD'VE STOPPED KOGA-SAN... WHEN HE INVITED ME TO RIDE THIS MORNING...
P-POOR TESHIMA-SAN...
NO... KOGA-SAN WOULDN'T HAVE STOPPED.
NOTHING COULD STOP HIM...
IN FACT, HE PROBABLY FORESAW THIS EXACT SCENARIO...
...AND TESHIMA-SAN ALREADY ACCEPTED THIS CHALLENGE.
WOOSH

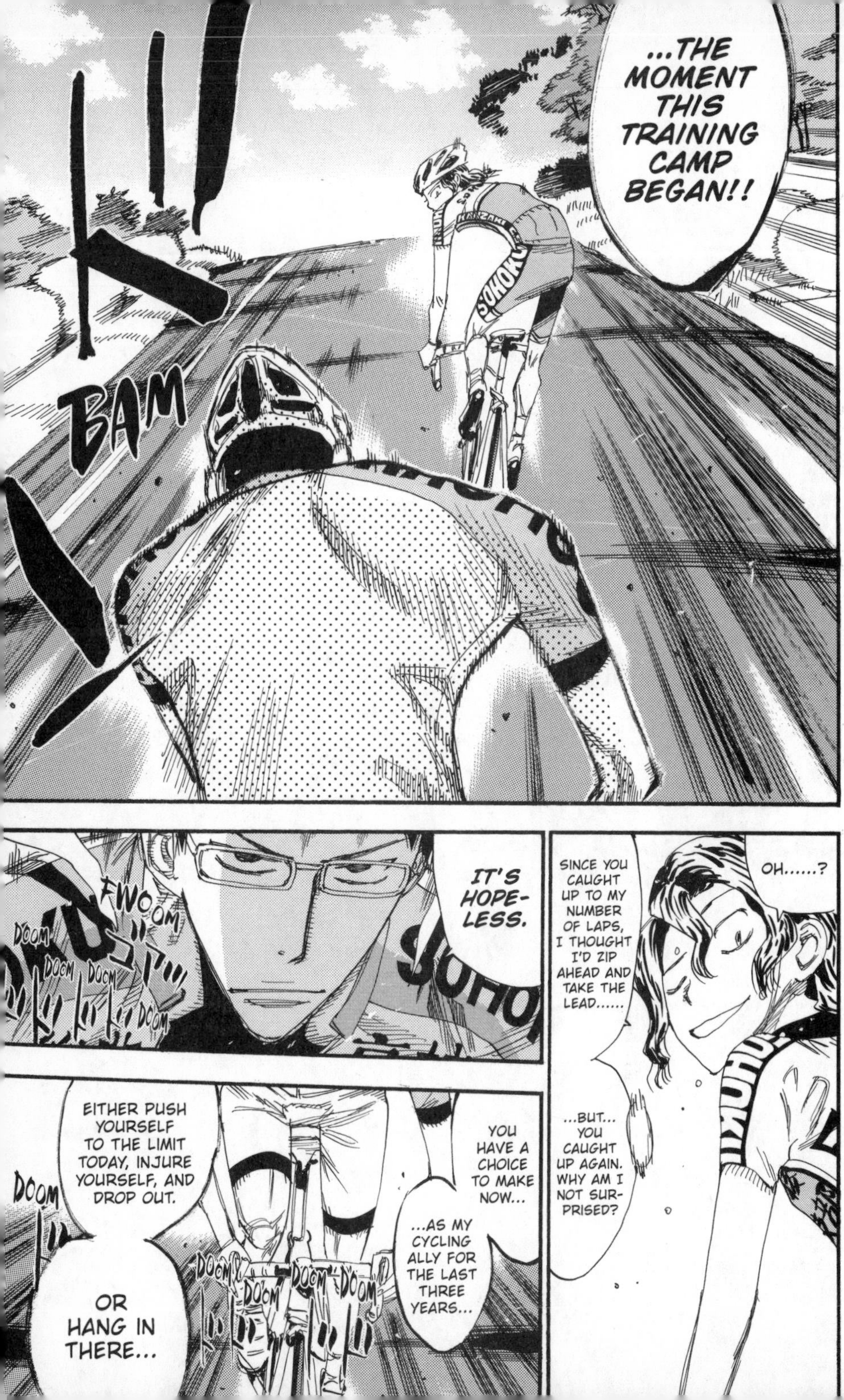
...THE MOMENT THIS TRAINING CAMP BEGAN!!
BAM
OH......?
SINCE YOU CAUGHT UP TO MY NUMBER OF LAPS, I THOUGHT I'D ZIP AHEAD AND TAKE THE LEAD......
...BUT... YOU CAUGHT UP AGAIN. WHY AM I NOT SURPRISED?
IT'S HOPELESS.
FWOOM
DOOM DOOM DOOM DOOM
YOU HAVE A CHOICE TO MAKE NOW...
...AS MY CYCLING ALLY FOR THE LAST THREE YEARS...
EITHER PUSH YOURSELF TO THE LIMIT TODAY, INJURE YOURSELF, AND DROP OUT.
OR HANG IN THERE...
DOOM DOOM DOOM DOOM DOOM

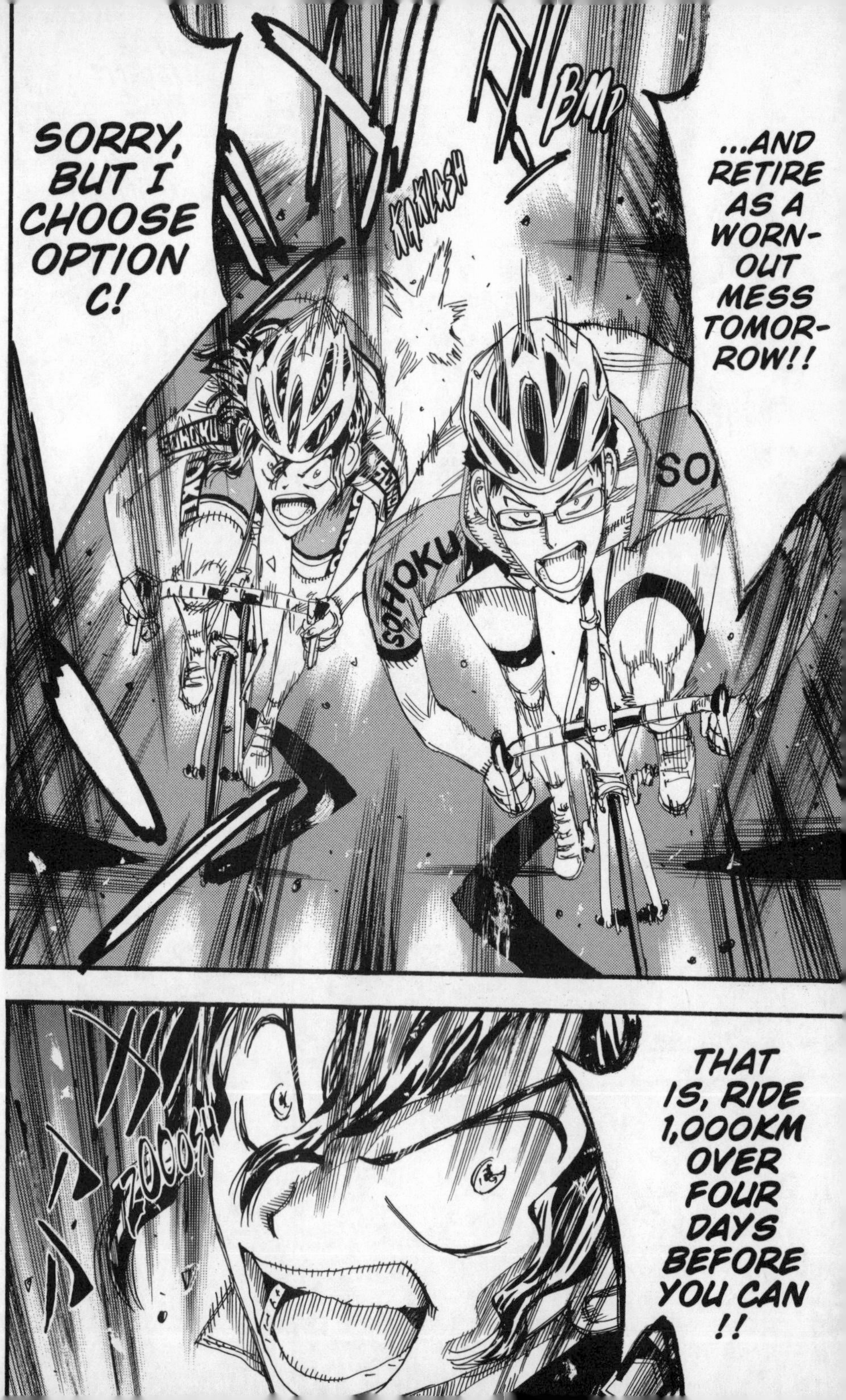

...AND RETIRE AS A WORN-OUT MESS TOMORROW!!
BMP
KAKLASH
SORRY, BUT I CHOOSE OPTION C!
THAT IS, RIDE 1,000KM OVER FOUR DAYS BEFORE YOU CAN!!
ZOOOSH

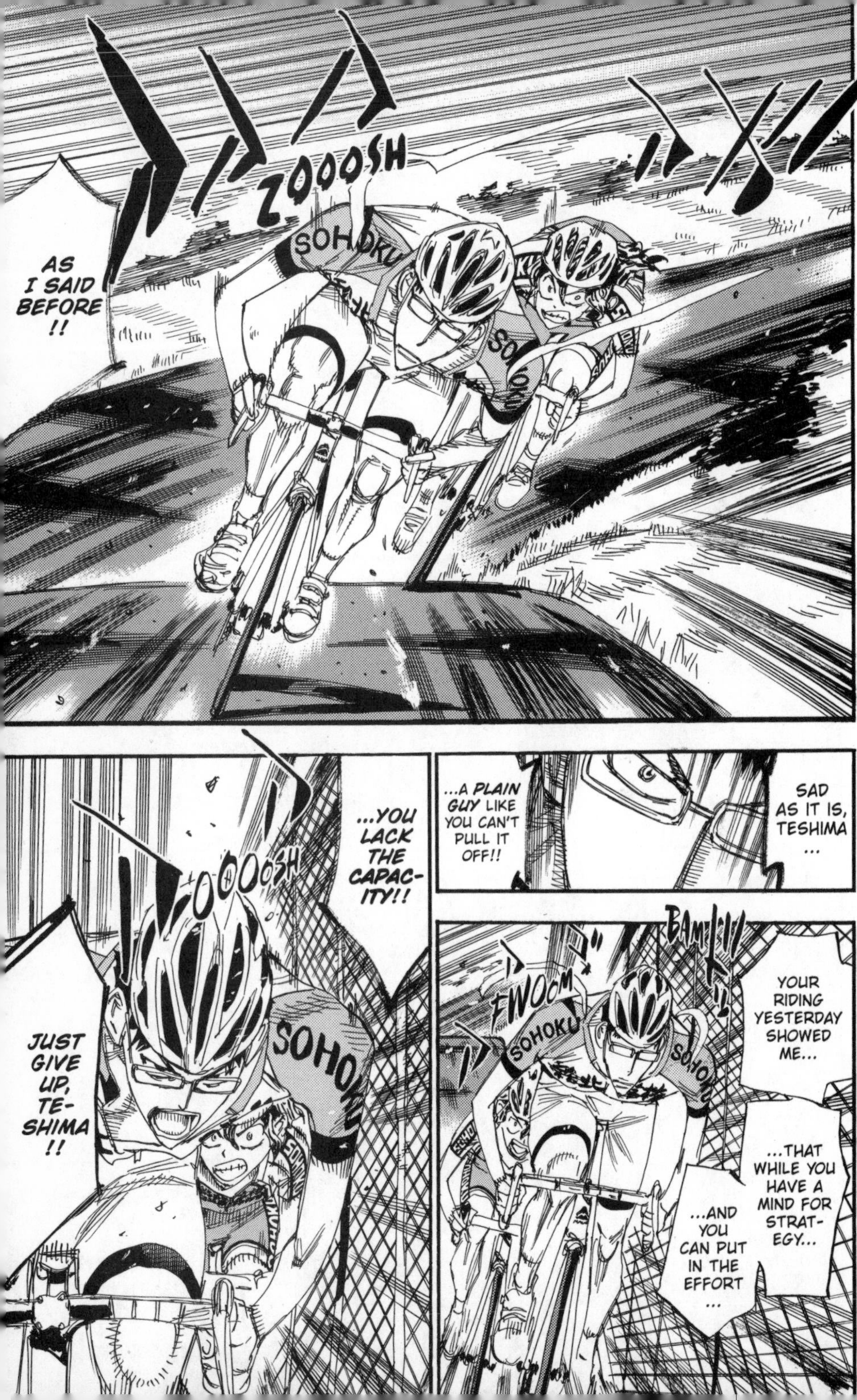
ZOOOSH
AS I SAID BEFORE!!
SAD AS IT IS, TESHIMA...
...A PLAIN GUY LIKE YOU CAN'T PULL IT OFF!!
BAM!!
FWOOM
YOUR RIDING YESTERDAY SHOWED ME...
...THAT WHILE YOU HAVE A MIND FOR STRATEGY...
...AND YOU CAN PUT IN THE EFFORT...
...YOU LACK THE CAPACITY!!
JUST GIVE UP, TESHIMA!!

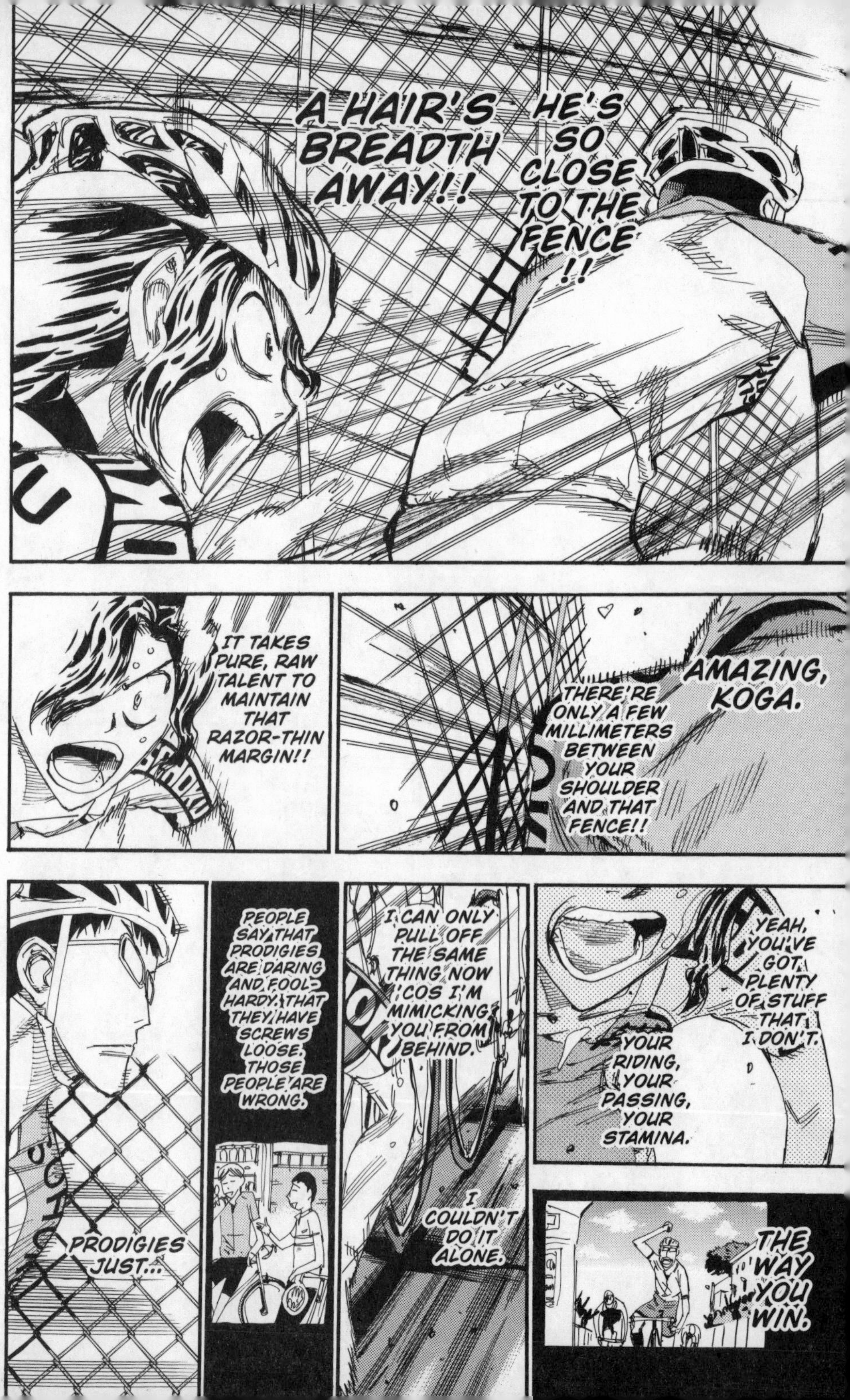
HE'S SO CLOSE TO THE FENCE!!
A HAIR'S BREADTH AWAY!!
AMAZING, KOGA.
THERE'RE ONLY A FEW MILLIMETERS BETWEEN YOUR SHOULDER AND THAT FENCE!!
IT TAKES PURE, RAW TALENT TO MAINTAIN THAT RAZOR-THIN MARGIN!!
YEAH, YOU'VE GOT PLENTY OF STUFF THAT I DON'T.
YOUR RIDING, YOUR PASSING, YOUR STAMINA.
THE WAY YOU WIN.
I CAN ONLY PULL OFF THE SAME THING NOW 'COS I'M MIMICKING YOU FROM BEHIND.
I COULDN'T DO IT ALONE.
PEOPLE SAY THAT PRODIGIES ARE DARING AND FOOL-HARDY, THAT THEY HAVE SCREWS LOOSE. THOSE PEOPLE ARE WRONG.
PRODIGIES JUST...

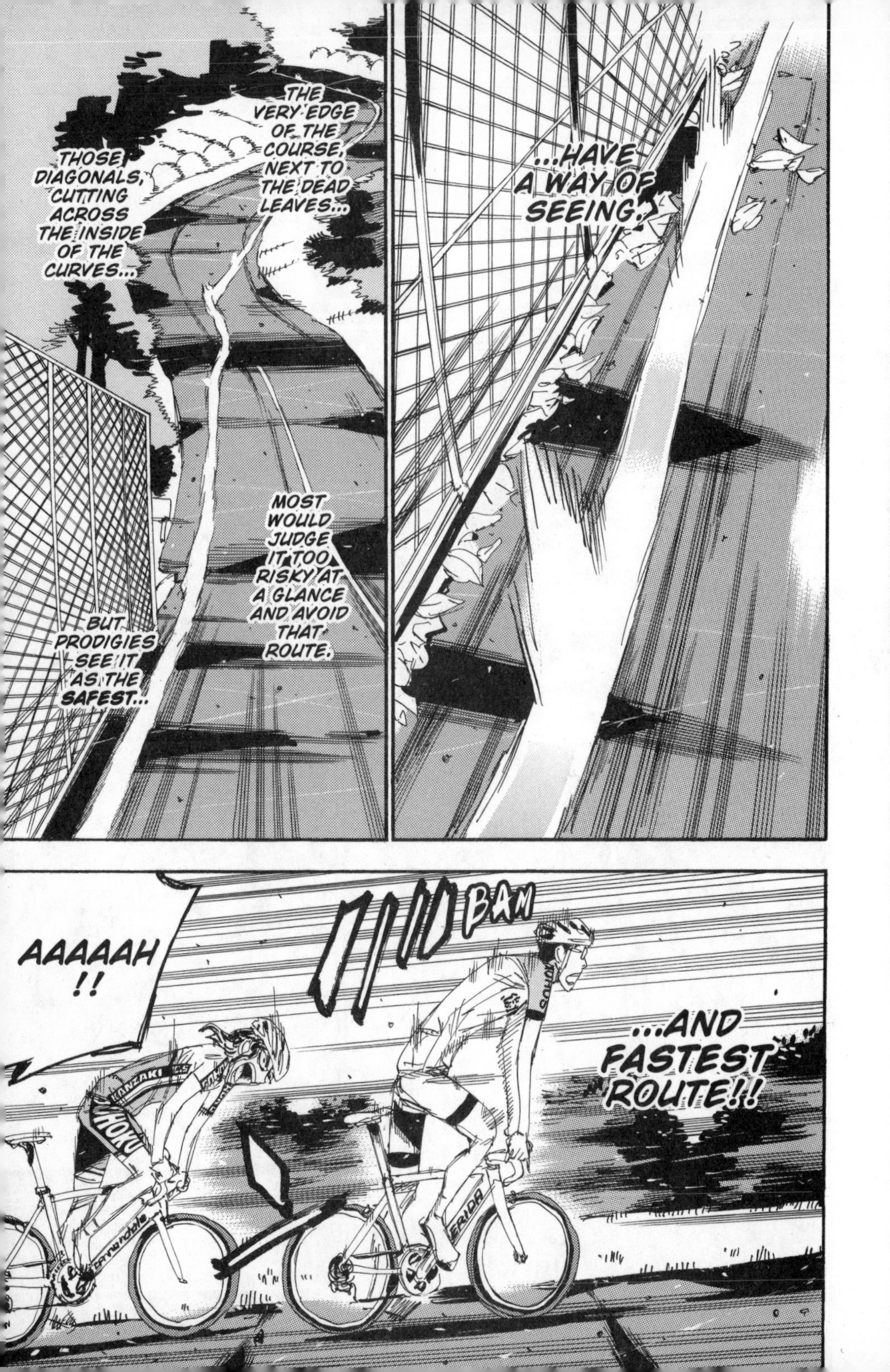
...HAVE A WAY OF SEEING.
THE VERY EDGE OF THE COURSE, NEXT TO THE DEAD LEAVES...
THOSE DIAGONALS, CUTTING ACROSS THE INSIDE OF THE CURVES...
MOST WOULD JUDGE IT TOO RISKY AT A GLANCE AND AVOID THAT ROUTE.
BUT PRODIGIES SEE IT AS THE SAFEST...
BAM
...AND FASTEST ROUTE!!
AAAAAH!!

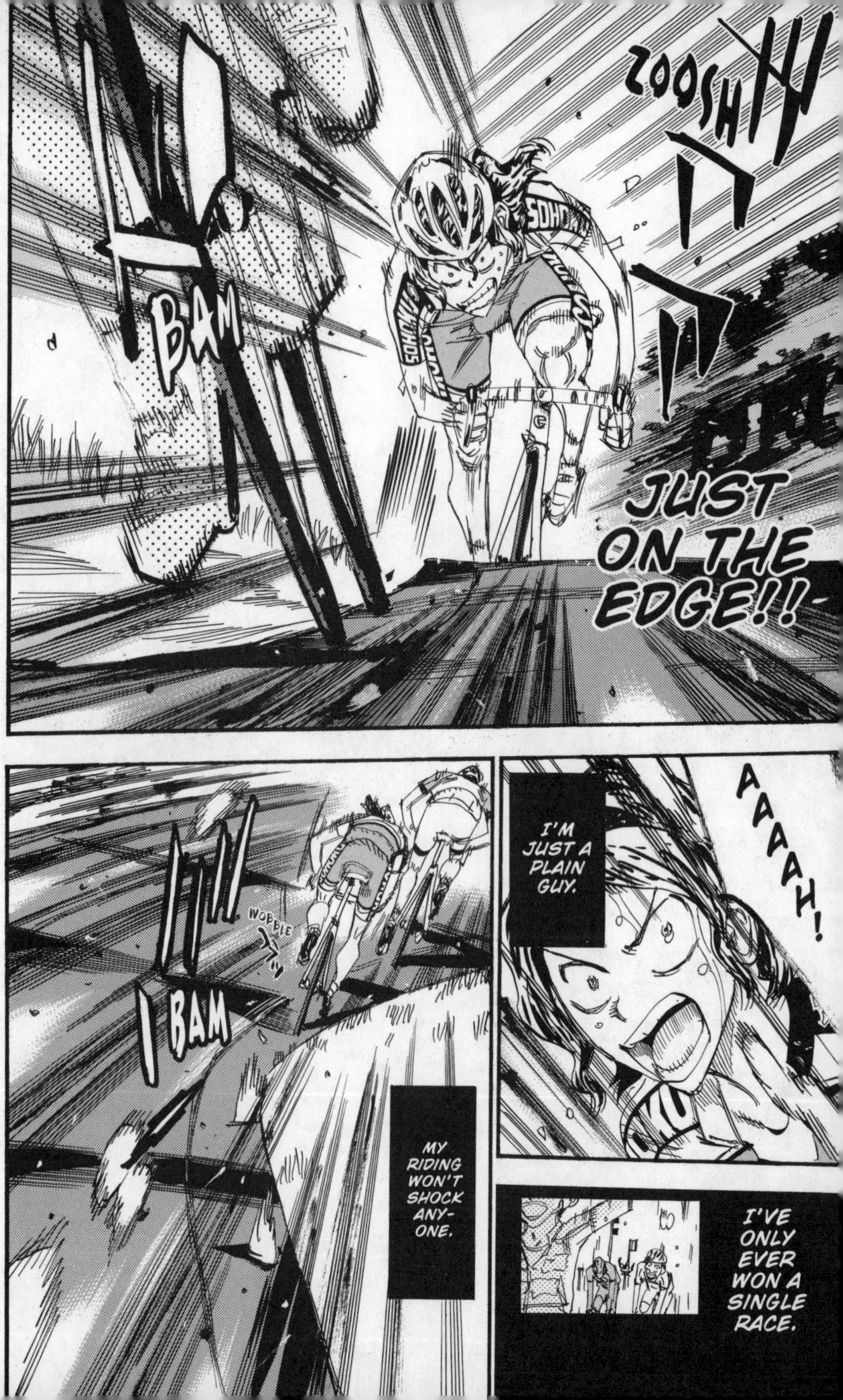
ZOOSH
JUST ON THE EDGE!!
BAM
I'M JUST A PLAIN GUY.
AAAAH!
I'VE ONLY EVER WON A SINGLE RACE.
WOBBLE
BAM
MY RIDING WON'T SHOCK ANYONE.

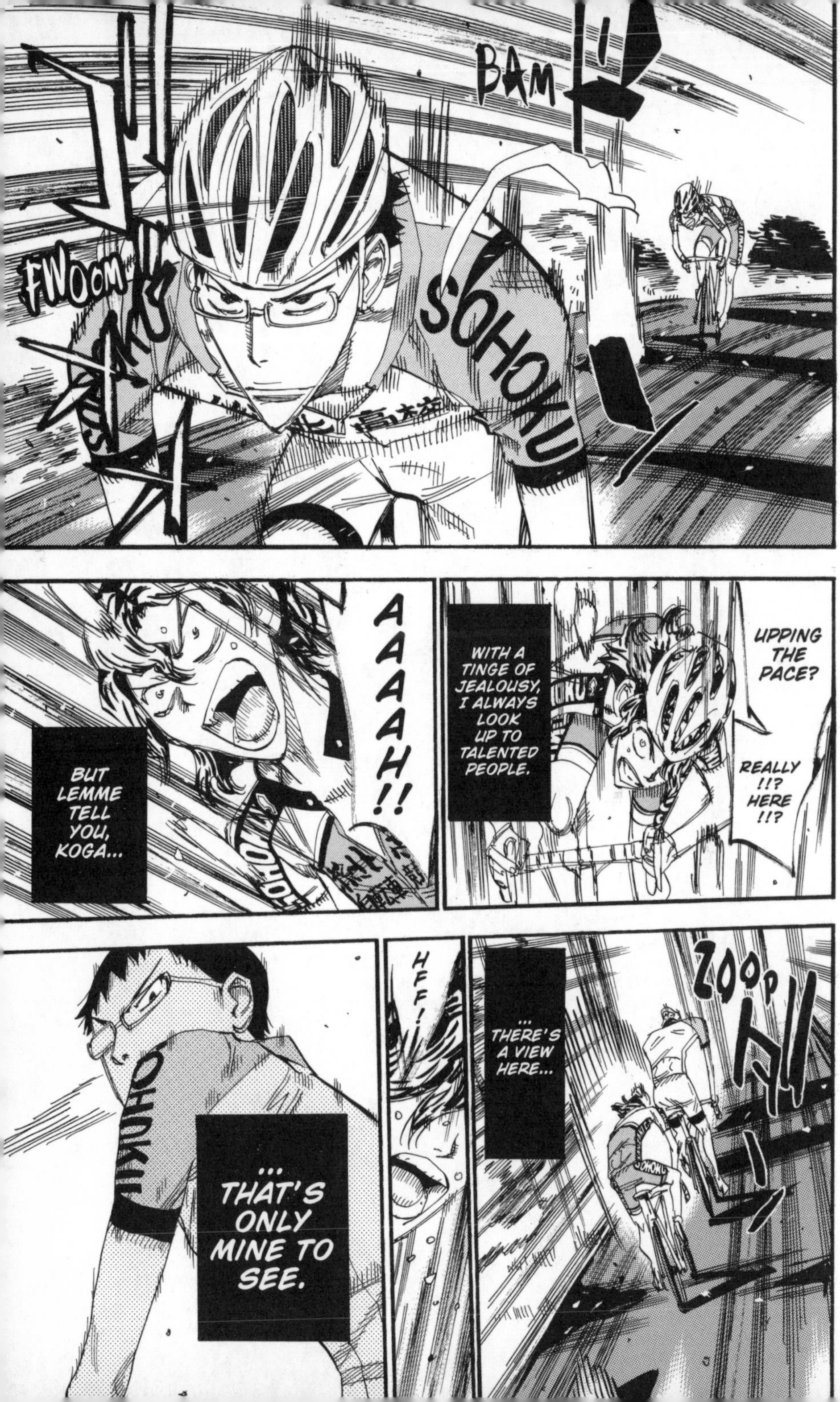
BAM
FWOOM
UPPING THE PACE?
WITH A TINGE OF JEALOUSY, I ALWAYS LOOK UP TO TALENTED PEOPLE.
REALLY !!? HERE !!?
AAAAAH!!
BUT LEMME TELL YOU, KOGA...
ZOOP
... THERE'S A VIEW HERE...
HFF!
... THAT'S ONLY MINE TO SEE.

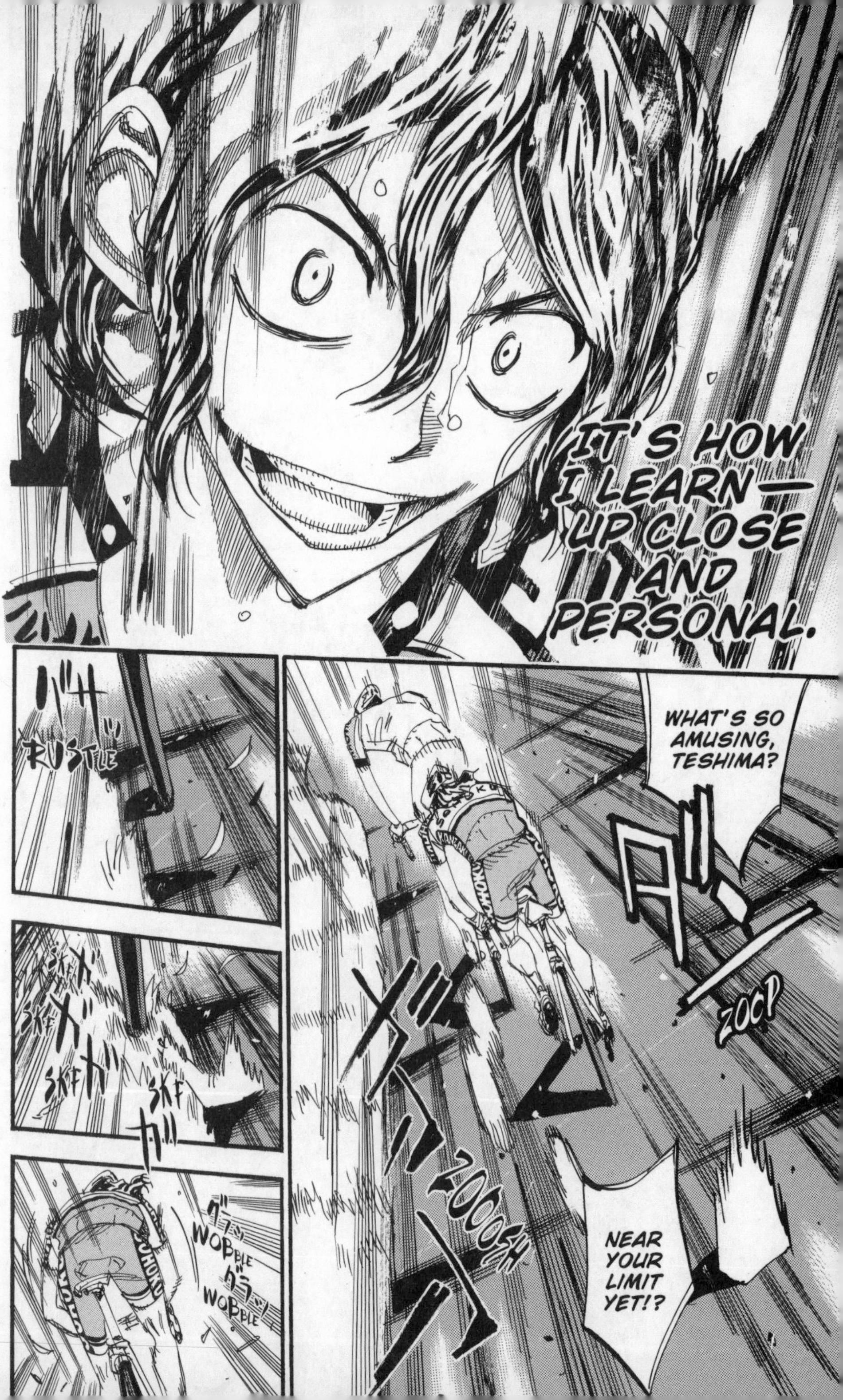
IT'S HOW I LEARN—UP CLOSE AND PERSONAL.
WHAT'S SO AMUSING, TESHIMA?
ZOOP
ZOOOSH
NEAR YOUR LIMIT YET!?
RUSTLE
SKF
SKF
SKF
SKF
WOBBLE
WOBBLE

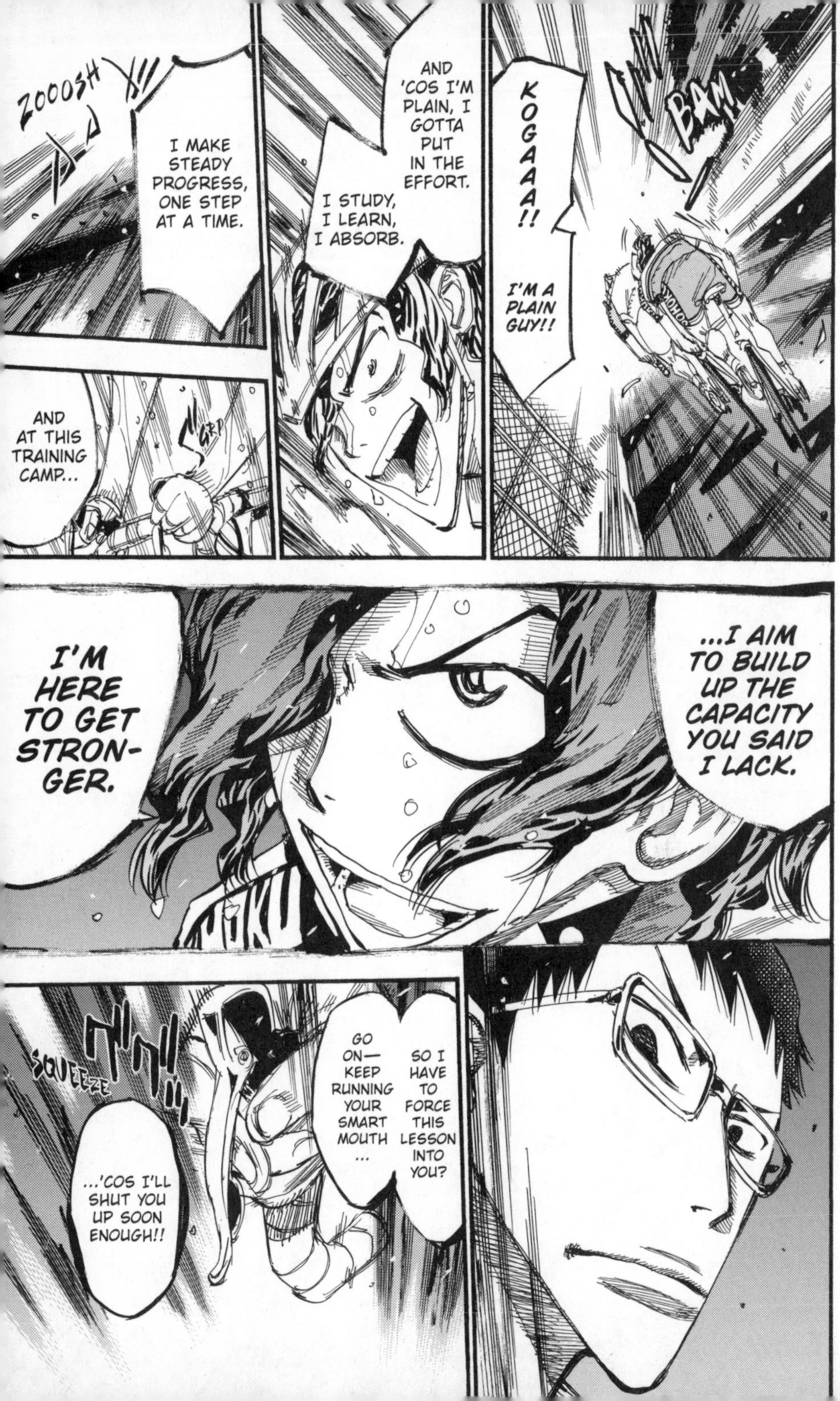
BAM
KOGAAAA!!
I'M A PLAIN GUY!!
AND 'COS I'M PLAIN, I GOTTA PUT IN THE EFFORT.
I STUDY, I LEARN, I ABSORB.
ZOOOSH
I MAKE STEADY PROGRESS, ONE STEP AT A TIME.
GRP
AND AT THIS TRAINING CAMP...
...I AIM TO BUILD UP THE CAPACITY YOU SAID I LACK.
I'M HERE TO GET STRONGER.
SO I HAVE TO FORCE THIS LESSON INTO YOU?
GO ON— KEEP RUNNING YOUR SMART MOUTH...
SQUEEZE
...'COS I'LL SHUT YOU UP SOON ENOUGH!!

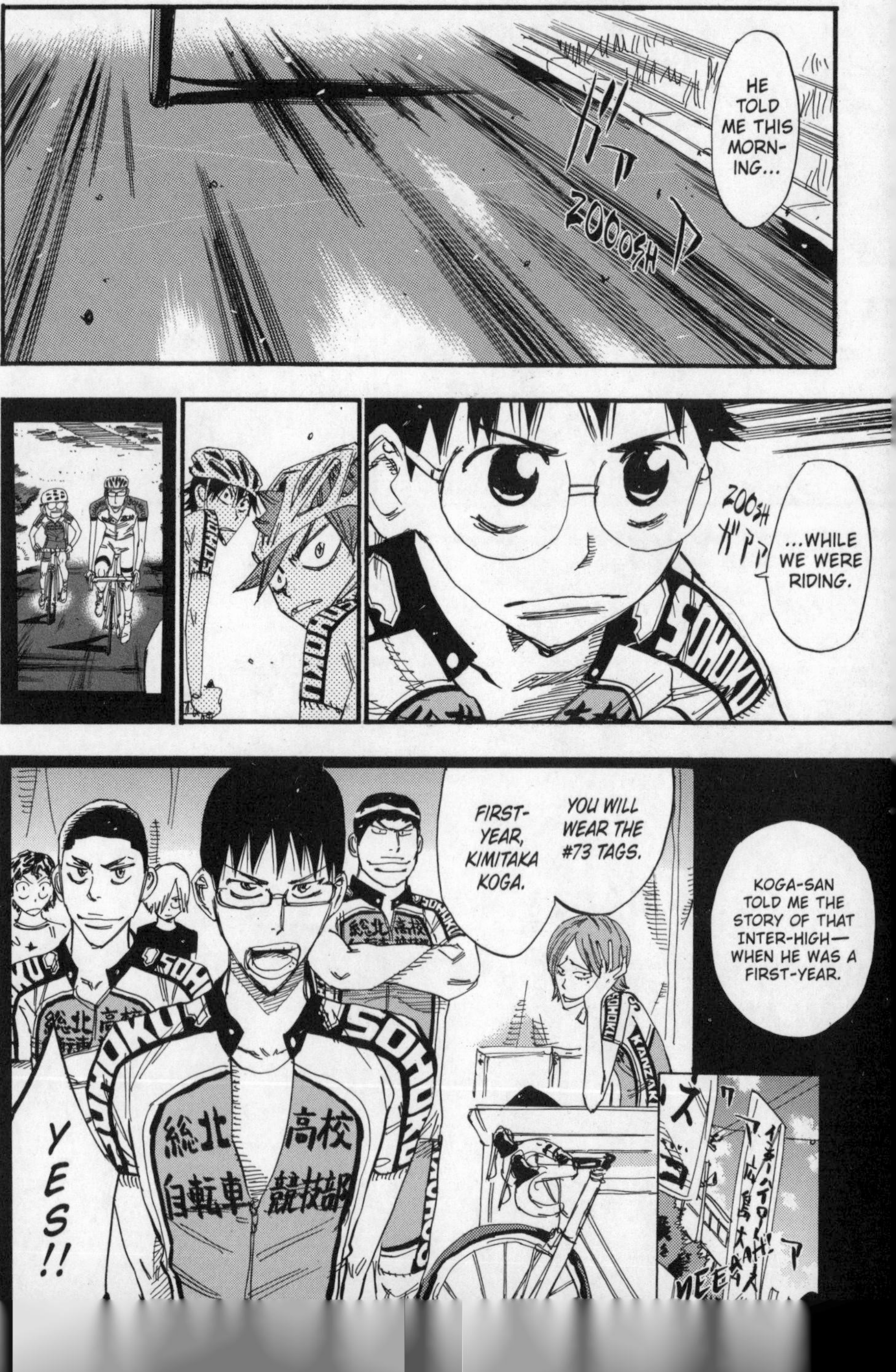
HE TOLD ME THIS MORNING...
ZOOOSH
ZOOSH
...WHILE WE WERE RIDING.
KOGA-SAN TOLD ME THE STORY OF THAT INTER-HIGH—WHEN HE WAS A FIRST-YEAR.
FIRST-YEAR, KIMITAKA KOGA. YOU WILL WEAR THE #73 TAGS.
YES!!

RIDE.287 THE FIRST-YEAR WITH THE #73 TAGS, KOGA

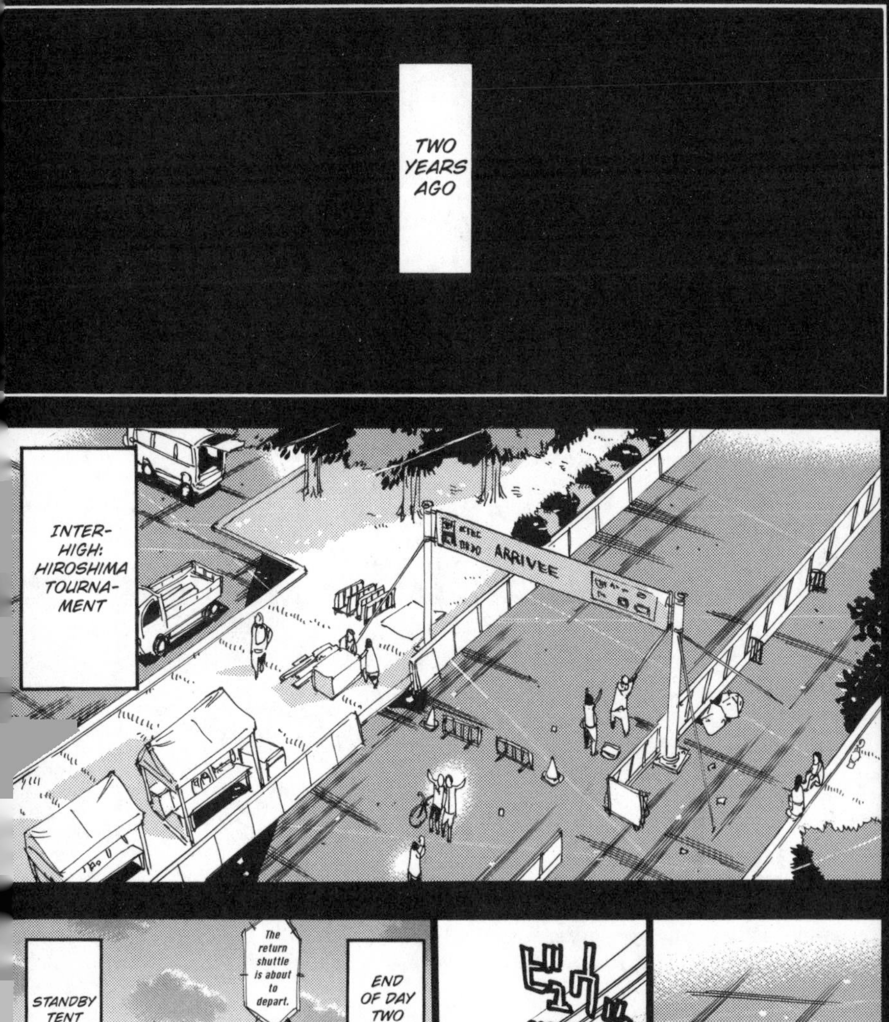
TWO YEARS AGO
INTER-HIGH: HIROSHIMA TOURNAMENT
ARRIVEE
INTER-HIGH ROAD RACE
HIROSHIMA TOURNAMENT
SPECIAL MAPLE LEAF MANJU
EXCLUSIVE
ONLY SOLD HERE!
INTER-HIGH
WHOOSH
END OF DAY TWO (THE SECOND STAGE)
The return shuttle is about to depart.
STANDBY TENT FOR CHIBA'S SOHOKU HIGH

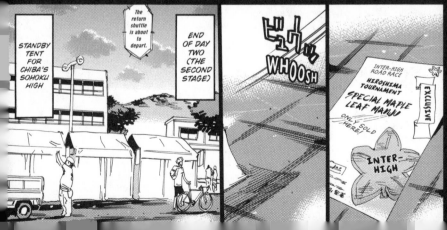

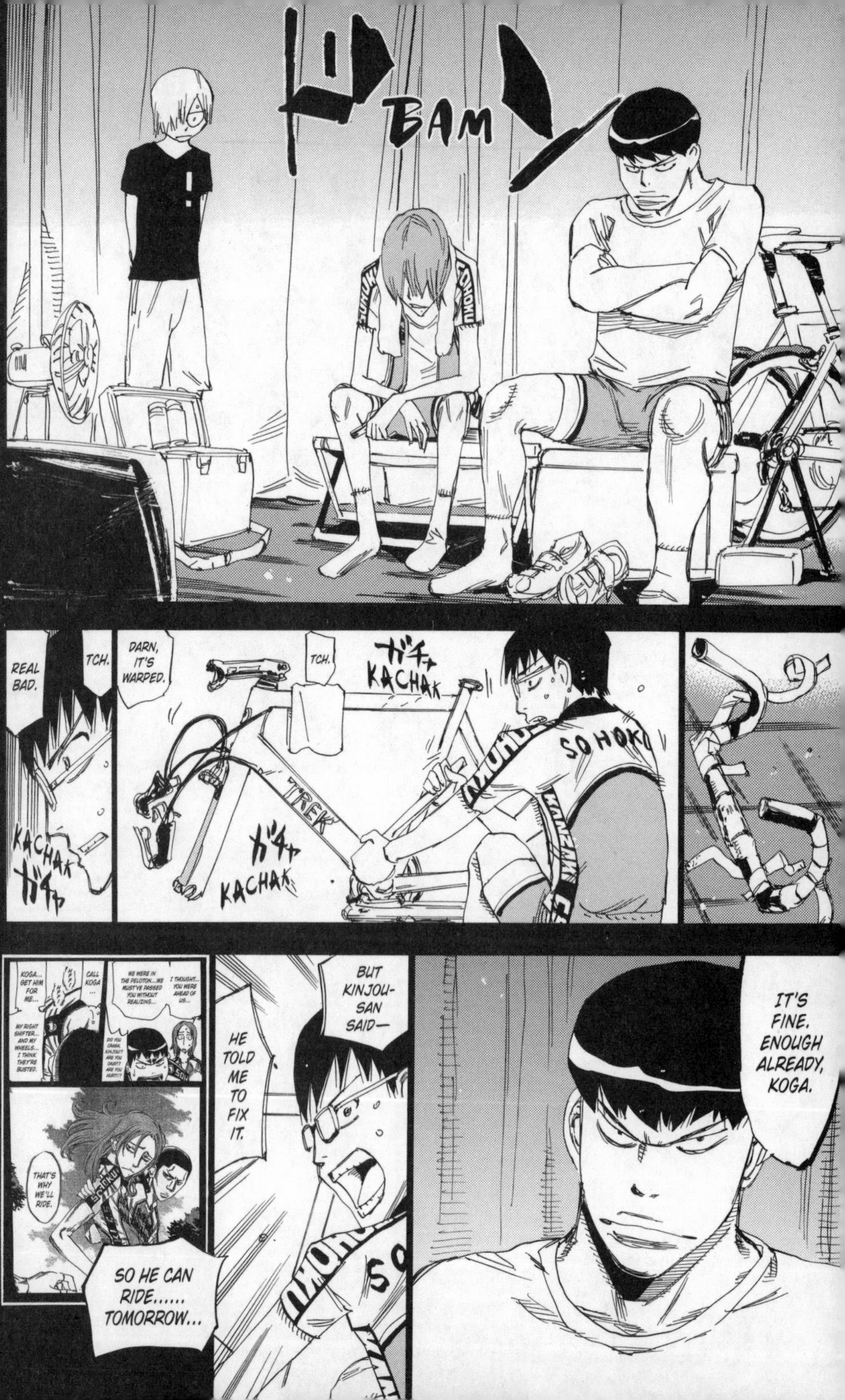
BAM
KACHA
TCH.
DARN, IT'S WARPED.
KACHA
TCH.
REAL BAD.
KACHA
IT'S FINE. ENOUGH ALREADY, KOGA.
BUT KINJOU-SAN SAID—
HE TOLD ME TO FIX IT.
I THOUGHT... YOU WERE AHEAD OF US...
WE WERE IN THE PELOTON...WE MUST'VE PASSED YOU WITHOUT REALIZING...
DID YOU CRASH, KINJOU!? ARE YOU OKAY!? ARE YOU HURT!?
CALL KOGA ...
HFF!
HFF!
KOGA... GET HIM FOR ME...
MY RIGHT SHIFTER... AND MY WHEELS... I THINK THEY'RE BUSTED.
THAT'S WHY WE'LL RIDE.
SO HE CAN RIDE...... TOMORROW...

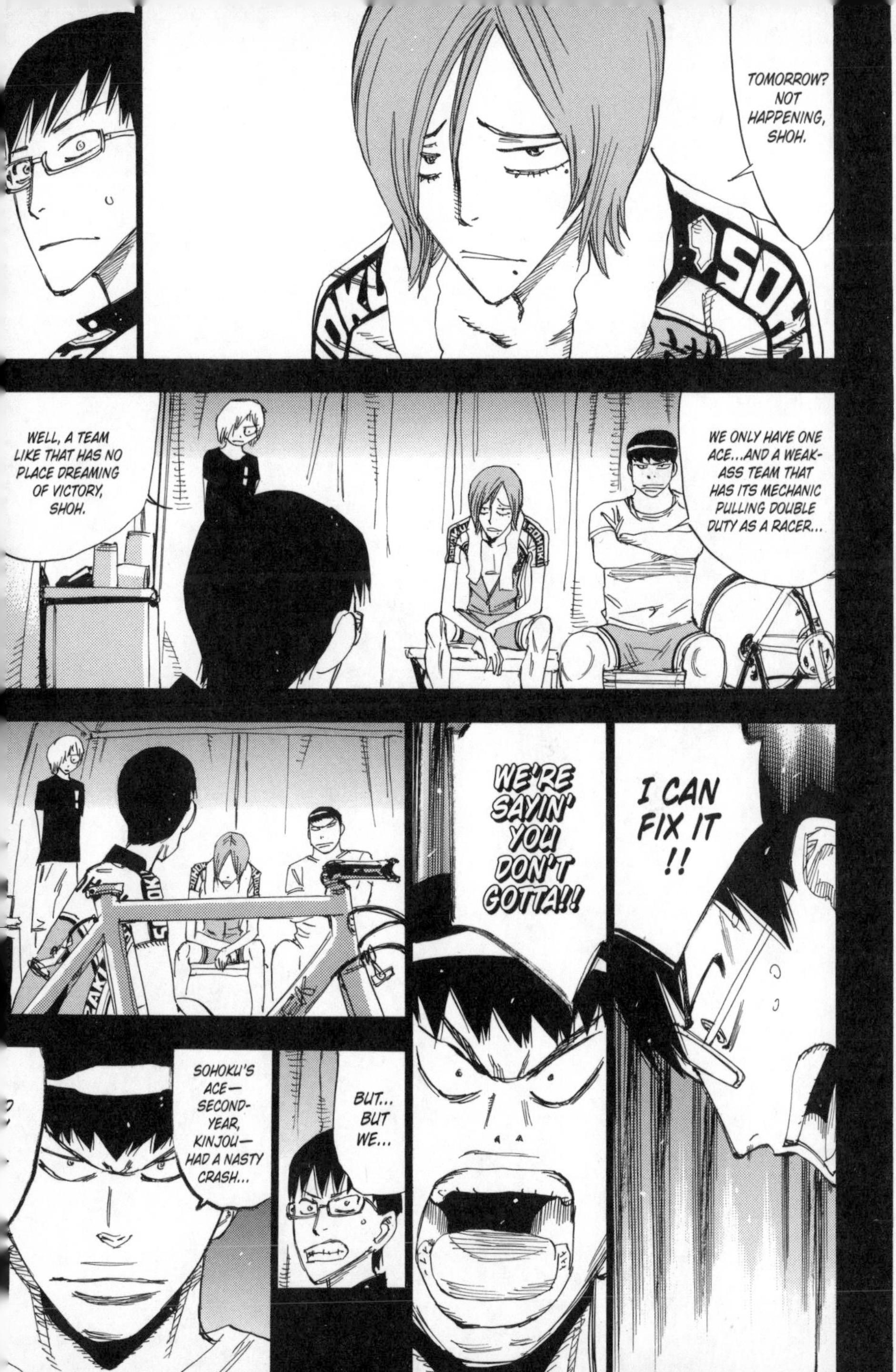
TOMORROW? NOT HAPPENING, SHOH.
WE ONLY HAVE ONE ACE...AND A WEAK-ASS TEAM THAT HAS ITS MECHANIC PULLING DOUBLE DUTY AS A RACER...
WELL, A TEAM LIKE THAT HAS NO PLACE DREAMING OF VICTORY, SHOH.
I CAN FIX IT !!
WE'RE SAYIN' YOU DON'T GOTTA!!
BUT... BUT WE...
SOHOKU'S ACE—SECOND-YEAR, KINJOU—HAD A NASTY CRASH...

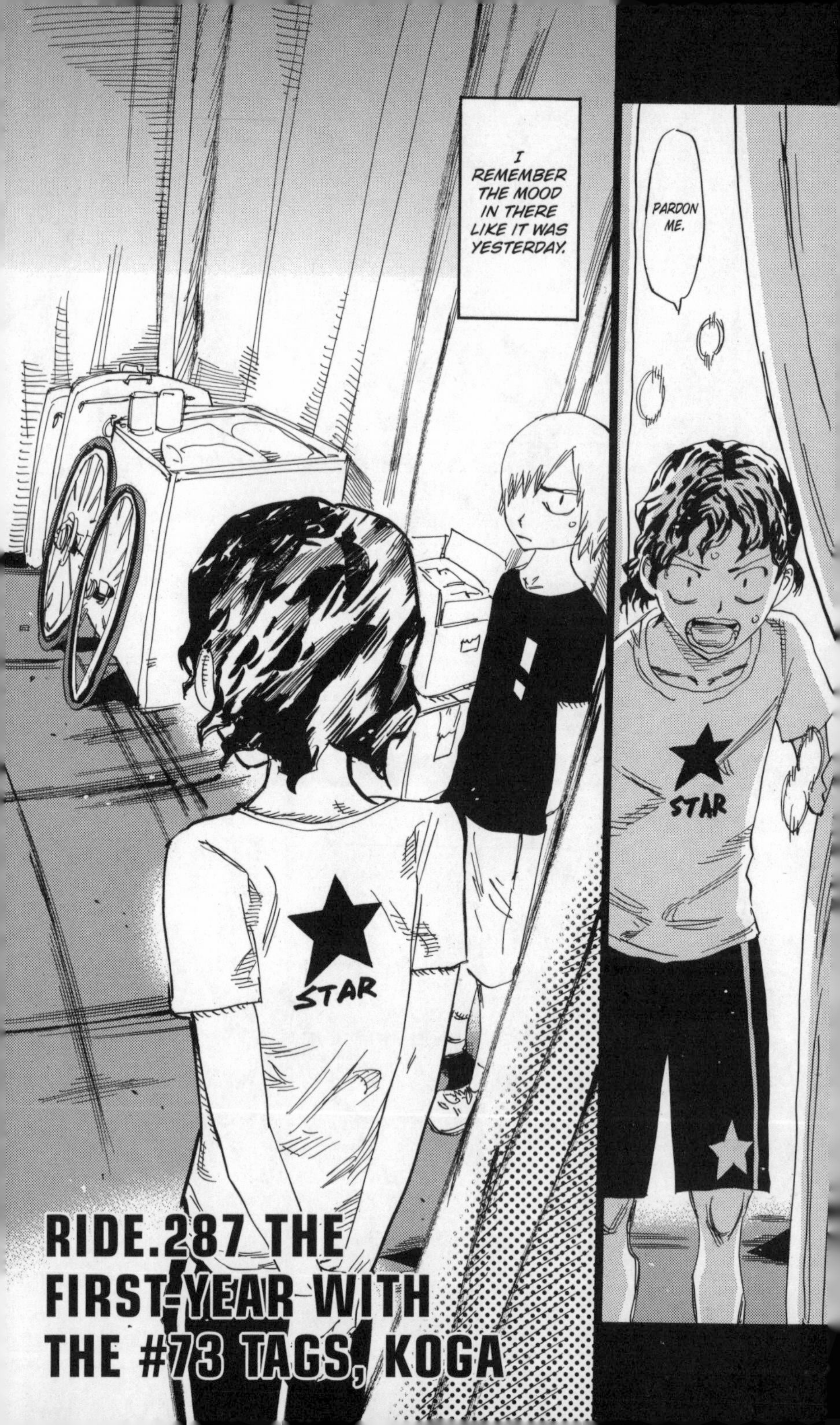
PARDON ME.
STAR
I REMEMBER THE MOOD IN THERE LIKE IT WAS YESTERDAY.
STAR
RIDE.287 THE FIRST-YEAR WITH THE #73 TAGS, KOGA

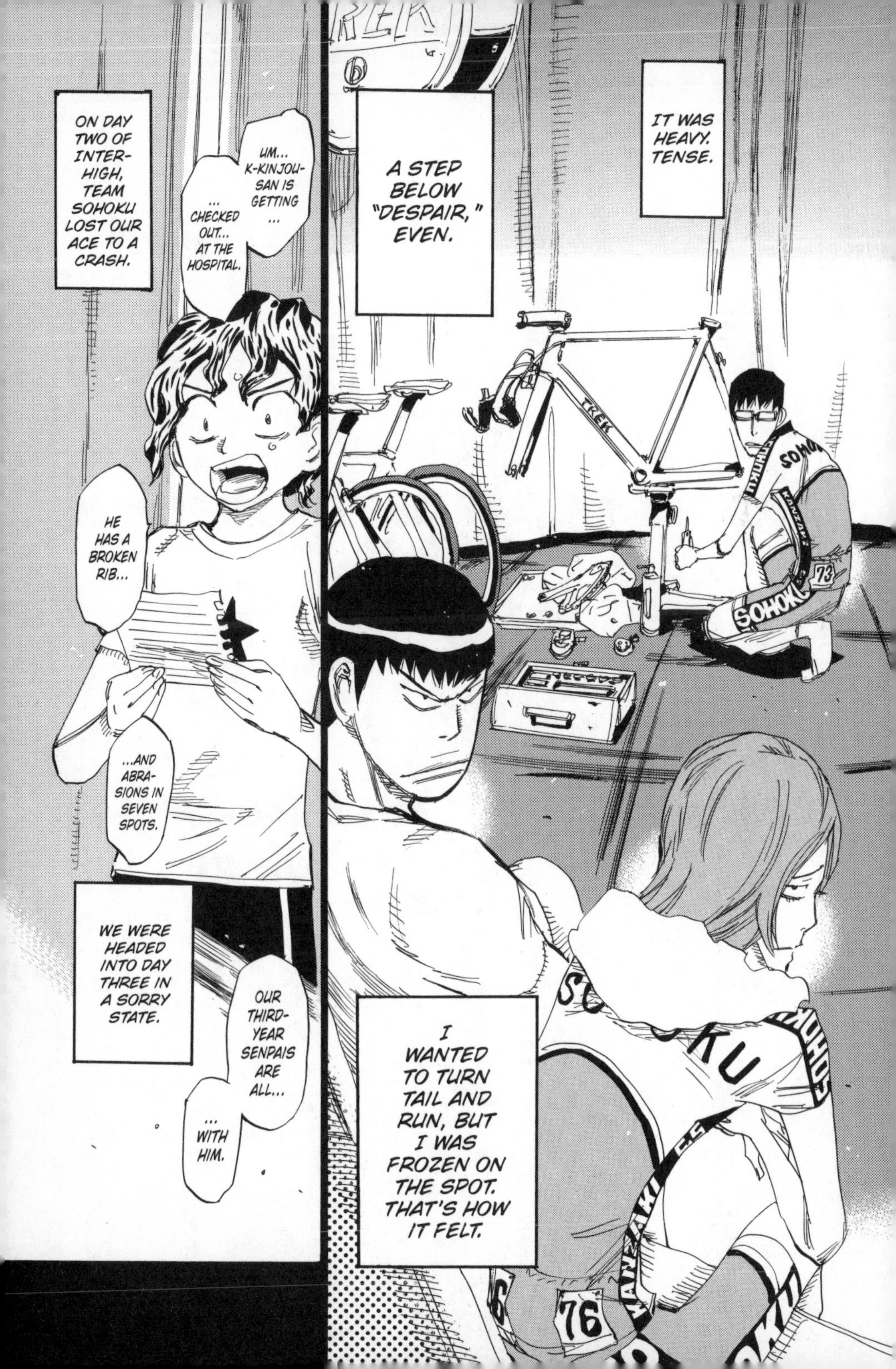
IT WAS HEAVY. TENSE.
A STEP BELOW "DESPAIR," EVEN.
I WANTED TO TURN TAIL AND RUN, BUT I WAS FROZEN ON THE SPOT. THAT'S HOW IT FELT.
UM... K-KINJOU-SAN IS GETTING ...
... CHECKED OUT... AT THE HOSPITAL.
ON DAY TWO OF INTER-HIGH, TEAM SOHOKU LOST OUR ACE TO A CRASH.
HE HAS A BROKEN RIB...
...AND ABRASIONS IN SEVEN SPOTS.
OUR THIRD-YEAR SENPAIS ARE ALL...
... WITH HIM.
WE WERE HEADED INTO DAY THREE IN A SORRY STATE.

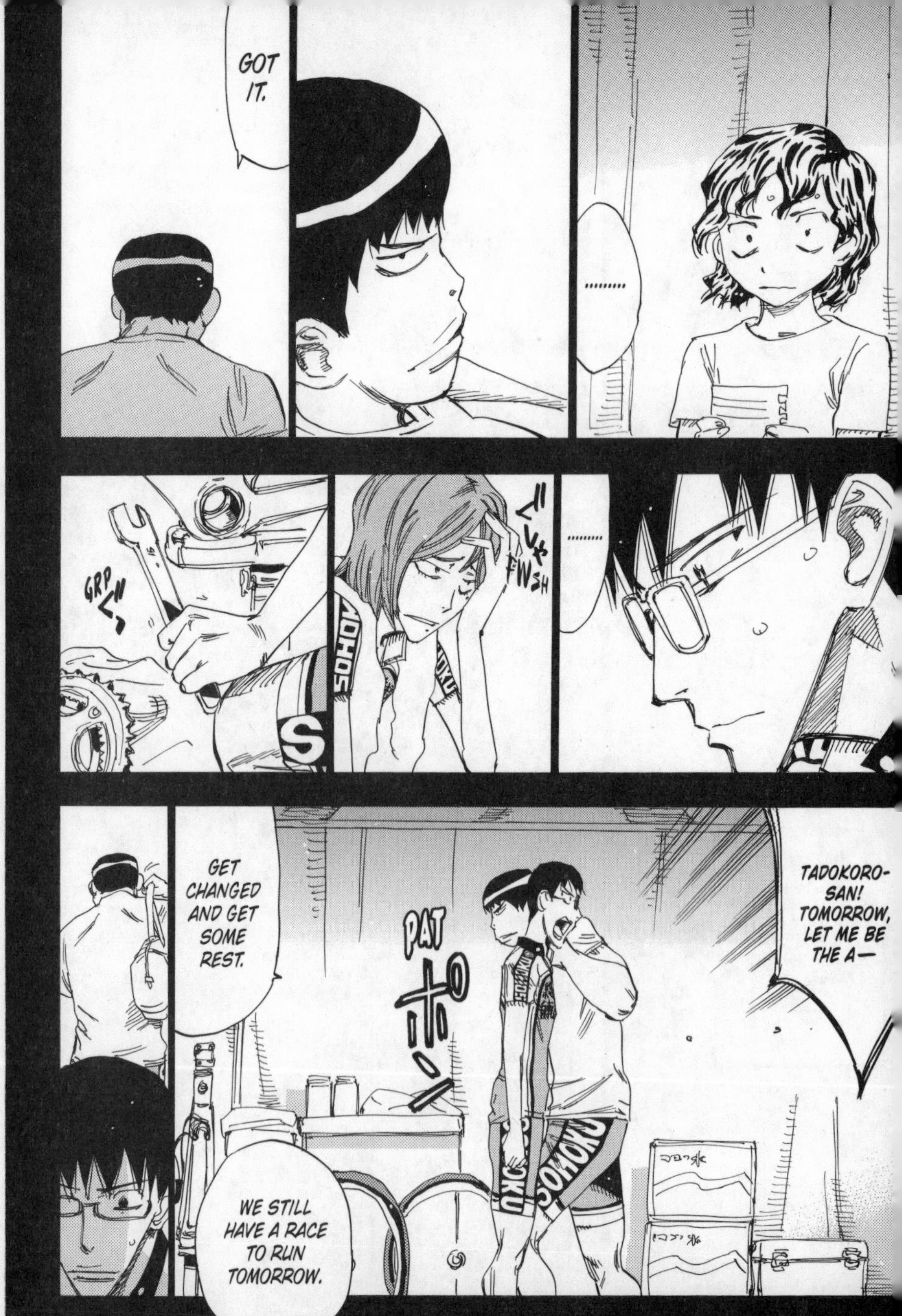
....
GOT IT.
....
FWSH
GRP
TADOKORO-SAN! TOMORROW, LET ME BE THE A—
PAT
GET CHANGED AND GET SOME REST.
WE STILL HAVE A RACE TO RUN TOMORROW.

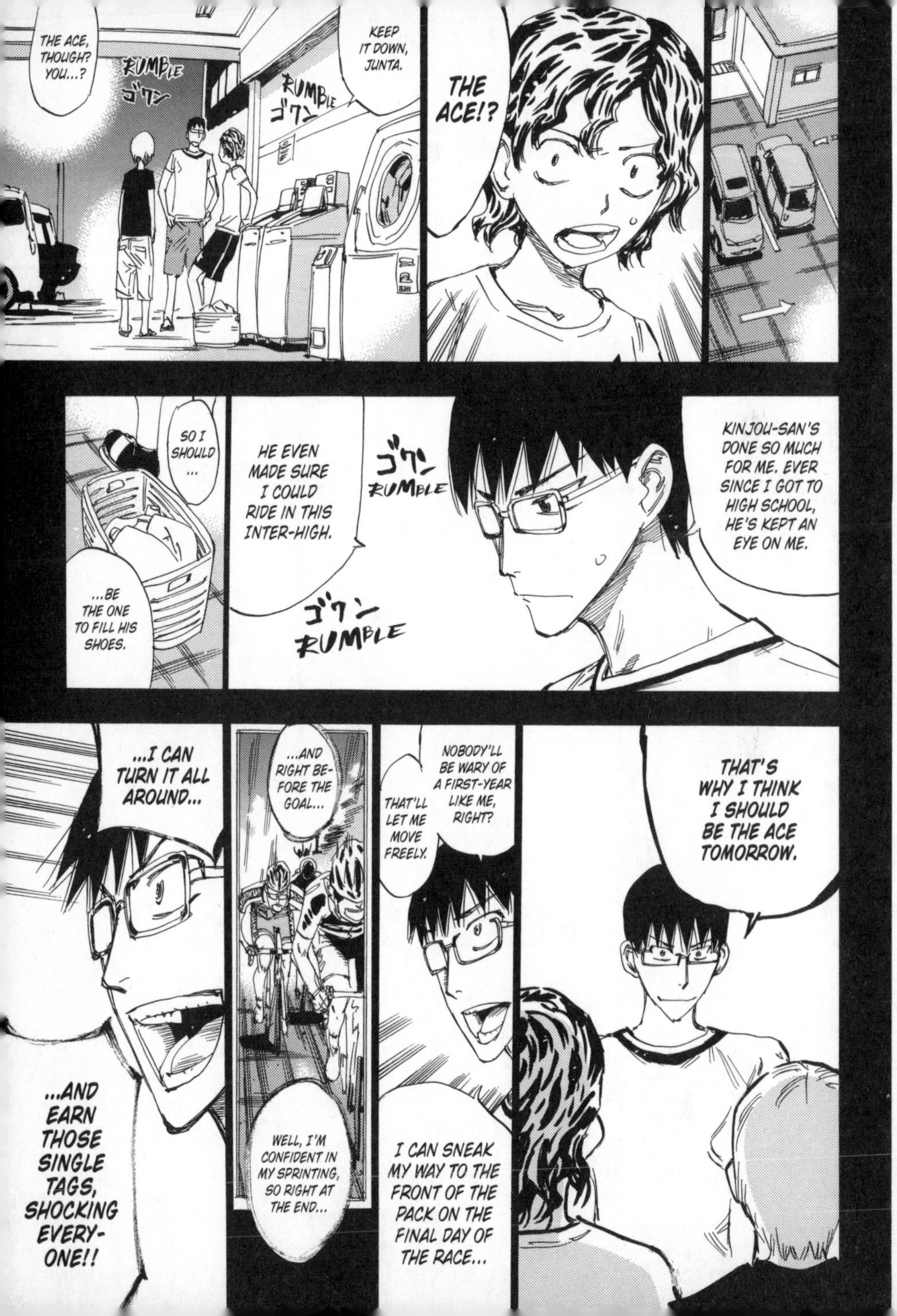
THE ACE!?
KEEP IT DOWN, JUNTA.
RUMBLE
ゴウン
THE ACE, THOUGH? YOU...?
RUMBLE
ゴウン
KINJOU-SAN'S DONE SO MUCH FOR ME. EVER SINCE I GOT TO HIGH SCHOOL, HE'S KEPT AN EYE ON ME.
ゴウン
RUMBLE
HE EVEN MADE SURE I COULD RIDE IN THIS INTER-HIGH.
ゴウン
RUMBLE
SO I SHOULD ...
...BE THE ONE TO FILL HIS SHOES.
THAT'S WHY I THINK I SHOULD BE THE ACE TOMORROW.
NOBODY'LL BE WARY OF A FIRST-YEAR LIKE ME, RIGHT?
THAT'LL LET ME MOVE FREELY.
I CAN SNEAK MY WAY TO THE FRONT OF THE PACK ON THE FINAL DAY OF THE RACE...
...AND RIGHT BEFORE THE GOAL...
WELL, I'M CONFIDENT IN MY SPRINTING, SO RIGHT AT THE END...
...I CAN TURN IT ALL AROUND...
...AND EARN THOSE SINGLE TAGS, SHOCKING EVERY-ONE!!

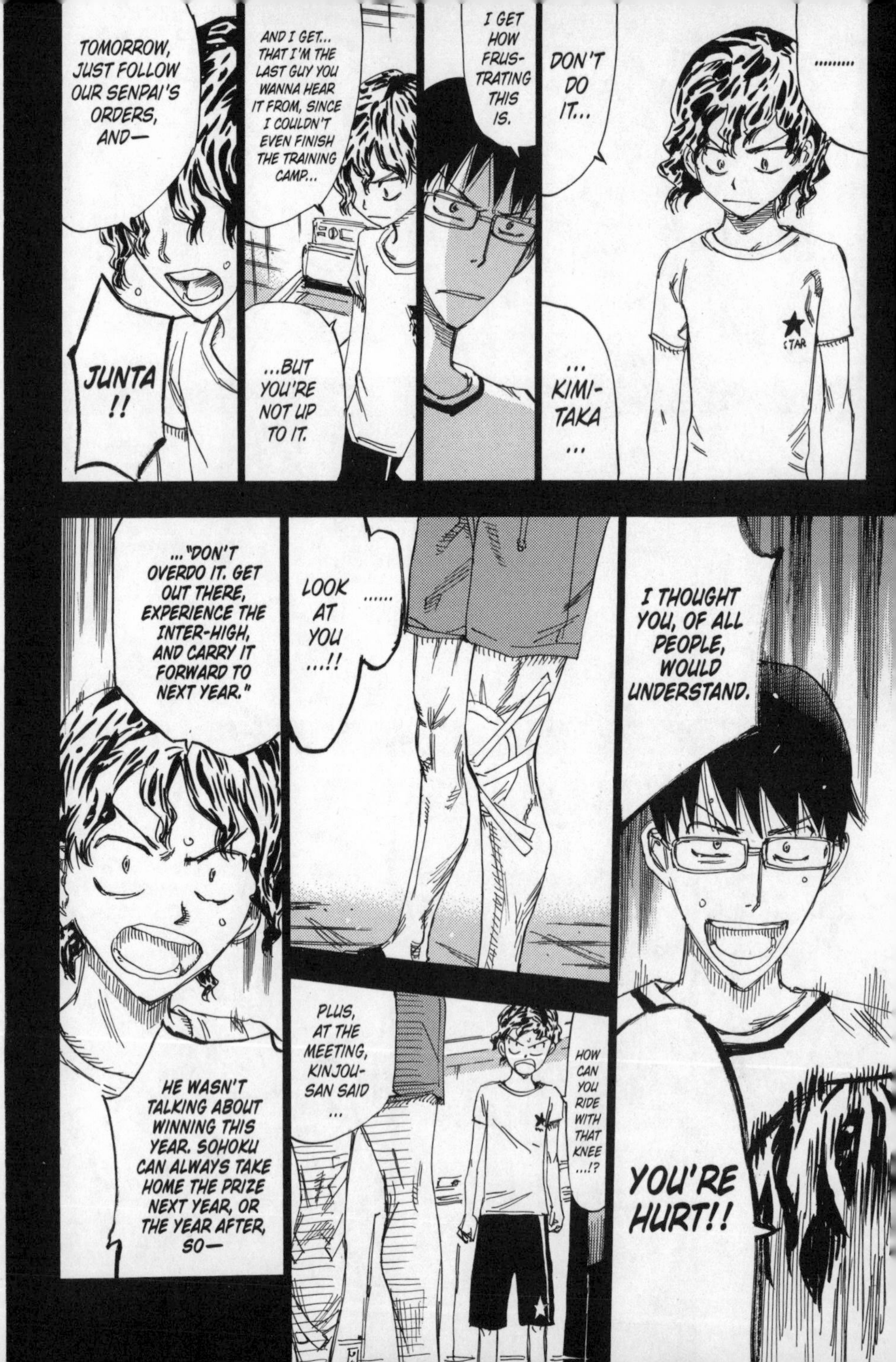
....
DON'T DO IT...
...KIMI-TAKA...
I GET HOW FRUS-TRATING THIS IS.
AND I GET... THAT I'M THE LAST GUY YOU WANNA HEAR IT FROM, SINCE I COULDN'T EVEN FINISH THE TRAINING CAMP...
...BUT YOU'RE NOT UP TO IT.
TOMORROW, JUST FOLLOW OUR SENPAI'S ORDERS, AND—
JUNTA!!
I THOUGHT YOU, OF ALL PEOPLE, WOULD UNDERSTAND.
YOU'RE HURT!!
LOOK AT YOU ...!!
......
HOW CAN YOU RIDE WITH THAT KNEE ...!?
PLUS, AT THE MEETING, KINJOU-SAN SAID ...
..."DON'T OVERDO IT. GET OUT THERE, EXPERIENCE THE INTER-HIGH, AND CARRY IT FORWARD TO NEXT YEAR."
HE WASN'T TALKING ABOUT WINNING THIS YEAR. SOHOKU CAN ALWAYS TAKE HOME THE PRIZE NEXT YEAR, OR THE YEAR AFTER, SO—

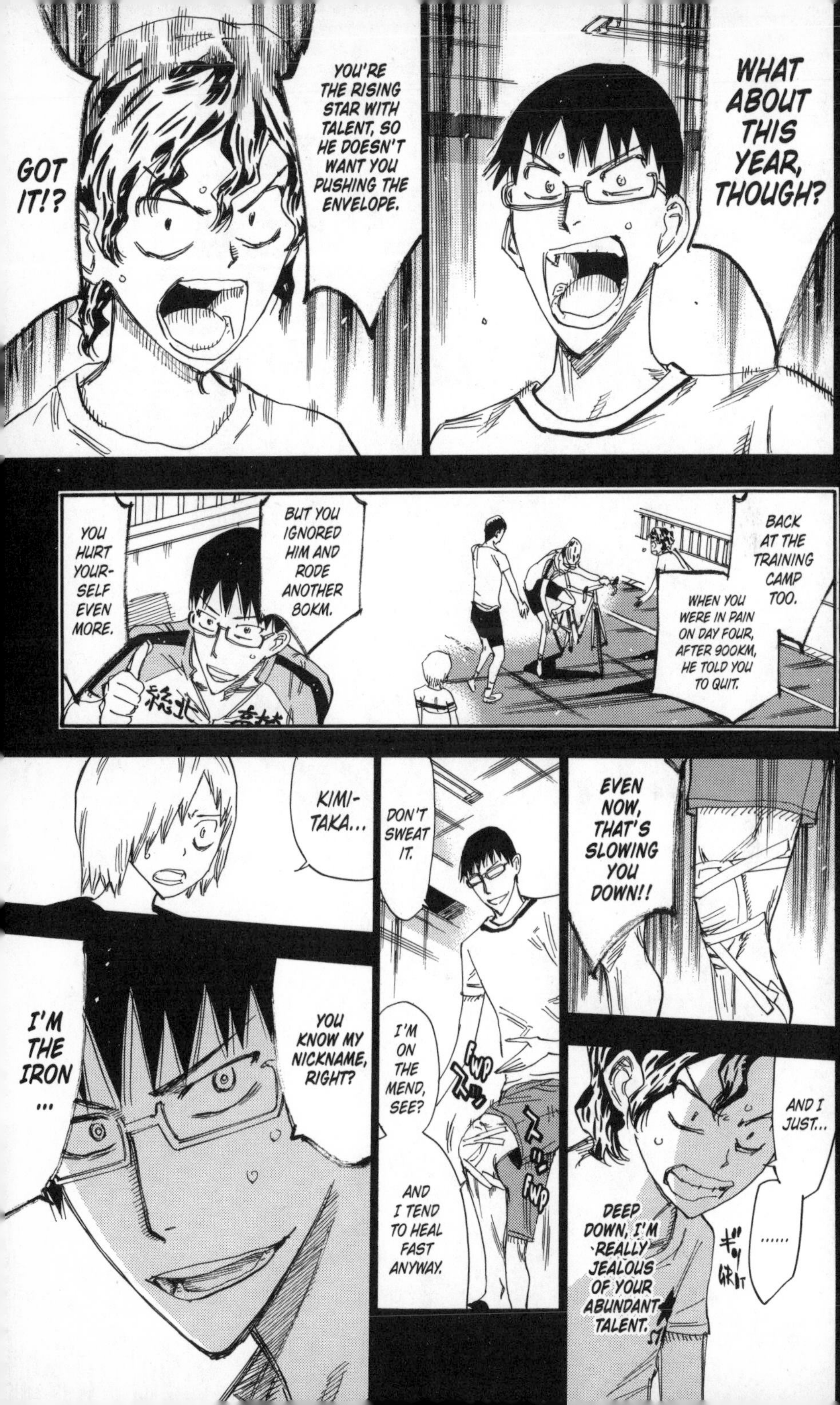
WHAT ABOUT THIS YEAR, THOUGH?
YOU'RE THE RISING STAR WITH TALENT, SO HE DOESN'T WANT YOU PUSHING THE ENVELOPE.
GOT IT!?
BACK AT THE TRAINING CAMP TOO.
WHEN YOU WERE IN PAIN ON DAY FOUR, AFTER 900KM, HE TOLD YOU TO QUIT.
BUT YOU IGNORED HIM AND RODE ANOTHER 80KM.
YOU HURT YOURSELF EVEN MORE.
EVEN NOW, THAT'S SLOWING YOU DOWN!!
AND I JUST...
DEEP DOWN, I'M REALLY JEALOUS OF YOUR ABUNDANT TALENT.
GRIT
......
DON'T SWEAT IT.
I'M ON THE MEND, SEE?
FWP
FWP
AND I TEND TO HEAL FAST ANYWAY.
KIMI-TAKA...
YOU KNOW MY NICKNAME, RIGHT?
I'M THE IRON ...

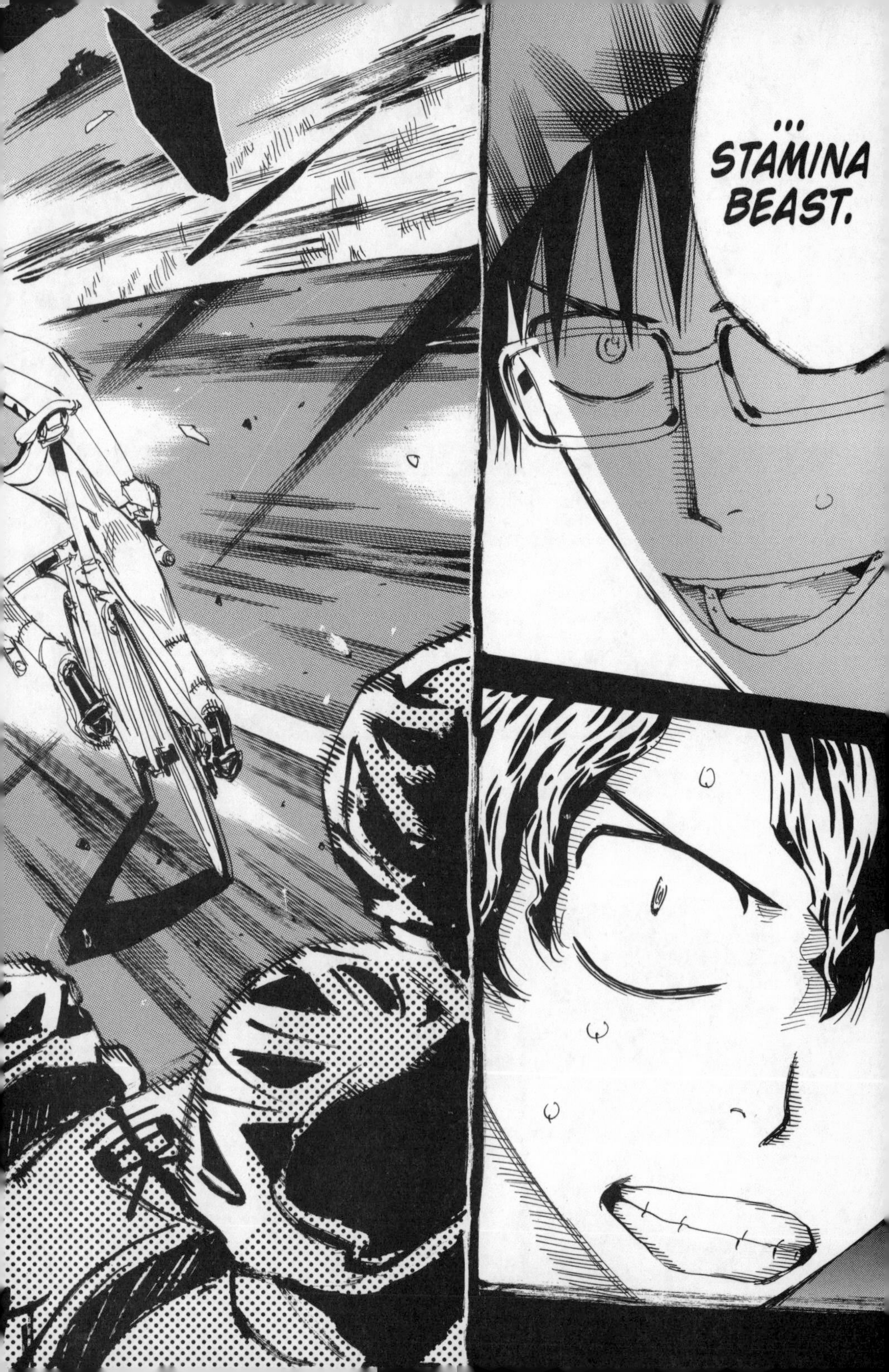
...
STÄMINA BEAST.

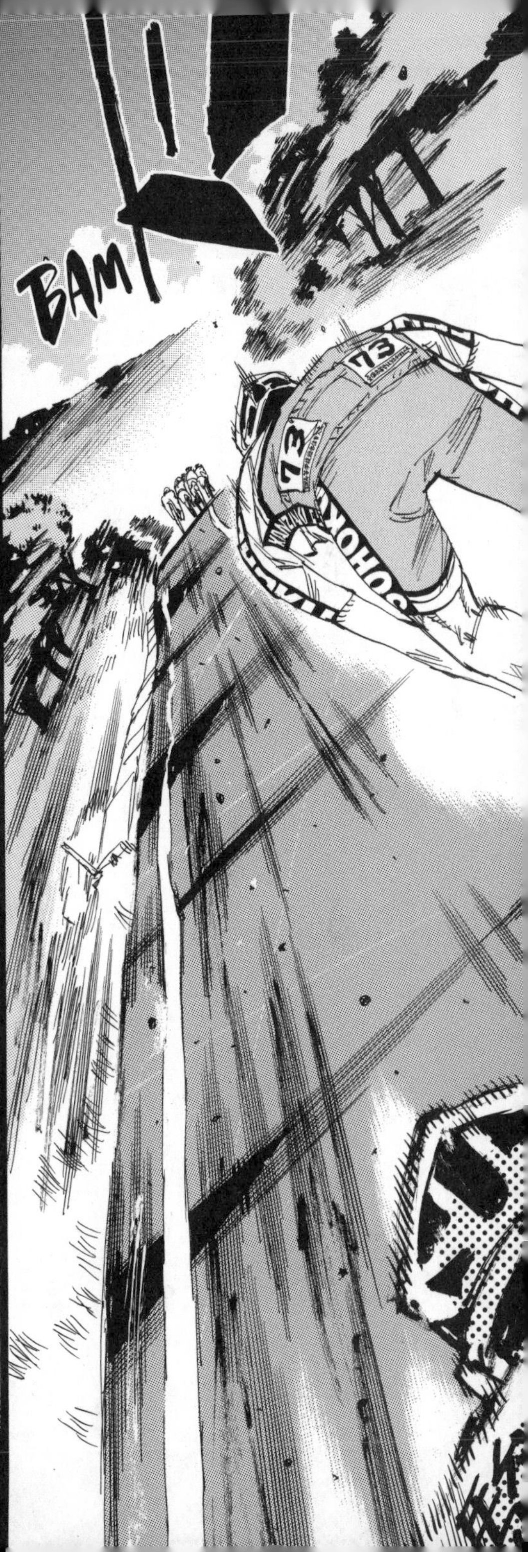
BAM

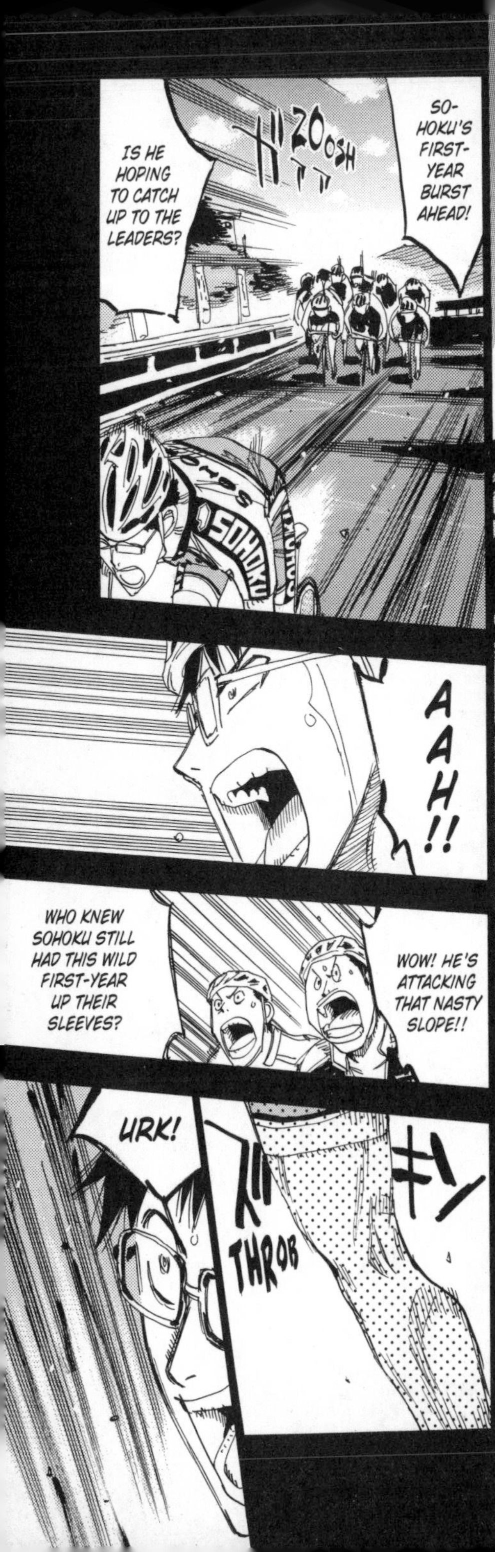
SO-HOKU'S FIRST-YEAR BURST AHEAD!
ZOOSH
IS HE HOPING TO CATCH UP TO THE LEADERS?
AAAH!!
WOW! HE'S ATTACKING THAT NASTY SLOPE!!
WHO KNEW SOHOKU STILL HAD THIS WILD FIRST-YEAR UP THEIR SLEEVES?
THROB
URK!

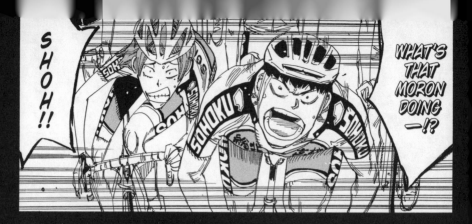

WHAT'S THAT MORON DOING—!?
SHOHH!!
WASN'T HE LISTENING TO OUR SENPAIS IN THIS MORNING'S MEETING?
SHOULD WE STOP HIM, TADO-KOROCCHI?
NAH, YOU GOTTA FOCUS ON THE RIDGE DURING LEG TWO.
AAAAAH!!
I'M THEIR HOPE.
KINJOU-SAN...
KINJOU-SAN IS...
AS YOU GROW, YOU'RE BOUND...
...TO GET A LOT STRONGER, KOGA.
I LOOK FORWARD TO NEXT YEAR'S INTER-HIGH.
HUH?

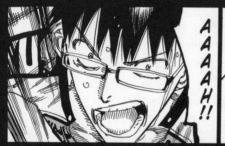

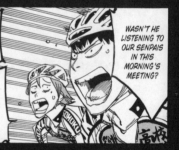

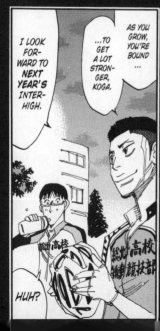

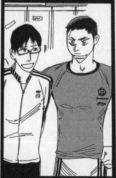

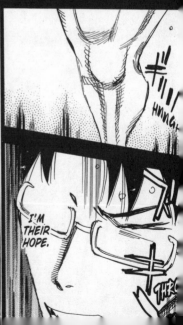

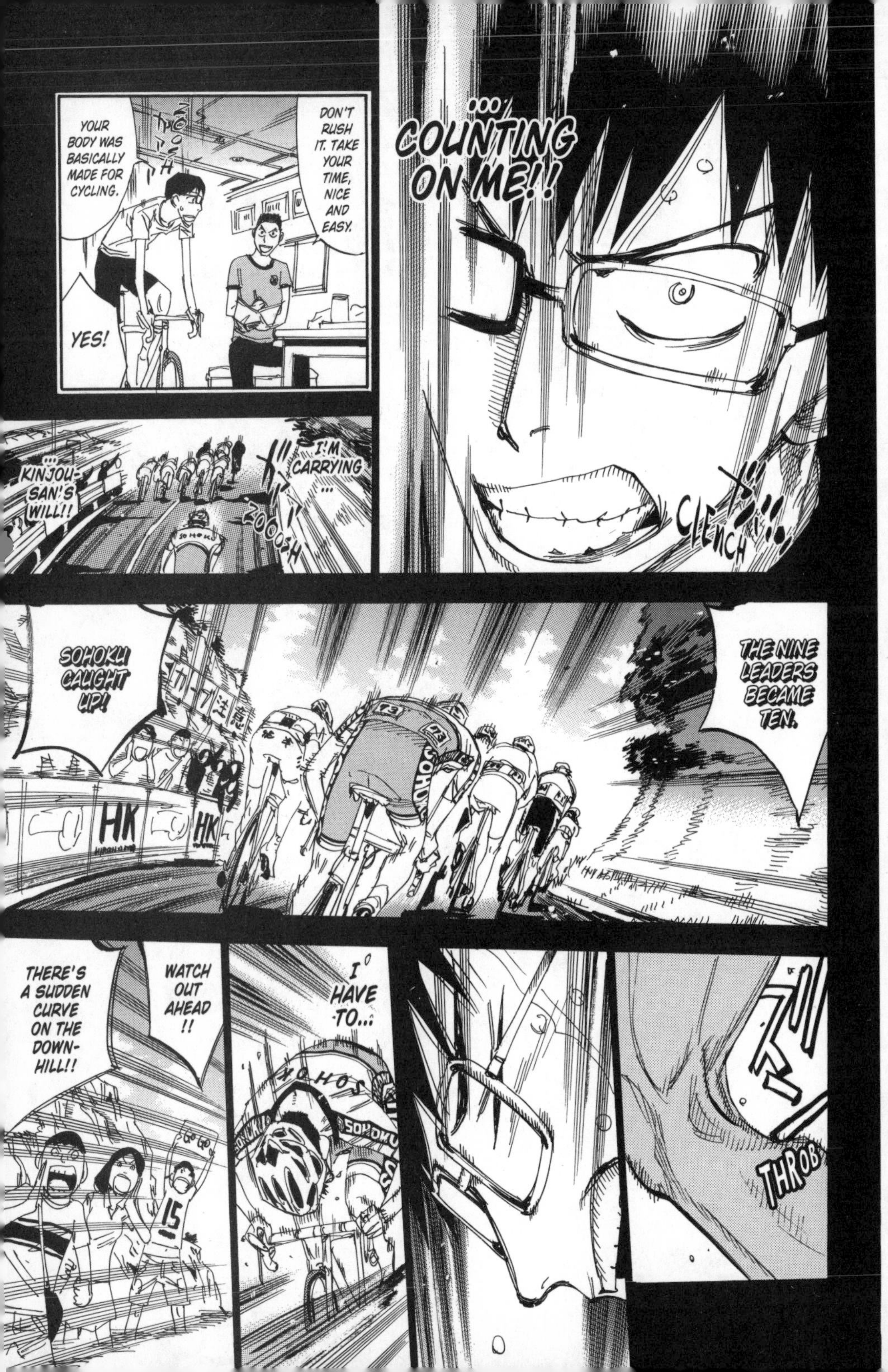

...COUNTING ON ME!!
CLENCH
DON'T RUSH IT. TAKE YOUR TIME, NICE AND EASY.
YOUR BODY WAS BASICALLY MADE FOR CYCLING.
YES!
I'M CARRYING...
...KINJOU-SAN'S WILL!!
ZOOOSH
THE NINE LEADERS BECAME TEN.
SOHOKU CAUGHT UP!
THROB
I HAVE TO...
WATCH OUT AHEAD!!
THERE'S A SUDDEN CURVE ON THE DOWN-HILL!!

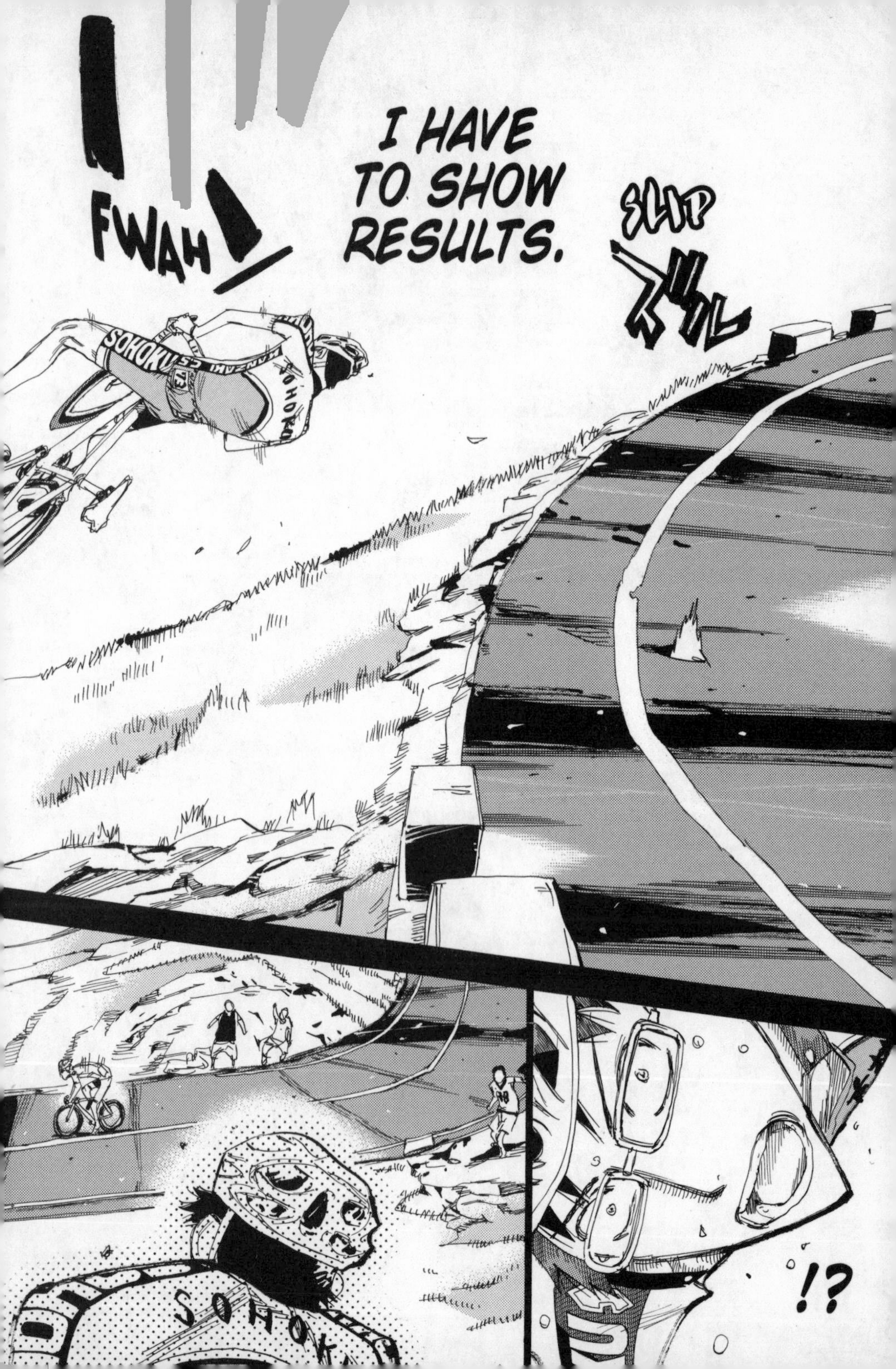
I HAVE TO SHOW RESULTS.
SLIP
FWAH
!?

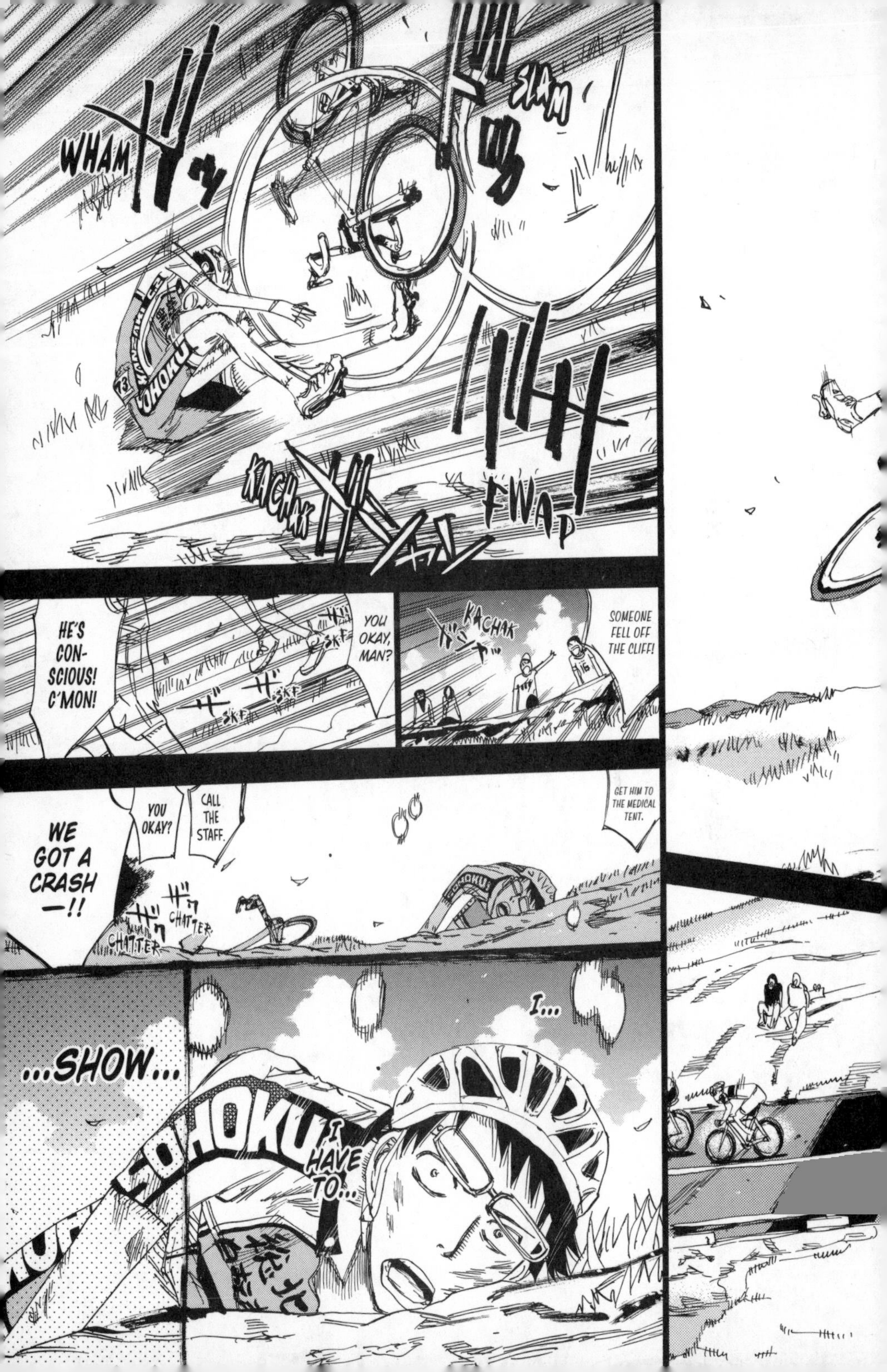
SLAM
WHAM
KACHAK
FWAP
KACHAK
SOMEONE FELL OFF THE CLIFF!
YOU OKAY, MAN?
SKF
SKF
SKF
HE'S CONSCIOUS! C'MON!
GET HIM TO THE MEDICAL TENT.
CALL THE STAFF.
YOU OKAY?
CHATTER
CHATTER
WE GOT A CRASH—!!
I...
I HAVE TO...
...SHOW...

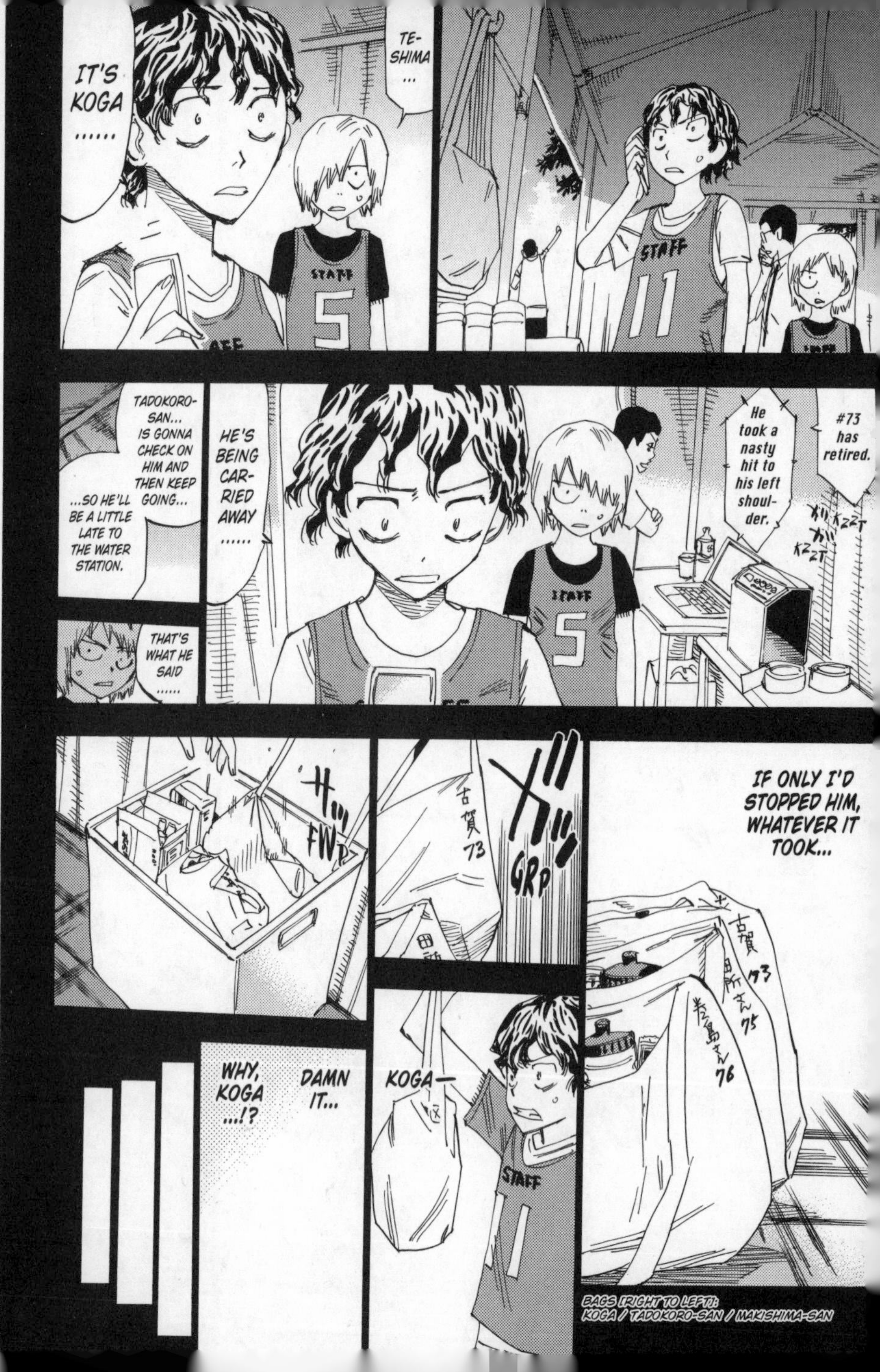
TE-SHIMA ...
IT'S KOGA ......
#73 has retired.
He took a nasty hit to his left shoulder.
KZZT KZZT
HE'S BEING CARRIED AWAY ......
TADOKORO-SAN... IS GONNA CHECK ON HIM AND THEN KEEP GOING...
...SO HE'LL BE A LITTLE LATE TO THE WATER STATION.
THAT'S WHAT HE SAID ......
IF ONLY I'D STOPPED HIM, WHATEVER IT TOOK...
古賀 73
田所さん 75
巻島さん 76
BAGS [RIGHT TO LEFT]: KOGA / TADOKORO-SAN / MAKISHIMA-SAN
古賀 73
GRP
FWP
KOGA—
DAMN IT...
WHY, KOGA ...!?

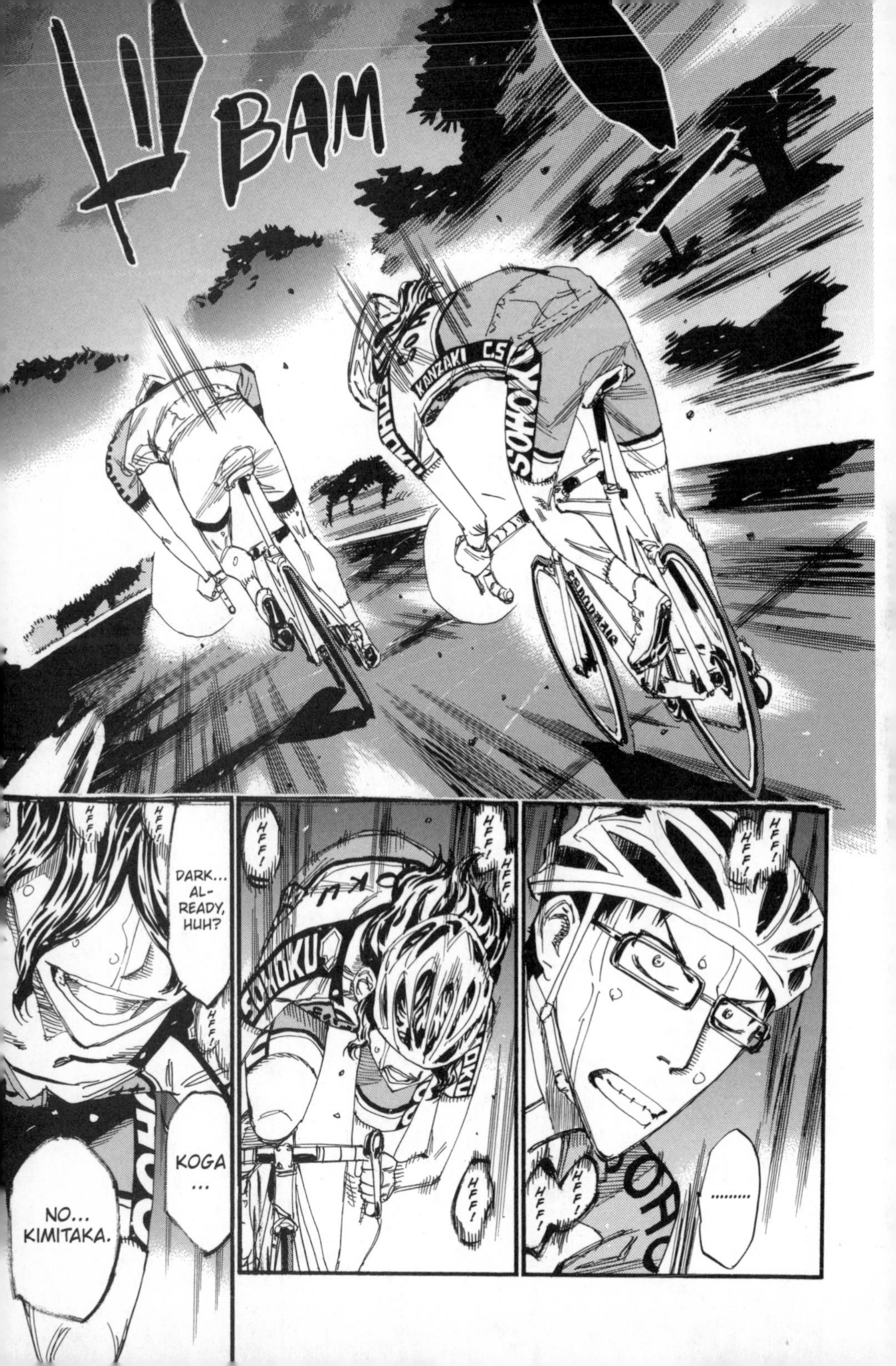
BAM
HFF! HFF!
....
HFF! HFF!
HFF! HFF!
HFF! HFF!
HFF! HFF!
DARK... AL-READY, HUH?
HFF!
KOGA...
NO... KIMITAKA.

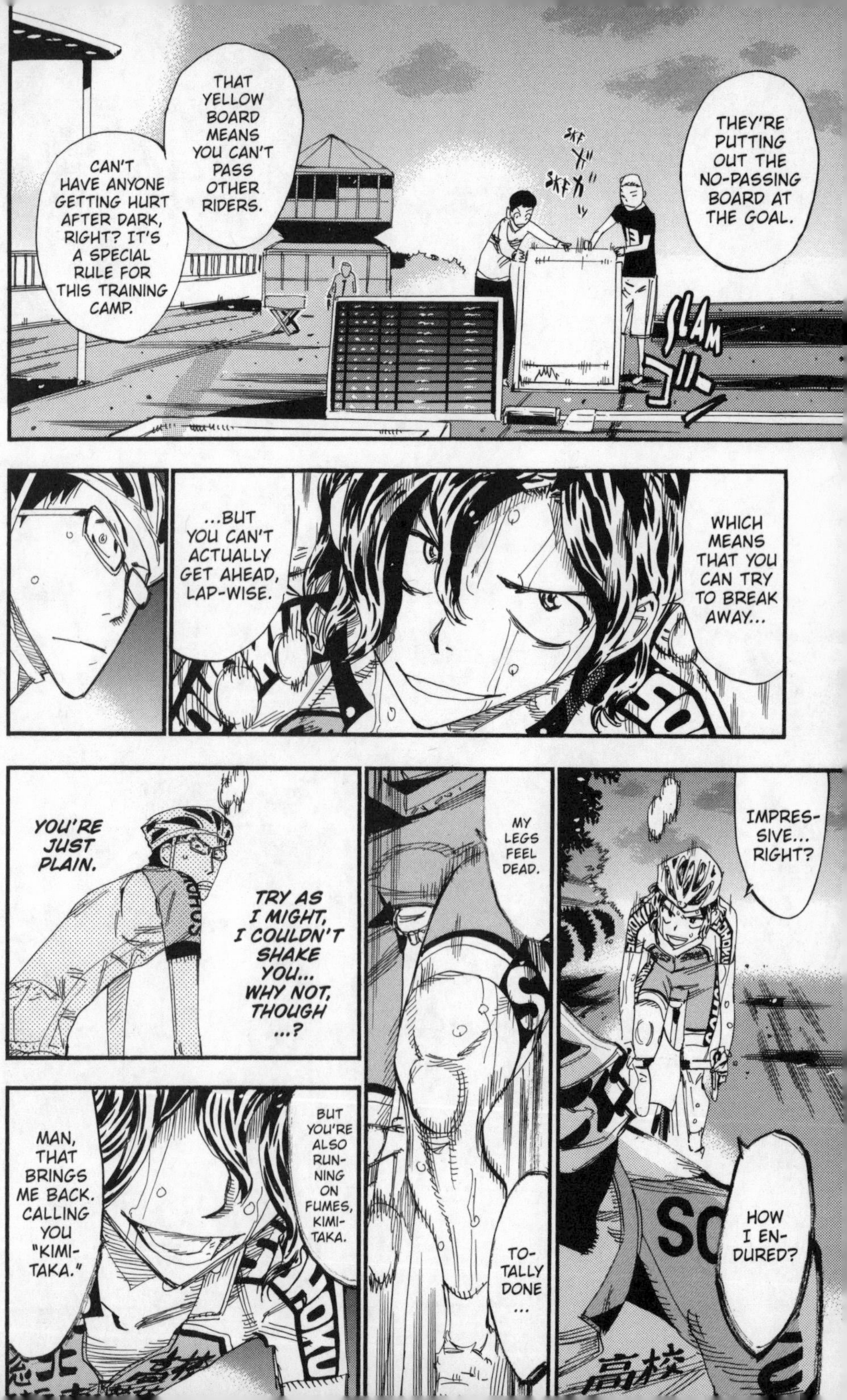
THEY'RE PUTTING OUT THE NO-PASSING BOARD AT THE GOAL.
SKF SKF
SLAM
THAT YELLOW BOARD MEANS YOU CAN'T PASS OTHER RIDERS.
CAN'T HAVE ANYONE GETTING HURT AFTER DARK, RIGHT? IT'S A SPECIAL RULE FOR THIS TRAINING CAMP.
WHICH MEANS THAT YOU CAN TRY TO BREAK AWAY...
...BUT YOU CAN'T ACTUALLY GET AHEAD, LAP-WISE.
IMPRESSIVE... RIGHT?
HOW I ENDURED?
MY LEGS FEEL DEAD.
TOTALLY DONE...
YOU'RE JUST PLAIN.
TRY AS I MIGHT, I COULDN'T SHAKE YOU... WHY NOT, THOUGH...?
BUT YOU'RE ALSO RUNNING ON FUMES, KIMITAKA.
MAN, THAT BRINGS ME BACK. CALLING YOU "KIMITAKA."

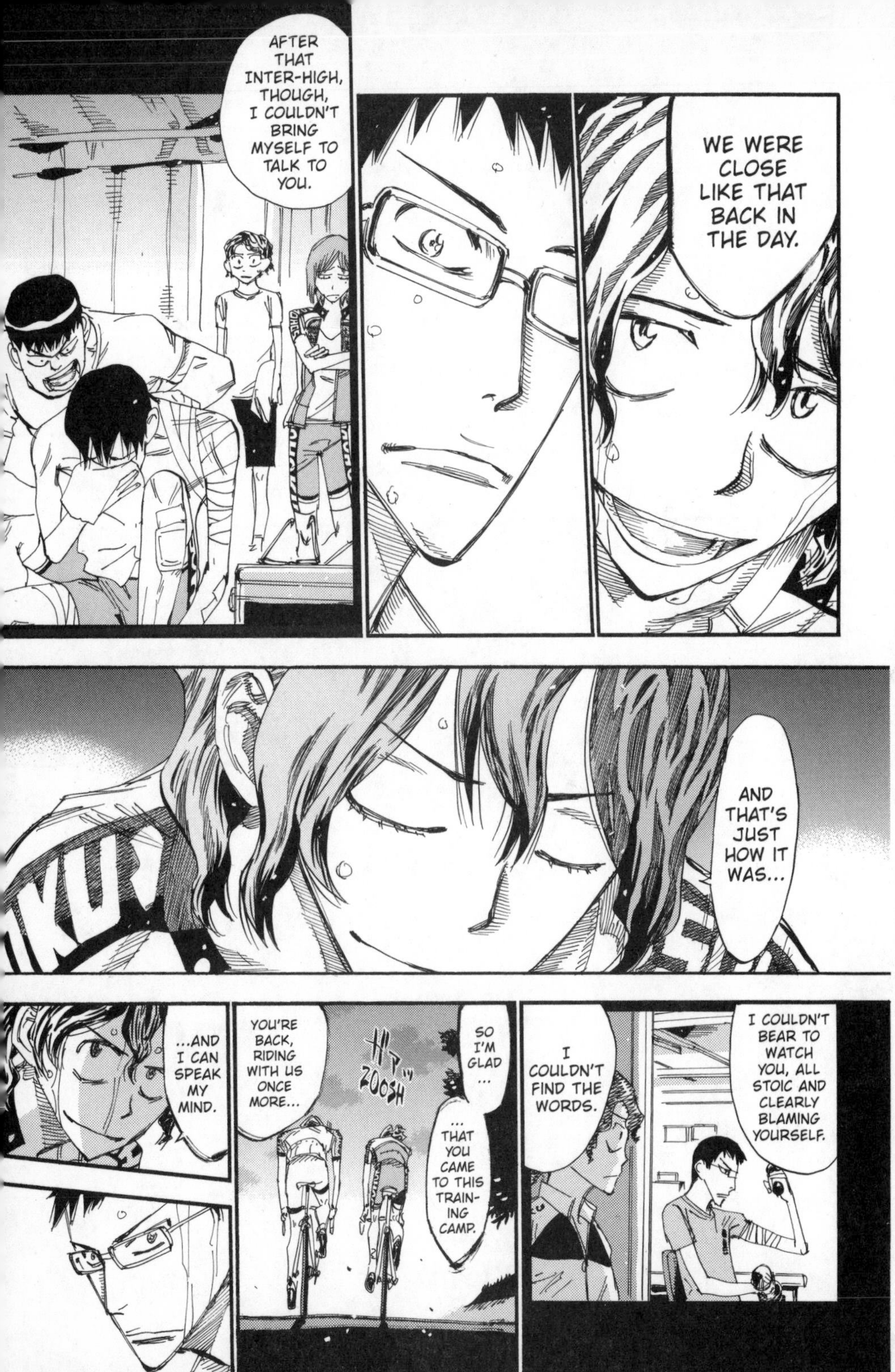
WE WERE CLOSE LIKE THAT BACK IN THE DAY.
AFTER THAT INTER-HIGH, THOUGH, I COULDN'T BRING MYSELF TO TALK TO YOU.
AND THAT'S JUST HOW IT WAS...
I COULDN'T BEAR TO WATCH YOU, ALL STOIC AND CLEARLY BLAMING YOURSELF.
I COULDN'T FIND THE WORDS.
SO I'M GLAD...
...THAT YOU CAME TO THIS TRAIN-ING CAMP.
ZOOSH
YOU'RE BACK, RIDING WITH US ONCE MORE...
...AND I CAN SPEAK MY MIND.

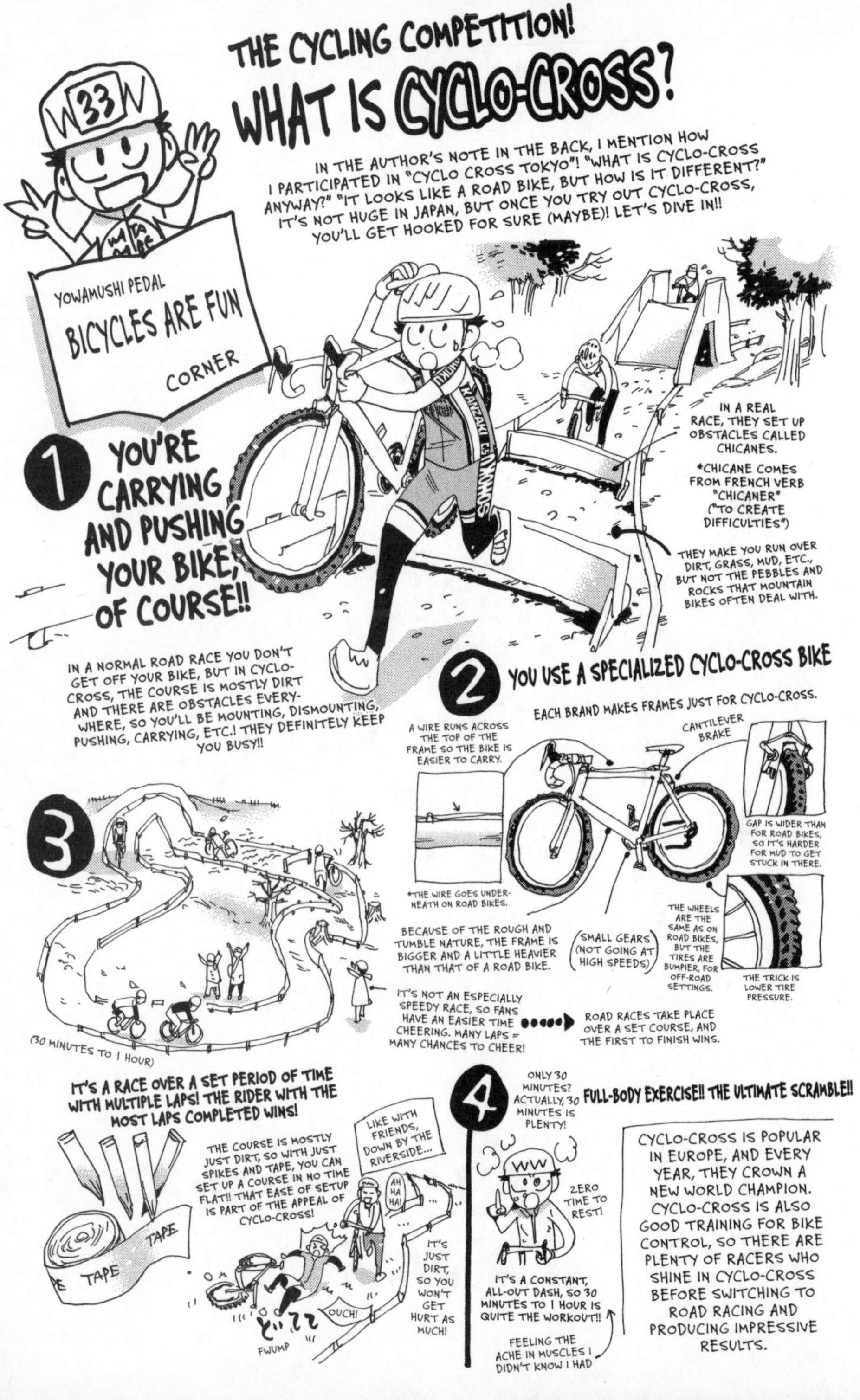
THE CYCLING COMPETITION!
WHAT IS CYCLO-CROSS?
33
YOWAMUSHI PEDAL
BICYCLES ARE FUN
CORNER
IN THE AUTHOR'S NOTE IN THE BACK, I MENTION HOW I PARTICIPATED IN "CYCLO CROSS TOKYO"! "WHAT IS CYCLO-CROSS ANYWAY?" "IT LOOKS LIKE A ROAD BIKE, BUT HOW IS IT DIFFERENT?" IT'S NOT HUGE IN JAPAN, BUT ONCE YOU TRY OUT CYCLO-CROSS, YOU'LL GET HOOKED FOR SURE (MAYBE)! LET'S DIVE IN!!
1 YOU'RE CARRYING AND PUSHING YOUR BIKE, OF COURSE!!
IN A REAL RACE, THEY SET UP OBSTACLES CALLED CHICANES.
*CHICANE COMES FROM FRENCH VERB "CHICANER" ("TO CREATE DIFFICULTIES")
THEY MAKE YOU RUN OVER DIRT, GRASS, MUD, ETC., BUT NOT THE PEBBLES AND ROCKS THAT MOUNTAIN BIKES OFTEN DEAL WITH.
IN A NORMAL ROAD RACE YOU DON'T GET OFF YOUR BIKE, BUT IN CYCLO-CROSS, THE COURSE IS MOSTLY DIRT AND THERE ARE OBSTACLES EVERYWHERE, SO YOU'LL BE MOUNTING, DISMOUNTING, PUSHING, CARRYING, ETC.! THEY DEFINITELY KEEP YOU BUSY!!
2 YOU USE A SPECIALIZED CYCLO-CROSS BIKE
EACH BRAND MAKES FRAMES JUST FOR CYCLO-CROSS.
A WIRE RUNS ACROSS THE TOP OF THE FRAME SO THE BIKE IS EASIER TO CARRY.
*THE WIRE GOES UNDERNEATH ON ROAD BIKES.
CANTILEVER BRAKE
GAP IS WIDER THAN FOR ROAD BIKES, SO IT'S HARDER FOR MUD TO GET STUCK IN THERE.
BECAUSE OF THE ROUGH AND TUMBLE NATURE, THE FRAME IS BIGGER AND A LITTLE HEAVIER THAN THAT OF A ROAD BIKE.
(SMALL GEARS (NOT GOING AT HIGH SPEEDS))
THE WHEELS ARE THE SAME AS ON ROAD BIKES, BUT THE TIRES ARE BUMPIER, FOR OFF-ROAD SETTINGS.
THE TRICK IS LOWER TIRE PRESSURE.
3
IT'S NOT AN ESPECIALLY SPEEDY RACE, SO FANS HAVE AN EASIER TIME CHEERING. MANY LAPS = MANY CHANCES TO CHEER!
ROAD RACES TAKE PLACE OVER A SET COURSE, AND THE FIRST TO FINISH WINS.
(30 MINUTES TO 1 HOUR)
IT'S A RACE OVER A SET PERIOD OF TIME WITH MULTIPLE LAPS! THE RIDER WITH THE MOST LAPS COMPLETED WINS!
THE COURSE IS MOSTLY JUST DIRT, SO WITH JUST SPIKES AND TAPE, YOU CAN SET UP A COURSE IN NO TIME FLAT!! THAT EASE OF SETUP IS PART OF THE APPEAL OF CYCLO-CROSS!
LIKE WITH FRIENDS, DOWN BY THE RIVERSIDE...
AH HA HA!
TAPE
TAPE
OUCH!
FWUMP
IT'S JUST DIRT, SO YOU WON'T GET HURT AS MUCH!
4
ONLY 30 MINUTES? ACTUALLY, 30 MINUTES IS PLENTY!
FULL-BODY EXERCISE!! THE ULTIMATE SCRAMBLE!!
ZERO TIME TO REST!
IT'S A CONSTANT, ALL-OUT DASH, SO 30 MINUTES TO 1 HOUR IS QUITE THE WORKOUT!!
FEELING THE ACHE IN MUSCLES I DIDN'T KNOW I HAD
CYCLO-CROSS IS POPULAR IN EUROPE, AND EVERY YEAR, THEY CROWN A NEW WORLD CHAMPION. CYCLO-CROSS IS ALSO GOOD TRAINING FOR BIKE CONTROL, SO THERE ARE PLENTY OF RACERS WHO SHINE IN CYCLO-CROSS BEFORE SWITCHING TO ROAD RACING AND PRODUCING IMPRESSIVE RESULTS.

YOWAMUSHI PEDAL

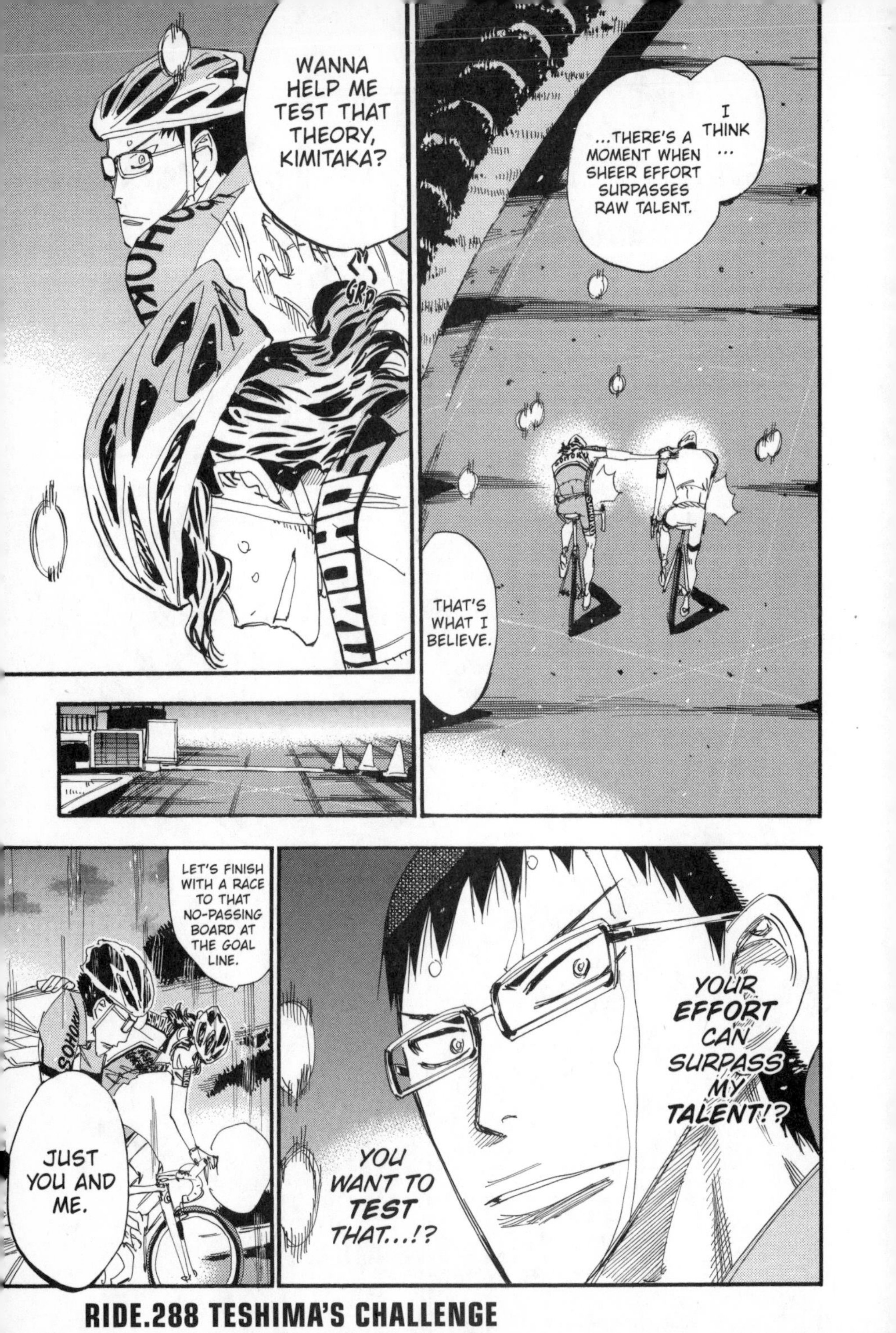
I THINK ...
...THERE'S A MOMENT WHEN SHEER EFFORT SURPASSES RAW TALENT.
THAT'S WHAT I BELIEVE.
WANNA HELP ME TEST THAT THEORY, KIMITAKA?
GRP
YOUR EFFORT CAN SURPASS MY TALENT!?
YOU WANT TO TEST THAT...!?
LET'S FINISH WITH A RACE TO THAT NO-PASSING BOARD AT THE GOAL LINE.
JUST YOU AND ME.

RIDE.288 TESHIMA'S CHALLENGE

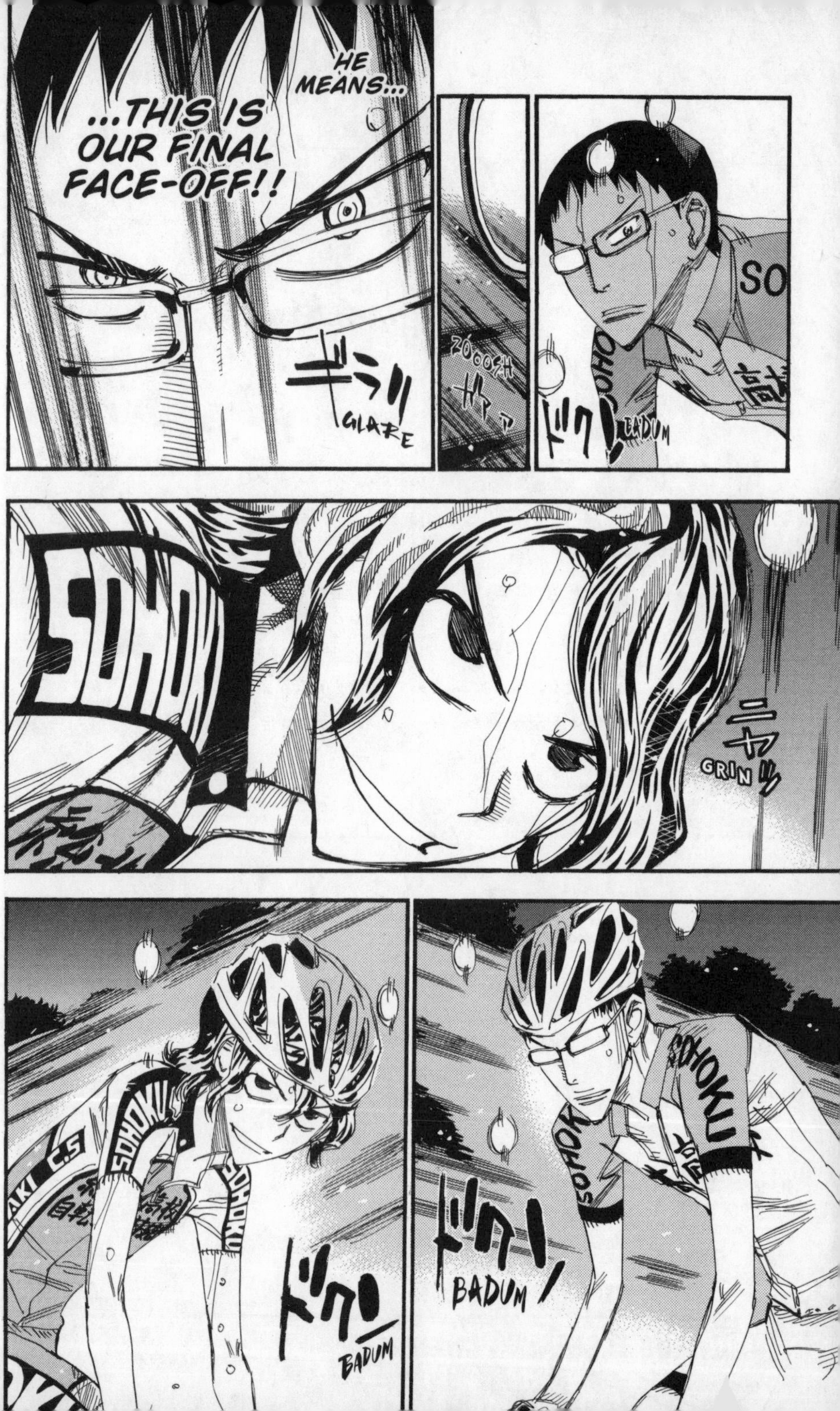

BADUM
ZOOOSH
HE MEANS...
...THIS IS OUR FINAL FACE-OFF!!
GLARE
GRIN
BADUM
BADUM

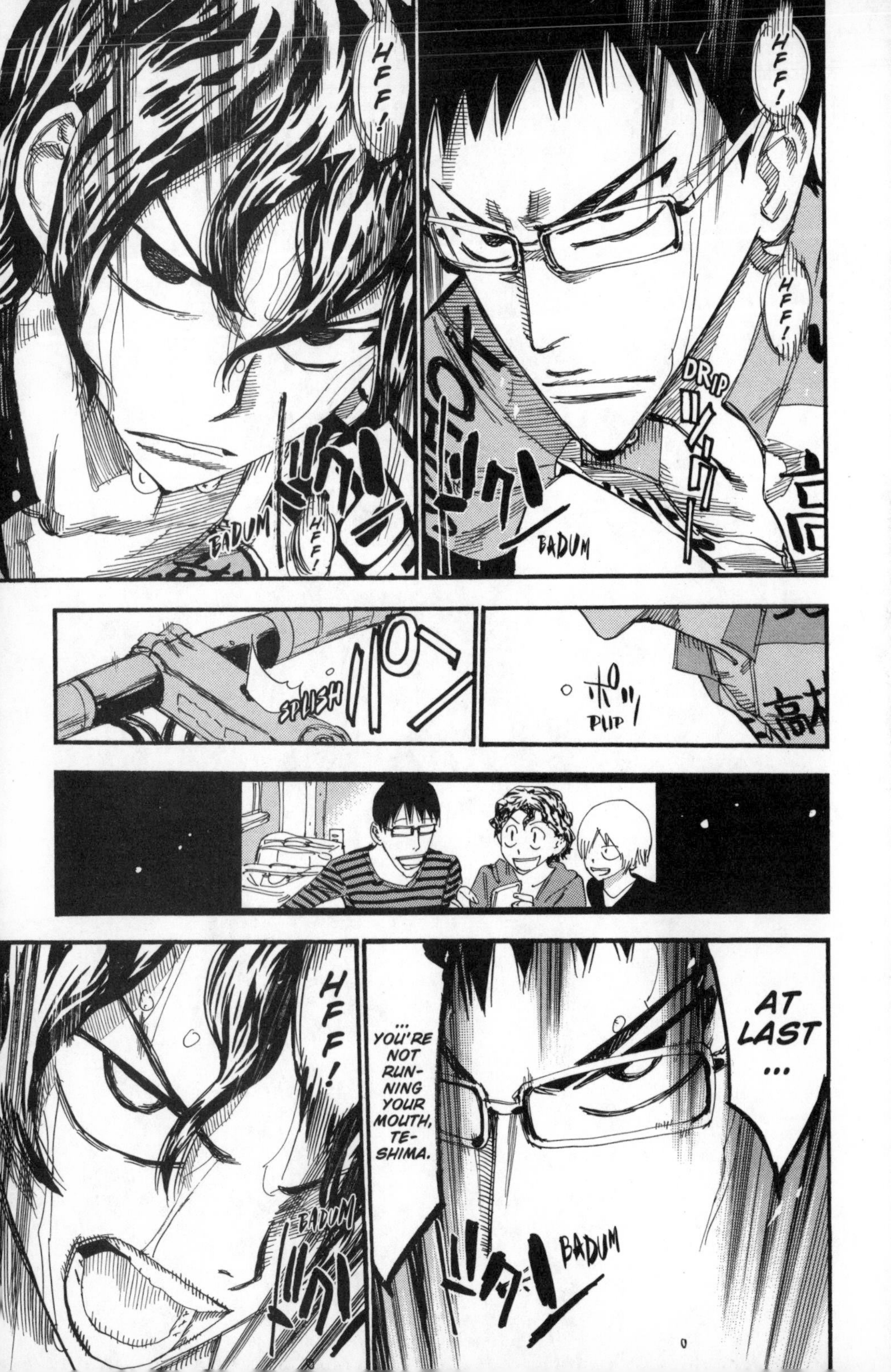
HFF!
HFF!
DRIP
BADUM
HFF!
BADUM
HFF!
PLIP
SPLISH
AT LAST...
...YOU'RE NOT RUN-NING YOUR MOUTH, TE-SHIMA.
BADUM
HFF!
BADUM

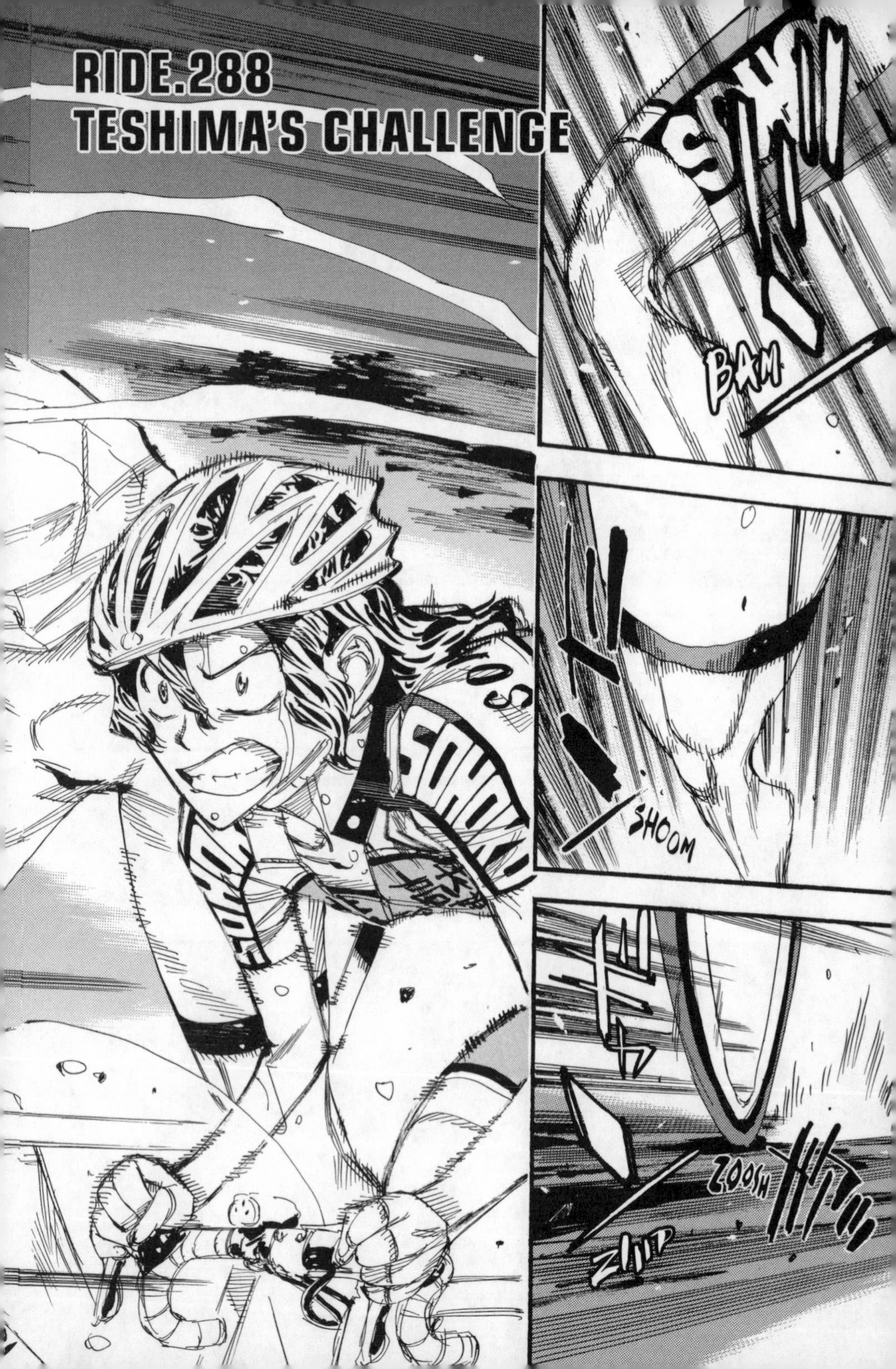
BAM
SHOOM
ZOOSH
ZIIIP
RIDE.288
TESHIMA'S CHALLENGE

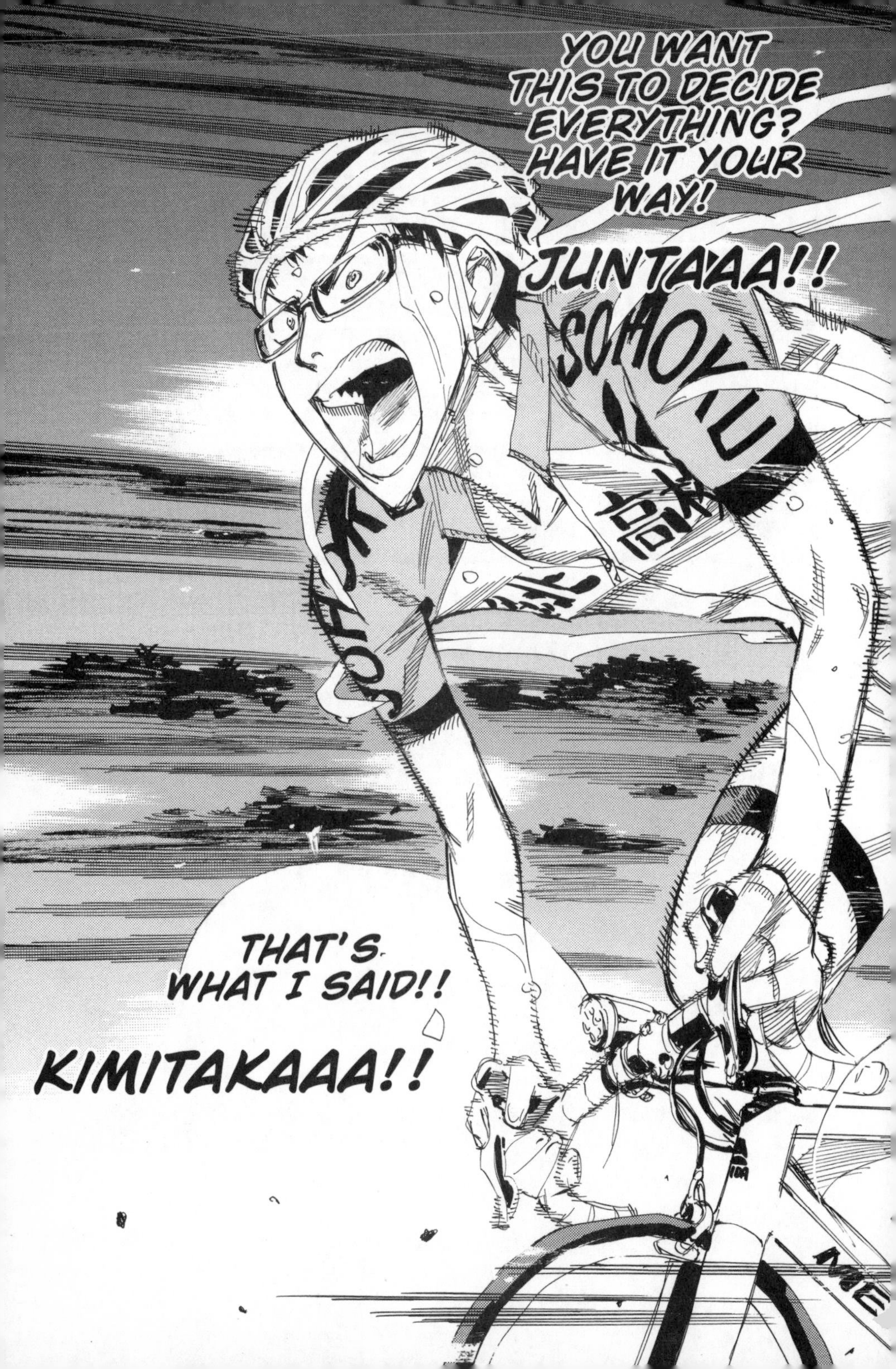

YOU WANT THIS TO DECIDE EVERYTHING? HAVE IT YOUR WAY!
JUNTAAA!!
SOHOKU
THAT'S WHAT I SAID!!
KIMITAKAAA!!

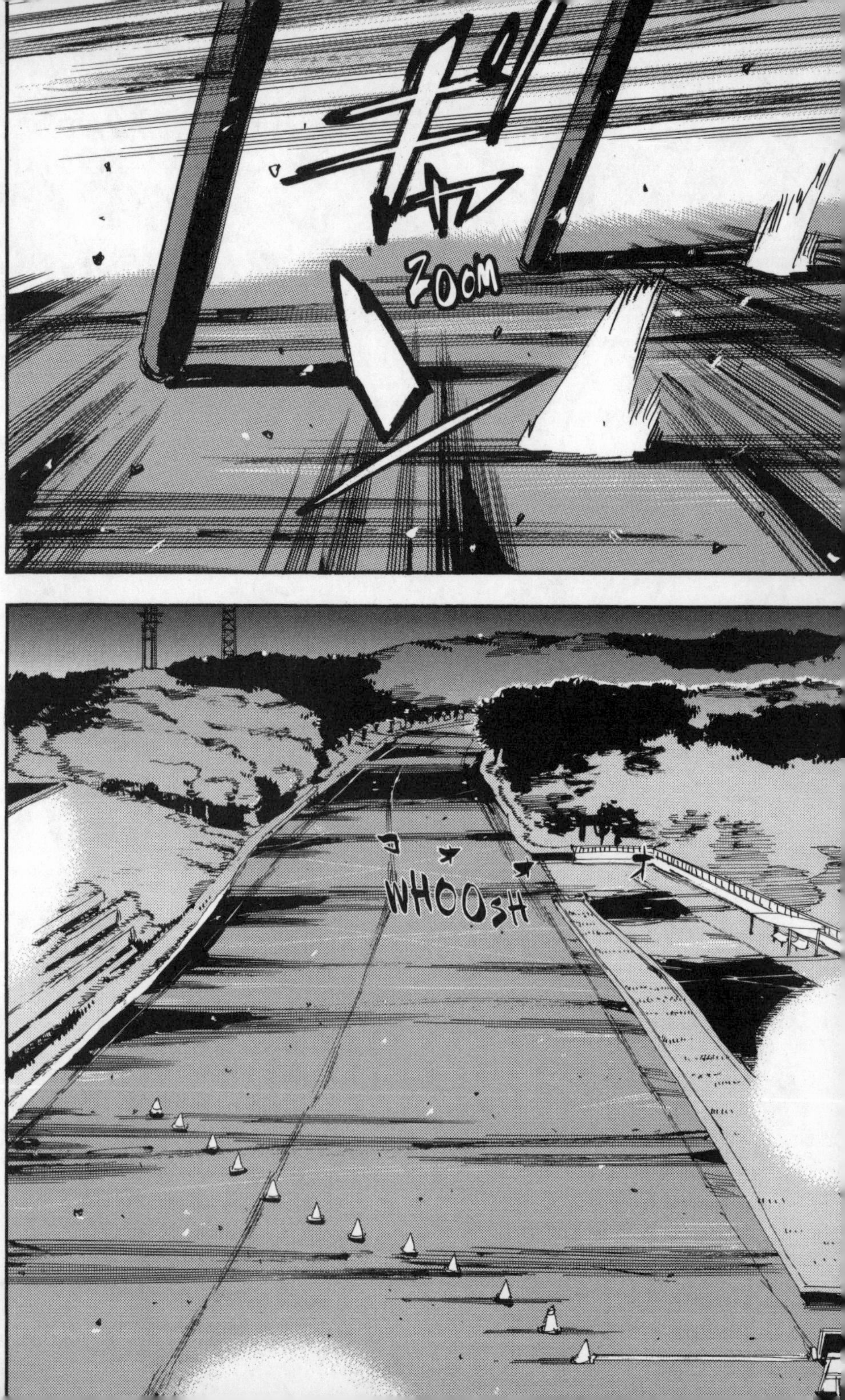
ZOOM
WHOOSH

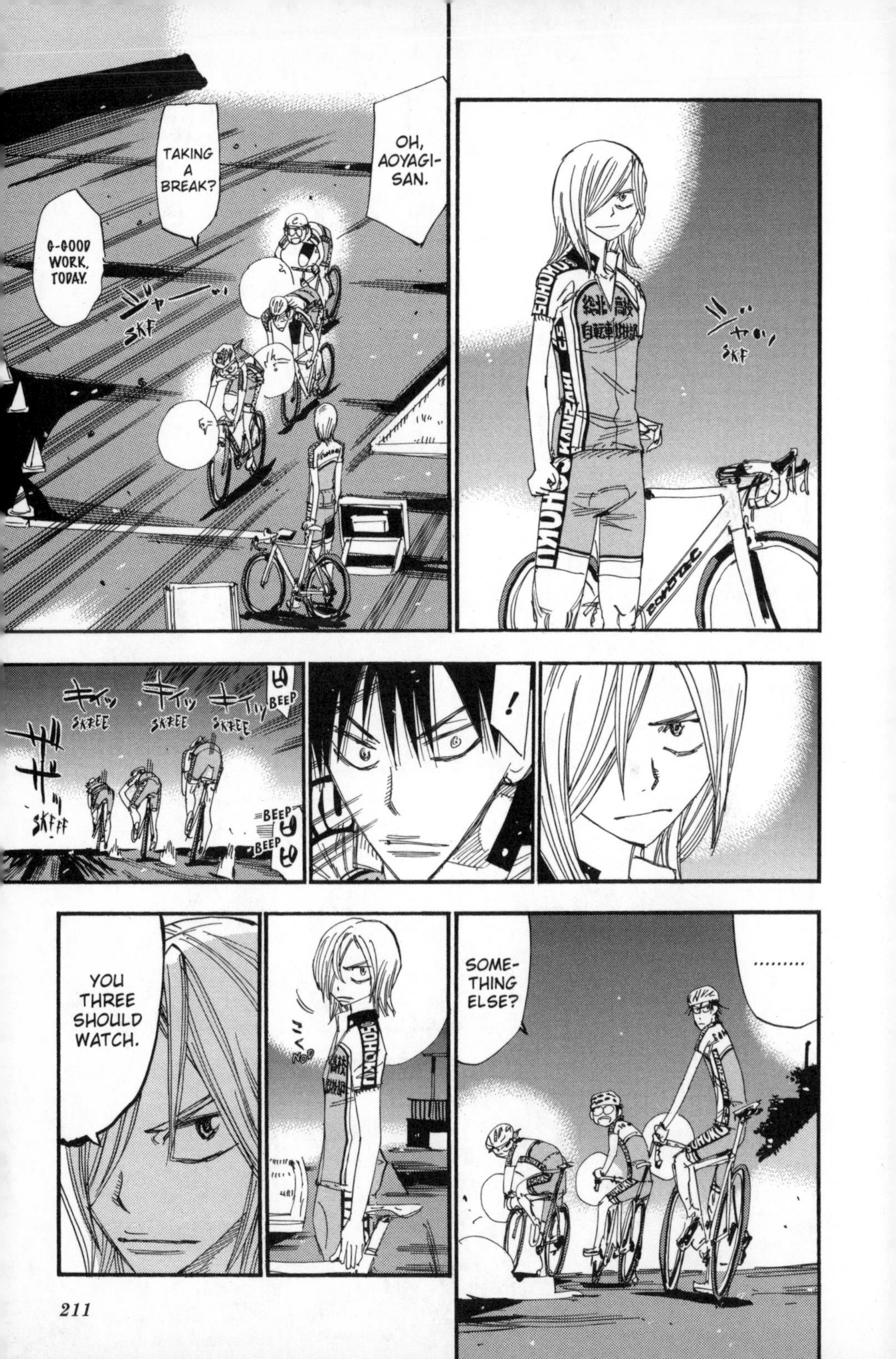

SKF
OH, AOYAGI-SAN.
TAKING A BREAK?
G-GOOD WORK, TODAY.
SKF
!
BEEP
SKREE
SKREE
SKREE
BEEP
BEEP
SKFFF
....
SOME-THING ELSE?
NOD
YOU THREE SHOULD WATCH.

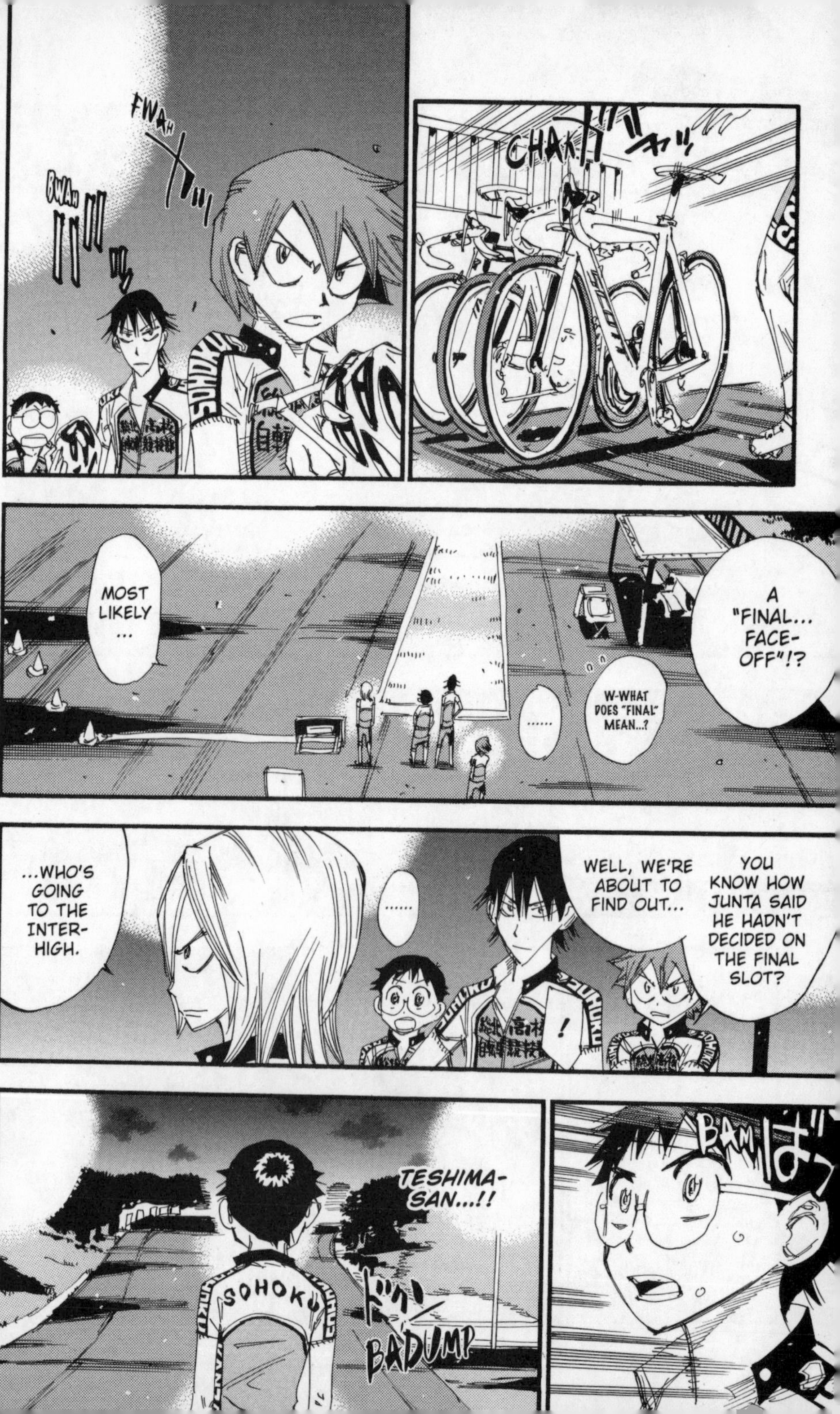
CHAK
FWAH
BWAH
A "FINAL... FACE-OFF"!?
W-WHAT DOES "FINAL" MEAN...?
......
MOST LIKELY ...
YOU KNOW HOW JUNTA SAID HE HADN'T DECIDED ON THE FINAL SLOT?
WELL, WE'RE ABOUT TO FIND OUT...
!
......
...WHO'S GOING TO THE INTER-HIGH.
BAM
TESHIMA-SAN...!!
BADUMP

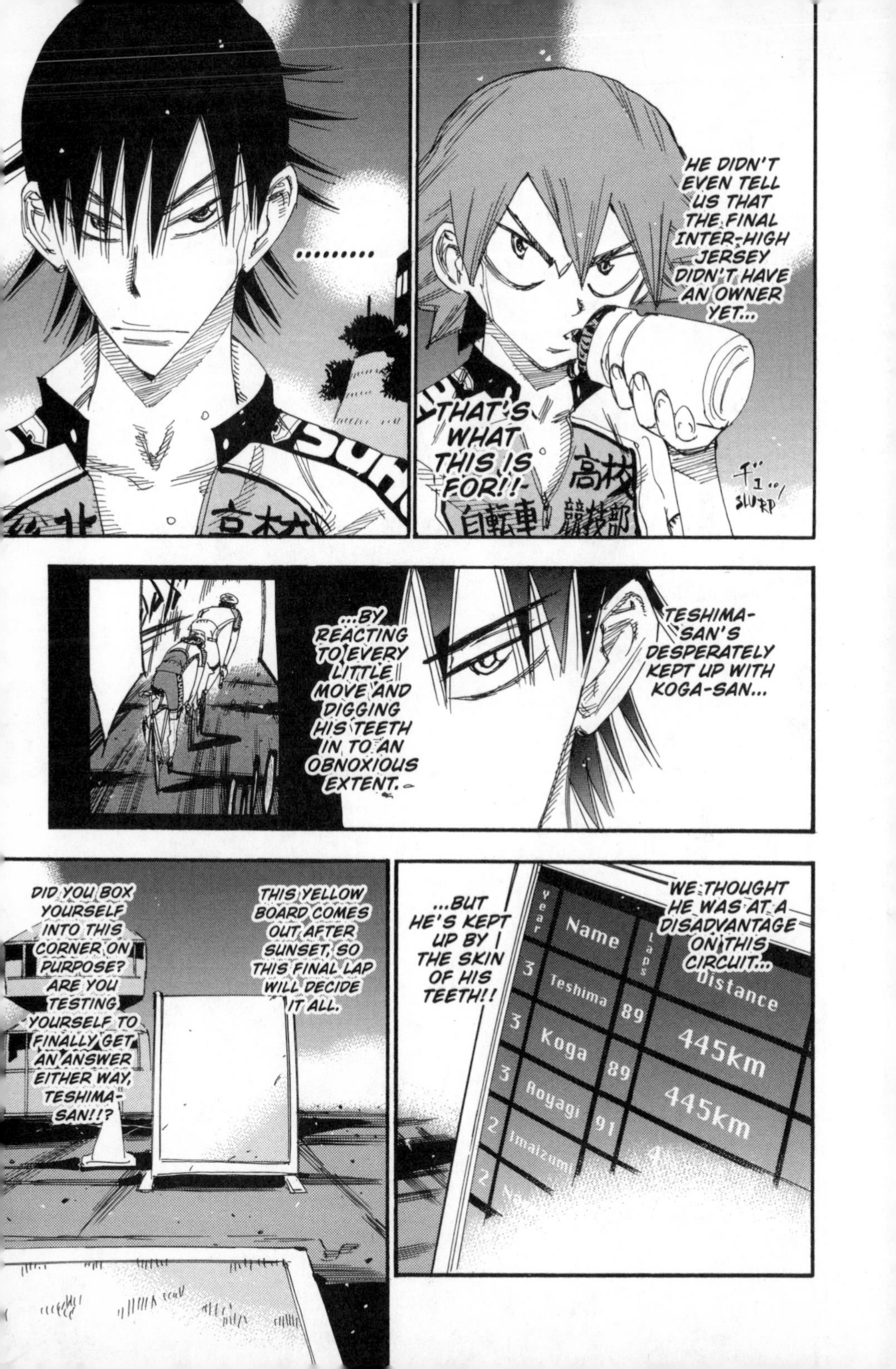
HE DIDN'T EVEN TELL US THAT THE FINAL INTER-HIGH JERSEY DIDN'T HAVE AN OWNER YET...
THAT'S WHAT THIS IS FOR!!
SLURP
....
TESHIMA-SAN'S DESPERATELY KEPT UP WITH KOGA-SAN...
...BY REACTING TO EVERY LITTLE MOVE AND DIGGING HIS TEETH IN TO AN OBNOXIOUS EXTENT.
WE THOUGHT HE WAS AT A DISADVANTAGE ON THIS CIRCUIT...
...BUT HE'S KEPT UP BY THE SKIN OF HIS TEETH!!
Year Name Laps Distance
3 Teshima 89
3 Koga 89 445km
3 Aoyagi 91 445km
2 Imaizumi
THIS YELLOW BOARD COMES OUT AFTER SUNSET, SO THIS FINAL LAP WILL DECIDE IT ALL.
DID YOU BOX YOURSELF INTO THIS CORNER ON PURPOSE? ARE YOU TESTING YOURSELF TO FINALLY GET AN ANSWER EITHER WAY, TESHIMA-SAN!!?

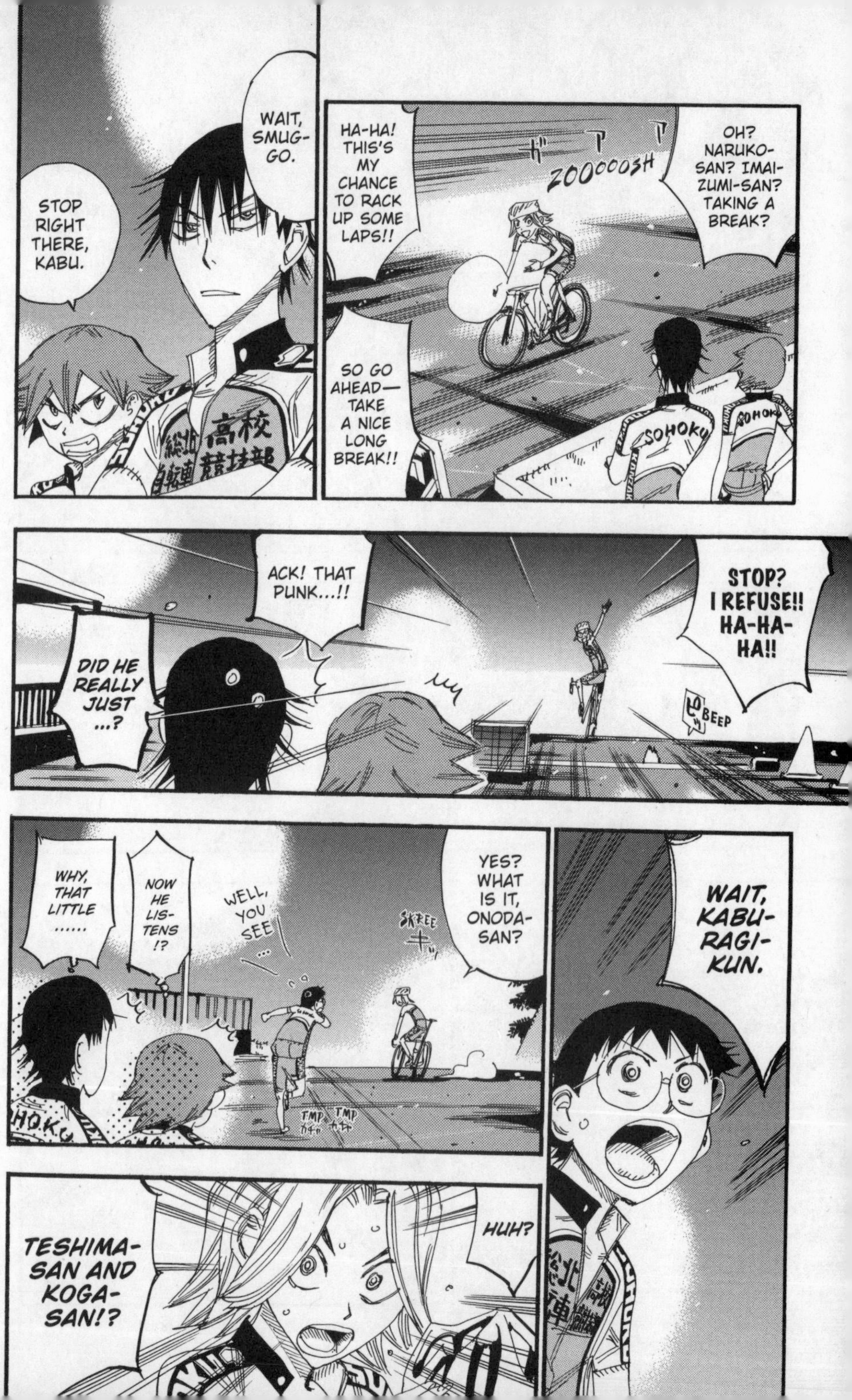
OH? NARUKO-SAN? IMAIZUMI-SAN? TAKING A BREAK?
ZOOOOOSH
HA-HA! THIS'S MY CHANCE TO RACK UP SOME LAPS!!
SO GO AHEAD—TAKE A NICE LONG BREAK!!
WAIT, SMUG-GO.
STOP RIGHT THERE, KABU.
STOP? I REFUSE!! HA-HA-HA!!
BEEP
ACK! THAT PUNK...!!
DID HE REALLY JUST ...?
WAIT, KABURAGI-KUN.
YES? WHAT IS IT, ONODA-SAN?
SKREE
WELL, YOU SEE ...
TMP
TMP
NOW HE LISTENS!?
WHY, THAT LITTLE ......
HUH?
TESHIMA-SAN AND KOGA-SAN!?

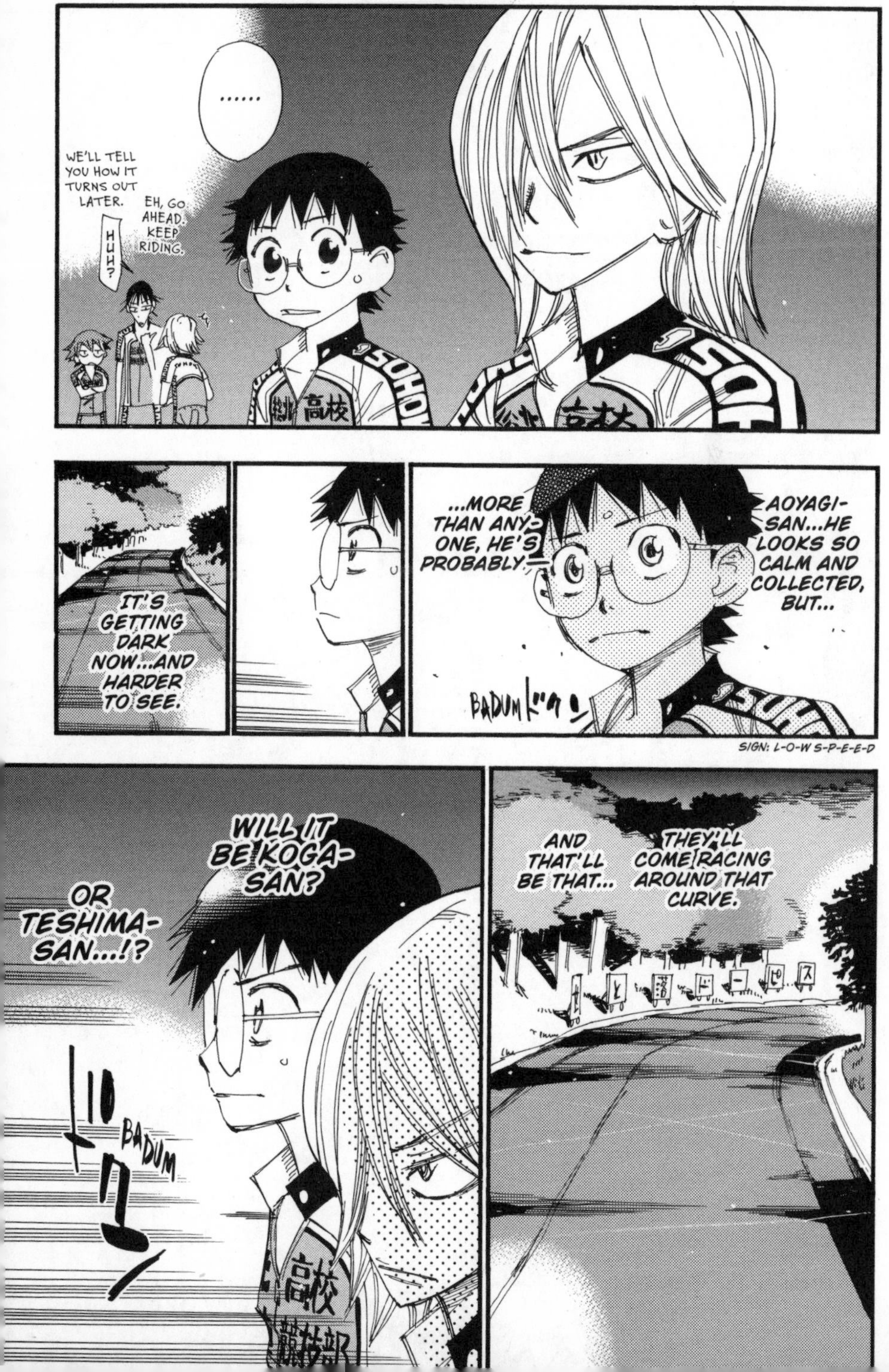
......
EH, GO AHEAD. KEEP RIDING.
HUH?
WE'LL TELL YOU HOW IT TURNS OUT LATER.
AOYAGI-SAN...HE LOOKS SO CALM AND COLLECTED, BUT...
...MORE THAN ANYONE, HE'S PROBABLY
BADUM
IT'S GETTING DARK NOW...AND HARDER TO SEE.
THEY'LL COME RACING AROUND THAT CURVE.
AND THAT'LL BE THAT...
WILL IT BE KOGA-SAN?
OR TESHIMA-SAN...!?
BADUM
SIGN: L-O-W S-P-E-E-D

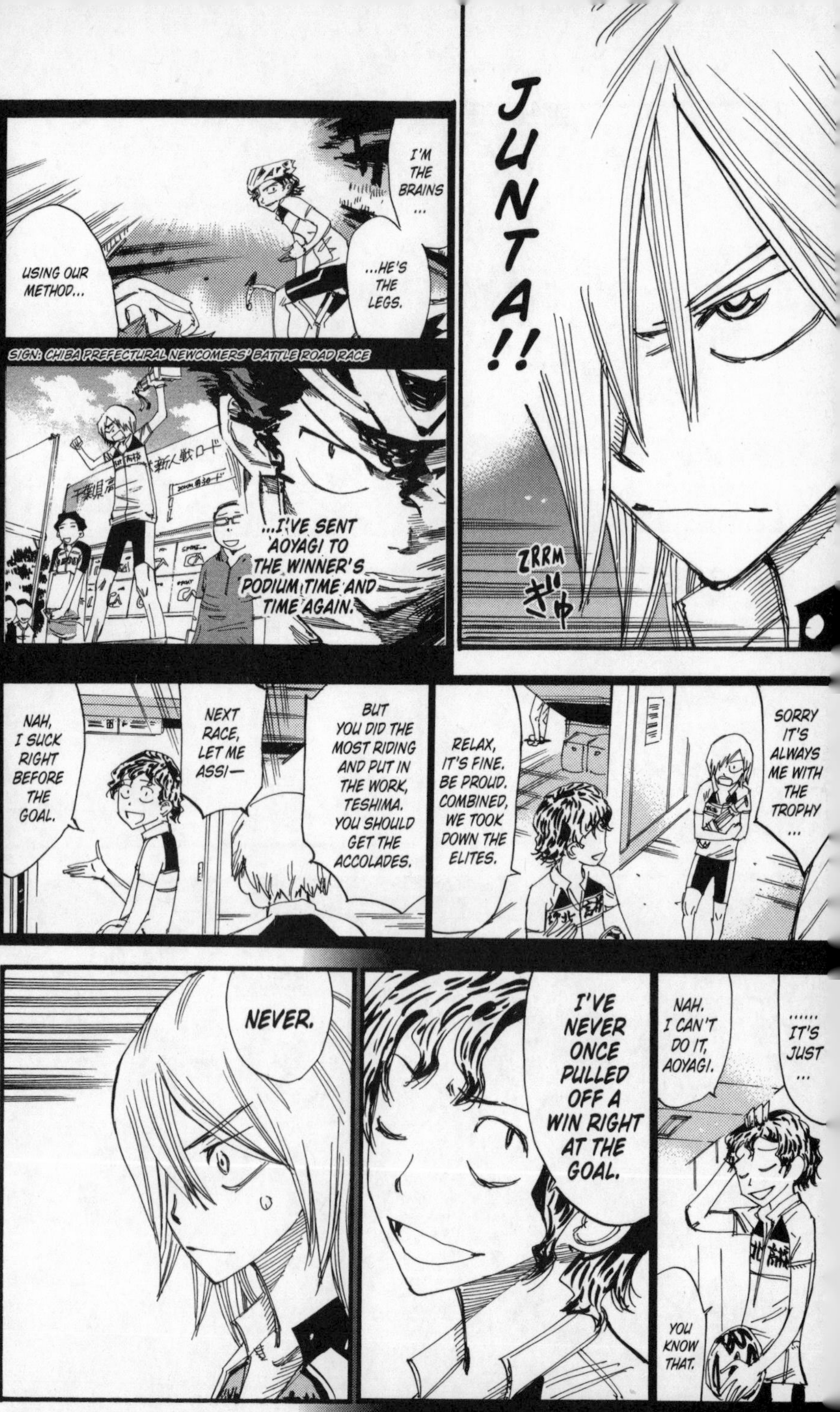
JUNTA!!
ZRRM
ぎゅ
I'M THE BRAINS...
...HE'S THE LEGS.
USING OUR METHOD...
SIGN: CHIBA PREFECTURAL NEWCOMERS' BATTLE ROAD RACE
...I'VE SENT AOYAGI TO THE WINNER'S PODIUM TIME AND TIME AGAIN.
SORRY IT'S ALWAYS ME WITH THE TROPHY...
RELAX, IT'S FINE. BE PROUD. COMBINED, WE TOOK DOWN THE ELITES.
BUT YOU DID THE MOST RIDING AND PUT IN THE WORK, TESHIMA. YOU SHOULD GET THE ACCOLADES.
NEXT RACE, LET ME ASSI—
NAH, I SUCK RIGHT BEFORE THE GOAL.
......IT'S JUST...
NAH. I CAN'T DO IT, AOYAGI.
YOU KNOW THAT.
I'VE NEVER ONCE PULLED OFF A WIN RIGHT AT THE GOAL.
NEVER.

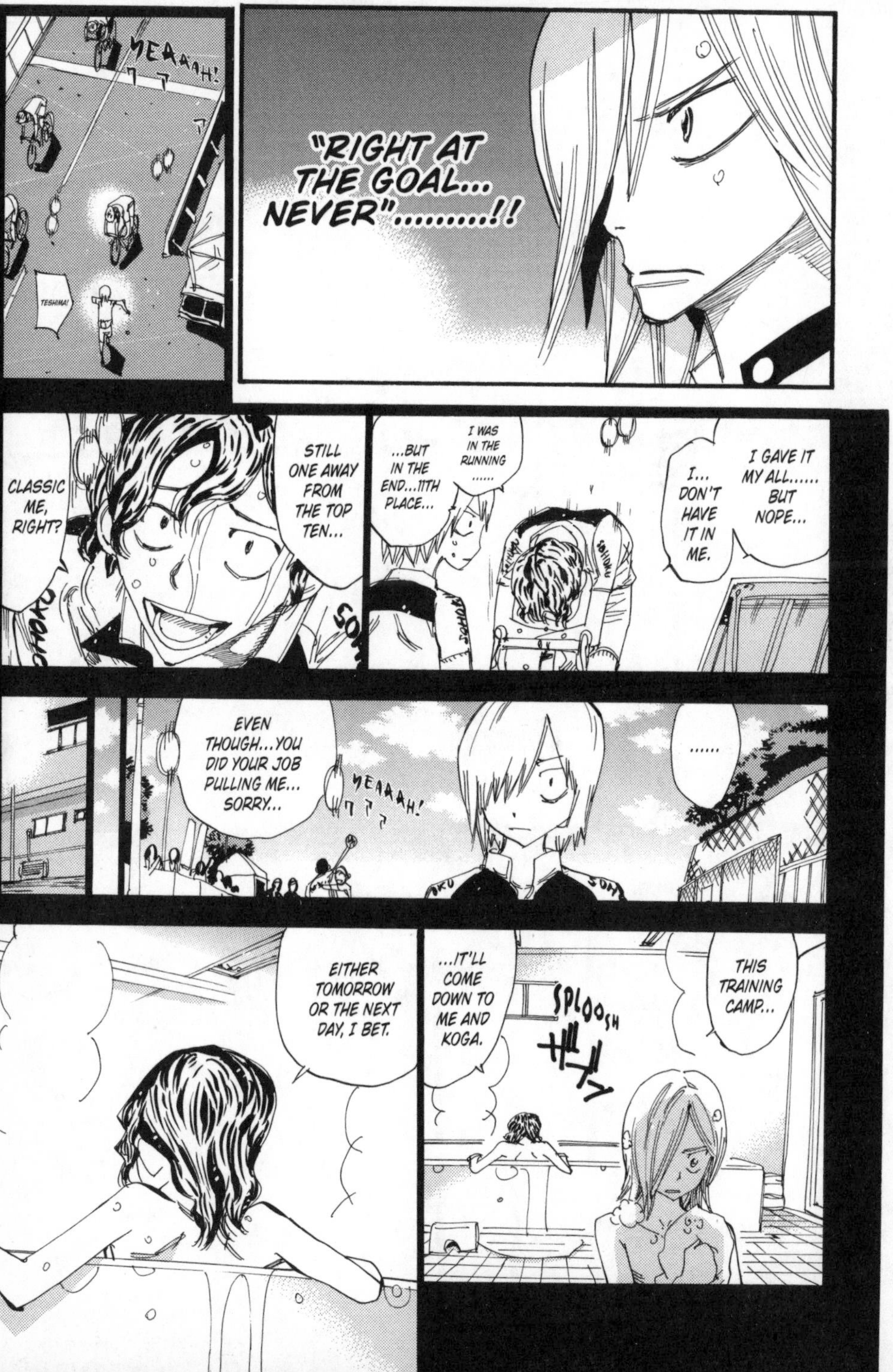
"RIGHT AT THE GOAL... NEVER"..........!!
YEAAAH!
TESHIMA!
I GAVE IT MY ALL...... BUT NOPE...
I... DON'T HAVE IT IN ME.
I WAS IN THE RUNNING ......
...BUT IN THE END...11TH PLACE...
STILL ONE AWAY FROM THE TOP TEN...
CLASSIC ME, RIGHT?
......
EVEN THOUGH...YOU DID YOUR JOB PULLING ME... SORRY...
YEAAAH!
THIS TRAINING CAMP...
SPLOOSH
...IT'LL COME DOWN TO ME AND KOGA.
EITHER TOMORROW OR THE NEXT DAY, I BET.

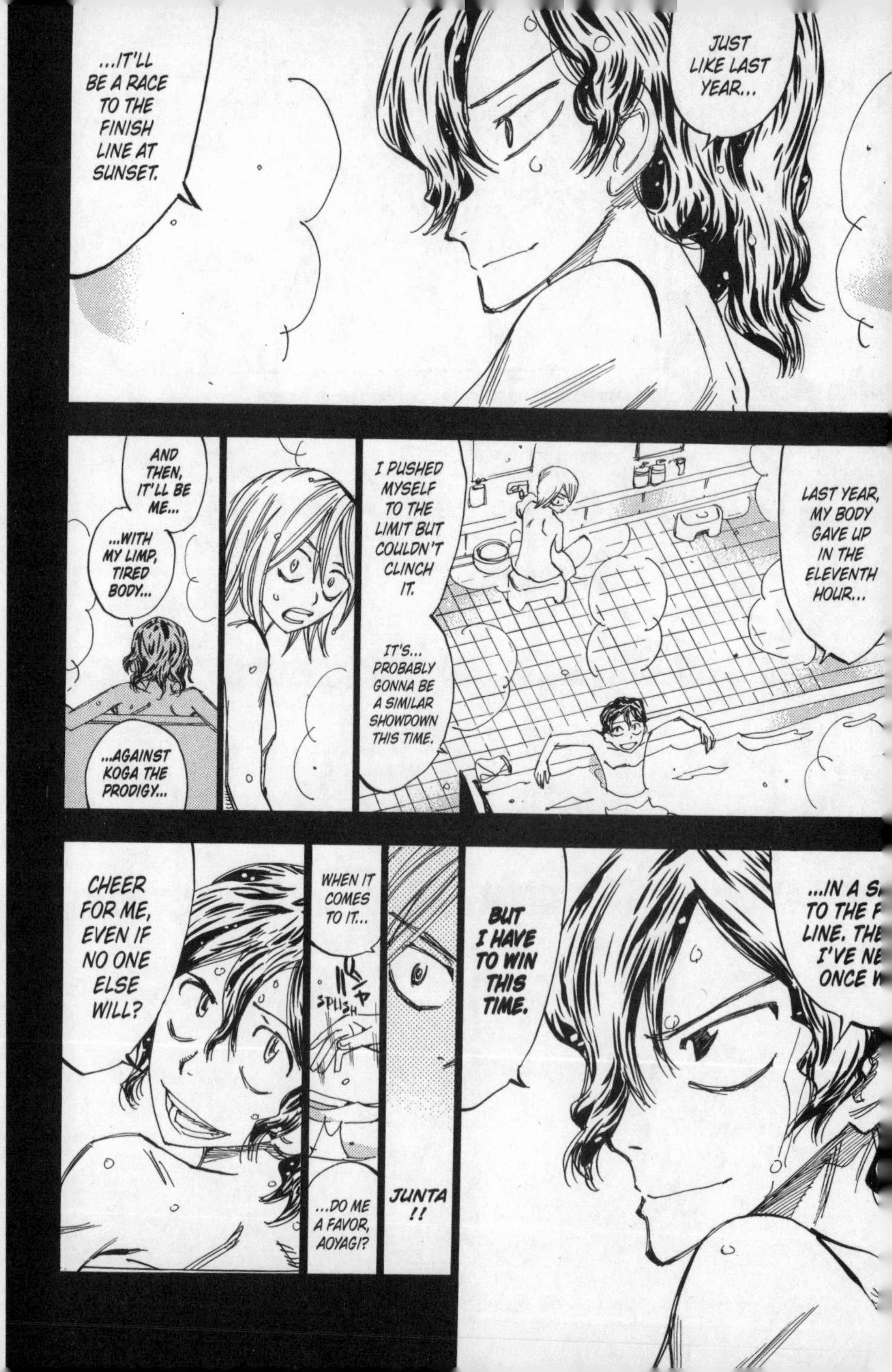
JUST LIKE LAST YEAR...
...IT'LL BE A RACE TO THE FINISH LINE AT SUNSET.
LAST YEAR, MY BODY GAVE UP IN THE ELEVENTH HOUR...
I PUSHED MYSELF TO THE LIMIT BUT COULDN'T CLINCH IT.
IT'S... PROBABLY GONNA BE A SIMILAR SHOWDOWN THIS TIME.
AND THEN, IT'LL BE ME...
...WITH MY LIMP, TIRED BODY...
...AGAINST KOGA THE PRODIGY...
BUT I HAVE TO WIN THIS TIME.
WHEN IT COMES TO IT...
SPLISH
JUNTA!!
...DO ME A FAVOR, AOYAGI?
CHEER FOR ME, EVEN IF NO ONE ELSE WILL?

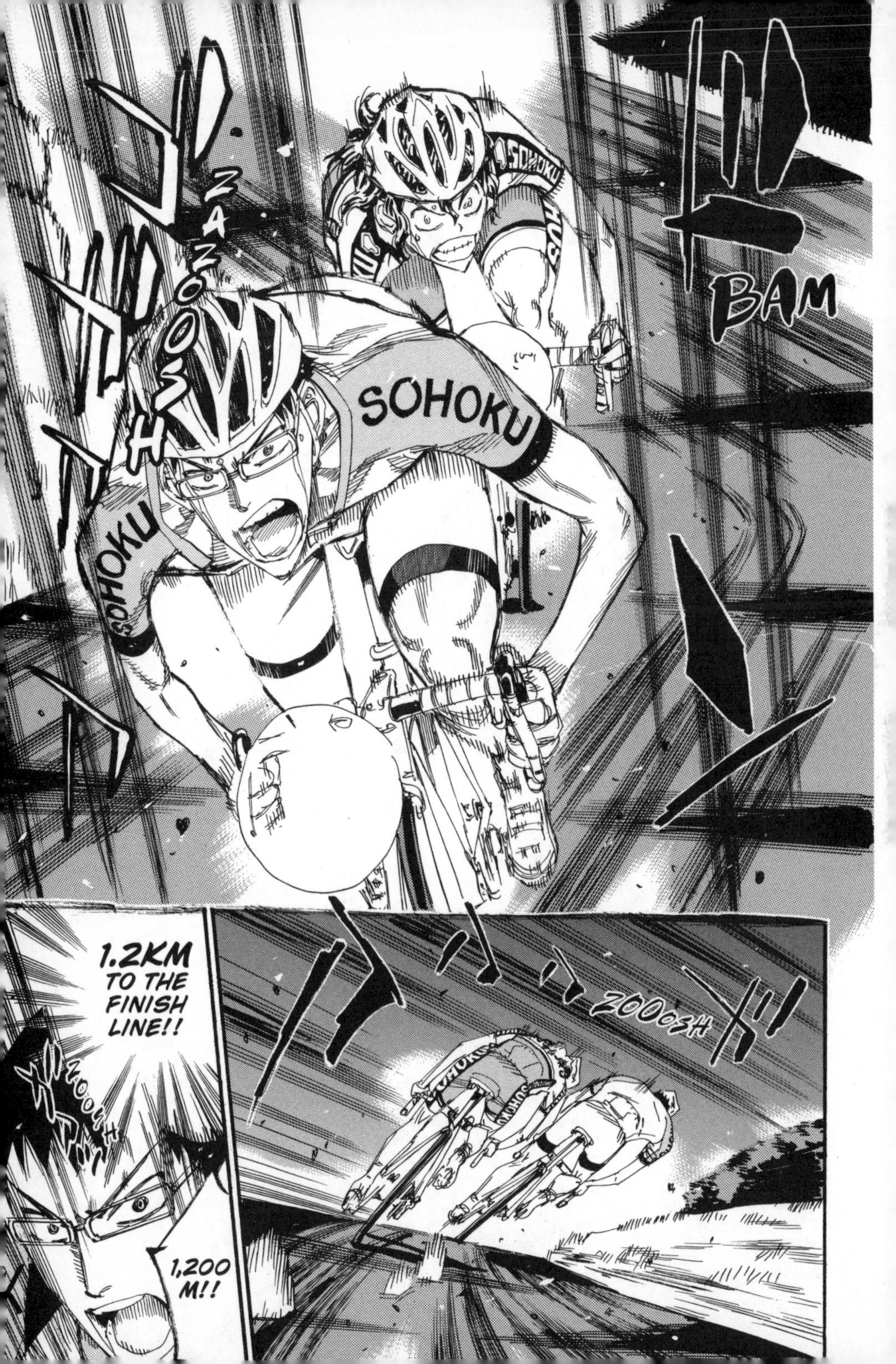

BAM
ZAZOOOSH
SOHOKU
ZOOOSH
1.2KM TO THE FINISH LINE!!
ZOOOSH
1,200 M!!

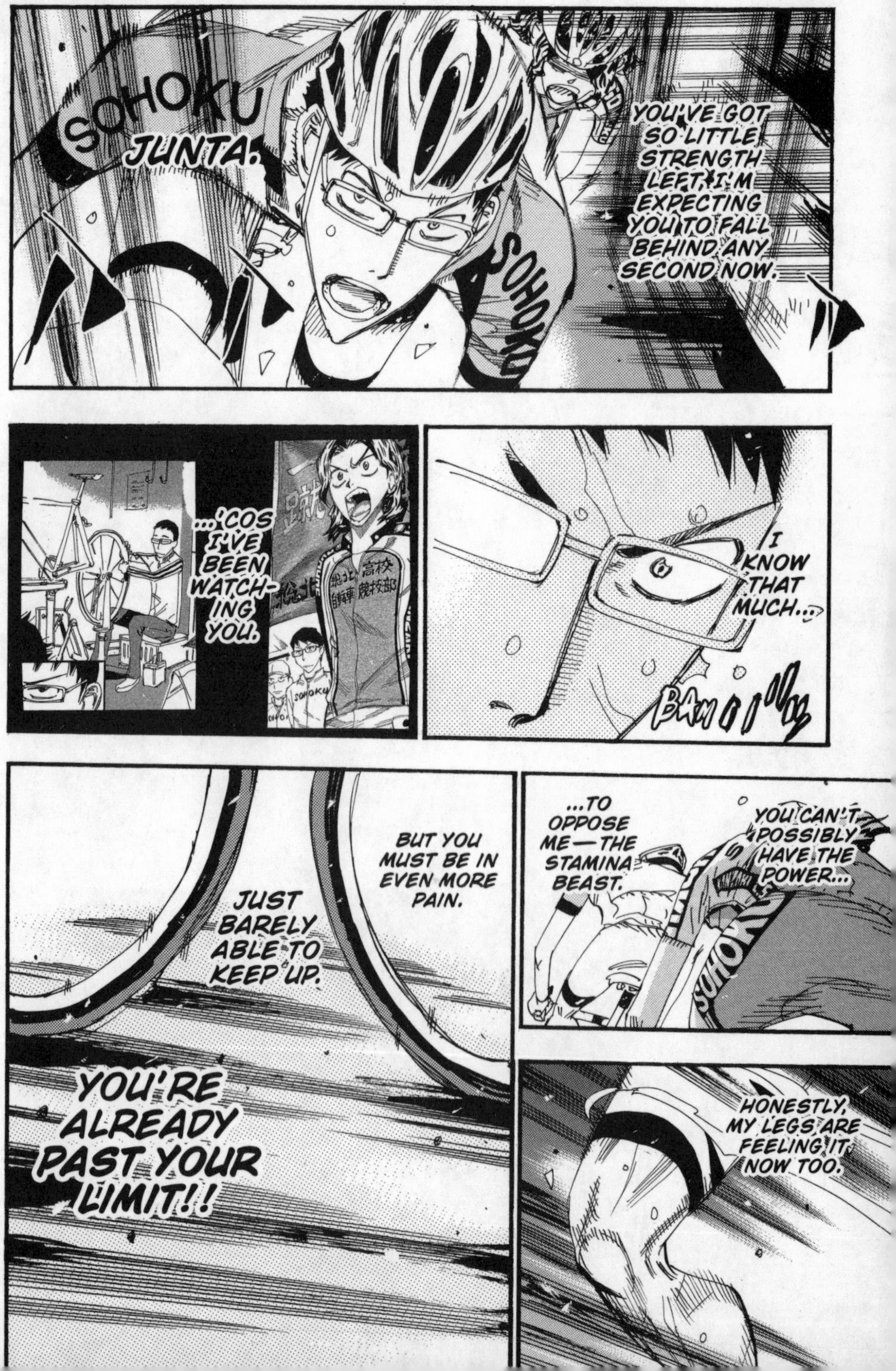
SOHOKU
JUNTA.
YOU'VE GOT SO LITTLE STRENGTH LEFT I'M EXPECTING YOU TO FALL BEHIND ANY SECOND NOW.
I KNOW THAT MUCH...
BAM!!
...'COS I'VE BEEN WATCHING YOU.
YOU CAN'T POSSIBLY HAVE THE POWER...
...TO OPPOSE ME—THE STAMINA BEAST.
HONESTLY, MY LEGS ARE FEELING IT NOW TOO.
BUT YOU MUST BE IN EVEN MORE PAIN.
JUST BARELY ABLE TO KEEP UP.
YOU'RE ALREADY PAST YOUR LIMIT!!

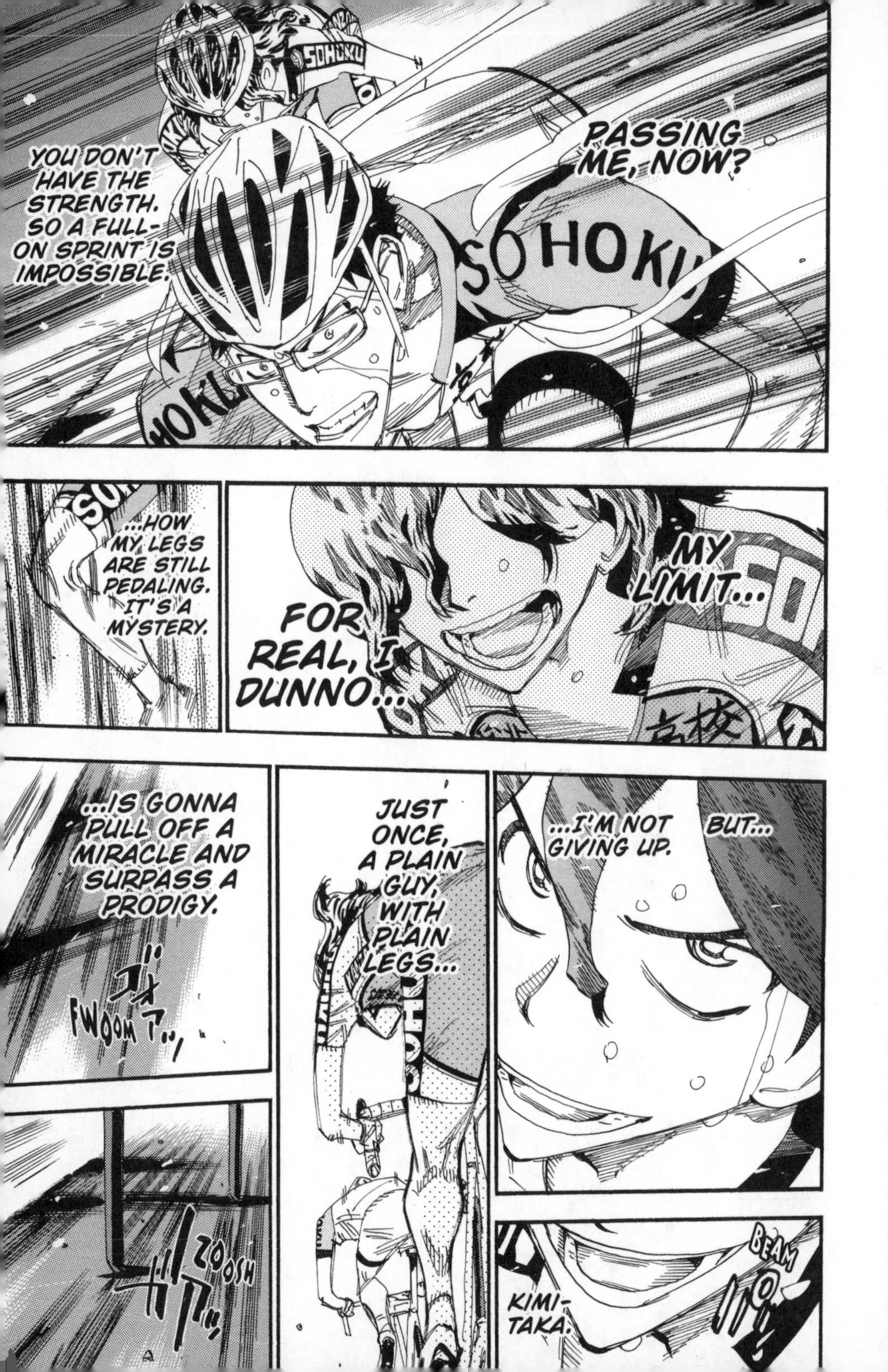
PASSING ME, NOW?
YOU DON'T HAVE THE STRENGTH. SO A FULL-ON SPRINT IS IMPOSSIBLE.
MY LIMIT...
FOR REAL, I DUNNO...
...HOW MY LEGS ARE STILL PEDALING. IT'S A MYSTERY.
BUT...
...I'M NOT GIVING UP.
BEAM
KIMI-TAKA.
JUST ONCE, A PLAIN GUY, WITH PLAIN LEGS...
...IS GONNA PULL OFF A MIRACLE AND SURPASS A PRODIGY.
FWOOM
ZOOSH

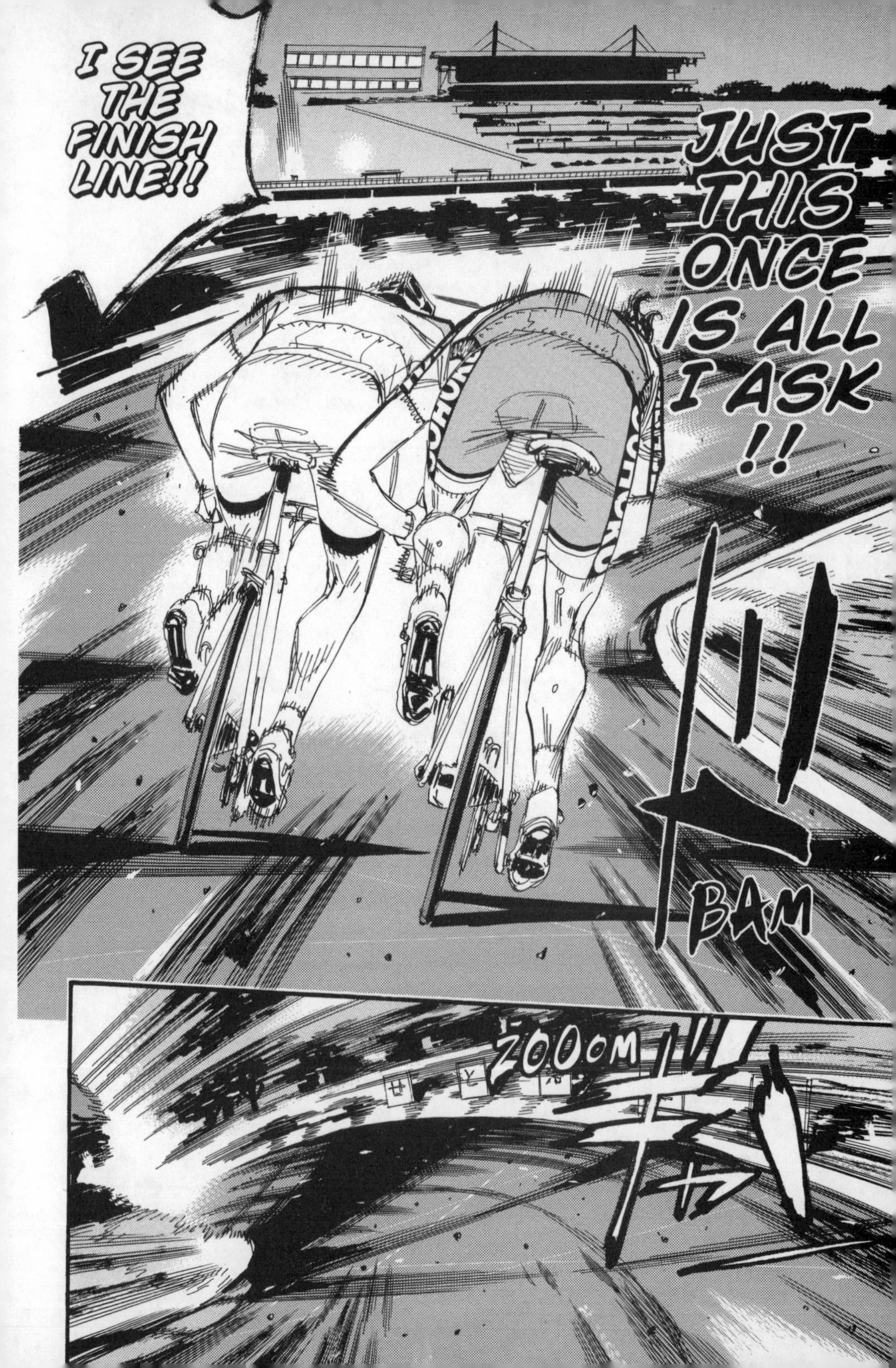
JUST THIS ONCE IS ALL I ASK!!
I SEE THE FINISH LINE!!
BAM
ZOOOM

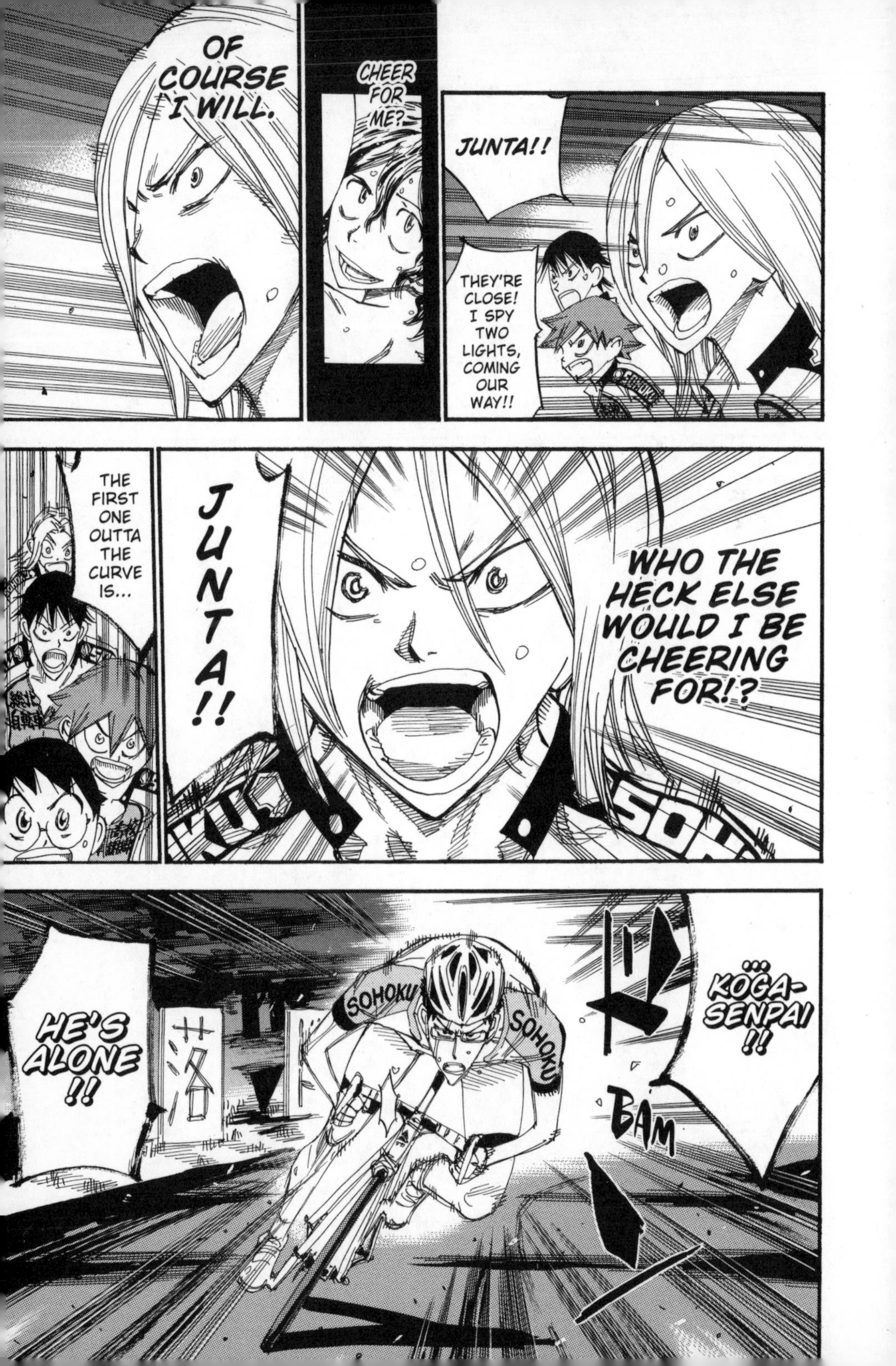
JUNTA!!
THEY'RE CLOSE! I SPY TWO LIGHTS, COMING OUR WAY!!
CHEER FOR ME?
OF COURSE I WILL.
WHO THE HECK ELSE WOULD I BE CHEERING FOR!?
JUNTA!!
THE FIRST ONE OUTTA THE CURVE IS...
...KŌGA-SENPAI!!
BAM
SOHOKU
SOHOKU
HE'S ALONE!!

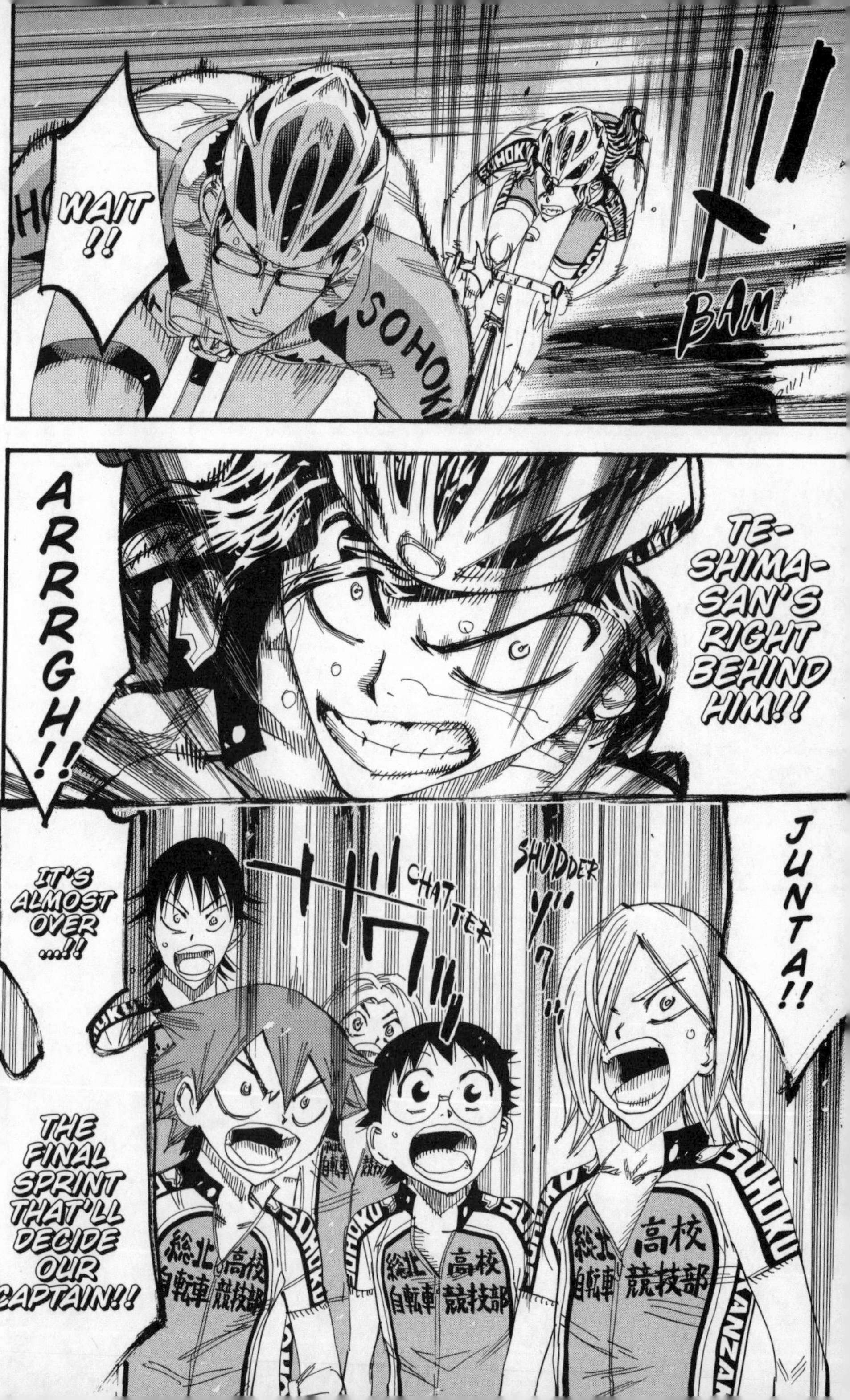
BAM
WAIT!!
TE-SHIMA-SAN'S RIGHT BEHIND HIM!!
ARRRGH!!
JUNTA!!
SHUDDER
CHATTER
IT'S ALMOST OVER...!!
THE FINAL SPRINT THAT'LL DECIDE OUR CAPTAIN!!

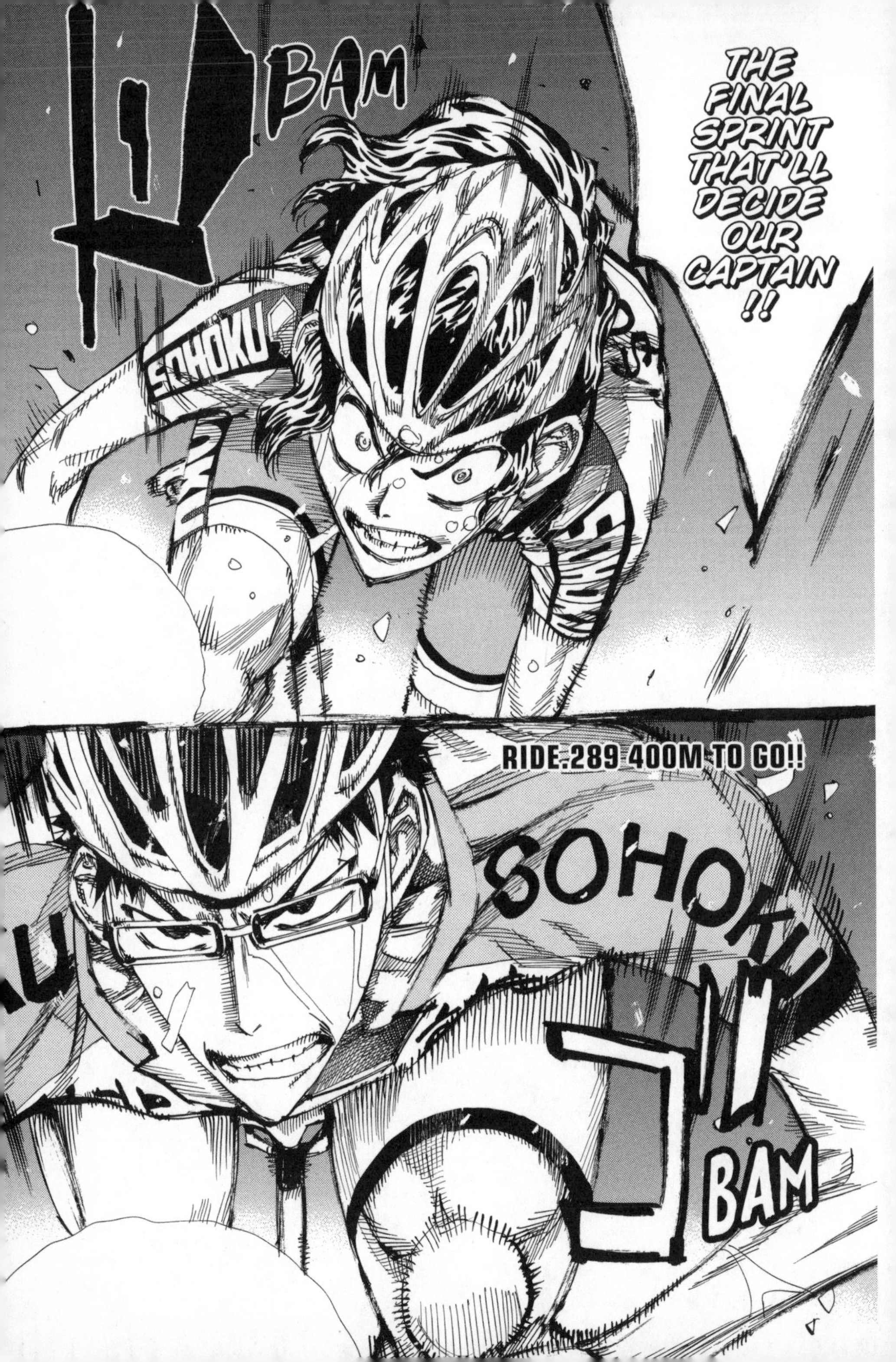
THE FINAL SPRINT THAT'LL DECIDE OUR CAPTAIN!!
BAM
SOHOKU
RIDE.289 400M TO GO!!
BAM

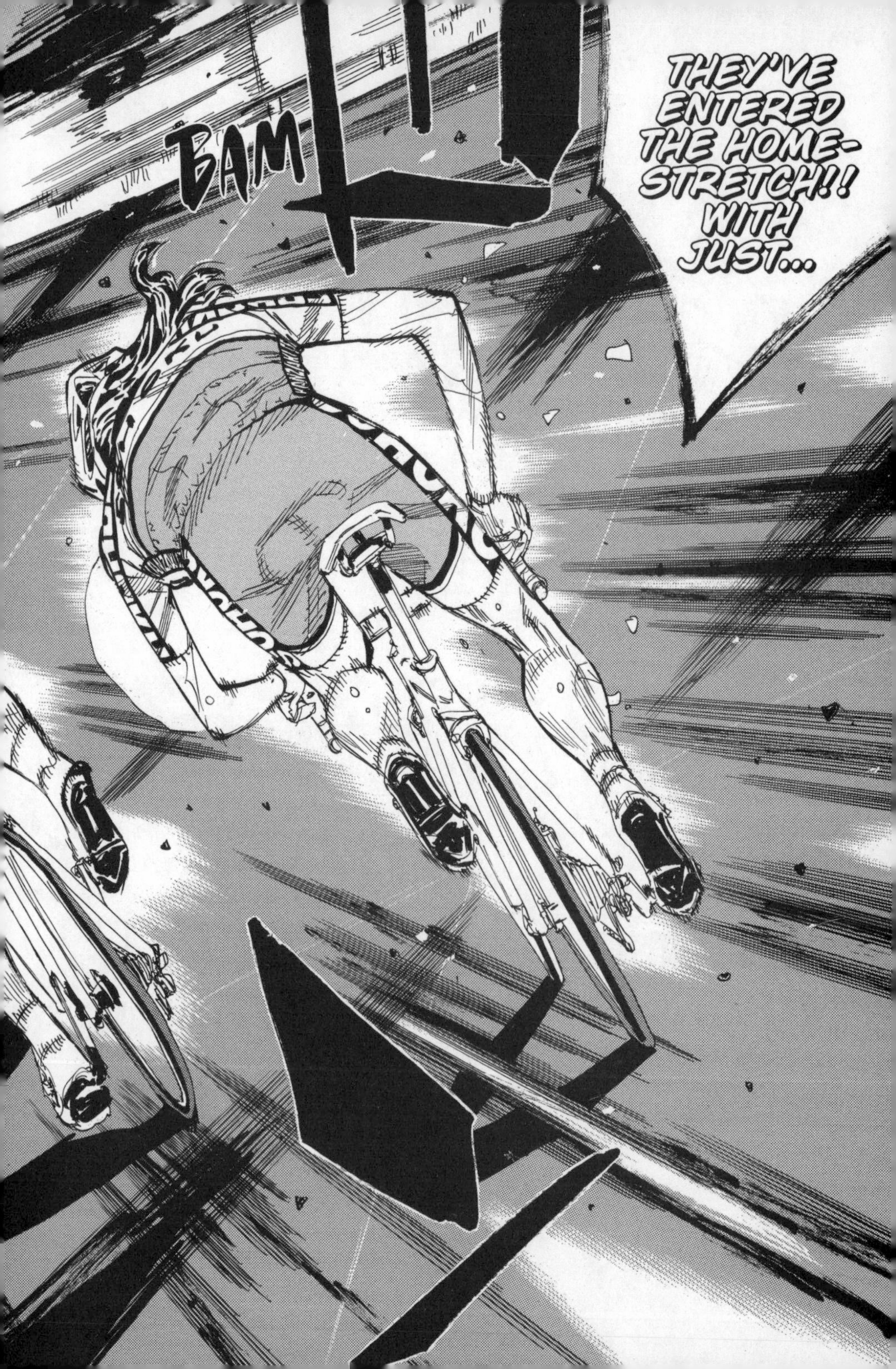
THEY'VE ENTERED THE HOME-STRETCH!! WITH JUST...
BAM

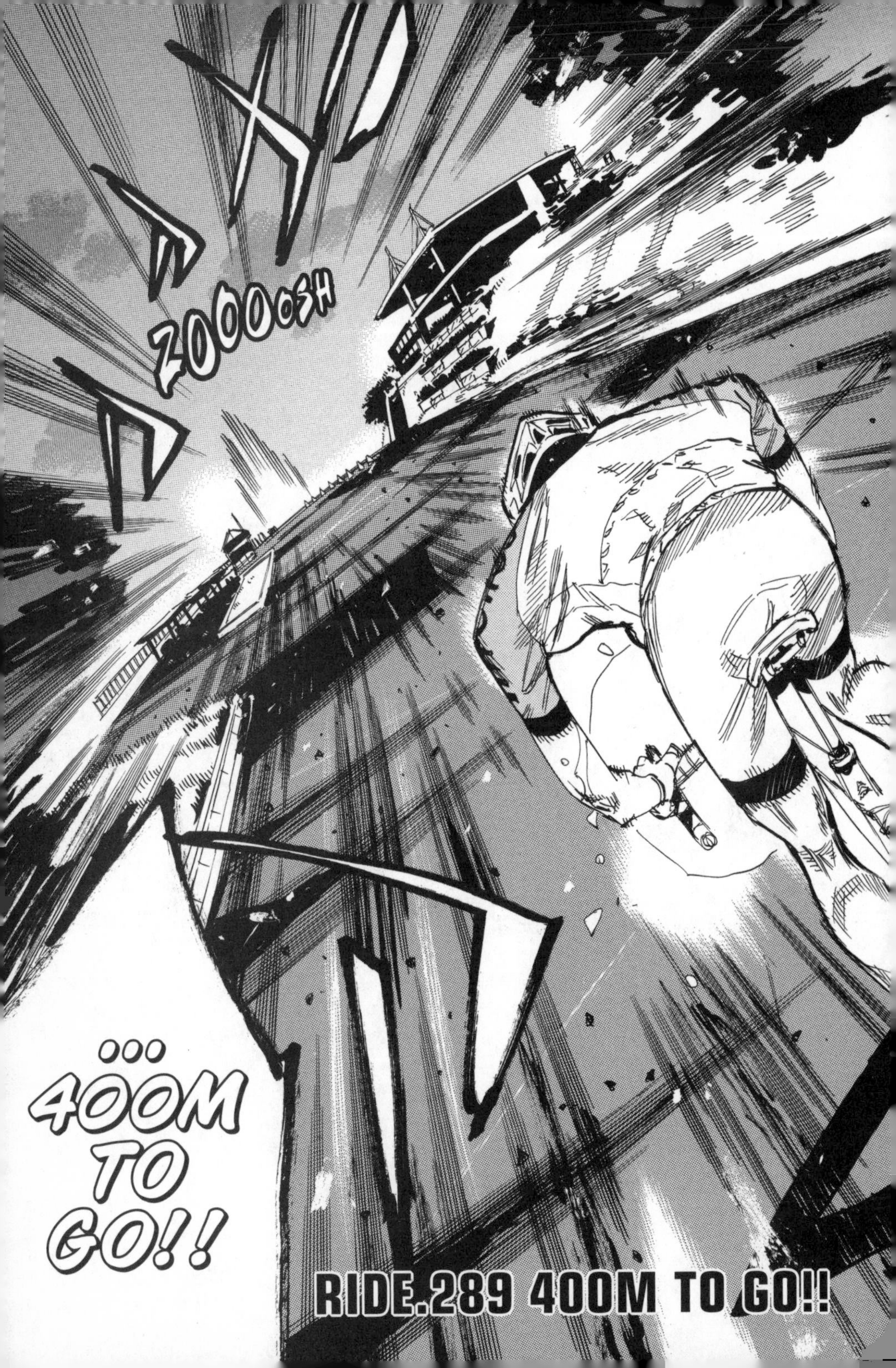ZOOOOSH
...400M TO GO!!
RIDE.289 400M TO GO!!

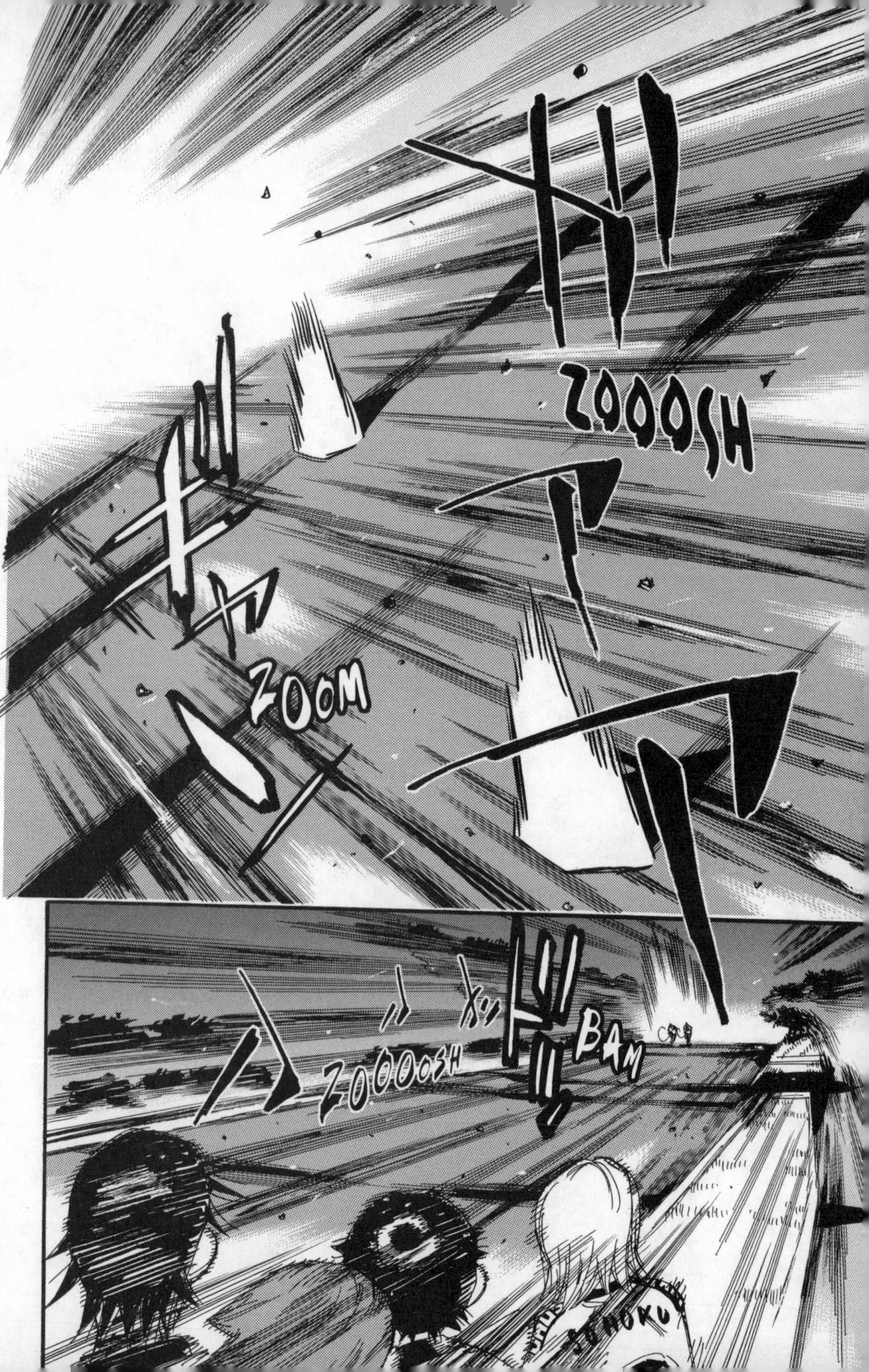
ZOOOSH
ZOOM
BAM
ZOOOOOSH
SOHOKU

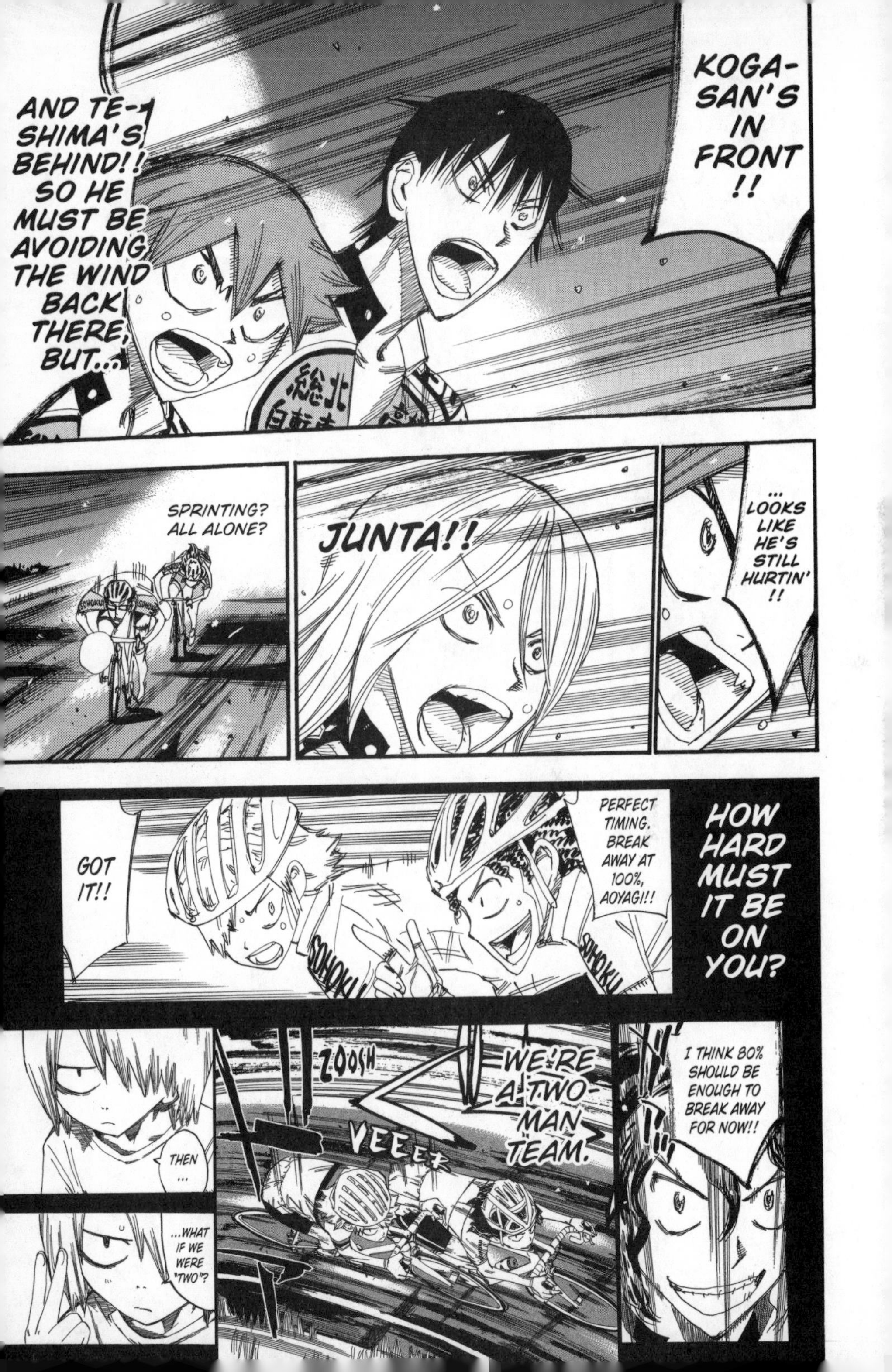
KOGA-SAN'S IN FRONT!!
AND TE-SHIMA'S BEHIND!! SO HE MUST BE AVOIDING THE WIND BACK THERE, BUT...
...LOOKS LIKE HE'S STILL HURTIN'!!
JUNTA!!
SPRINTING? ALL ALONE?
HOW HARD MUST IT BE ON YOU?
PERFECT TIMING. BREAK AWAY AT 100%, AOYAGI!!
GOT IT!!
I THINK 80% SHOULD BE ENOUGH TO BREAK AWAY FOR NOW!!
WE'RE A TWO-MAN TEAM.
ZOOSH
VEEEE
THEN...
...WHAT IF WE WERE "TWO"?

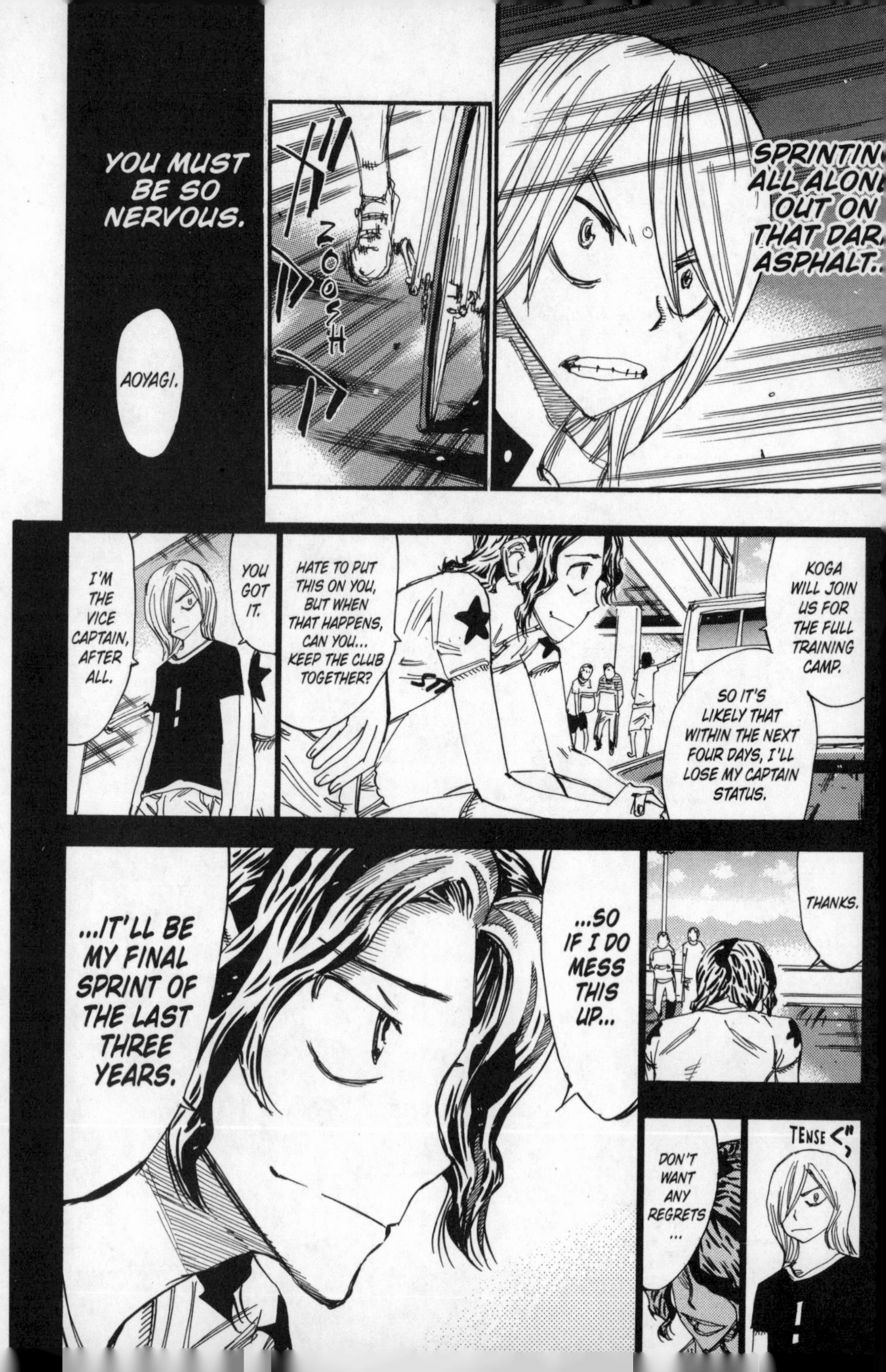
SPRINTIN ALL ALON OUT ON THAT DAR ASPHALT..
ZOOSH
YOU MUST BE SO NERVOUS.
AOYAGI.
KOGA WILL JOIN US FOR THE FULL TRAINING CAMP.
SO IT'S LIKELY THAT WITHIN THE NEXT FOUR DAYS, I'LL LOSE MY CAPTAIN STATUS.
HATE TO PUT THIS ON YOU, BUT WHEN THAT HAPPENS, CAN YOU... KEEP THE CLUB TOGETHER?
YOU GOT IT.
I'M THE VICE CAPTAIN, AFTER ALL.
THANKS.
TENSE
DON'T WANT ANY REGRETS ...
...SO IF I DO MESS THIS UP...
...IT'LL BE MY FINAL SPRINT OF THE LAST THREE YEARS.

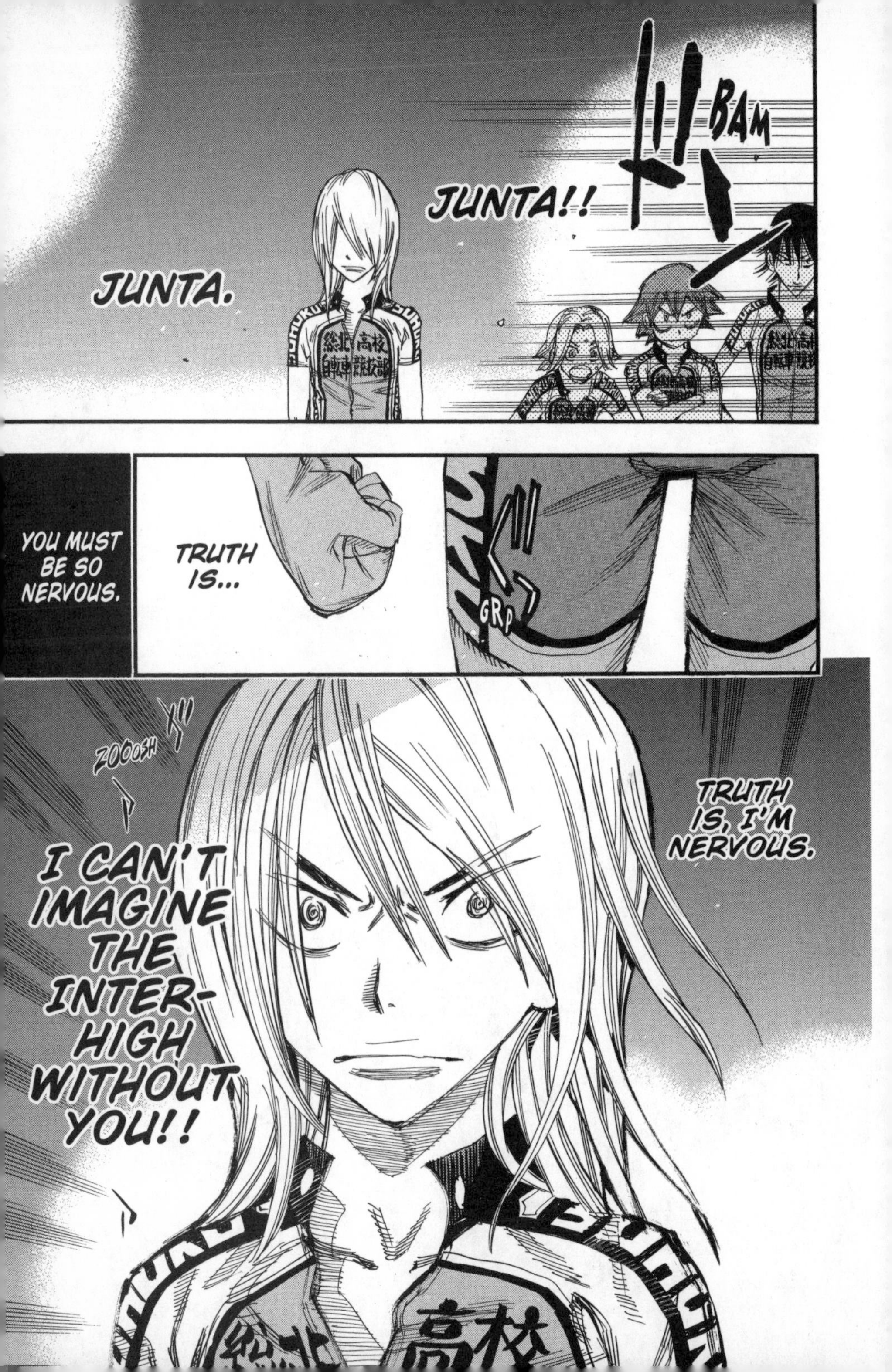
BAM
JUNTA!!
JUNTA.
GRP
TRUTH IS...
YOU MUST BE SO NERVOUS.
TRUTH IS, I'M NERVOUS.
ZOOOSH
I CAN'T IMAGINE THE INTER-HIGH WITHOUT YOU!!

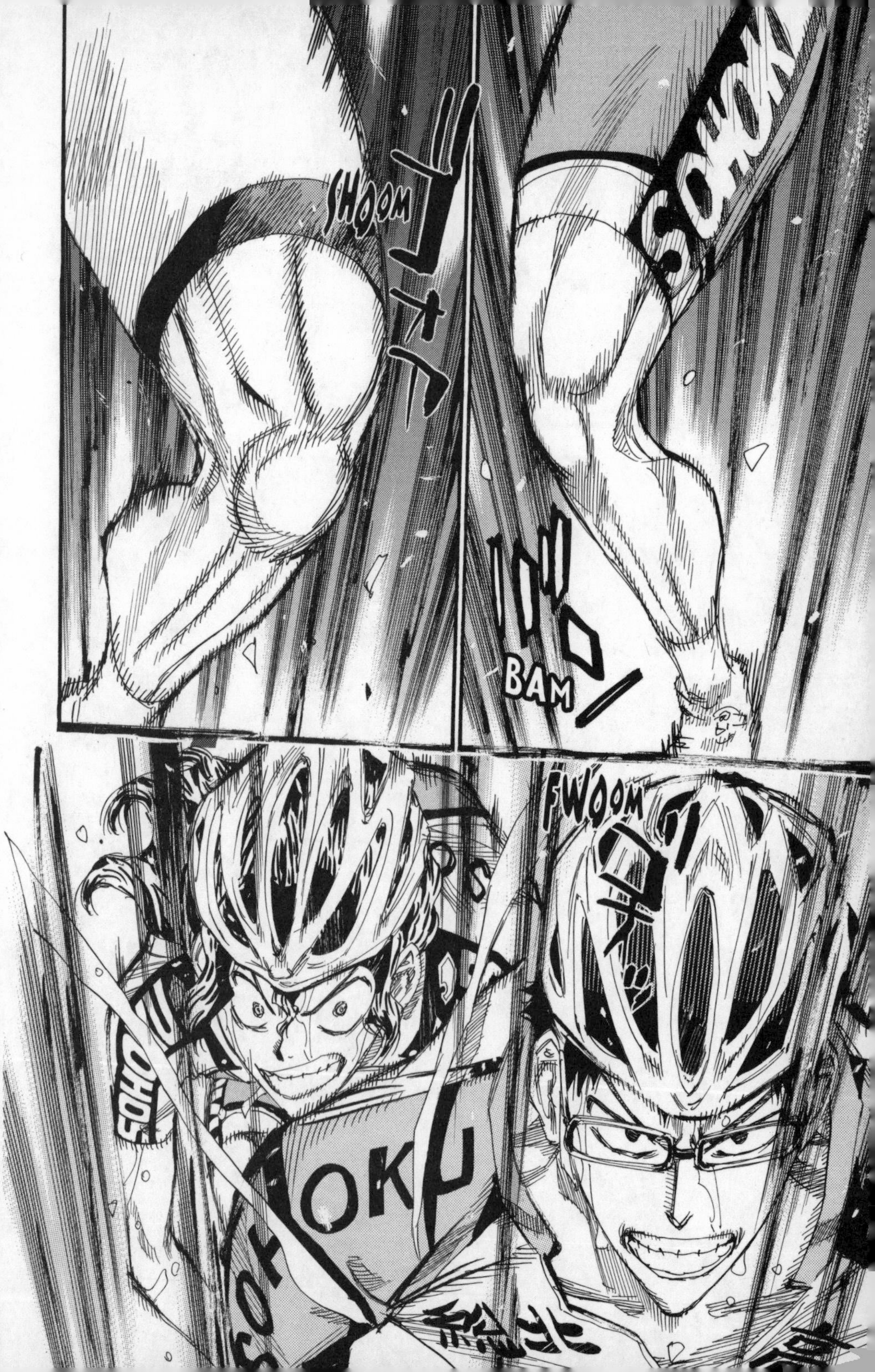
BAM
SHOOM
FWOOM

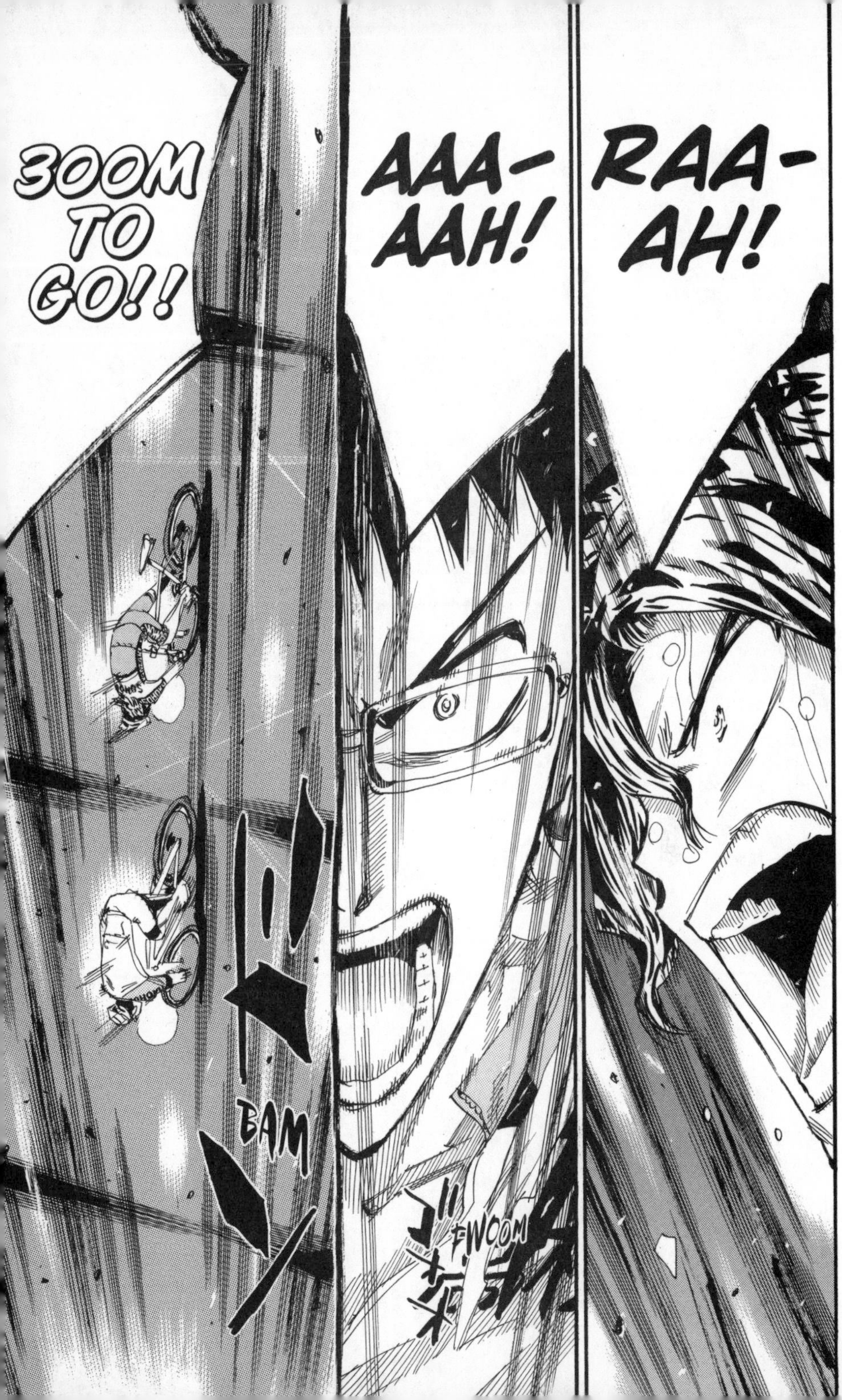
RAA-
AH!
AAA-
AAH!
FWOOM
300M
TO
GO!!
BAM

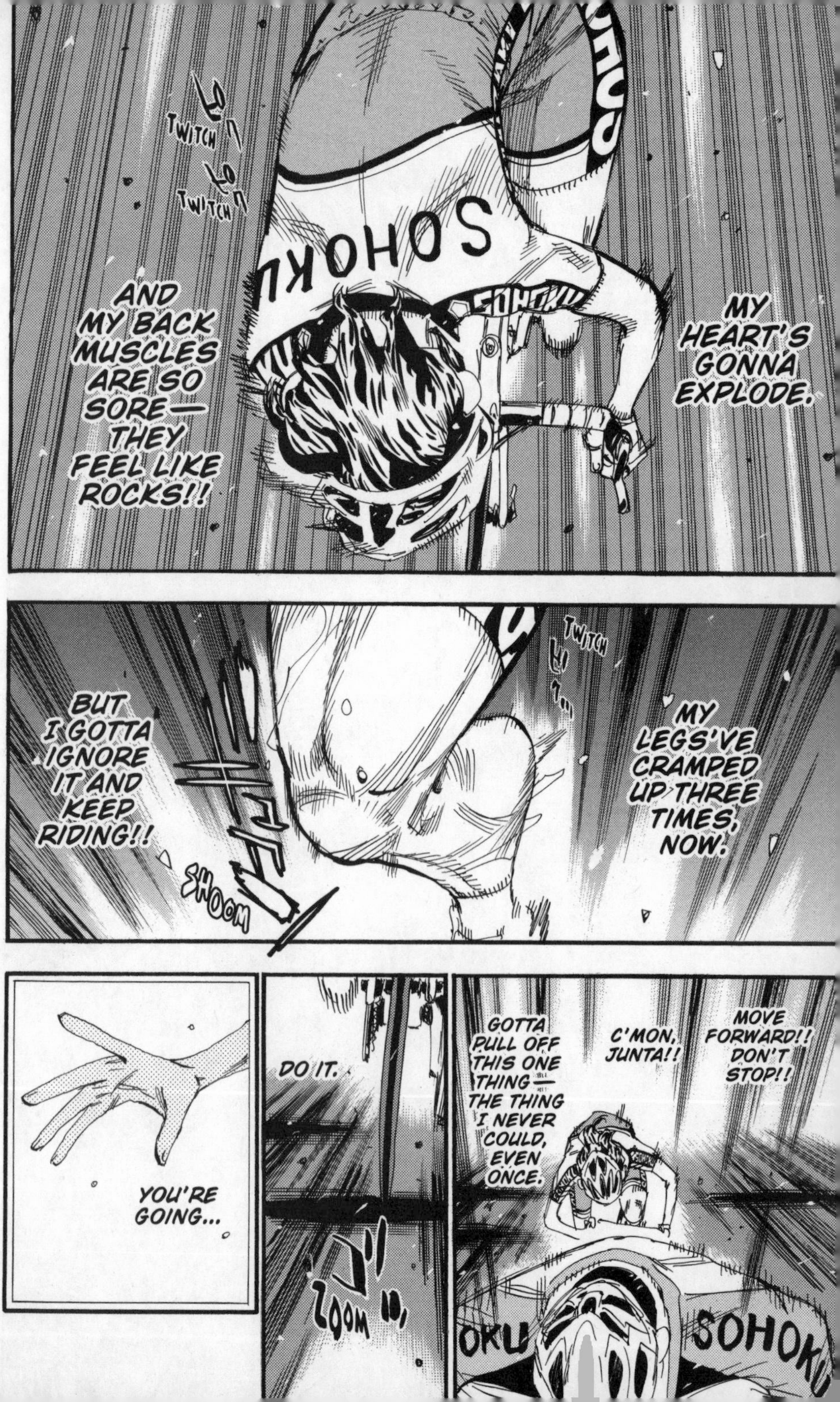
MY HEART'S GONNA EXPLODE.
TWITCH
TWITCH
AND MY BACK MUSCLES ARE SO SORE— THEY FEEL LIKE ROCKS!!
TWITCH
MY LEGS'VE CRAMPED UP THREE TIMES, NOW.
BUT I GOTTA IGNORE IT AND KEEP RIDING!!
SHOOM
MOVE FORWARD!! DON'T STOP!!
C'MON, JUNTA!!
GOTTA PULL OFF THIS ONE THING— THE THING I NEVER COULD, EVEN ONCE.
DO IT.
ZOOM
YOU'RE GOING...

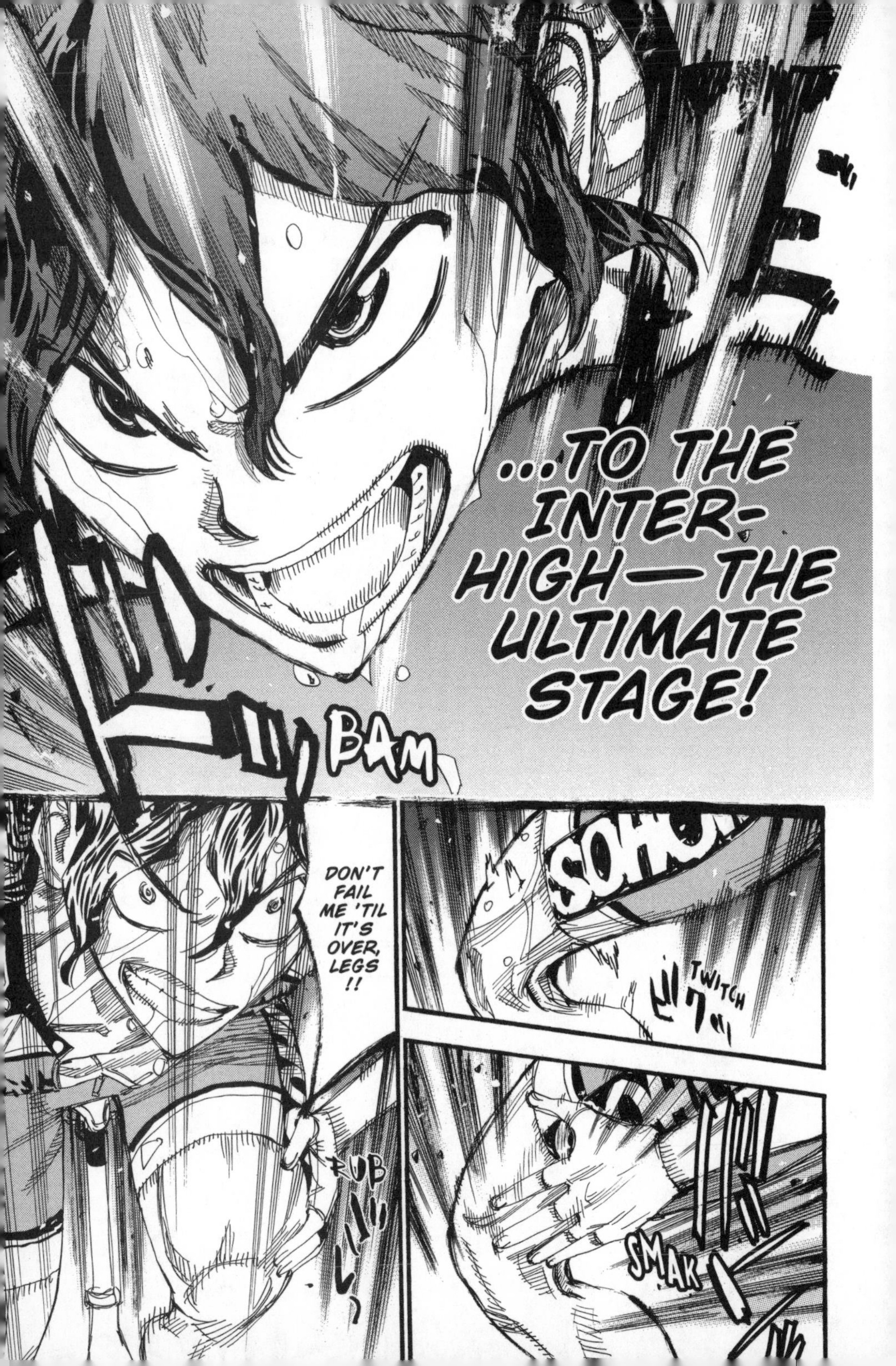
...TO THE INTER-HIGH—THE ULTIMATE STAGE!
BAM
TWITCH
SMAK
DON'T FAIL ME 'TIL IT'S OVER, LEGS!!
RUB

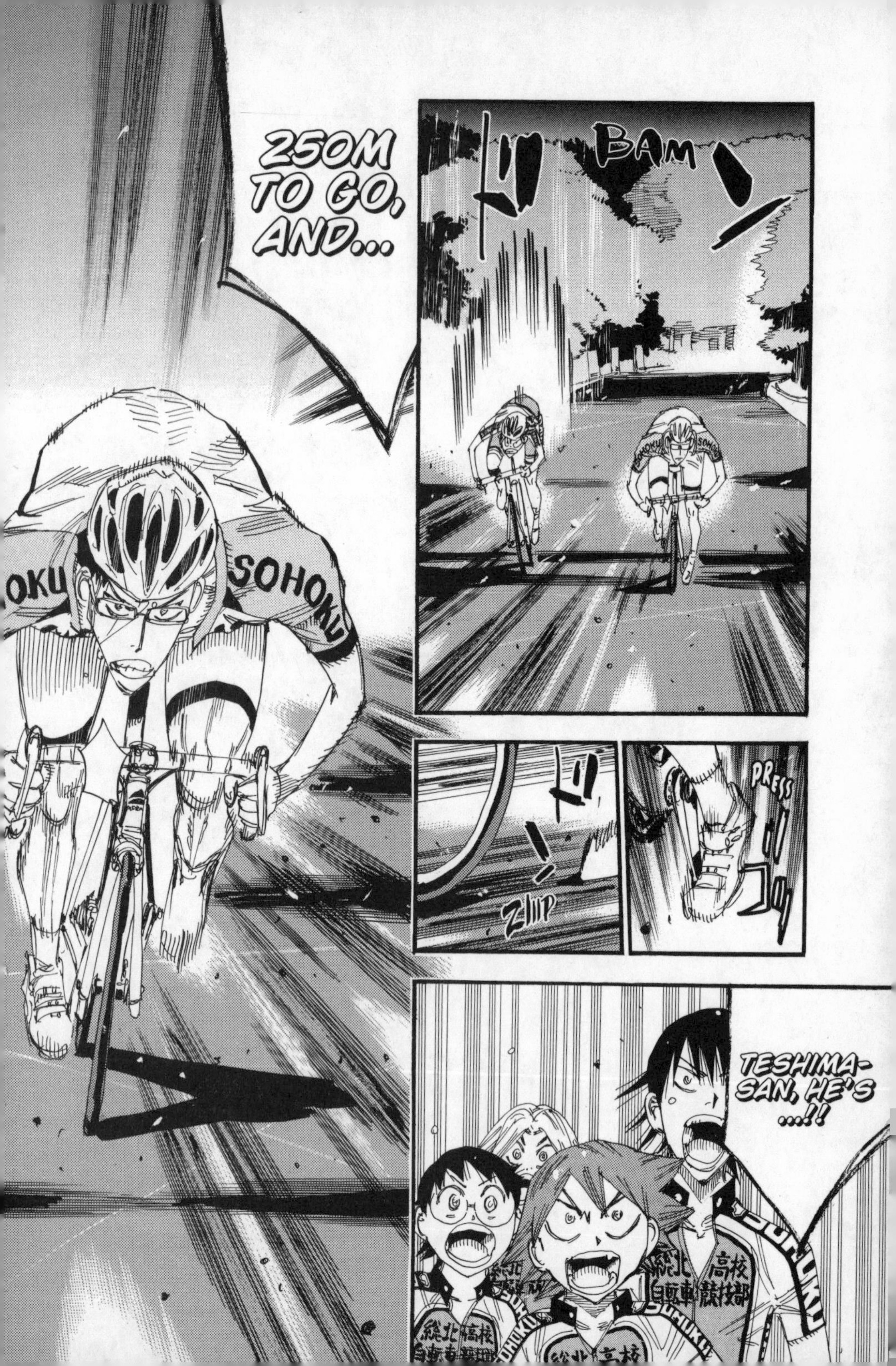
BAM
PRESS
ZIIP
TESHIMA-SAN, HE'S ...!!
250M TO GO, AND...

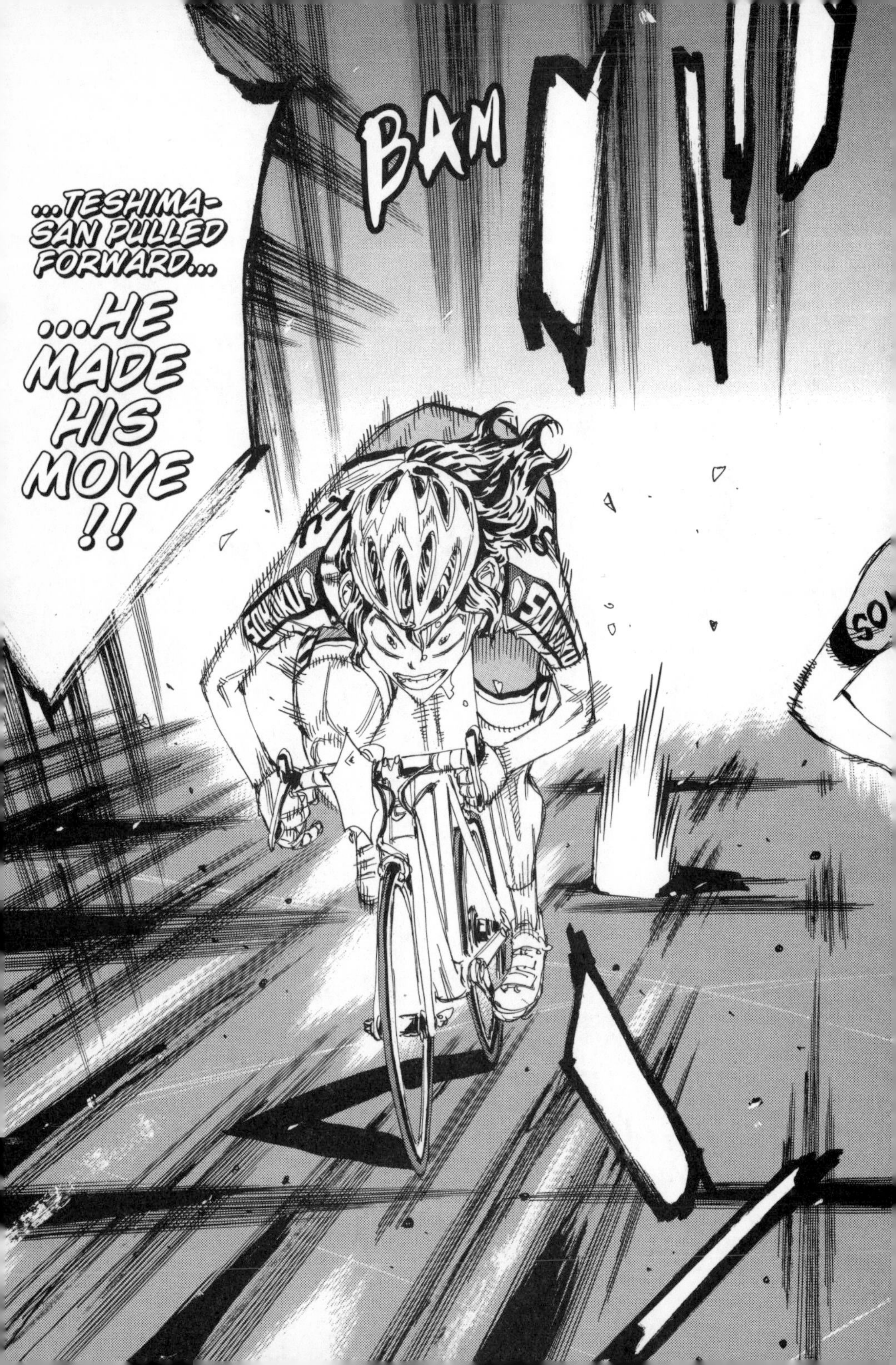
BAM
...TESHIMA-SAN PULLED FORWARD...
...HE MADE HIS MOVE!!

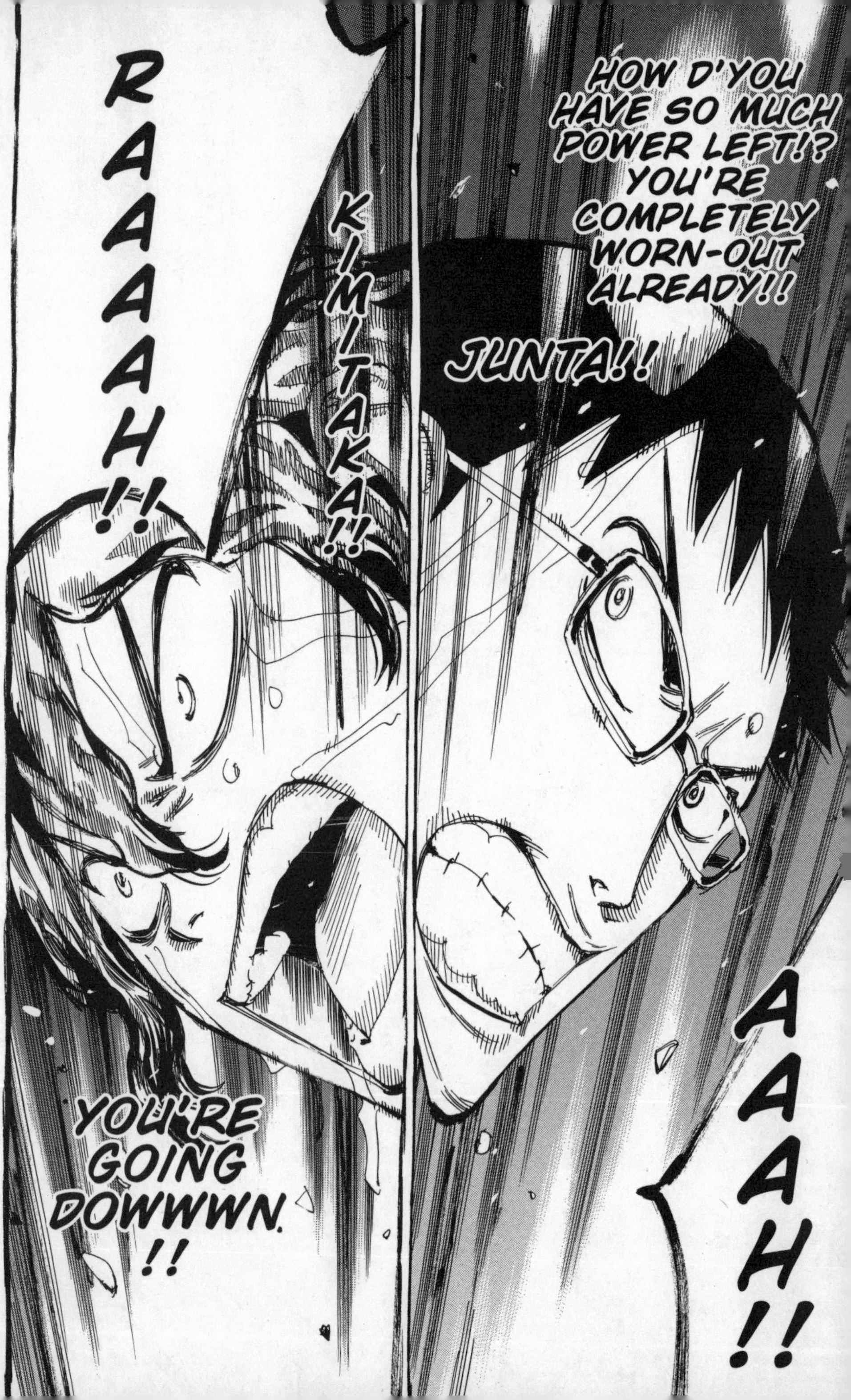
HOW D'YOU HAVE SO MUCH POWER LEFT!? YOU'RE COMPLETELY WORN-OUT ALREADY!!
JUNTA!!
AAAAH!!
KIMITAKA!!
RAAAAH!!
YOU'RE GOING DOWWWN.!!

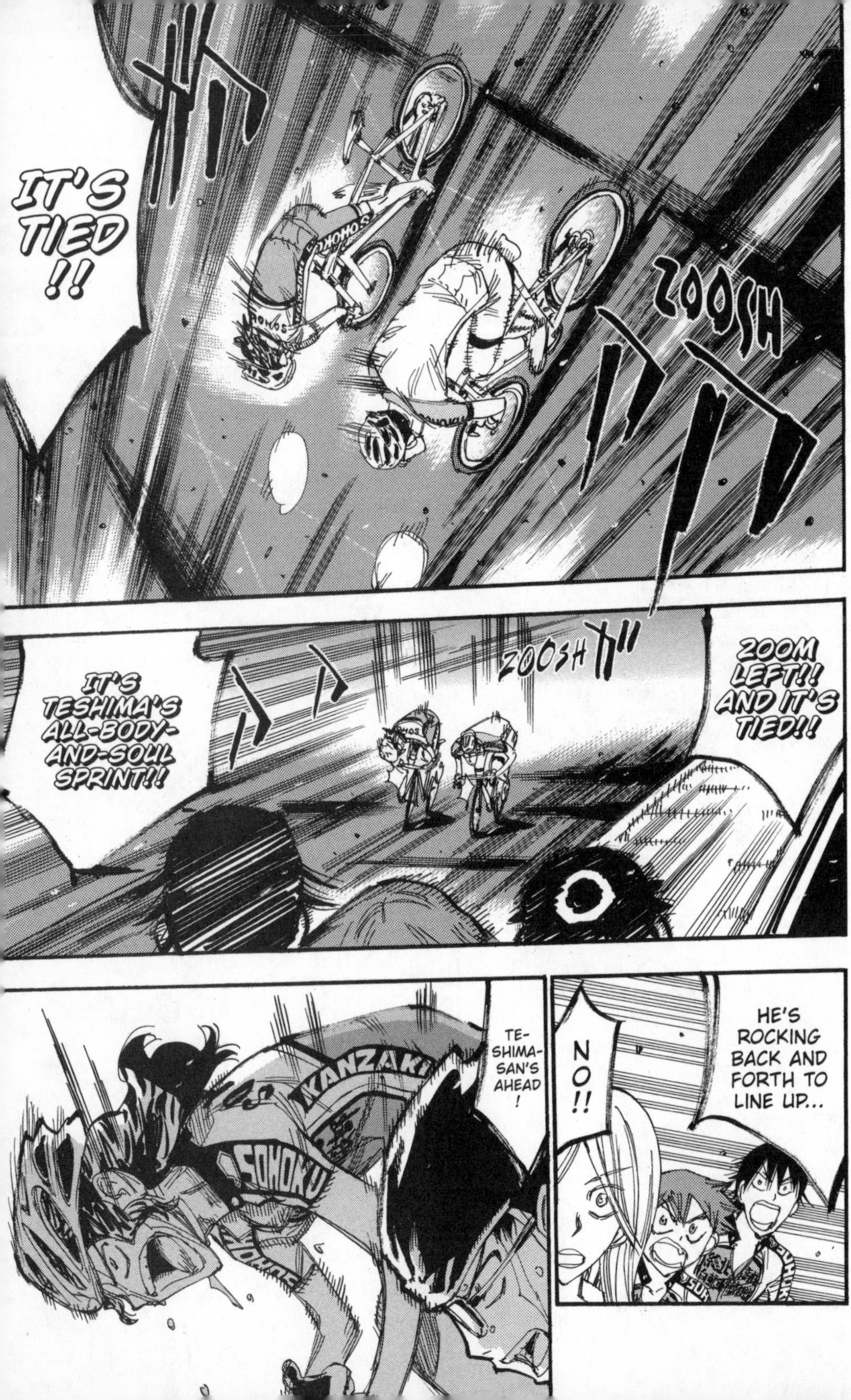
ZOOSH
IT'S TIED!!
ZOOM LEFT!! AND IT'S TIED!!
ZOOSH
IT'S TESHIMA'S ALL-BODY-AND-SOUL SPRINT!!
HE'S ROCKING BACK AND FORTH TO LINE UP...
NO!!
TE-SHIMA-SAN'S AHEAD!

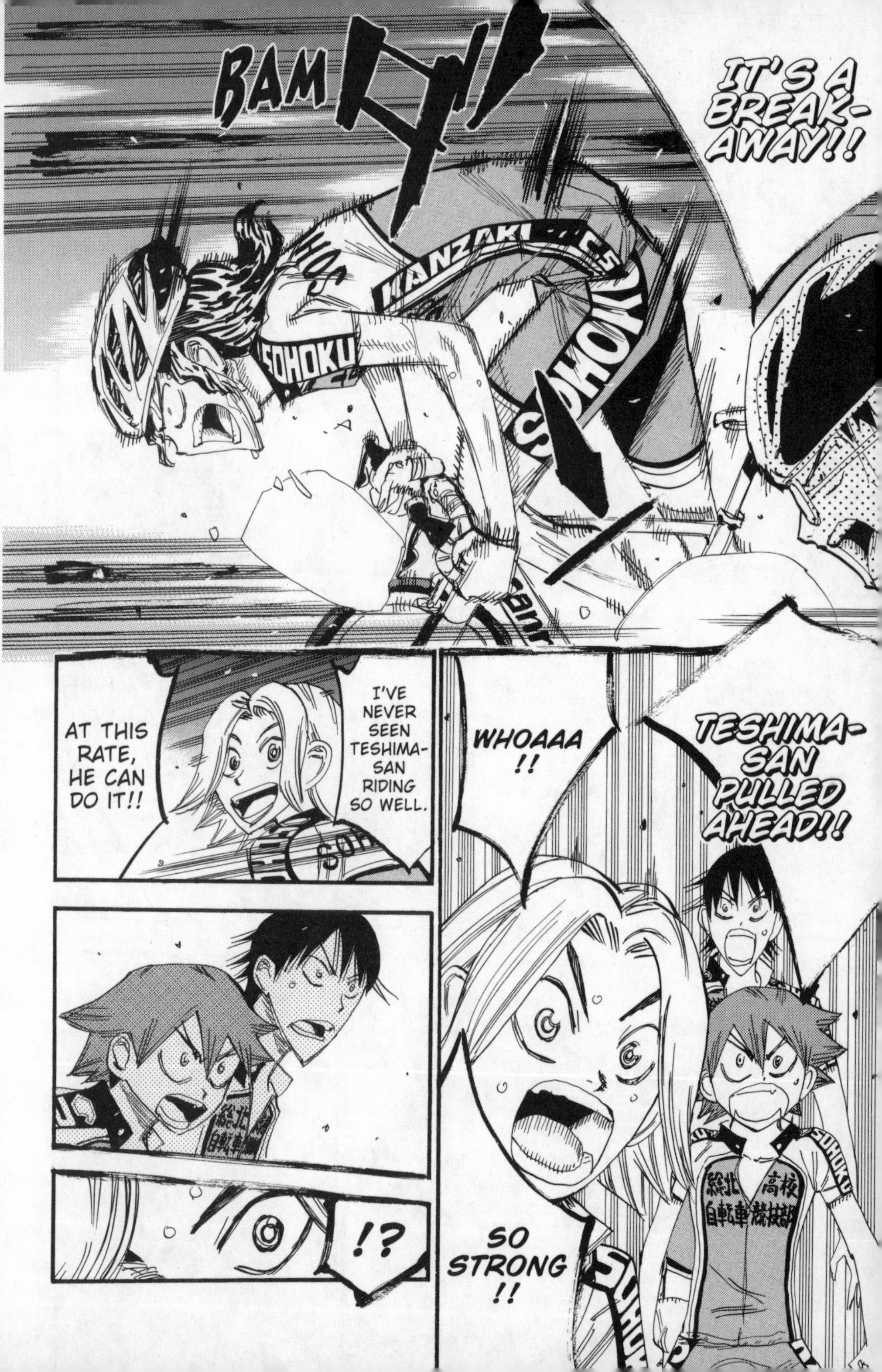
IT'S A BREAKAWAY!!
BAM
TESHIMA-SAN PULLED AHEAD!!
WHOAAA!!
SO STRONG!!
I'VE NEVER SEEN TESHIMA-SAN RIDING SO WELL.
AT THIS RATE, HE CAN DO IT!!
!?

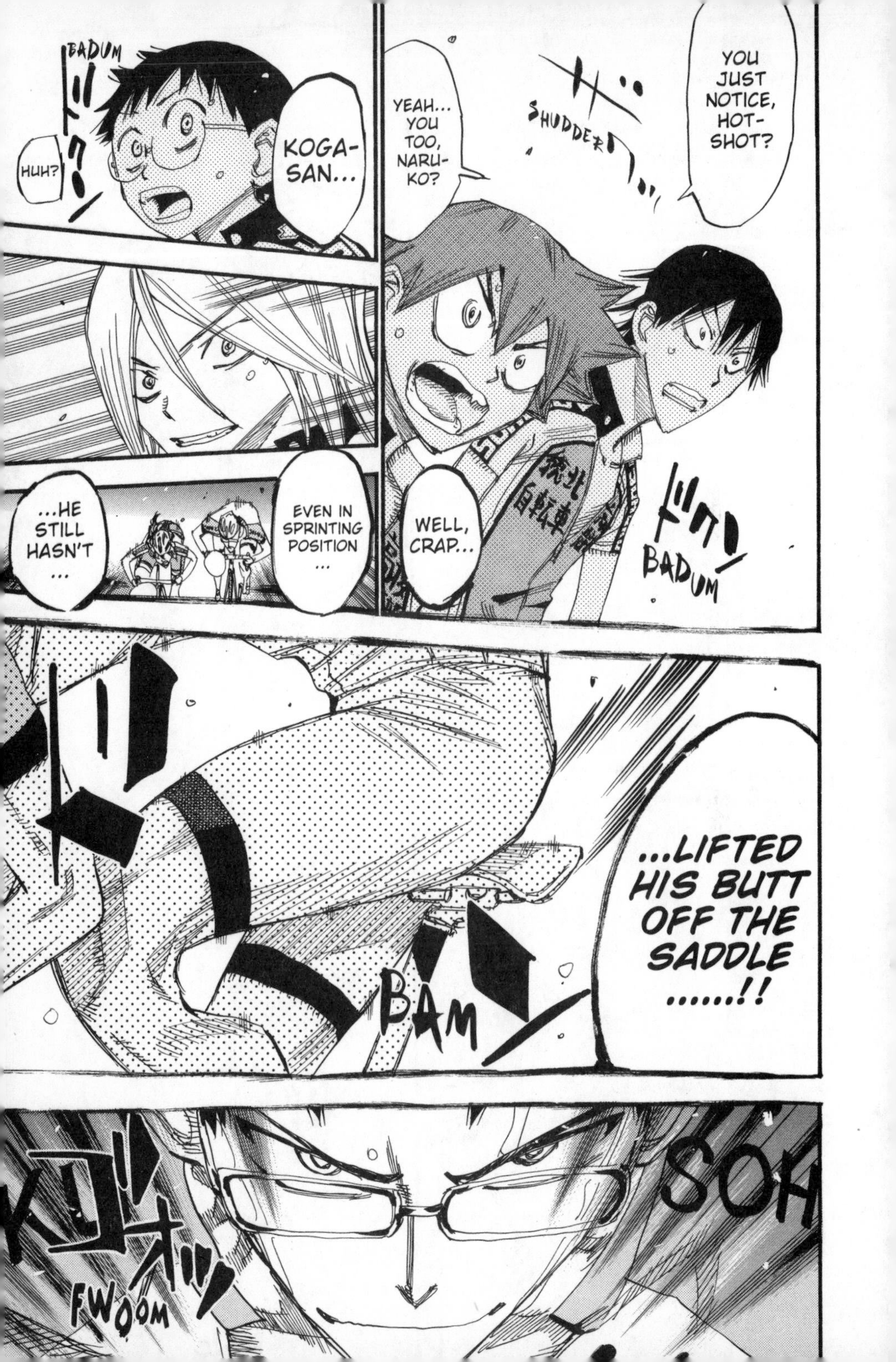

YOU JUST NOTICE, HOT-SHOT?
SHUDDER
YEAH... YOU TOO, NARUKO?
WELL, CRAP...
BADUM
BADUM
KOGA-SAN...
HUH?
EVEN IN SPRINTING POSITION ...
...HE STILL HASN'T ...
...LIFTED HIS BUTT OFF THE SADDLE ......!!
BAM
SOH
FWOOM

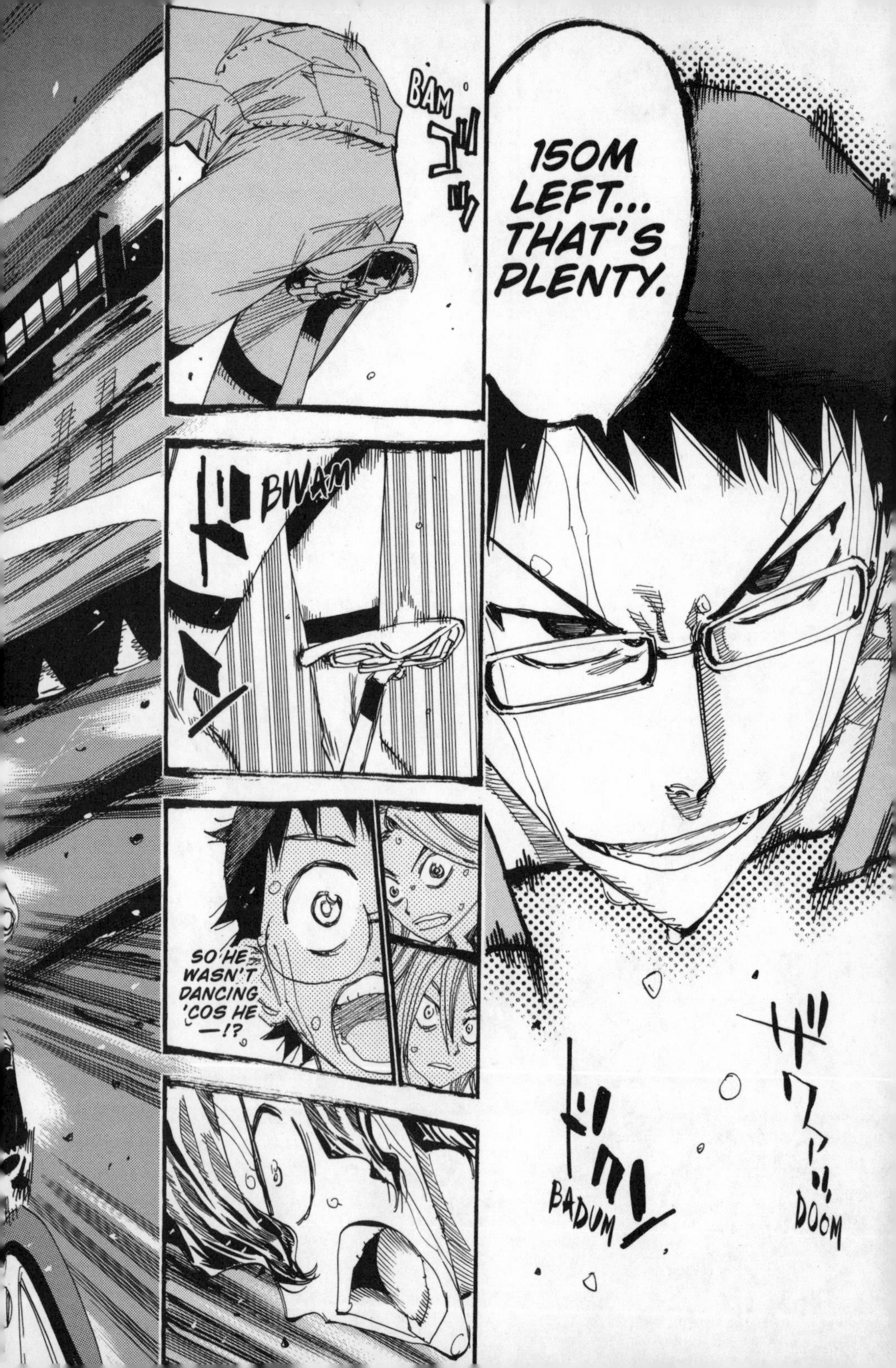
150M LEFT... THAT'S PLENTY.
DOOM
BADUM
BAM
BWAM
SO HE WASN'T DANCING 'COS HE—!?

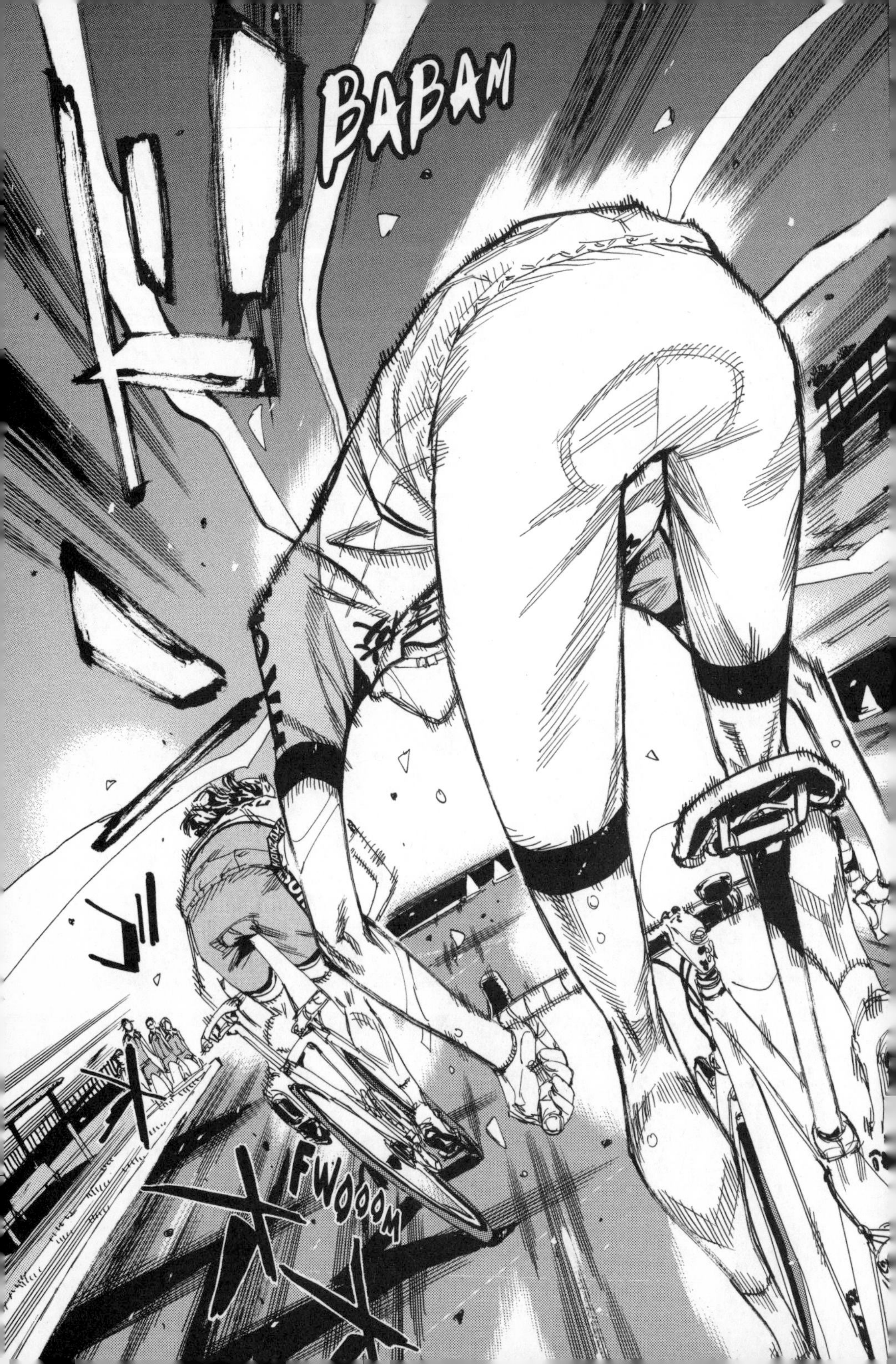
BABAM
FWOOOM

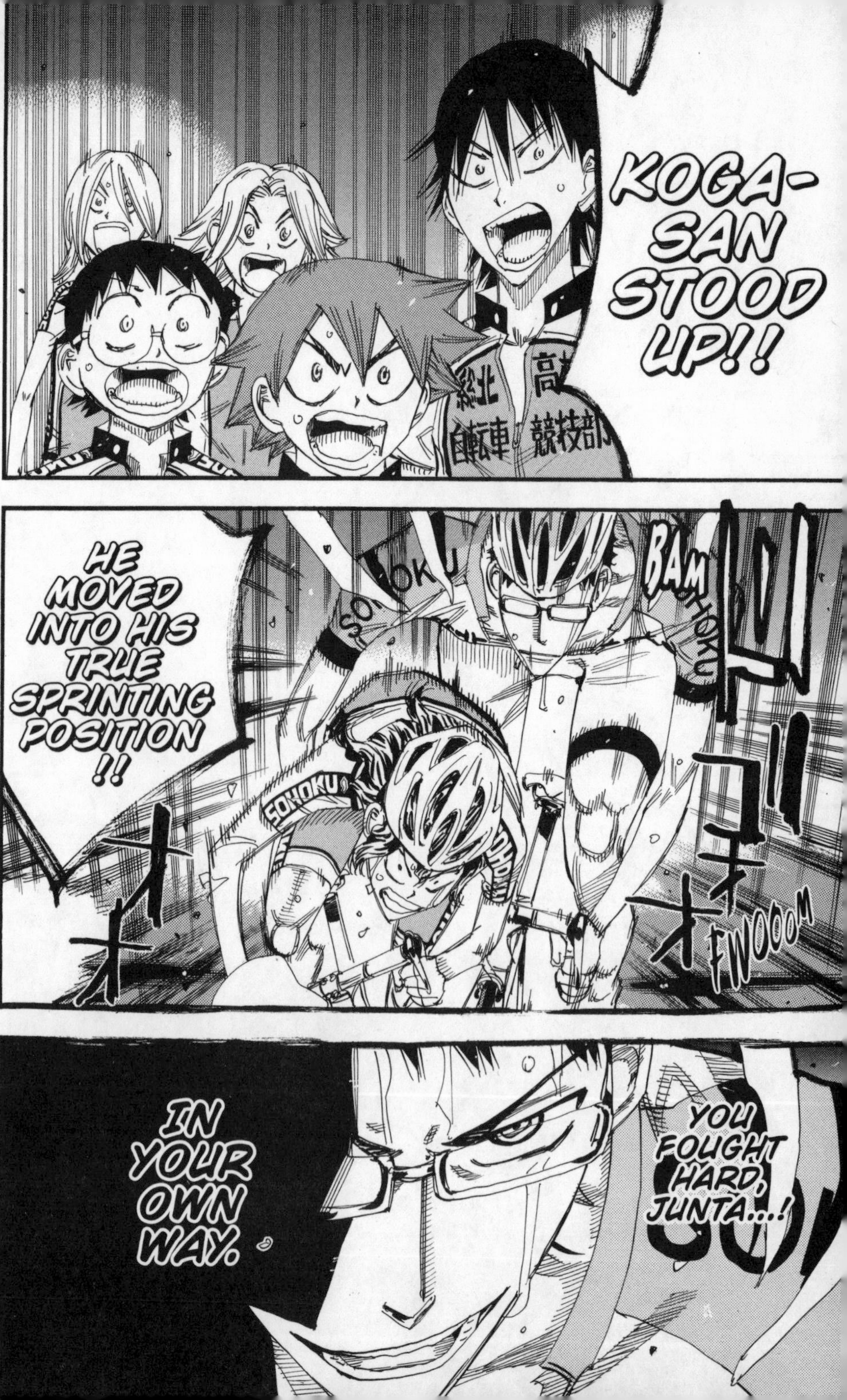
KOGA-SAN STOOD UP!!
BAM
HE MOVED INTO HIS TRUE SPRINTING POSITION!!
FWOOOM
YOU FOUGHT HARD, JUNTA...!
IN YOUR OWN WAY.

RIDE.290 THE PLAIN AND THE PRODIGIOUS

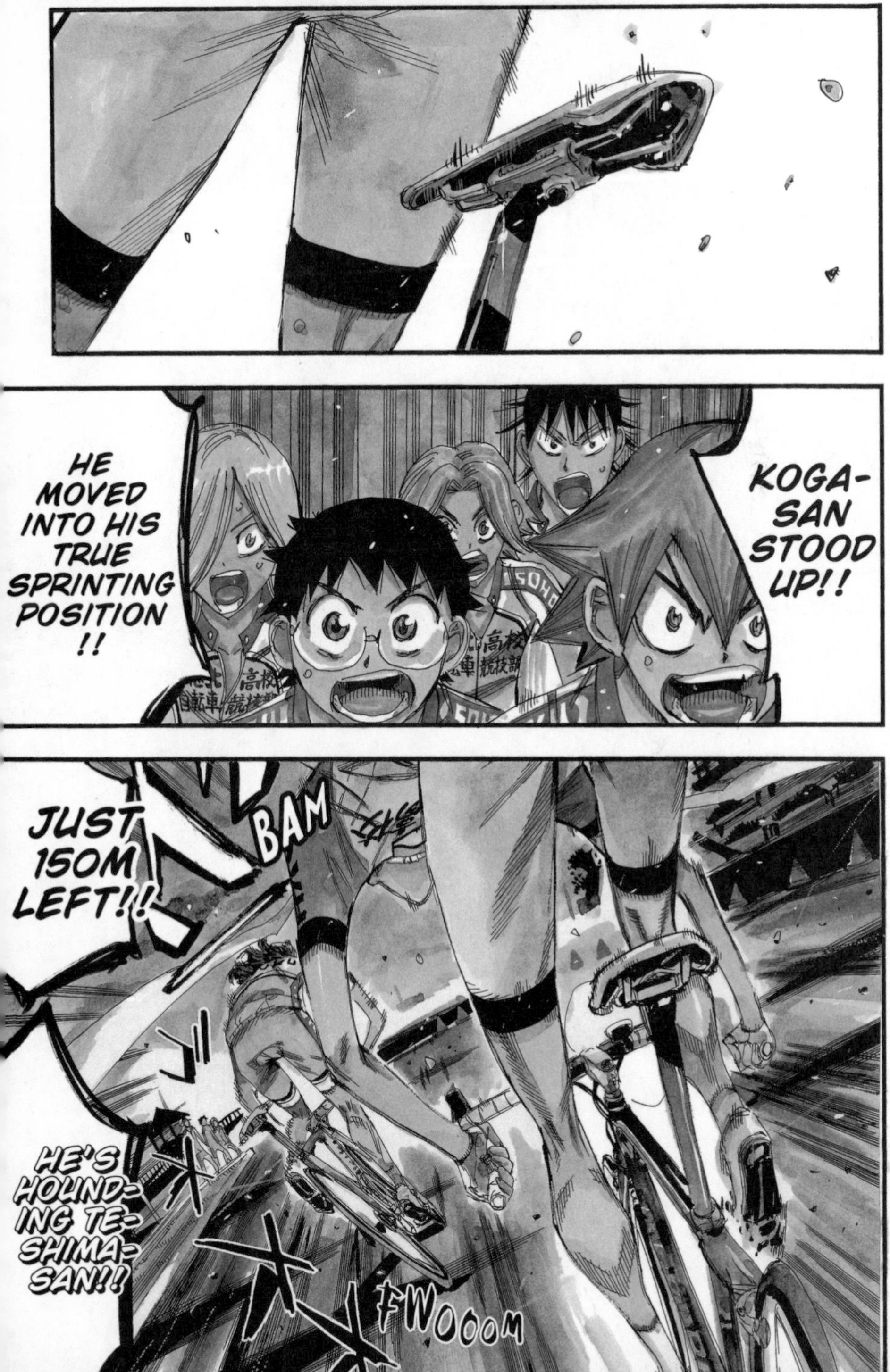
KOGA-SAN STOOD UP!!
HE MOVED INTO HIS TRUE SPRINTING POSITION!!
BAM
JUST 150M LEFT!!
HE'S HOUNDING TESHIMA-SAN!!
FWOOOM

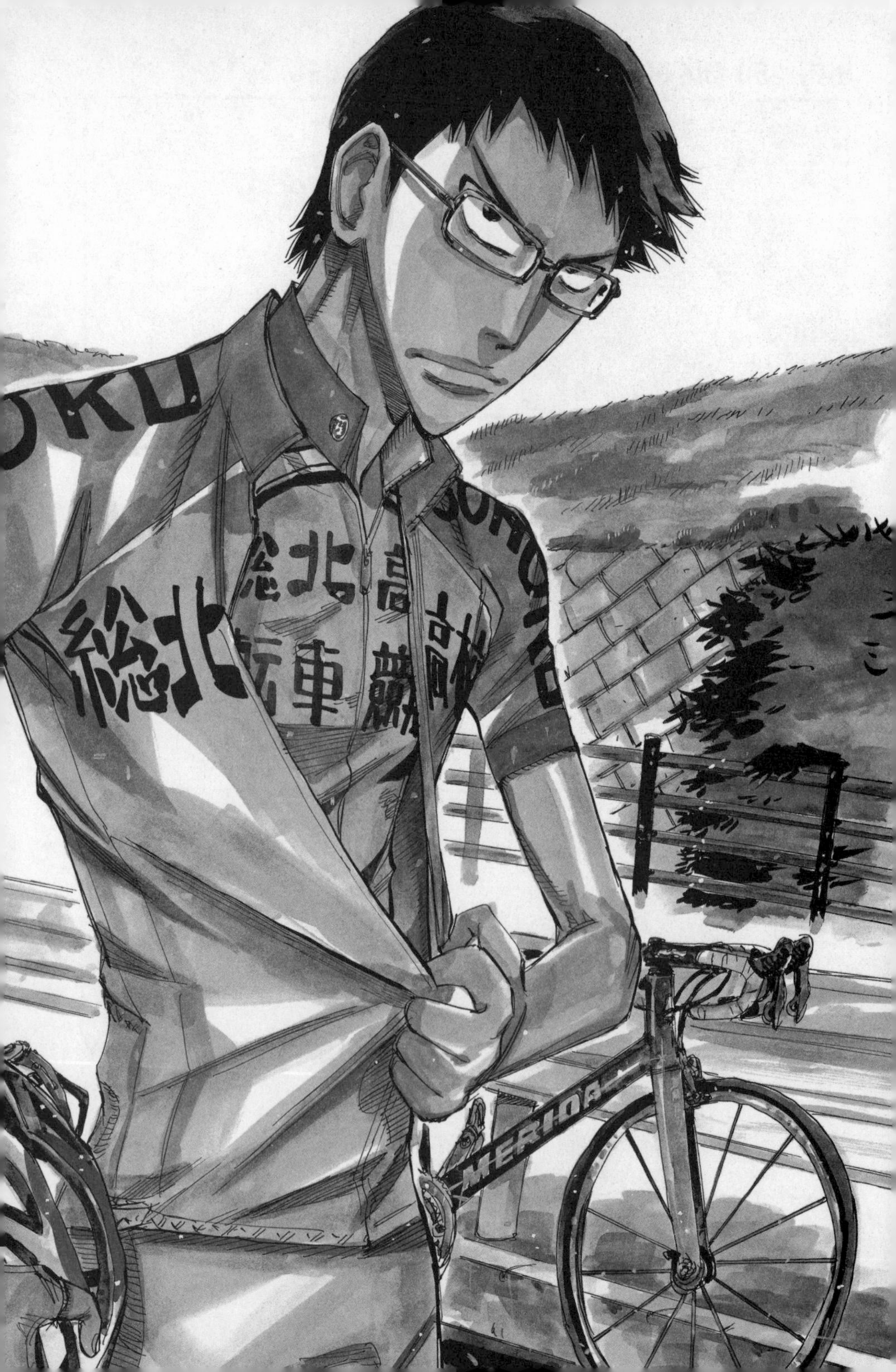
総北
MERIDA

RIDE.290
THE PLAIN AND THE PRODIGIOUS

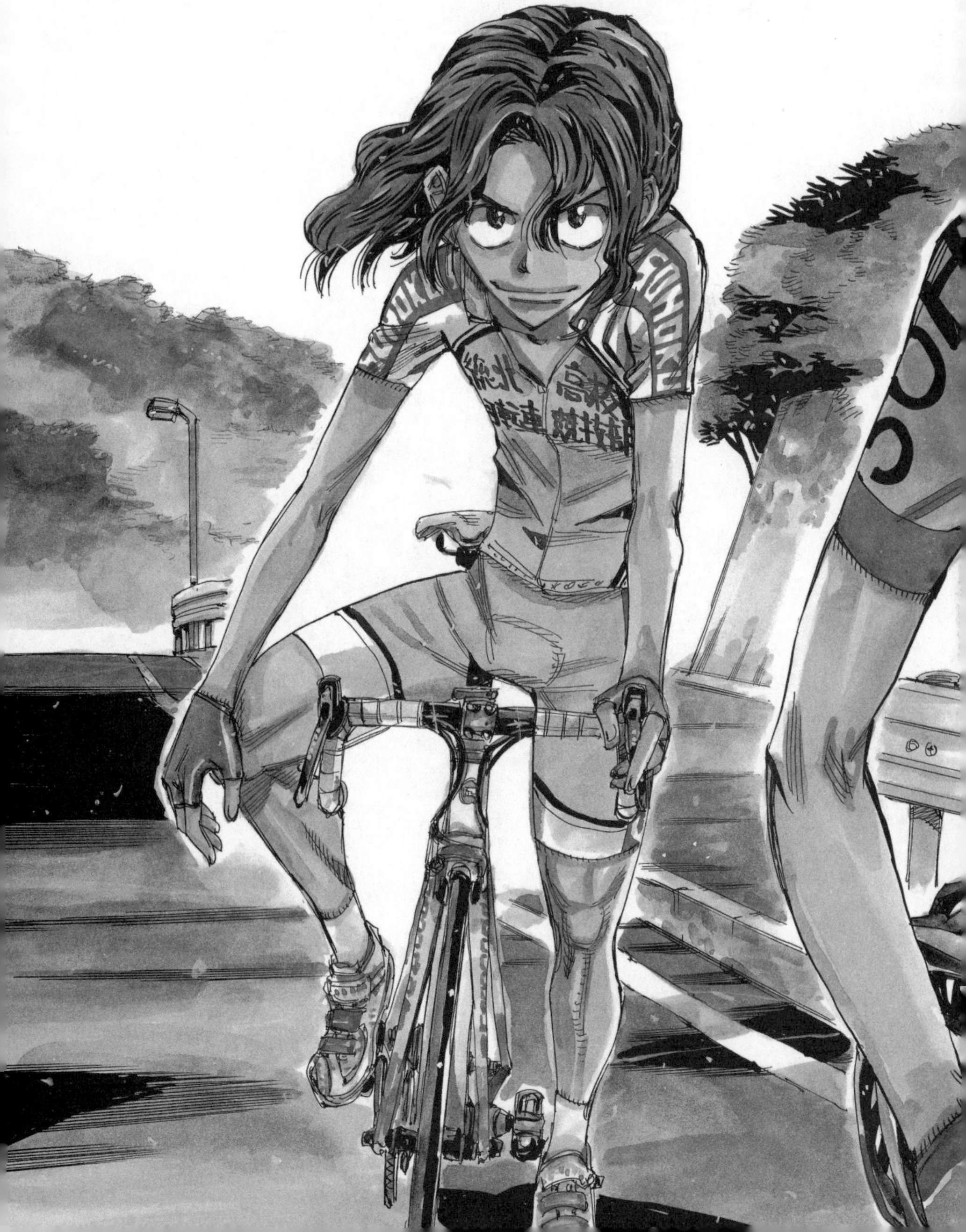

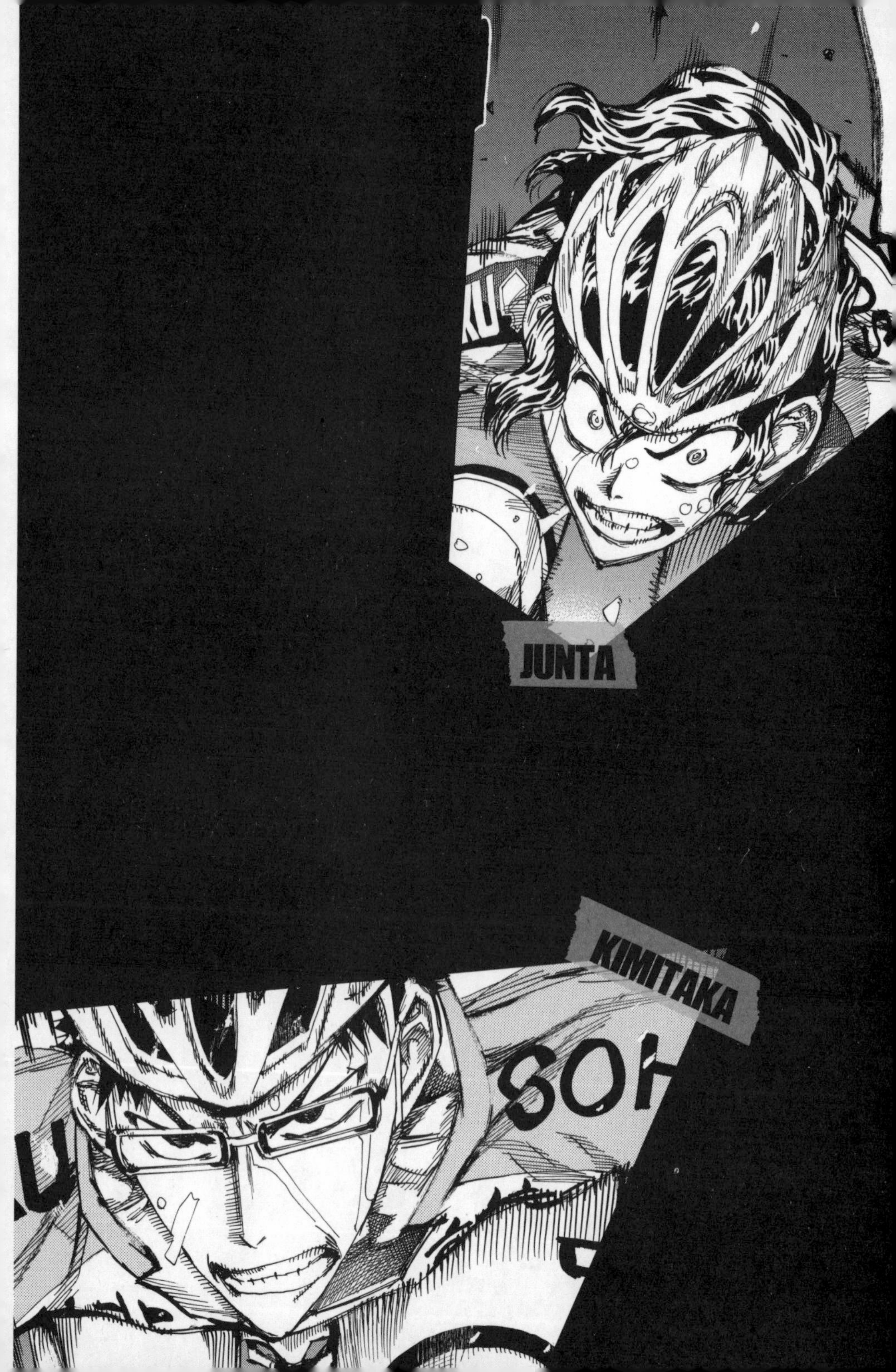
JUNTA
KIMITAKA

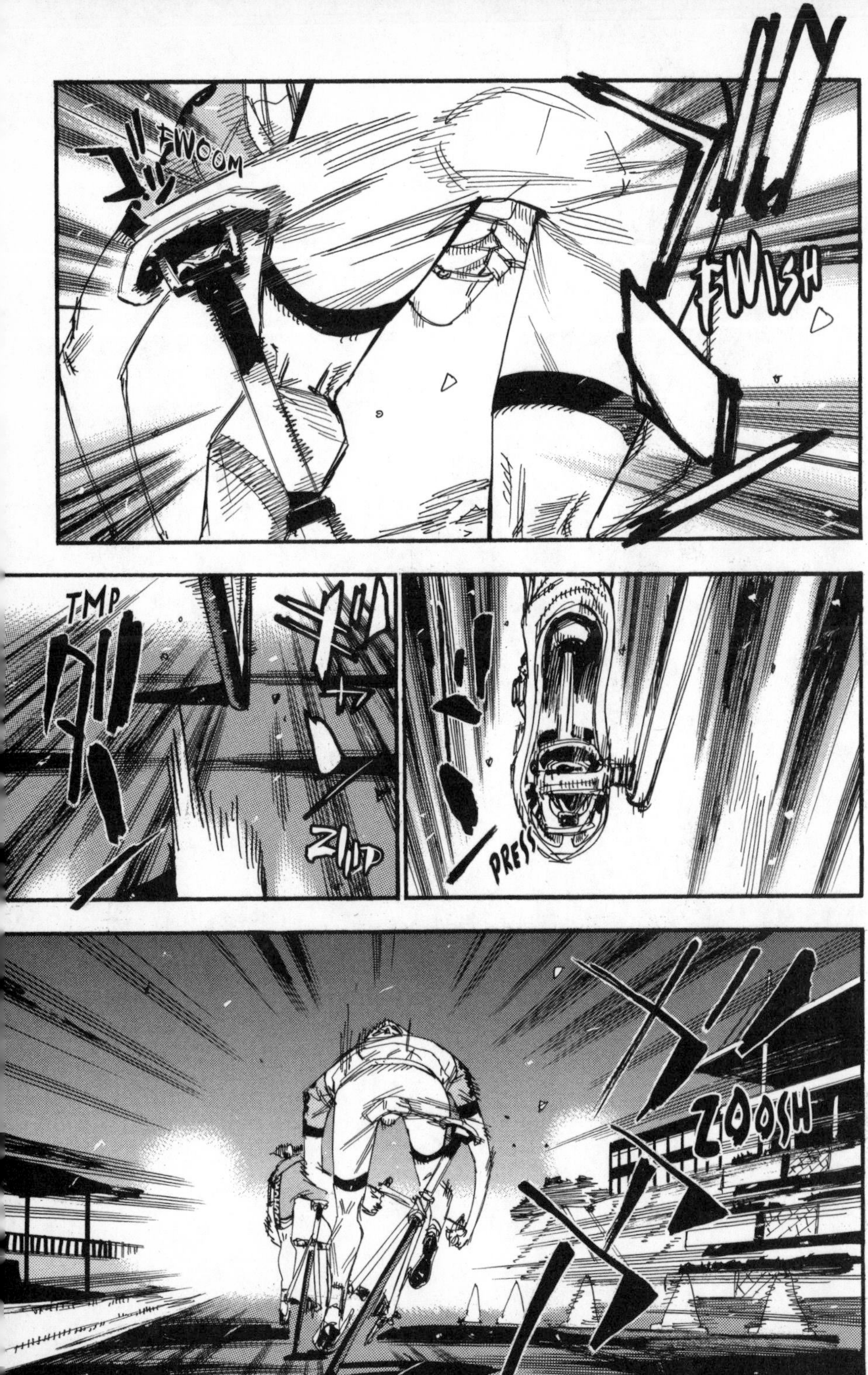
FWISH
FWOOM
PRESS
TMP
ZWIP
ZOOSH

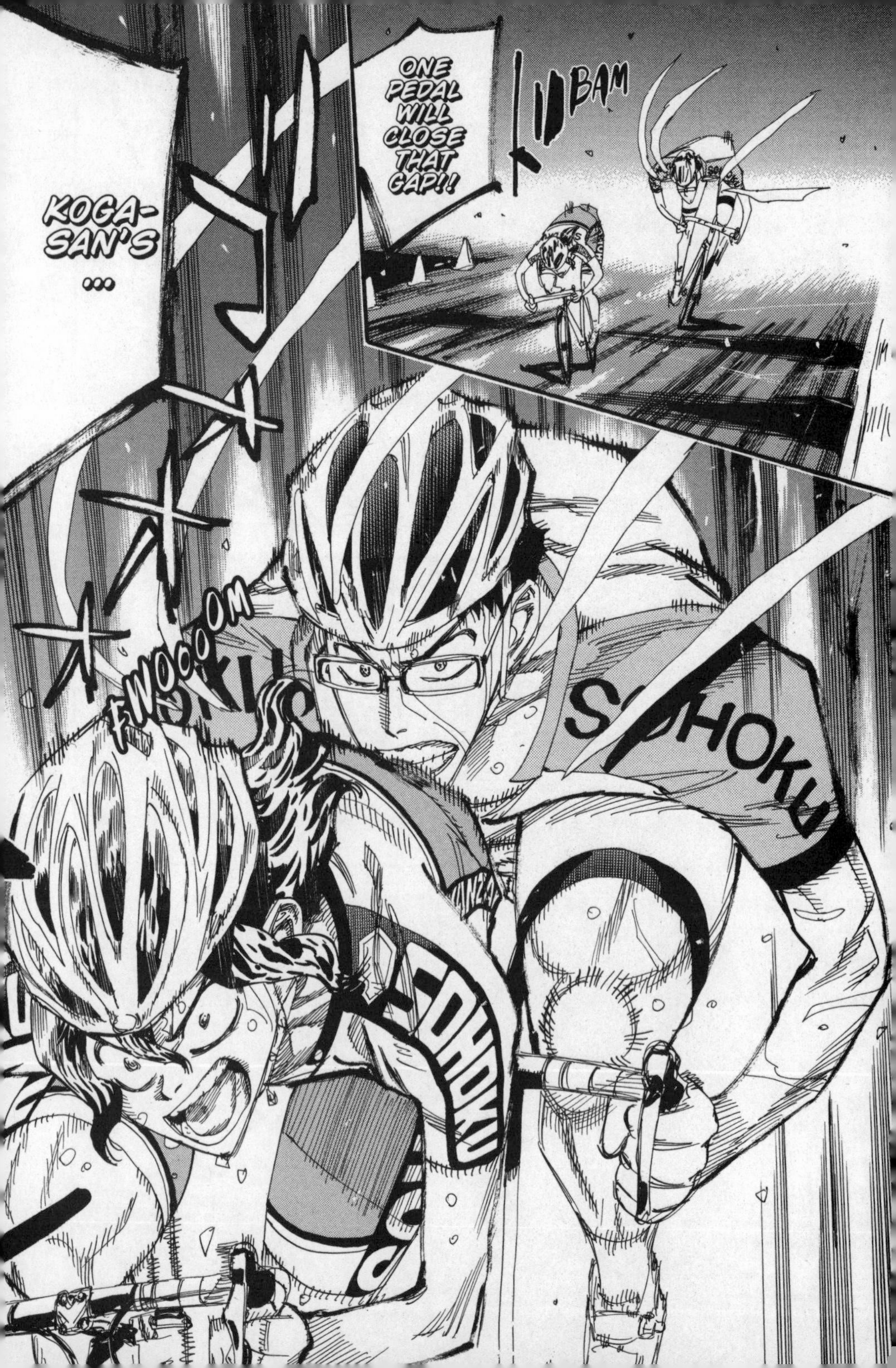
ONE PEDAL WILL CLOSE THAT GAP!!
BAM
KOGA-SAN'S ...
FWOOOOM

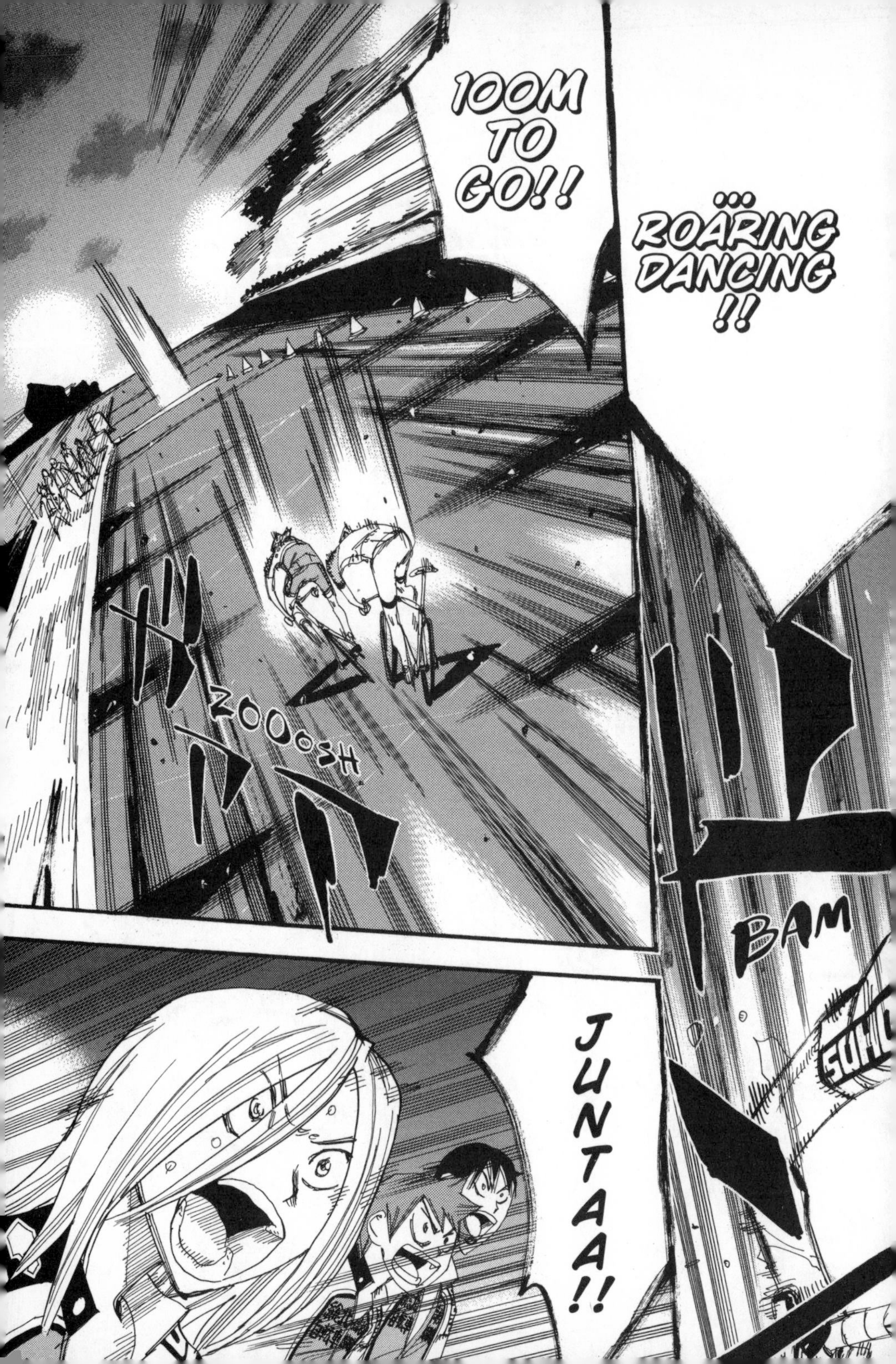
...ROARING DANCING!!
100M TO GO!!
ZOOOSH
BAM
JUNTAAA!!

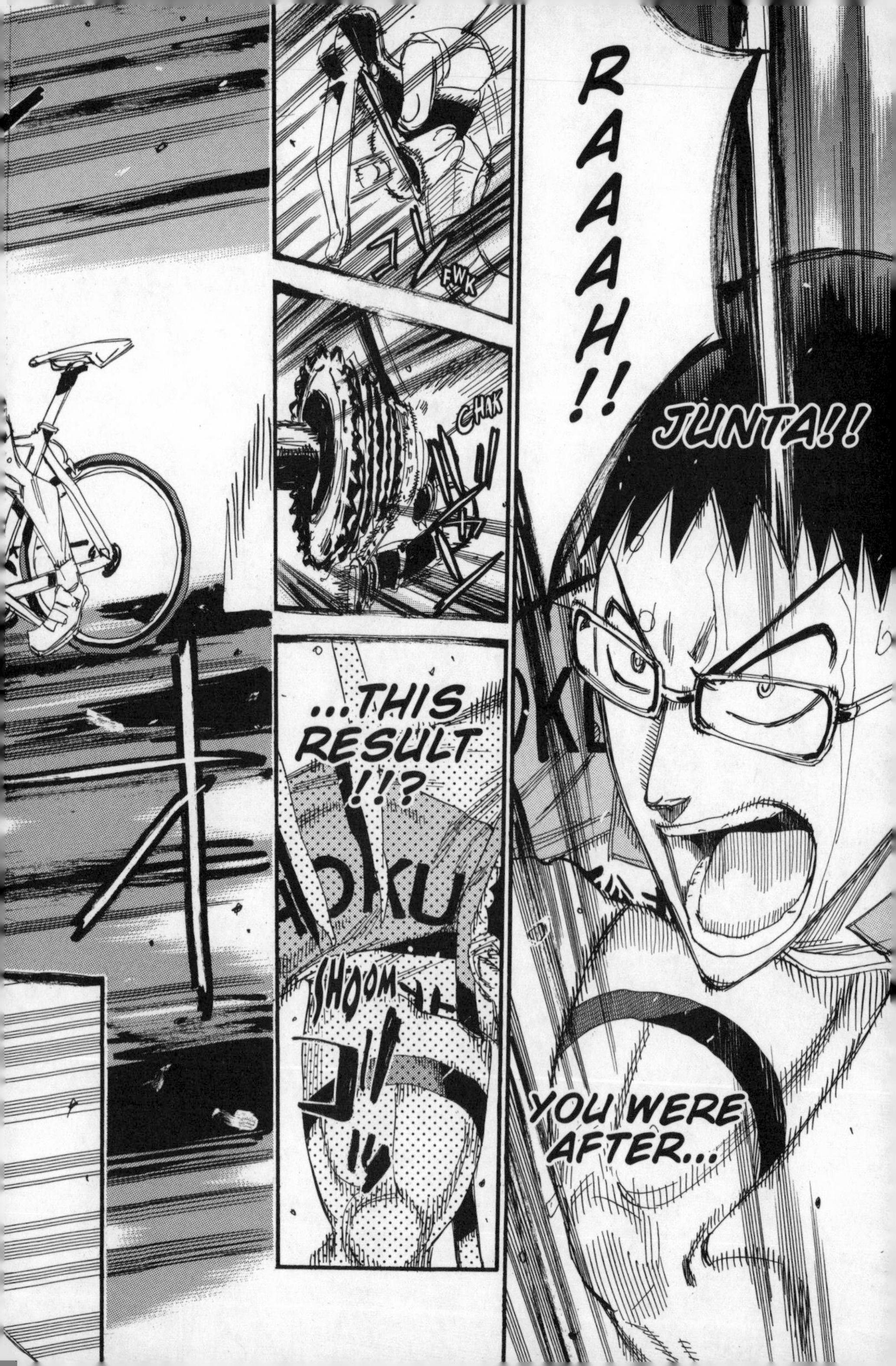
RAAAH!!
JUNTA!!
YOU WERE AFTER...
FWK
CHAK
...THIS RESULT!!?
SHOOM

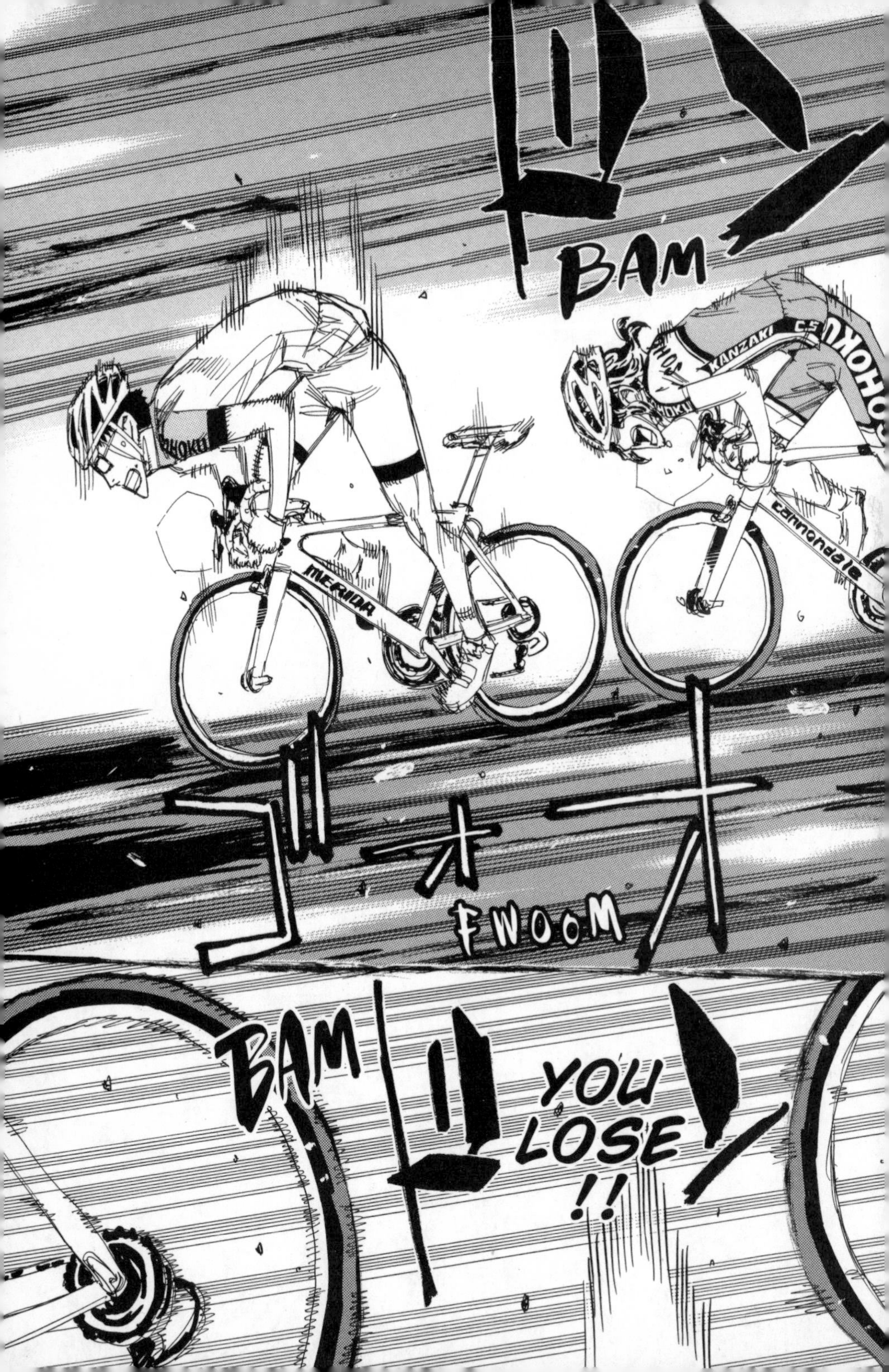
BAM
FWOOM
YOU LOSE!!
BAM

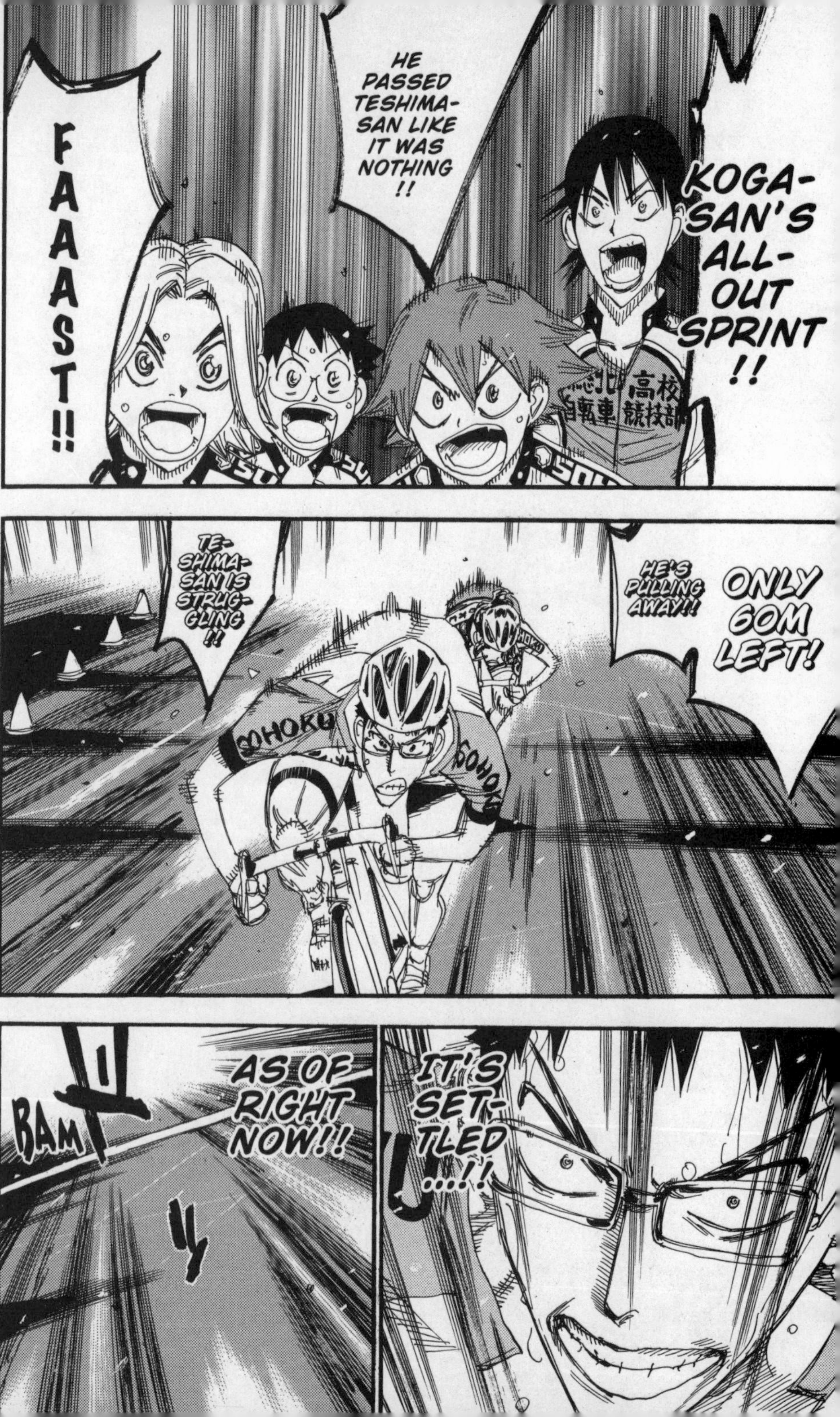
KOGA-SAN'S ALL-OUT SPRINT!!
HE PASSED TESHIMA-SAN LIKE IT WAS NOTHING!!
FAAAST!!
ONLY 60M LEFT!
HE'S PULLING AWAY!!
TE-SHIMA-SAN IS STRUG-GLING!!
SOHOKU
SOHOKU
IT'S SET-TLED...!!
AS OF RIGHT NOW!!
BAM

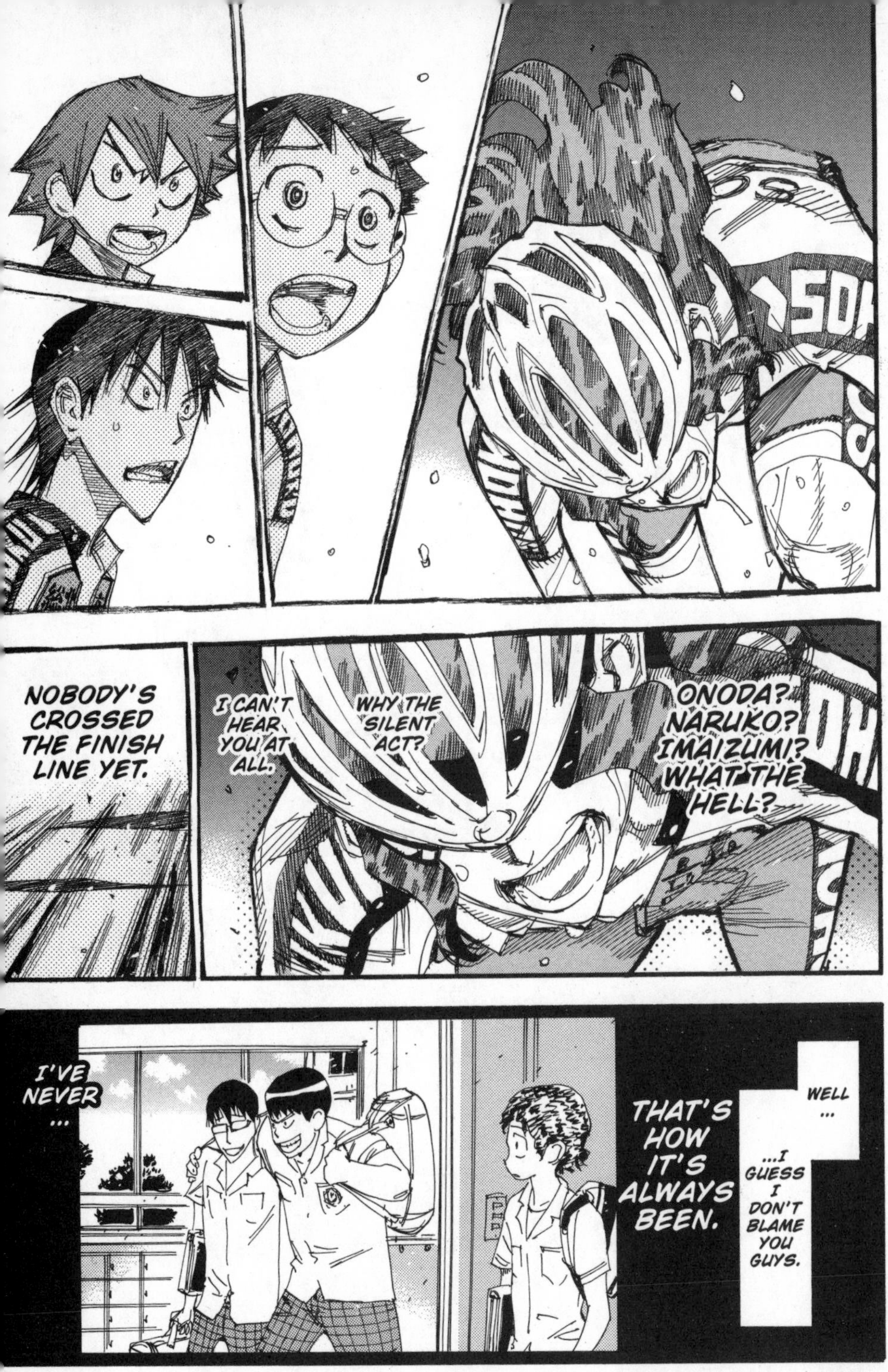
ONODA? NARUKO? IMAIZUMI? WHAT THE HELL?
WHY THE SILENT ACT?
I CAN'T HEAR YOU AT ALL.
NOBODY'S CROSSED THE FINISH LINE YET.
WELL ...
...I GUESS I DON'T BLAME YOU GUYS.
THAT'S HOW IT'S ALWAYS BEEN.
I'VE NEVER ...

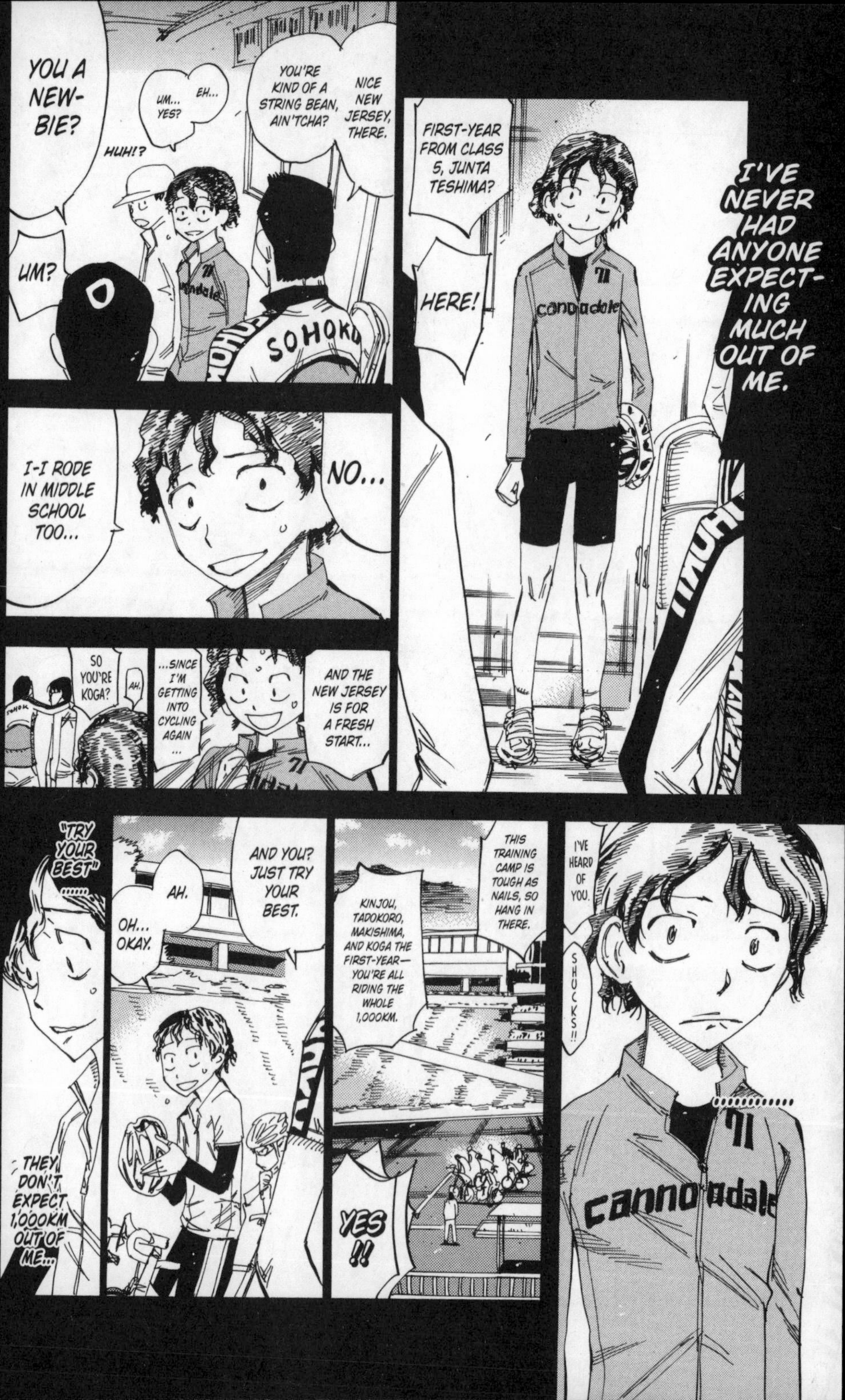
FIRST-YEAR FROM CLASS 5, JUNTA TESHIMA?
HERE!
I'VE NEVER HAD ANYONE EXPECTING MUCH OUT OF ME.
NICE NEW JERSEY, THERE.
YOU'RE KIND OF A STRING BEAN, AIN'TCHA?
EH...
UM... YES?
YOU A NEW-BIE?
HUH!?
UM?
SOHOKU
NO...
I-I RODE IN MIDDLE SCHOOL TOO...
AND THE NEW JERSEY IS FOR A FRESH START...
...SINCE I'M GETTING INTO CYCLING AGAIN...
AH.
SO YOU'RE KOGA?
I'VE HEARD OF YOU.
SHUCKS!!
....
THIS TRAINING CAMP IS TOUGH AS NAILS, SO HANG IN THERE.
KINJOU, TADOKORO, MAKISHIMA, AND KOGA THE FIRST-YEAR—YOU'RE ALL RIDING THE WHOLE 1,000KM.
YES!!
AND YOU? JUST TRY YOUR BEST.
AH.
OH... OKAY.
"TRY YOUR BEST" ......
THEY DON'T EXPECT 1,000KM OUT OF ME...

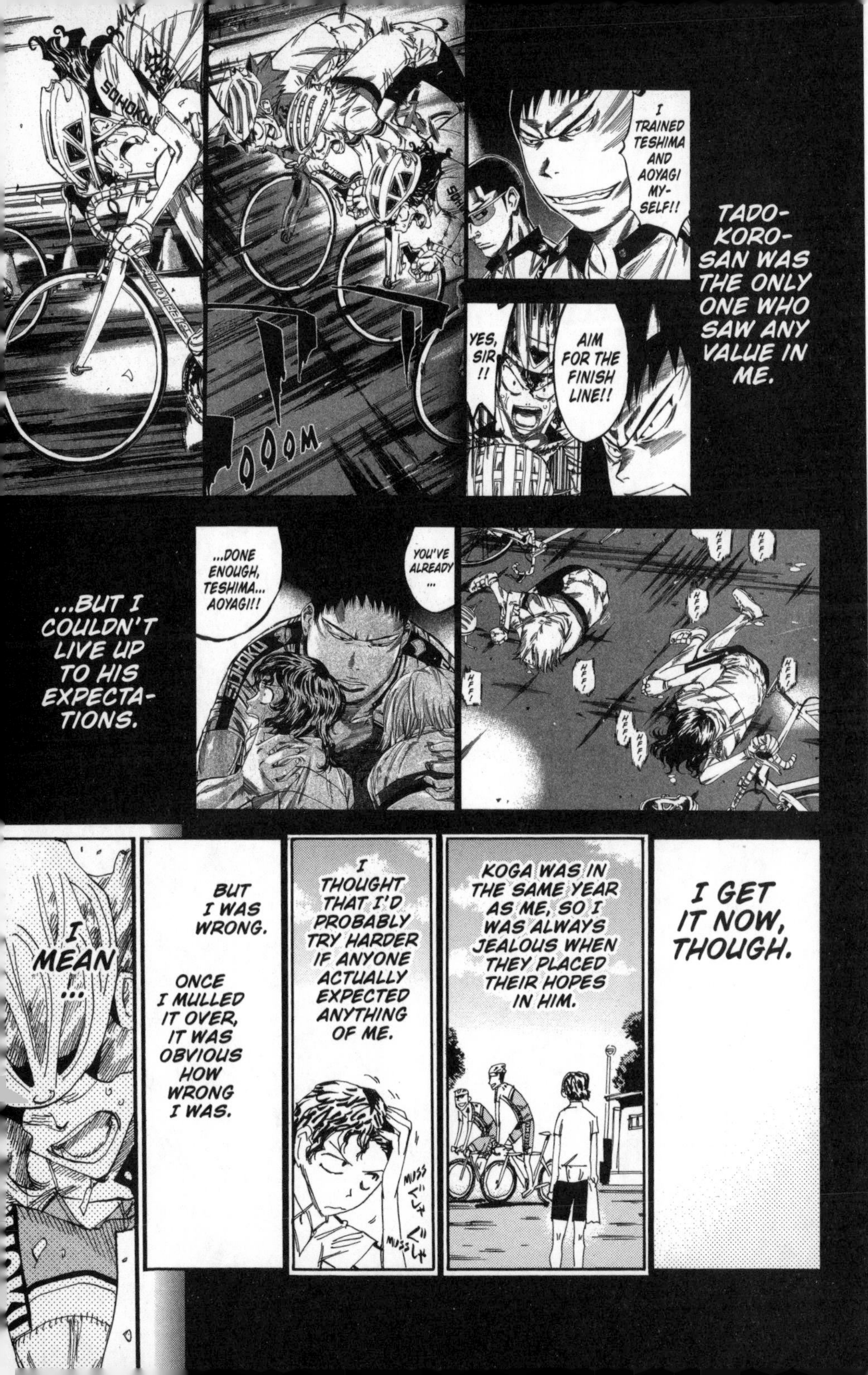
TADOKORO-SAN WAS THE ONLY ONE WHO SAW ANY VALUE IN ME.
I TRAINED TESHIMA AND AOYAGI MYSELF!!
AIM FOR THE FINISH LINE!!
YES, SIR!!
OOOM
HFF!
HFF!
HFF!
HFF!
HFF!
HFF!
HFF!
YOU'VE ALREADY ...
...DONE ENOUGH, TESHIMA... AOYAGI!!
...BUT I COULDN'T LIVE UP TO HIS EXPECTATIONS.
I GET IT NOW, THOUGH.
KOGA WAS IN THE SAME YEAR AS ME, SO I WAS ALWAYS JEALOUS WHEN THEY PLACED THEIR HOPES IN HIM.
I THOUGHT THAT I'D PROBABLY TRY HARDER IF ANYONE ACTUALLY EXPECTED ANYTHING OF ME.
MUSS
MUSS
BUT I WAS WRONG.
ONCE I MULLED IT OVER, IT WAS OBVIOUS HOW WRONG I WAS.
I MEAN ...

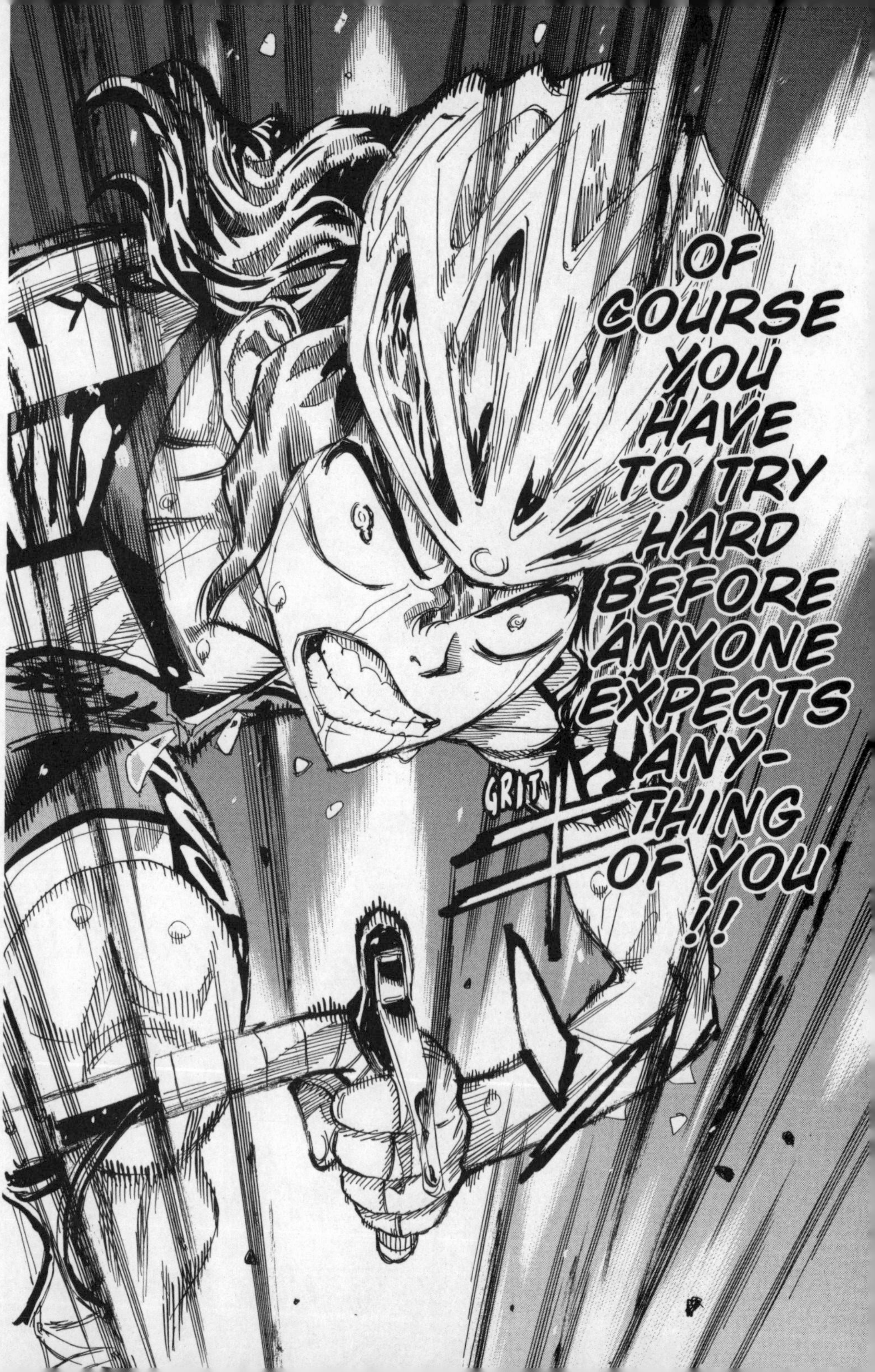
OF COURSE YOU HAVE TO TRY HARD BEFORE ANYONE EXPECTS ANY-THING OF YOU!!
GRIT

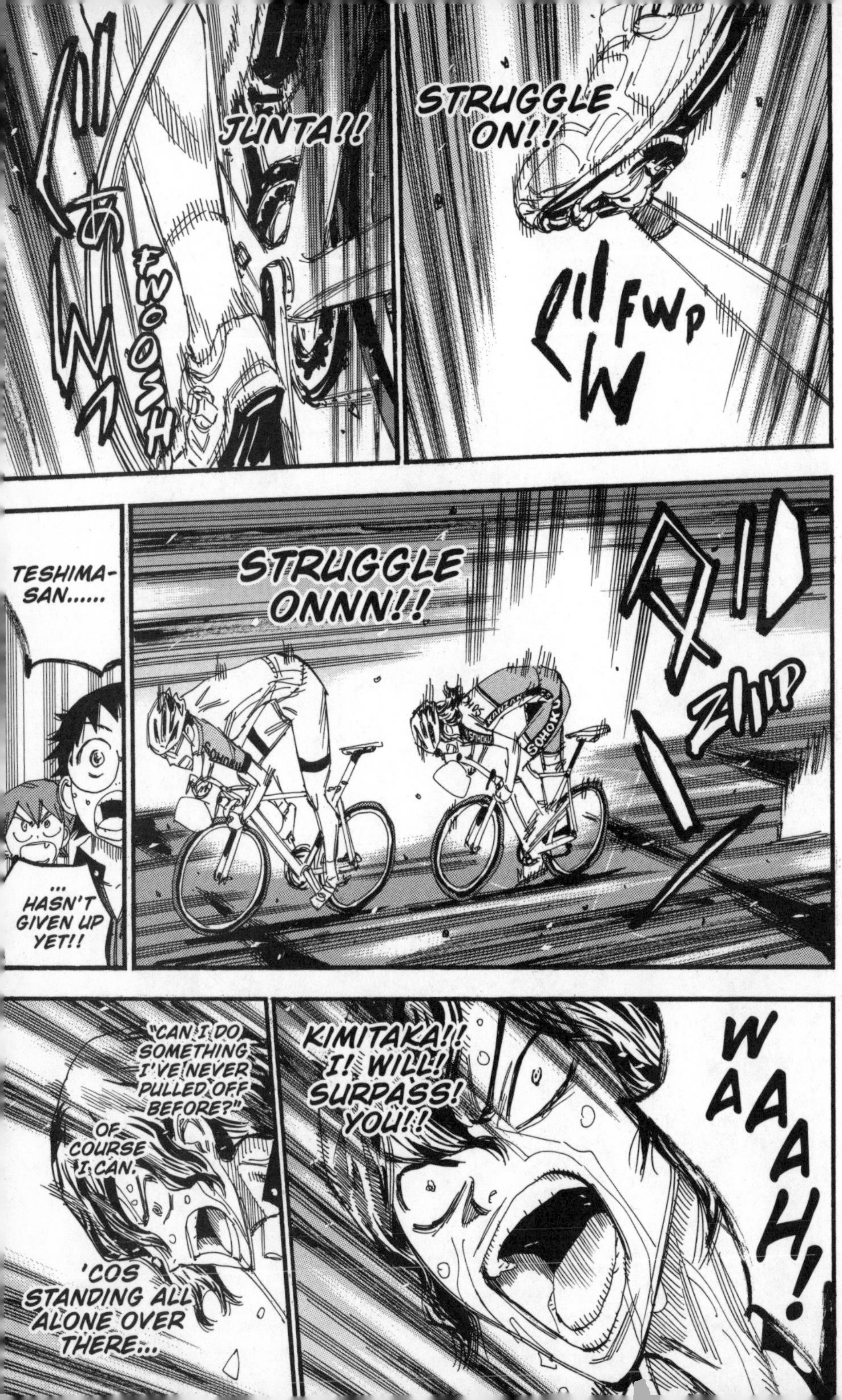
STRUGGLE ON!!
FWP
JUNTA!!
FWOOSH
STRUGGLE ONNN!!
ZIIIP
TESHIMA-SAN......
...HASN'T GIVEN UP YET!!
WAAAH!
KIMITAKA!! I! WILL! SURPASS! YOU!!
"CAN I DO SOMETHING I'VE NEVER PULLED OFF BEFORE?"
OF COURSE I CAN.
'COS STANDING ALL ALONE OVER THERE...

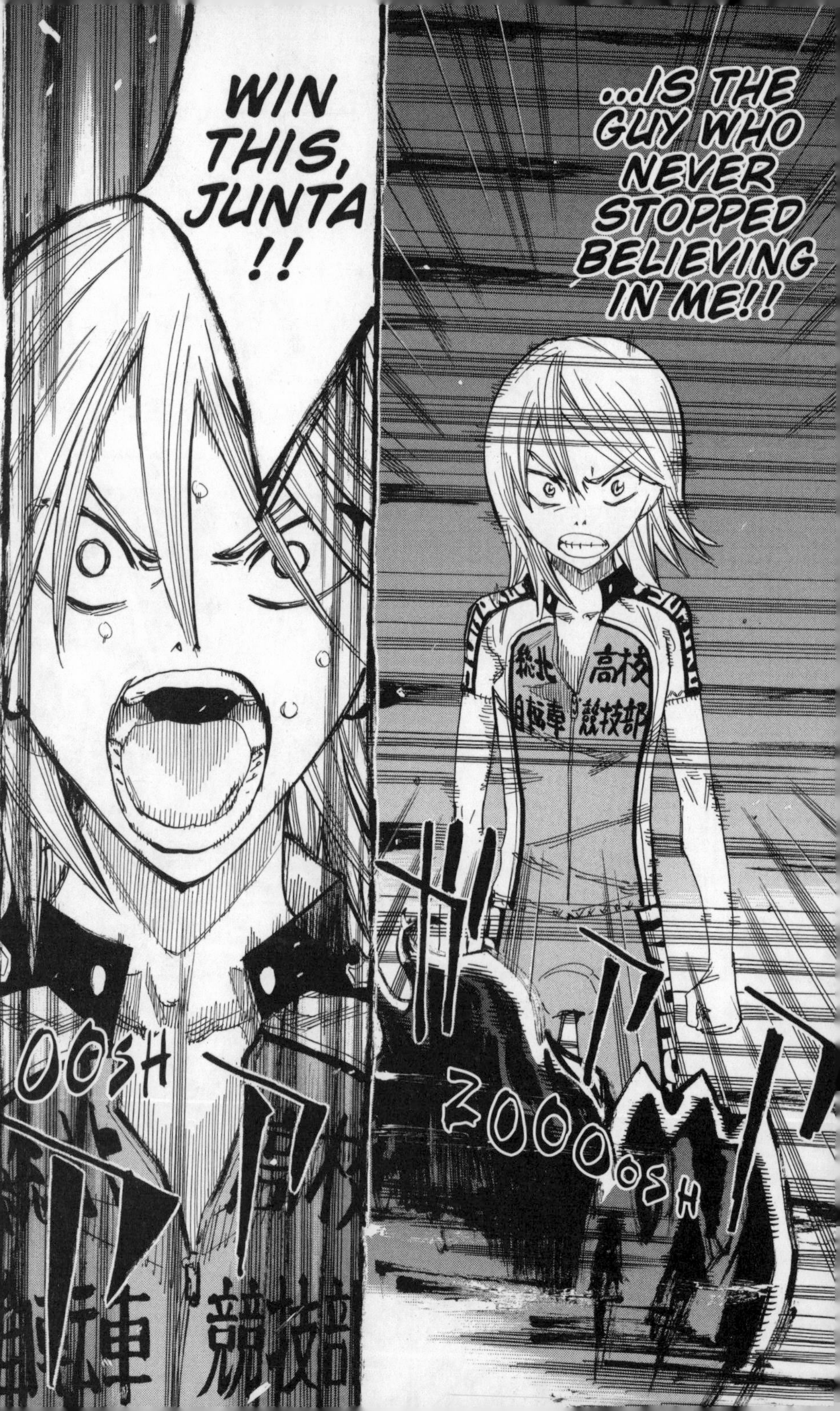
...IS THE GUY WHO NEVER STOPPED BELIEVING IN ME!!
総北 高校
自転車 競技部
ZOOOOoosh
WIN THIS, JUNTA!!
OOSH

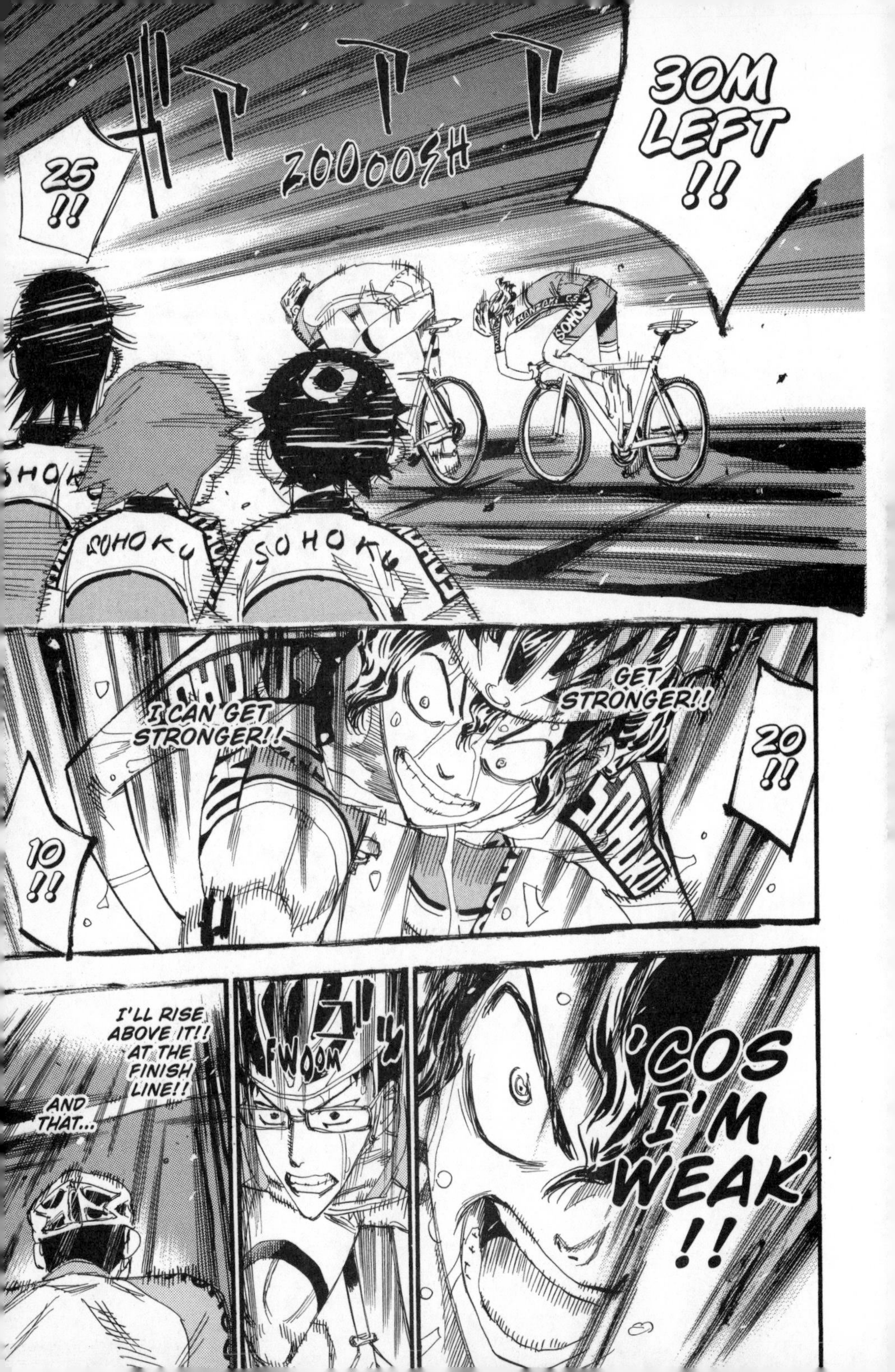
30M LEFT!!
ZOOOOOSH
25!!
20!!
GET STRONGER!!
I CAN GET STRONGER!!
10!!
'COS I'M WEAK!!
FWOOM
I'LL RISE ABOVE IT!! AT THE FINISH LINE!!
AND THAT...

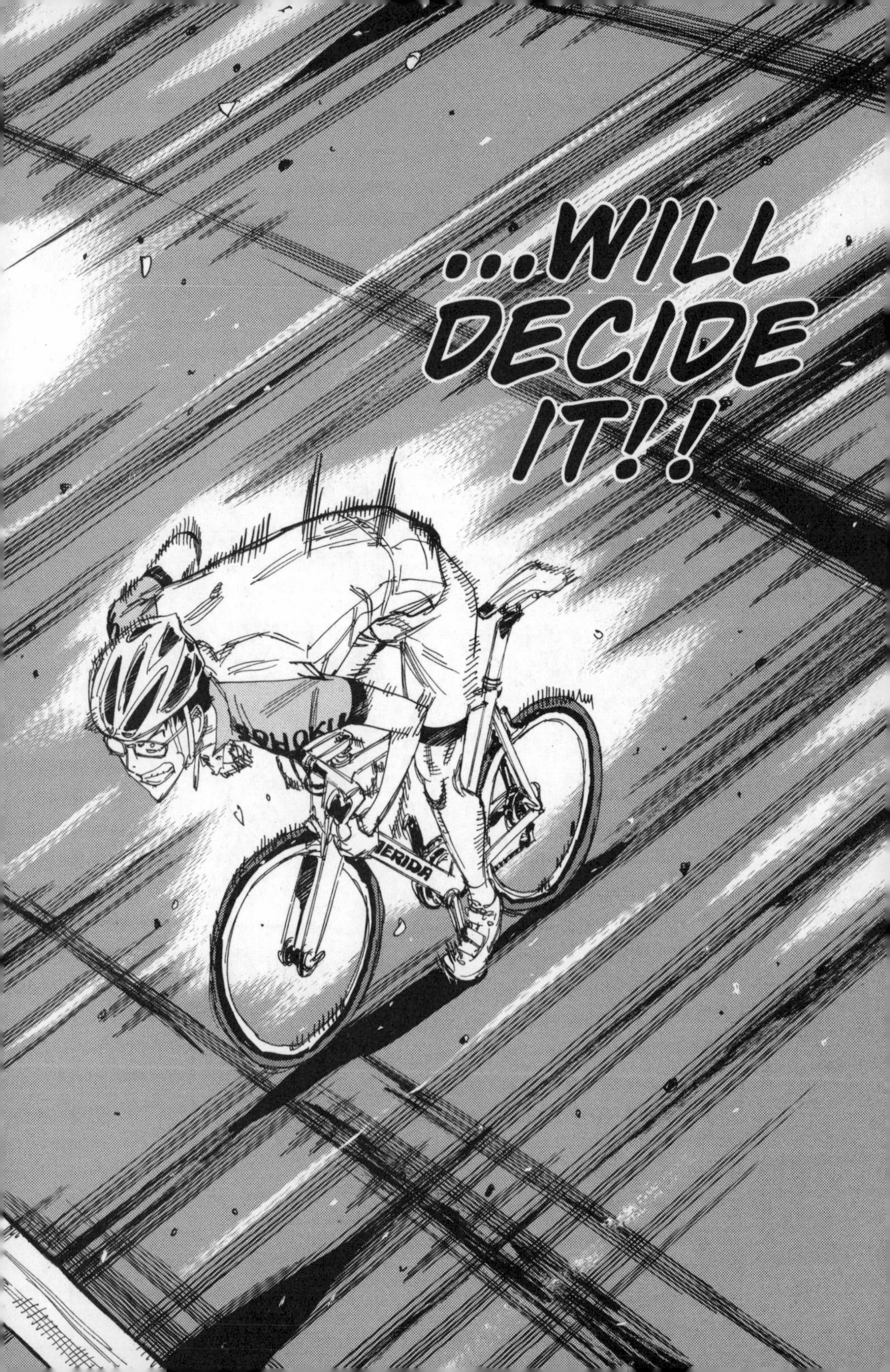
...WILL DECIDE IT!!
SOHOKU
MERIDA

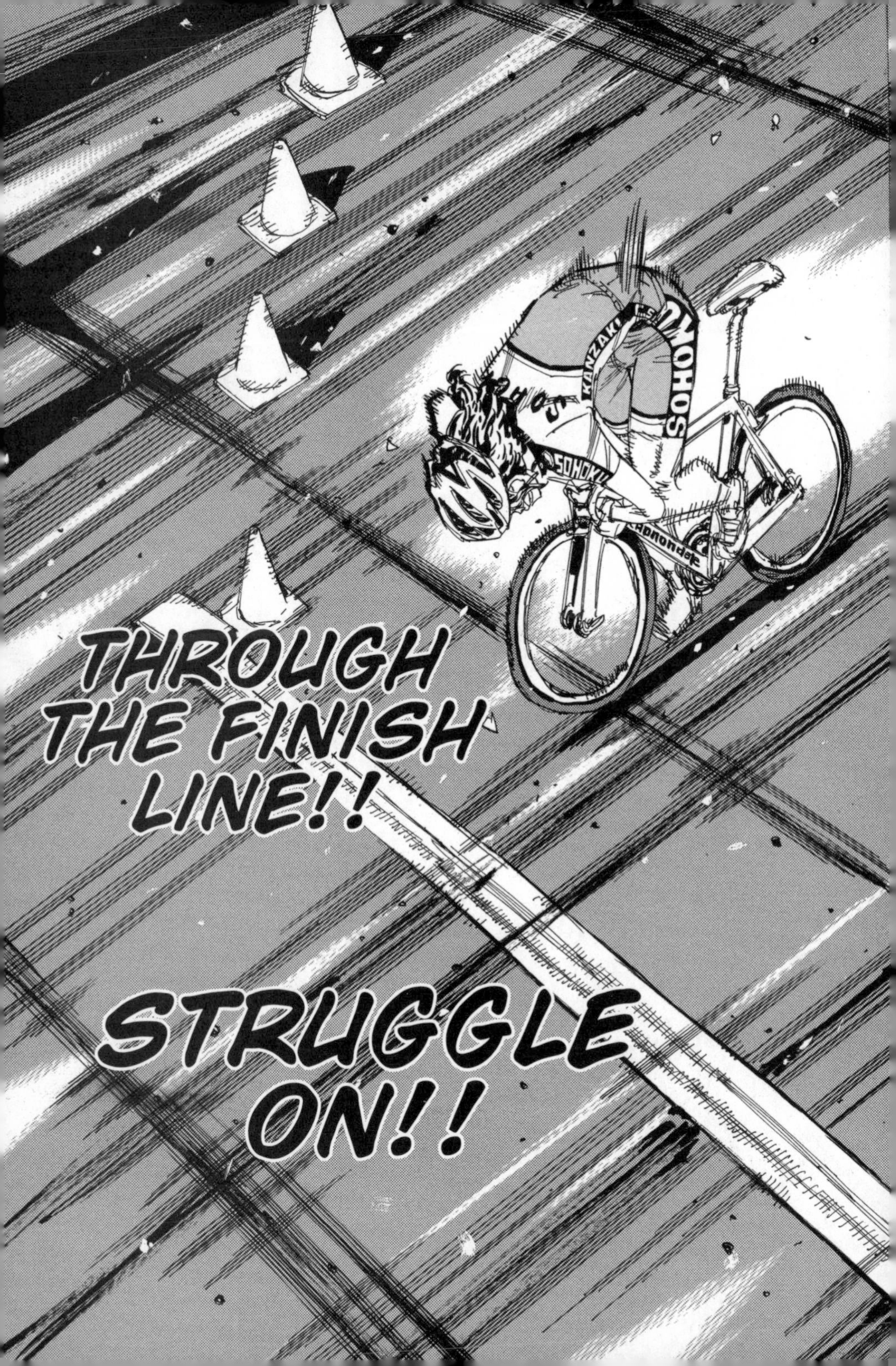
THROUGH THE FINISH LINE!!
STRUGGLE ON!!

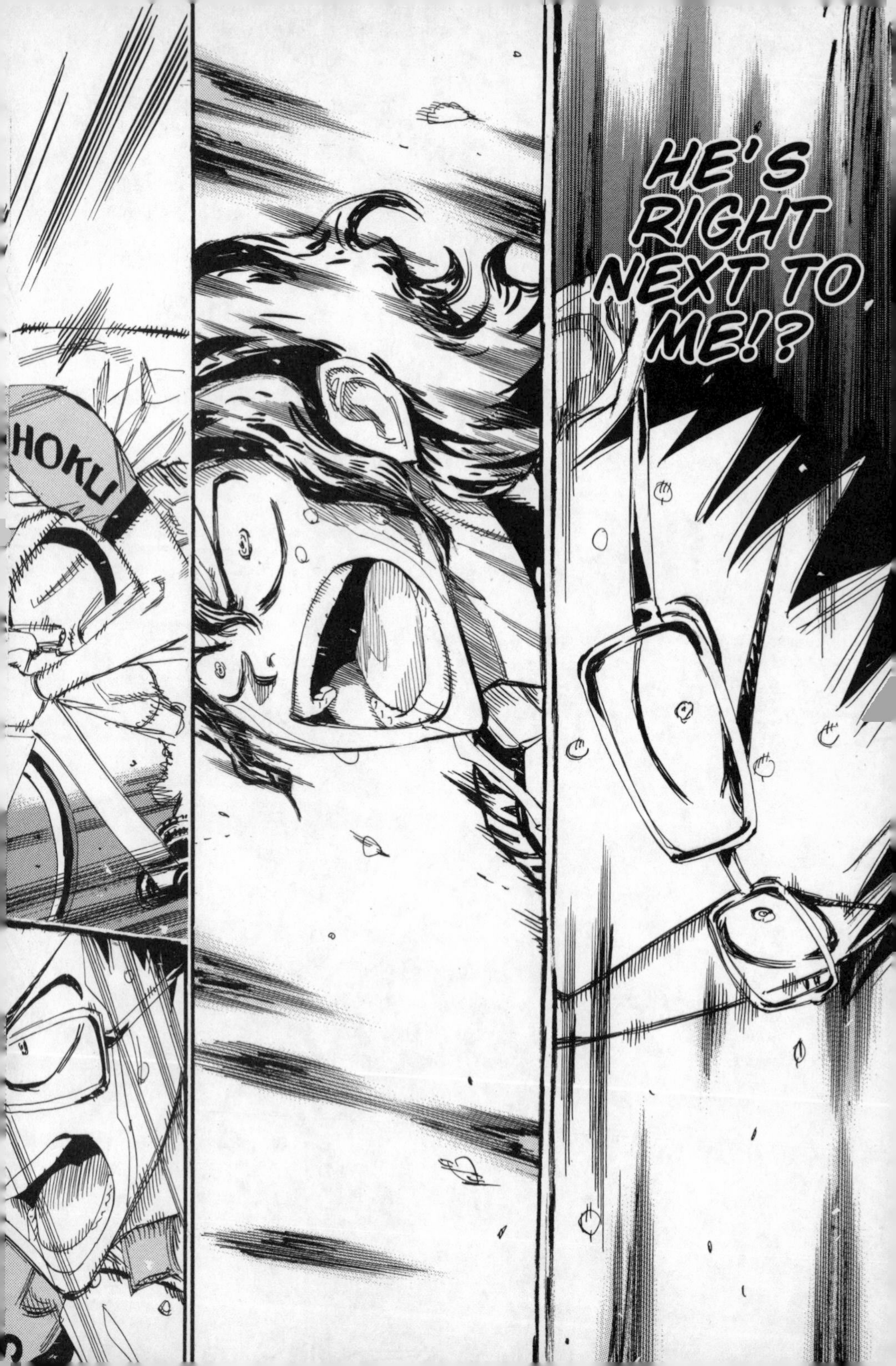
HE'S RIGHT NEXT TO ME!?
HOKU

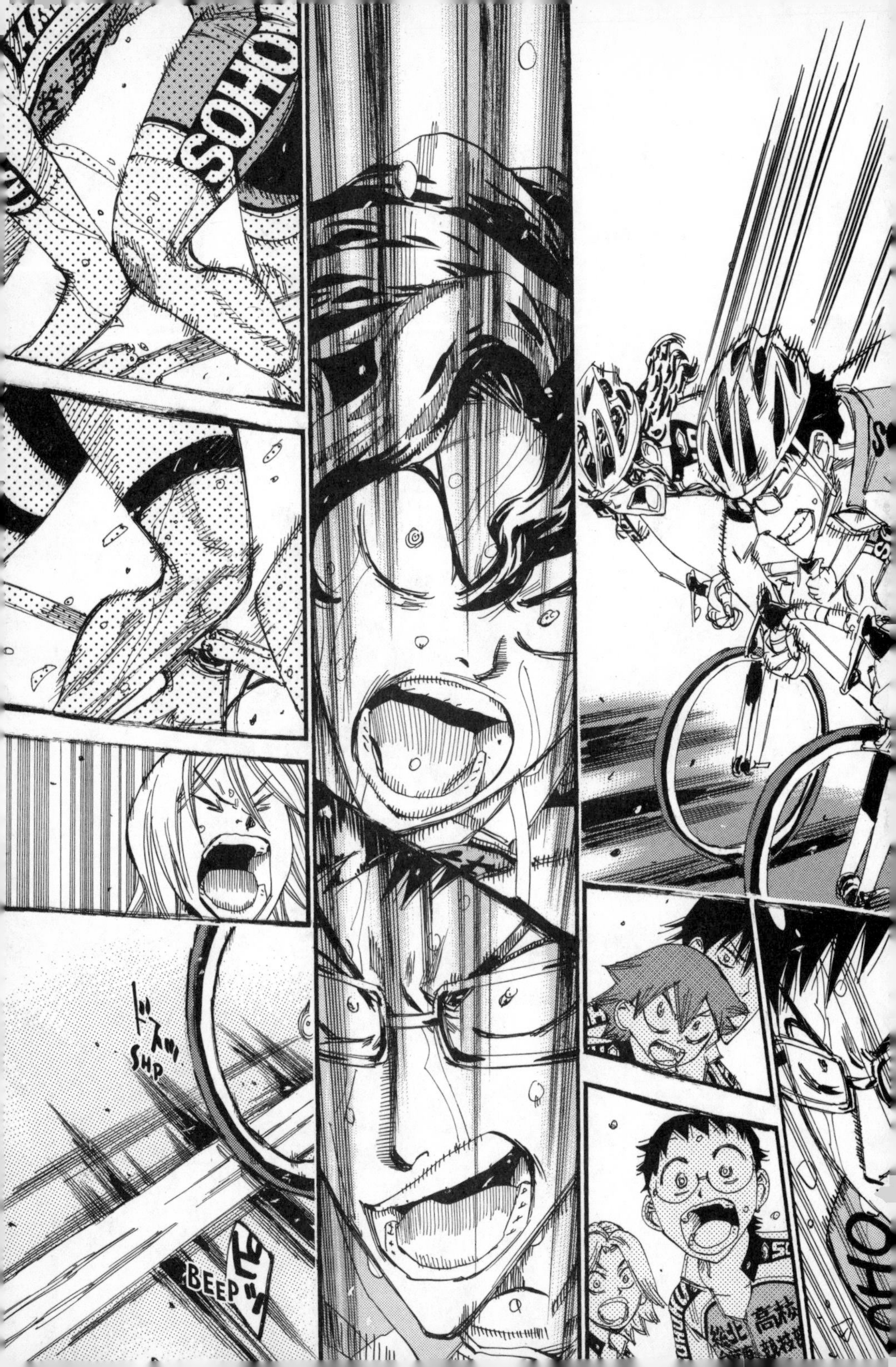
ドスッ
SHP
ピッ
BEEP

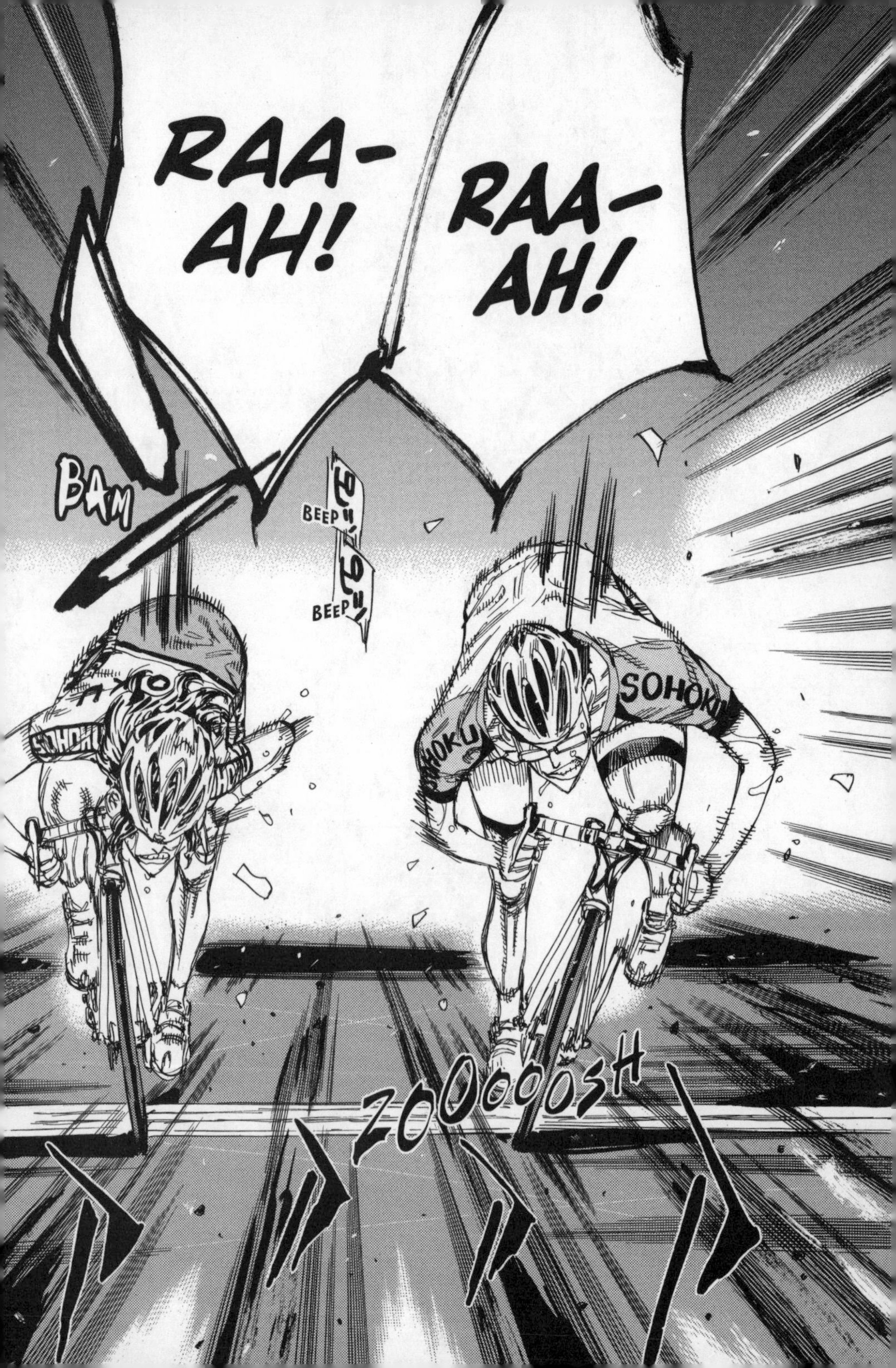
RAA-AH!
RAA-AH!
BEEP
BEEP
BAM
SOHOKU
ZOOOOOSH

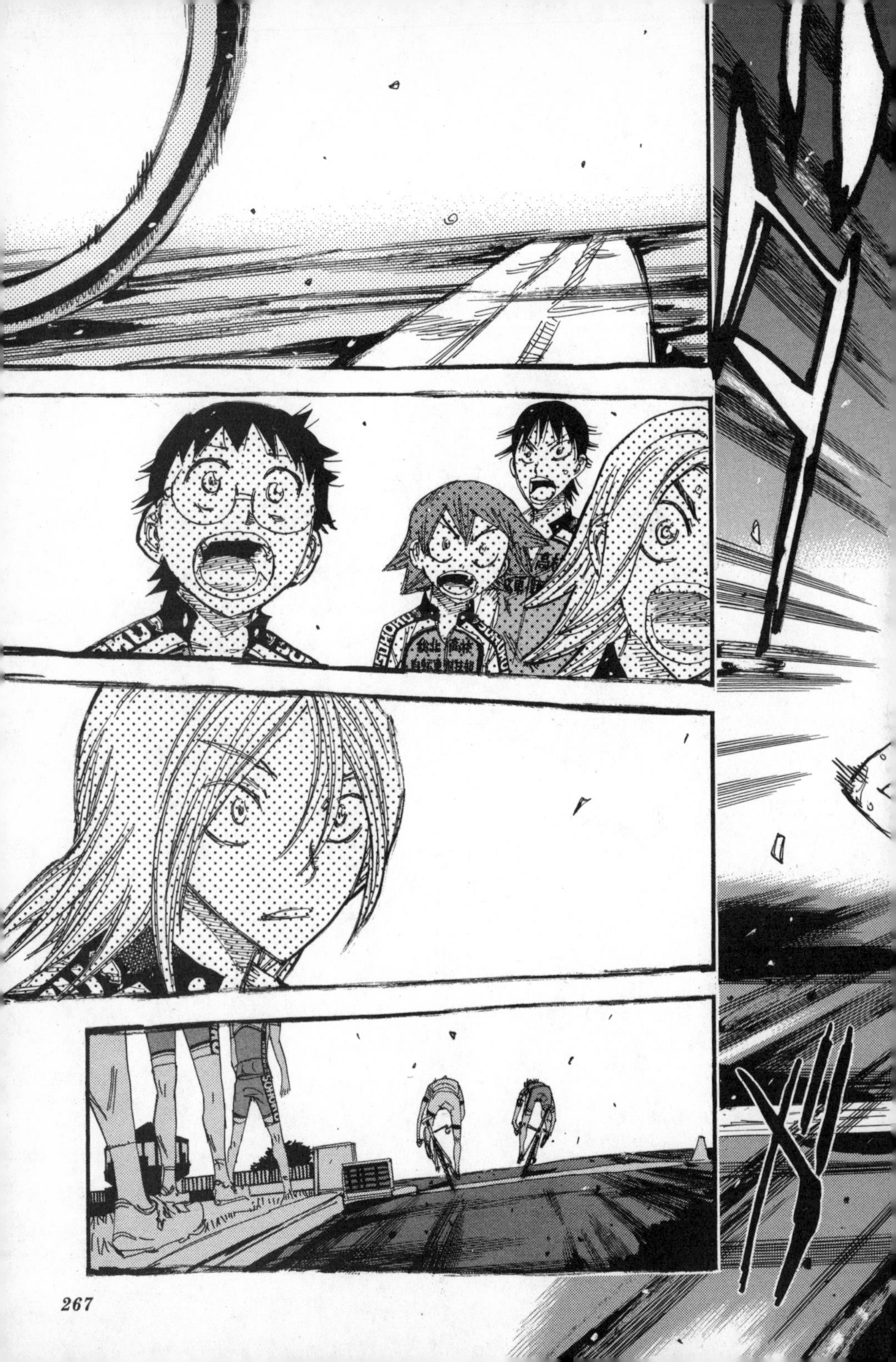

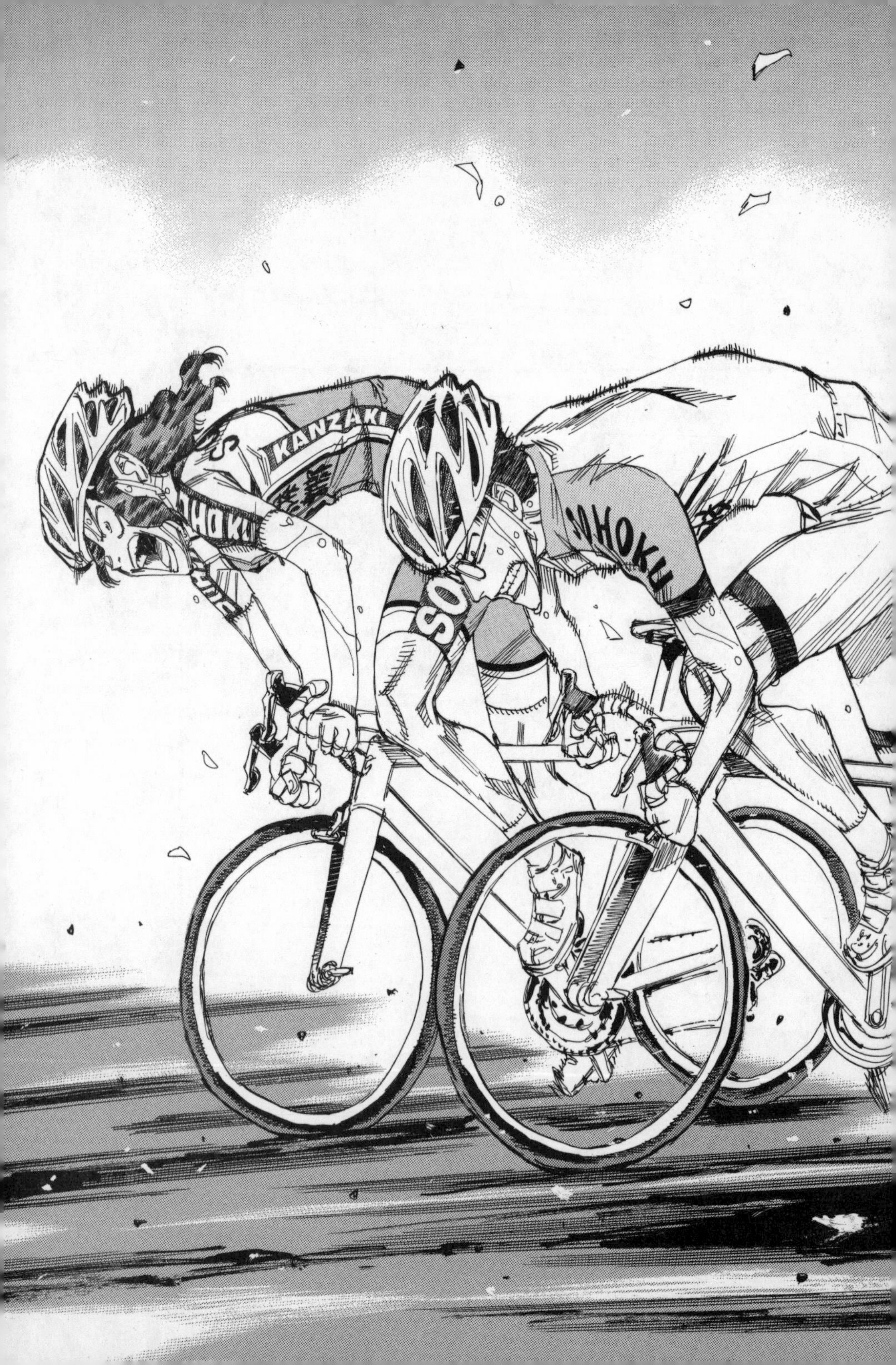
KANZAKI
SOHOKU

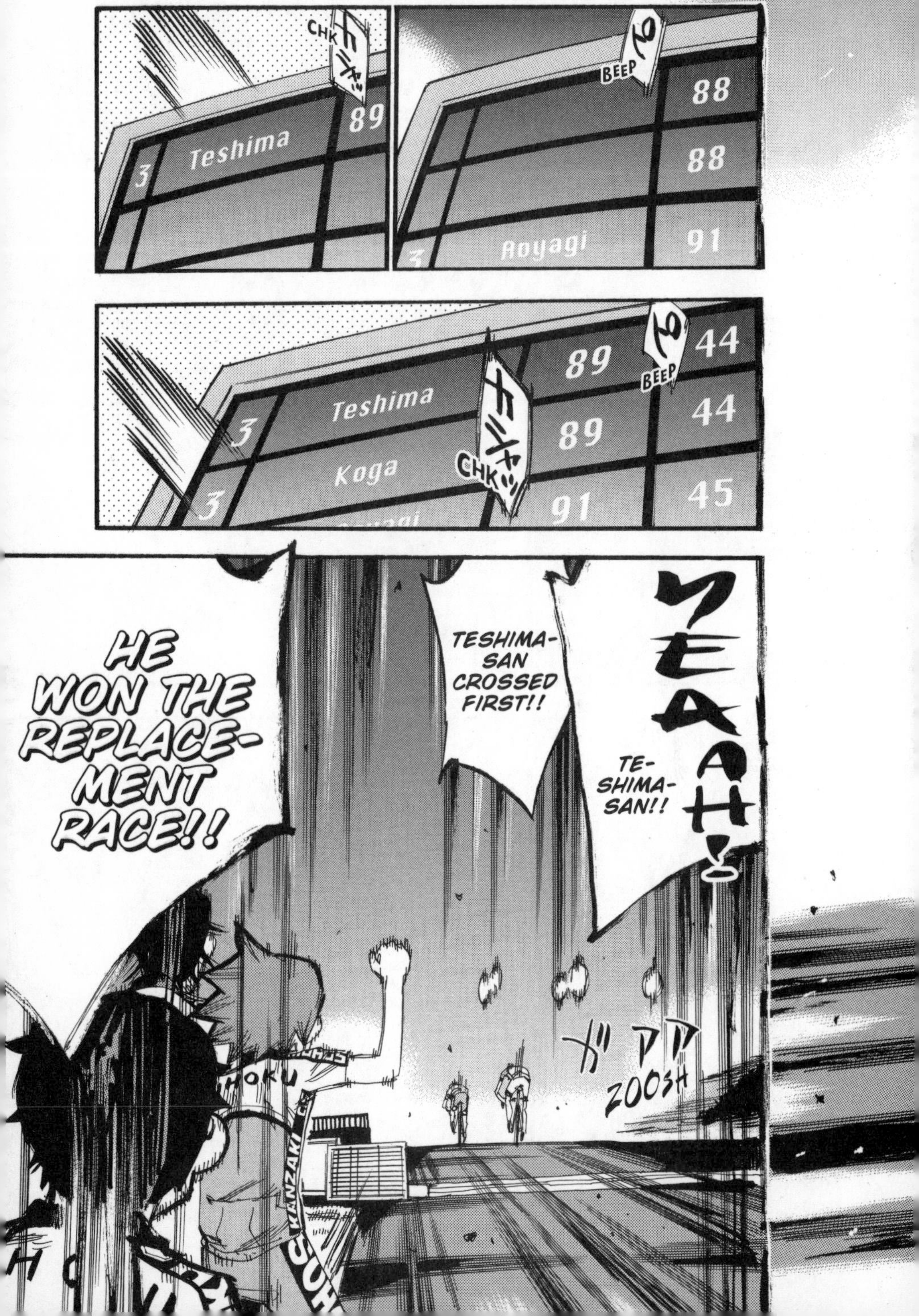

BEEP
88
88
3 Aoyagi 91
CHK
3 Teshima 89
BEEP
CHK
3 Teshima 89 44
3 Koga 89 44
91 45
YEAAAH!
TESHIMA-SAN CROSSED FIRST!!
TE-SHIMA-SAN!!
HE WON THE REPLACEMENT RACE!!
ZOOSH

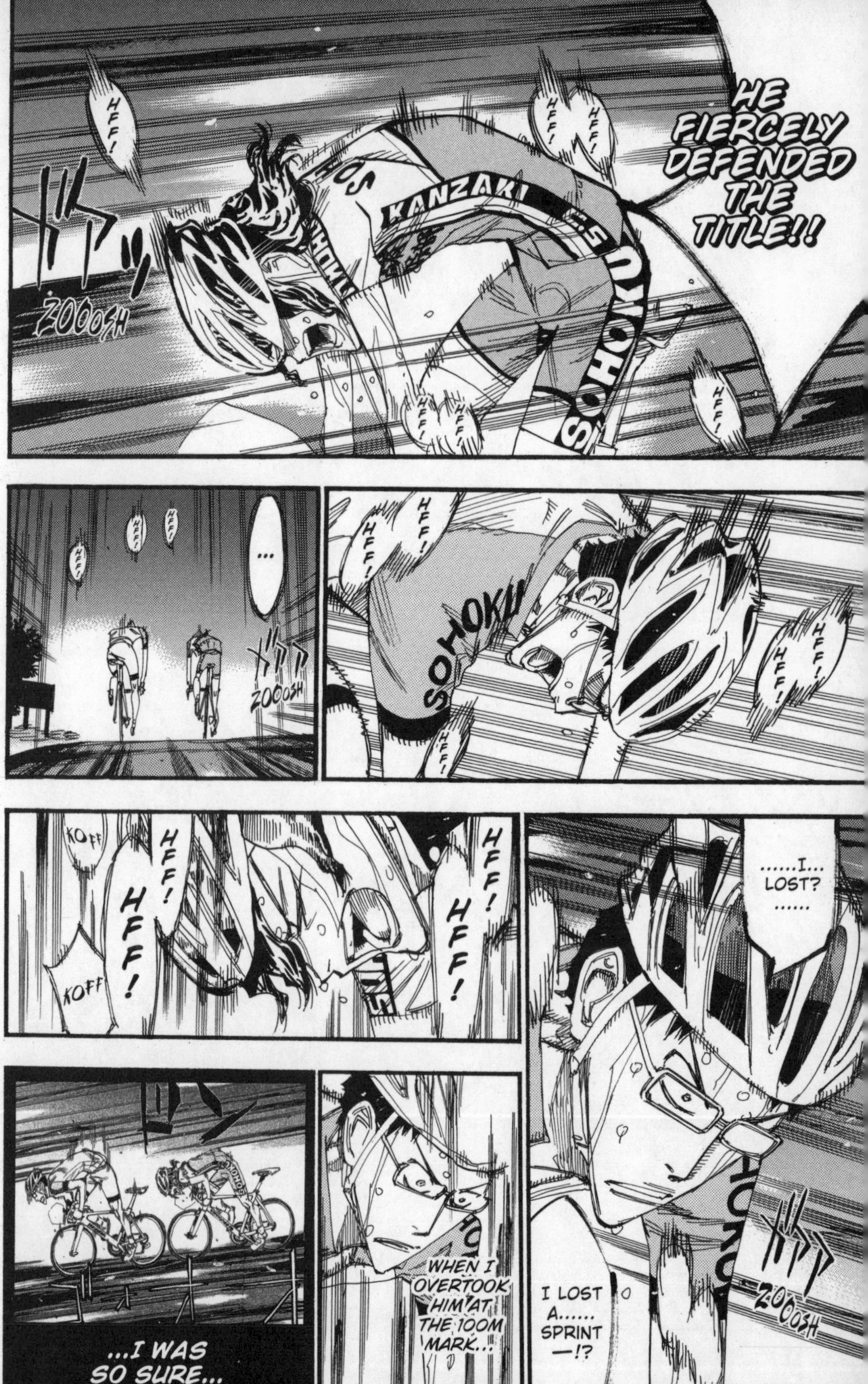
HE FIERCELY DEFENDED THE TITLE!!
HFF!
HFF!
HFF!
HFF!
ZOOOSH
HFF!
HFF!
HFF!
HFF!
HFF!
HFF!
HFF!
HFF!
HFF!
HFF!
HFF!
...
HFF!
ZOOOSH
......I... LOST? ......
I LOST A...... SPRINT —!?
ZOOOSH
HFF!
HFF!
HFF!
HFF!
KOFF
KOFF
WHEN I OVERTOOK HIM AT THE 100M MARK...
...I WAS SO SURE...

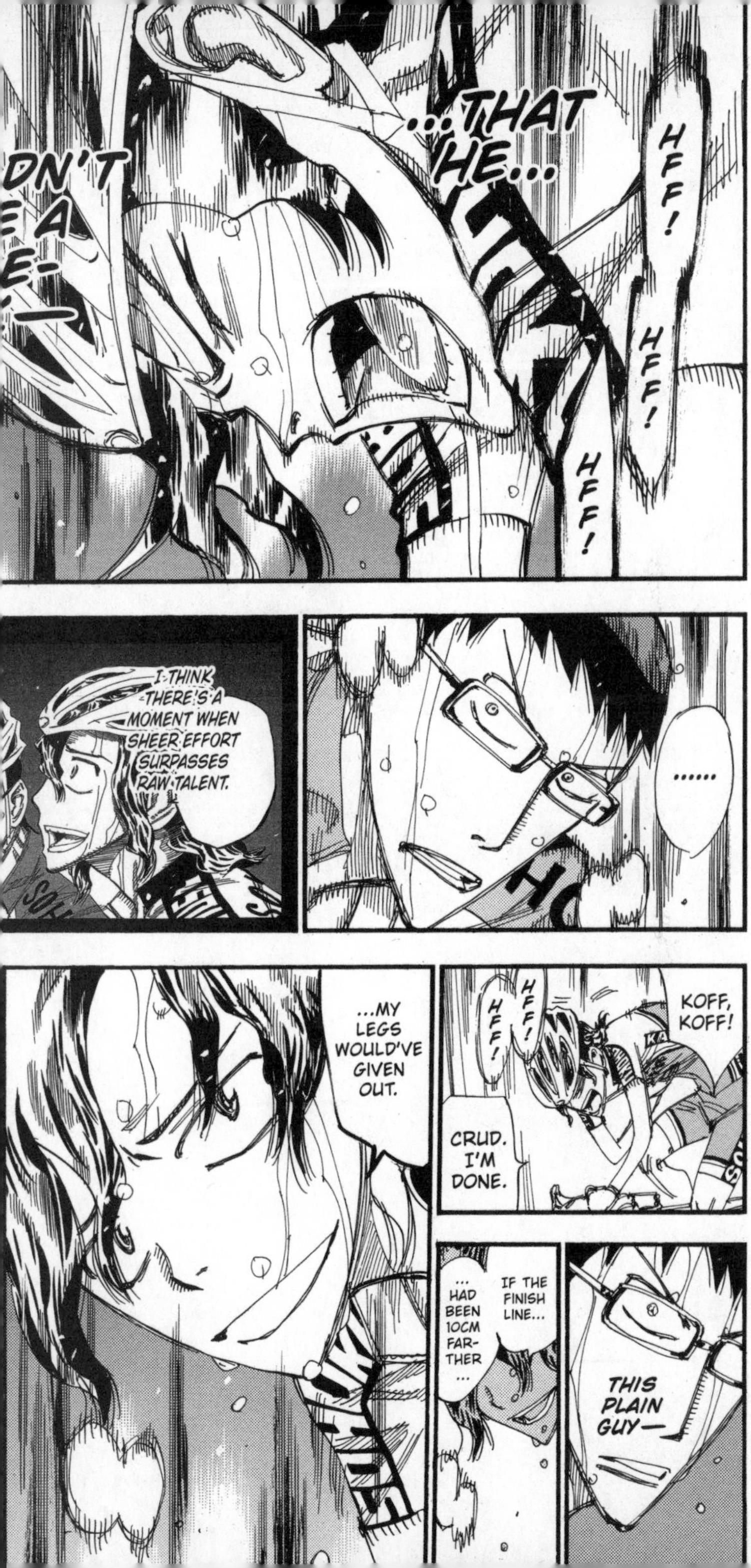
HFF! HFF! HFF!
...THAT HE...
......
I THINK THERE'S A MOMENT WHEN SHEER EFFORT SURPASSES RAW TALENT.
KOFF, KOFF!
HFF! HFF!
CRUD. I'M DONE.
THIS PLAIN GUY—
IF THE FINISH LINE...
...HAD BEEN 10CM FARTHER...
...MY LEGS WOULD'VE GIVEN OUT.

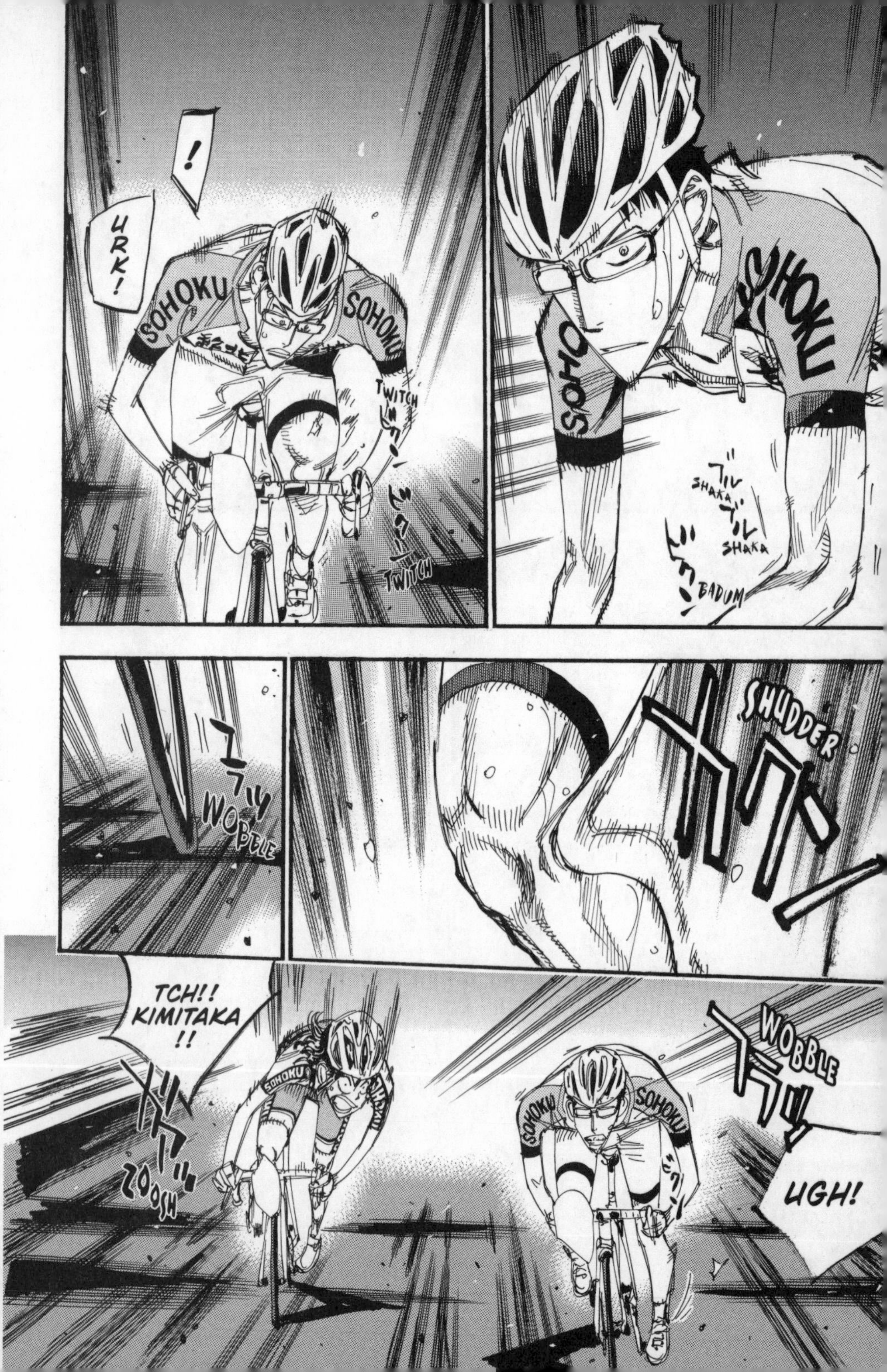
SHAKA
SHAKA
BADUM
!
URK!
TWITCH
TWITCH
SHUDDER
WOBBLE
WOBBLE
UGH!
TCH!! KIMITAKA!!
ZOOSH

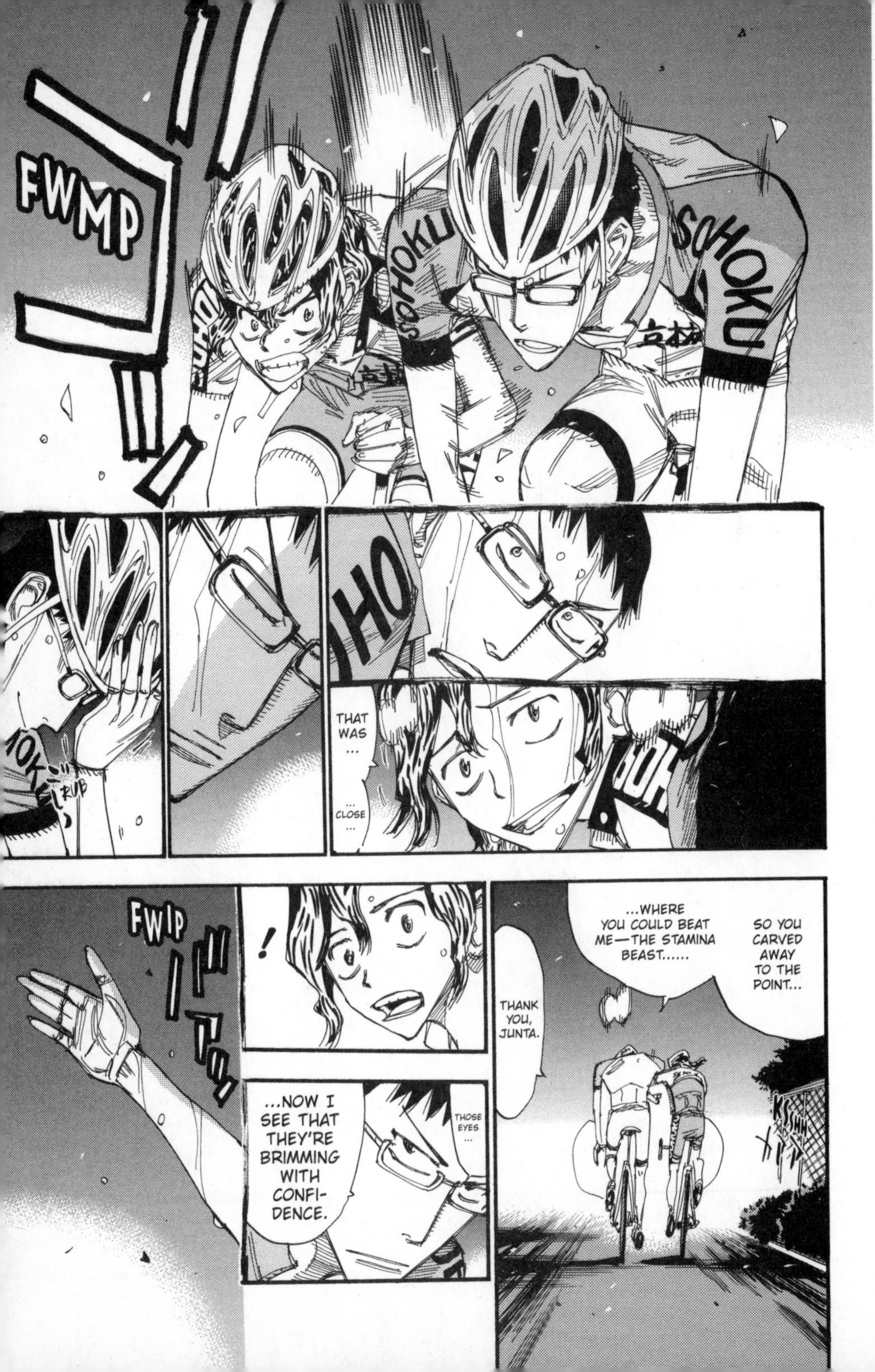
FWMP
THAT WAS ...
... CLOSE ...
RUB
SO YOU CARVED AWAY TO THE POINT...
...WHERE YOU COULD BEAT ME—THE STAMINA BEAST......
THANK YOU, JUNTA.
KSHHH
!
THOSE EYES ...
...NOW I SEE THAT THEY'RE BRIMMING WITH CONFI-DENCE.
FWIP

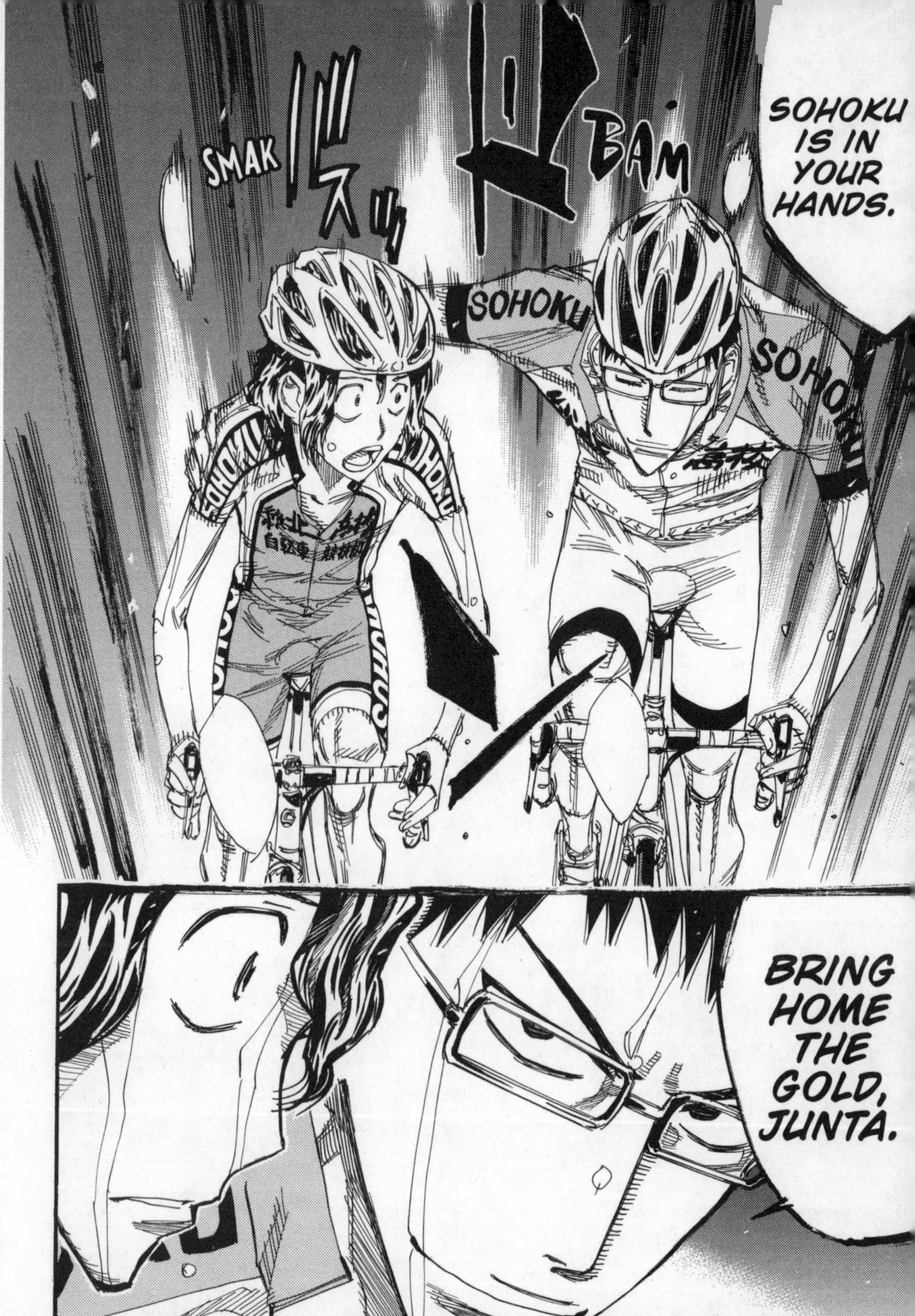
SOHOKU IS IN YOUR HANDS.
BAM
SMAK
BRING HOME THE GOLD, JUNTA.

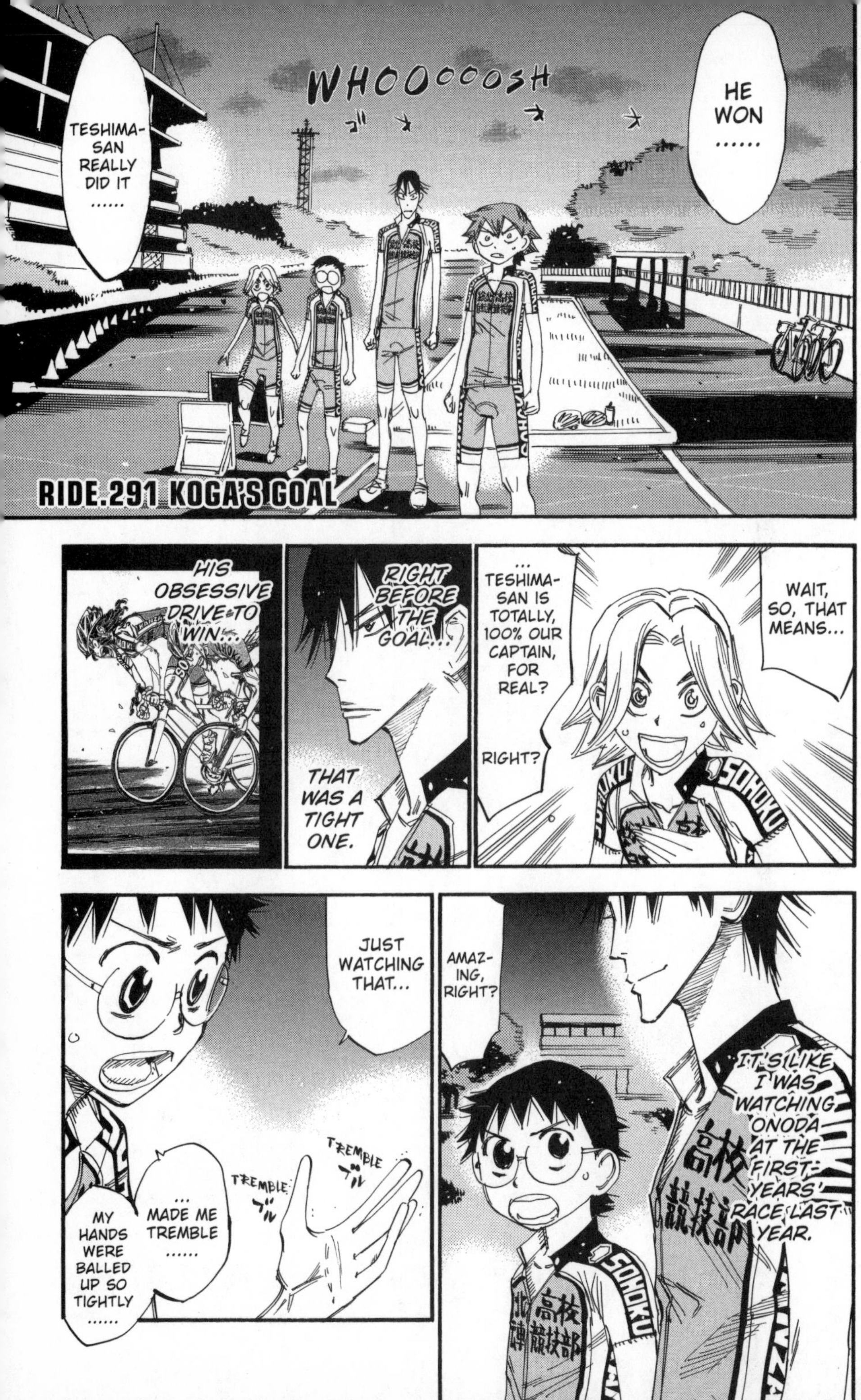
HE WON ......
WHOOOOOOSH
TESHIMA-SAN REALLY DID IT ......
RIDE.291 KOGA'S GOAL
WAIT, SO, THAT MEANS...
... TESHIMA-SAN IS TOTALLY, 100% OUR CAPTAIN, FOR REAL?
RIGHT?
RIGHT BEFORE THE GOAL...
THAT WAS A TIGHT ONE.
HIS OBSESSIVE DRIVE TO WIN...
IT'S LIKE I WAS WATCHING ONODA AT THE FIRST-YEARS' RACE LAST YEAR.
AMAZ-ING, RIGHT?
JUST WATCHING THAT...
TREMBLE
TREMBLE
... MADE ME TREMBLE ......
MY HANDS WERE BALLED UP SO TIGHTLY ......

RIDE.291 KOGA'S GOAL

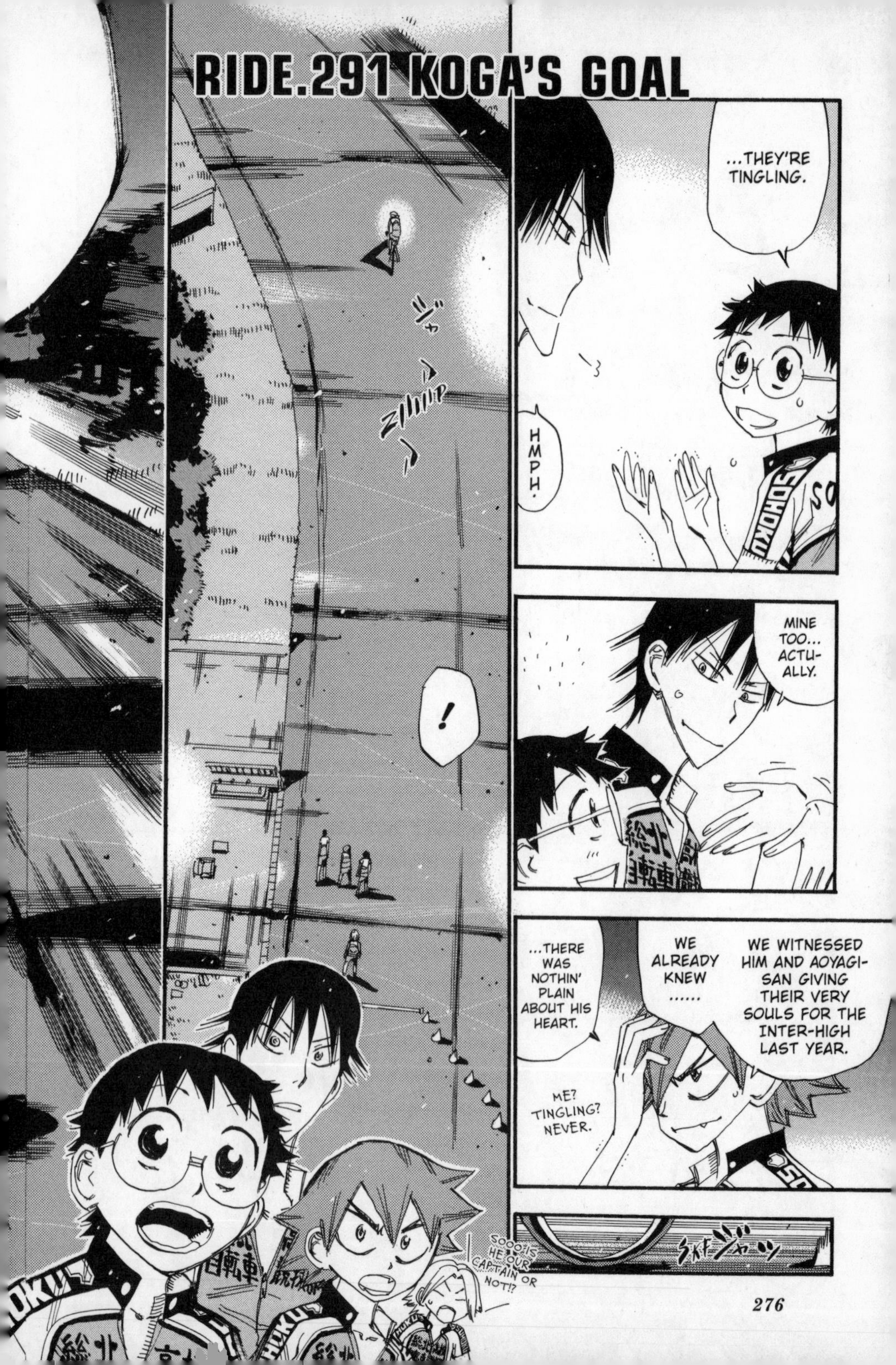
...THEY'RE TINGLING.
HMPH.
MINE TOO... ACTUALLY.
WE WITNESSED HIM AND AOYAGI-SAN GIVING THEIR VERY SOULS FOR THE INTER-HIGH LAST YEAR.
WE ALREADY KNEW ......
...THERE WAS NOTHIN' PLAIN ABOUT HIS HEART.
ME? TINGLING? NEVER.
!
SOOO, IS HE OUR CAPTAIN OR NOT!?

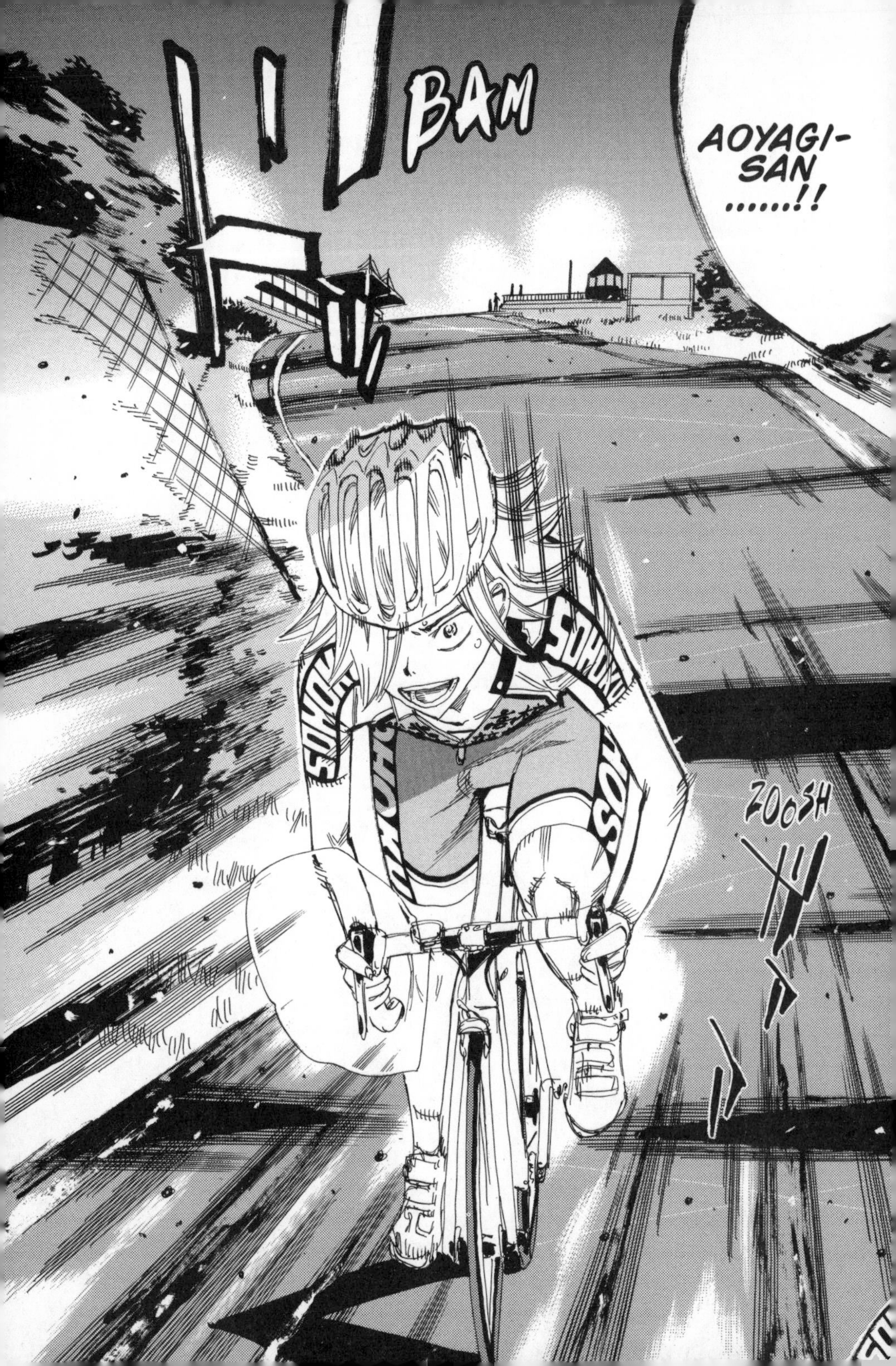
BAM
AOYAGI-SAN ......!!
ZOOSH

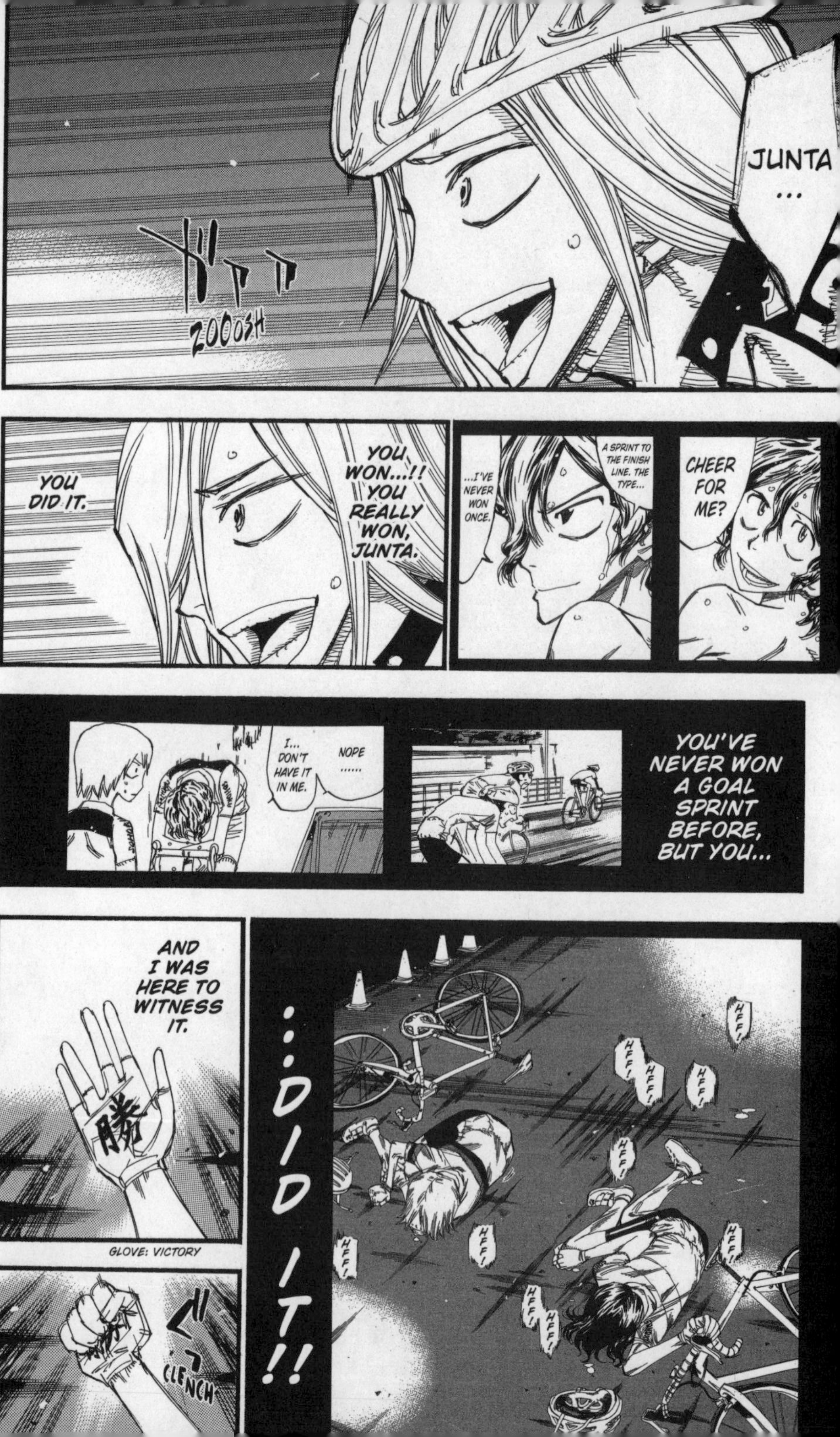
JUNTA ...
ザァァ
ZOOOSH
CHEER FOR ME?
A SPRINT TO THE FINISH LINE. THE TYPE...
...I'VE NEVER WON ONCE.
YOU WON...!! YOU REALLY WON, JUNTA.
YOU DID IT.
YOU'VE NEVER WON A GOAL SPRINT BEFORE, BUT YOU...
NOPE ......
I... DON'T HAVE IT IN ME.
...DID IT!!
HFF!
HFF!
HFF!
HFF!
HFF!
HFF!
HFF!
HFF!
HFF!
HFF!
AND I WAS HERE TO WITNESS IT.
勝
GLOVE: VICTORY
ぐっ
CLENCH

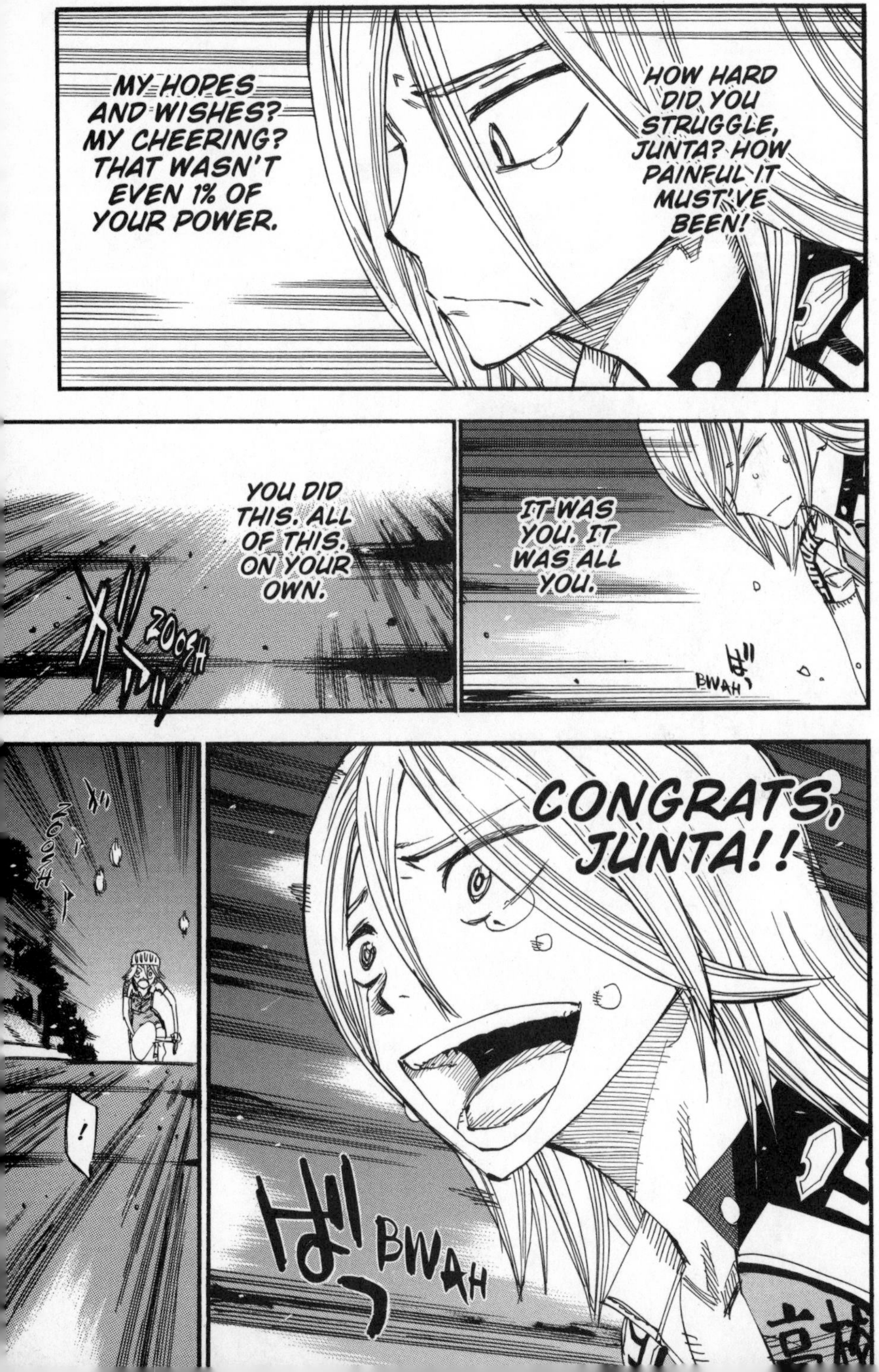
HOW HARD DID YOU STRUGGLE, JUNTA? HOW PAINFUL IT MUST'VE BEEN!
MY HOPES AND WISHES? MY CHEERING? THAT WASN'T EVEN 1% OF YOUR POWER.
IT WAS YOU. IT WAS ALL YOU.
BWAH
YOU DID THIS. ALL OF THIS. ON YOUR OWN.
ZOOSH
CONGRATS, JUNTA!!
BWAH
ZOOSH
!

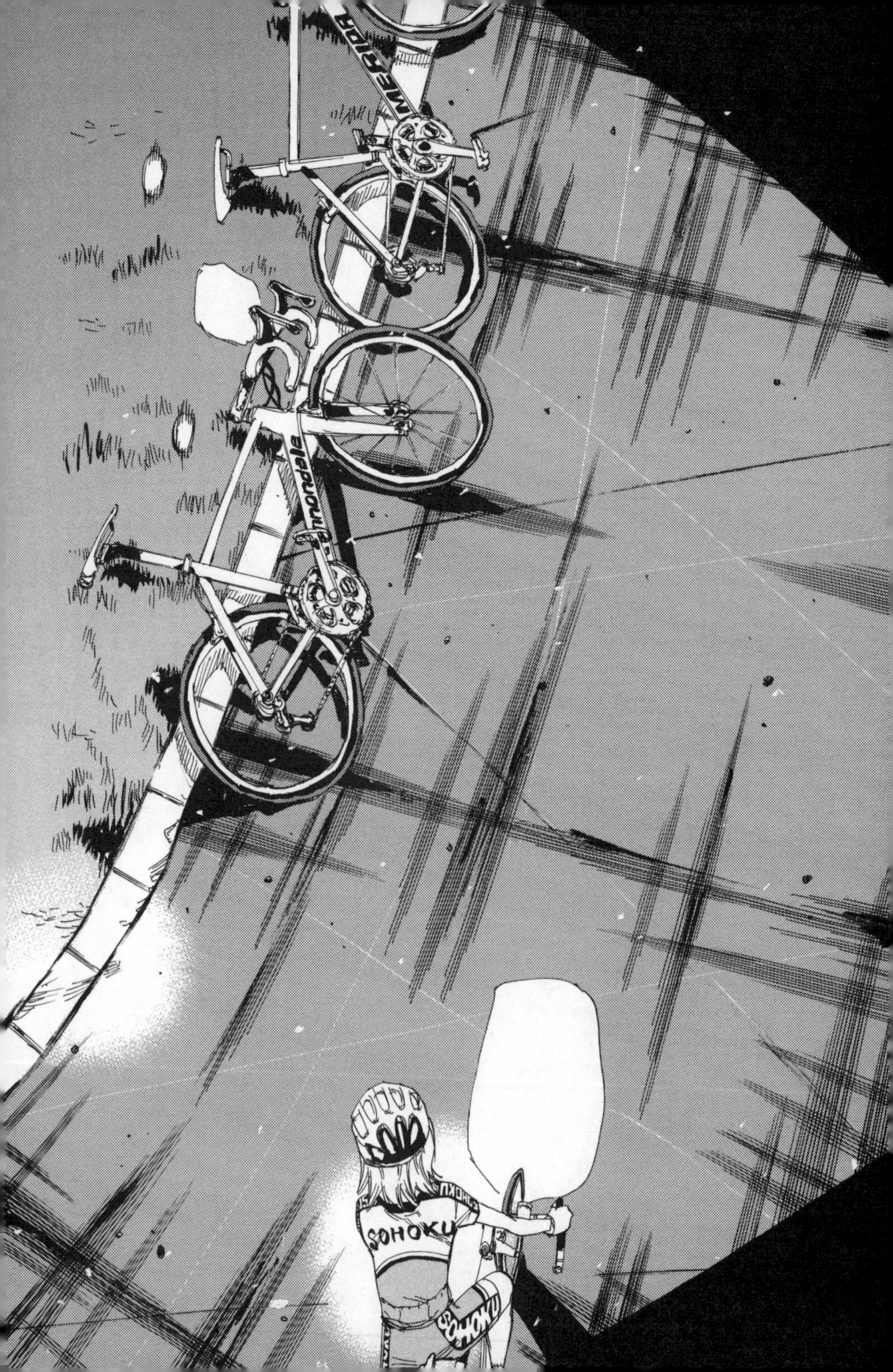
SOHOKU

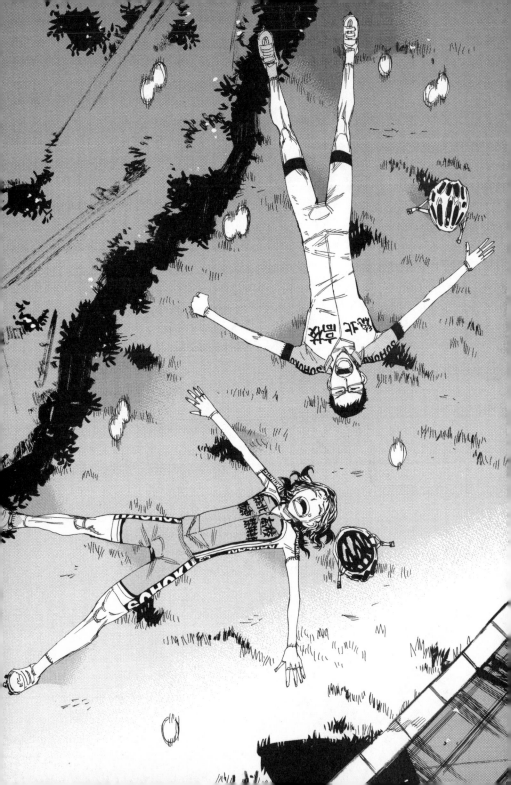

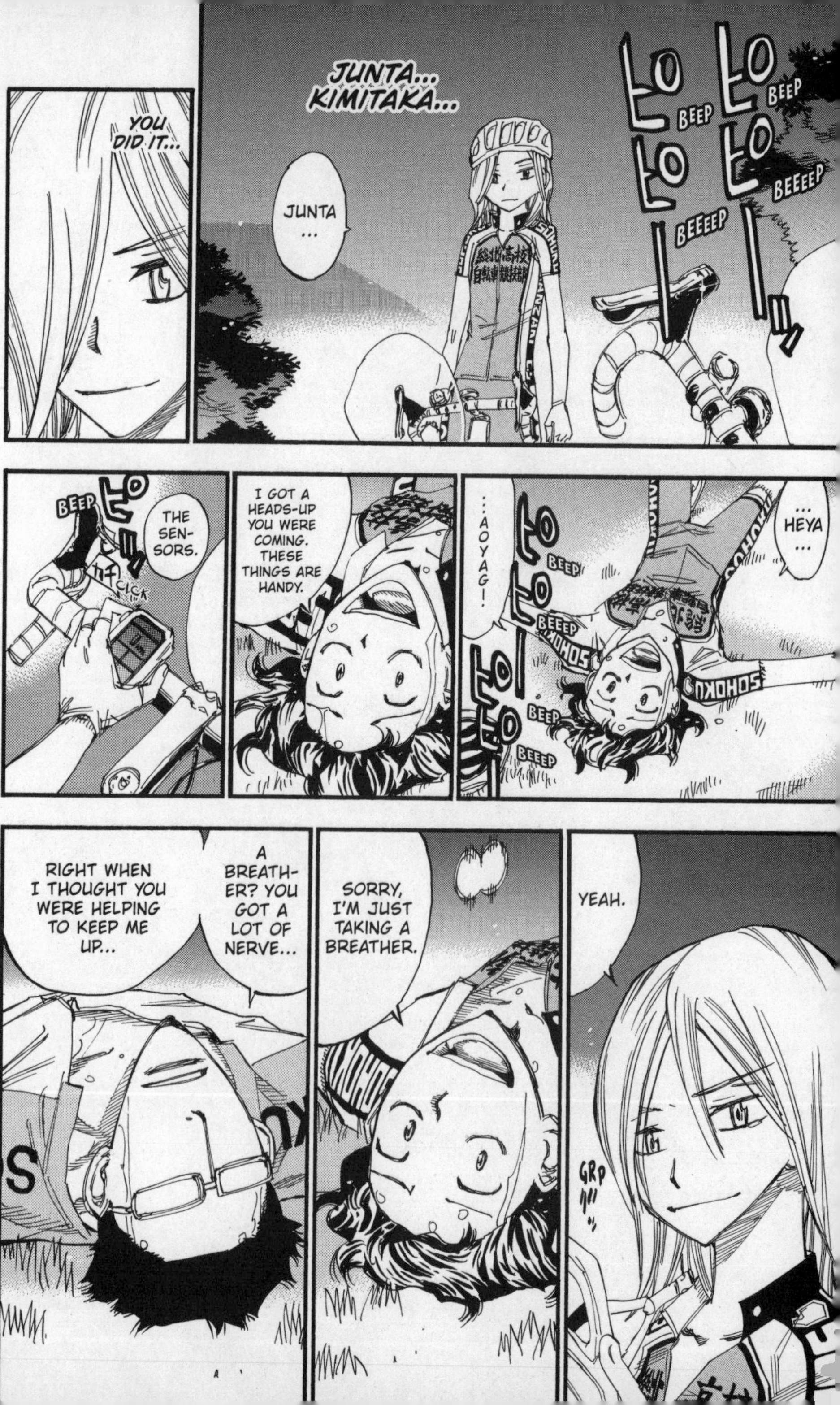
JUNTA... KIMITAKA...
BEEP
BEEP
BEEEEP
BEEEEP
JUNTA ...
YOU DID IT...
... HEYA ...
...AOYAGI!
BEEP
BEEEP
BEEP
BEEEP
I GOT A HEADS-UP YOU WERE COMING. THESE THINGS ARE HANDY.
BEEP
THE SEN-SORS.
CLICK
YEAH.
GRP
SORRY, I'M JUST TAKING A BREATHER.
A BREATHER? YOU GOT A LOT OF NERVE...
RIGHT WHEN I THOUGHT YOU WERE HELPING TO KEEP ME UP...

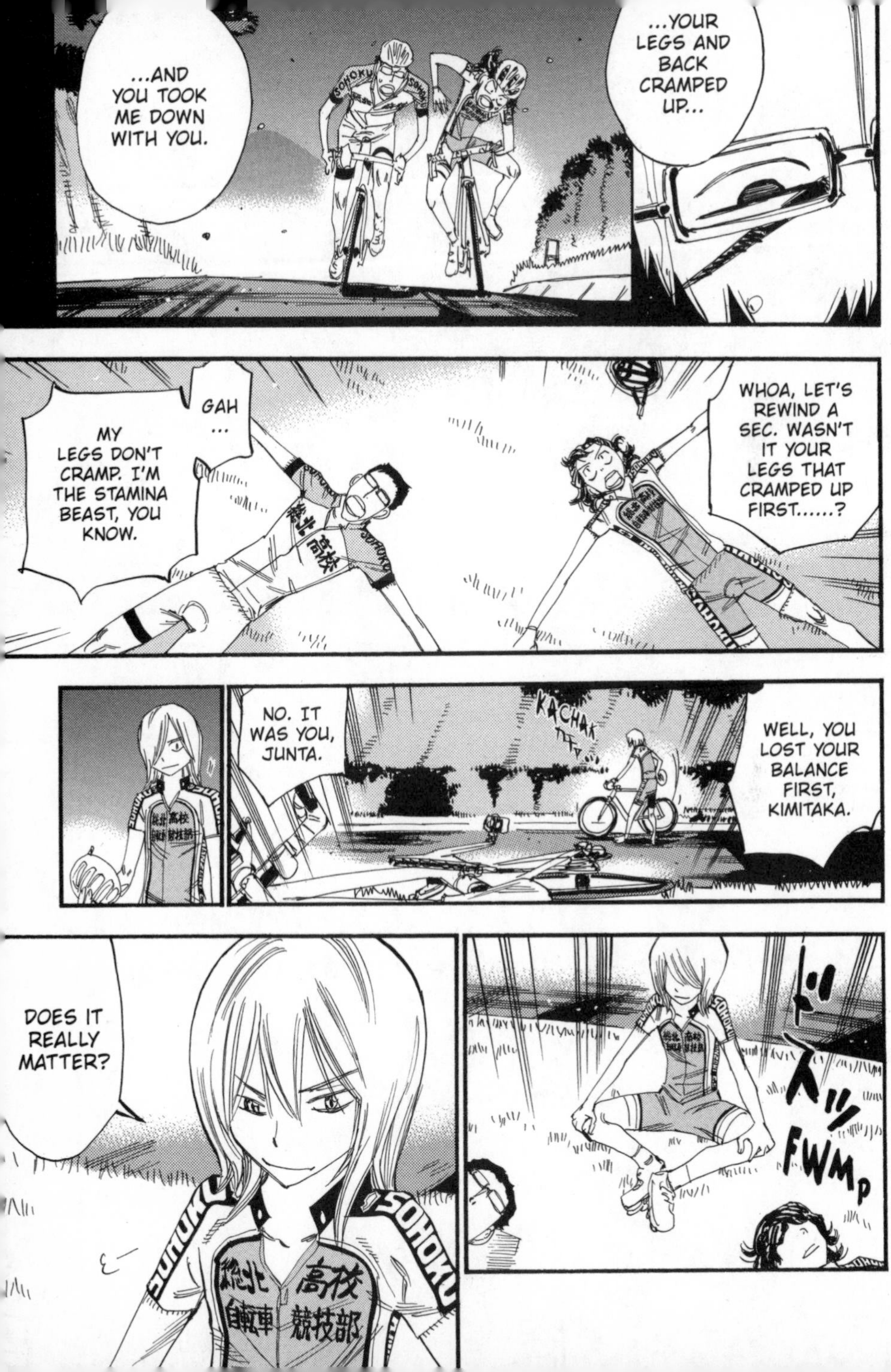
...YOUR LEGS AND BACK CRAMPED UP...
...AND YOU TOOK ME DOWN WITH YOU.
WHOA, LET'S REWIND A SEC. WASN'T IT YOUR LEGS THAT CRAMPED UP FIRST......?
GAH ...
MY LEGS DON'T CRAMP. I'M THE STAMINA BEAST, YOU KNOW.
WELL, YOU LOST YOUR BALANCE FIRST, KIMITAKA.
KACHAK
NO. IT WAS YOU, JUNTA.
FWMP
DOES IT REALLY MATTER?

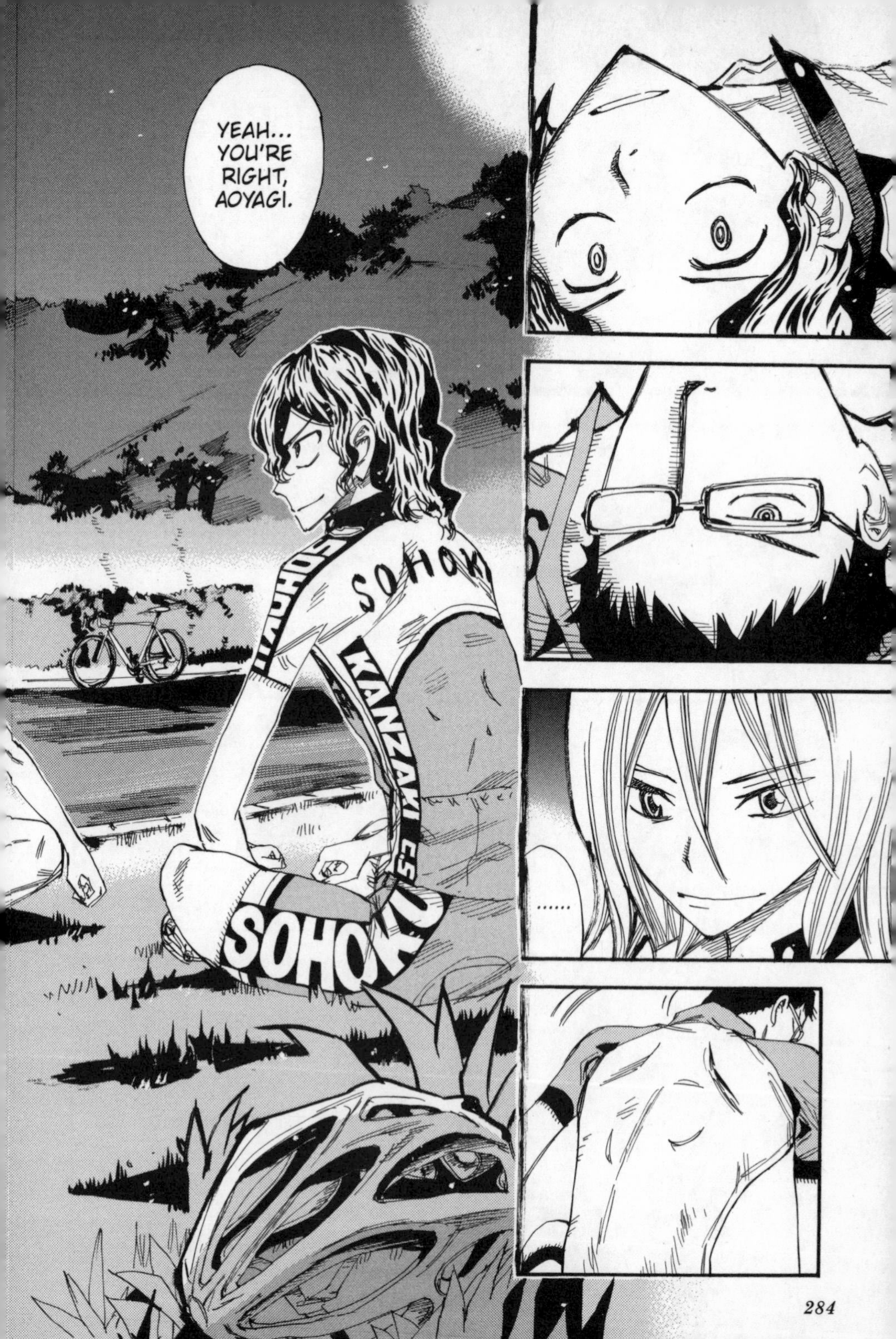
......
YEAH... YOU'RE RIGHT, AOYAGI.

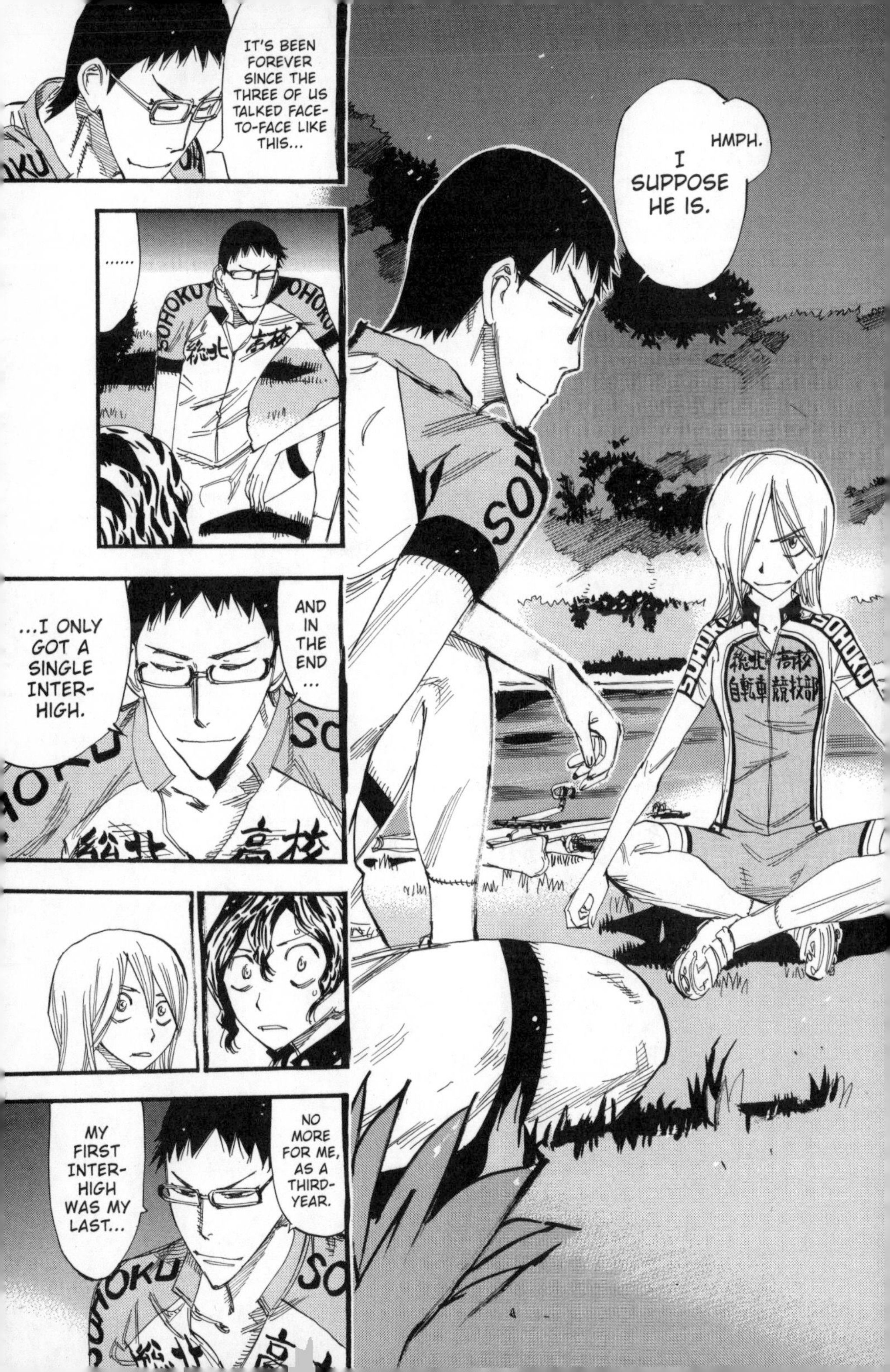
HMPH. I SUPPOSE HE IS.
IT'S BEEN FOREVER SINCE THE THREE OF US TALKED FACE-TO-FACE LIKE THIS...
......
AND IN THE END...
...I ONLY GOT A SINGLE INTER-HIGH.
NO MORE FOR ME, AS A THIRD-YEAR.
MY FIRST INTER-HIGH WAS MY LAST...

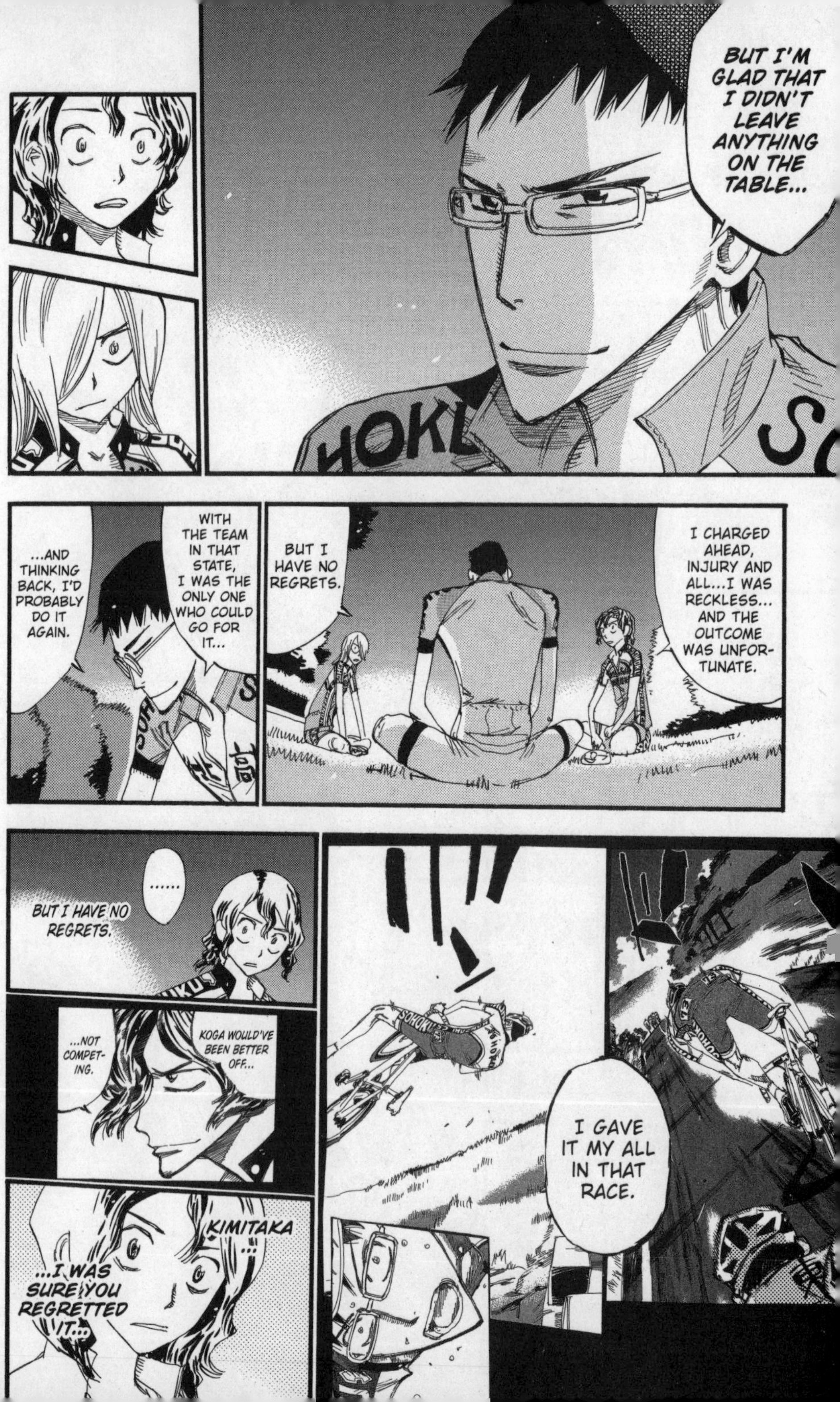
BUT I'M GLAD THAT I DIDN'T LEAVE ANYTHING ON THE TABLE...
I CHARGED AHEAD, INJURY AND ALL...I WAS RECKLESS... AND THE OUTCOME WAS UNFORTUNATE.
BUT I HAVE NO REGRETS.
WITH THE TEAM IN THAT STATE, I WAS THE ONLY ONE WHO COULD GO FOR IT...
...AND THINKING BACK, I'D PROBABLY DO IT AGAIN.
I GAVE IT MY ALL IN THAT RACE.
......
BUT I HAVE NO REGRETS.
KOGA WOULD'VE BEEN BETTER OFF...
...NOT COMPETING.
KIMITAKA...
...I WAS SURE YOU REGRETTED IT...

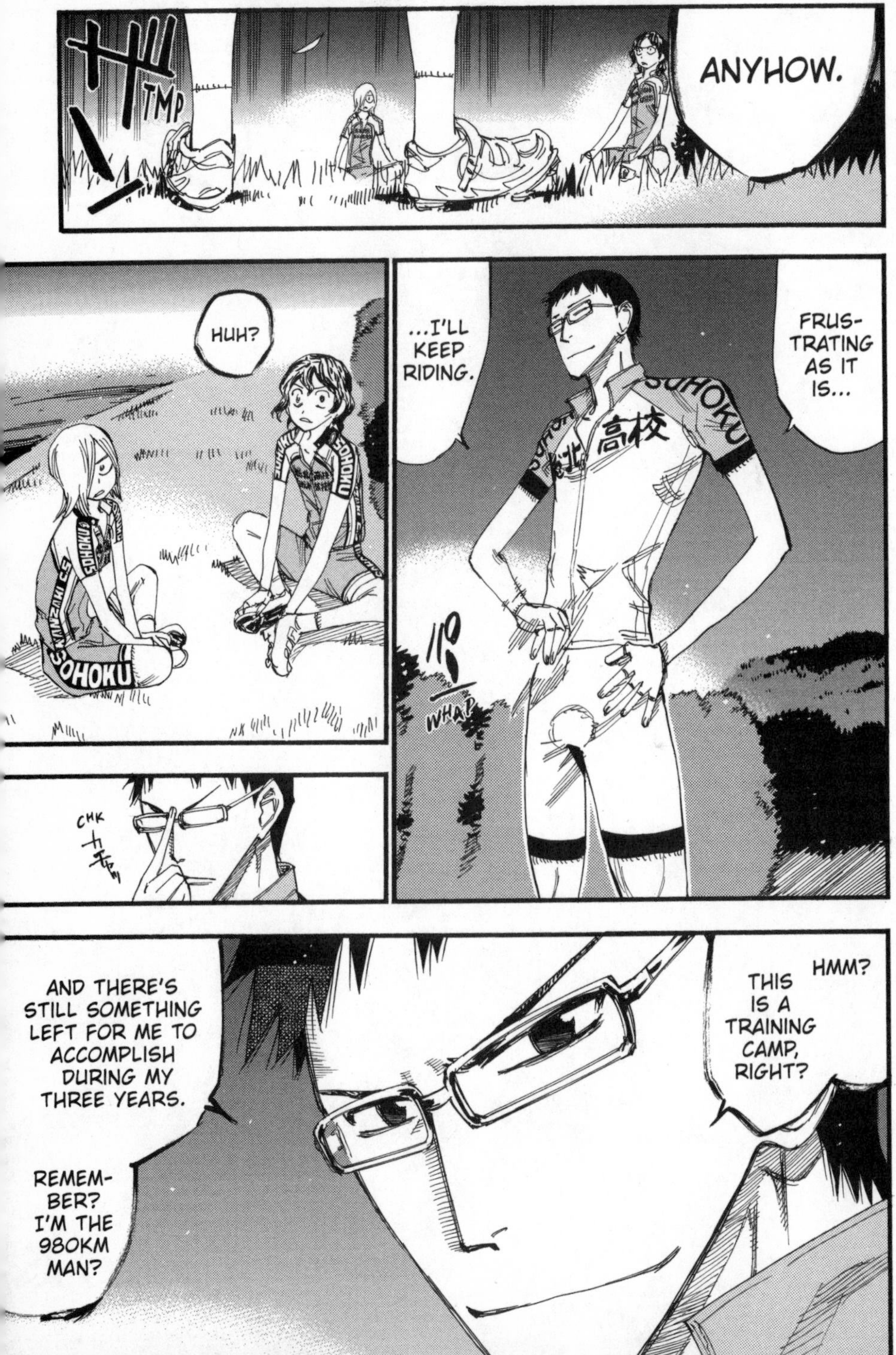
ANYHOW.
TMP
FRUS-TRATING AS IT IS...
...I'LL KEEP RIDING.
WHAP
HUH?
CHK
HMM?
THIS IS A TRAINING CAMP, RIGHT?
AND THERE'S STILL SOMETHING LEFT FOR ME TO ACCOMPLISH DURING MY THREE YEARS.
REMEM-BER? I'M THE 980KM MAN?

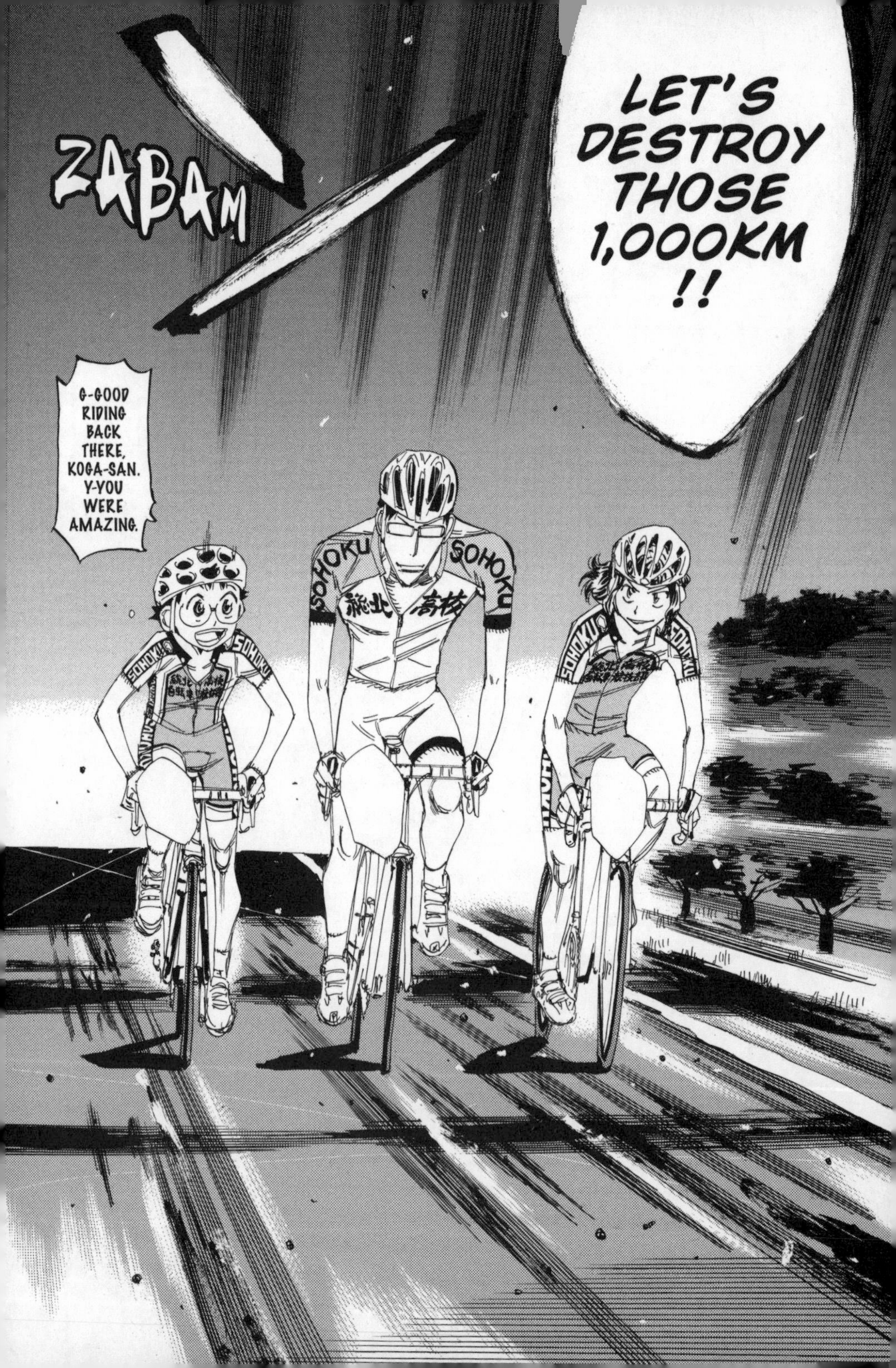
LET'S DESTROY THOSE 1,000KM !!
ZABAM
G-GOOD RIDING BACK THERE, KOGA-SAN. Y-YOU WERE AMAZING.

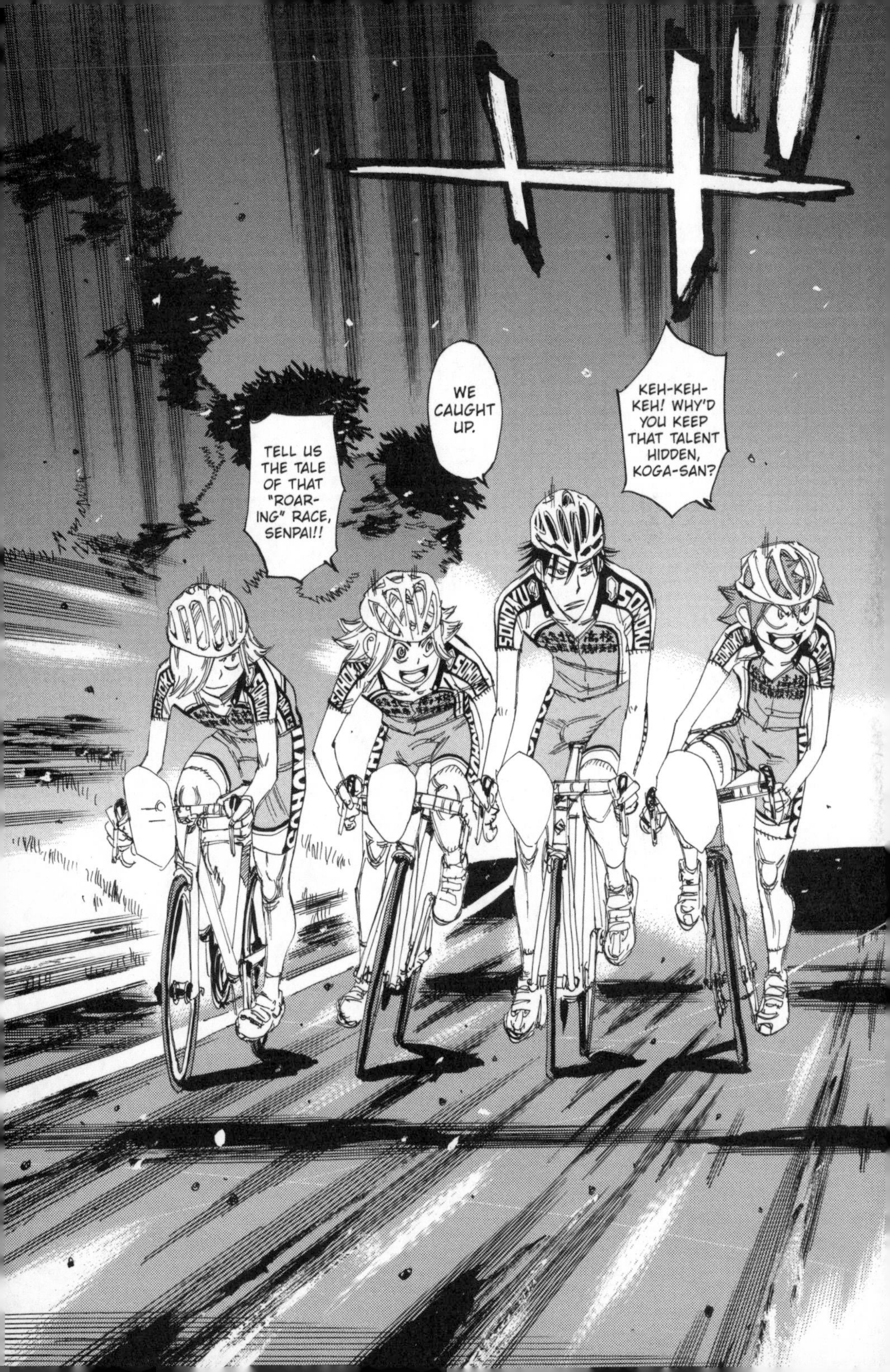
KEH-KEH-KEH! WHY'D YOU KEEP THAT TALENT HIDDEN, KOGA-SAN?
WE CAUGHT UP.
TELL US THE TALE OF THAT "ROAR-ING" RACE, SENPAI!!

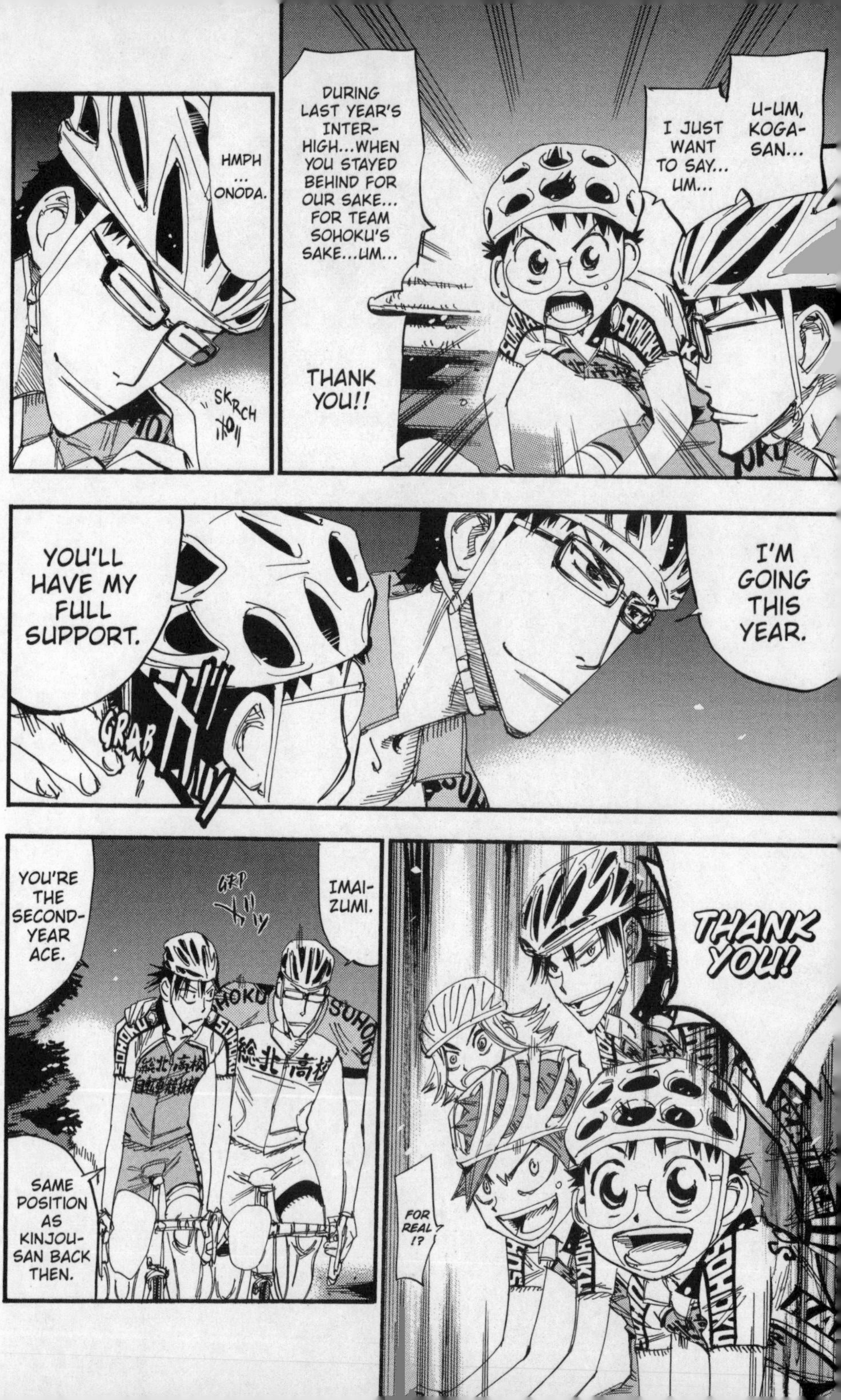
U-UM, KOGA-SAN...
I JUST WANT TO SAY... UM...
DURING LAST YEAR'S INTER-HIGH...WHEN YOU STAYED BEHIND FOR OUR SAKE... FOR TEAM SOHOKU'S SAKE...UM...
THANK YOU!!
HMPH ... ONODA.
SKRCH
I'M GOING THIS YEAR.
YOU'LL HAVE MY FULL SUPPORT.
GRAB
THANK YOU!
FOR REAL!?
IMAI-ZUMI.
GRP
YOU'RE THE SECOND-YEAR ACE.
SAME POSITION AS KINJOU-SAN BACK THEN.

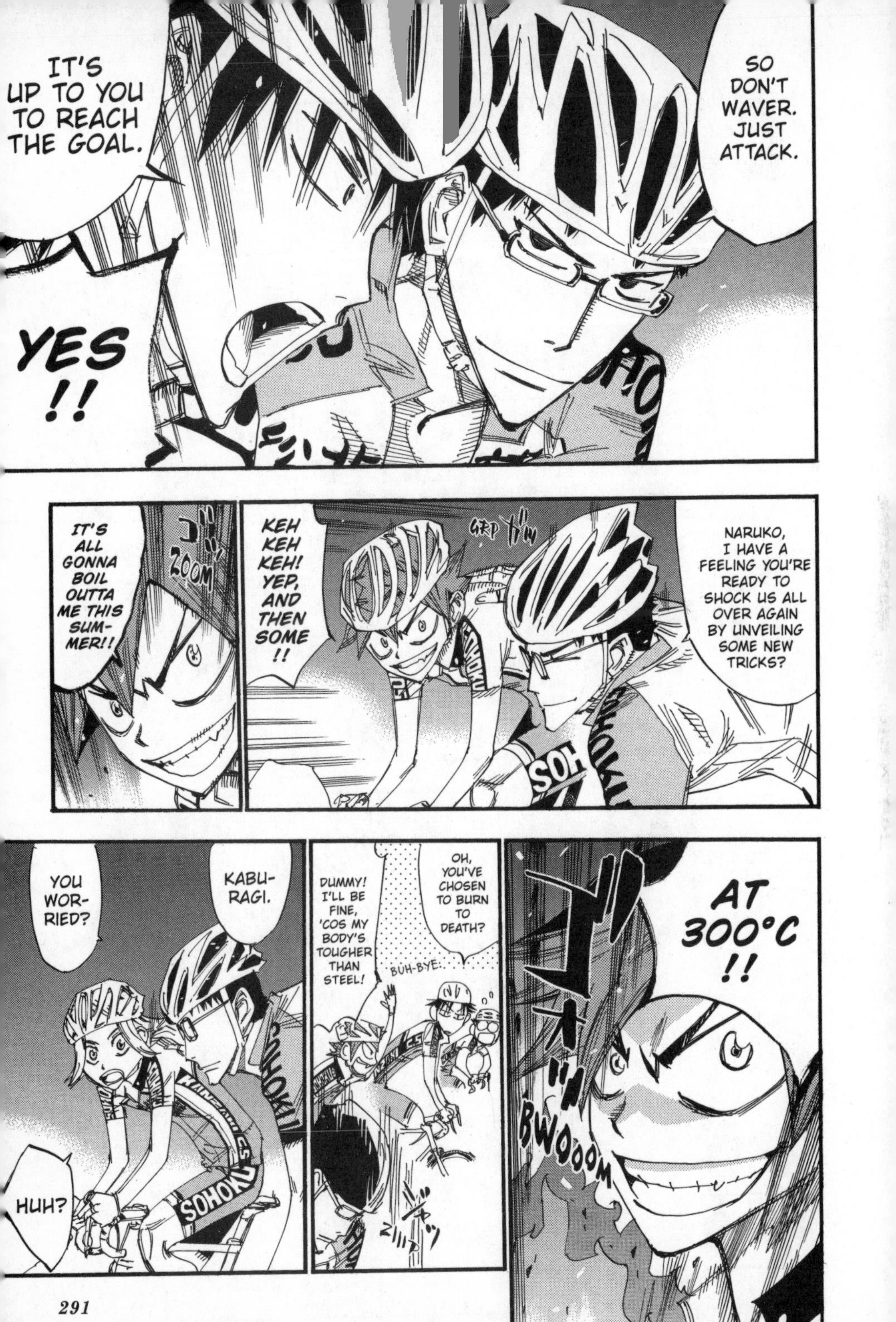
SO DON'T WAVER. JUST ATTACK.
IT'S UP TO YOU TO REACH THE GOAL.
YES!!
NARUKO, I HAVE A FEELING YOU'RE READY TO SHOCK US ALL OVER AGAIN BY UNVEILING SOME NEW TRICKS?
GRP
KEH KEH KEH! YEP, AND THEN SOME!!
ZOOM
IT'S ALL GONNA BOIL OUTTA ME THIS SUMMER!!
AT 300°C!!
BWOOOM
OH, YOU'VE CHOSEN TO BURN TO DEATH?
DUMMY! I'LL BE FINE, 'COS MY BODY'S TOUGHER THAN STEEL!
BUH-BYE.
ZIIIP
KABU-RAGI.
YOU WOR-RIED?
HUH?

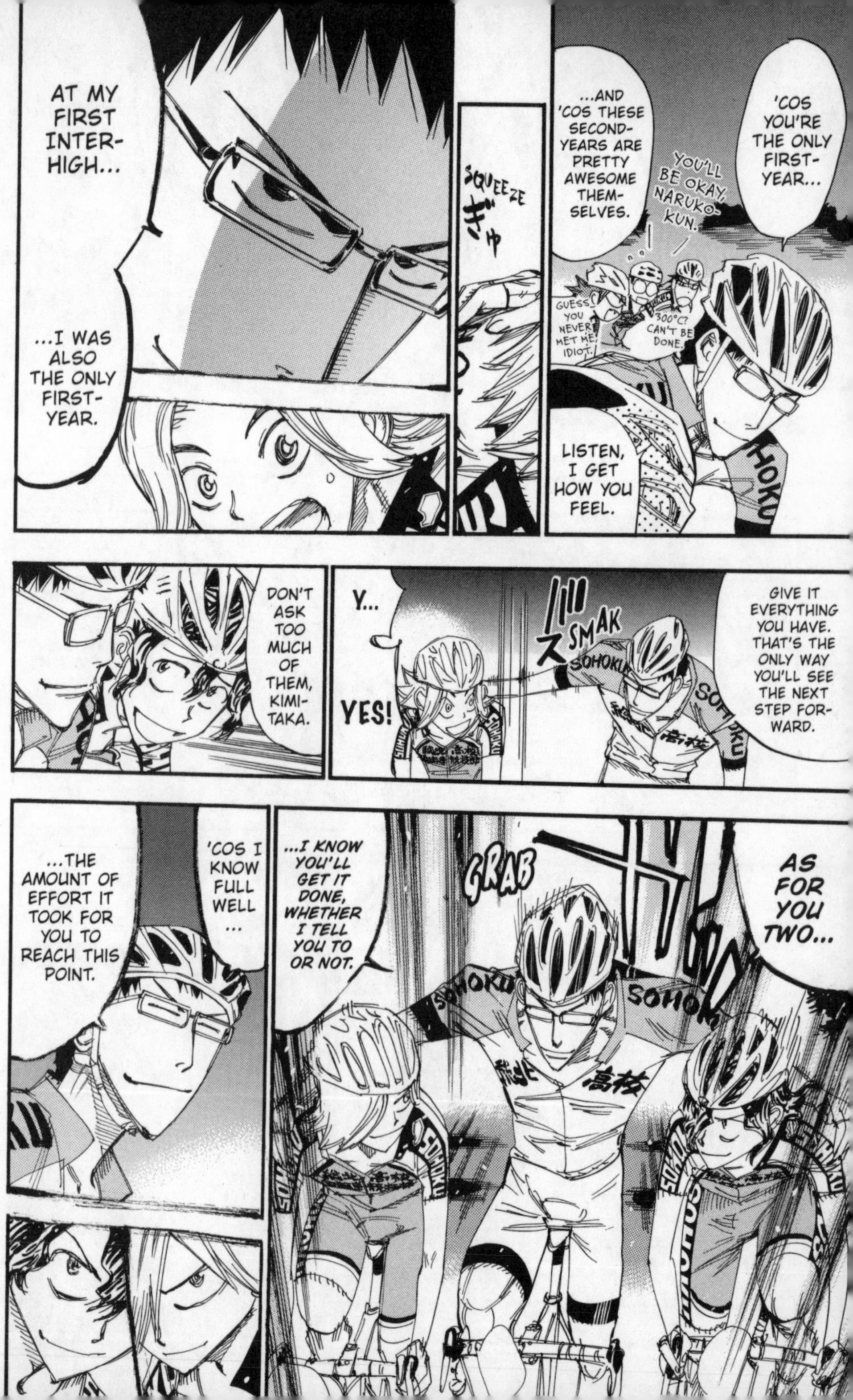
'COS YOU'RE THE ONLY FIRST-YEAR...
YOU'LL BE OKAY, NARUKO-KUN.
...AND 'COS THESE SECOND-YEARS ARE PRETTY AWESOME THEMSELVES.
300°C? CAN'T BE DONE.
GUESS YOU NEVER MET ME, IDIOT.
LISTEN, I GET HOW YOU FEEL.
SQUEEZE
ぎゅ
AT MY FIRST INTER-HIGH...
...I WAS ALSO THE ONLY FIRST-YEAR.
GIVE IT EVERYTHING YOU HAVE. THAT'S THE ONLY WAY YOU'LL SEE THE NEXT STEP FORWARD.
ドス
SMAK
Y...
YES!
DON'T ASK TOO MUCH OF THEM, KIMITAKA.
AS FOR YOU TWO...
GRAB
...I KNOW YOU'LL GET IT DONE, WHETHER I TELL YOU TO OR NOT.
'COS I KNOW FULL WELL...
...THE AMOUNT OF EFFORT IT TOOK FOR YOU TO REACH THIS POINT.

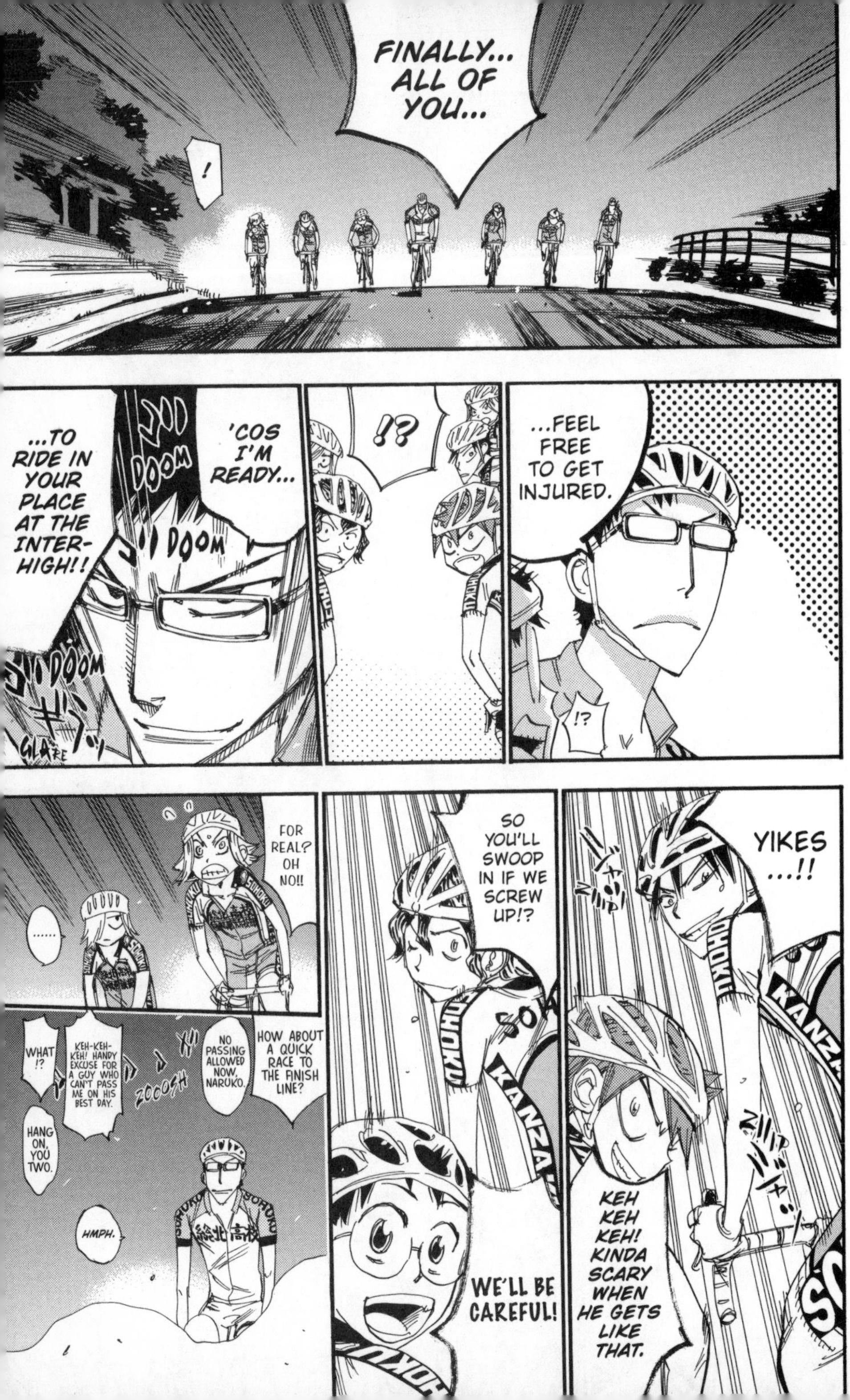

FINALLY... ALL OF YOU...
!
...FEEL FREE TO GET INJURED.
!?
!?
'COS I'M READY...
...TO RIDE IN YOUR PLACE AT THE INTER-HIGH!!
DOOM
DOOM
DOOM
GLARE
YIKES ...!!
KEH KEH KEH! KINDA SCARY WHEN HE GETS LIKE THAT.
SO YOU'LL SWOOP IN IF WE SCREW UP!?
WE'LL BE CAREFUL!
FOR REAL? OH NO!!
......
HOW ABOUT A QUICK RACE TO THE FINISH LINE?
NO PASSING ALLOWED NOW, NARUKO.
KEH-KEH-KEH! HANDY EXCUSE FOR A GUY WHO CAN'T PASS ME ON HIS BEST DAY.
WHAT !?
ZOOOSH
HANG ON, YOU TWO.
HMPH.

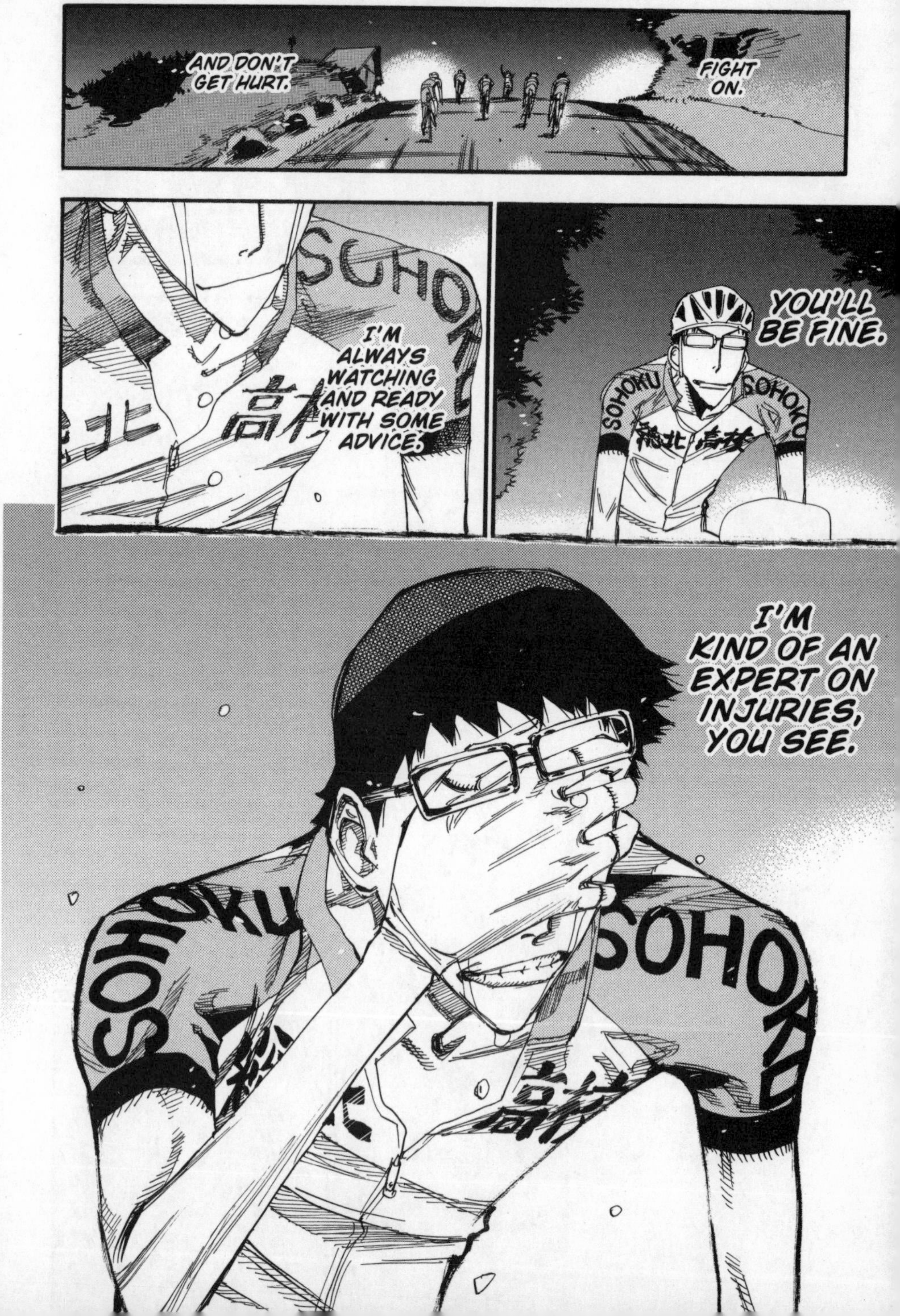
FIGHT ON.
AND DON'T GET HURT.
YOU'LL BE FINE.
I'M ALWAYS WATCHING AND READY WITH SOME ADVICE.
I'M KIND OF AN EXPERT ON INJURIES, YOU SEE.

RIDE.292 DEEP WHEELS

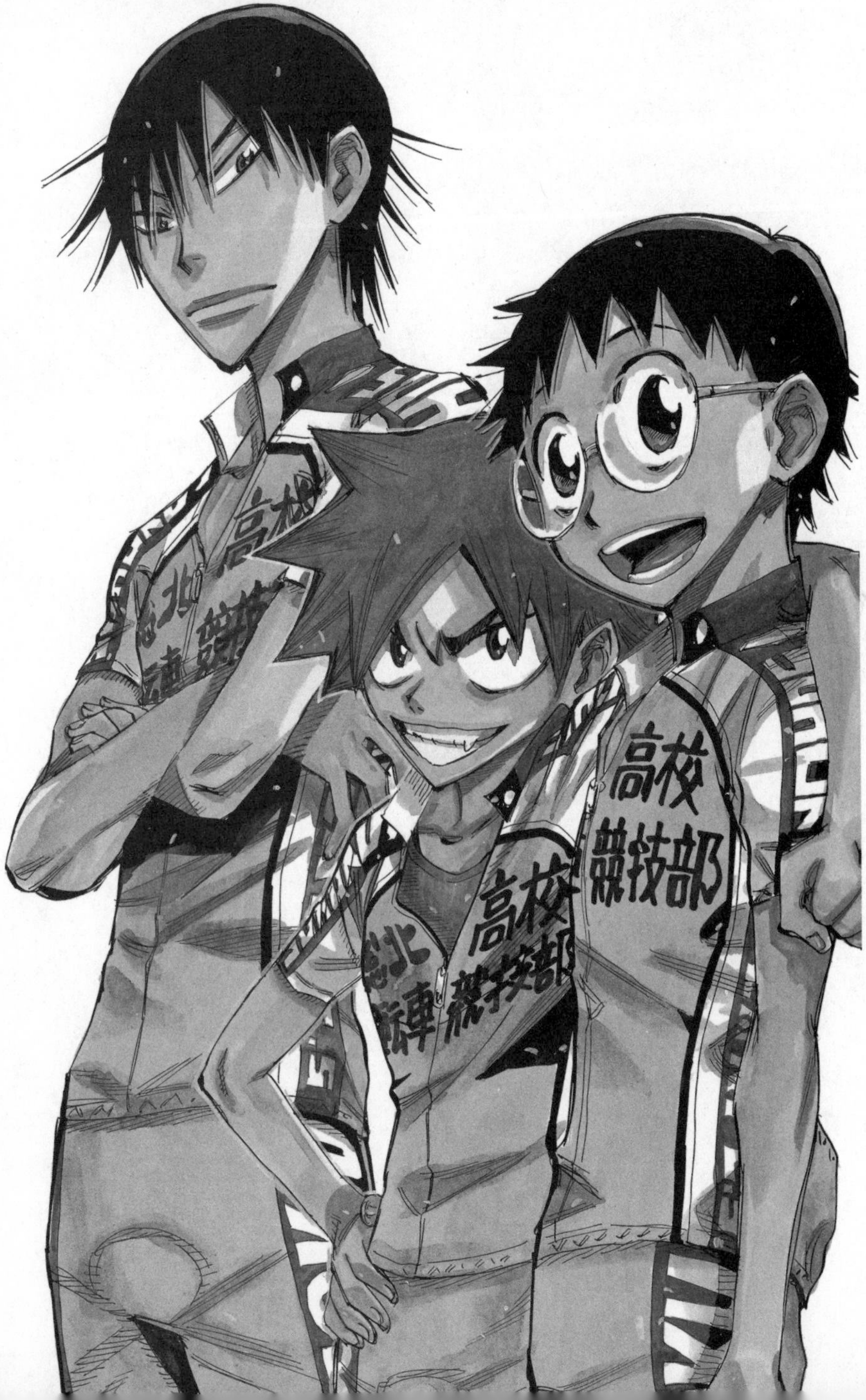
高校
競技部

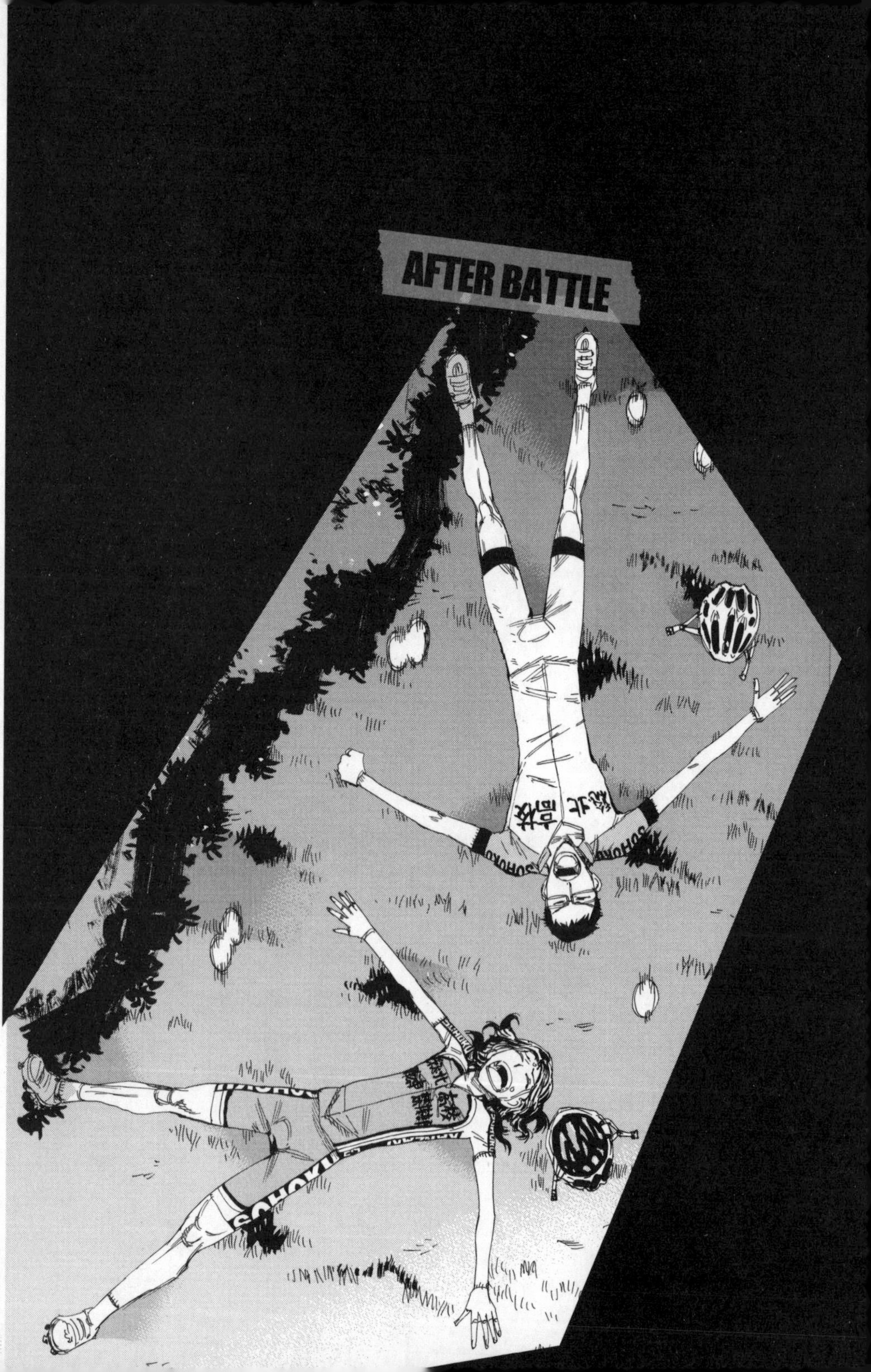
AFTER BATTLE

SIGN: BICYCLE FOREST / CSP: CYCLING SPORTS PARK

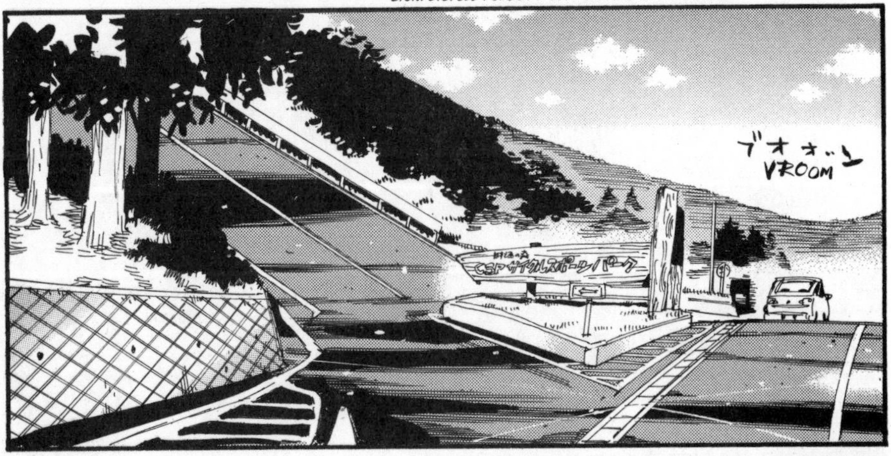
ブオオッ
VROOM
CSPサイクルスポーツパーク

BIG SIGN: BICYCLE FOREST / CYCLING SPORTS PARK / CSP

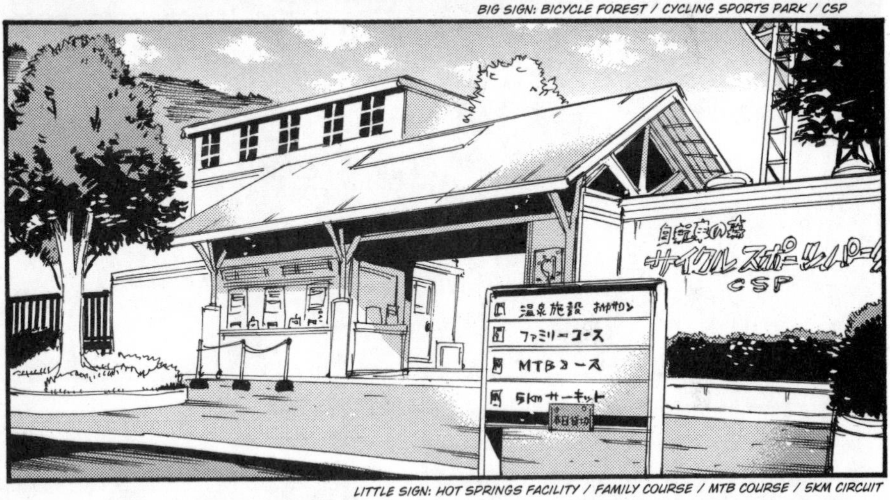
サイクルスポーツパーク
CSP
ファミリーコース
MTBコース
5kmサーキット

LITTLE SIGN: HOT SPRINGS FACILITY / FAMILY COURSE / MTB COURSE / 5KM CIRCUIT

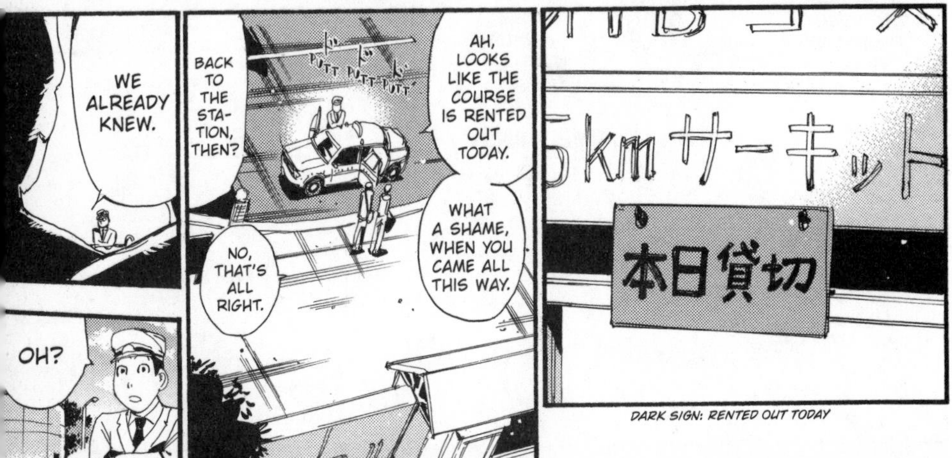
5kmサーキット
本日貸切
AH, LOOKS LIKE THE COURSE IS RENTED OUT TODAY.
PUTT PUTT PUTT
BACK TO THE STATION, THEN?
WHAT A SHAME, WHEN YOU CAME ALL THIS WAY.
NO, THAT'S ALL RIGHT.
WE ALREADY KNEW.
OH?

DARK SIGN: RENTED OUT TODAY

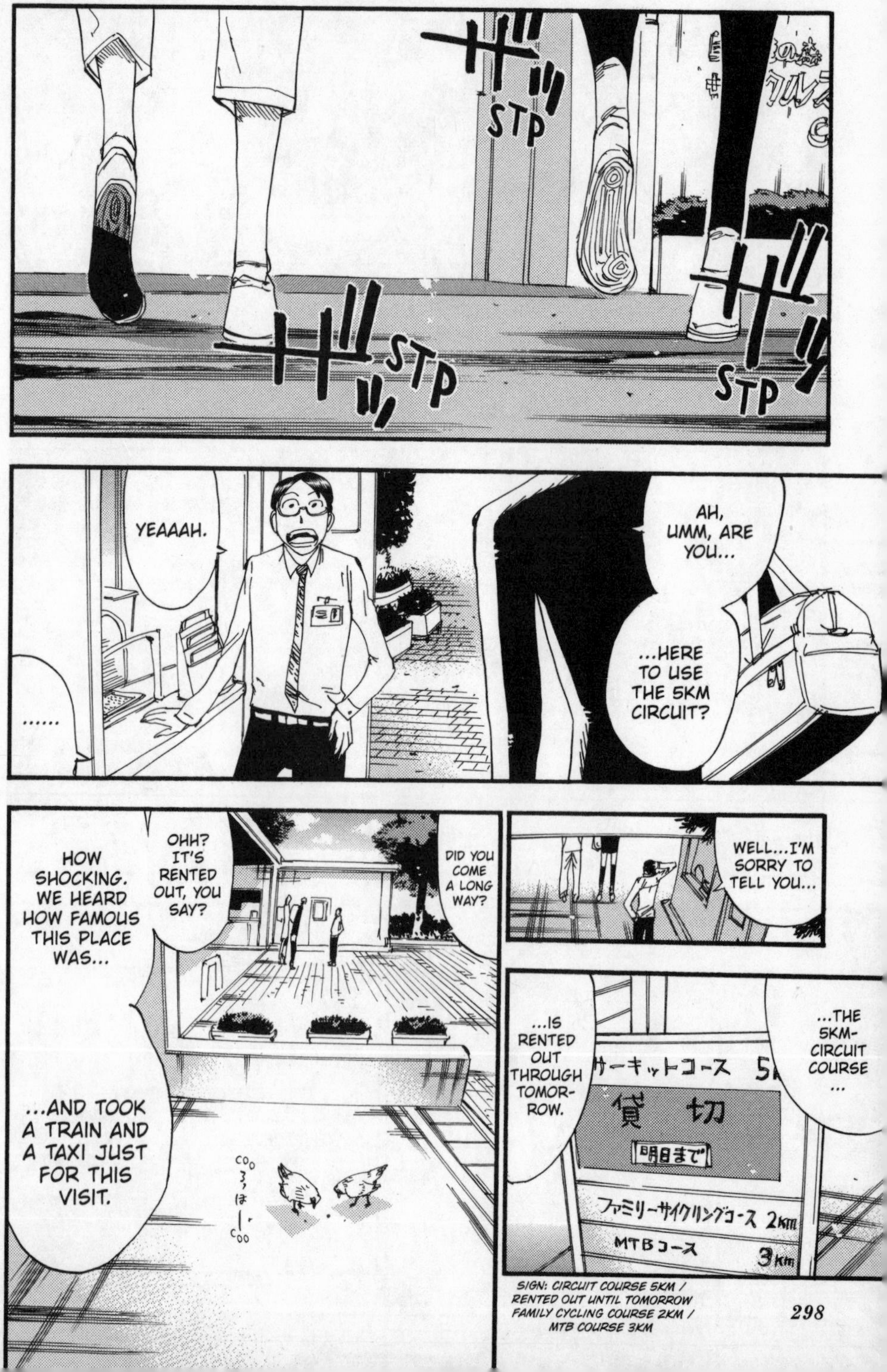
ザッ
STP
ザッ
STP
ザッ
STP
AH, UMM, ARE YOU...
...HERE TO USE THE 5KM CIRCUIT?
YEAAAH.
......
WELL...I'M SORRY TO TELL YOU...
...THE 5KM-CIRCUIT COURSE ...
...IS RENTED OUT THROUGH TOMORROW.
サーキットコース 5k
貸切
明日まで
ファミリーサイクリングコース 2km
MTBコース 3km
DID YOU COME A LONG WAY?
OHH? IT'S RENTED OUT, YOU SAY?
HOW SHOCKING. WE HEARD HOW FAMOUS THIS PLACE WAS...
...AND TOOK A TRAIN AND A TAXI JUST FOR THIS VISIT.
COO
COO

SIGN: CIRCUIT COURSE 5KM / RENTED OUT UNTIL TOMORROW FAMILY CYCLING COURSE 2KM / MTB COURSE 3KM

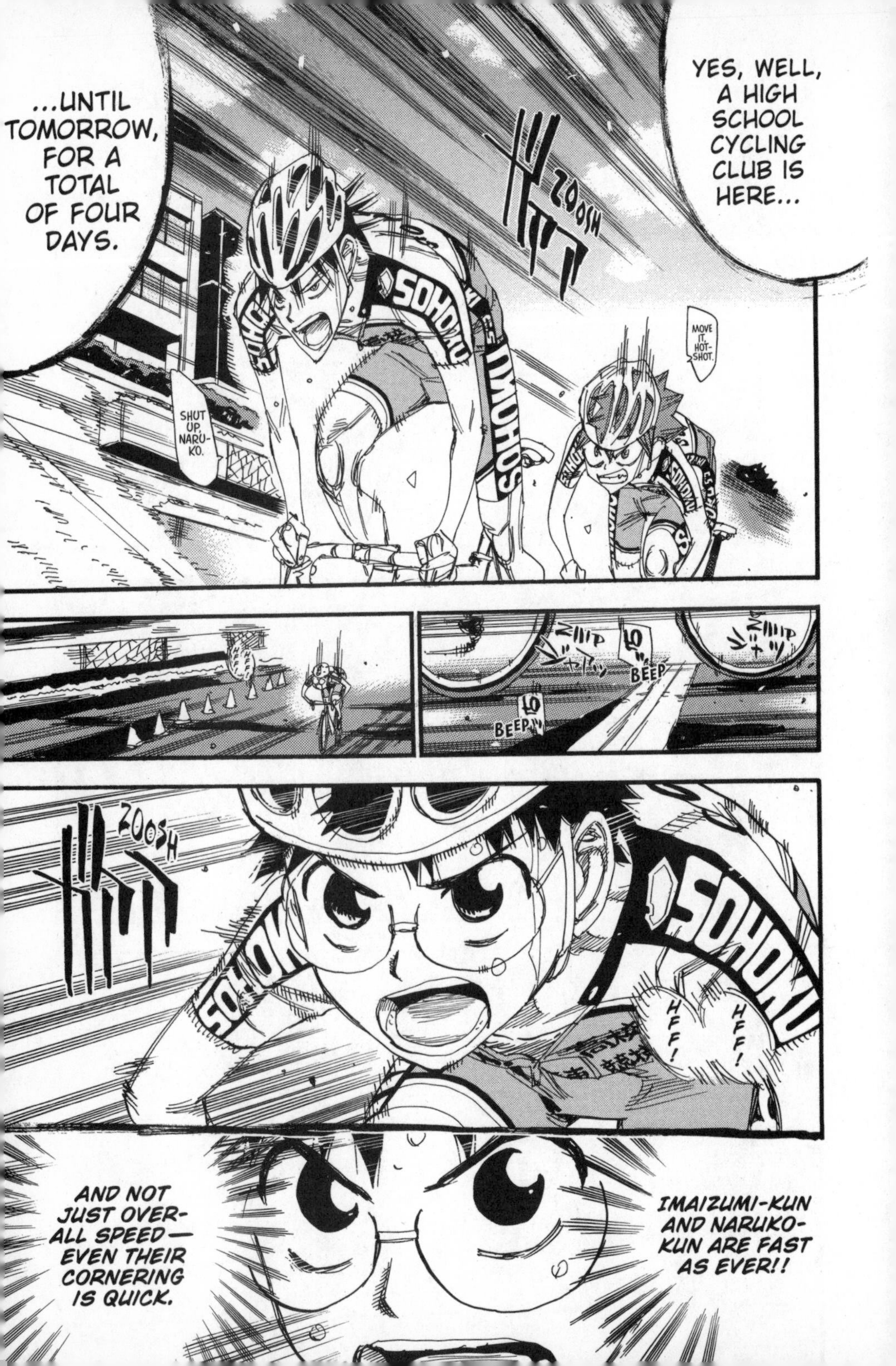
YES, WELL, A HIGH SCHOOL CYCLING CLUB IS HERE...
...UNTIL TOMORROW, FOR A TOTAL OF FOUR DAYS.
ZOOSH
MOVE IT, HOT-SHOT.
SHUT UP, NARU-KO.
ZIIIP
BEEP
ZIIIP
BEEP
HFF HFF
ZOOSH
HFF!
HFF!
IMAIZUMI-KUN AND NARUKO-KUN ARE FAST AS EVER!!
AND NOT JUST OVER-ALL SPEED—EVEN THEIR CORNERING IS QUICK.

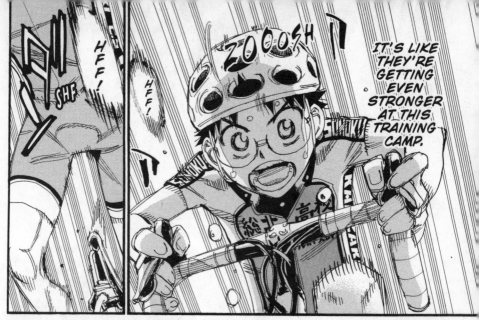

HFF! SHF

HFF!

ZOOOSH

IT'S LIKE THEY'RE GETTING EVEN STRONGER AT THIS TRAINING CAMP.

BUZZ OFF.

MOVE IT.

ZOOOSH

FWOOOSH

ON THE CORNERS...

RAAAH!

TCH.

HFF! HFF!

SO COOL!!

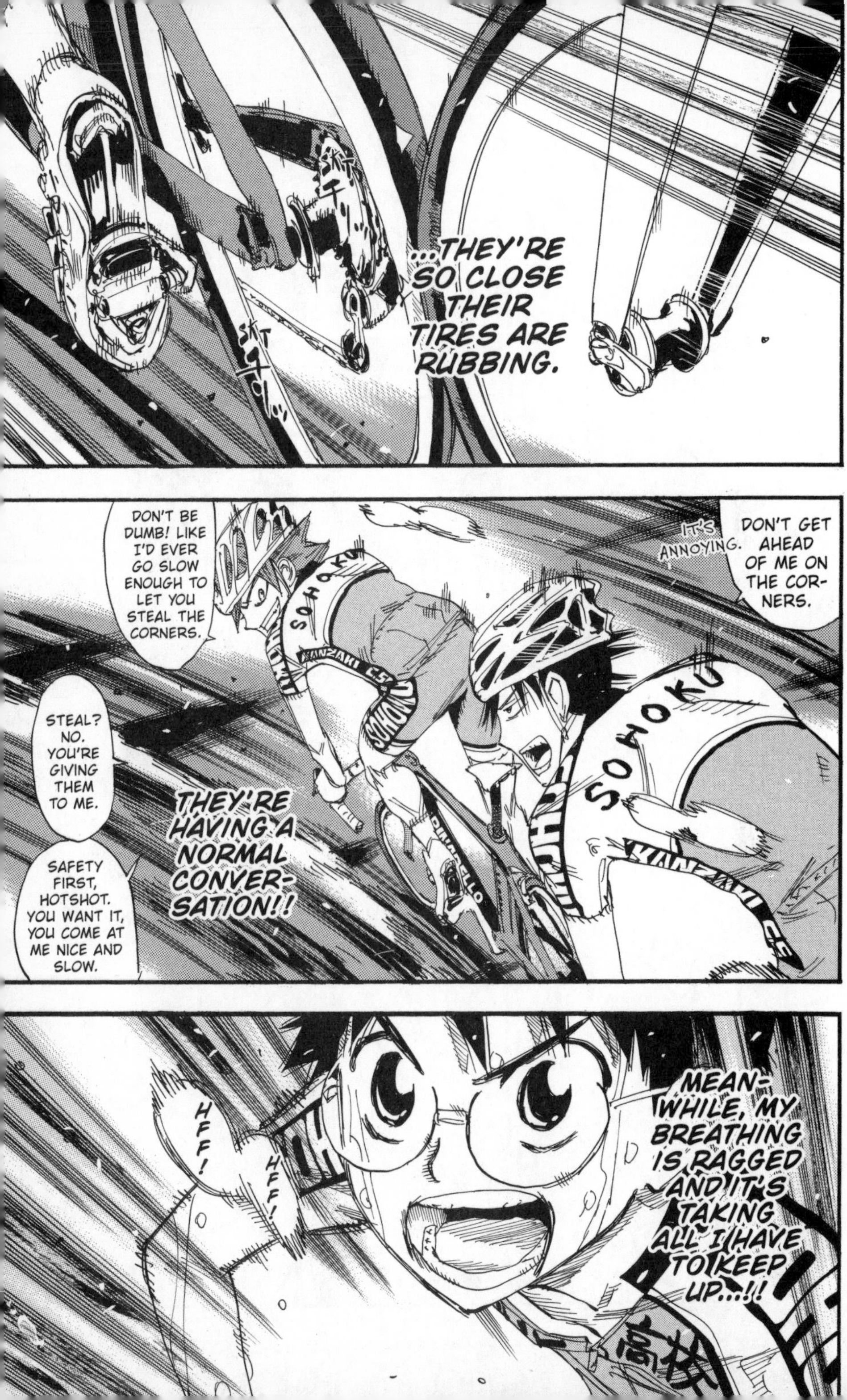
...THEY'RE SO CLOSE THEIR TIRES ARE RUBBING.
SKT
SKT
DON'T GET AHEAD OF ME ON THE CORNERS.
IT'S ANNOYING.
DON'T BE DUMB! LIKE I'D EVER GO SLOW ENOUGH TO LET YOU STEAL THE CORNERS.
THEY'RE HAVING A NORMAL CONVERSATION!!
STEAL? NO. YOU'RE GIVING THEM TO ME.
SAFETY FIRST, HOTSHOT. YOU WANT IT, YOU COME AT ME NICE AND SLOW.
MEANWHILE, MY BREATHING IS RAGGED AND IT'S TAKING ALL I HAVE TO KEEP UP...!!
HFF!
HFF!
高校

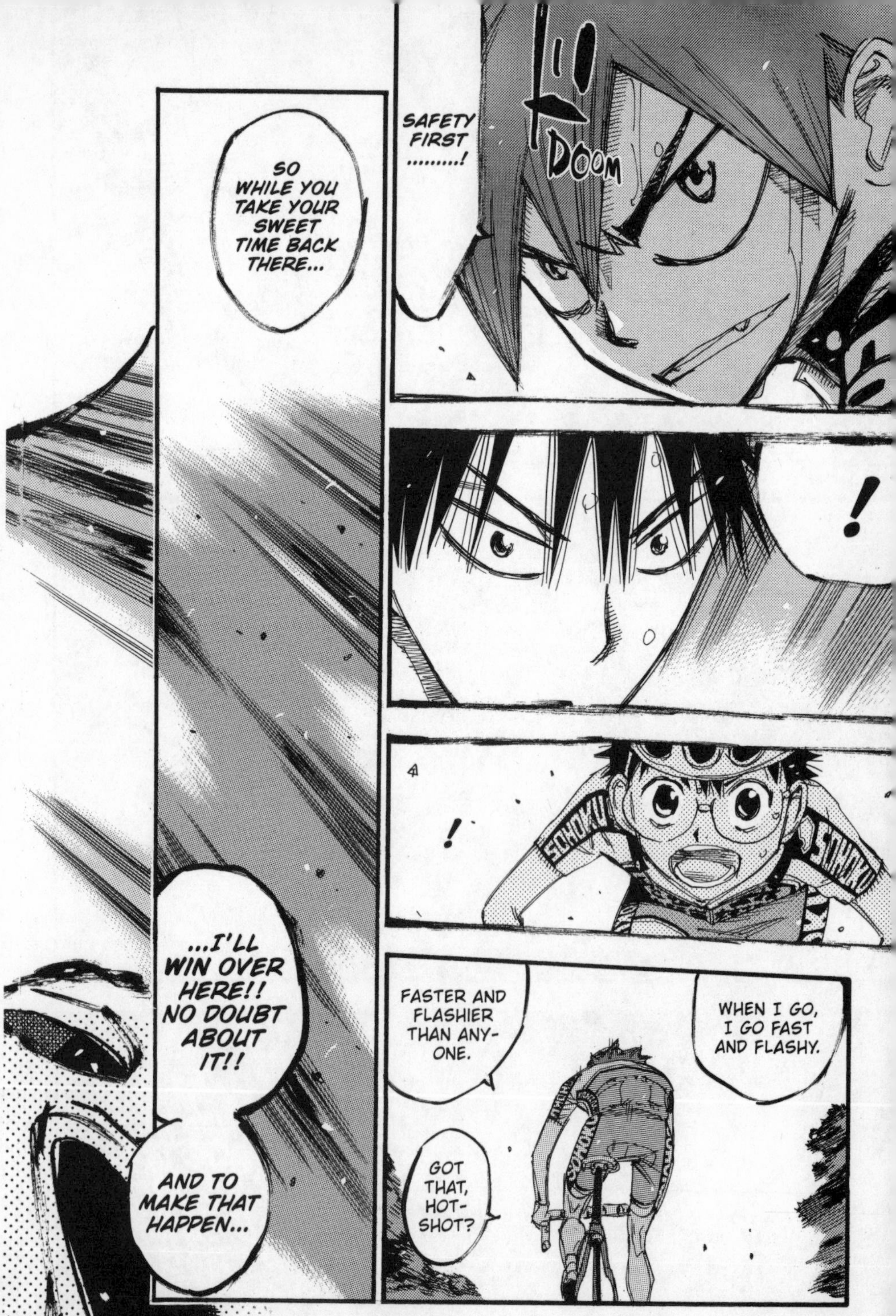
SAFETY FIRST ....!
DOOM
!
!
WHEN I GO, I GO FAST AND FLASHY.
FASTER AND FLASHIER THAN ANY-ONE.
GOT THAT, HOT-SHOT?
SO WHILE YOU TAKE YOUR SWEET TIME BACK THERE...
...I'LL WIN OVER HERE!! NO DOUBT ABOUT IT!!
AND TO MAKE THAT HAPPEN...

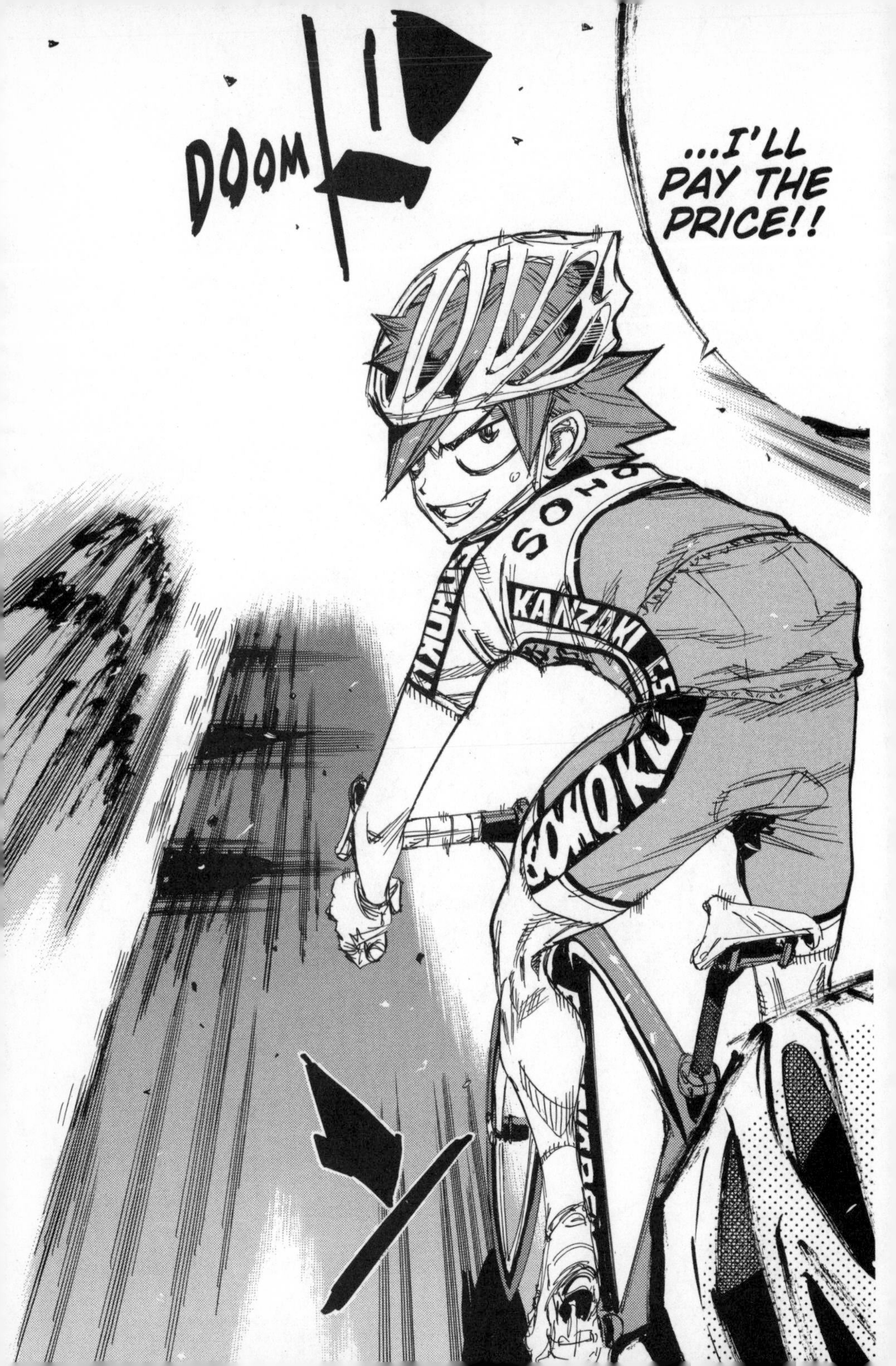
...I'LL PAY THE PRICE!!
DOOM

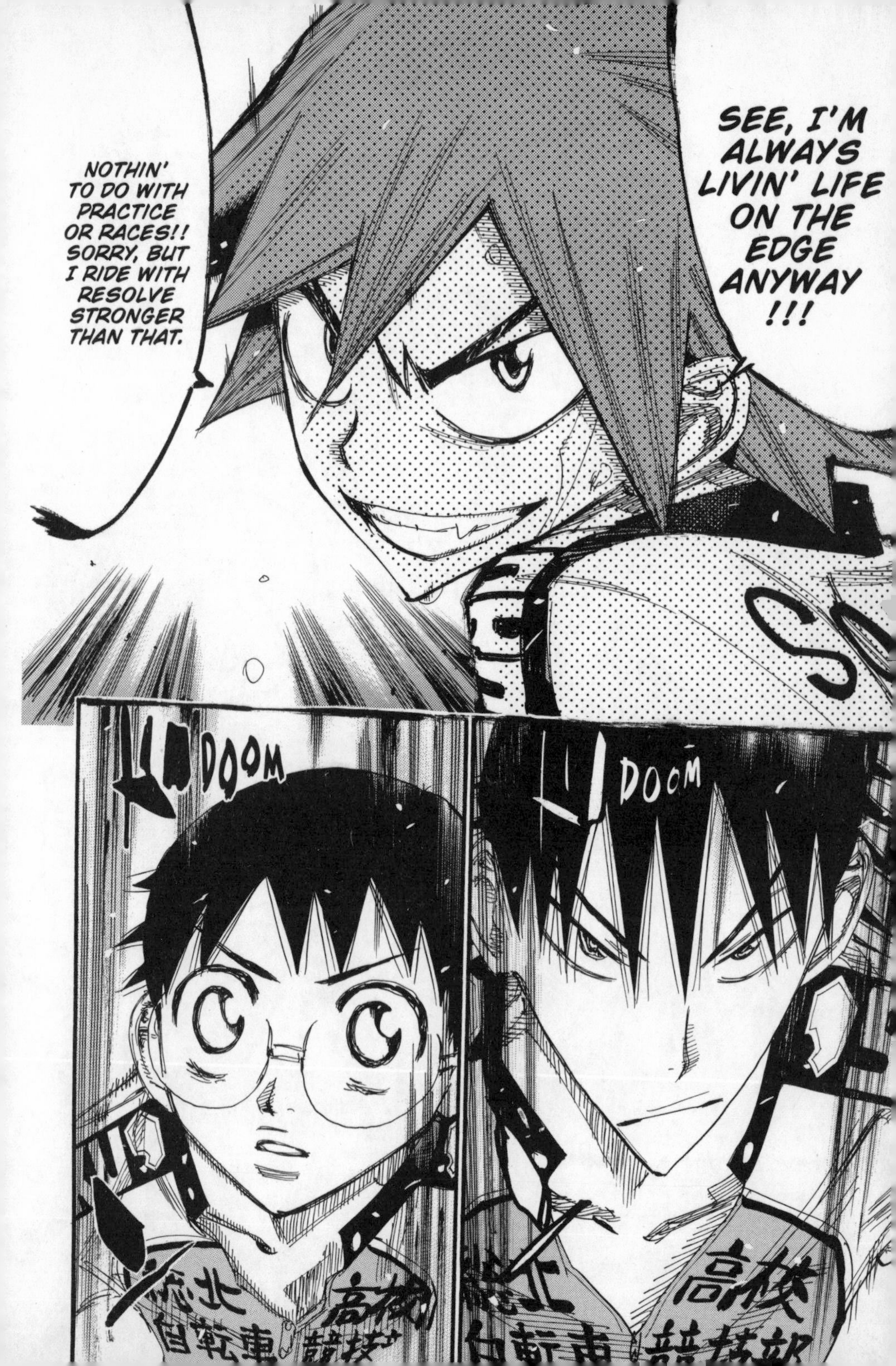
SEE, I'M ALWAYS LIVIN' LIFE ON THE EDGE ANYWAY!!!
NOTHIN' TO DO WITH PRACTICE OR RACES!! SORRY, BUT I RIDE WITH RESOLVE STRONGER THAN THAT.
DOOM
DOOM

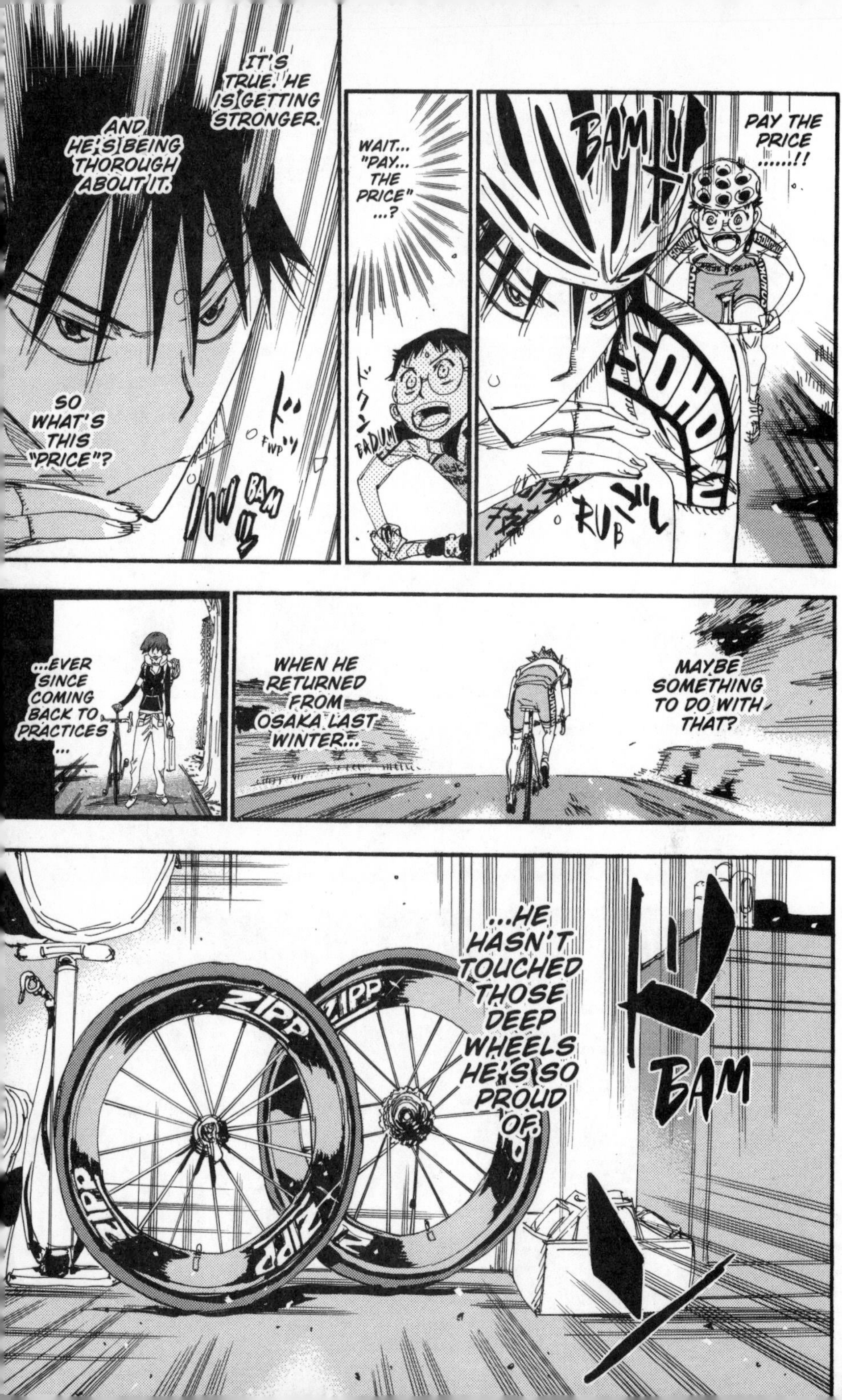
BAM
PAY THE PRICE ......!!
RUB
WAIT... "PAY... THE PRICE" ...?
BADUM
IT'S TRUE. HE IS GETTING STRONGER.
AND HE'S BEING THOROUGH ABOUT IT.
SO WHAT'S THIS "PRICE"?
FWP
BAM
WHEN HE RETURNED FROM OSAKA LAST WINTER...
MAYBE SOMETHING TO DO WITH THAT?
...EVER SINCE COMING BACK TO PRACTICES...
...HE HASN'T TOUCHED THOSE DEEP WHEELS HE'S SO PROUD OF.
BAM
ZIPP

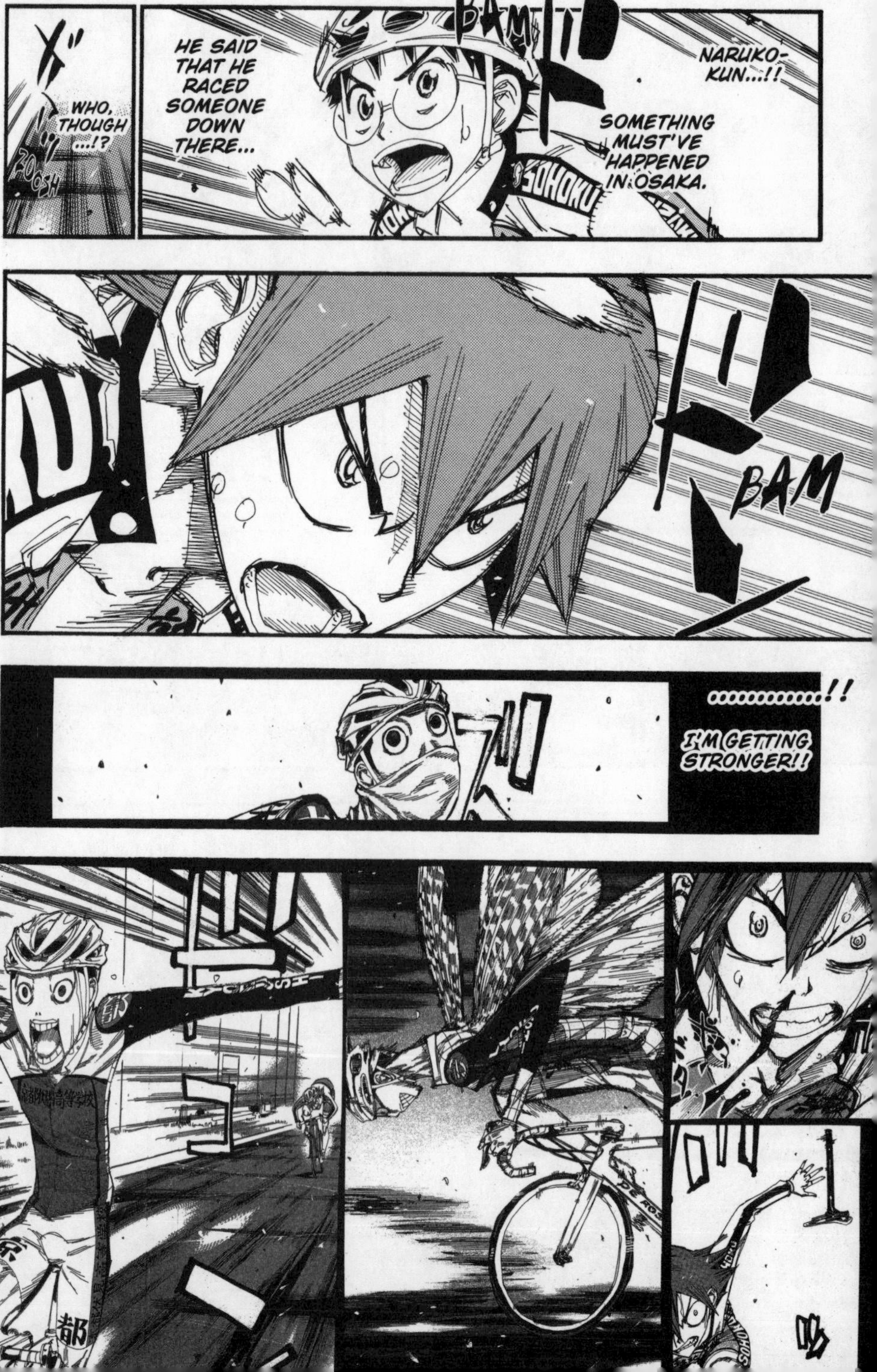
BAM
NARUKO-KUN...!!
SOMETHING MUST'VE HAPPENED IN OSAKA.
HE SAID THAT HE RACED SOMEONE DOWN THERE...
WHO, THOUGH ...!?
ZOOSH
BAM
..............!!
I'M GETTING STRONGER!!

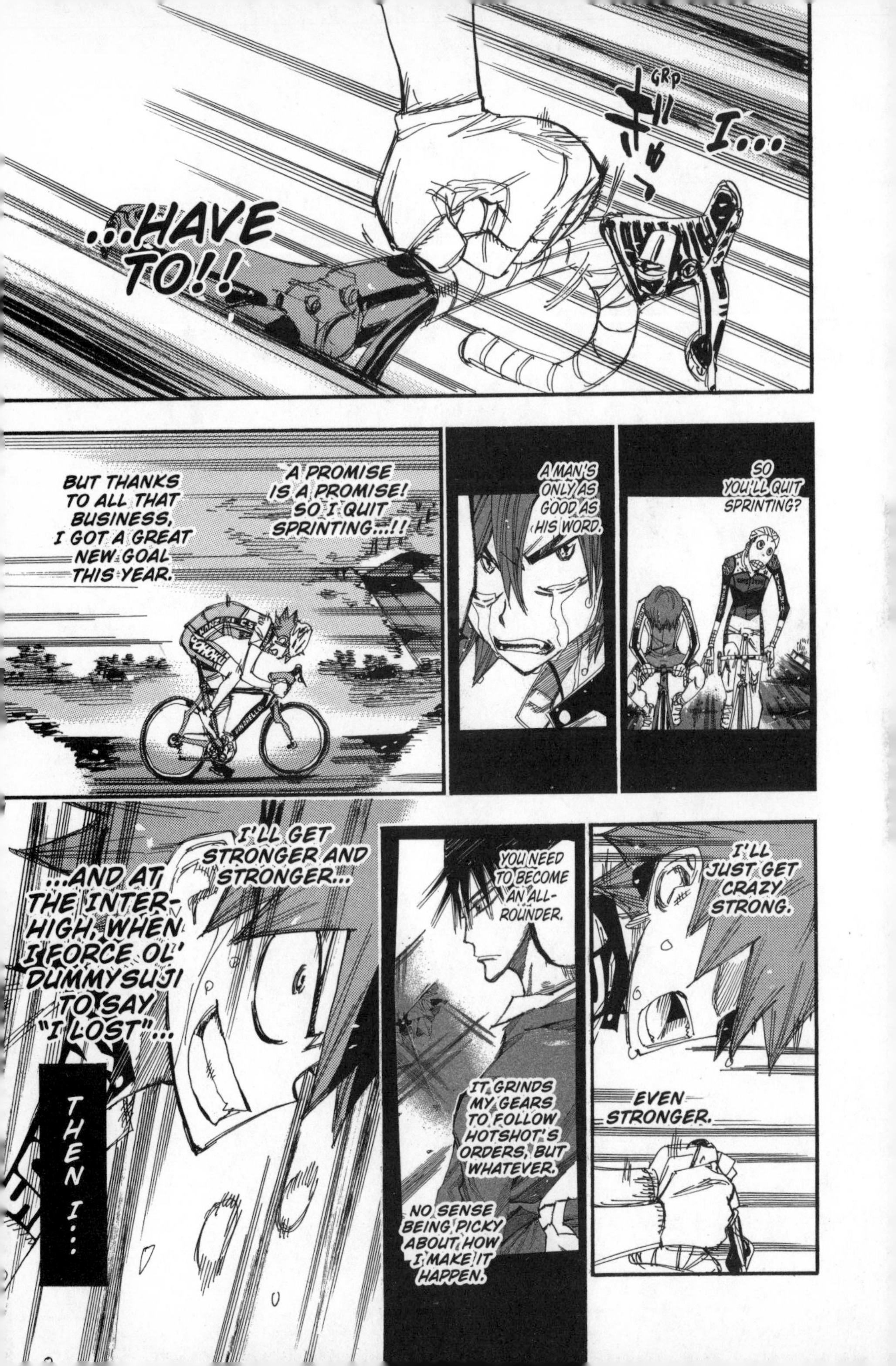
GRP
I...
...HAVE TO!!
SO YOU'LL QUIT SPRINTING?
A MAN'S ONLY AS GOOD AS HIS WORD.
A PROMISE IS A PROMISE! SO I QUIT SPRINTING...!!
BUT THANKS TO ALL THAT BUSINESS, I GOT A GREAT NEW GOAL THIS YEAR.
I'LL JUST GET CRAZY STRONG.
EVEN STRONGER.
YOU NEED TO BECOME AN ALL-ROUNDER.
IT GRINDS MY GEARS TO FOLLOW HOTSHOT'S ORDERS, BUT WHATEVER.
NO SENSE BEING PICKY ABOUT HOW I MAKE IT HAPPEN.
I'LL GET STRONGER AND STRONGER...
...AND AT THE INTER-HIGH, WHEN I FORCE OL' DUMMYSUJI TO SAY "I LOST"...
THEN I...

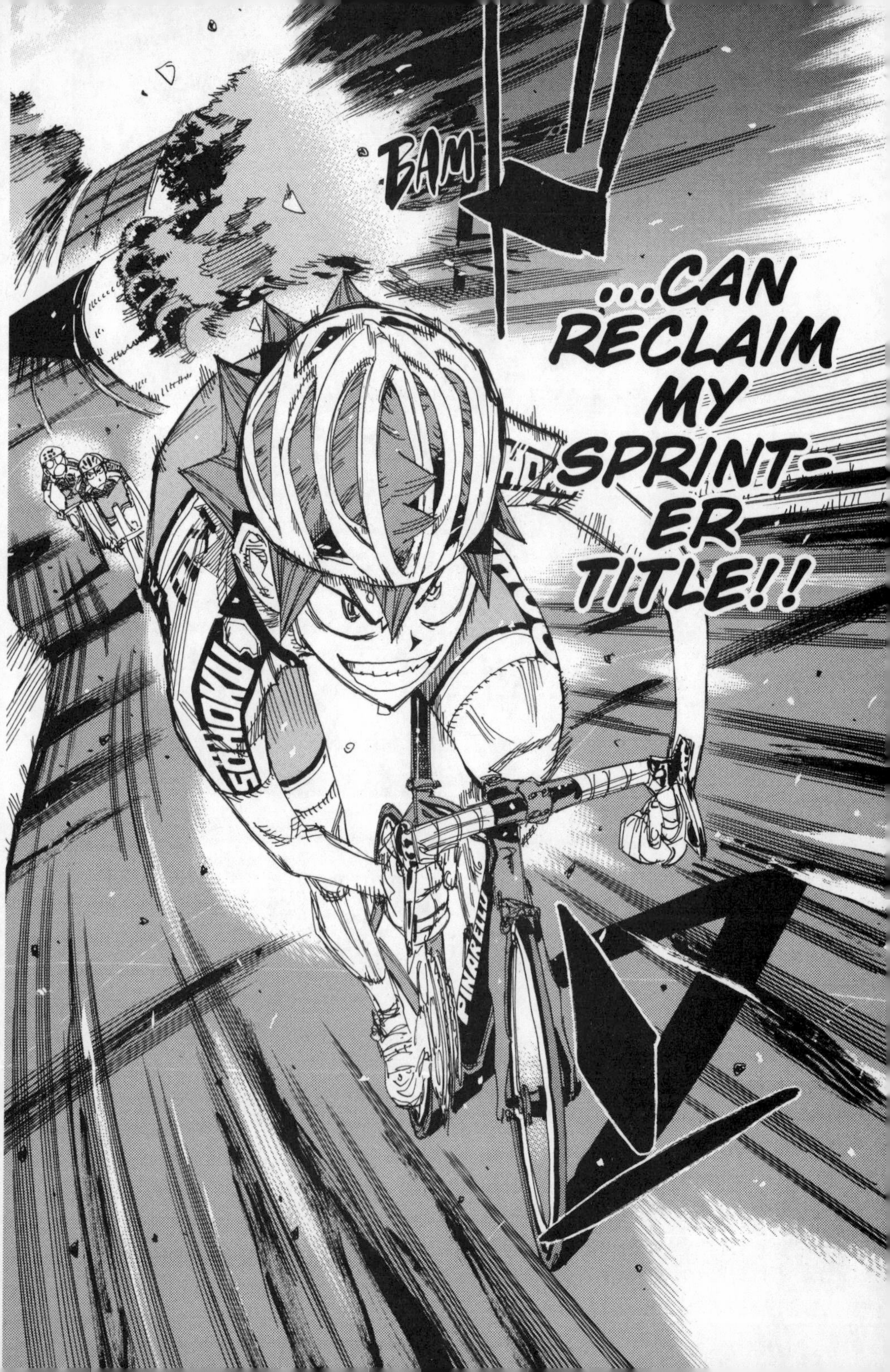
BAM
...CAN RECLAIM MY SPRINT-ER TITLE!!
SOHOKU
PINARELLO

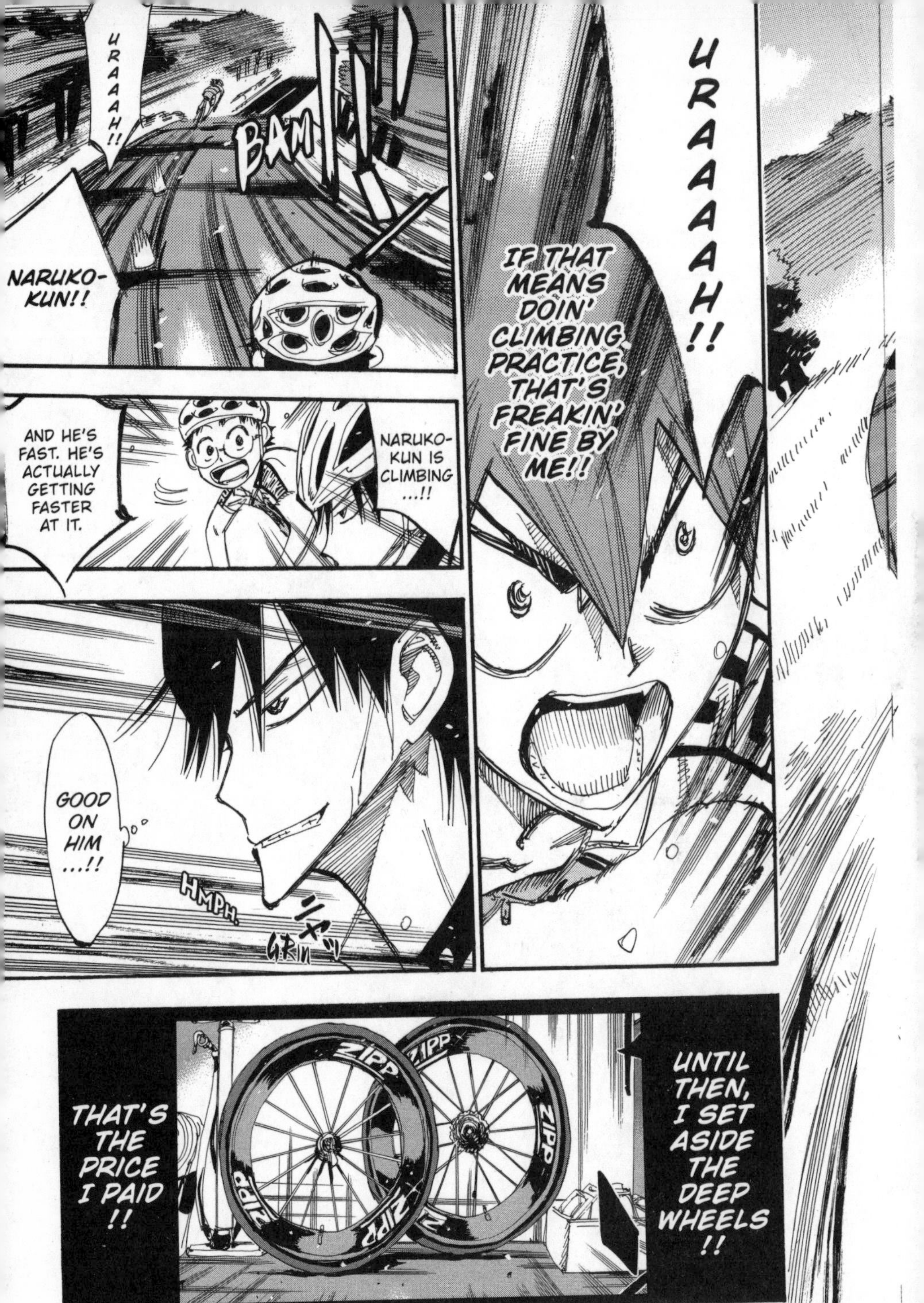
URAAAAAH!!
IF THAT MEANS DOIN' CLIMBING PRACTICE, THAT'S FREAKIN' FINE BY ME!!
URAAAAH!!
BAM
NARUKO-KUN!!
NARUKO-KUN IS CLIMBING ...!!
AND HE'S FAST. HE'S ACTUALLY GETTING FASTER AT IT.
GOOD ON HIM ...!!
HMPH.
GRIN
UNTIL THEN, I SET ASIDE THE DEEP WHEELS!!
THAT'S THE PRICE I PAID!!
ZIPP

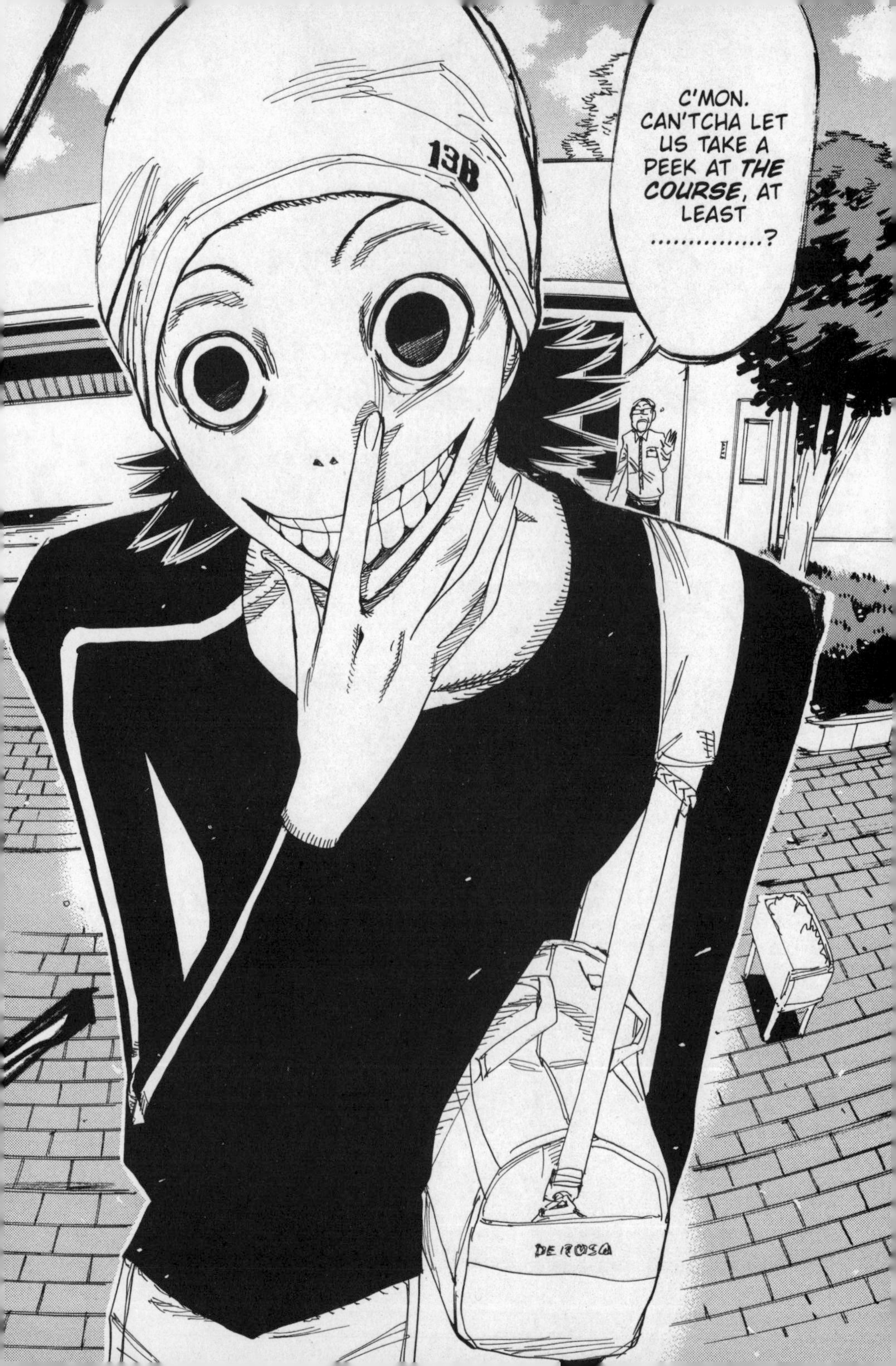
C'MON. CAN'TCHA LET US TAKE A PEEK AT *THE COURSE*, AT LEAST ....?
13B
DE ROSA

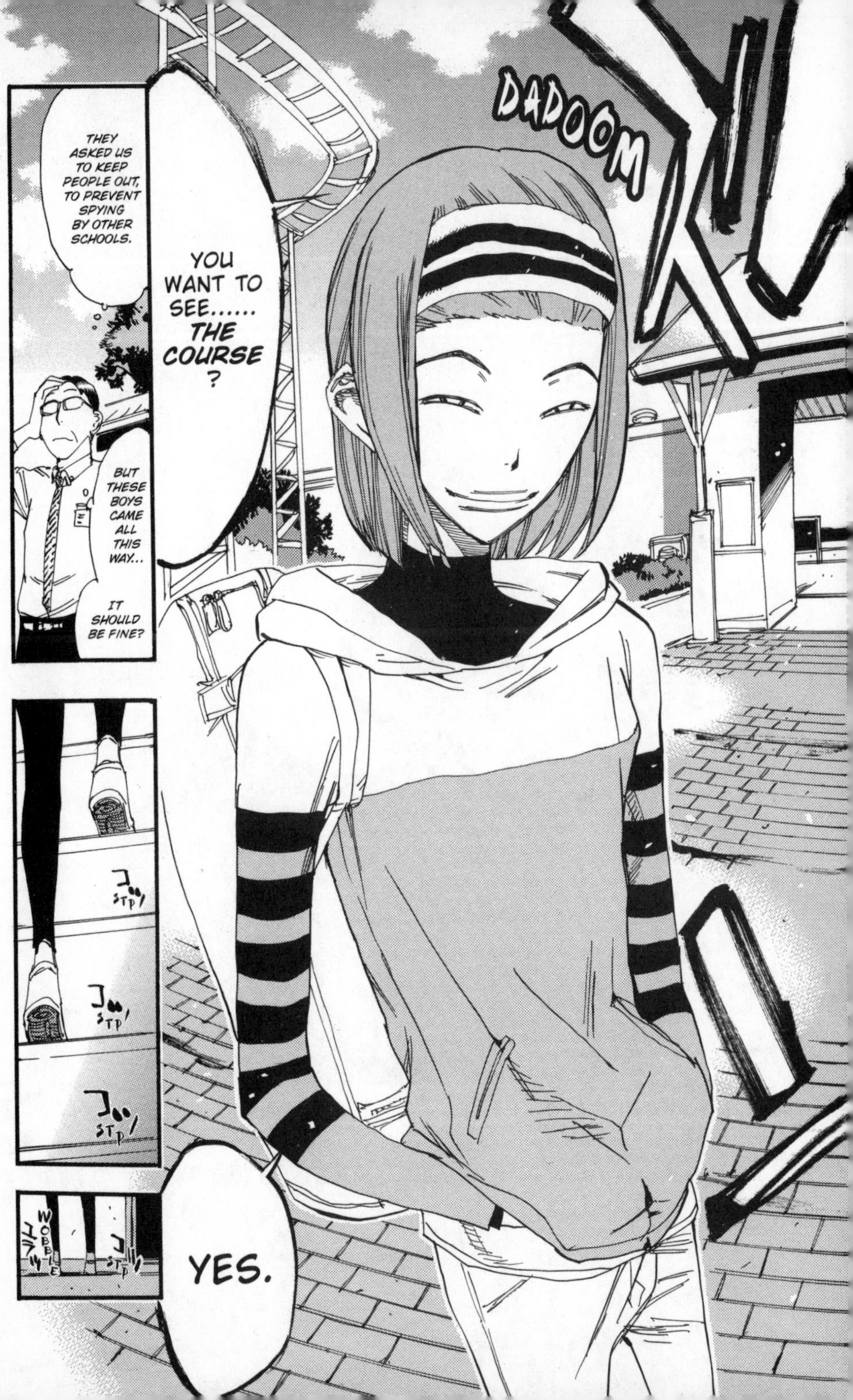
DADOOM
YOU WANT TO SEE...... THE COURSE?
YES.
THEY ASKED US TO KEEP PEOPLE OUT, TO PREVENT SPYING BY OTHER SCHOOLS.
BUT THESE BOYS CAME ALL THIS WAY...
IT SHOULD BE FINE?
STP
STP
STP
STP
WOBBLE

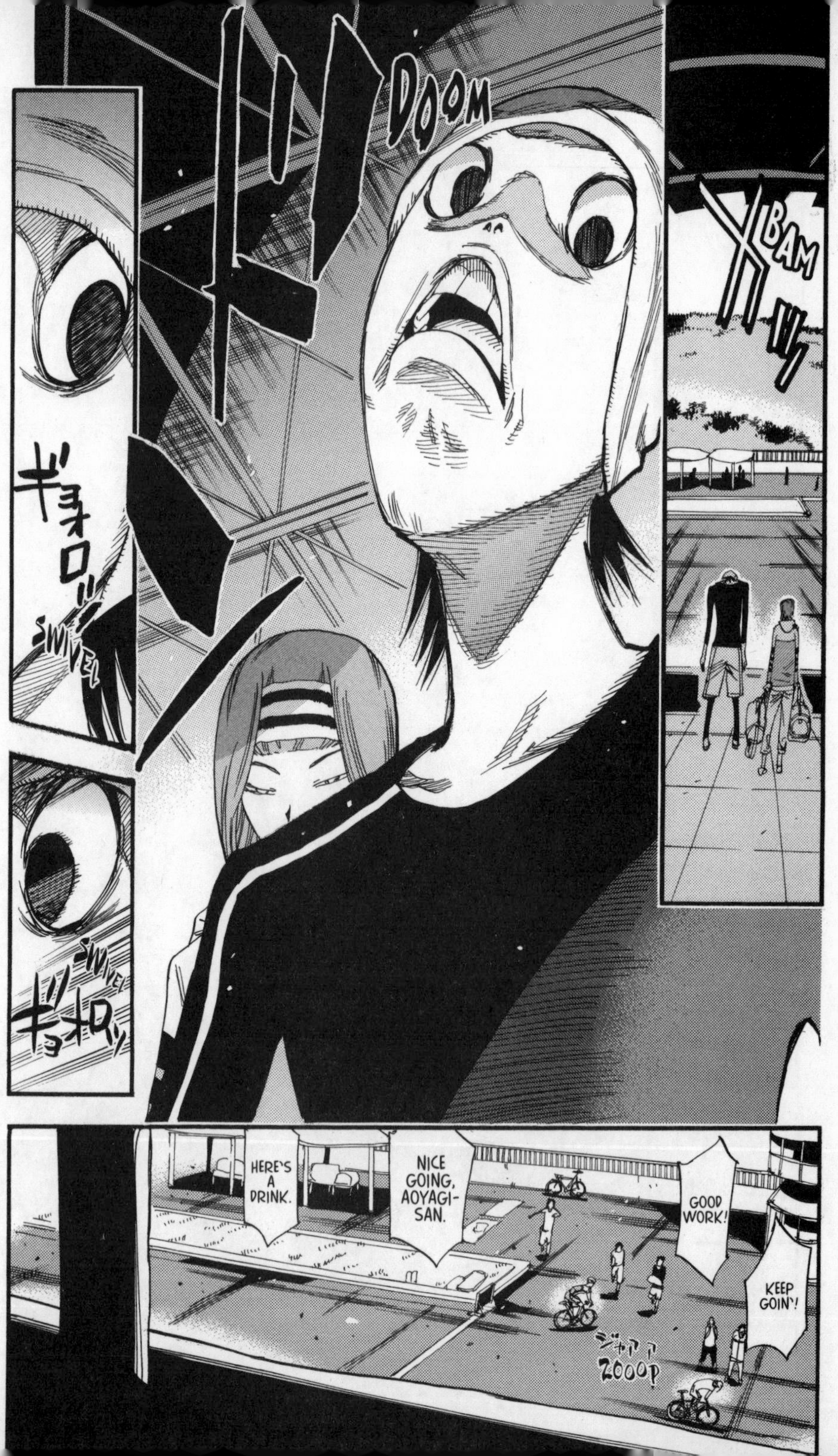
BAM
DOOM
SWIVEL
SWIVEL
GOOD WORK!
KEEP GOIN'!
NICE GOING, AOYAGI-SAN.
HERE'S A DRINK.
ZOOOP

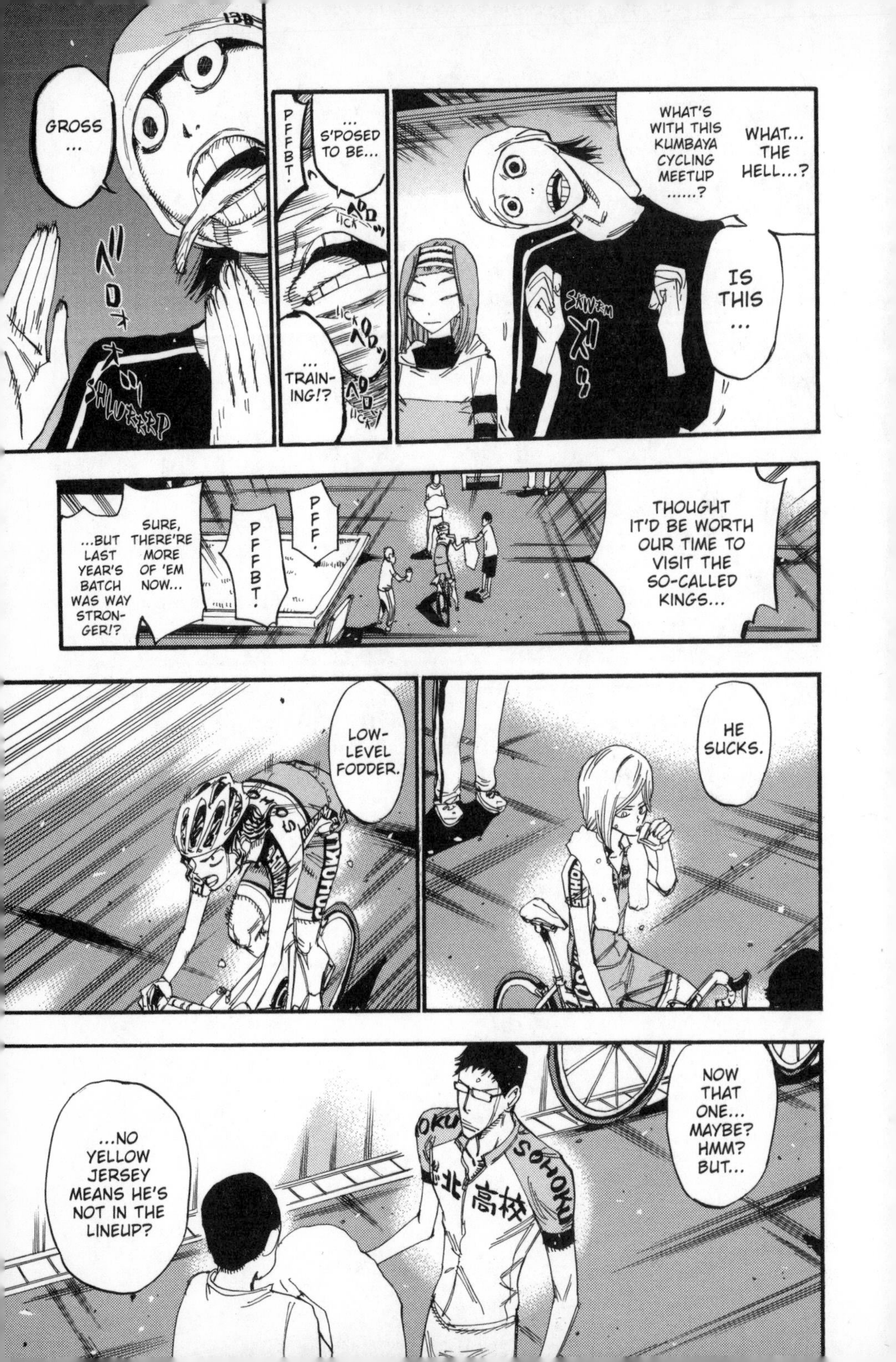
WHAT... THE HELL...?
WHAT'S WITH THIS KUMBAYA CYCLING MEETUP ......?
IS THIS ...
SKWRM
... S'POSED TO BE...
PFFBT.
LICK
LICK
... TRAINING!?
LICK
GROSS ...
SHLURRRP
THOUGHT IT'D BE WORTH OUR TIME TO VISIT THE SO-CALLED KINGS...
PFF.
PFFBT.
SURE, THERE'RE MORE OF 'EM NOW...
...BUT LAST YEAR'S BATCH WAS WAY STRONGER!?
HE SUCKS.
LOW-LEVEL FODDER.
NOW THAT ONE... MAYBE? HMM? BUT...
...NO YELLOW JERSEY MEANS HE'S NOT IN THE LINEUP?

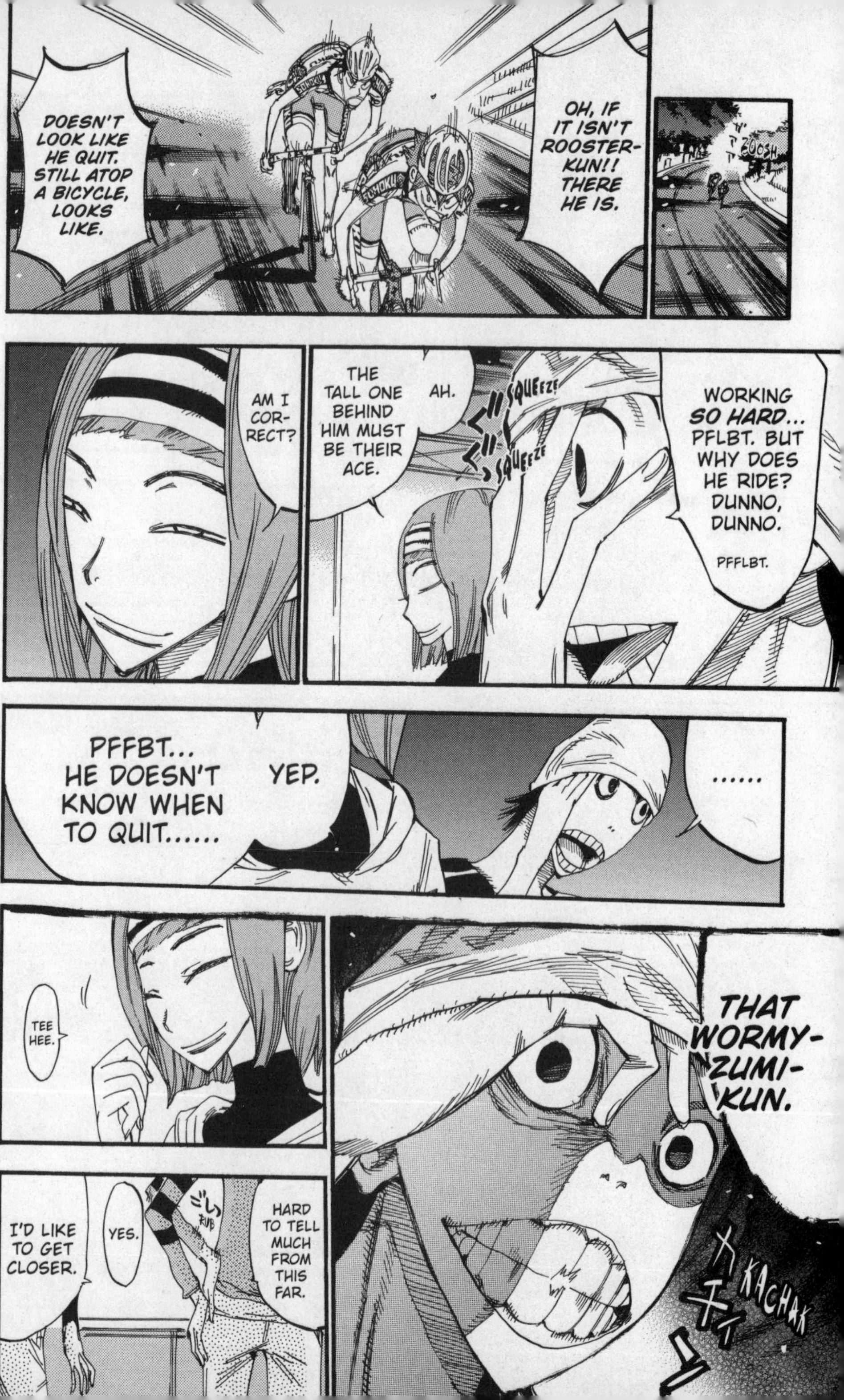

ZOOSH
OH, IF IT ISN'T ROOSTER-KUN!! THERE HE IS.
DOESN'T LOOK LIKE HE QUIT. STILL ATOP A BICYCLE, LOOKS LIKE.
WORKING SO HARD... PFLBT. BUT WHY DOES HE RIDE? DUNNO, DUNNO.
PFFLBT.
SQUEEZE
SQUEEZE
AH.
THE TALL ONE BEHIND HIM MUST BE THEIR ACE.
AM I COR-RECT?
......
YEP.
PFFBT... HE DOESN'T KNOW WHEN TO QUIT......
THAT WORMY-ZUMI-KUN.
KACHAK
TEE HEE.
HARD TO TELL MUCH FROM THIS FAR.
RUB
YES.
I'D LIKE TO GET CLOSER.

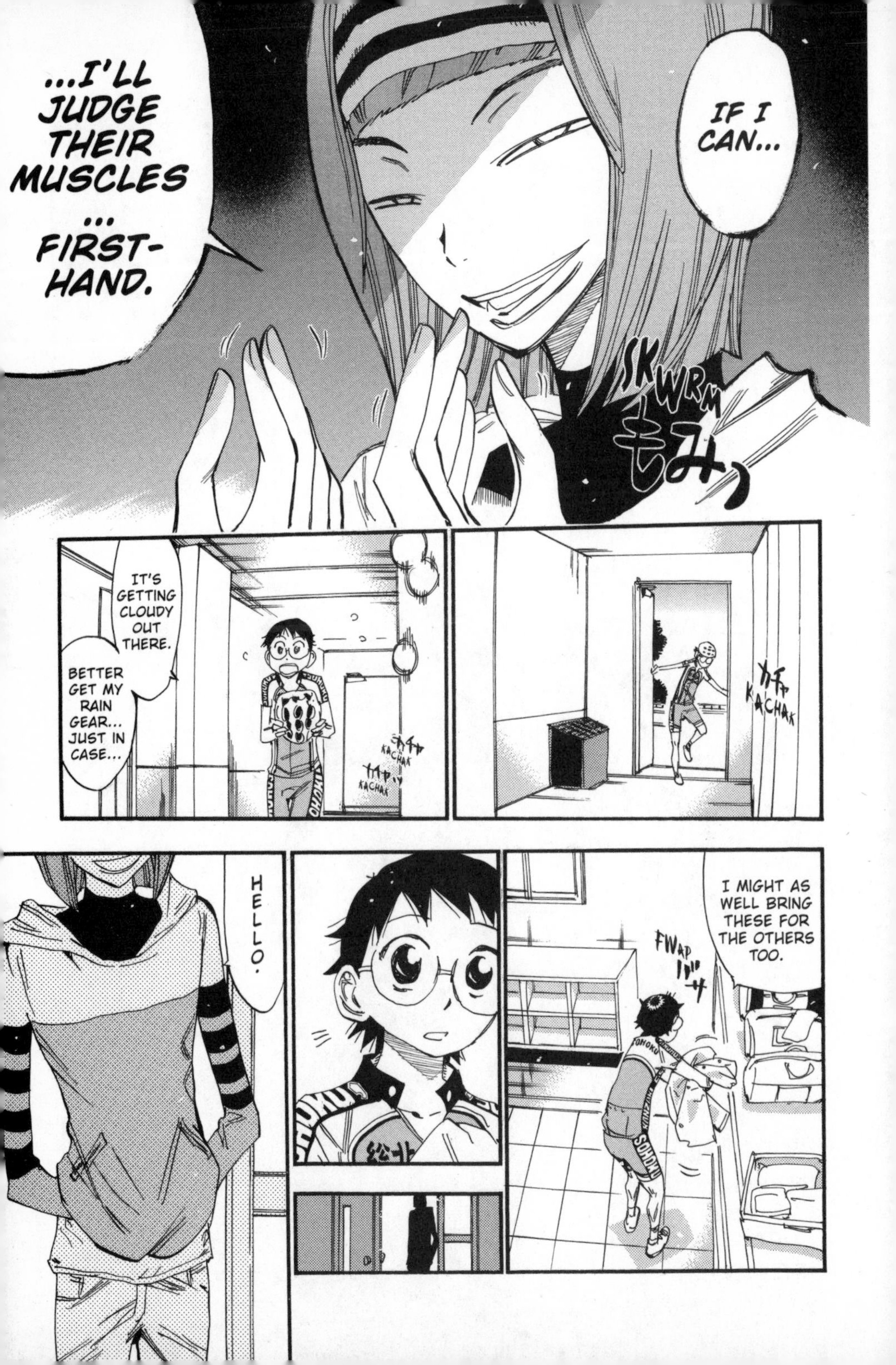
IF I CAN...
...I'LL JUDGE THEIR MUSCLES ... FIRST-HAND.
SKWRM
KACHAK
IT'S GETTING CLOUDY OUT THERE.
BETTER GET MY RAIN GEAR... JUST IN CASE...
KACHAK
KACHAK
I MIGHT AS WELL BRING THESE FOR THE OTHERS TOO.
FWAP
HELLO.

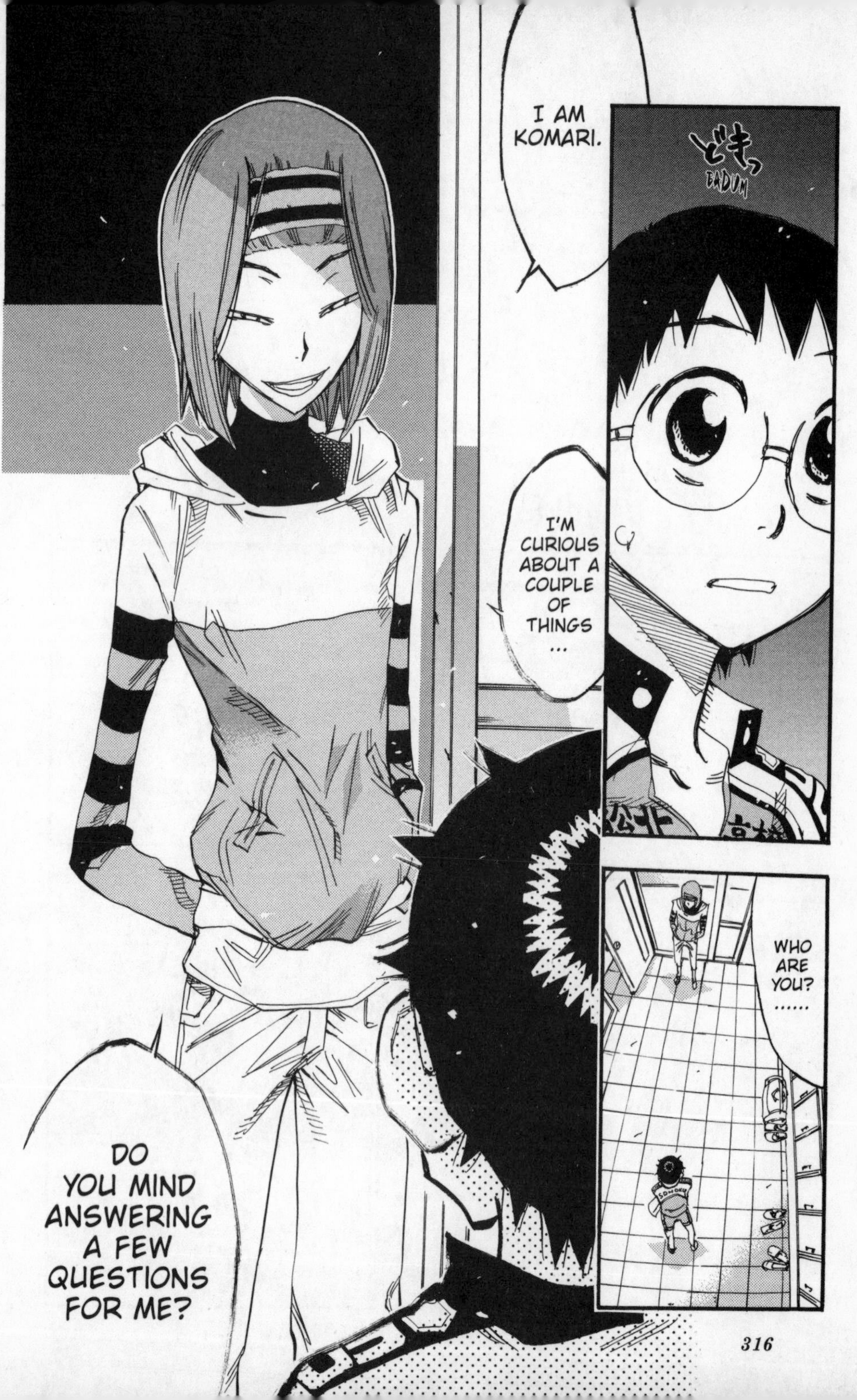
どきっ
BADUM
WHO ARE YOU? ......
I AM KOMARI.
I'M CURIOUS ABOUT A COUPLE OF THINGS ...
DO YOU MIND ANSWERING A FEW QUESTIONS FOR ME?

RIDE.293 FINGERTIPS

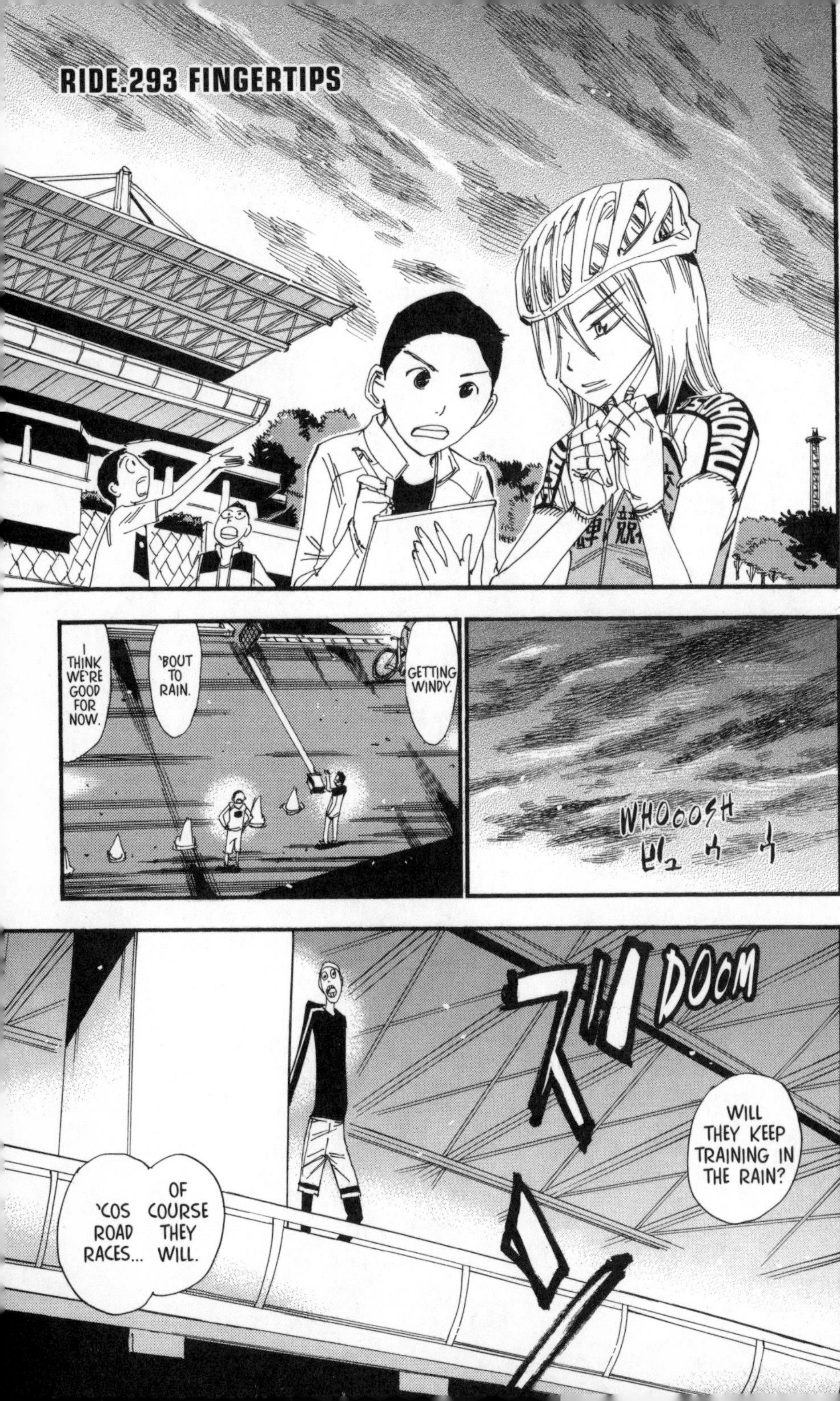
WHOOOSH
GETTING WINDY.
'BOUT TO RAIN.
I THINK WE'RE GOOD FOR NOW.
DOOM
WILL THEY KEEP TRAINING IN THE RAIN?
OF COURSE THEY WILL. 'COS ROAD RACES...

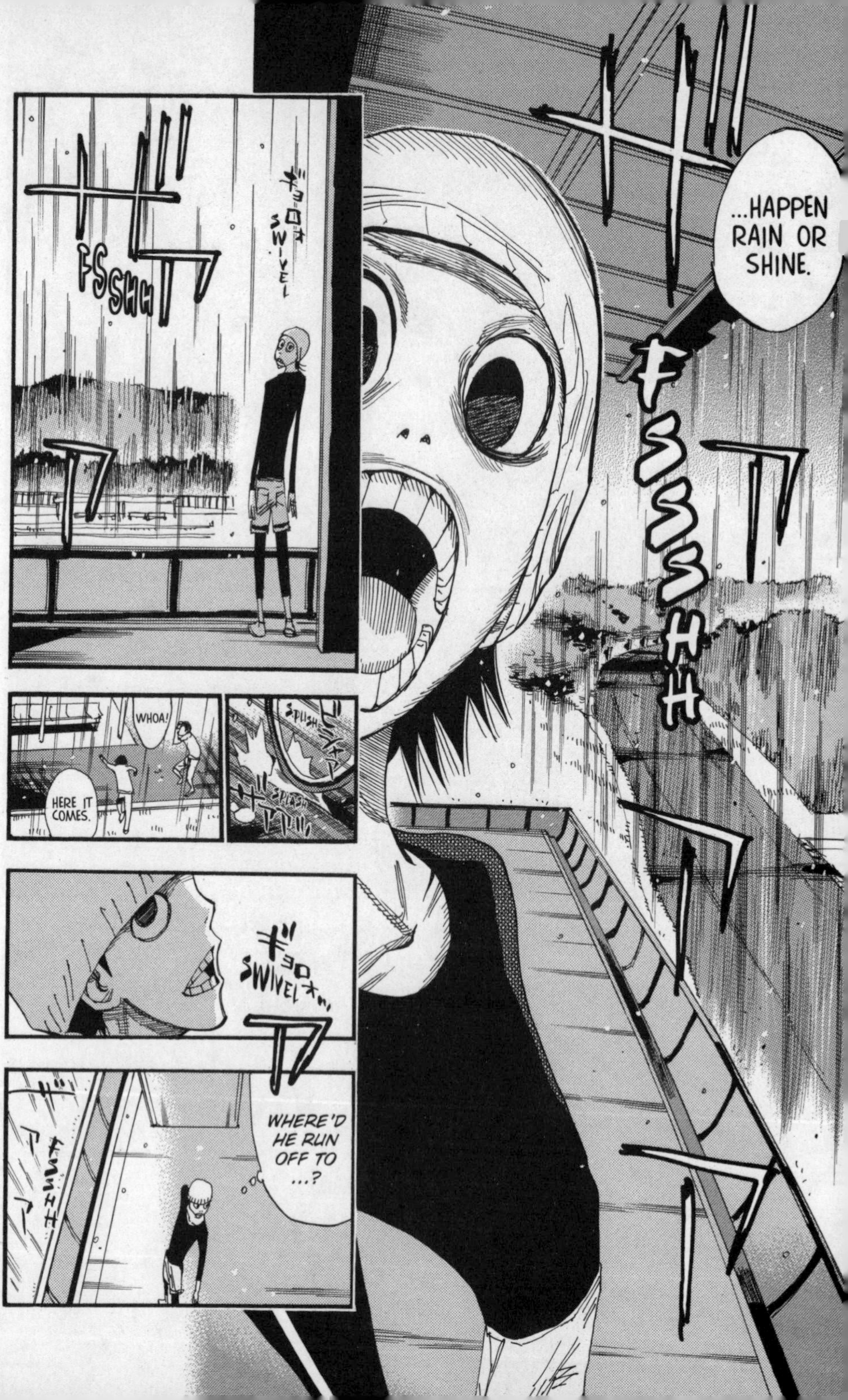
...HAPPEN RAIN OR SHINE.
FSSHHH
SWIVEL
FSSHH
SPLISH
SPLASH
WHOA!
HERE IT COMES.
SWIVEL
WHERE'D HE RUN OFF TO ...?

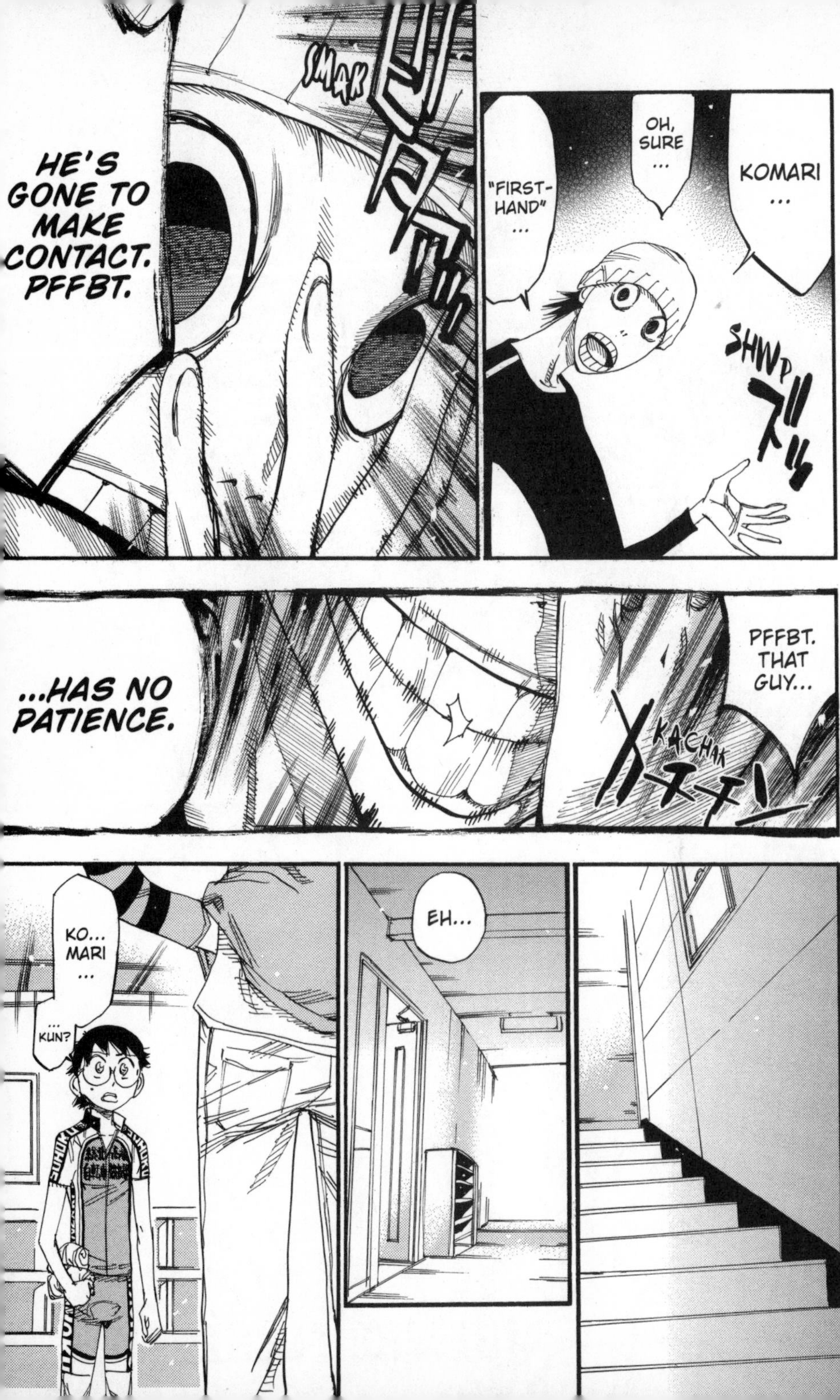
KOMARI …
OH, SURE …
"FIRST-HAND" …
SHWP
SMAK
HE'S GONE TO MAKE CONTACT. PFFBT.
PFFBT. THAT GUY…
KACHAK
…HAS NO PATIENCE.
EH…
KO… MARI …
… KUN?

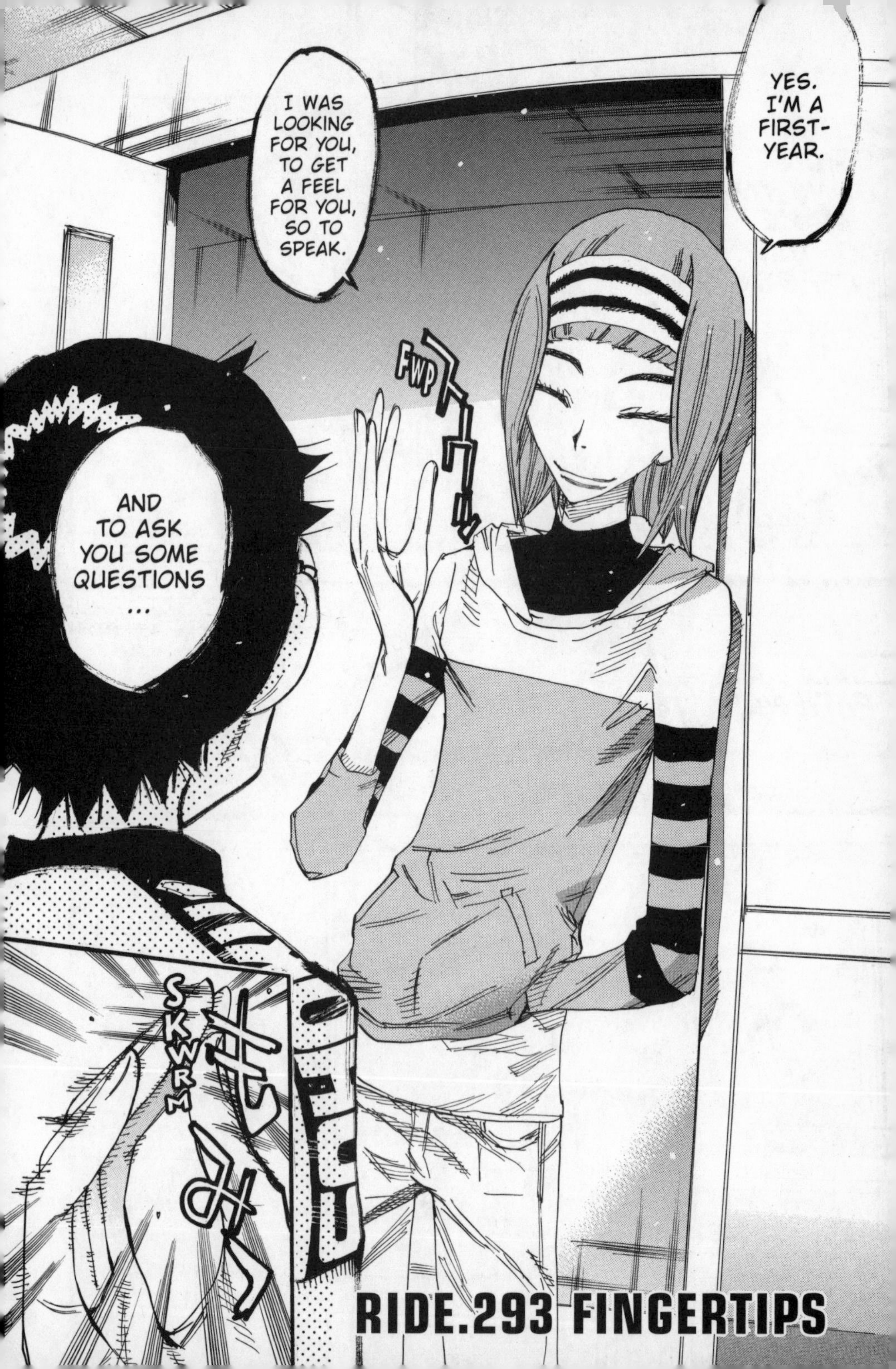
YES. I'M A FIRST-YEAR.
I WAS LOOKING FOR YOU, TO GET A FEEL FOR YOU, SO TO SPEAK.
FWP
AND TO ASK YOU SOME QUESTIONS ...
SKWRM

RIDE.293 FINGERTIPS

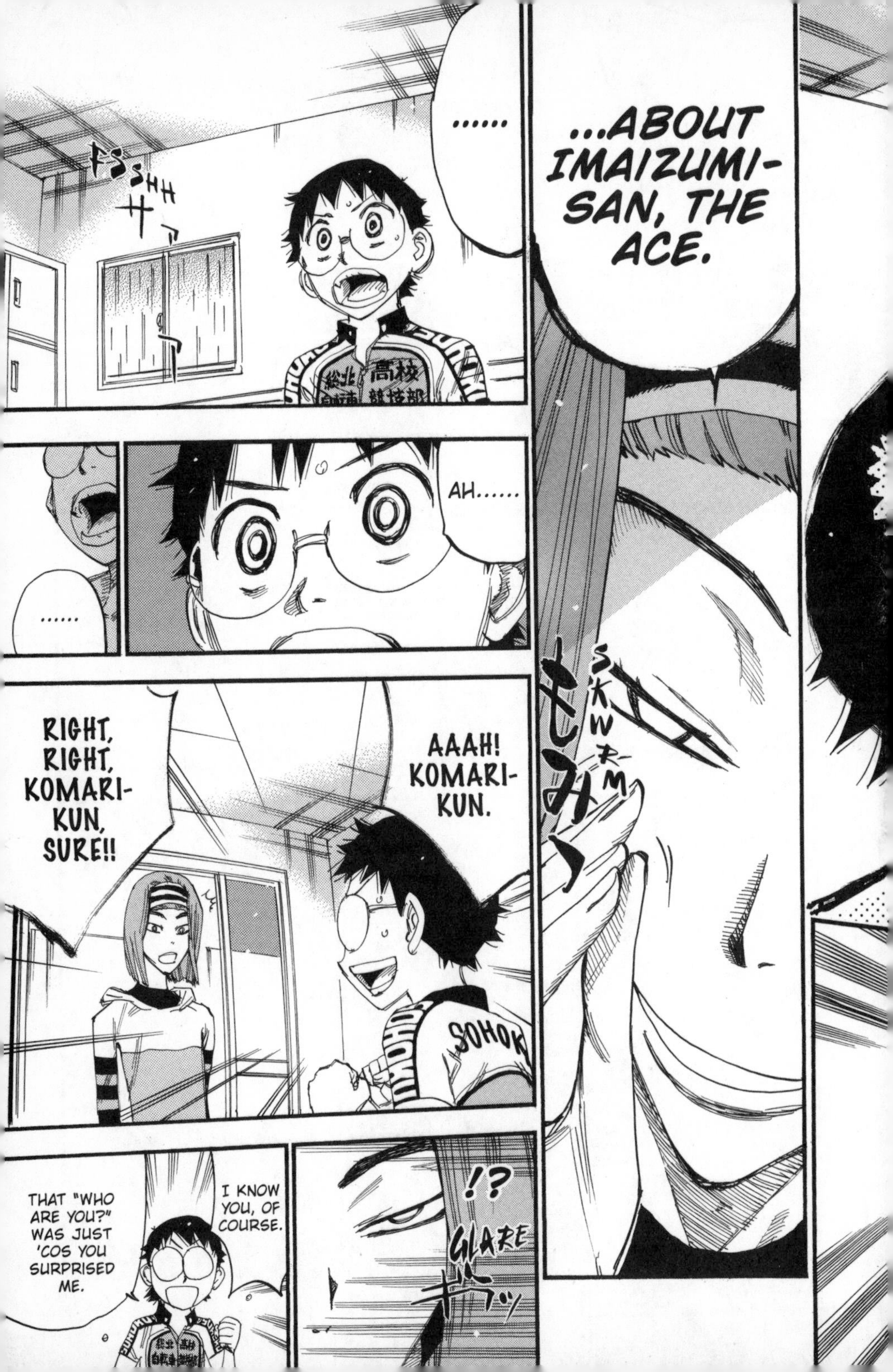
...ABOUT IMAIZUMI-SAN, THE ACE.
SKWRM
......
FSSHH
AH......
......
AAAH! KOMARI-KUN.
RIGHT, RIGHT, KOMARI-KUN, SURE!!
SOHOK
!?
GLARE
I KNOW YOU, OF COURSE.
THAT "WHO ARE YOU?" WAS JUST 'COS YOU SURPRISED ME.

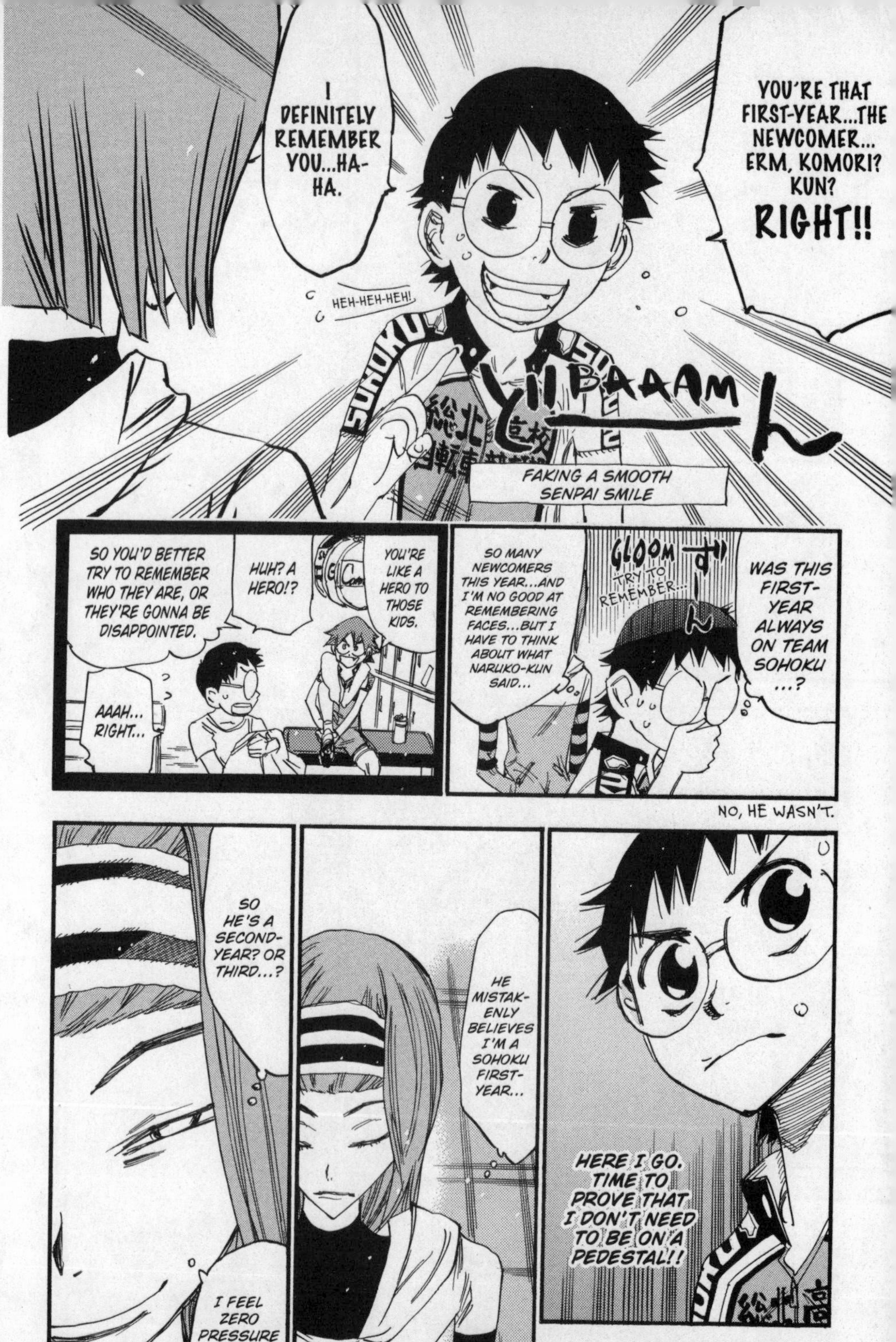
YOU'RE THAT FIRST-YEAR...THE NEWCOMER... ERM, KOMORI? KUN? RIGHT!!
I DEFINITELY REMEMBER YOU...HA-HA.
HEH-HEH-HEH!
YIIBAAAM
FAKING A SMOOTH SENPAI SMILE
WAS THIS FIRST-YEAR ALWAYS ON TEAM SOHOKU ...?
GLOOM
TRY TO REMEMBER...
SO MANY NEWCOMERS THIS YEAR...AND I'M NO GOOD AT REMEMBERING FACES...BUT I HAVE TO THINK ABOUT WHAT NARUKO-KUN SAID...
YOU'RE LIKE A HERO TO THOSE KIDS.
HUH? A HERO!?
SO YOU'D BETTER TRY TO REMEMBER WHO THEY ARE, OR THEY'RE GONNA BE DISAPPOINTED.
AAAH... RIGHT...
NO, HE WASN'T.
HERE I GO. TIME TO PROVE THAT I DON'T NEED TO BE ON A PEDESTAL!!
HE MISTAKENLY BELIEVES I'M A SOHOKU FIRST-YEAR...
SO HE'S A SECOND-YEAR? OR THIRD...?
I FEEL ZERO PRESSURE FROM THIS ONE.

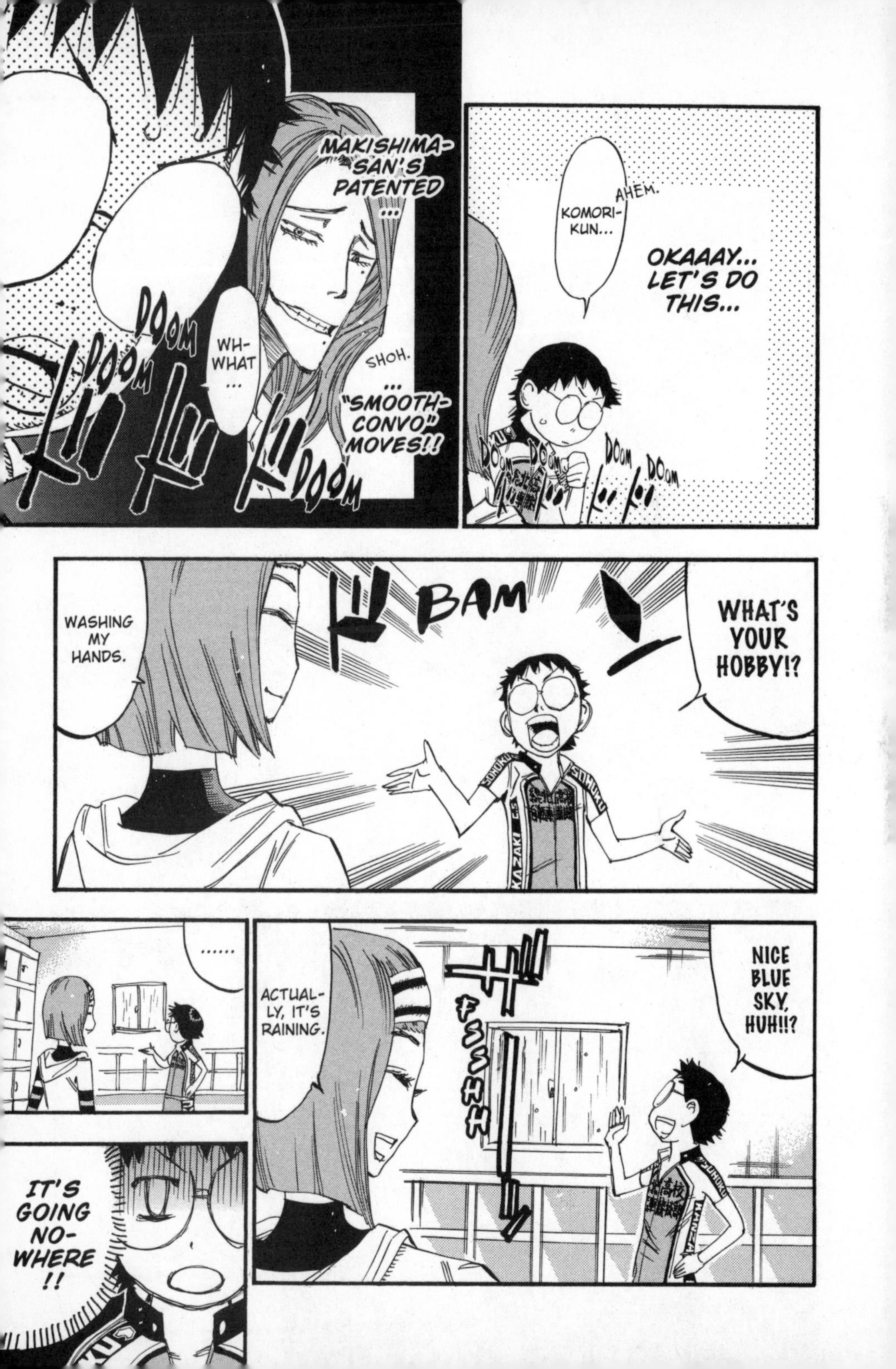
AHEM.
KOMORI-KUN...
OKAAAY... LET'S DO THIS...
DOOM DOOM DOOM DOOM
MAKISHIMA-SAN'S PATENTED...
SHOH.
..."SMOOTH-CONVO" MOVES!!
WH-WHAT...
DOOM DOOM KUDOOM
WHAT'S YOUR HOBBY!?
BAM
WASHING MY HANDS.
NICE BLUE SKY, HUH!!?
FSSHH
ACTUALLY, IT'S RAINING.
......
IT'S GOING NOWHERE!!

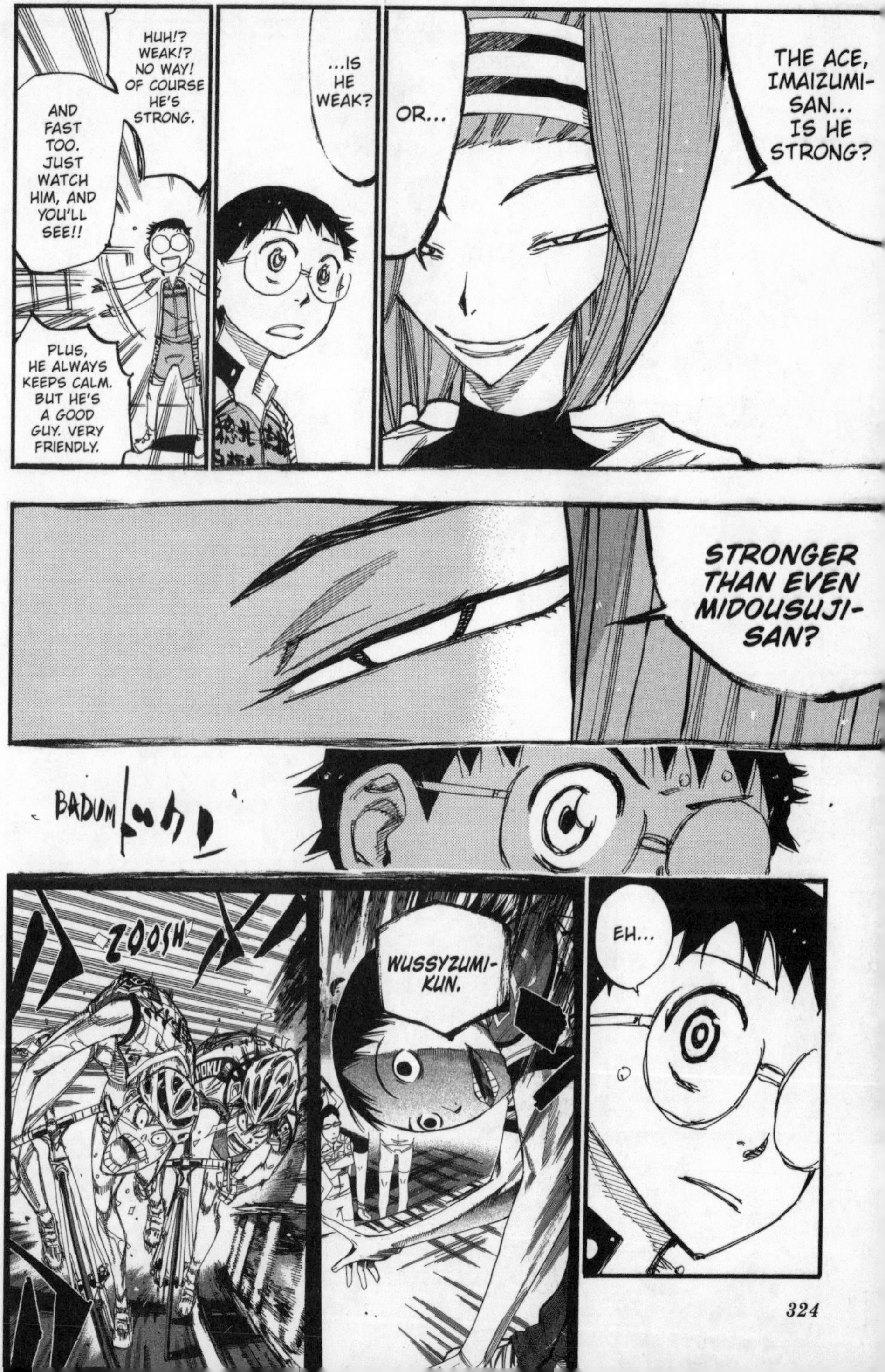
THE ACE, IMAIZUMI-SAN... IS HE STRONG?
OR...
...IS HE WEAK?
HUH!? WEAK!? NO WAY! OF COURSE HE'S STRONG.
AND FAST TOO. JUST WATCH HIM, AND YOU'LL SEE!!
PLUS, HE ALWAYS KEEPS CALM. BUT HE'S A GOOD GUY. VERY FRIENDLY.
STRONGER THAN EVEN MIDOUSUJI-SAN?
BADUM
EH...
WUSSYZUMI-KUN.
ZOOSH

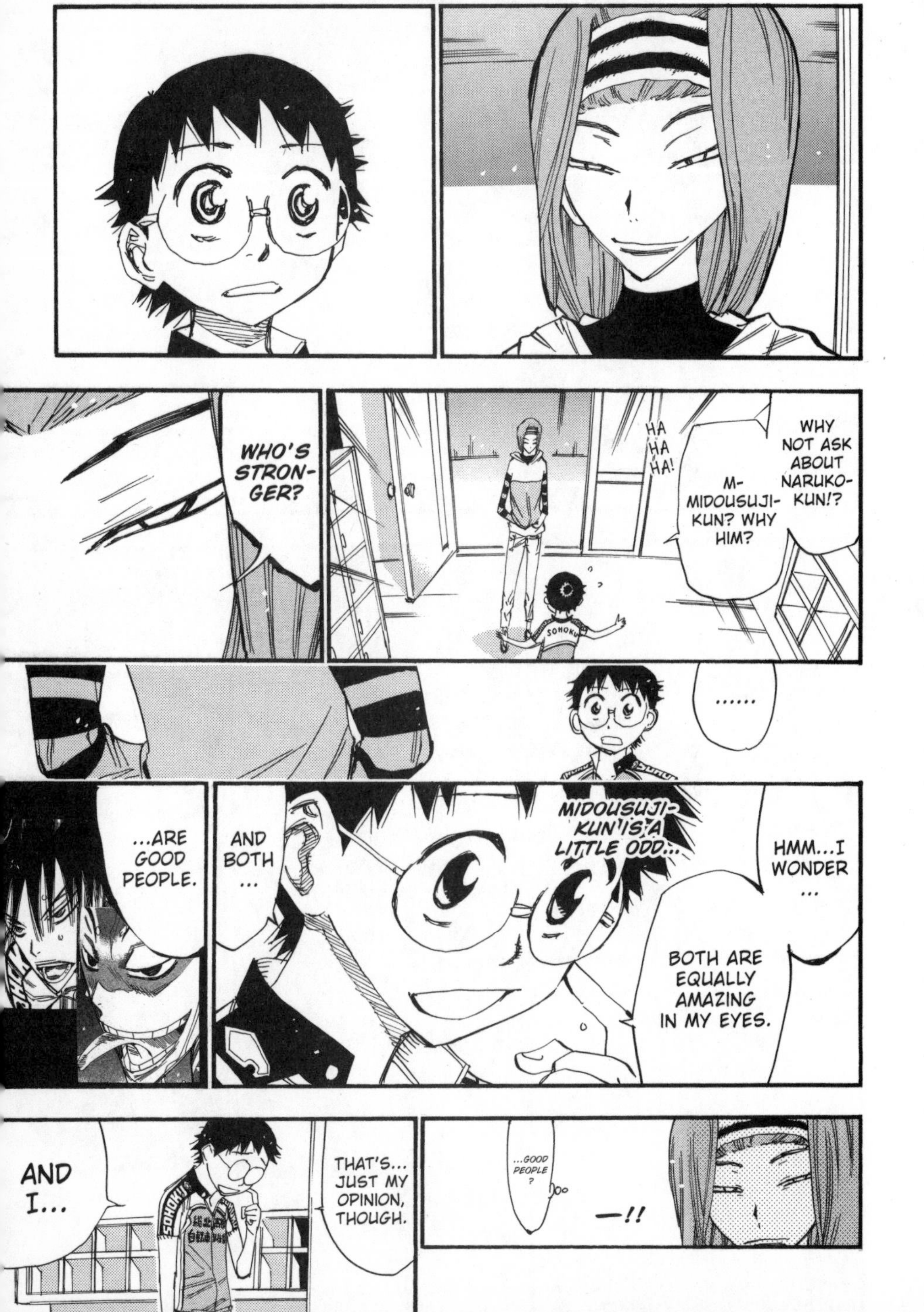
WHY NOT ASK ABOUT NARUKO-KUN!?
M-MIDOUSUJI-KUN? WHY HIM?
HA HA HA!
WHO'S STRON-GER?
......
HMM...I WONDER...
MIDOUSUJI-KUN IS A LITTLE ODD...
BOTH ARE EQUALLY AMAZING IN MY EYES.
AND BOTH...
...ARE GOOD PEOPLE.
...GOOD PEOPLE?
—!!
THAT'S... JUST MY OPINION, THOUGH.
AND I...

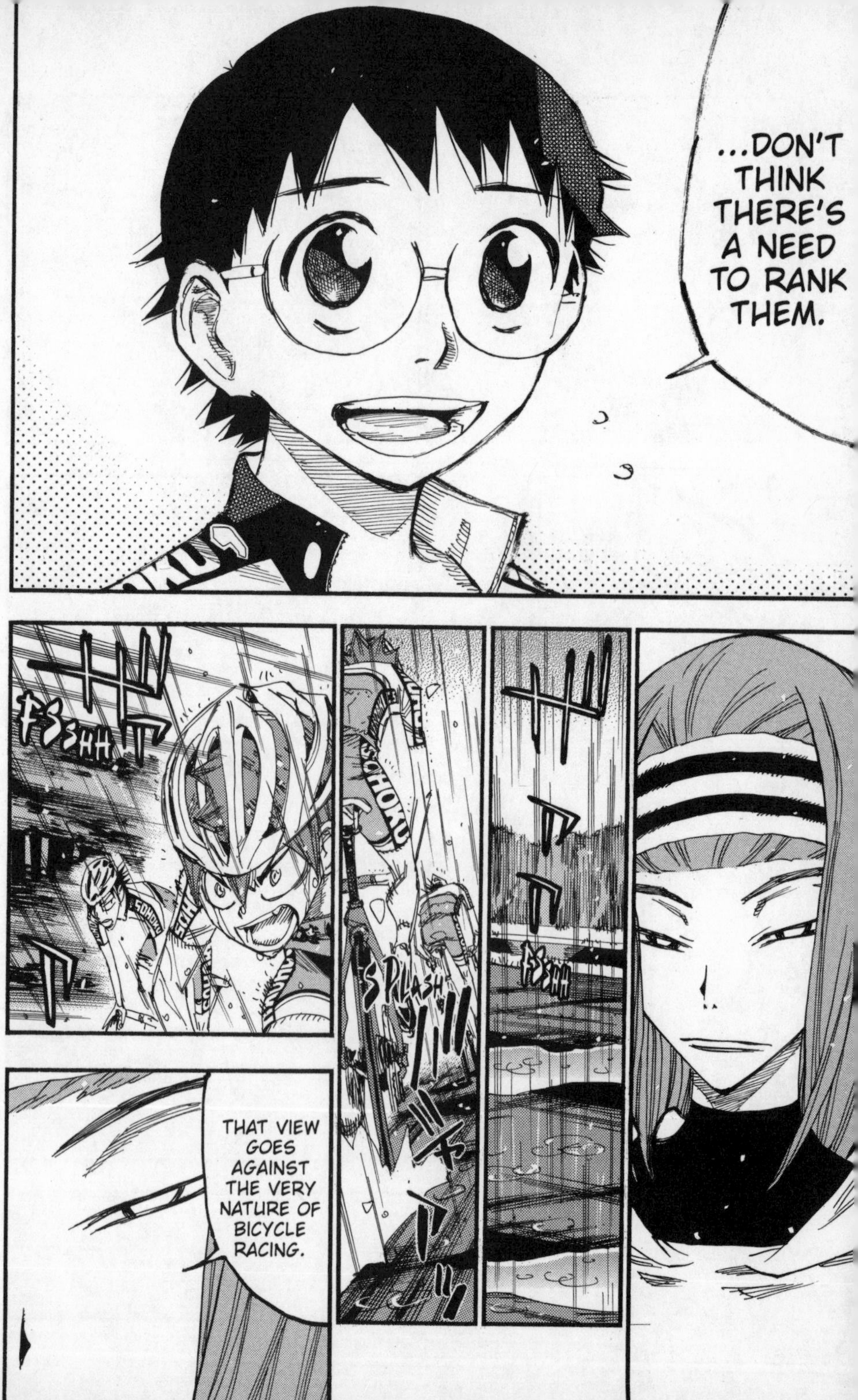
...DON'T THINK THERE'S A NEED TO RANK THEM.
FSSHH
SPLASH
FSSHH
THAT VIEW GOES AGAINST THE VERY NATURE OF BICYCLE RACING.

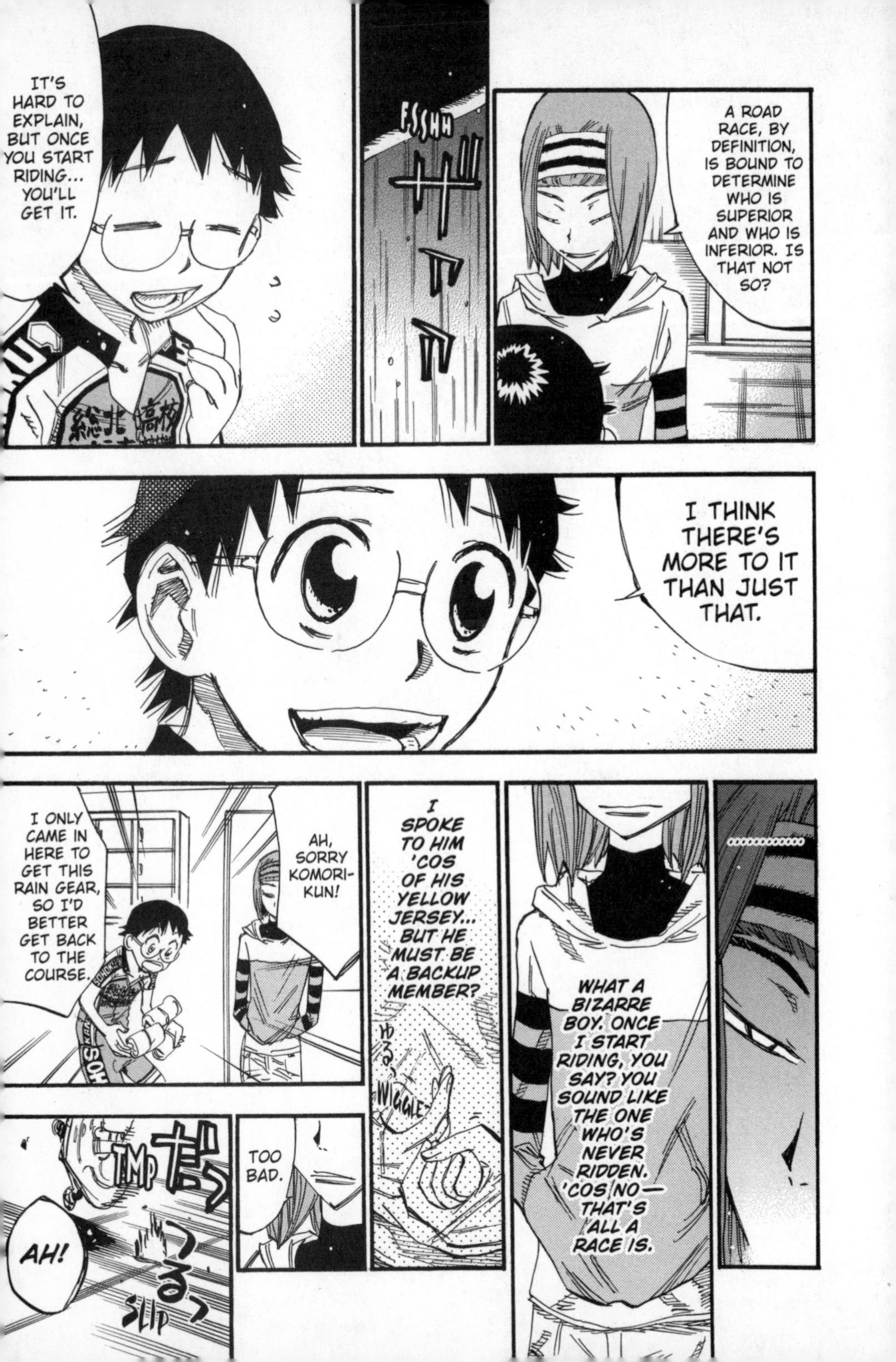
A ROAD RACE, BY DEFINITION, IS BOUND TO DETERMINE WHO IS SUPERIOR AND WHO IS INFERIOR. IS THAT NOT SO?
FSSHH
IT'S HARD TO EXPLAIN, BUT ONCE YOU START RIDING... YOU'LL GET IT.
I THINK THERE'S MORE TO IT THAN JUST THAT.
....
WHAT A BIZARRE BOY. ONCE I START RIDING, YOU SAY? YOU SOUND LIKE THE ONE WHO'S NEVER RIDDEN. 'COS NO— THAT'S ALL A RACE IS.
I SPOKE TO HIM 'COS OF HIS YELLOW JERSEY... BUT HE MUST BE A BACKUP MEMBER?
WIGGLE
AH, SORRY KOMORI-KUN!
I ONLY CAME IN HERE TO GET THIS RAIN GEAR, SO I'D BETTER GET BACK TO THE COURSE.
TOO BAD.
TMP
AH!
SLIP

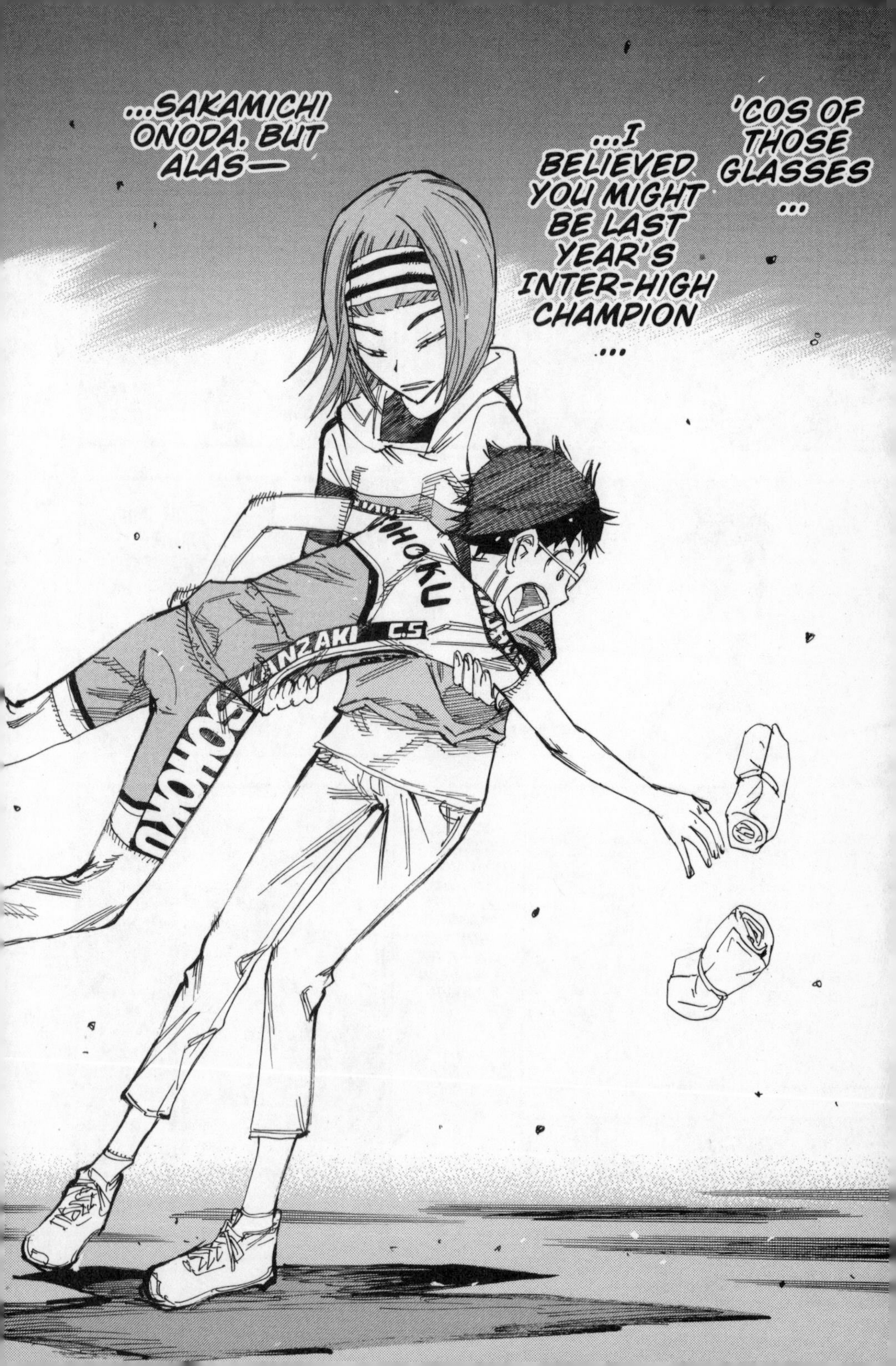
'COS OF THOSE GLASSES ...
...I BELIEVED YOU MIGHT BE LAST YEAR'S INTER-HIGH CHAMPION ...
...SAKAMICHI ONODA. BUT ALAS—
SOHOKU
KANZAKI C.S
SOHOKU

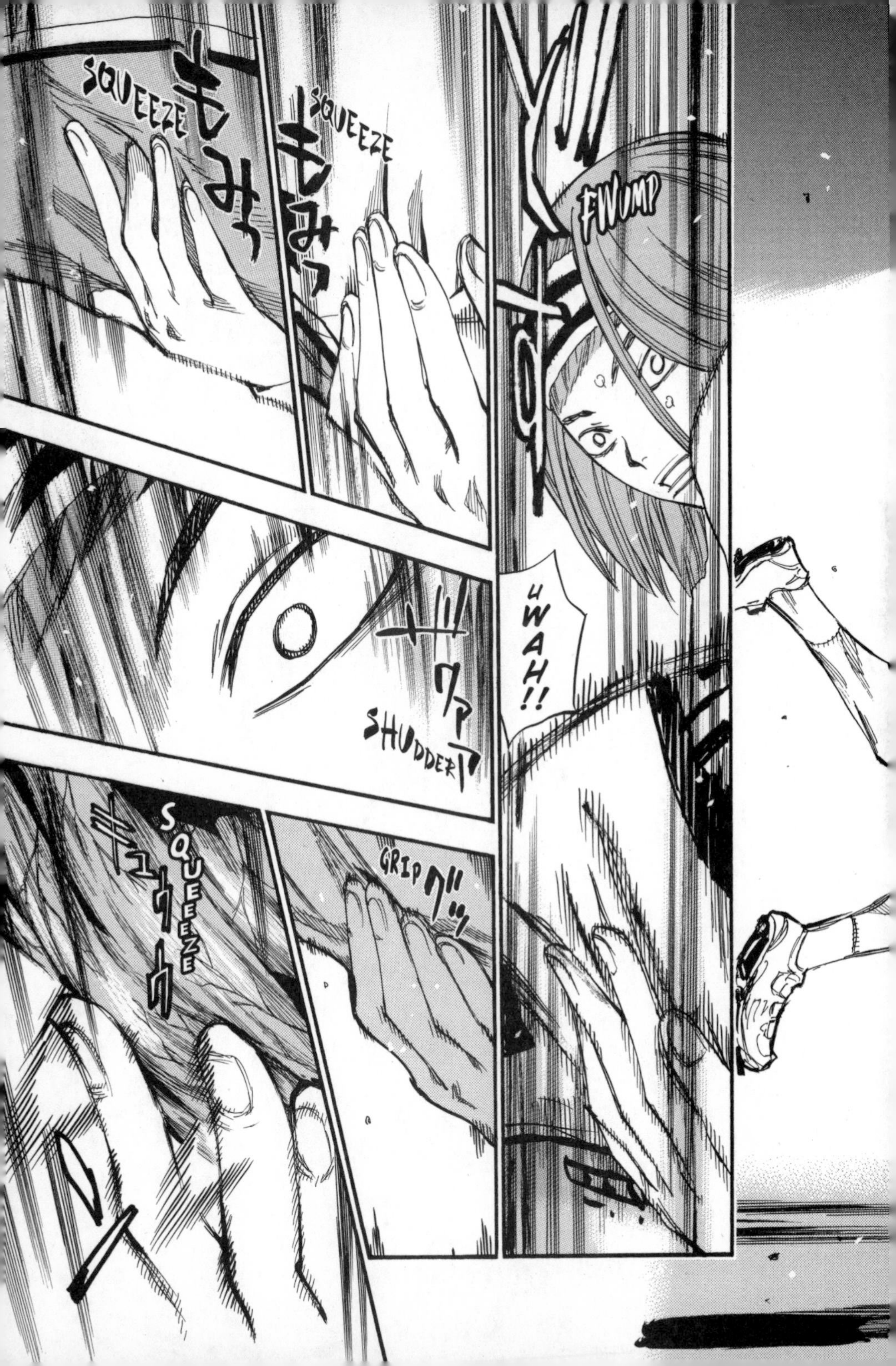

FWUMP
UWAH!!
SQUEEZE
もみっ
SQUEEZE
もみっ
SHUDDER
GRIP
グッ
SQUEEZE

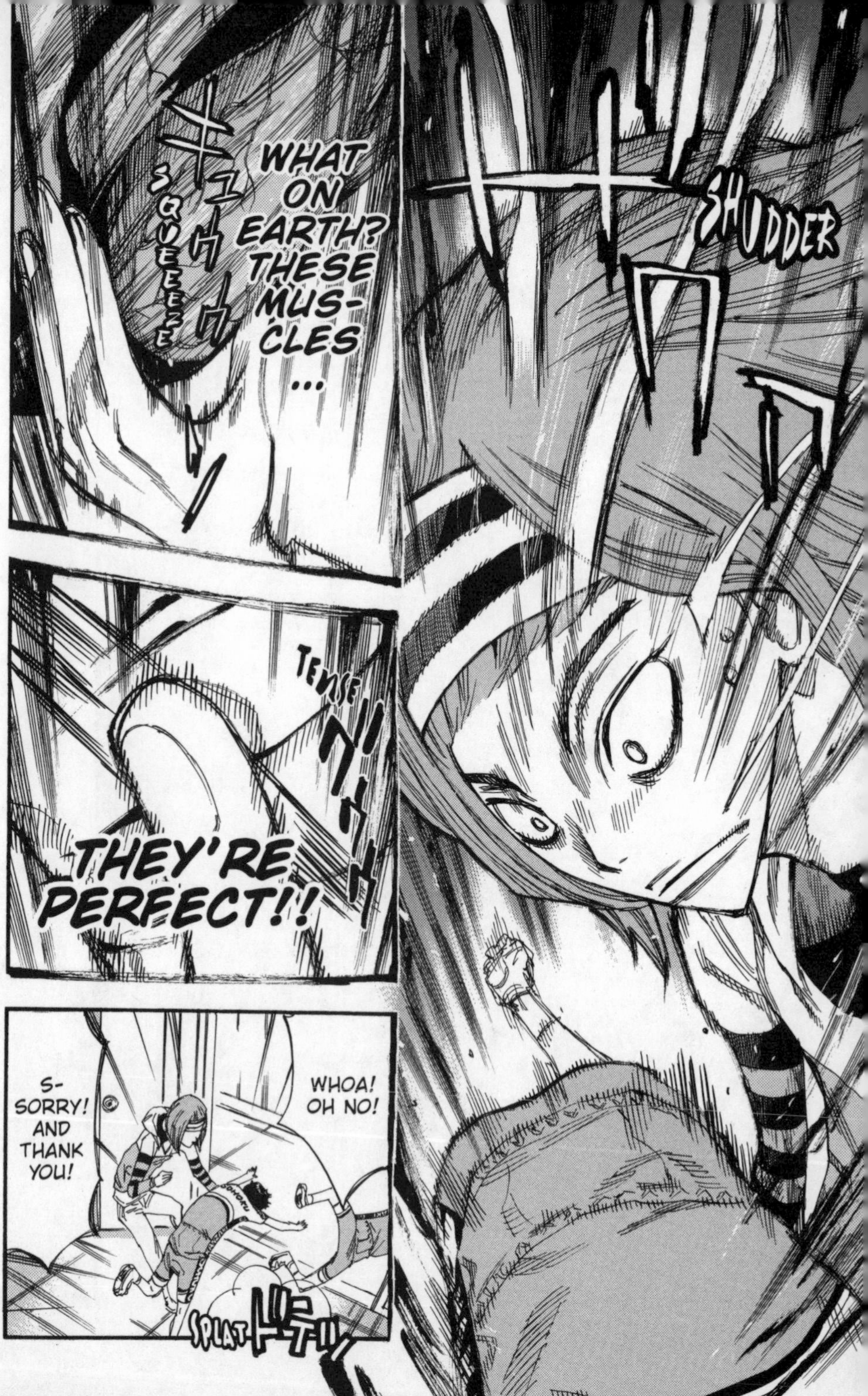
SHUDDER
SQUEEEEZE
WHAT ON EARTH? THESE MUS-CLES...
TENSE
THEY'RE PERFECT!!
WHOA! OH NO!
S-SORRY! AND THANK YOU!
SPLAT

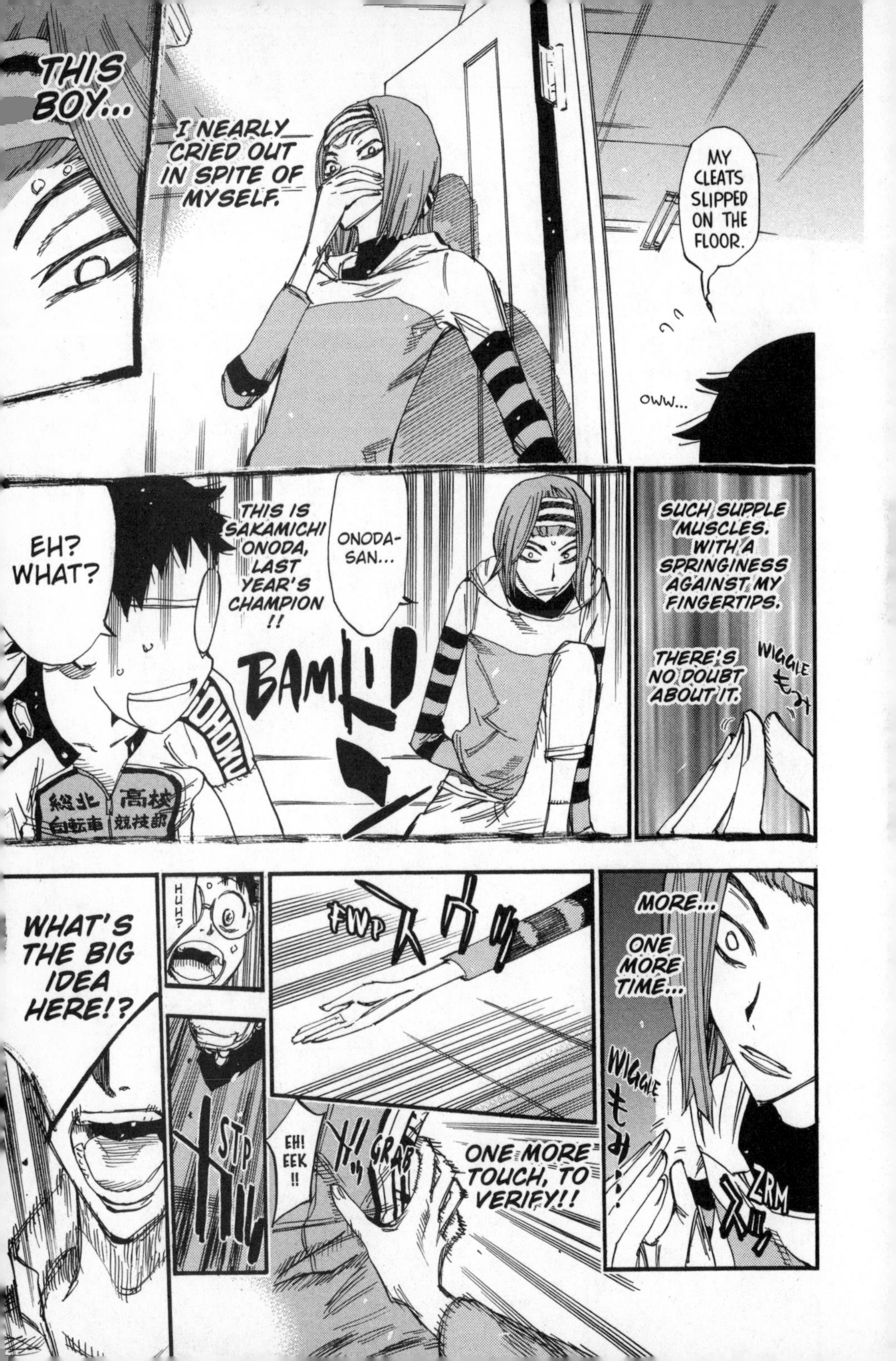

MY CLEATS SLIPPED ON THE FLOOR.
OWW...
I NEARLY CRIED OUT IN SPITE OF MYSELF.
THIS BOY...
SUCH SUPPLE MUSCLES. WITH A SPRINGINESS AGAINST MY FINGERTIPS.
THERE'S NO DOUBT ABOUT IT.
WIGGLE
ONODA-SAN...
THIS IS SAKAMICHI ONODA, LAST YEAR'S CHAMPION!!
BAM
EH? WHAT?
総北高校
自転車競技部
MORE...
ONE MORE TIME...
WIGGLE
ZRM
FWIP
HUH?
WHAT'S THE BIG IDEA HERE!?
ONE MORE TOUCH, TO VERIFY!!
GRAB
EH! EEK!!
STP

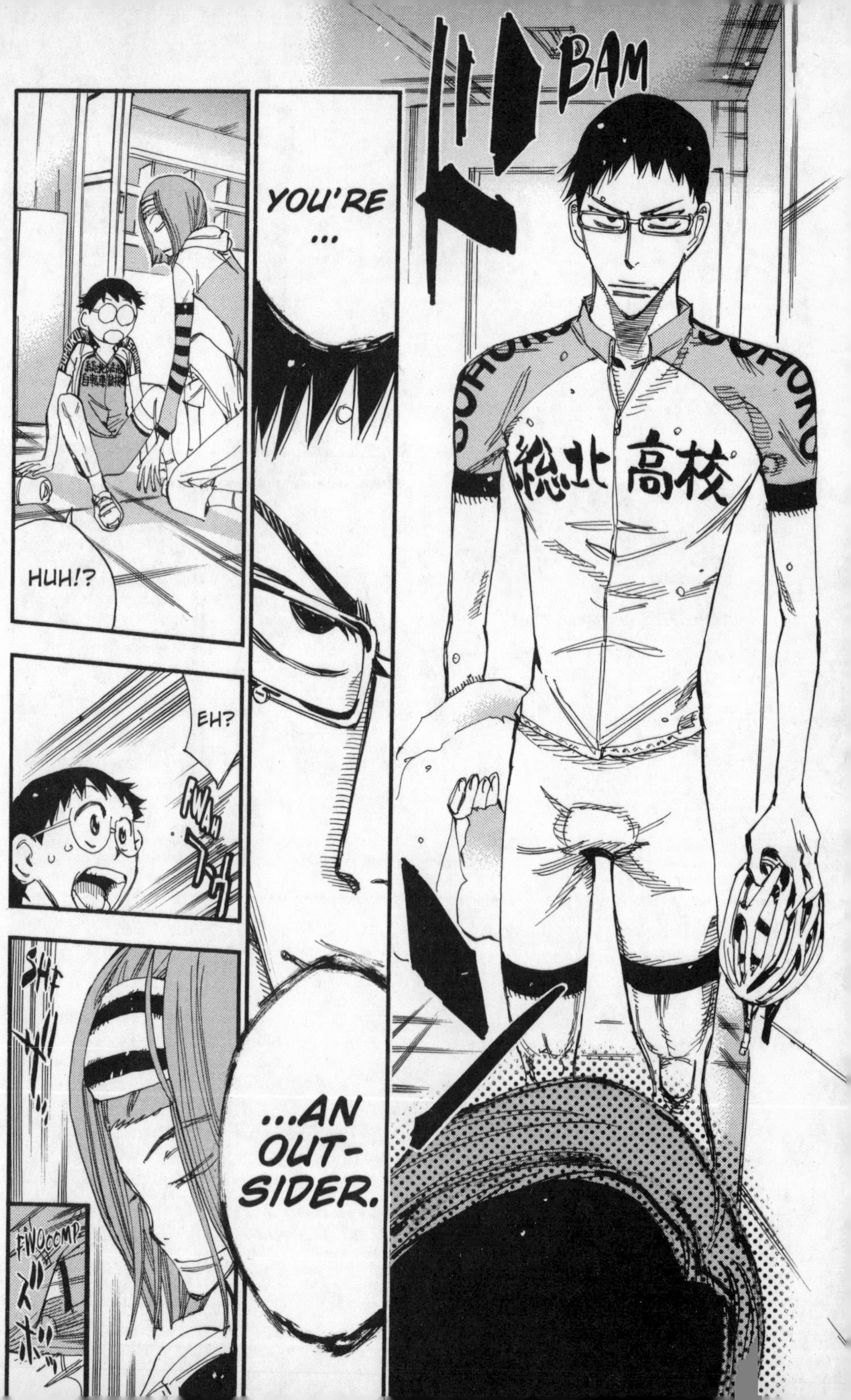
BAM
総北高校
YOU'RE ...
...AN OUT-SIDER.
HUH!?
EH?
FWAH
SHF
FWOOOMP

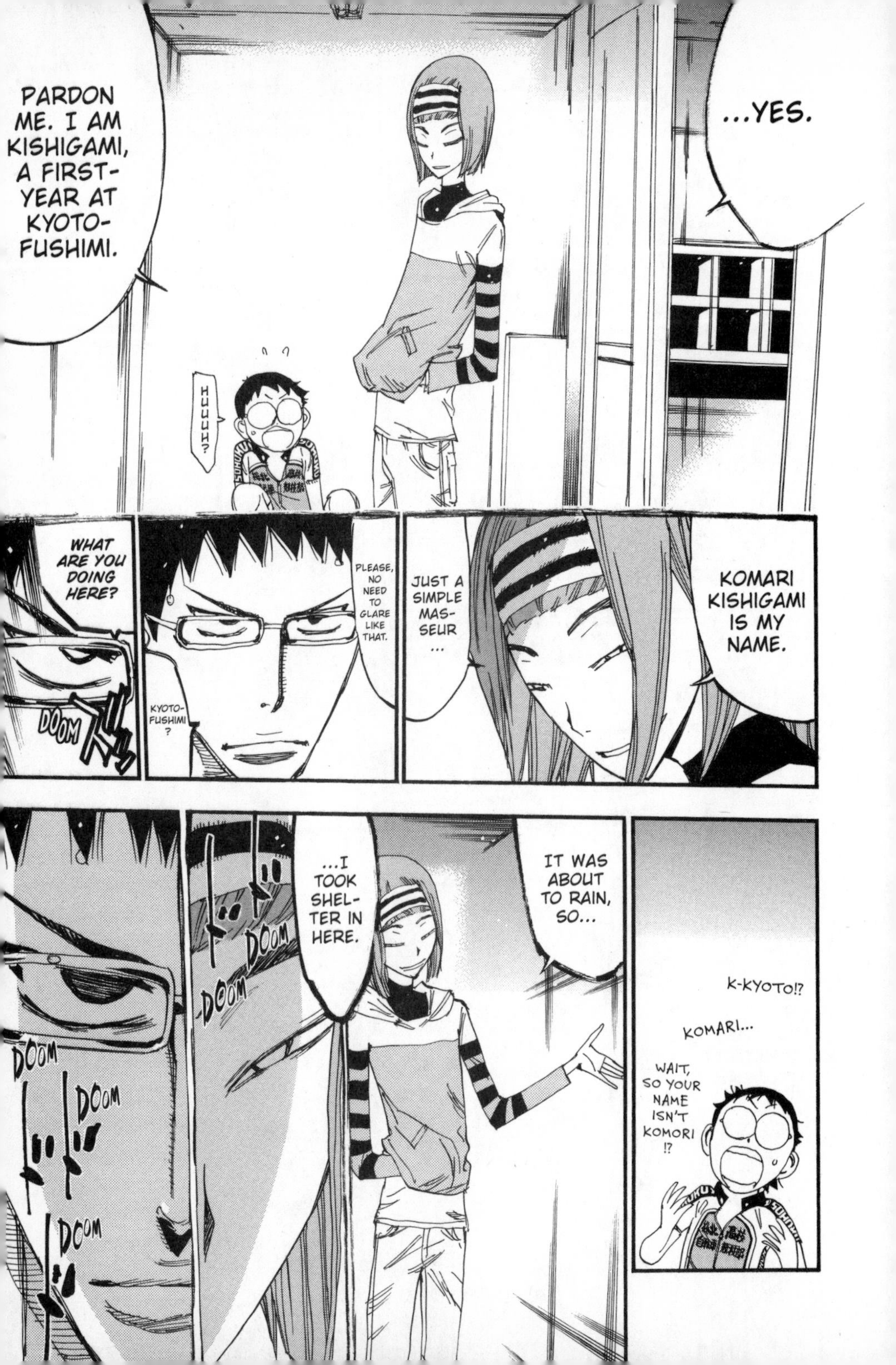
...YES.
PARDON ME. I AM KISHIGAMI, A FIRST-YEAR AT KYOTO-FUSHIMI.
HUUUH?
KOMARI KISHIGAMI IS MY NAME.
JUST A SIMPLE MAS-SEUR...
PLEASE, NO NEED TO GLARE LIKE THAT.
KYOTO-FUSHIMI?
WHAT ARE YOU DOING HERE?
DOOM
K-KYOTO!?
KOMARI...
WAIT, SO YOUR NAME ISN'T KOMORI!?
IT WAS ABOUT TO RAIN, SO...
...I TOOK SHEL-TER IN HERE.
DOOM
DOOM
DOOM
DOOM
DOOM

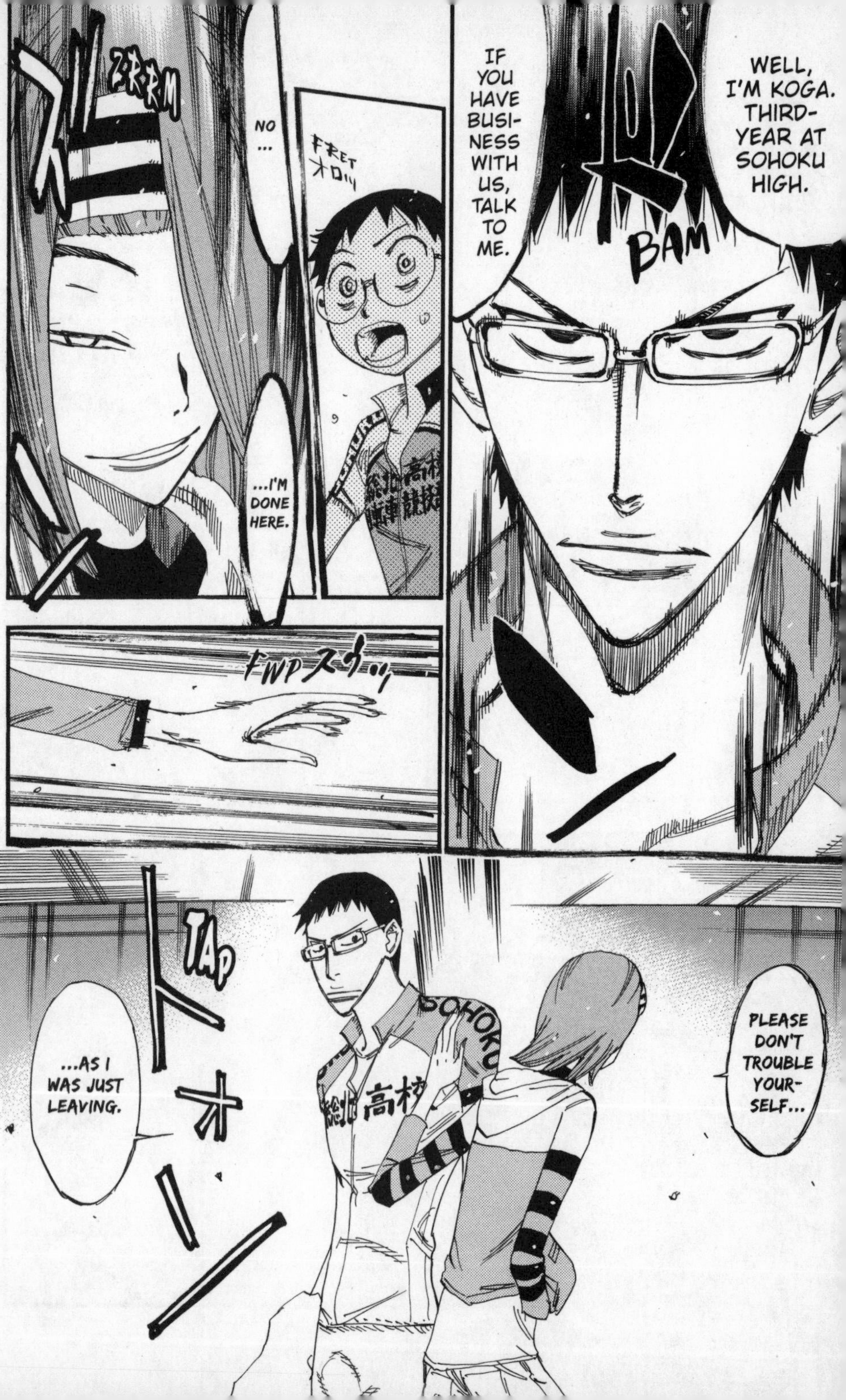

WELL, I'M KOGA. THIRD-YEAR AT SOHOKU HIGH.
BAM
IF YOU HAVE BUSINESS WITH US, TALK TO ME.
FRET
NO ...
ZRRM
...I'M DONE HERE.
FWP
PLEASE DON'T TROUBLE YOURSELF...
TAP
...AS I WAS JUST LEAVING.

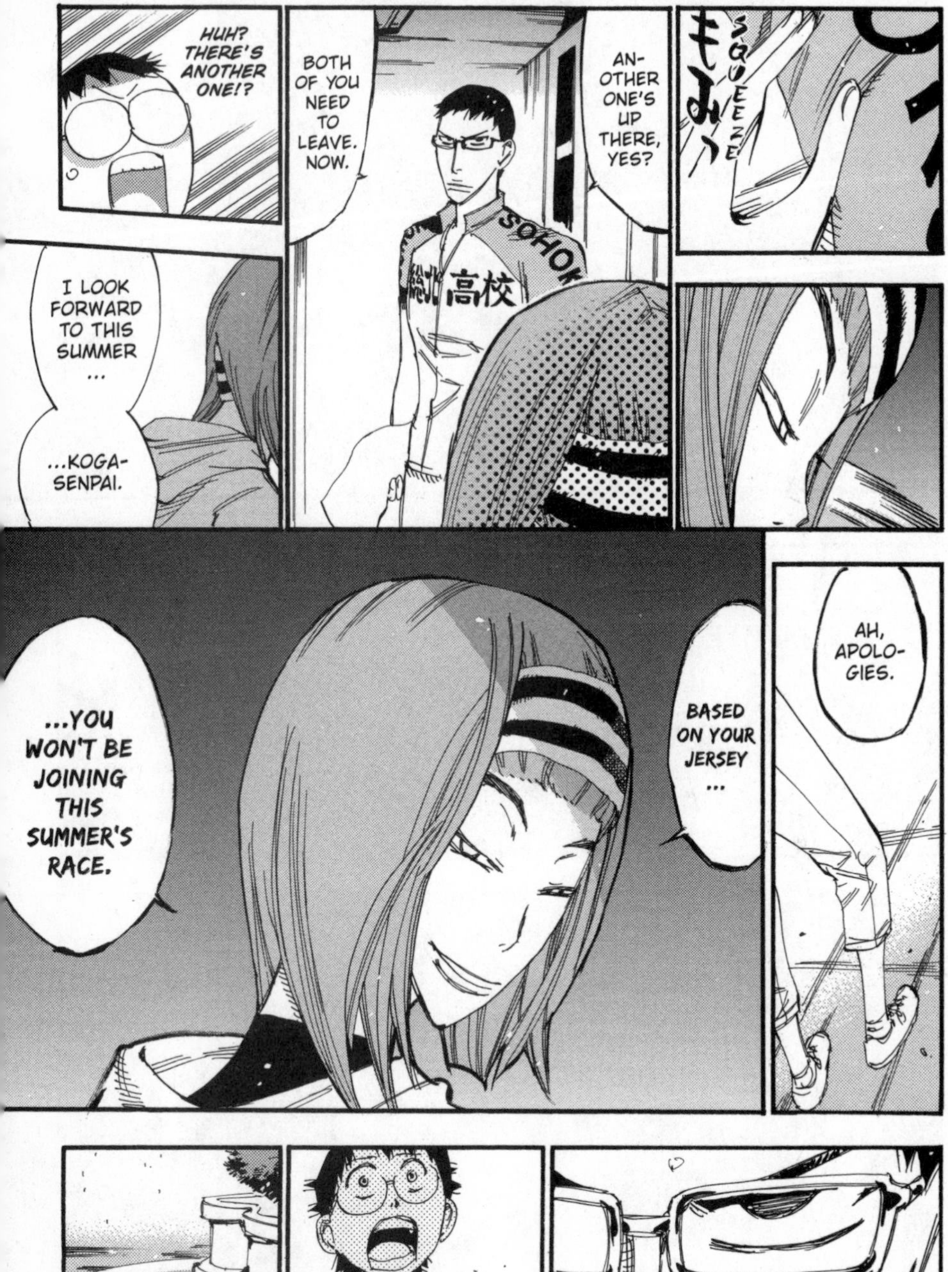
SQUEEZE
もみっ
AN-OTHER ONE'S UP THERE, YES?
BOTH OF YOU NEED TO LEAVE. NOW.
HUH? THERE'S ANOTHER ONE!?
SOHOKU
総北高校
I LOOK FORWARD TO THIS SUMMER ...
...KOGA-SENPAI.
AH, APOLOGIES.
BASED ON YOUR JERSEY ...
...YOU WON'T BE JOINING THIS SUMMER'S RACE.

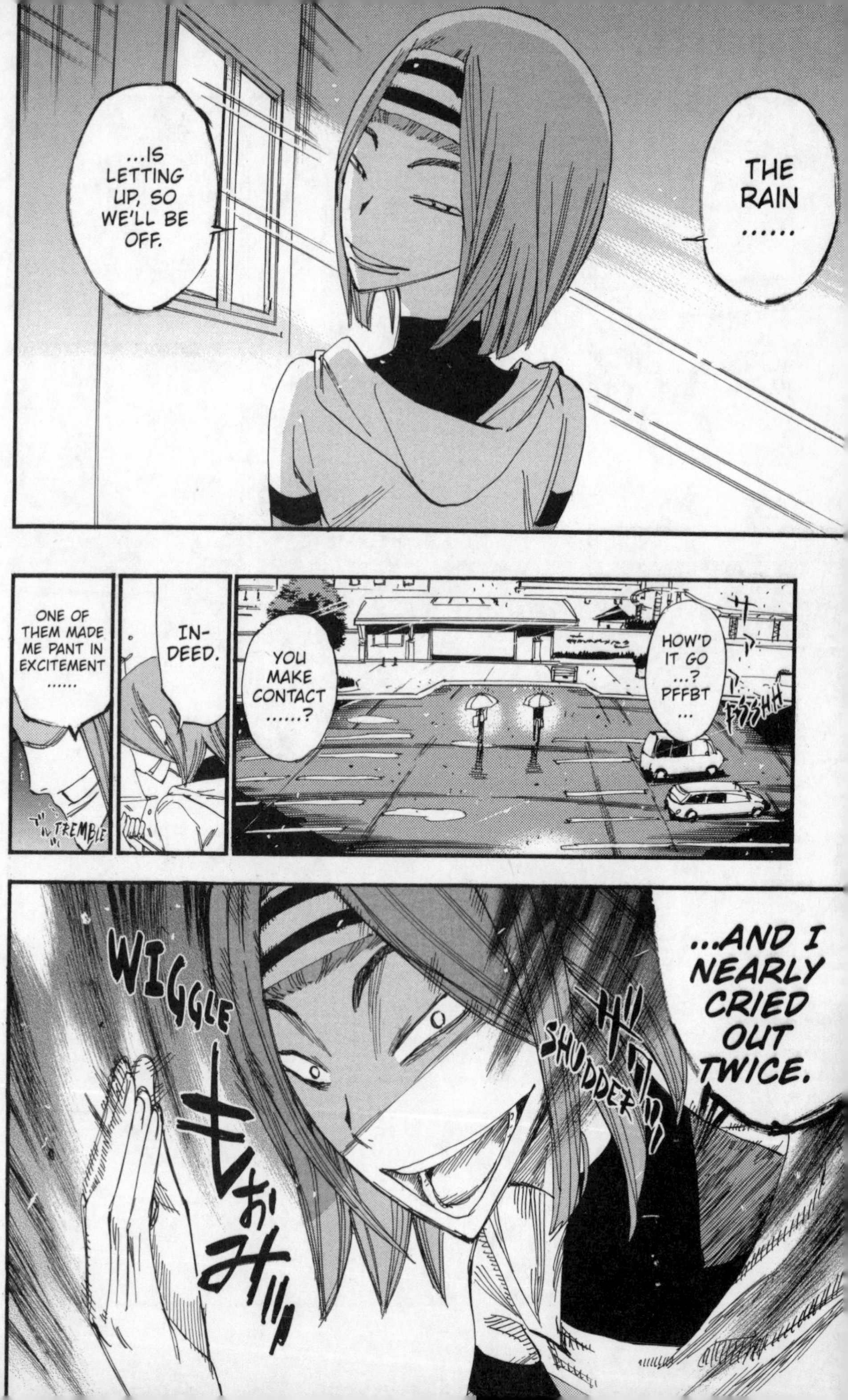
THE RAIN ......
...IS LETTING UP, SO WE'LL BE OFF.
HOW'D IT GO ...? PFFBT ...
FSSHH
YOU MAKE CONTACT ......?
IN-DEED.
ONE OF THEM MADE ME PANT IN EXCITEMENT ......
TREMBLE
...AND I NEARLY CRIED OUT TWICE.
SHUDDER!!
WIGGLE

RIDE.294 1,000KM!

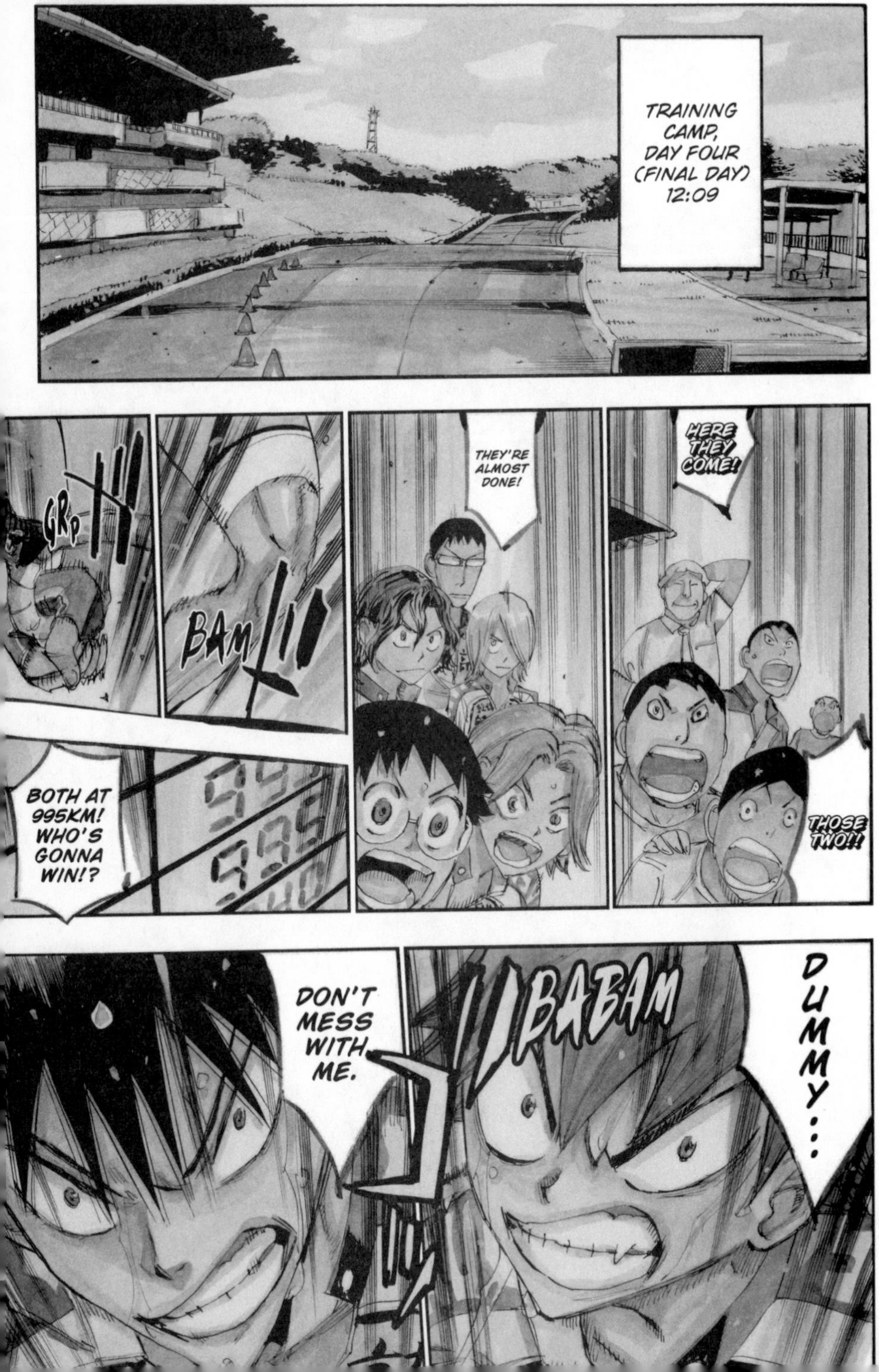
TRAINING CAMP, DAY FOUR (FINAL DAY) 12:09
HERE THEY COME!
THOSE TWO!!
THEY'RE ALMOST DONE!
BAM
GRP
BOTH AT 995KM! WHO'S GONNA WIN!?
DUMMY...
BABAM
DON'T MESS WITH ME.

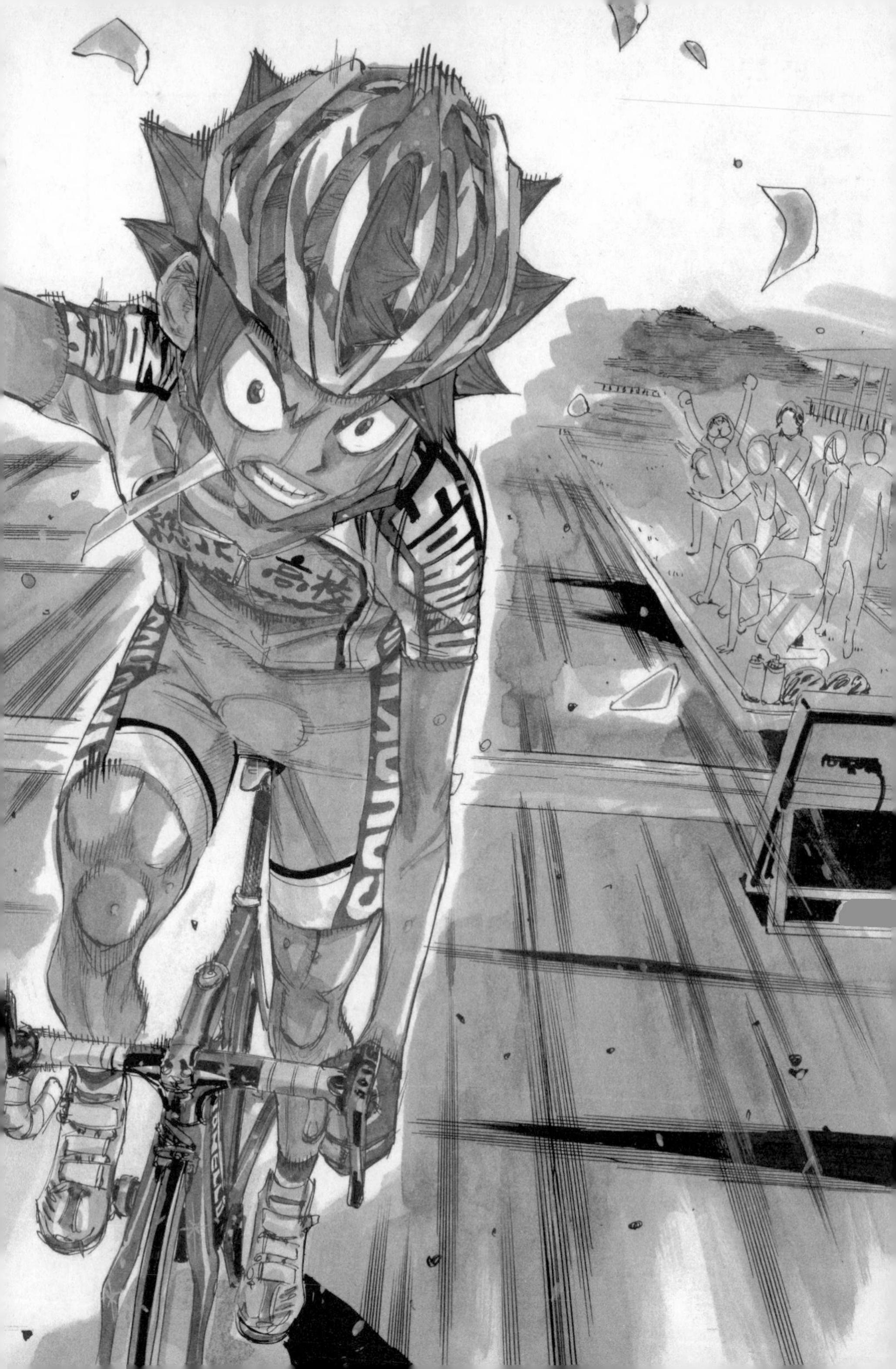

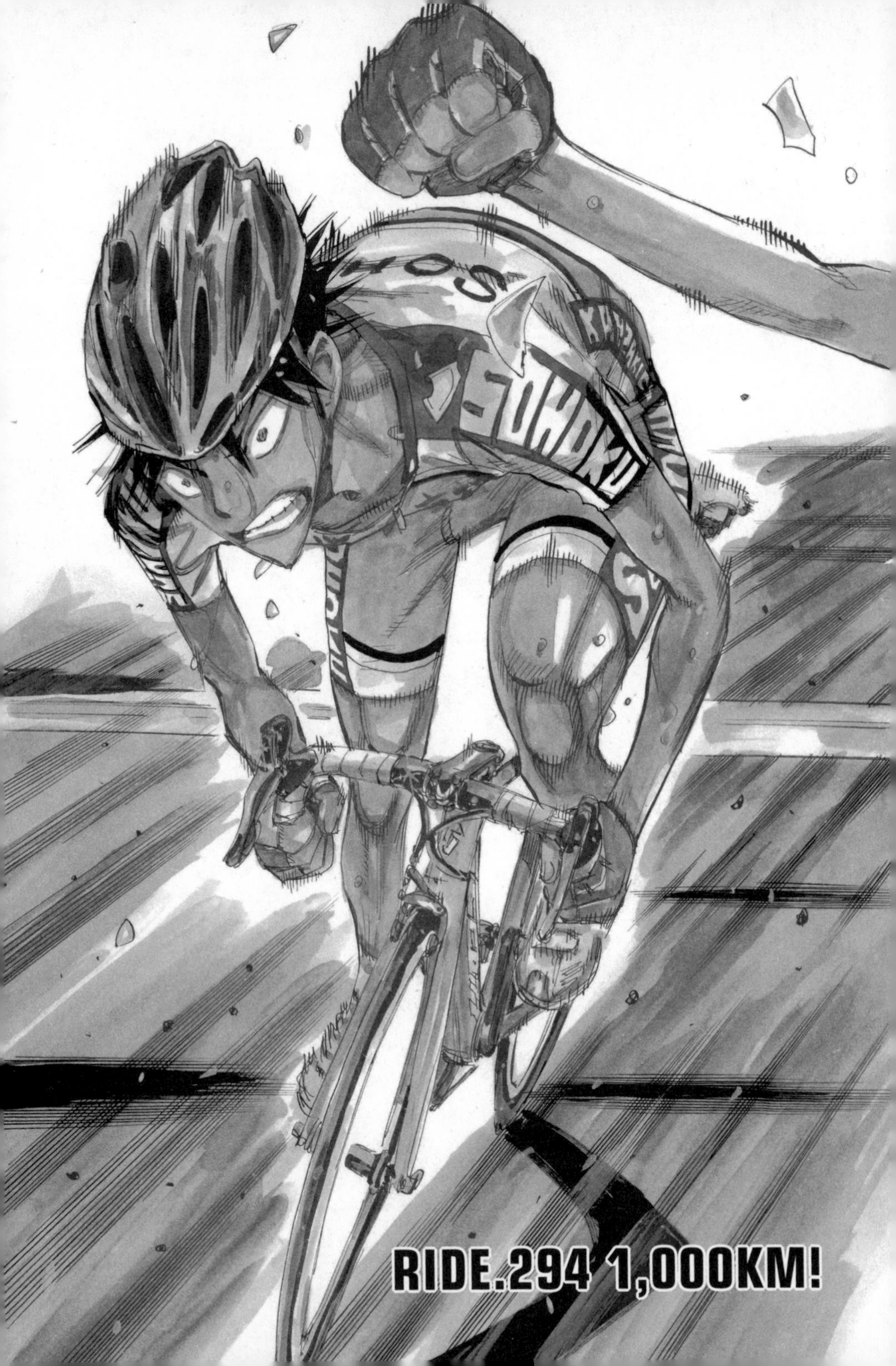
RIDE.294 1,000KM!

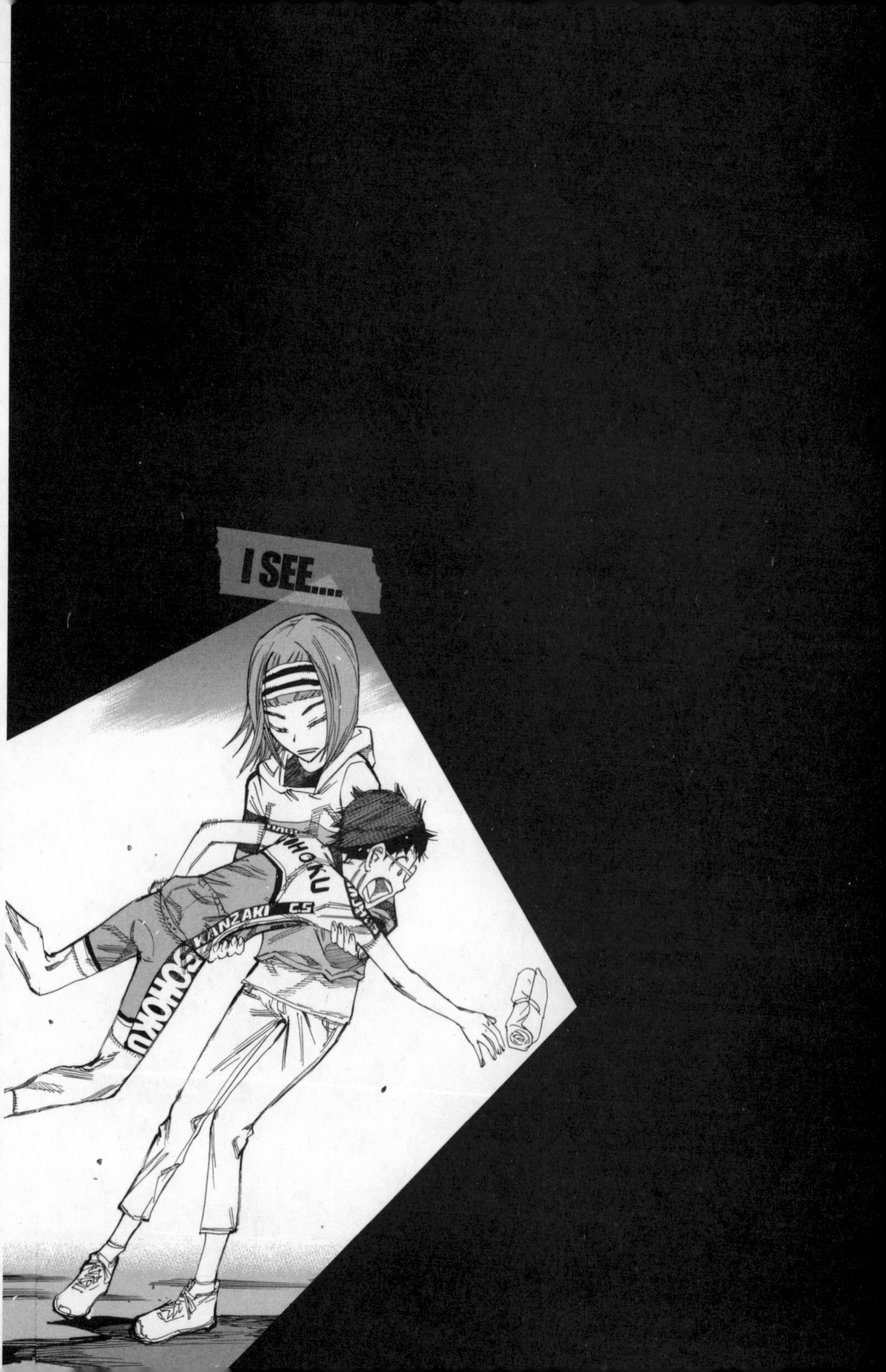
I SEE....
SOHOKU
KANZAKI
C.5

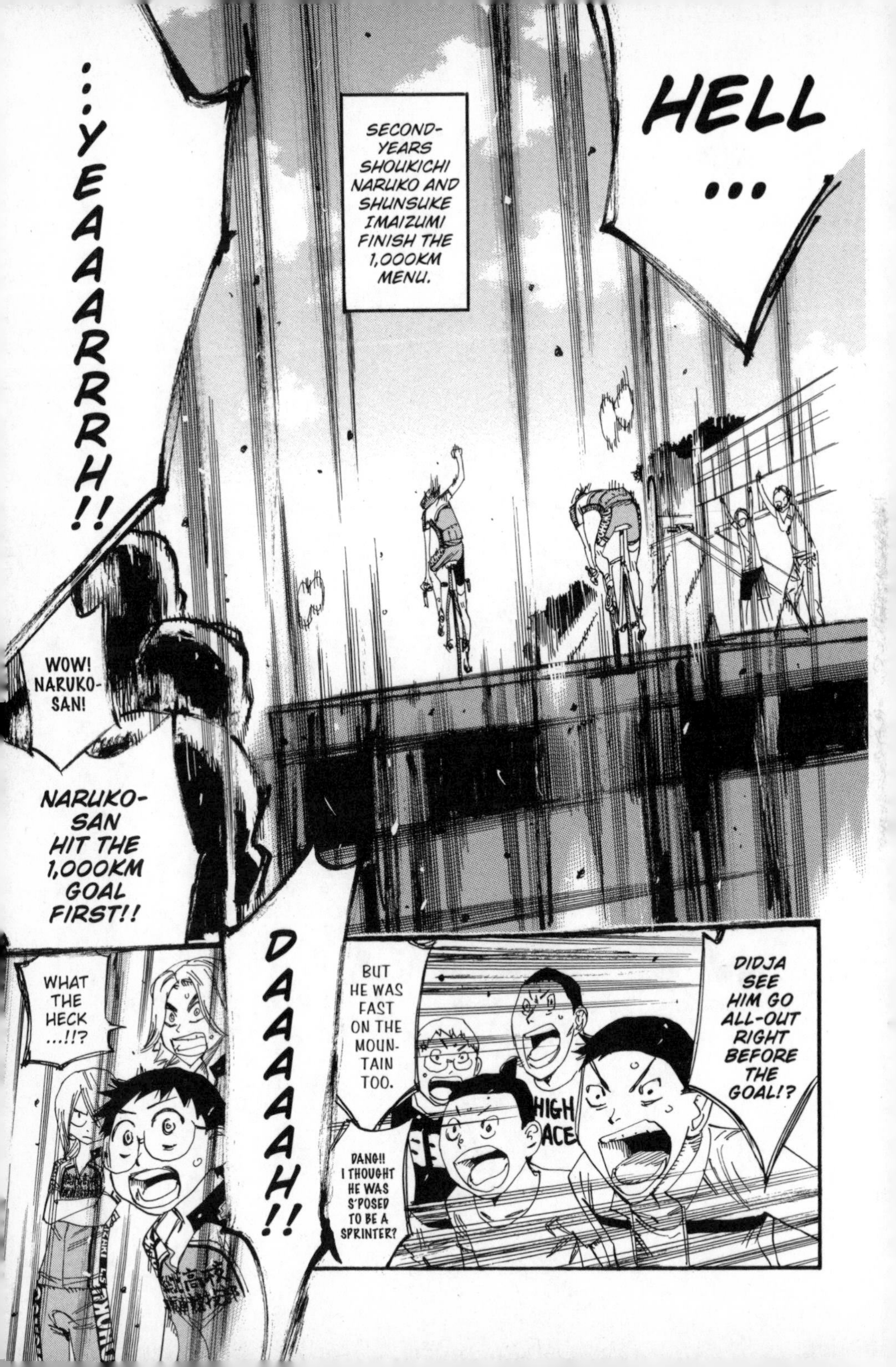
HELL...
SECOND-YEARS SHOUKICHI NARUKO AND SHUNSUKE IMAIZUMI FINISH THE 1,000KM MENU.
...YEAAAARRRRH!!
WOW! NARUKO-SAN!
NARUKO-SAN HIT THE 1,000KM GOAL FIRST!!
DIDJA SEE HIM GO ALL-OUT RIGHT BEFORE THE GOAL!?
BUT HE WAS FAST ON THE MOUNTAIN TOO.
DANG!! I THOUGHT HE WAS S'POSED TO BE A SPRINTER?
DAAAAAAAH!!
WHAT THE HECK ...!!?

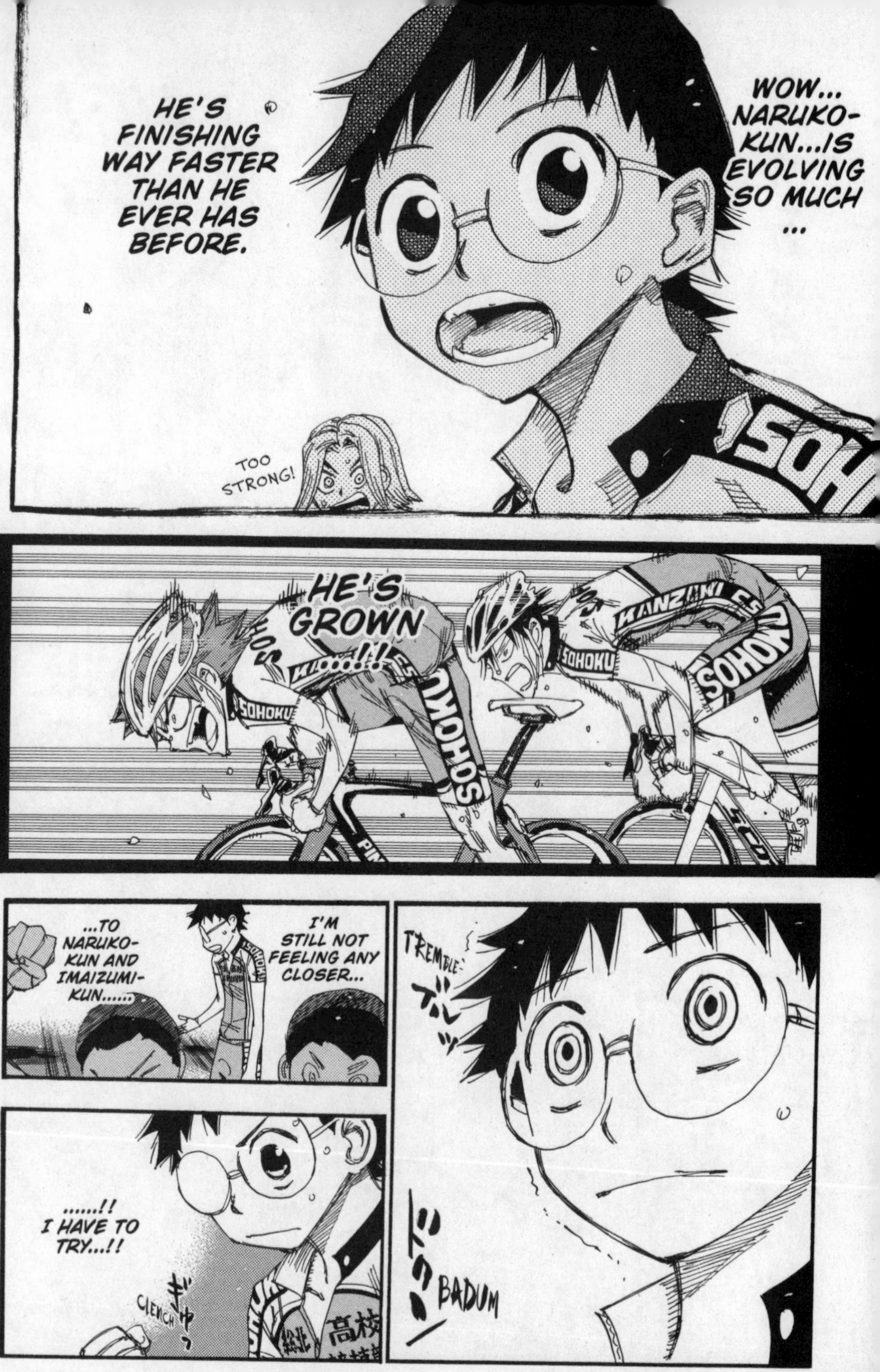
WOW... NARUKO-KUN...IS EVOLVING SO MUCH ...
HE'S FINISHING WAY FASTER THAN HE EVER HAS BEFORE.
TOO STRONG!
HE'S GROWN ......!!
TREMBLE
BADUM
I'M STILL NOT FEELING ANY CLOSER...
...TO NARUKO-KUN AND IMAIZUMI-KUN......
......!! I HAVE TO TRY...!!
CLENCH

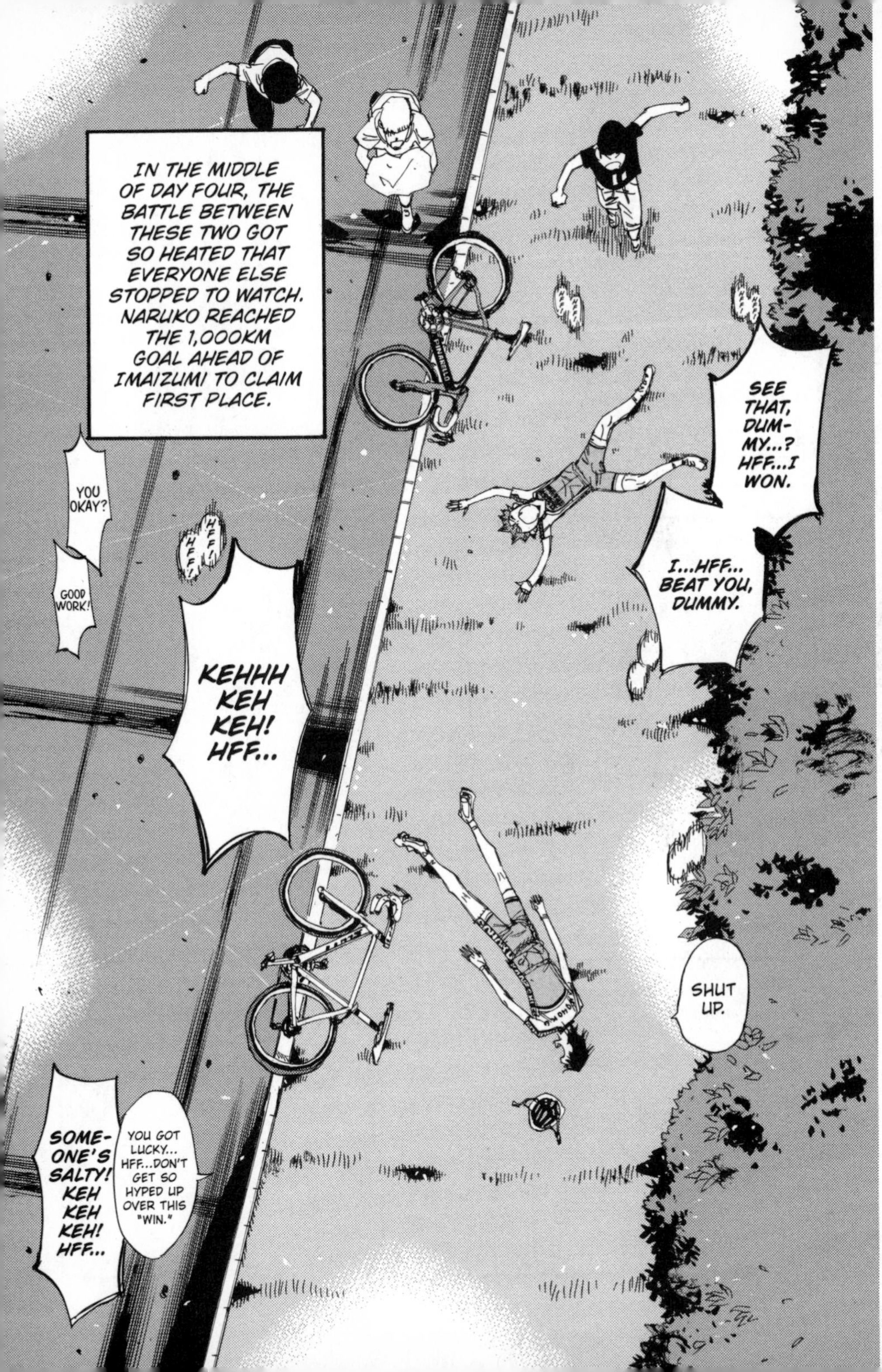
IN THE MIDDLE OF DAY FOUR, THE BATTLE BETWEEN THESE TWO GOT SO HEATED THAT EVERYONE ELSE STOPPED TO WATCH. NARUKO REACHED THE 1,000KM GOAL AHEAD OF IMAIZUMI TO CLAIM FIRST PLACE.
SEE THAT, DUM-MY...? HFF...I WON.
I...HFF... BEAT YOU, DUMMY.
YOU OKAY?
GOOD WORK!
HFF! HFF!
KEHHH KEH KEH! HFF...
SHUT UP.
YOU GOT LUCKY... HFF...DON'T GET SO HYPED UP OVER THIS "WIN."
SOME-ONE'S SALTY! KEH KEH KEH! HFF...

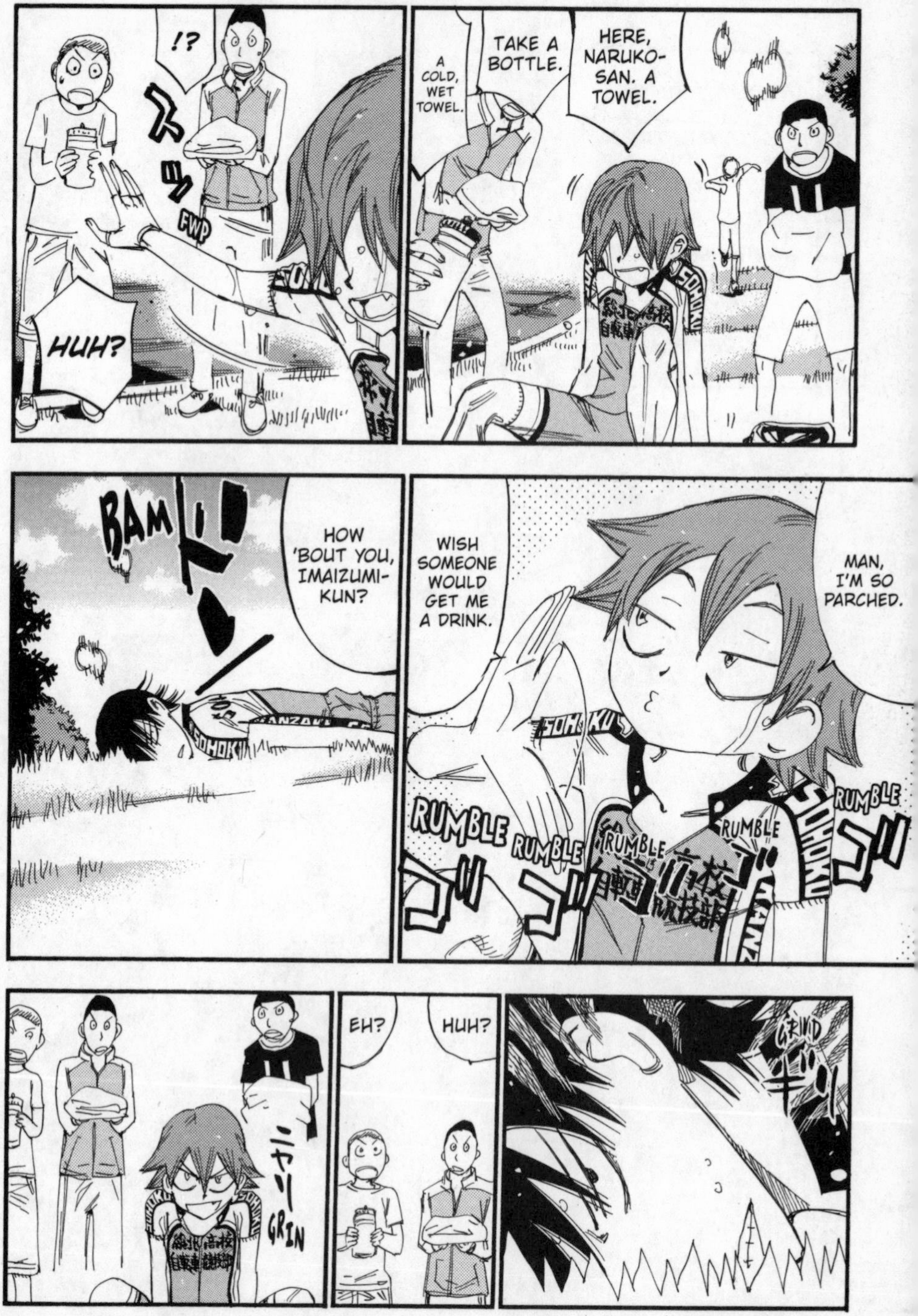
HERE, NARUKO-SAN. A TOWEL.
TAKE A BOTTLE.
A COLD, WET TOWEL.
!?
FWP
HUH?
MAN, I'M SO PARCHED.
RUMBLE
RUMBLE
RUMBLE
RUMBLE
RUMBLE
WISH SOMEONE WOULD GET ME A DRINK.
HOW 'BOUT YOU, IMAIZUMI-KUN?
BAM
GRIND
HUH?
EH?
GRIN

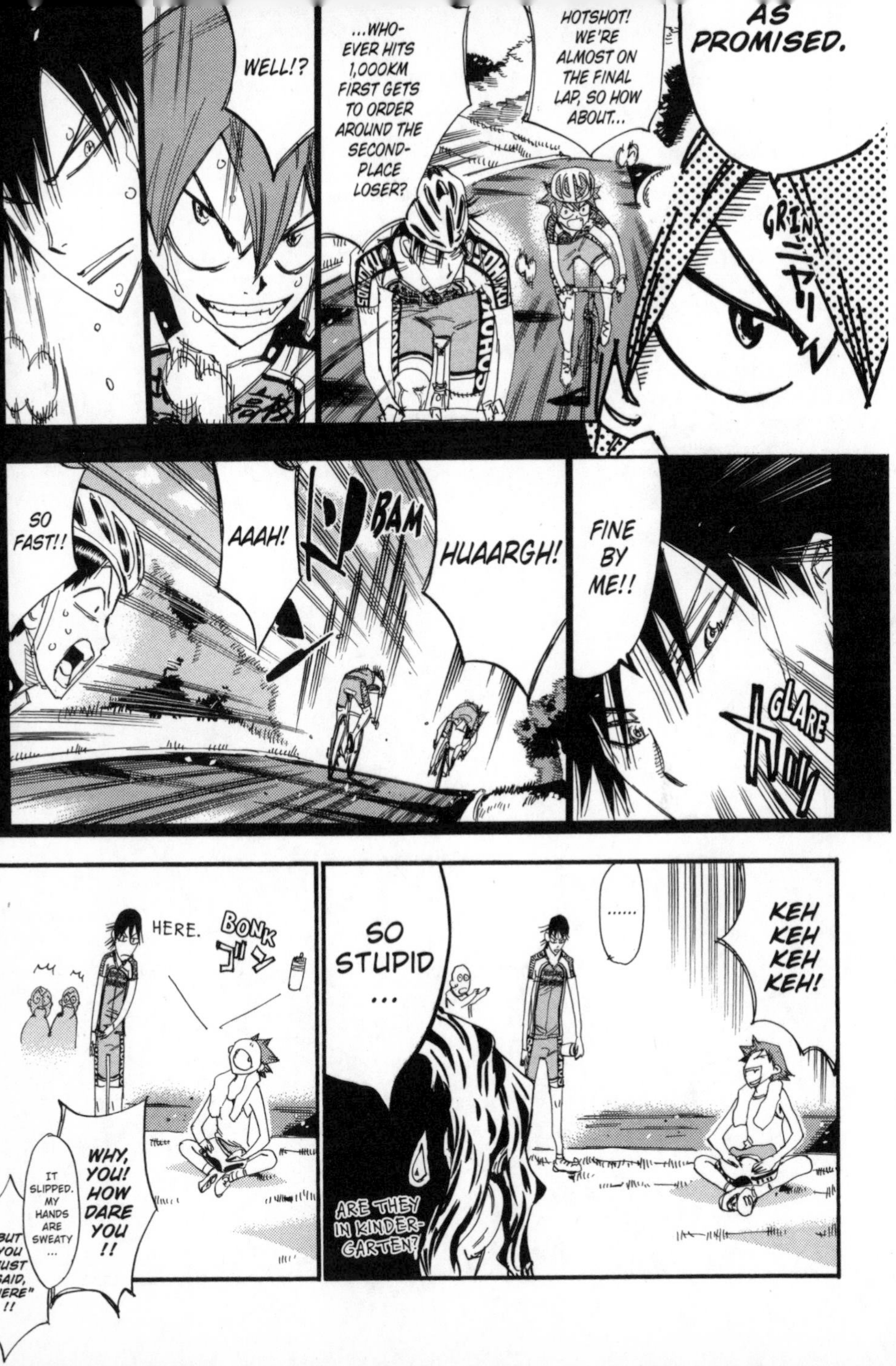
AS PROMISED.
GRIN
HOTSHOT! WE'RE ALMOST ON THE FINAL LAP, SO HOW ABOUT...
...WHO-EVER HITS 1,000KM FIRST GETS TO ORDER AROUND THE SECOND-PLACE LOSER?
WELL!?
FINE BY ME!!
GLARE
HUAARGH!
BAM
AAAH!
SO FAST!!
KEH KEH KEH KEH!
......
SO STUPID...
ARE THEY IN KINDER-GARTEN?
HERE.
BONK
WHY, YOU! HOW DARE YOU!!
IT SLIPPED. MY HANDS ARE SWEATY...
BUT YOU JUST SAID, "HERE"!!

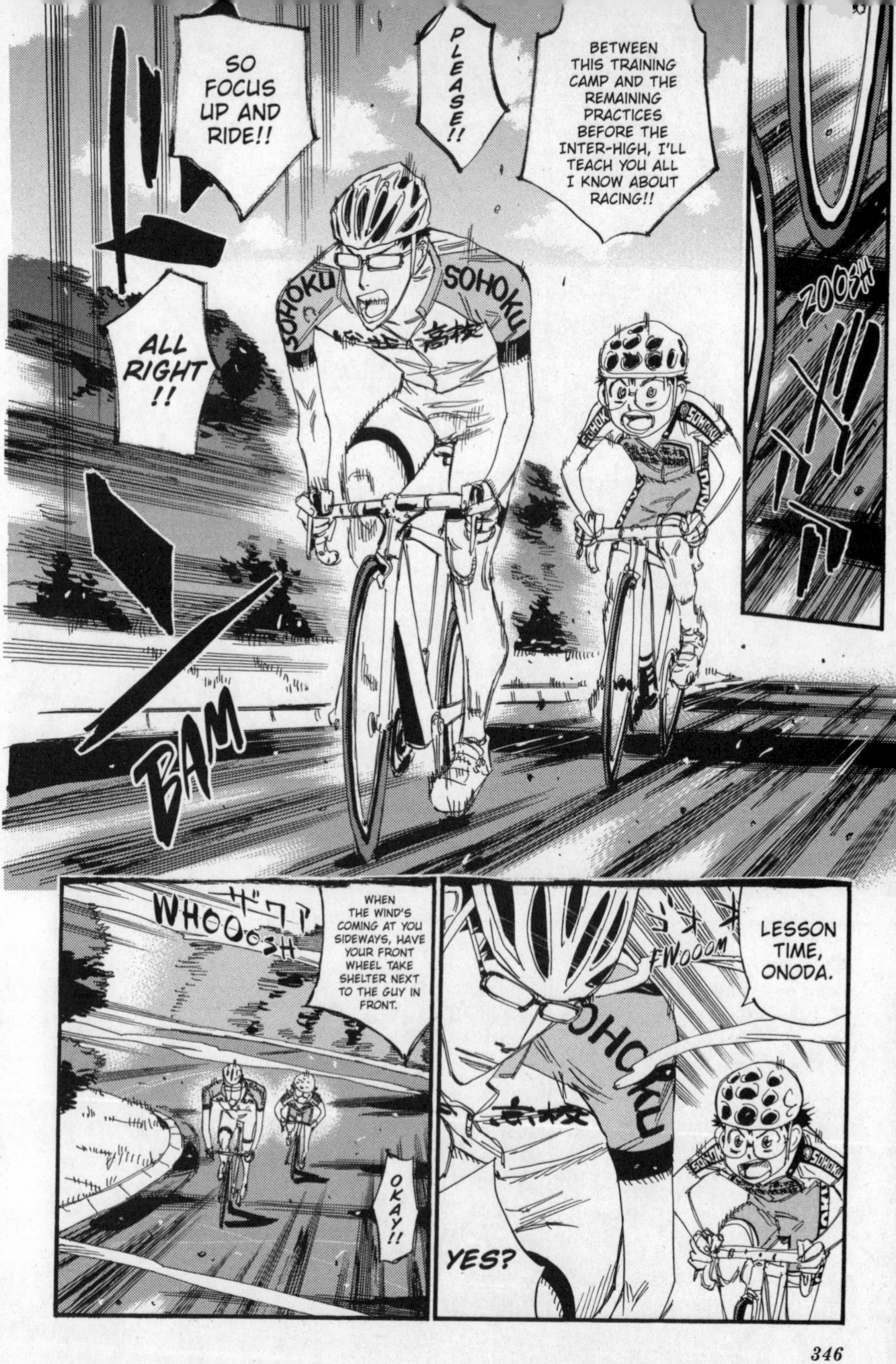
ZOOSH
BETWEEN THIS TRAINING CAMP AND THE REMAINING PRACTICES BEFORE THE INTER-HIGH, I'LL TEACH YOU ALL I KNOW ABOUT RACING!!
PLEASE!!
SO FOCUS UP AND RIDE!!
ALL RIGHT!!
BAM
LESSON TIME, ONODA.
FWOOOM
YES?
WHEN THE WIND'S COMING AT YOU SIDEWAYS, HAVE YOUR FRONT WHEEL TAKE SHELTER NEXT TO THE GUY IN FRONT.
WHOOOOSH
OKAY!!

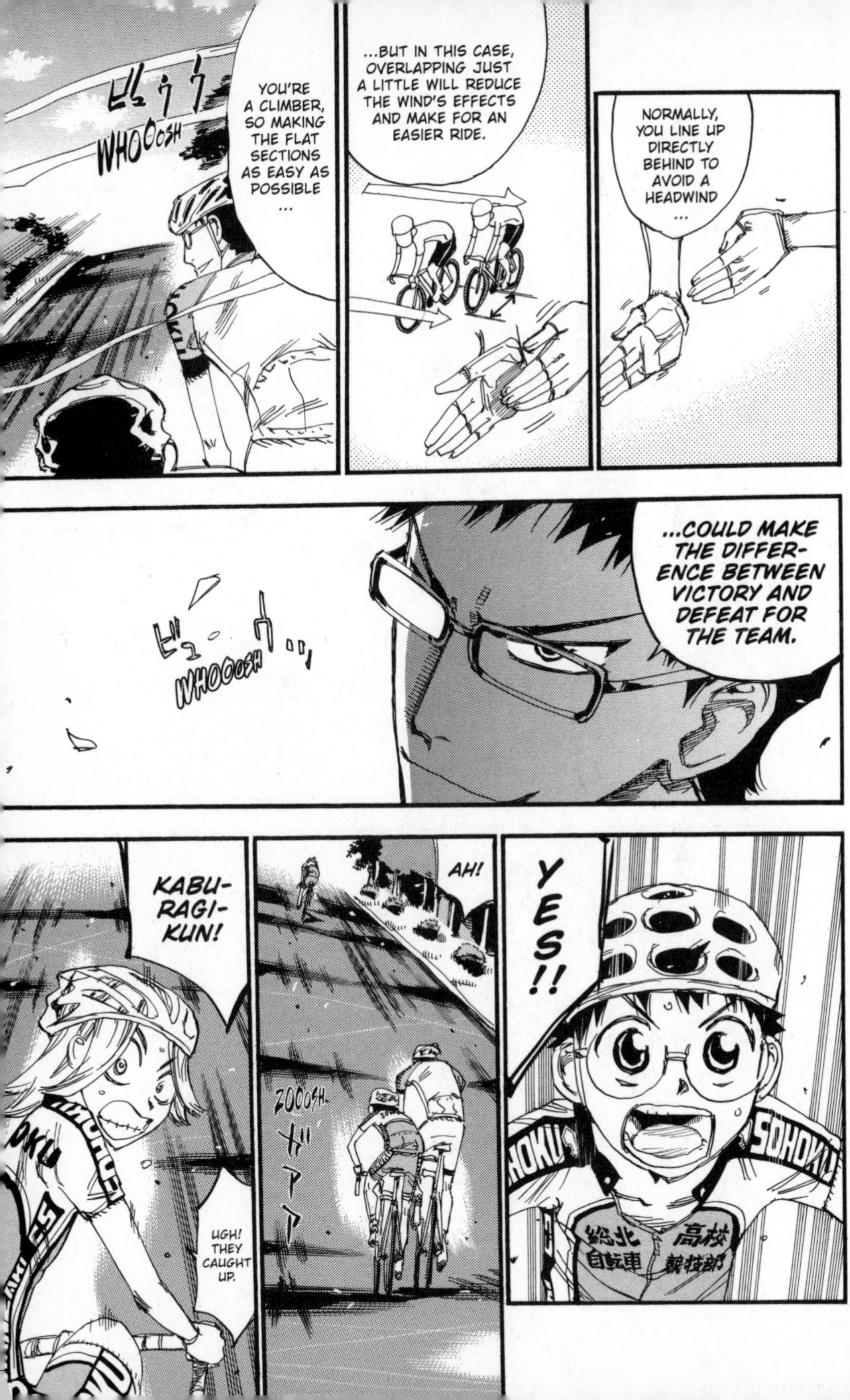
NORMALLY, YOU LINE UP DIRECTLY BEHIND TO AVOID A HEADWIND...
...BUT IN THIS CASE, OVERLAPPING JUST A LITTLE WILL REDUCE THE WIND'S EFFECTS AND MAKE FOR AN EASIER RIDE.
YOU'RE A CLIMBER, SO MAKING THE FLAT SECTIONS AS EASY AS POSSIBLE...
WHOOOSH
...COULD MAKE THE DIFFERENCE BETWEEN VICTORY AND DEFEAT FOR THE TEAM.
WHOOOSH
YES!!
SOHOKU
AH!
ZOOOSH
KABURAGI-KUN!
UGH! THEY CAUGHT UP.

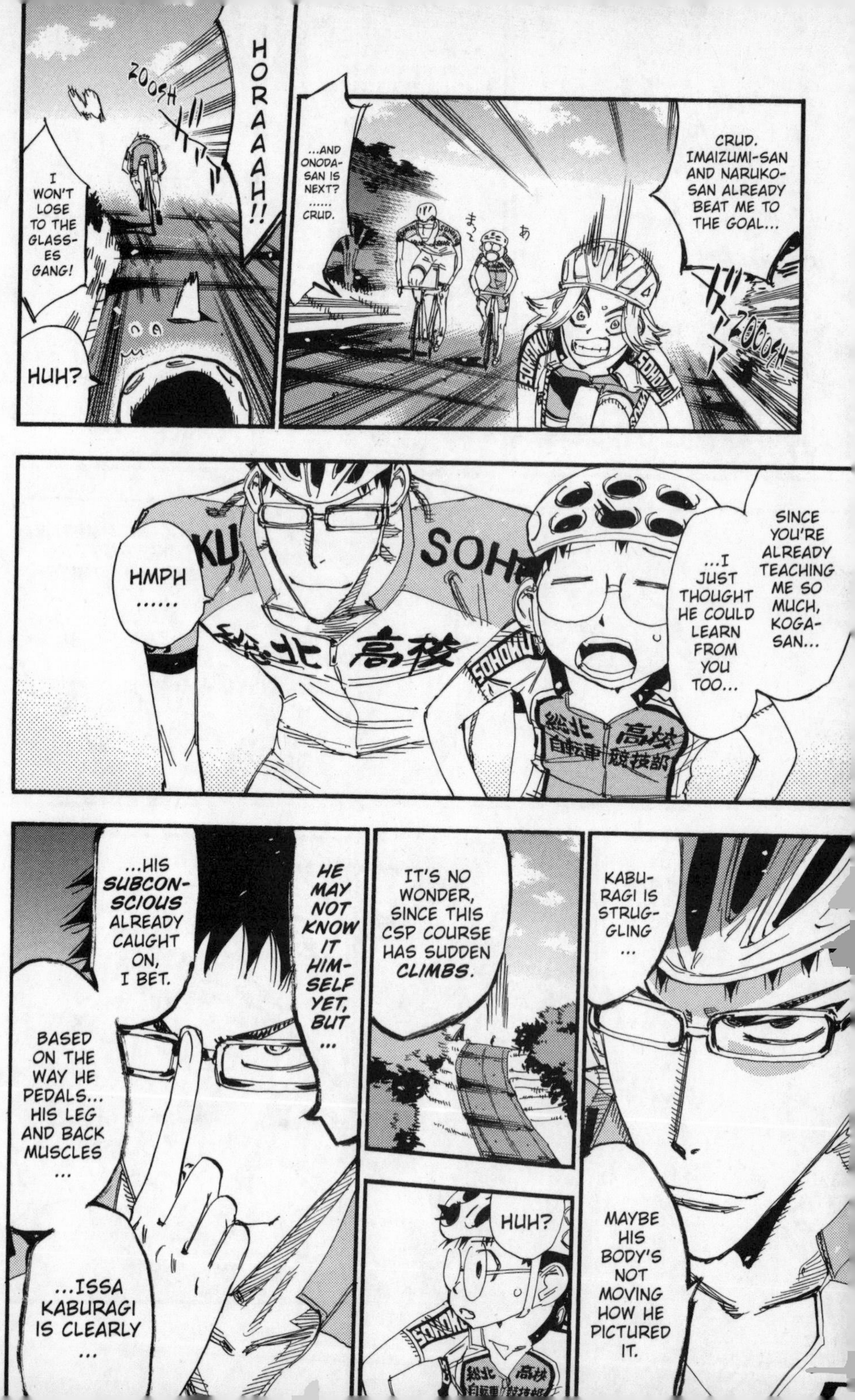
CRUD. IMAIZUMI-SAN AND NARUKO-SAN ALREADY BEAT ME TO THE GOAL...
ZOOOSH
あ
まって
...AND ONODA-SAN IS NEXT? ...... CRUD.
HORAAAAH!!
ZOOSH
I WON'T LOSE TO THE GLASSES GANG!
HUH?
SINCE YOU'RE ALREADY TEACHING ME SO MUCH, KOGA-SAN...
...I JUST THOUGHT HE COULD LEARN FROM YOU TOO...
HMPH ......
KABURAGI IS STRUGGLING ...
MAYBE HIS BODY'S NOT MOVING HOW HE PICTURED IT.
IT'S NO WONDER, SINCE THIS CSP COURSE HAS SUDDEN CLIMBS.
HUH?
HE MAY NOT KNOW IT HIMSELF YET, BUT ...
...HIS SUBCONSCIOUS ALREADY CAUGHT ON, I BET.
BASED ON THE WAY HE PEDALS... HIS LEG AND BACK MUSCLES ...
...ISSA KABURAGI IS CLEARLY ...

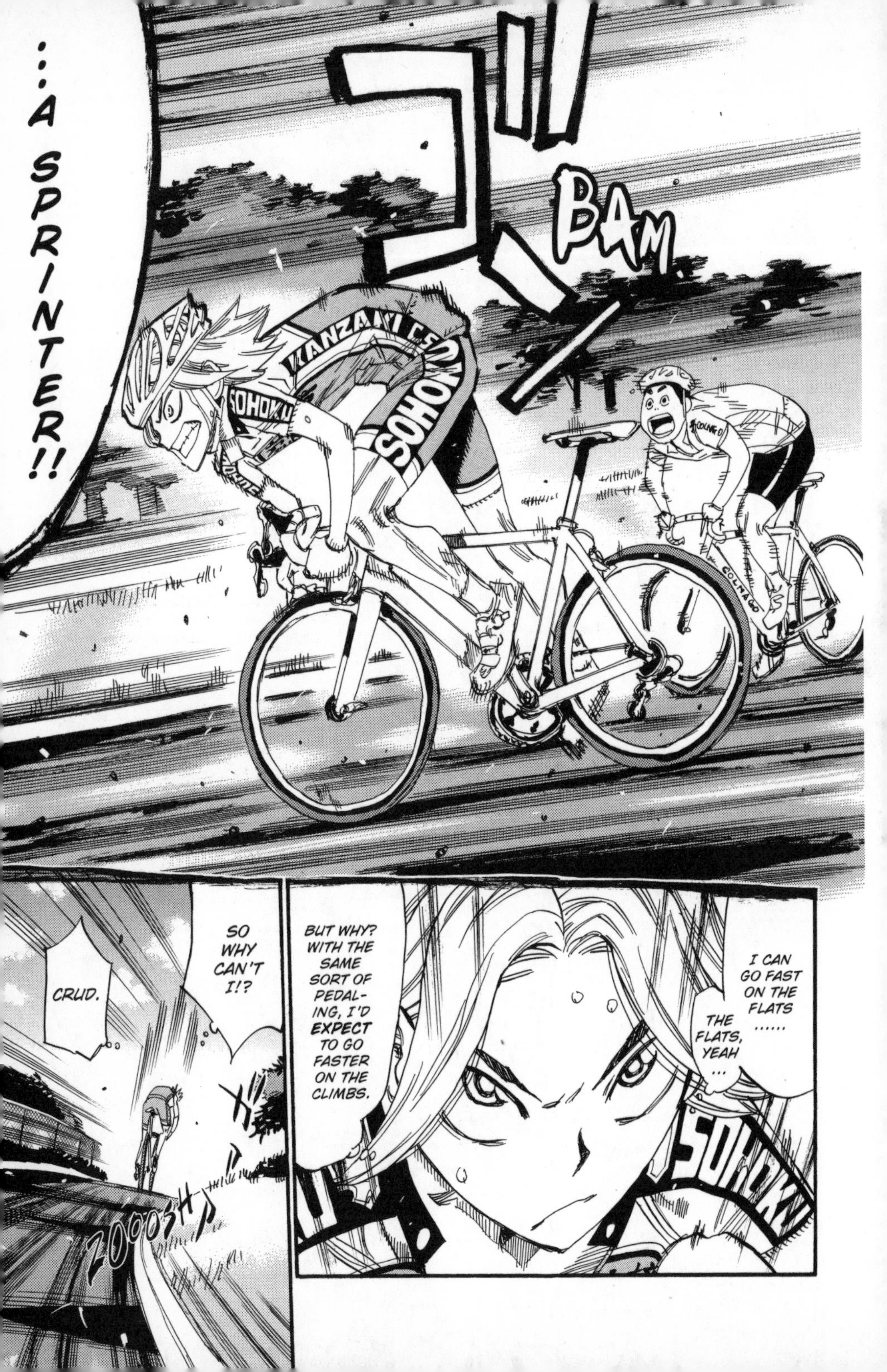
BAM
...A SPRINTER!!
I CAN GO FAST ON THE FLATS ......
THE FLATS, YEAH ...
BUT WHY? WITH THE SAME SORT OF PEDAL-ING, I'D EXPECT TO GO FASTER ON THE CLIMBS.
SO WHY CAN'T I!?
CRUD.
ZOOOSH

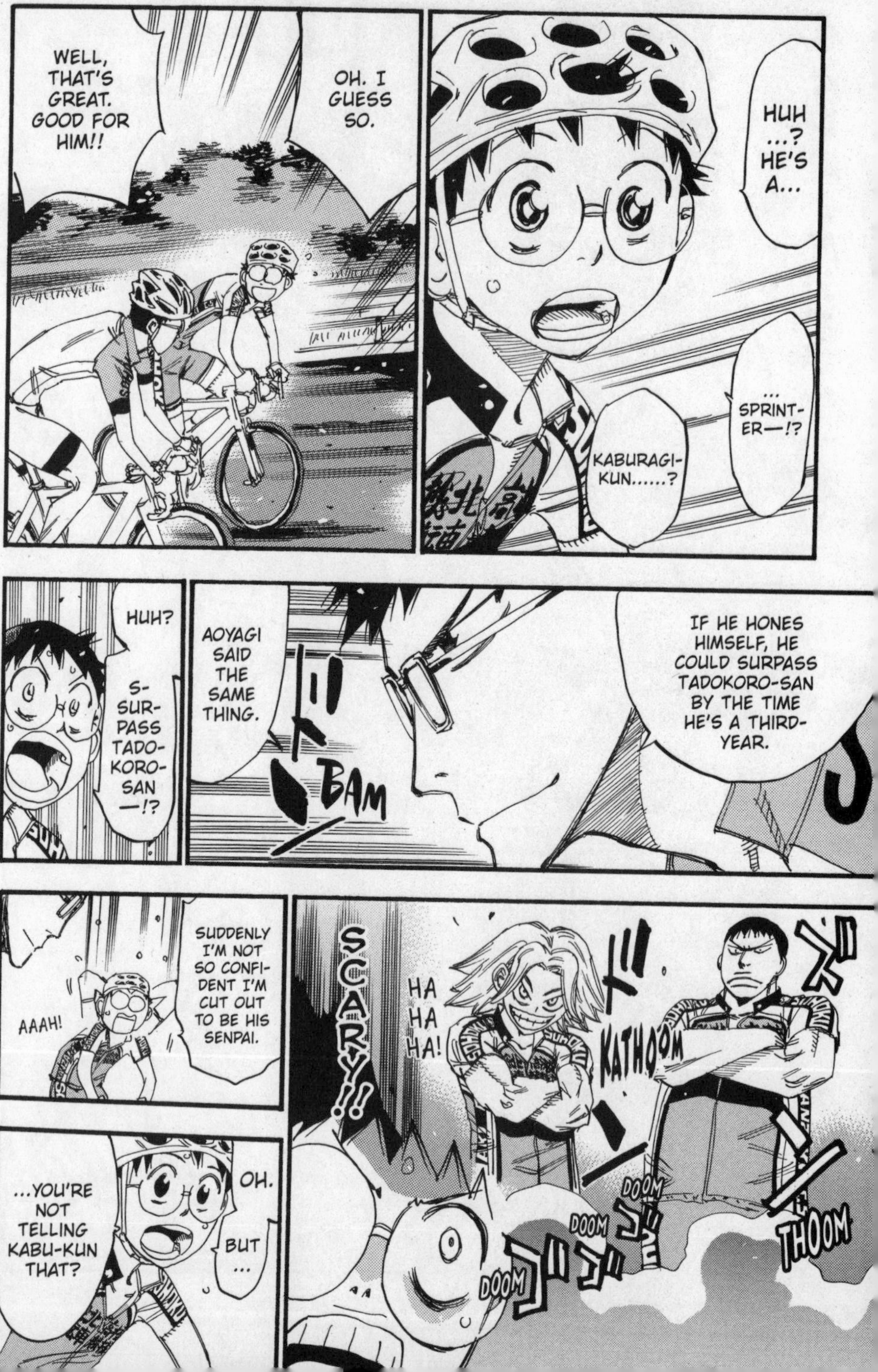
HUH ...? HE'S A...
... SPRINTER—!?
KABURAGI-KUN......?
OH. I GUESS SO.
WELL, THAT'S GREAT. GOOD FOR HIM!!
IF HE HONES HIMSELF, HE COULD SURPASS TADOKORO-SAN BY THE TIME HE'S A THIRD-YEAR.
AOYAGI SAID THE SAME THING.
BAM
HUH?
S-SURPASS TADOKORO-SAN—!?
SCARY!!
HA HA HA!
KATHOOM
THOOM
DOOM
DOOM
DOOM
SUDDENLY I'M NOT SO CONFIDENT I'M CUT OUT TO BE HIS SENPAI.
AAAH!
OH.
BUT ...
...YOU'RE NOT TELLING KABU-KUN THAT?

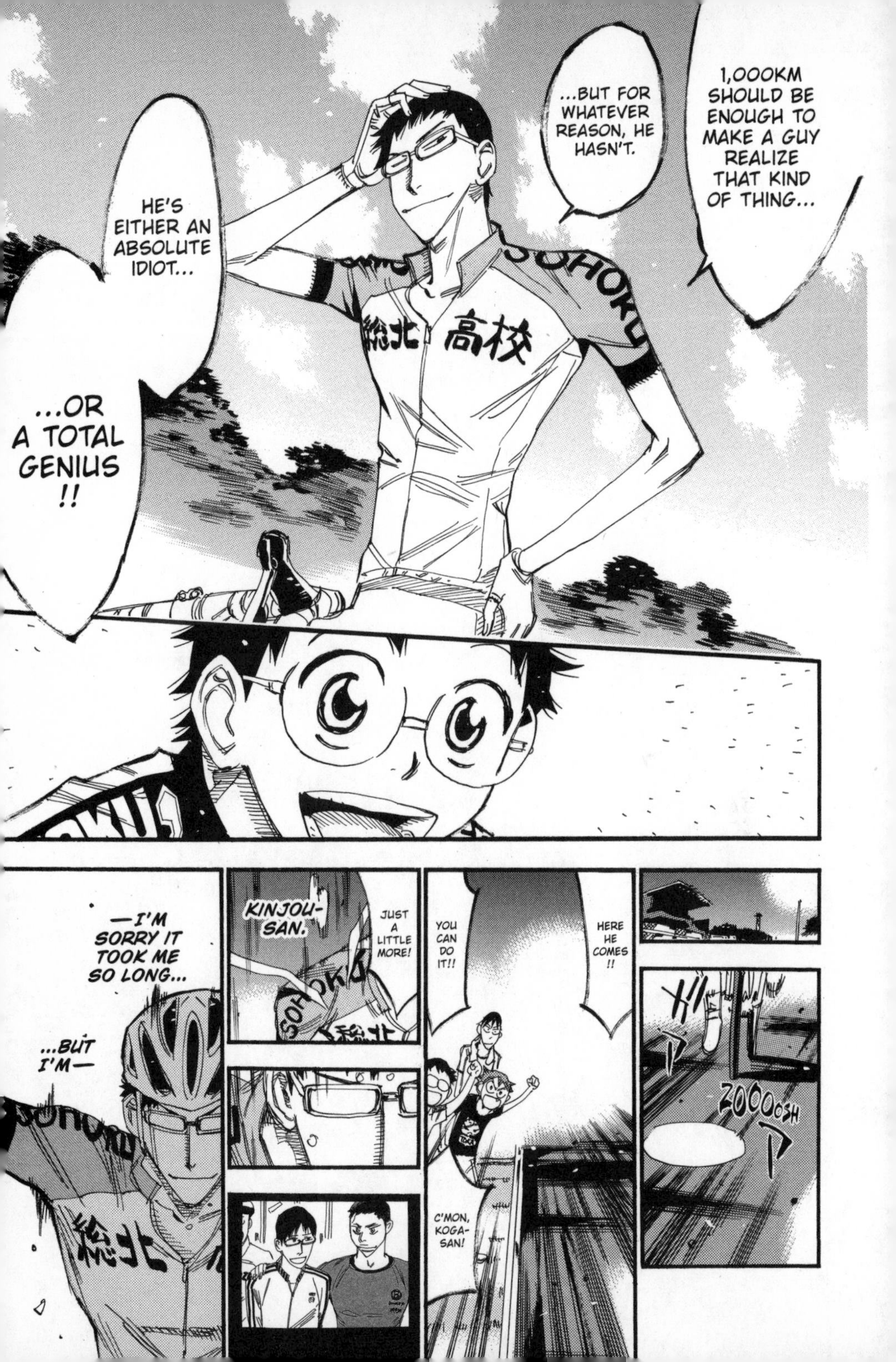
1,000KM SHOULD BE ENOUGH TO MAKE A GUY REALIZE THAT KIND OF THING...
...BUT FOR WHATEVER REASON, HE HASN'T.
HE'S EITHER AN ABSOLUTE IDIOT...
...OR A TOTAL GENIUS !!
ZOOOOSH
HERE HE COMES !!
YOU CAN DO IT!!
C'MON, KOGA-SAN!
JUST A LITTLE MORE!
KINJOU-SAN.
—I'M SORRY IT TOOK ME SO LONG...
...BUT I'M—

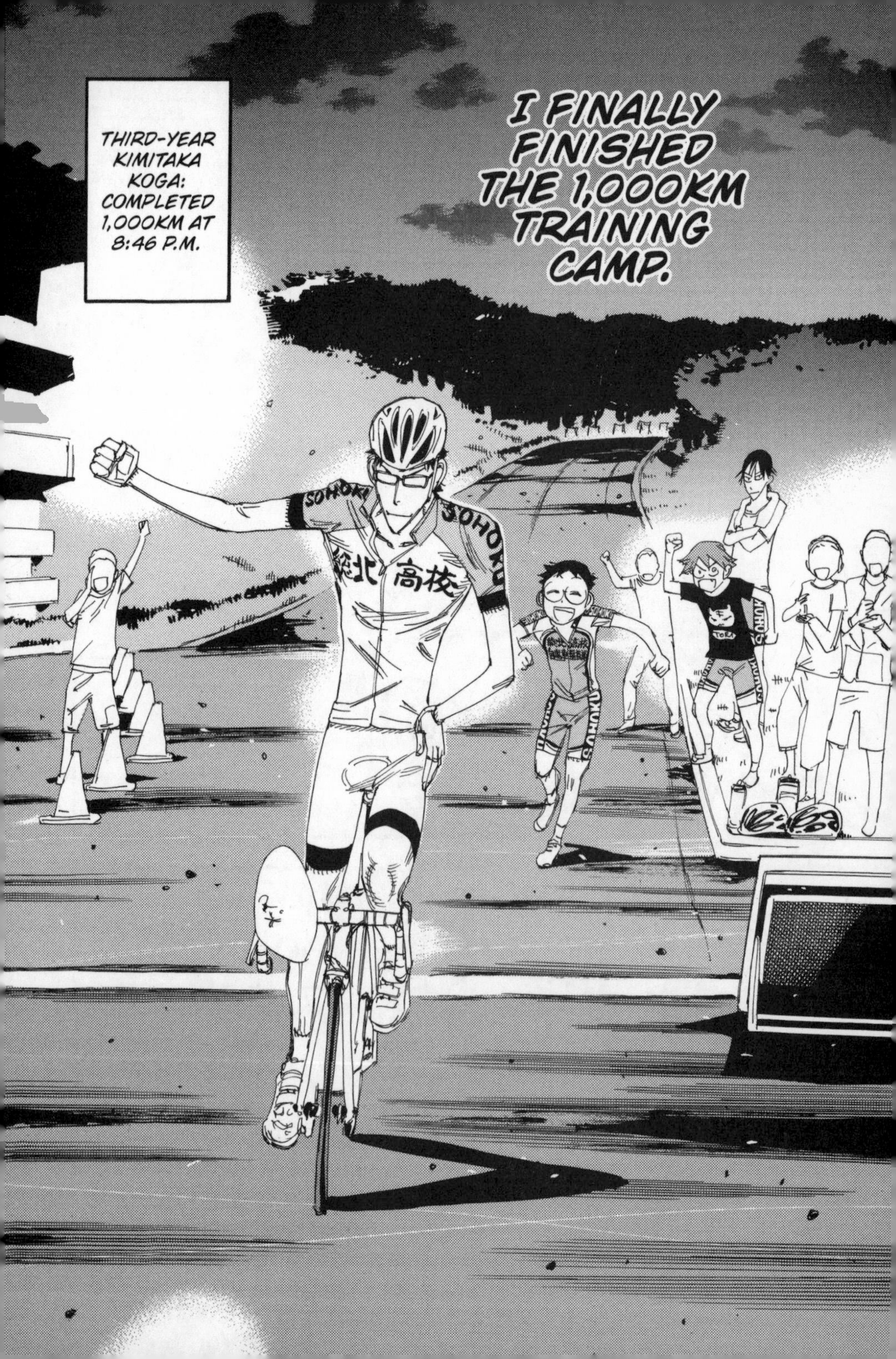
I FINALLY FINISHED THE 1,000KM TRAINING CAMP.
THIRD-YEAR KIMITAKA KOGA: COMPLETED 1,000KM AT 8:46 P.M.
SOHOKU
総北高校
TORA

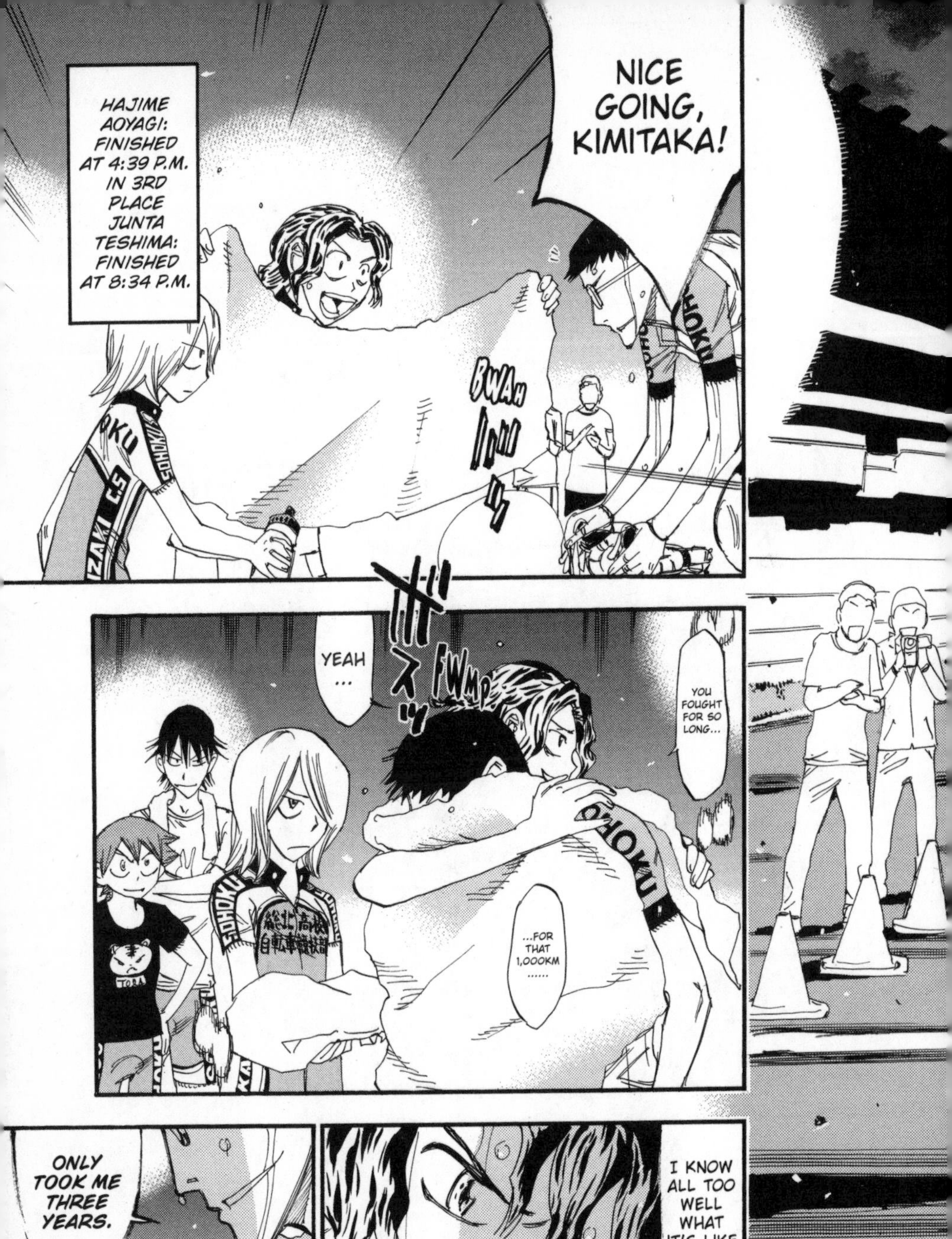
NICE GOING, KIMITAKA!
HAJIME AOYAGI: FINISHED AT 4:39 P.M. IN 3RD PLACE
JUNTA TESHIMA: FINISHED AT 8:34 P.M.
BWAH
FWMP
YOU FOUGHT FOR SO LONG...
...FOR THAT 1,000KM ......
YEAH ...
I KNOW ALL TOO WELL WHAT IT'S LIKE ....
ONLY TOOK ME THREE YEARS.

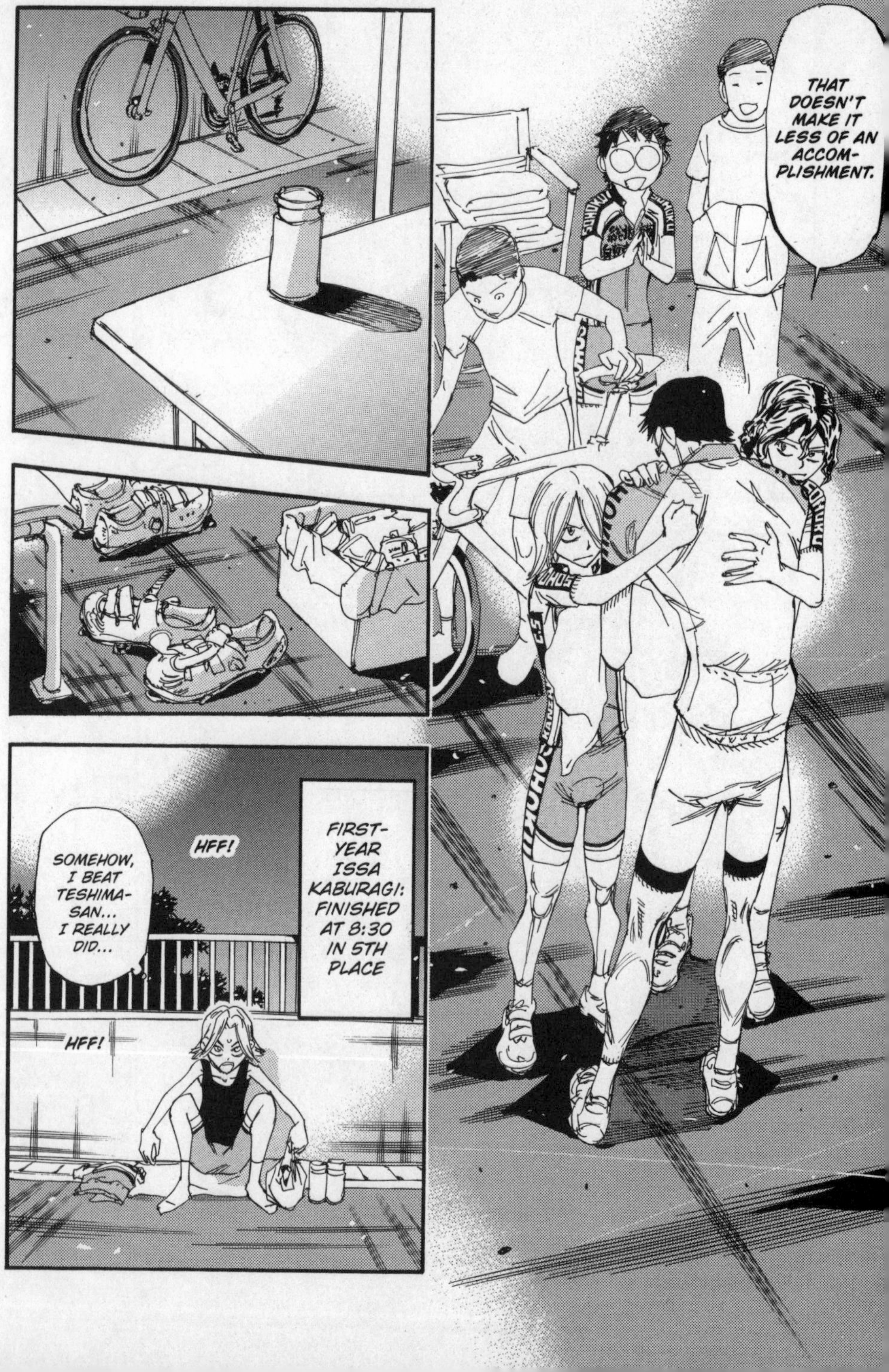
THAT DOESN'T MAKE IT LESS OF AN ACCOM-PLISHMENT.
FIRST-YEAR ISSA KABURAGI: FINISHED AT 8:30 IN 5TH PLACE
HFF!
SOMEHOW, I BEAT TESHIMA-SAN... I REALLY DID...
HFF!

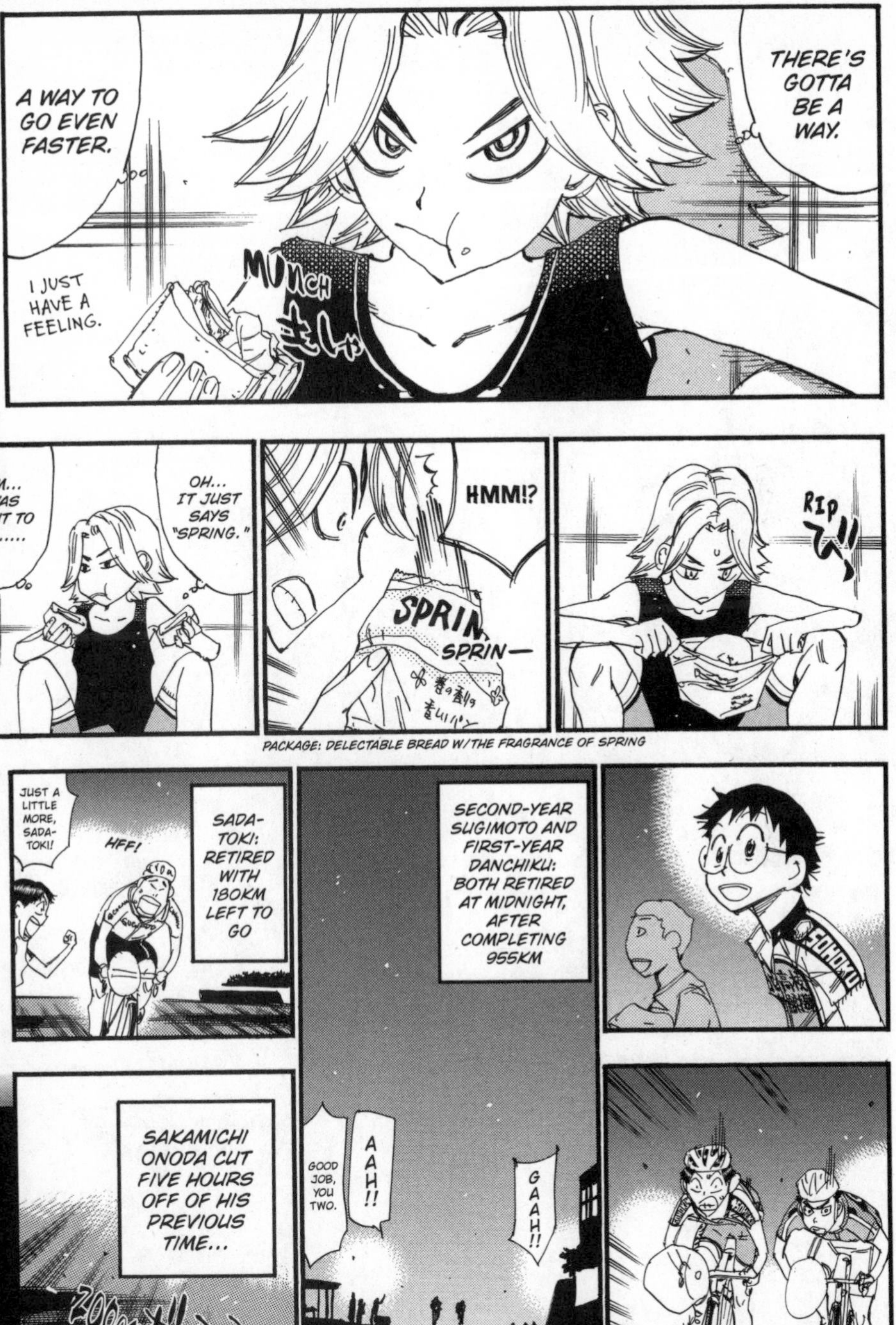
THERE'S GOTTA BE A WAY.
A WAY TO GO EVEN FASTER.
MUNCH
I JUST HAVE A FEELING.
RIP
HMM!?
SPRIN
SPRIN—
OH... IT JUST SAYS "SPRING."
HMM... I WAS ABOUT TO SAY......
PACKAGE: DELECTABLE BREAD W/THE FRAGRANCE OF SPRING
SECOND-YEAR SUGIMOTO AND FIRST-YEAR DANCHIKU: BOTH RETIRED AT MIDNIGHT, AFTER COMPLETING 955KM
GAAH!!
AAH!!
GOOD JOB, YOU TWO.
SADATOKI: RETIRED WITH 180KM LEFT TO GO
HFF!
JUST A LITTLE MORE, SADATOKI!
SAKAMICHI ONODA CUT FIVE HOURS OFF OF HIS PREVIOUS TIME...
ZOOOSH

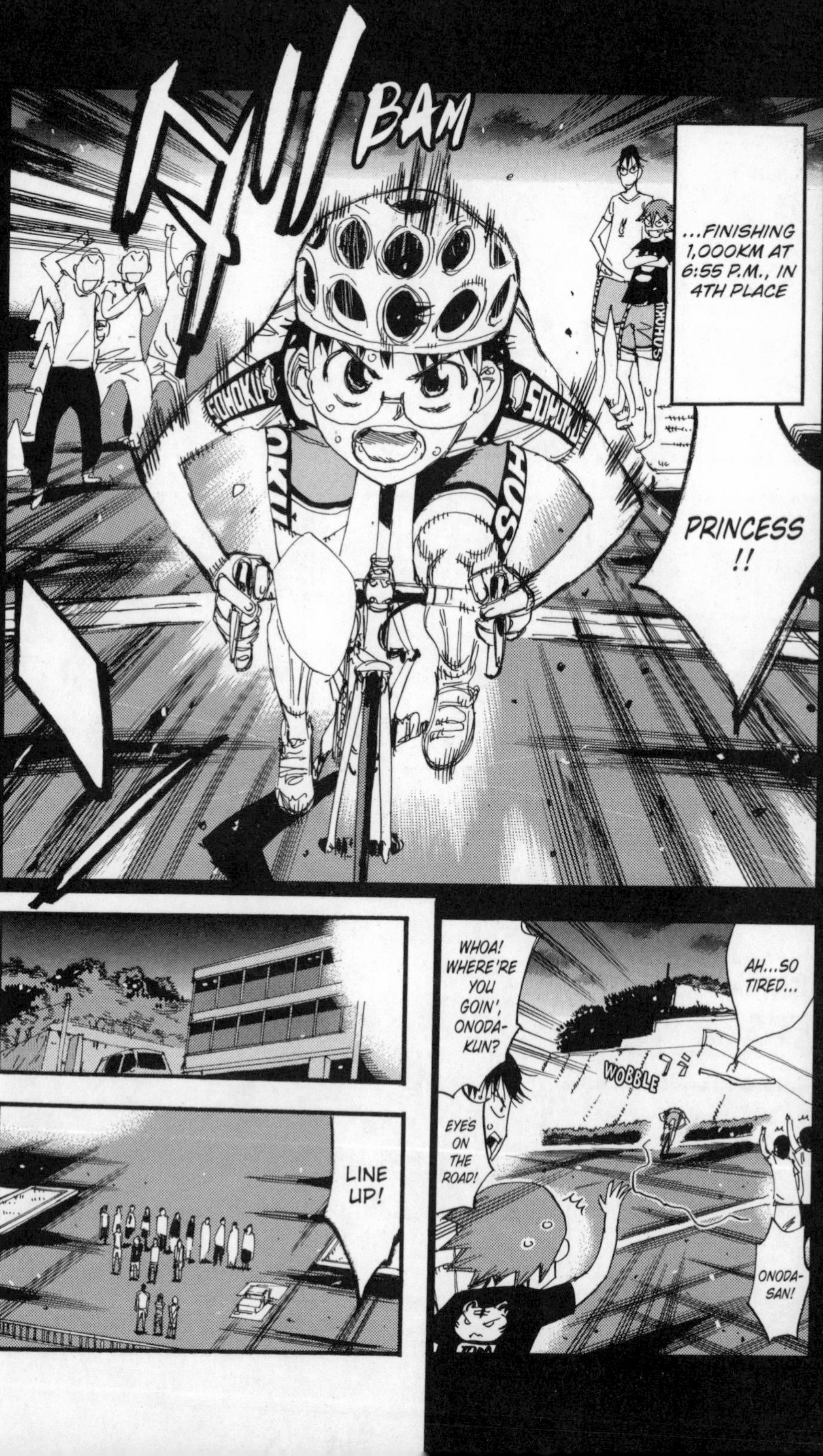

...FINISHING 1,000KM AT 6:55 P.M., IN 4TH PLACE
BAM
PRINCESS !!
AH...SO TIRED...
WHOA! WHERE'RE YOU GOIN', ONODA-KUN?
WOBBLE
EYES ON THE ROAD!
ONODA-SAN!
LINE UP!

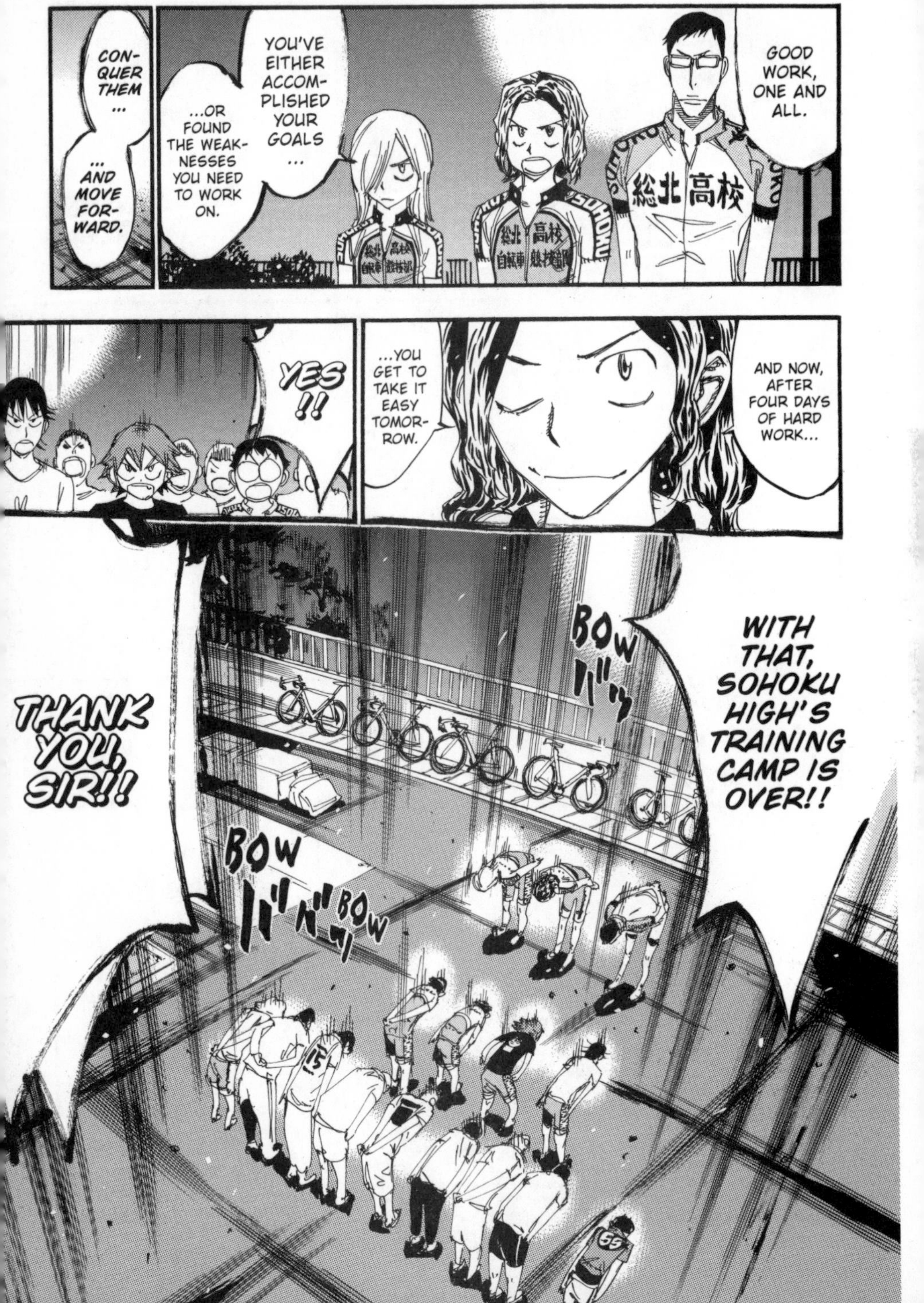
GOOD WORK, ONE AND ALL.
YOU'VE EITHER ACCOMPLISHED YOUR GOALS...
...OR FOUND THE WEAKNESSES YOU NEED TO WORK ON.
CONQUER THEM...
...AND MOVE FORWARD.
AND NOW, AFTER FOUR DAYS OF HARD WORK...
...YOU GET TO TAKE IT EASY TOMORROW.
YES!!
WITH THAT, SOHOKU HIGH'S TRAINING CAMP IS OVER!!
BOW
THANK YOU, SIR!!
BOW
BOW

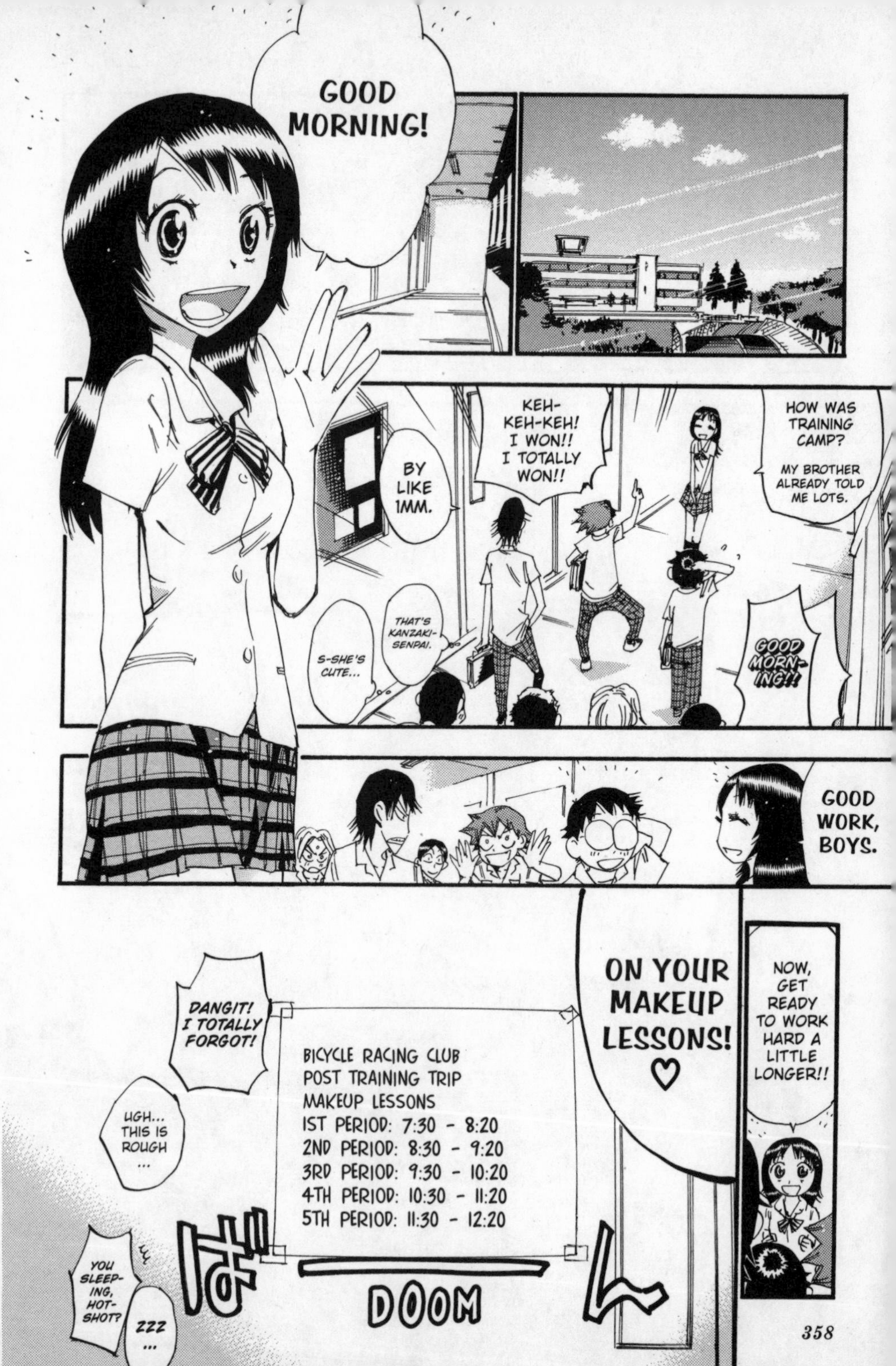
GOOD MORNING!
HOW WAS TRAINING CAMP?
MY BROTHER ALREADY TOLD ME LOTS.
GOOD MORN-ING!!
KEH-KEH-KEH! I WON!! I TOTALLY WON!!
BY LIKE 1MM.
THAT'S KANZAKI-SENPAI.
S-SHE'S CUTE...
GOOD WORK, BOYS.
NOW, GET READY TO WORK HARD A LITTLE LONGER!!
ON YOUR MAKEUP LESSONS! ♡
BICYCLE RACING CLUB
POST TRAINING TRIP
MAKEUP LESSONS
1ST PERIOD: 7:30 - 8:20
2ND PERIOD: 8:30 - 9:20
3RD PERIOD: 9:30 - 10:20
4TH PERIOD: 10:30 - 11:20
5TH PERIOD: 11:30 - 12:20
DANGIT! I TOTALLY FORGOT!
ばーん
DOOM
UGH... THIS IS ROUGH...
YOU SLEEPING, HOT-SHOT?
ZZZ...

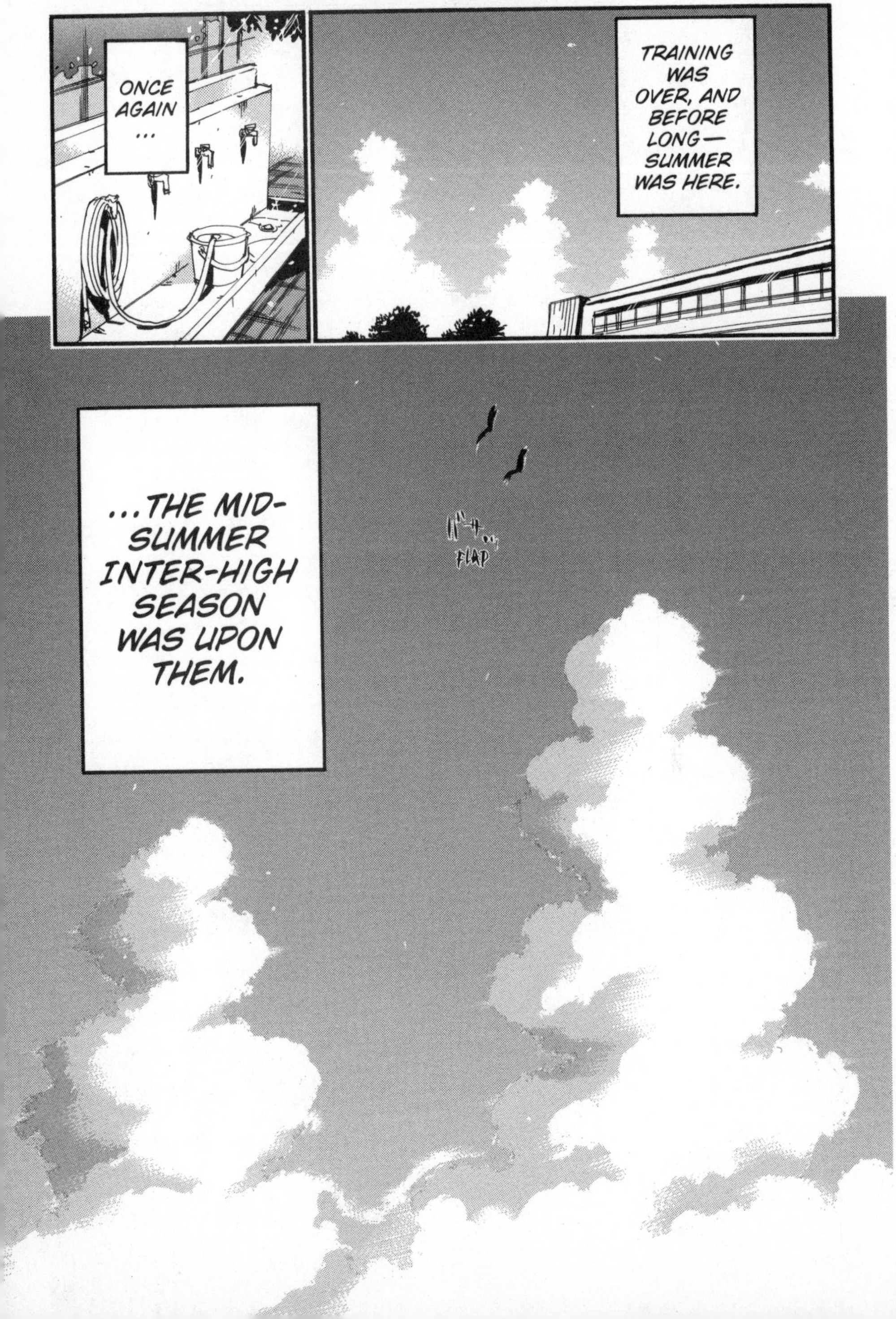
TRAINING WAS OVER, AND BEFORE LONG—SUMMER WAS HERE.
ONCE AGAIN...
...THE MID-SUMMER INTER-HIGH SEASON WAS UPON THEM.
FLAP

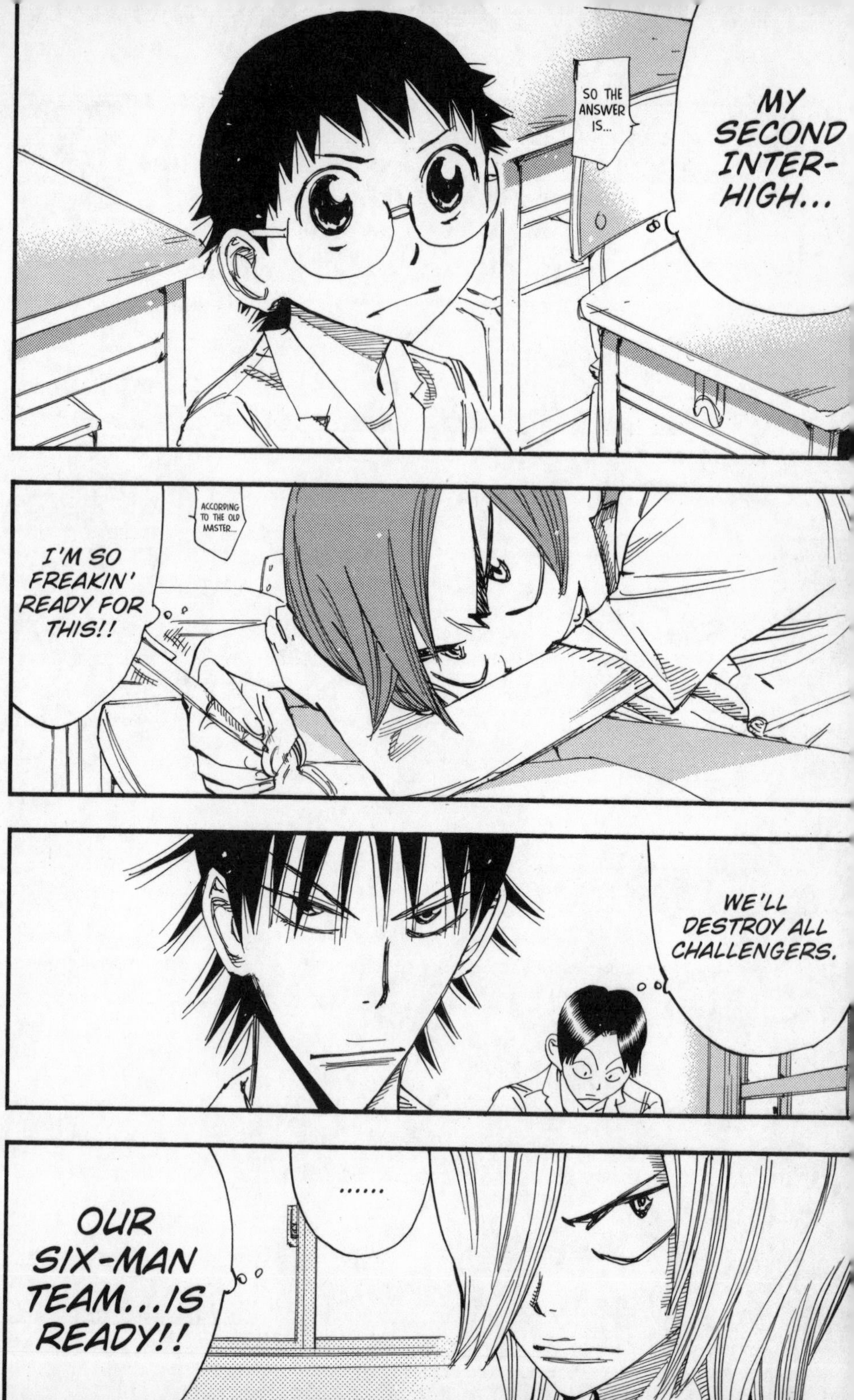
MY SECOND INTER-HIGH...
SO THE ANSWER IS...
ACCORDING TO THE OLD MASTER...
I'M SO FREAKIN' READY FOR THIS!!
WE'LL DESTROY ALL CHALLENGERS.
......
OUR SIX-MAN TEAM...IS READY!!

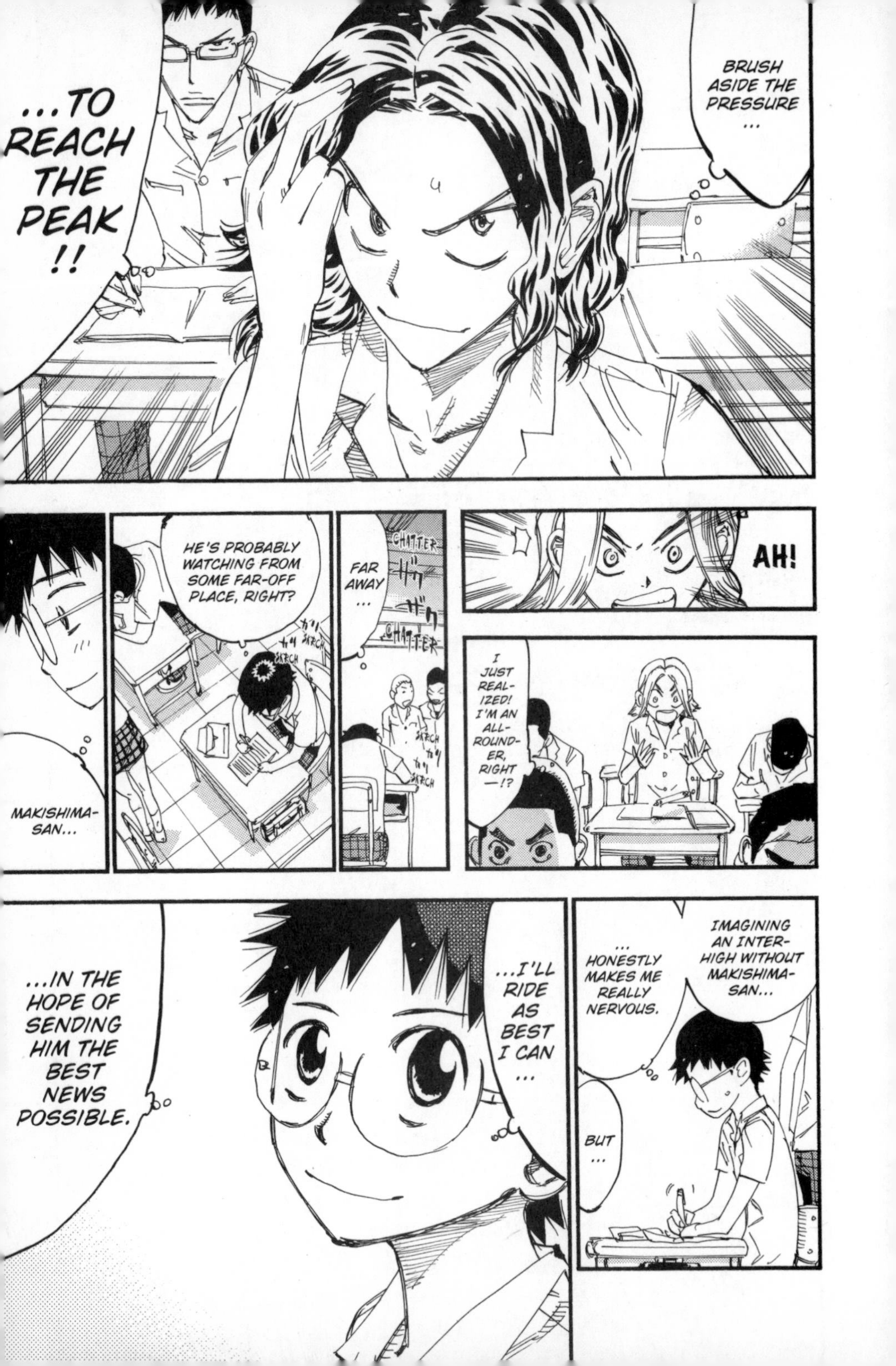
BRUSH ASIDE THE PRESSURE...
...TO REACH THE PEAK!!
AH!
I JUST REALIZED! I'M AN ALL-ROUNDER, RIGHT—!?
CHATTER
CHATTER
FAR AWAY...
SKRCH
SKRCH
HE'S PROBABLY WATCHING FROM SOME FAR-OFF PLACE, RIGHT?
SKRCH
SKRCH
MAKISHIMA-SAN...
IMAGINING AN INTER-HIGH WITHOUT MAKISHIMA-SAN...
...HONESTLY MAKES ME REALLY NERVOUS.
BUT...
...I'LL RIDE AS BEST I CAN...
...IN THE HOPE OF SENDING HIM THE BEST NEWS POSSIBLE.

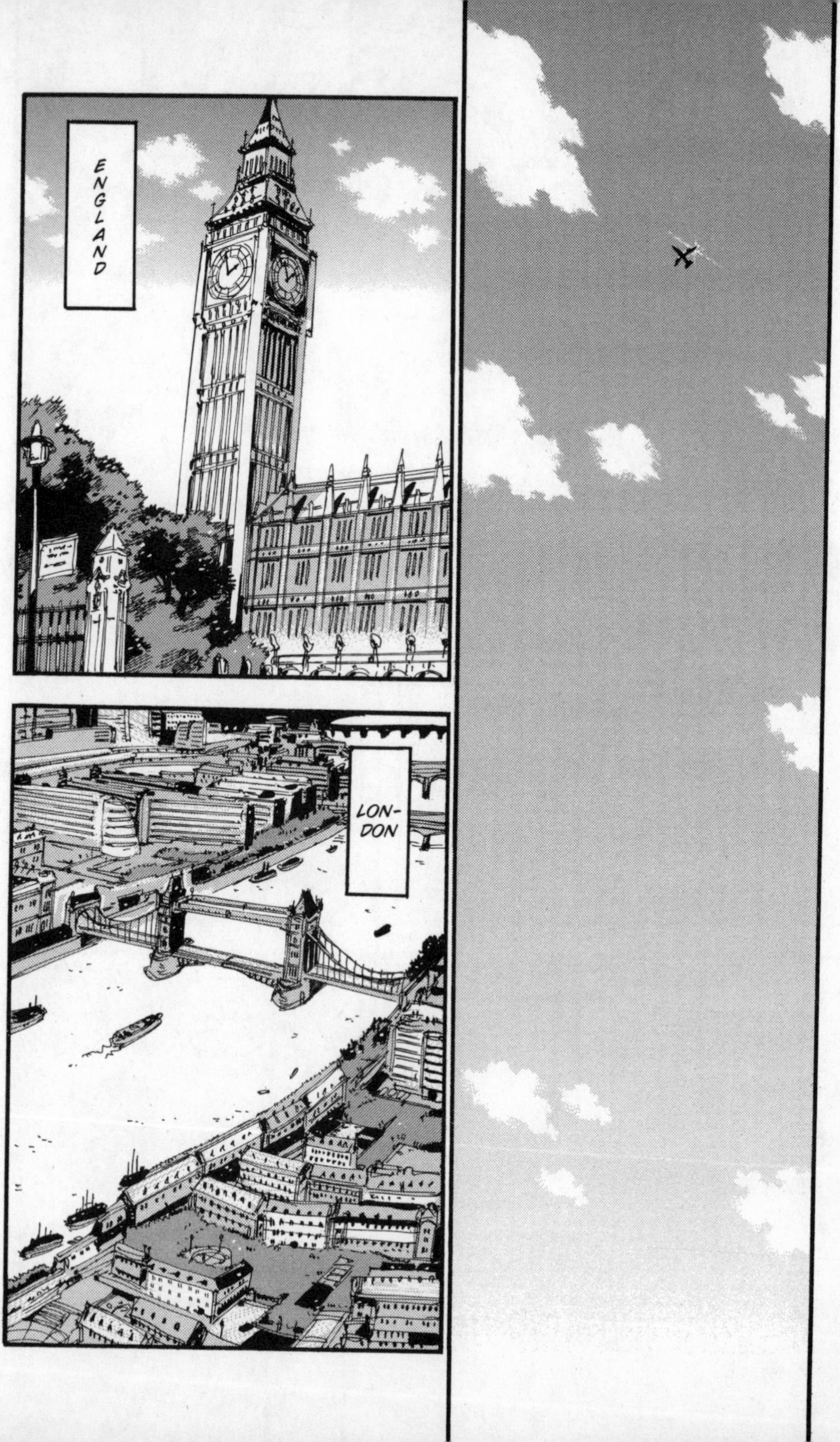
ENGLAND
LON-DON

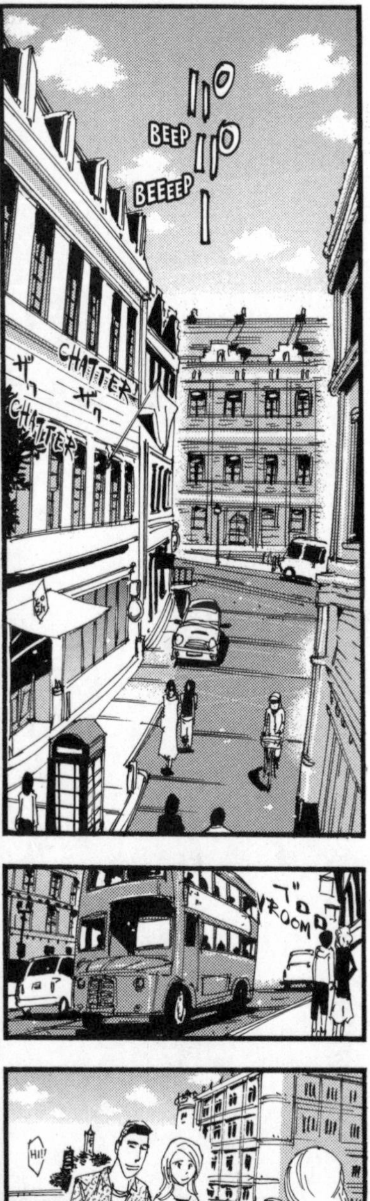
BEEP
BEEEP
CHATTER
CHATTER
VROOM
HI!!
SNAP

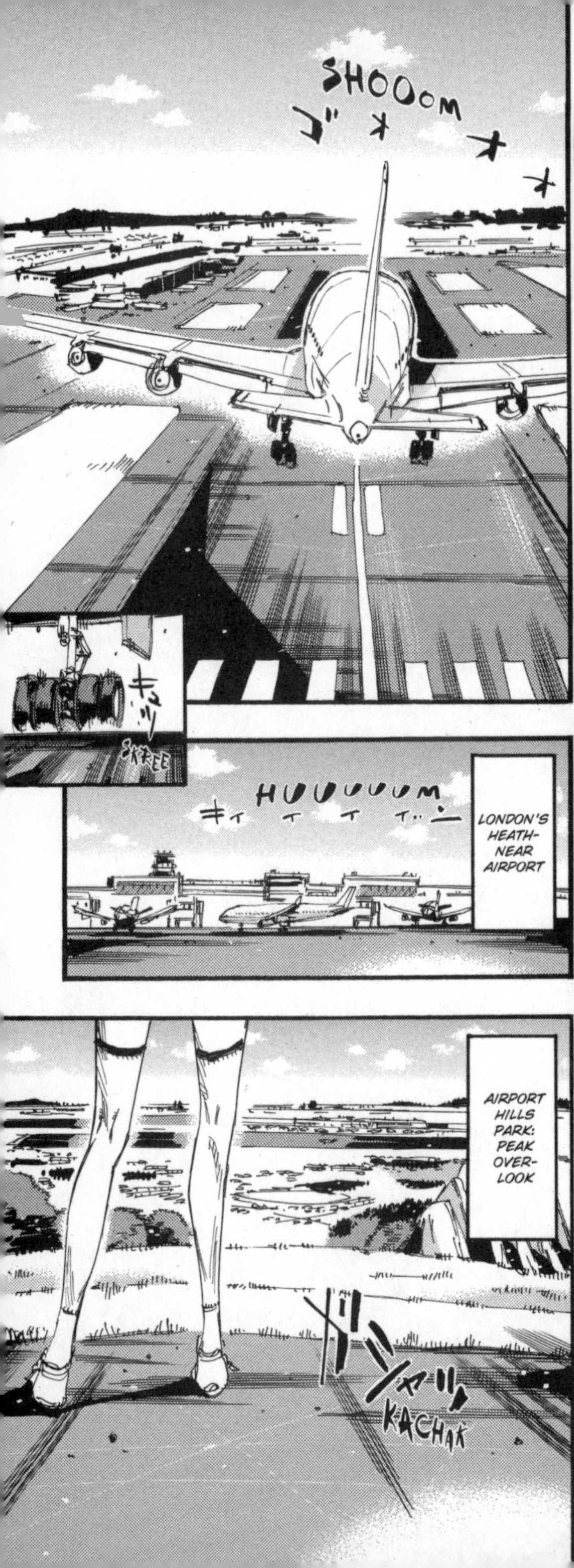
SHOOOM
SKREE
LONDON'S HEATH-NEAR AIRPORT
HUUUUUM
AIRPORT HILLS PARK: PEAK OVERLOOK
KACHAK

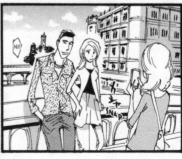

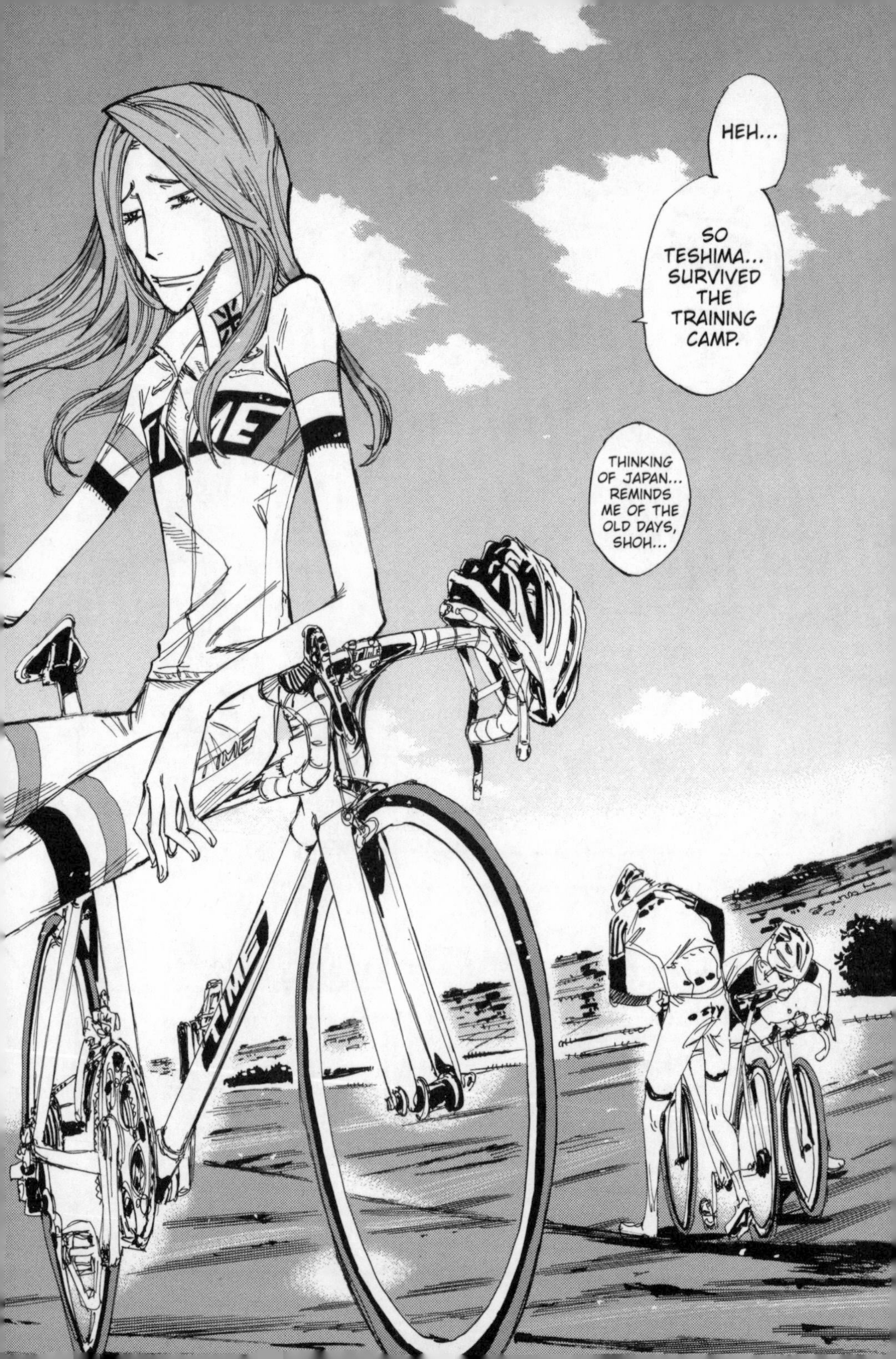
HEH...
SO TESHIMA... SURVIVED THE TRAINING CAMP.
THINKING OF JAPAN... REMINDS ME OF THE OLD DAYS, SHOH...

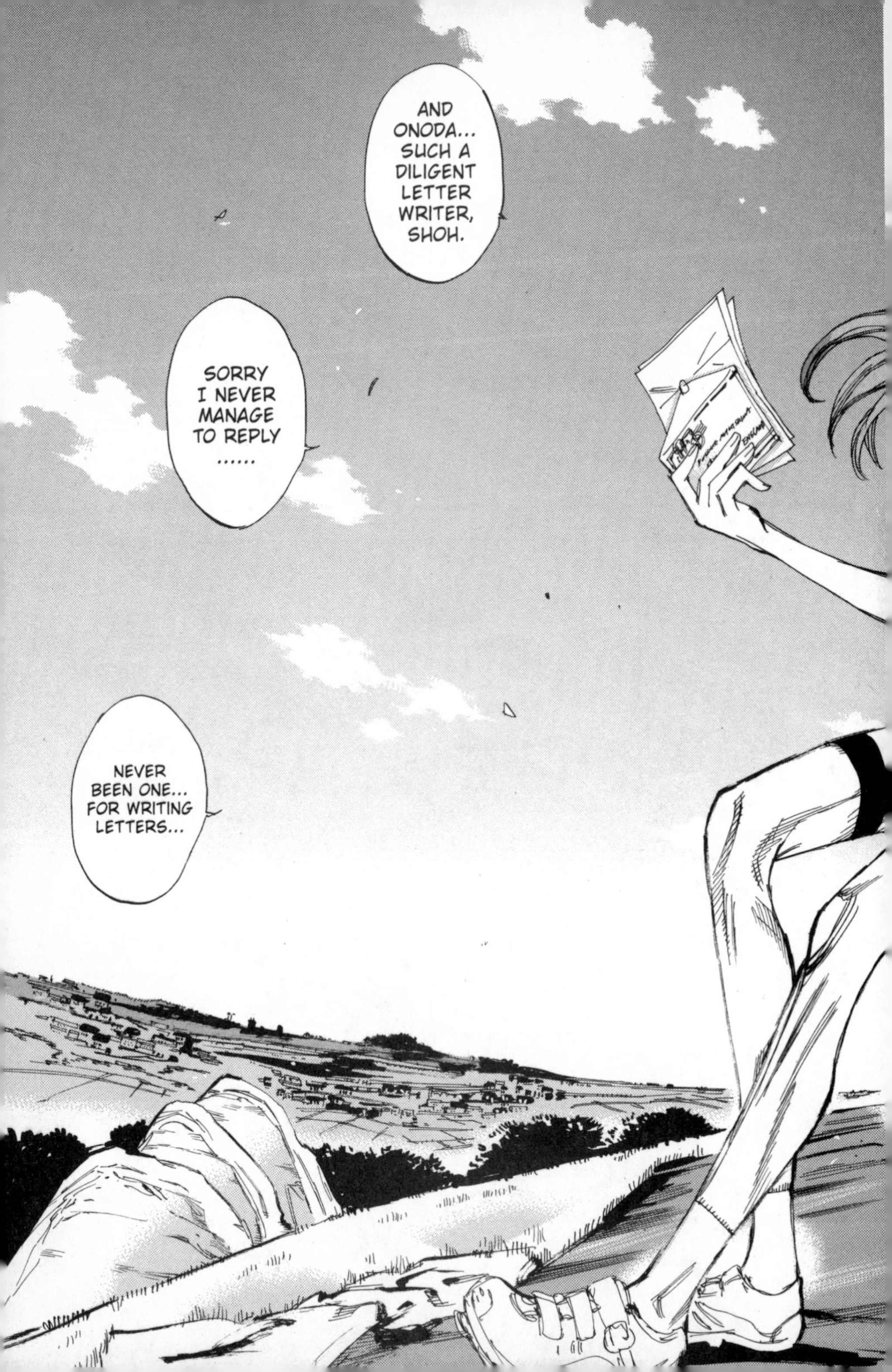
AND ONODA... SUCH A DILIGENT LETTER WRITER, SHOH.
SORRY I NEVER MANAGE TO REPLY ......
NEVER BEEN ONE... FOR WRITING LETTERS...

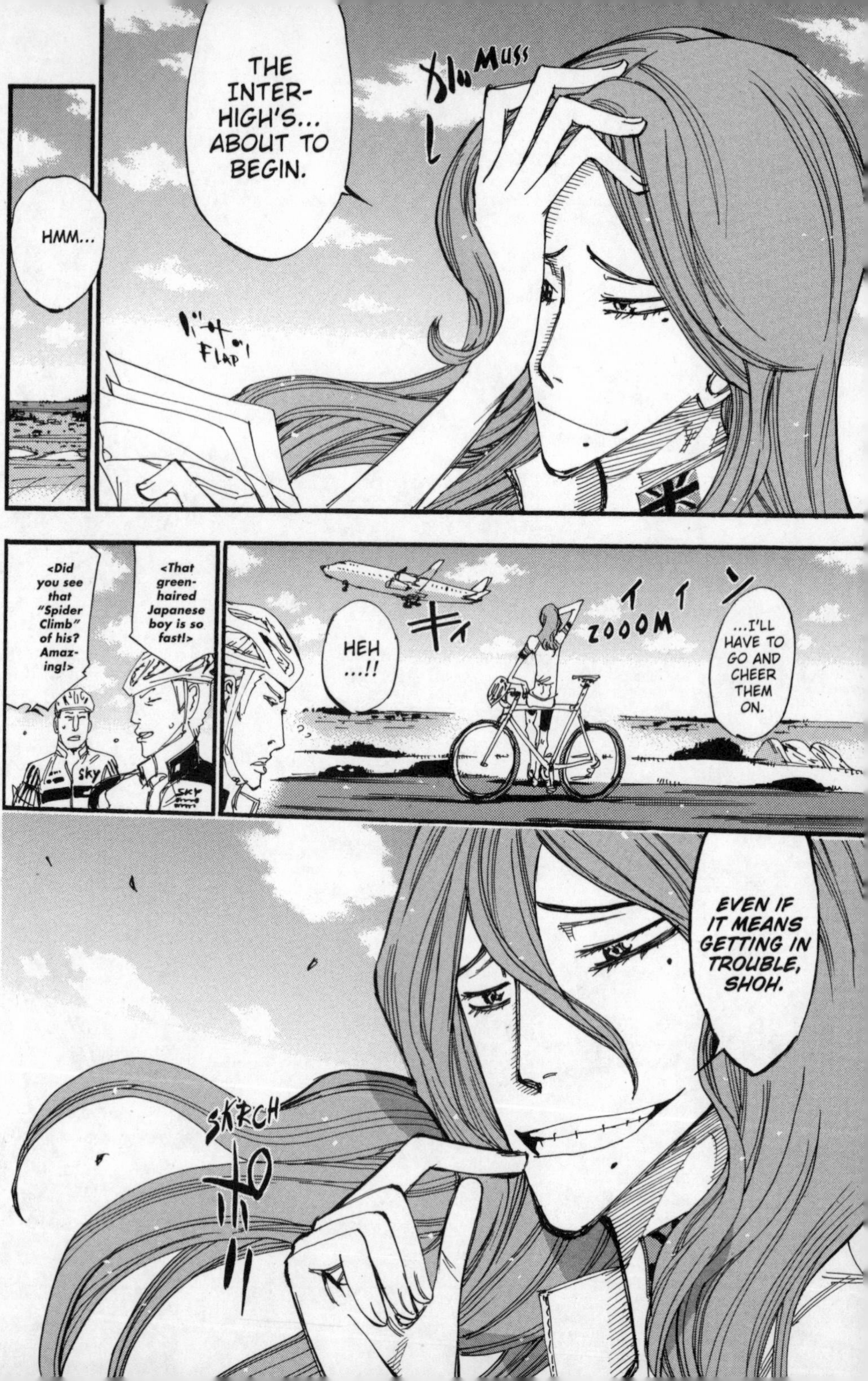
MUSS
THE INTER-HIGH'S... ABOUT TO BEGIN.
FLAP!
HMM...
...I'LL HAVE TO GO AND CHEER THEM ON.
ZOOOM
HEH ...!!
<That green-haired Japanese boy is so fast!>
<Did you see that "Spider Climb" of his? Amazing!>
EVEN IF IT MEANS GETTING IN TROUBLE, SHOH.
SKRCH

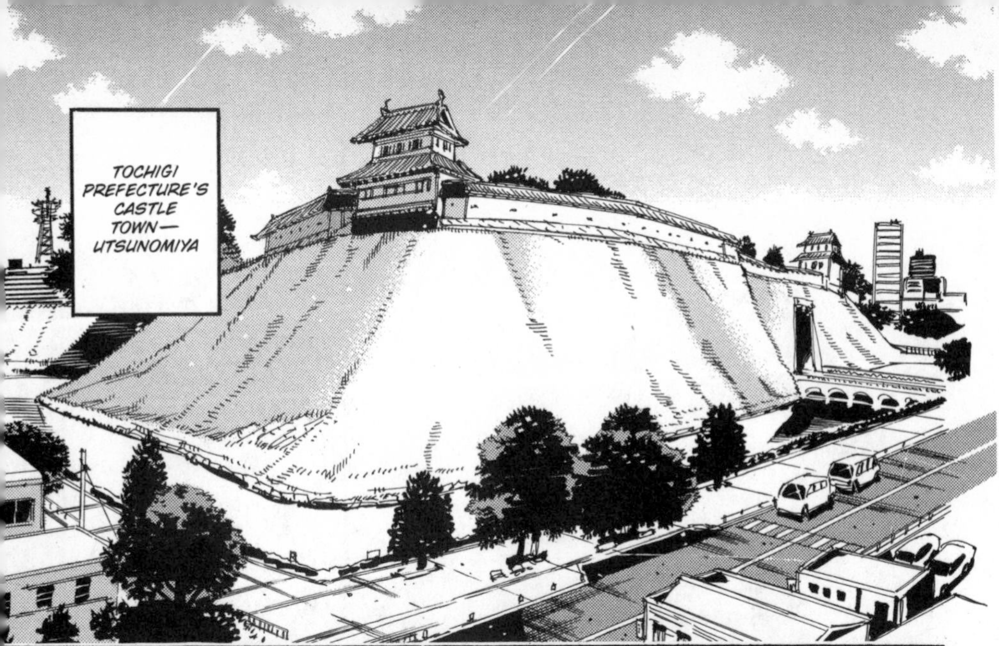
TOCHIGI PREFECTURE'S CASTLE TOWN— UTSUNOMIYA

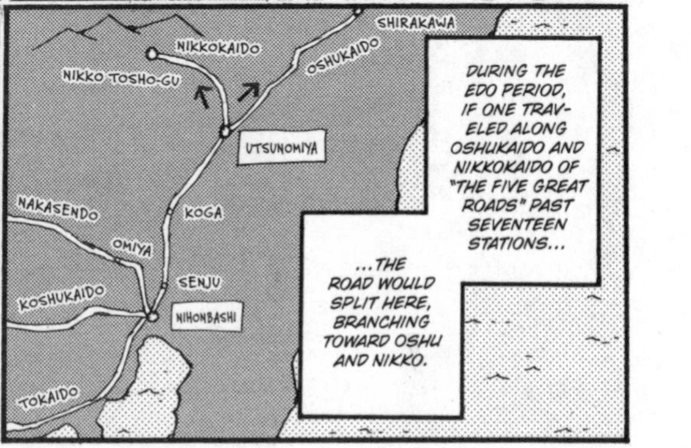
DURING THE EDO PERIOD, IF ONE TRAVELED ALONG OSHUKAIDO AND NIKKOKAIDO OF "THE FIVE GREAT ROADS" PAST SEVENTEEN STATIONS...
...THE ROAD WOULD SPLIT HERE, BRANCHING TOWARD OSHU AND NIKKO.
SHIRAKAWA
NIKKOKAIDO
OSHUKAIDO
NIKKO TOSHO-GU
UTSUNOMIYA
NAKASENDO
KOGA
OMIYA
SENJU
KOSHUKAIDO
NIHONBASHI
TOKAIDO

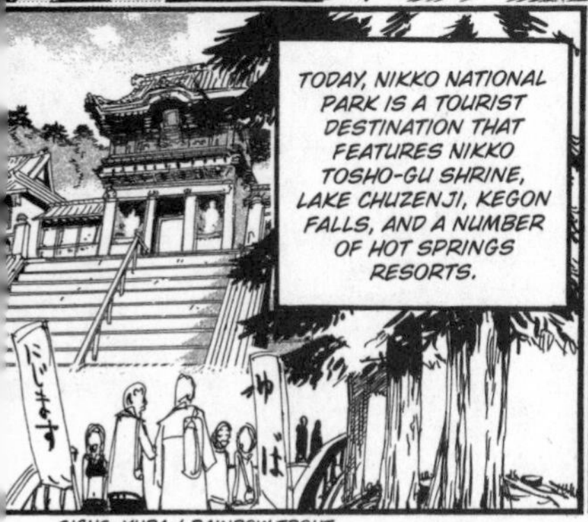
TODAY, NIKKO NATIONAL PARK IS A TOURIST DESTINATION THAT FEATURES NIKKO TOSHO-GU SHRINE, LAKE CHUZENJI, KEGON FALLS, AND A NUMBER OF HOT SPRINGS RESORTS.
ゆば
にじます

SIGNS: YUBA / RAINBOW TROUT

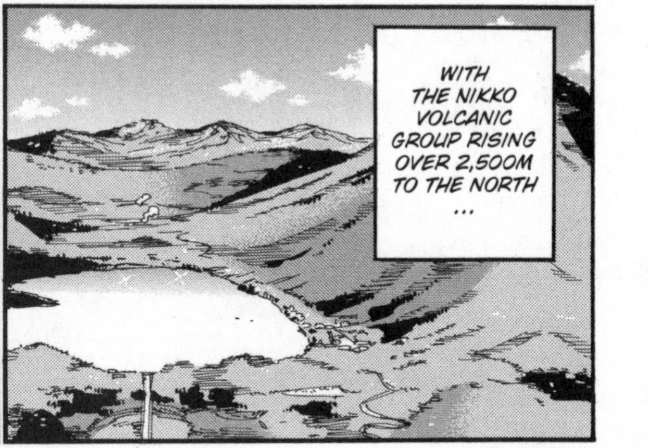
WITH THE NIKKO VOLCANIC GROUP RISING OVER 2,500M TO THE NORTH ...

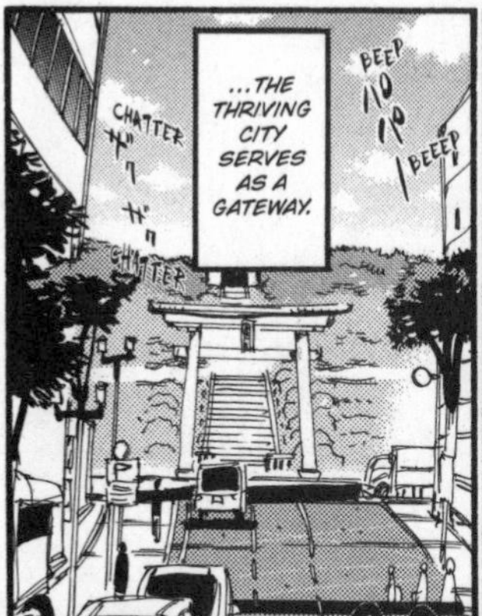
...THE THRIVING CITY SERVES AS A GATEWAY.
BEEP
BEEEP
CHATTER
CHATTER

RIDE.295 START!!!

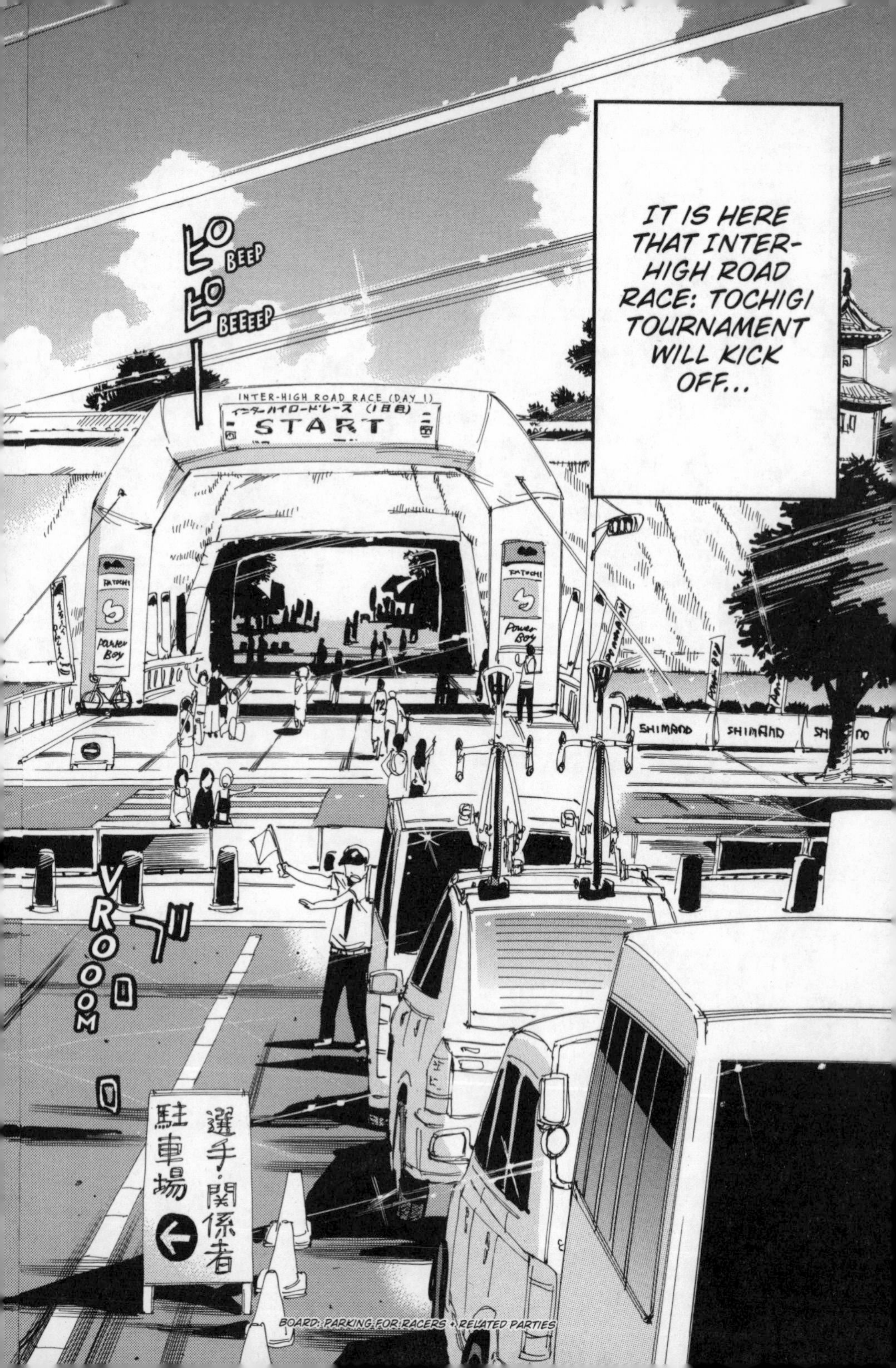
IT IS HERE THAT INTER-HIGH ROAD RACE: TOCHIGI TOURNAMENT WILL KICK OFF...
ピーピー
BEEP
BEEEEP
INTER-HIGH ROAD RACE (DAY 1)
インターハイロードレース (1日目)
START
SHIMANO
ブロロ
VROOOOM
選手・関係者
駐車場
BOARD: PARKING FOR RACERS + RELATED PARTIES

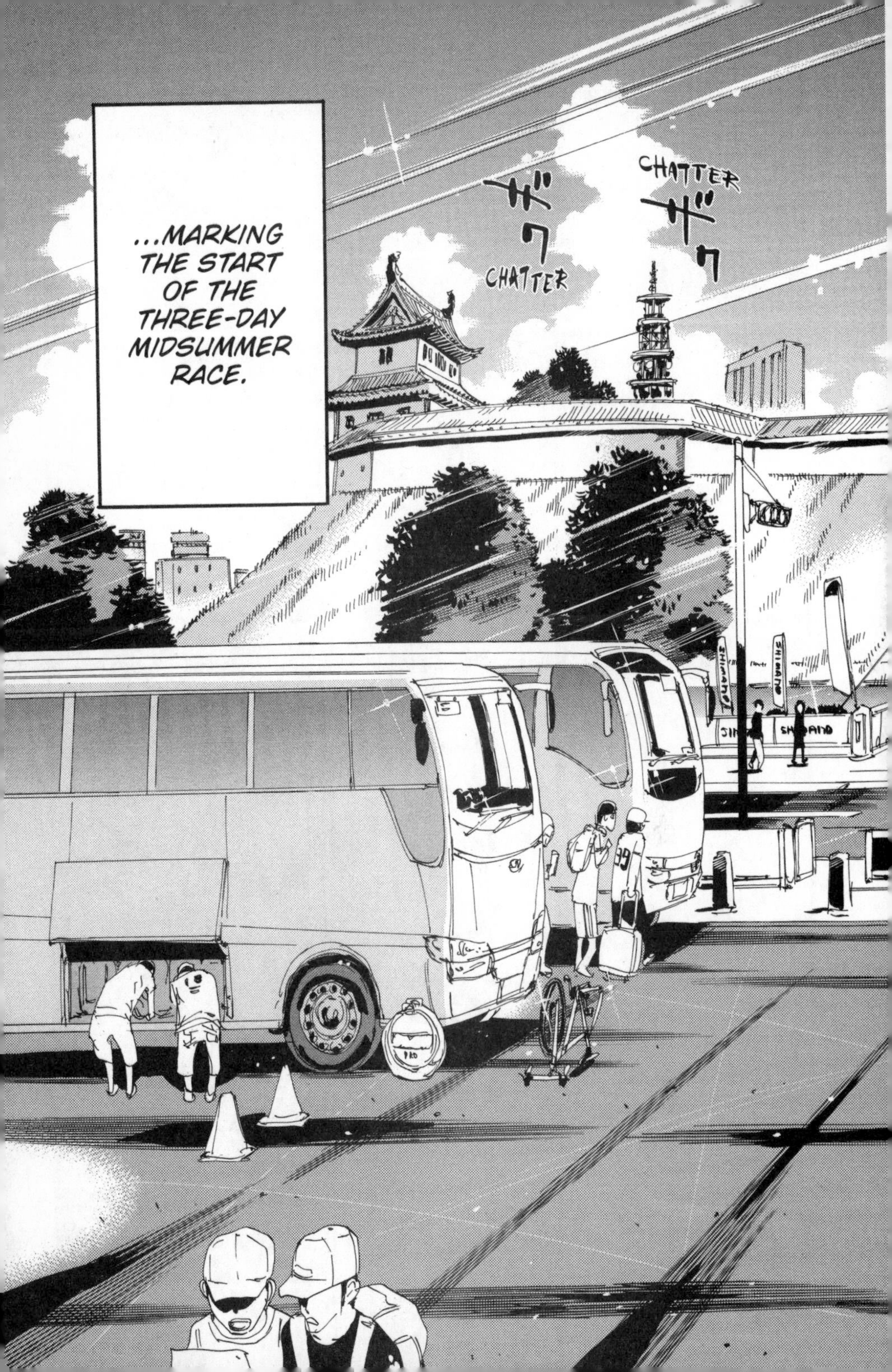
CHATTER
ザワ
ザワ
CHATTER
...MARKING THE START OF THE THREE-DAY MIDSUMMER RACE.

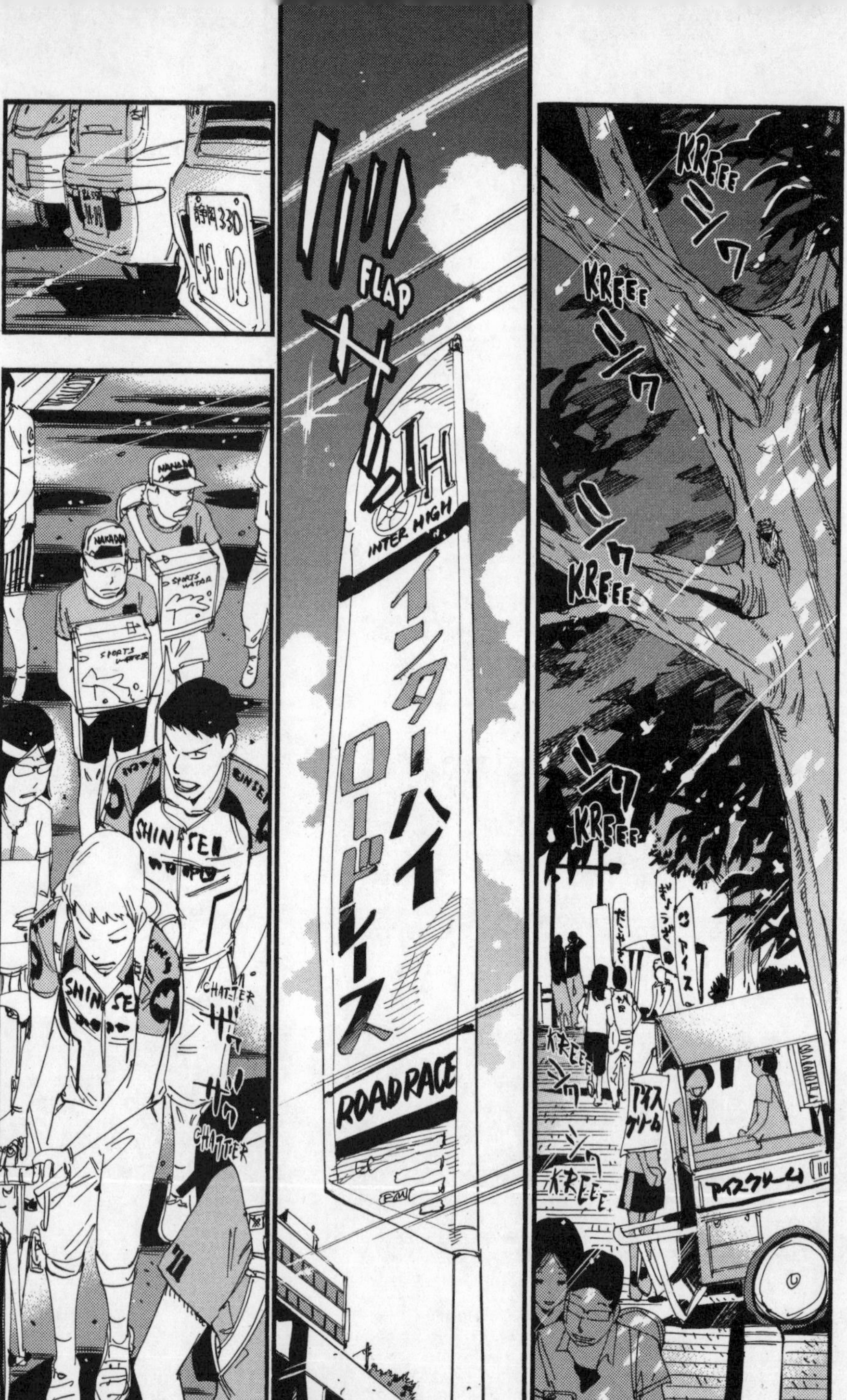
KREEE
KREEE
KREEE
KREEE
KREEE
KREEE
アイスクリーム
アイスクリーム
FLAP
IH
INTER HIGH
インターハイ
ロードレース
ROAD RACE
SPORTS WATER
SPORTS WATER
SHIN SEI
SHIN SEI
CHATTER
CHATTER

SIGN: INTER-HIGH ROAD RACE

SIGNS: ICE CREAM / GYOZA / TAKOYAKI
CART: ICE CREAM

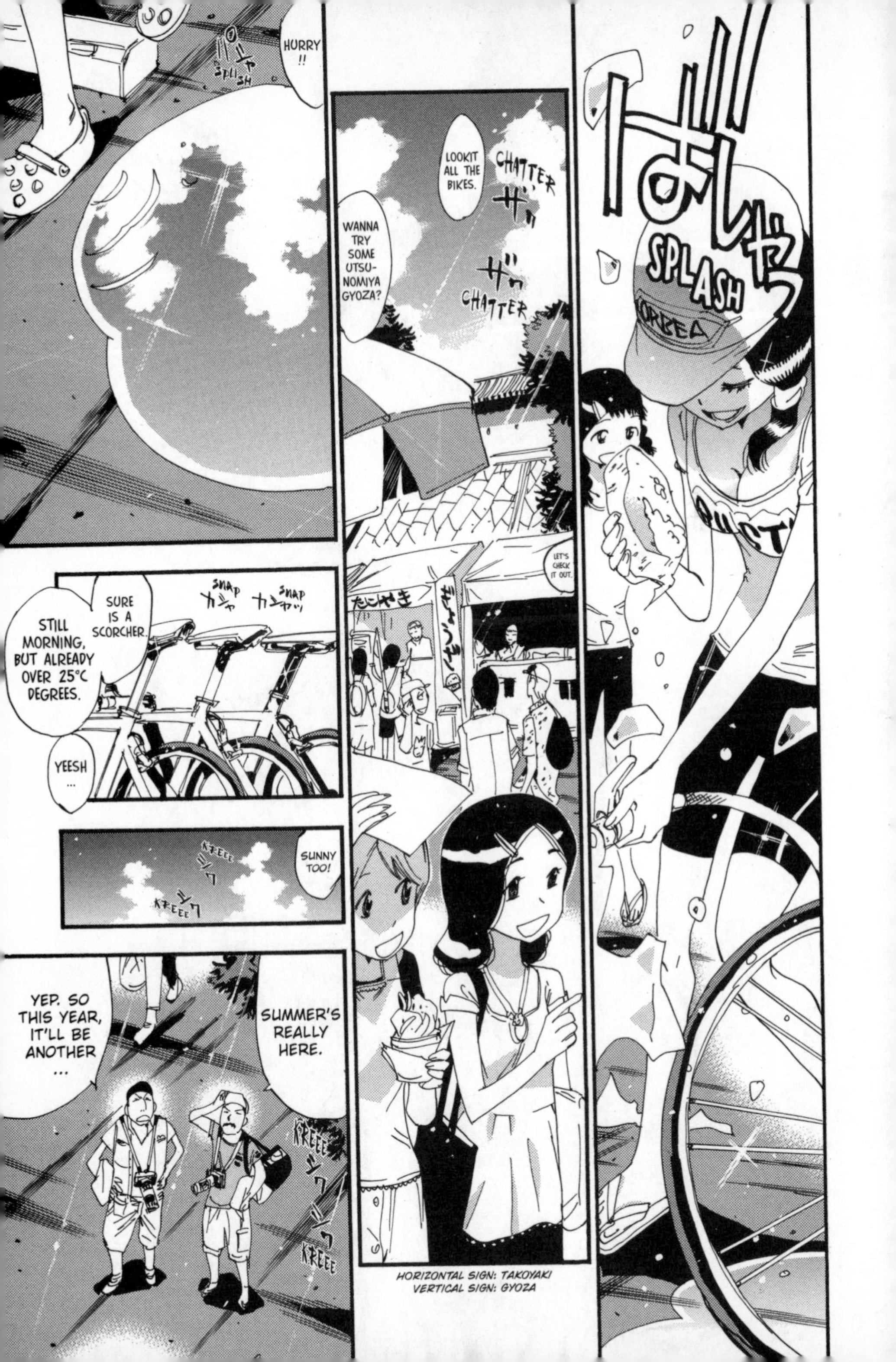

はしゃっ
SPLASH
LOOKIT ALL THE BIKES.
CHATTER
ザワ
WANNA TRY SOME UTSU-NOMIYA GYOZA?
ザワ
CHATTER
LET'S CHECK IT OUT.
たこやき
ぎょうざ
HURRY!!
パシャ
SPLASH
SURE IS A SCORCHER.
STILL MORNING, BUT ALREADY OVER 25°C DEGREES.
カシャ
SNAP
カシャッ
SNAP
YEESH ...
SUNNY TOO!
シワ
KREEEE
シワ
KREEEE
SUMMER'S REALLY HERE.
YEP. SO THIS YEAR, IT'LL BE ANOTHER ...
シワシワ
KREEEE

HORIZONTAL SIGN: TAKOYAKI
VERTICAL SIGN: GYOZA

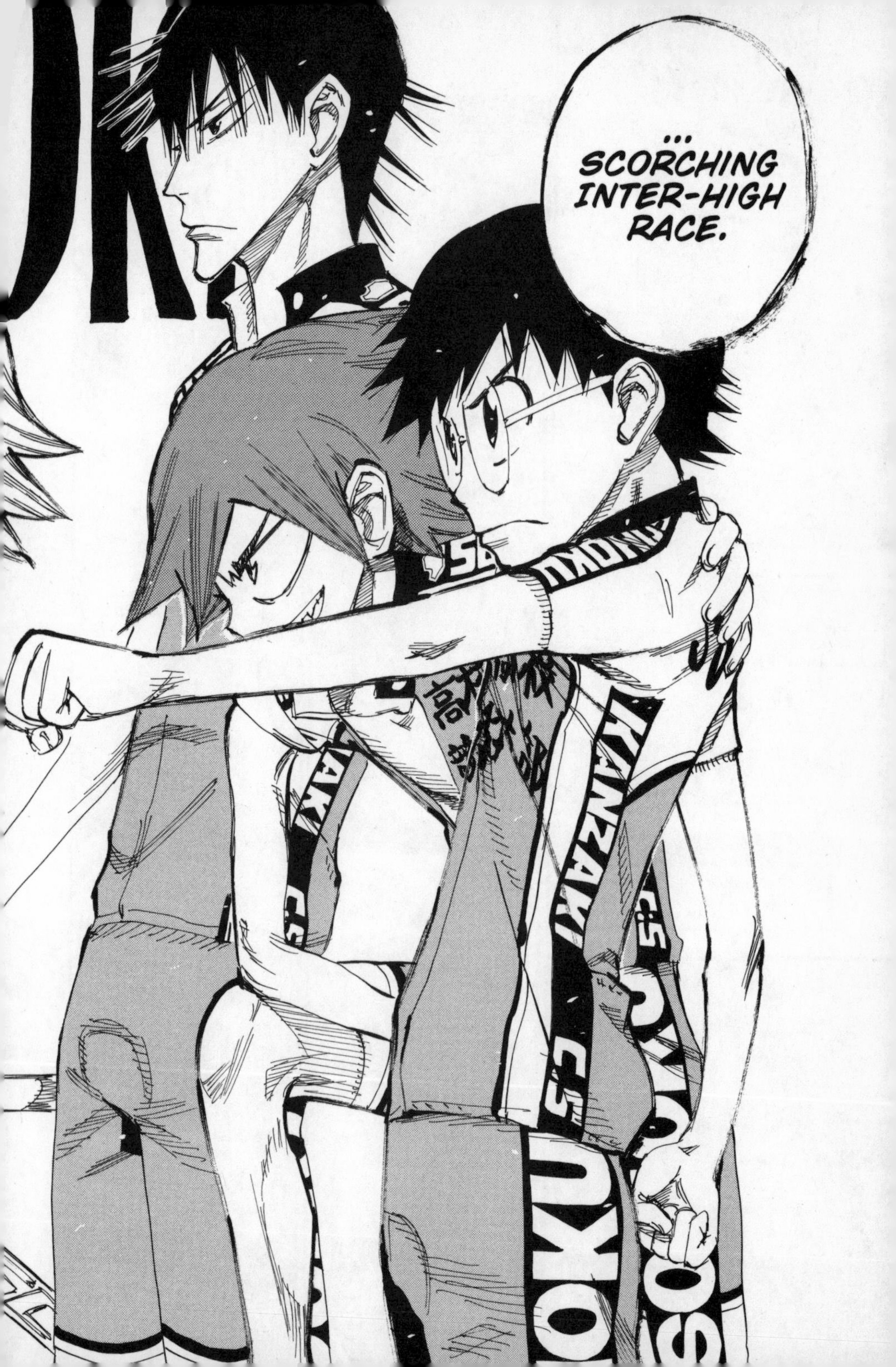
... SCORCHING INTER-HIGH RACE.

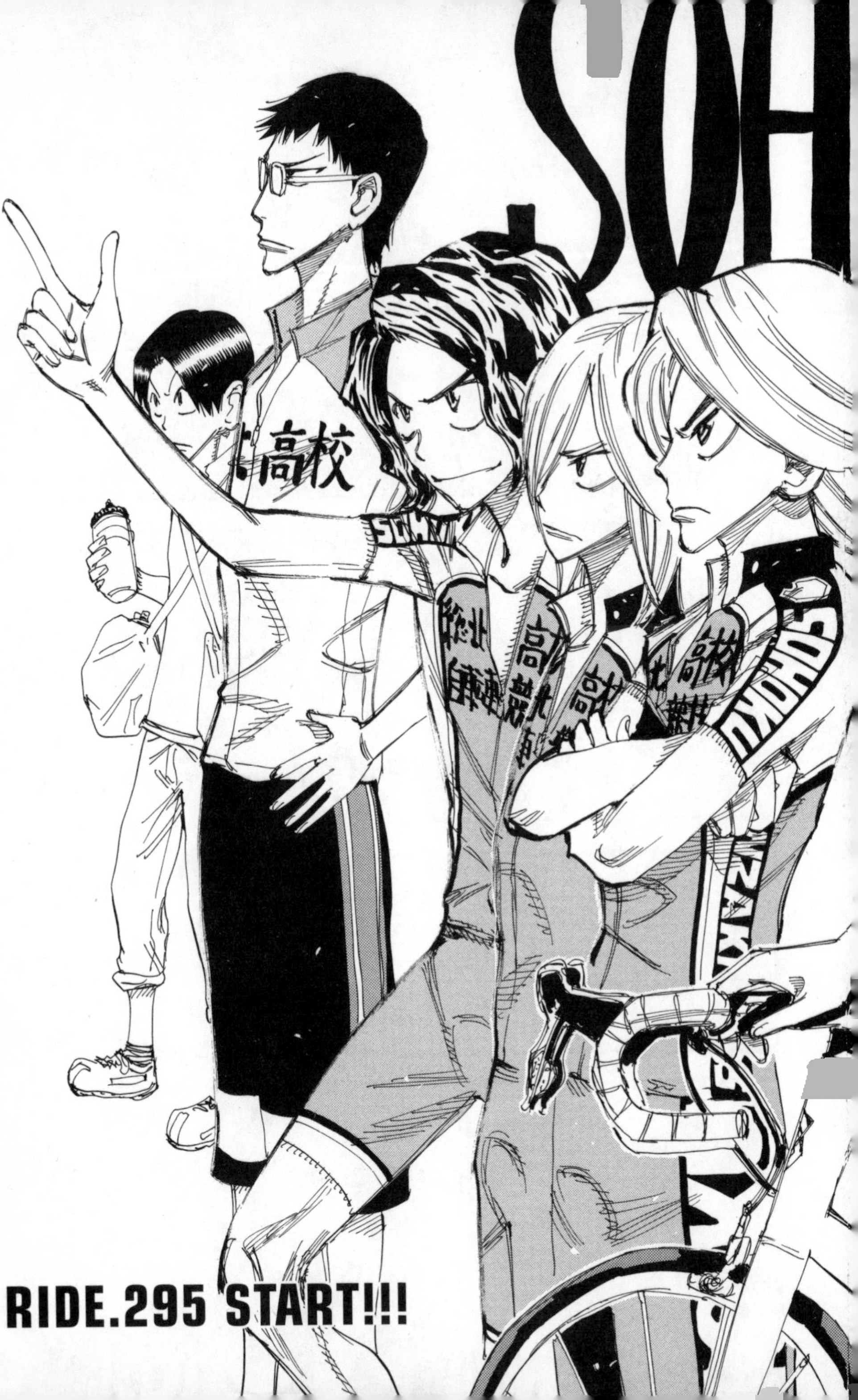

RIDE.295 START!!!

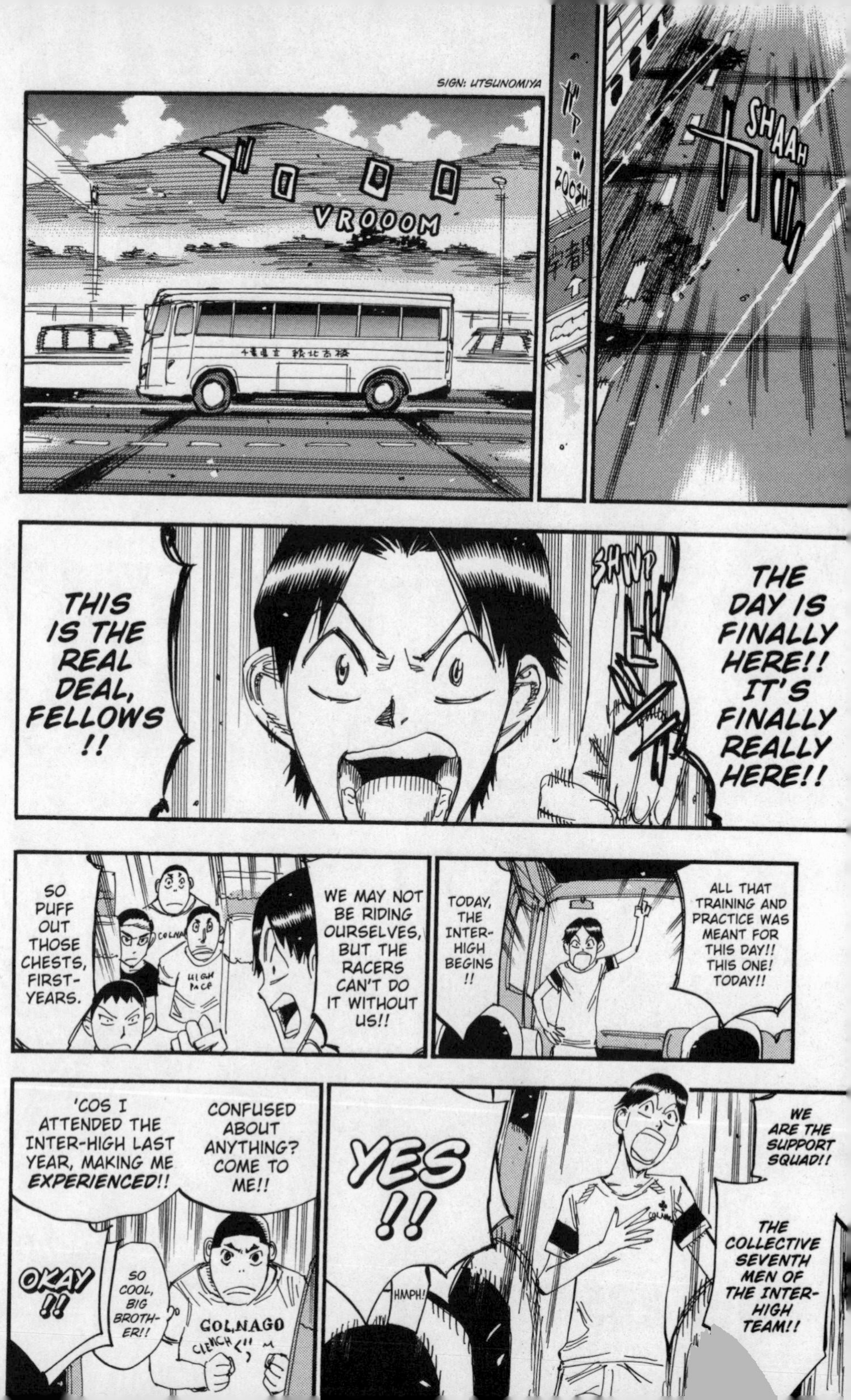
SIGN: UTSUNOMIYA
SHAAH
ZOOSH
VROOOM
THE DAY IS FINALLY HERE!! IT'S FINALLY REALLY HERE!!
SHWP
THIS IS THE REAL DEAL, FELLOWS!!
ALL THAT TRAINING AND PRACTICE WAS MEANT FOR THIS DAY!! THIS ONE! TODAY!!
TODAY, THE INTER-HIGH BEGINS!!
WE MAY NOT BE RIDING OURSELVES, BUT THE RACERS CAN'T DO IT WITHOUT US!!
SO PUFF OUT THOSE CHESTS, FIRST-YEARS.
WE ARE THE SUPPORT SQUAD!!
THE COLLECTIVE SEVENTH MEN OF THE INTER-HIGH TEAM!!
YES!!
HMPH!
CONFUSED ABOUT ANYTHING? COME TO ME!!
'COS I ATTENDED THE INTER-HIGH LAST YEAR, MAKING ME EXPERIENCED!!
SO COOL, BIG BROTHER!!
OKAY!!
CLENCH

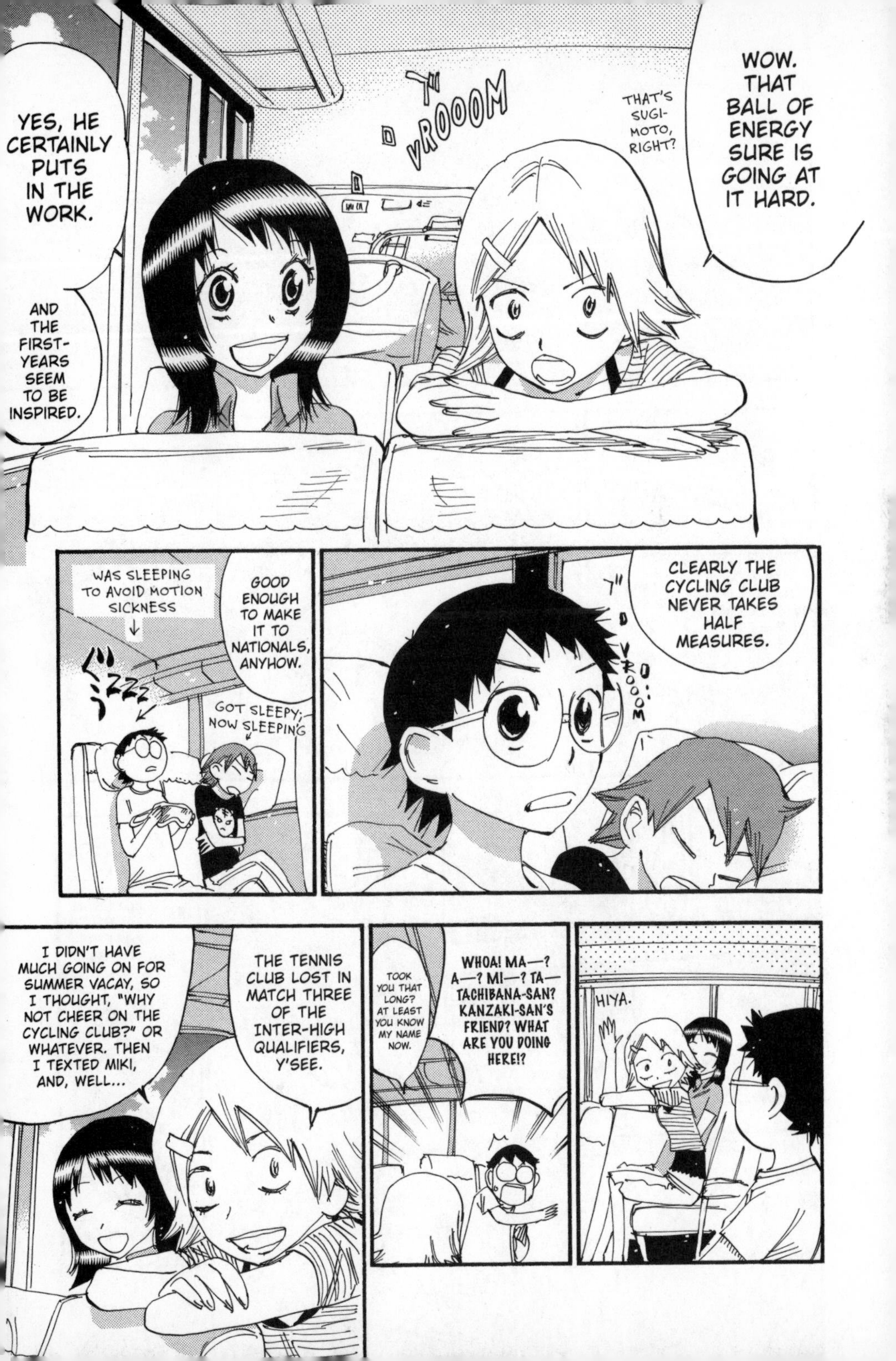
WOW. THAT BALL OF ENERGY SURE IS GOING AT IT HARD.
THAT'S SUGI-MOTO, RIGHT?
VROOOM
YES, HE CERTAINLY PUTS IN THE WORK.
AND THE FIRST-YEARS SEEM TO BE INSPIRED.
CLEARLY THE CYCLING CLUB NEVER TAKES HALF MEASURES.
VROOOM
GOOD ENOUGH TO MAKE IT TO NATIONALS, ANYHOW.
WAS SLEEPING TO AVOID MOTION SICKNESS
ZZZ
GOT SLEEPY; NOW SLEEPING
HIYA.
WHOA! MA—? A—? MI—? TA—TACHIBANA-SAN? KANZAKI-SAN'S FRIEND? WHAT ARE YOU DOING HERE!?
TOOK YOU THAT LONG? AT LEAST YOU KNOW MY NAME NOW.
THE TENNIS CLUB LOST IN MATCH THREE OF THE INTER-HIGH QUALIFIERS, Y'SEE.
I DIDN'T HAVE MUCH GOING ON FOR SUMMER VACAY, SO I THOUGHT, "WHY NOT CHEER ON THE CYCLING CLUB?" OR WHATEVER. THEN I TEXTED MIKI, AND, WELL...

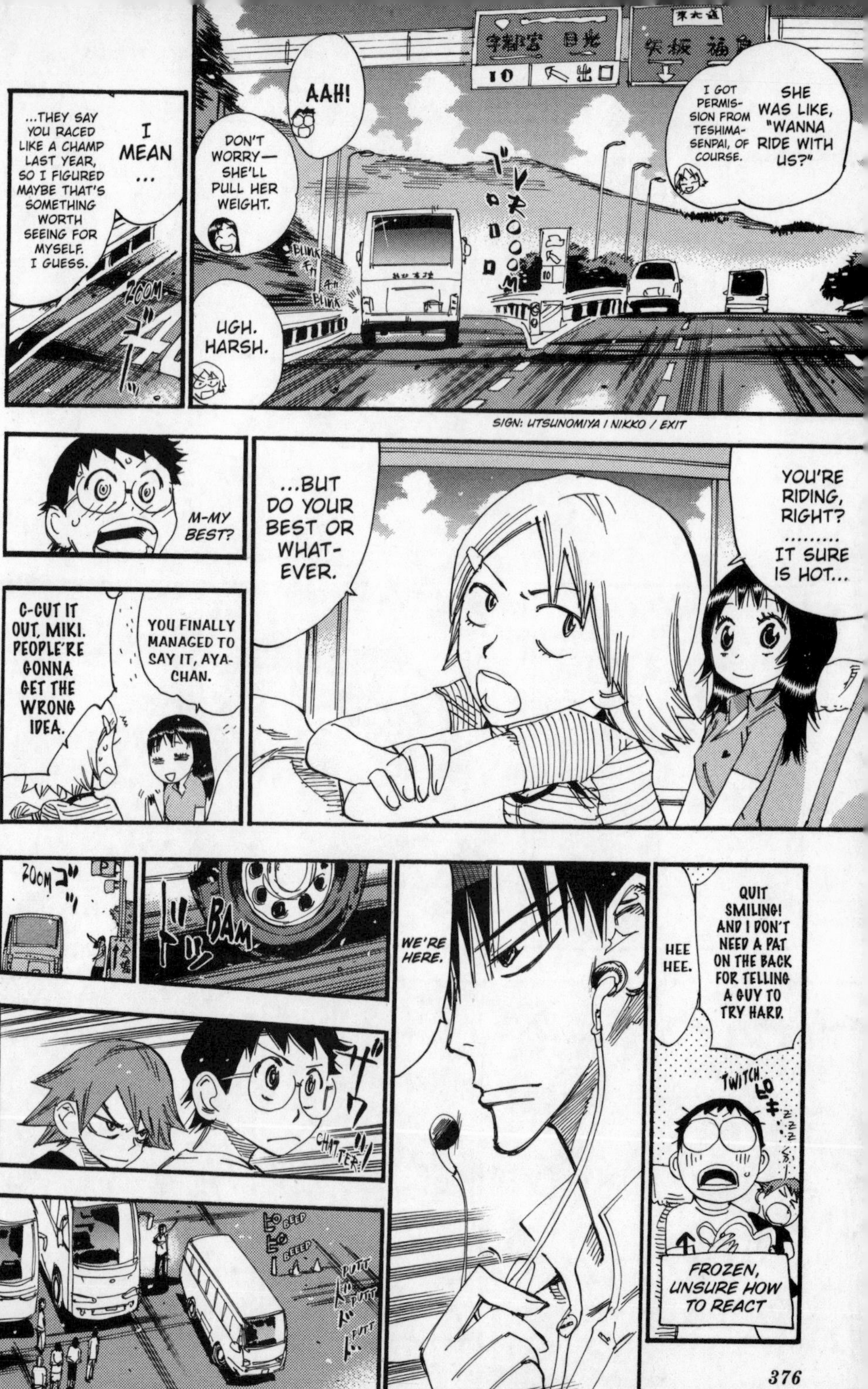
SHE WAS LIKE, "WANNA RIDE WITH US?"
I GOT PERMISSION FROM TESHIMA-SENPAI, OF COURSE.
AAH!
DON'T WORRY—SHE'LL PULL HER WEIGHT.
VROOOOM
BLINK BLINK
UGH. HARSH.
I MEAN...
...THEY SAY YOU RACED LIKE A CHAMP LAST YEAR, SO I FIGURED MAYBE THAT'S SOMETHING WORTH SEEING FOR MYSELF. I GUESS.
ZOOM
SIGN: UTSUNOMIYA / NIKKO / EXIT
YOU'RE RIDING, RIGHT? .... IT SURE IS HOT...
...BUT DO YOUR BEST OR WHATEVER.
M-MY BEST?
YOU FINALLY MANAGED TO SAY IT, AYA-CHAN.
C-CUT IT OUT, MIKI. PEOPLE'RE GONNA GET THE WRONG IDEA.
QUIT SMILING! AND I DON'T NEED A PAT ON THE BACK FOR TELLING A GUY TO TRY HARD.
HEE HEE.
TWITCH
FROZEN, UNSURE HOW TO REACT
WE'RE HERE.
BAM
ZOOM
CHATTER
BEEP
BEEEP
PUTT
PUTT
PUTT

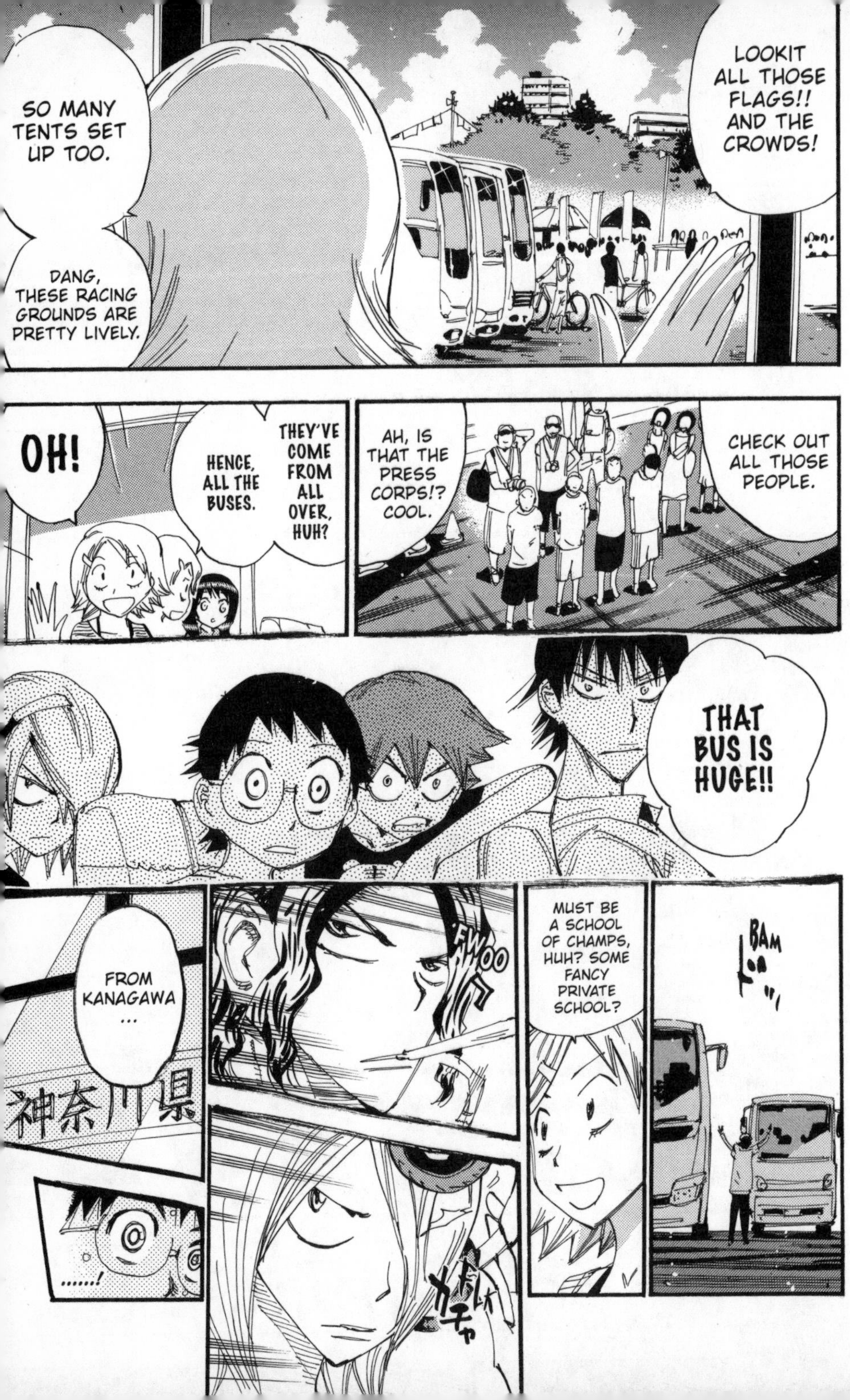

LOOKIT ALL THOSE FLAGS!! AND THE CROWDS!
SO MANY TENTS SET UP TOO.
DANG, THESE RACING GROUNDS ARE PRETTY LIVELY.
CHECK OUT ALL THOSE PEOPLE.
AH, IS THAT THE PRESS CORPS!? COOL.
THEY'VE COME FROM ALL OVER, HUH?
HENCE, ALL THE BUSES.
OH!
THAT BUS IS HUGE!!
BAM
MUST BE A SCHOOL OF CHAMPS, HUH? SOME FANCY PRIVATE SCHOOL?
FWOO
FROM KANAGAWA ...
神奈川県
カチャ
......!

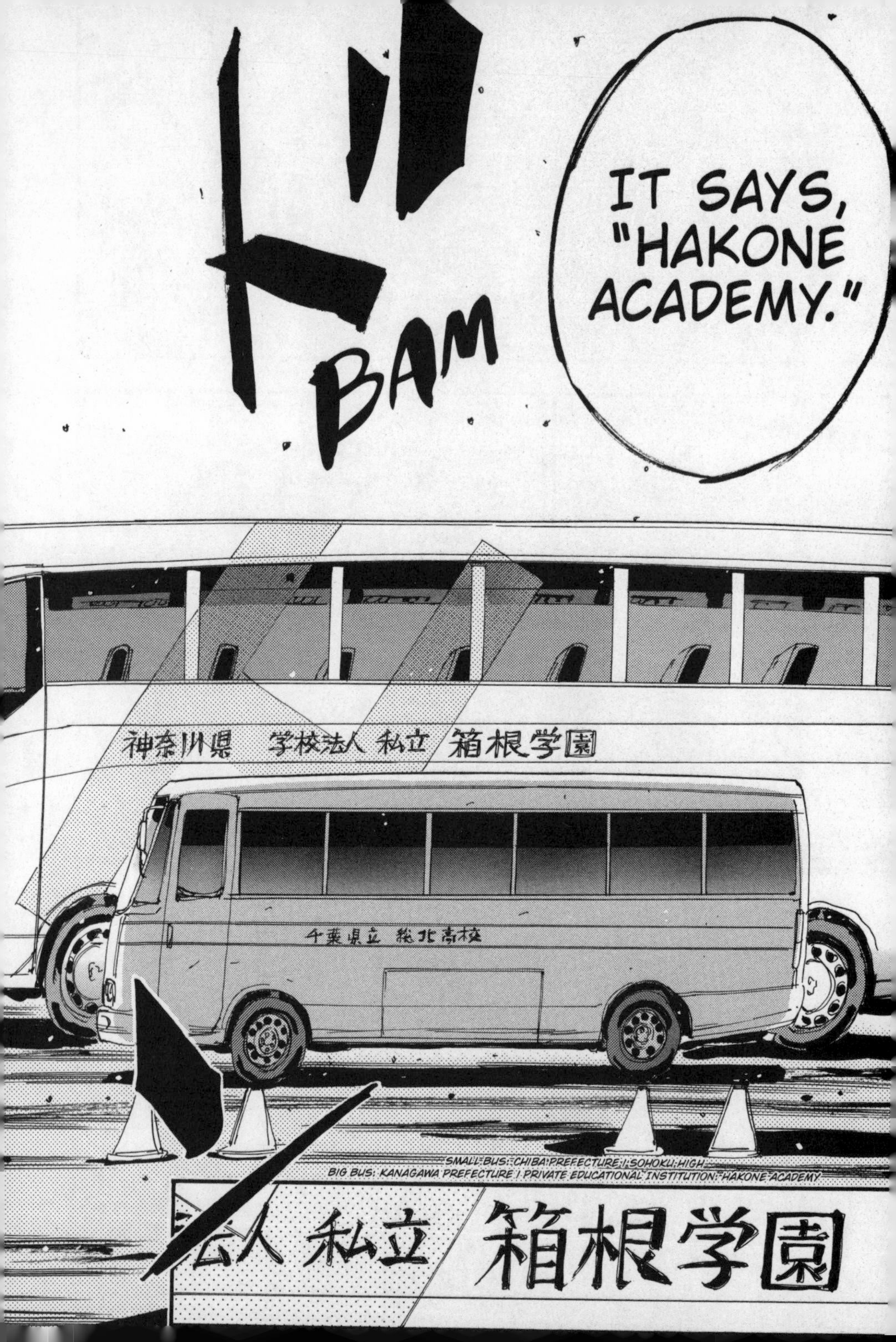
IT SAYS, "HAKONE ACADEMY."
ドン
BAM
神奈川県 学校法人 私立 箱根学園
千葉県立 総北高校
SMALL BUS: CHIBA PREFECTURE / SOHOKU HIGH
BIG BUS: KANAGAWA PREFECTURE / PRIVATE EDUCATIONAL INSTITUTION: HAKONE ACADEMY
法人 私立 箱根学園

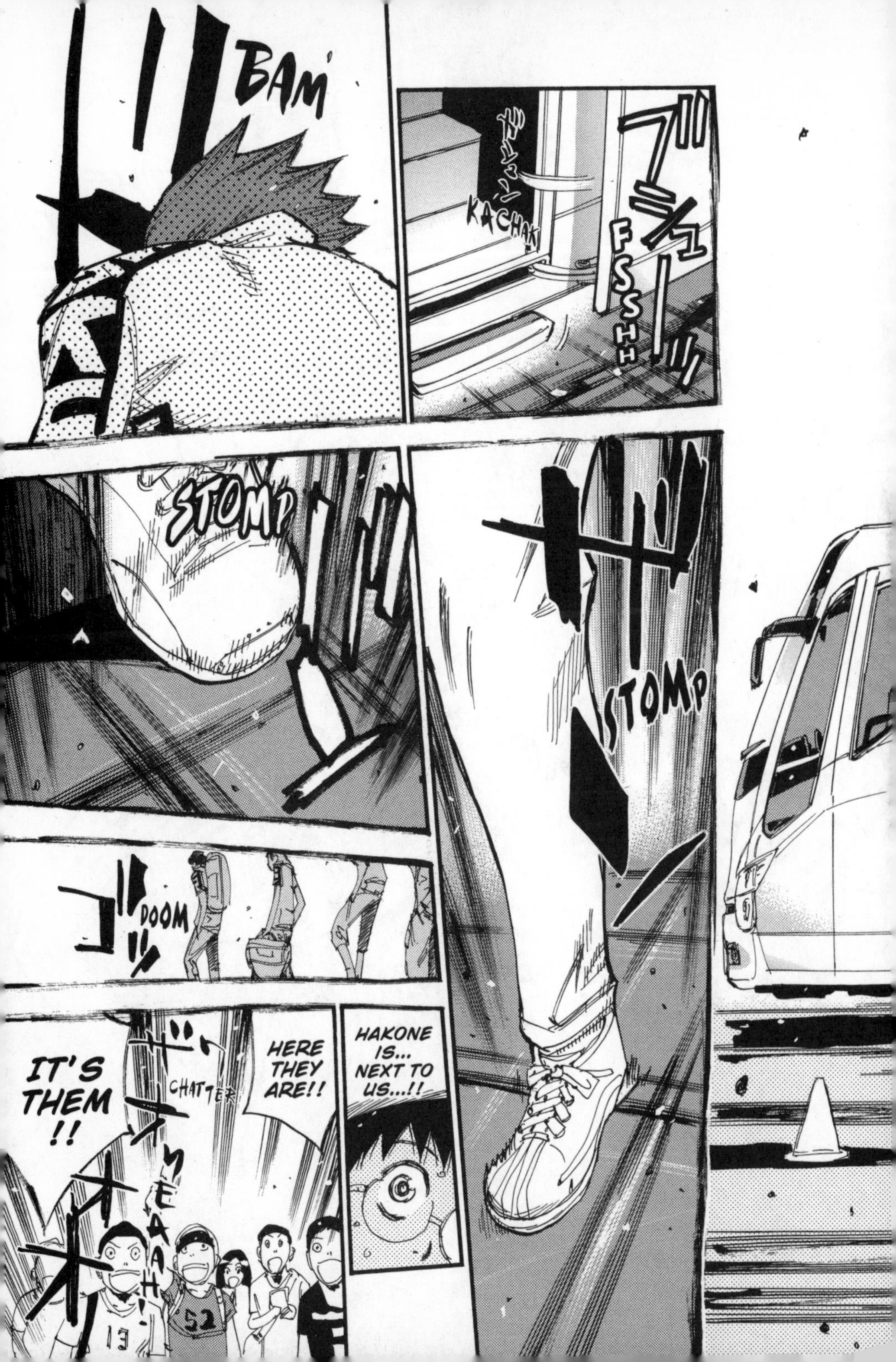
FSSHH
KACHAK
BAM
STOMP
STOMP
DOOM
HAKONE IS... NEXT TO US...!!
HERE THEY ARE!!
CHATTER
IT'S THEM!!
YEAAAH!

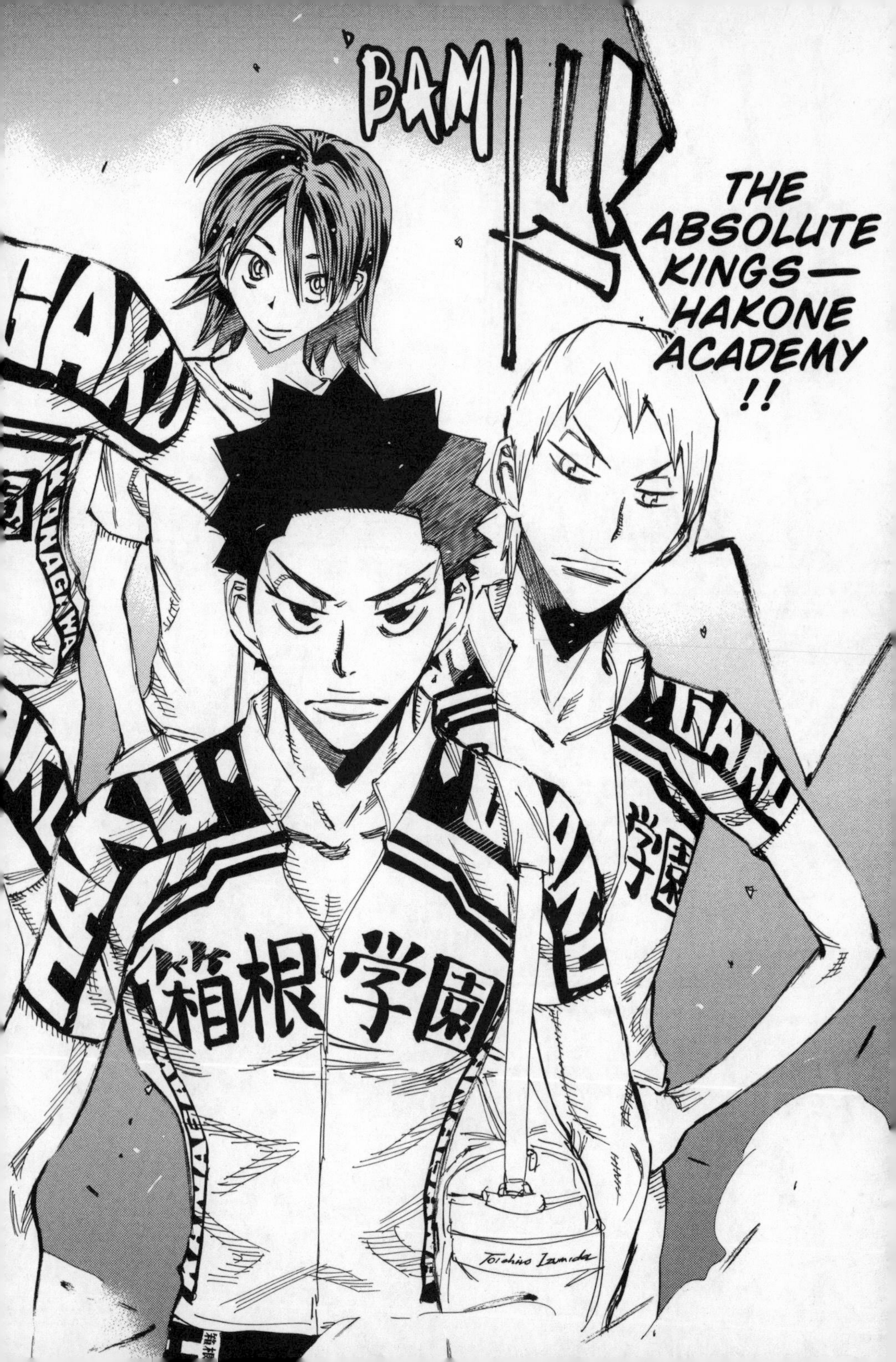
BAM
THE ABSOLUTE KINGS— HAKONE ACADEMY!!
箱根学園
Toshiro Izumida

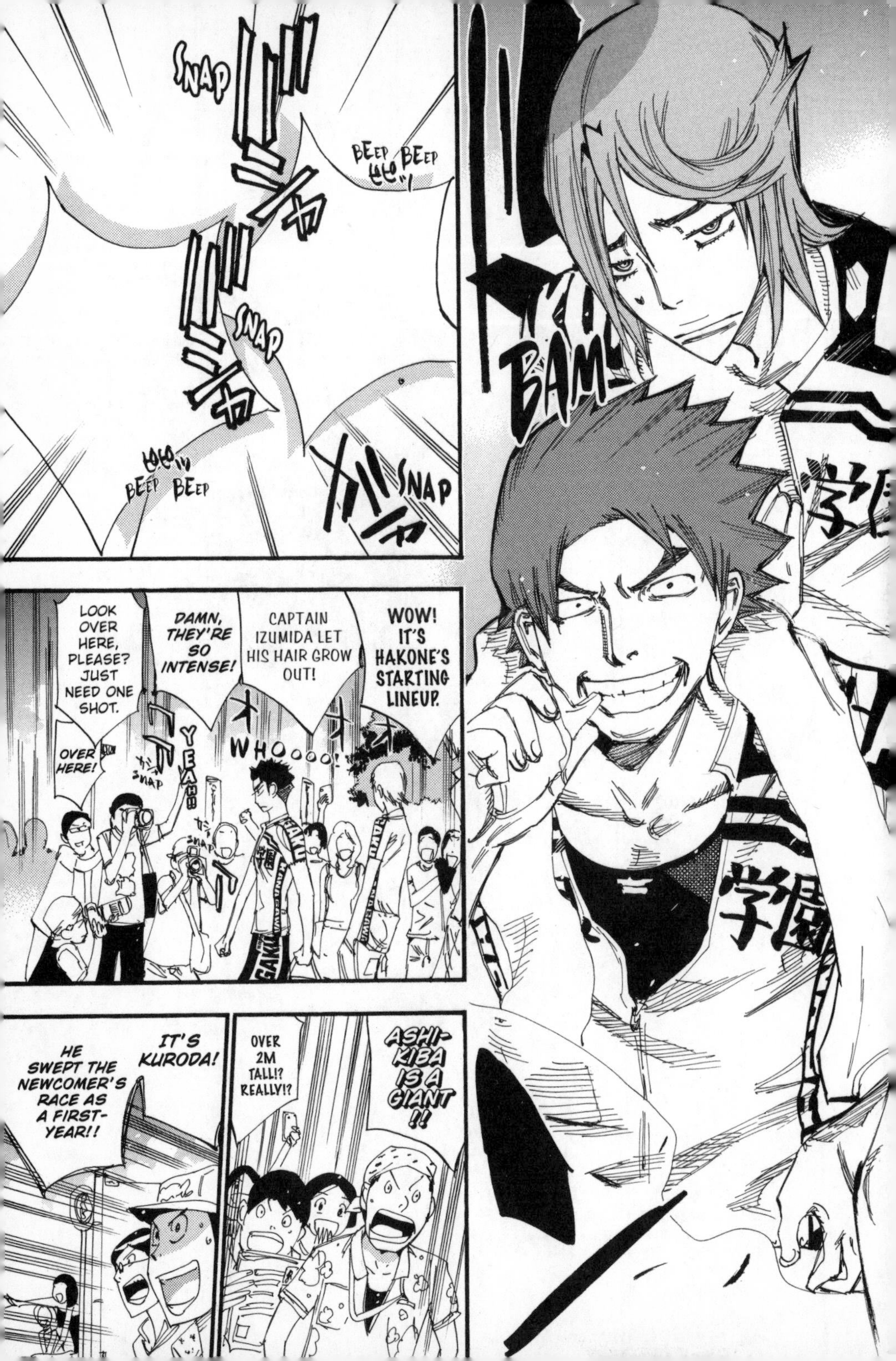
BAM
BEEP BEEP
SNAP
SNAP
SNAP
BEEP BEEP
WOW! IT'S HAKONE'S STARTING LINEUP.
CAPTAIN IZUMIDA LET HIS HAIR GROW OUT!
DAMN, THEY'RE SO INTENSE!
LOOK OVER HERE, PLEASE? JUST NEED ONE SHOT.
WHOOOOO!
YEAH!!
SNAP
OVER HERE!
SNAP
ASHIKIBA IS A GIANT!!
OVER 2M TALL!? REALLY!?
IT'S KURODA!
HE SWEPT THE NEWCOMER'S RACE AS A FIRST-YEAR!!

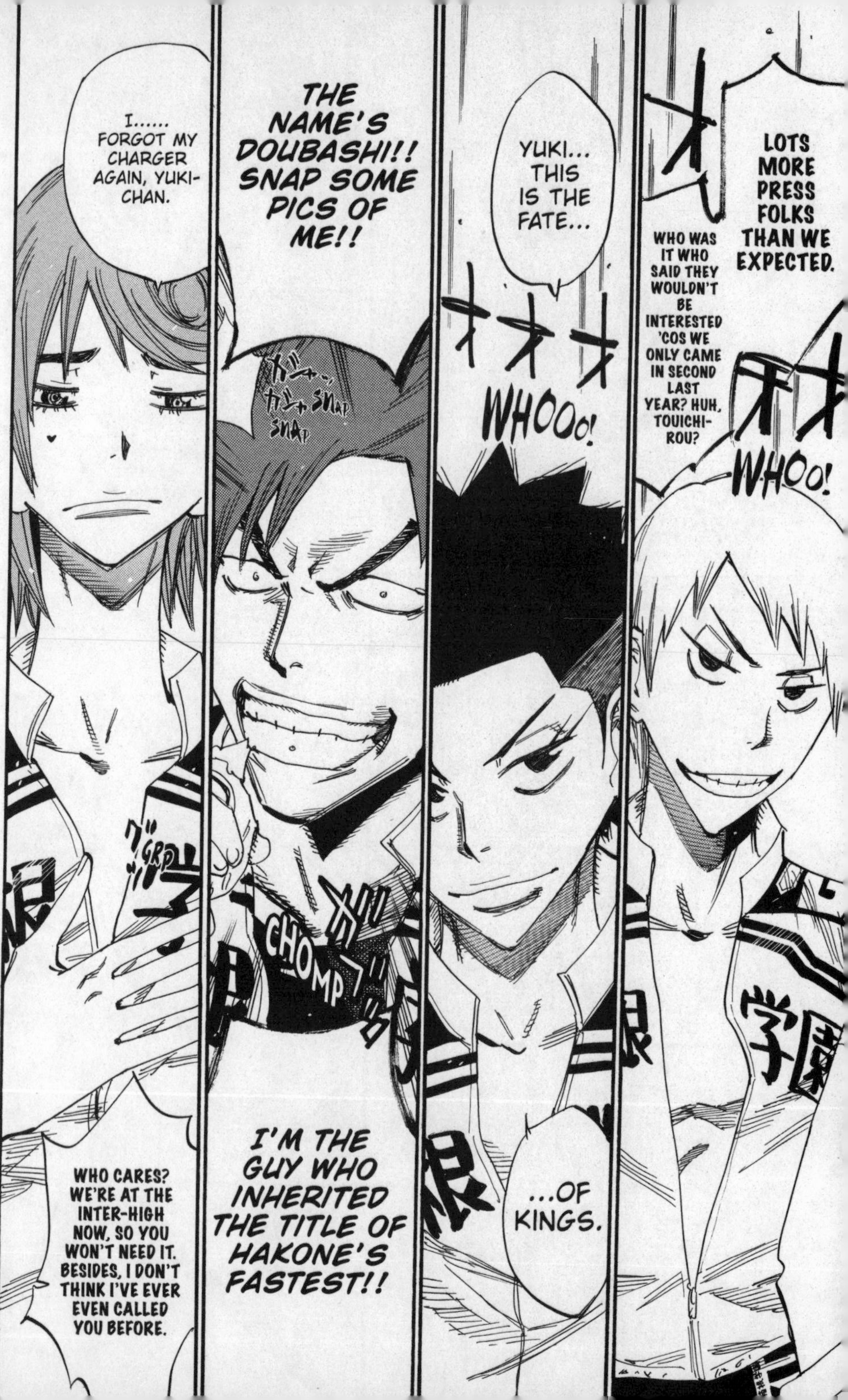
LOTS MORE PRESS FOLKS THAN WE EXPECTED.
WHO WAS IT WHO SAID THEY WOULDN'T BE INTERESTED 'COS WE ONLY CAME IN SECOND LAST YEAR? HUH, TOUICHIROU?
WHOO!
YUKI... THIS IS THE FATE...
WHOOo!
...OF KINGS.
THE NAME'S DOUBASHI!! SNAP SOME PICS OF ME!!
SNAP SNAP
CHOMP
I'M THE GUY WHO INHERITED THE TITLE OF HAKONE'S FASTEST!!
I...... FORGOT MY CHARGER AGAIN, YUKI-CHAN.
GRP
WHO CARES? WE'RE AT THE INTER-HIGH NOW, SO YOU WON'T NEED IT. BESIDES, I DON'T THINK I'VE EVER EVEN CALLED YOU BEFORE.

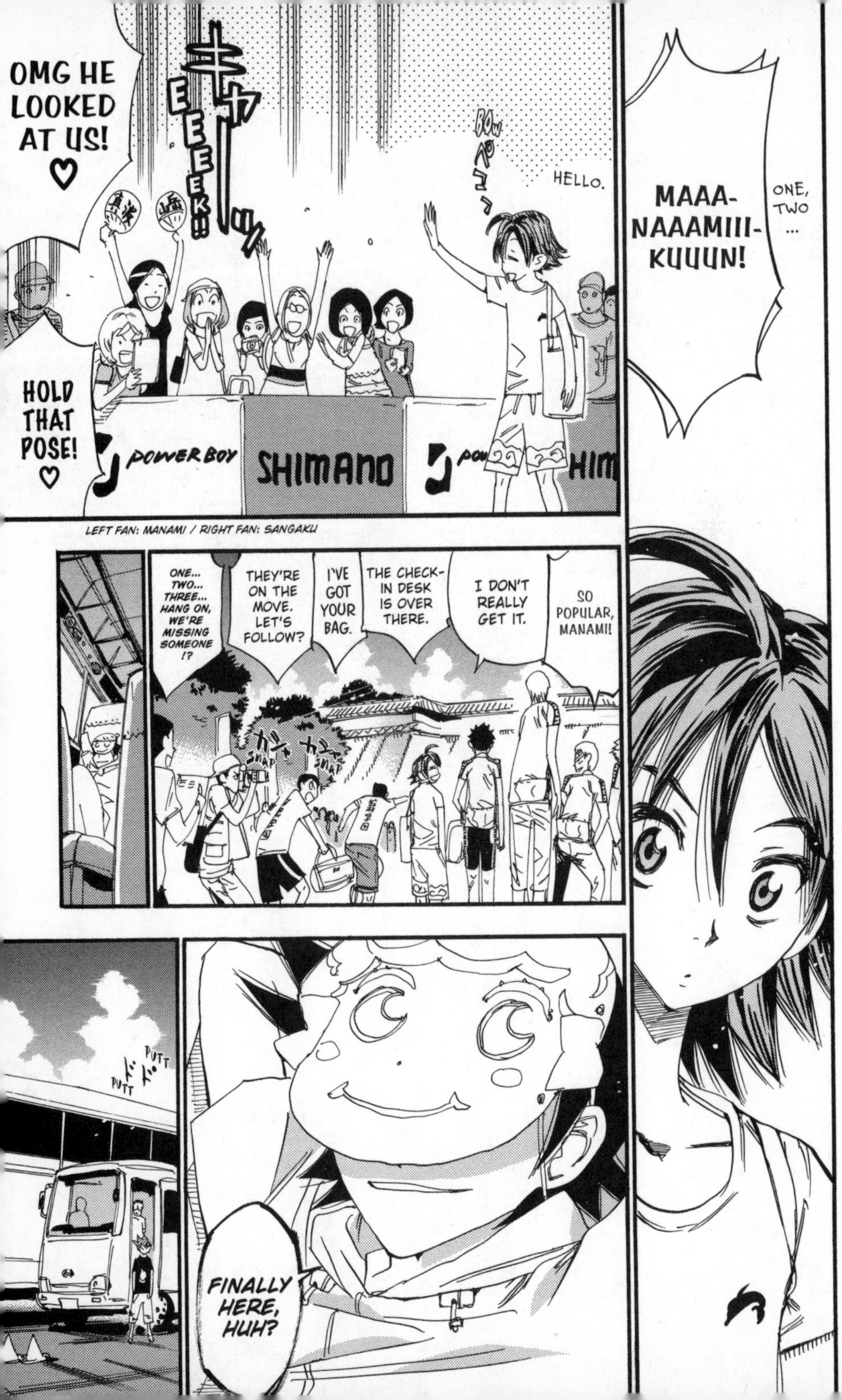
MAAA-NAAAMIII-KUUUN!
ONE, TWO ...
HELLO.
BOW
EEEEEK!!
OMG HE LOOKED AT US! ♡
HOLD THAT POSE! ♡
POWER BOY
SHIMANO
LEFT FAN: MANAMI / RIGHT FAN: SANGAKU
SO POPULAR, MANAMI!
I DON'T REALLY GET IT.
THE CHECK-IN DESK IS OVER THERE.
I'VE GOT YOUR BAG.
THEY'RE ON THE MOVE. LET'S FOLLOW?
ONE... TWO... THREE... HANG ON, WE'RE MISSING SOMEONE!?
SNAP
SNAP
FINALLY HERE, HUH?
PUTT
PUTT

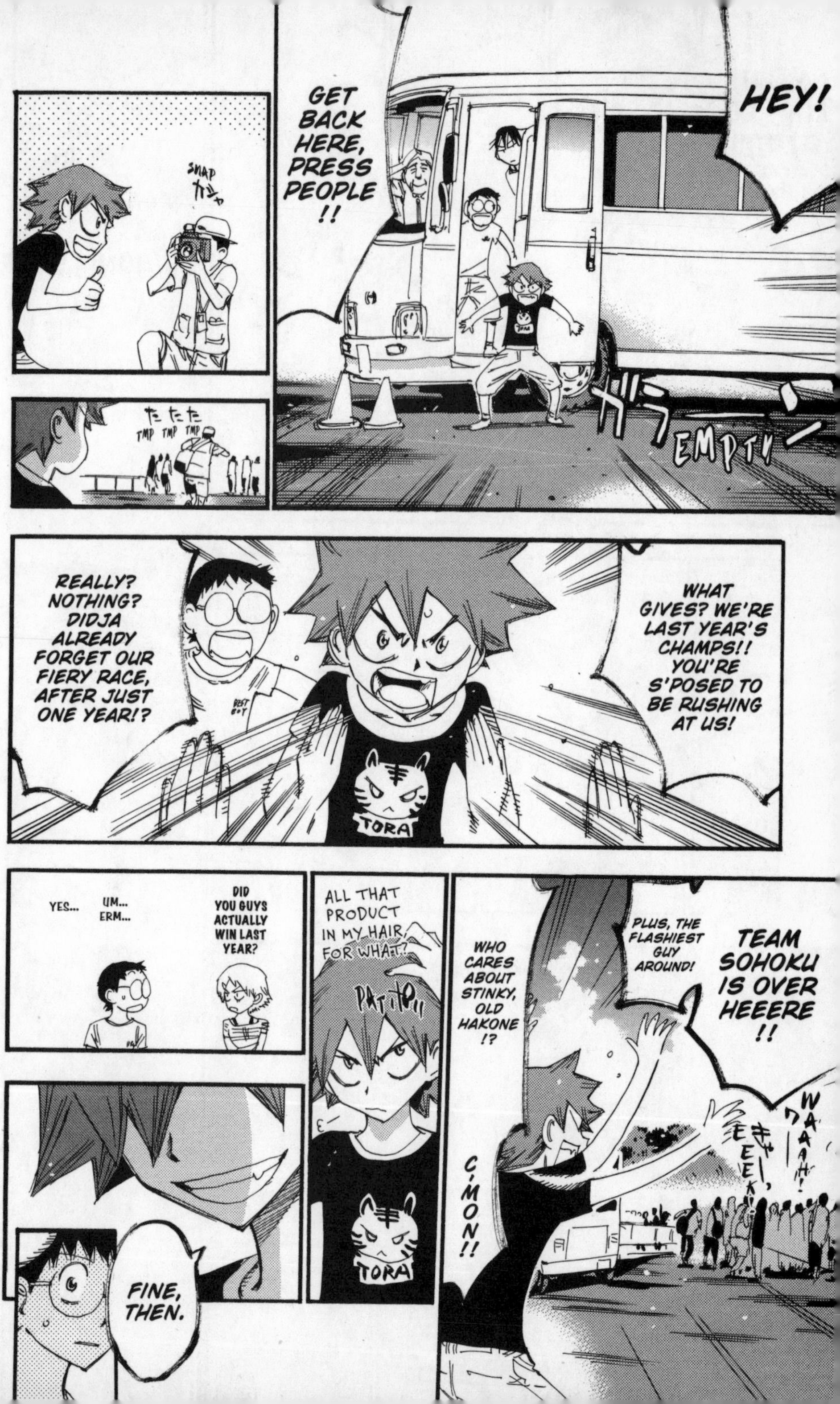
HEY!
GET BACK HERE, PRESS PEOPLE!!
EMPTY
SNAP
カシャ
たたた
TMP TMP TMP
WHAT GIVES? WE'RE LAST YEAR'S CHAMPS!! YOU'RE S'POSED TO BE RUSHING AT US!
REALLY? NOTHING? DIDJA ALREADY FORGET OUR FIERY RACE, AFTER JUST ONE YEAR!?
TEAM SOHOKU IS OVER HEEERE!!
PLUS, THE FLASHIEST GUY AROUND!
WHO CARES ABOUT STINKY, OLD HAKONE!?
C'MON!!
WAAAH!
EEEK!
ALL THAT PRODUCT IN MY HAIR, FOR WHAT!?
DID YOU GUYS ACTUALLY WIN LAST YEAR?
UM... ERM...
YES...
FINE, THEN.

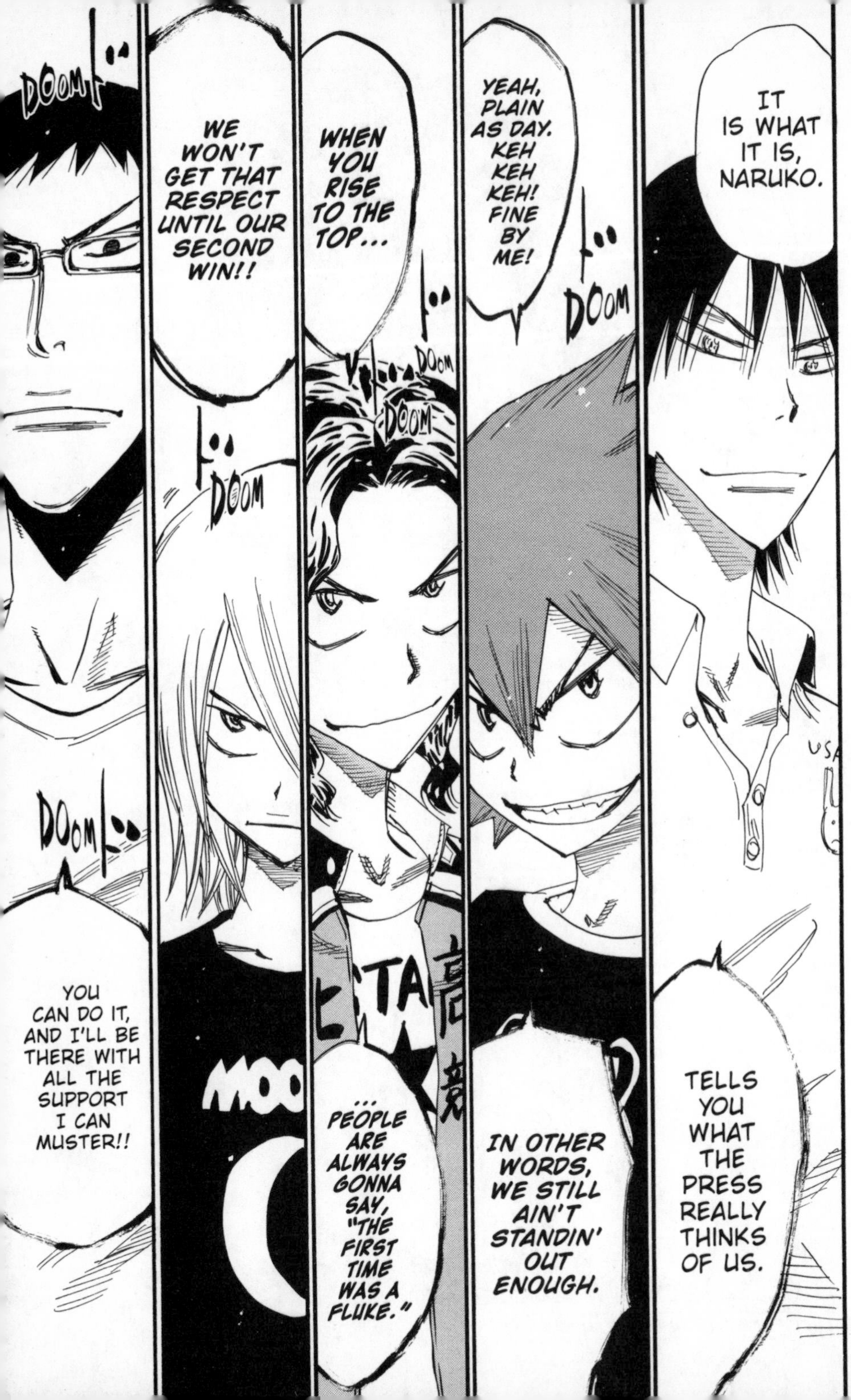
IT IS WHAT IT IS, NARUKO.
TELLS YOU WHAT THE PRESS REALLY THINKS OF US.
YEAH, PLAIN AS DAY. KEH KEH KEH! FINE BY ME!
DOOM
IN OTHER WORDS, WE STILL AIN'T STANDIN' OUT ENOUGH.
WHEN YOU RISE TO THE TOP...
DOOM
DOOM
...PEOPLE ARE ALWAYS GONNA SAY, "THE FIRST TIME WAS A FLUKE."
WE WON'T GET THAT RESPECT UNTIL OUR SECOND WIN!!
DOOM
DOOM
DOOM
YOU CAN DO IT, AND I'LL BE THERE WITH ALL THE SUPPORT I CAN MUSTER!!

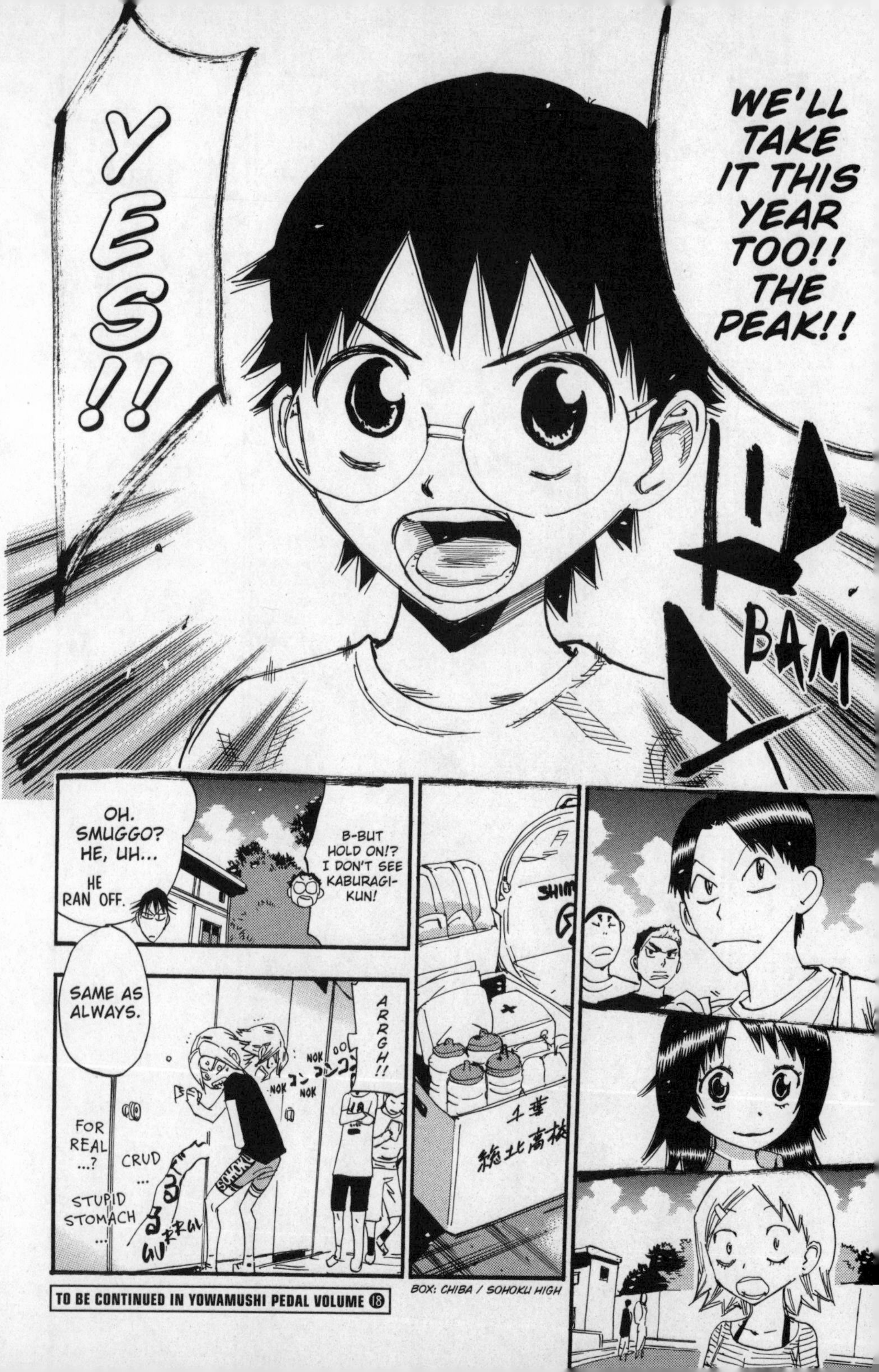
WE'LL TAKE IT THIS YEAR TOO!! THE PEAK!!
BAM
YES!!
B-BUT HOLD ON!? I DON'T SEE KABURAGI-KUN!
OH. SMUGGO? HE, UH...
HE RAN OFF.
SAME AS ALWAYS.
ARRGH!!
NOK NOK NOK NOK
FOR REAL ...?
CRUD ...
STUPID STOMACH ...
GURRGL

BOX: CHIBA / SOHOKU HIGH

TO BE CONTINUED IN YOWAMUSHI PEDAL VOLUME 18

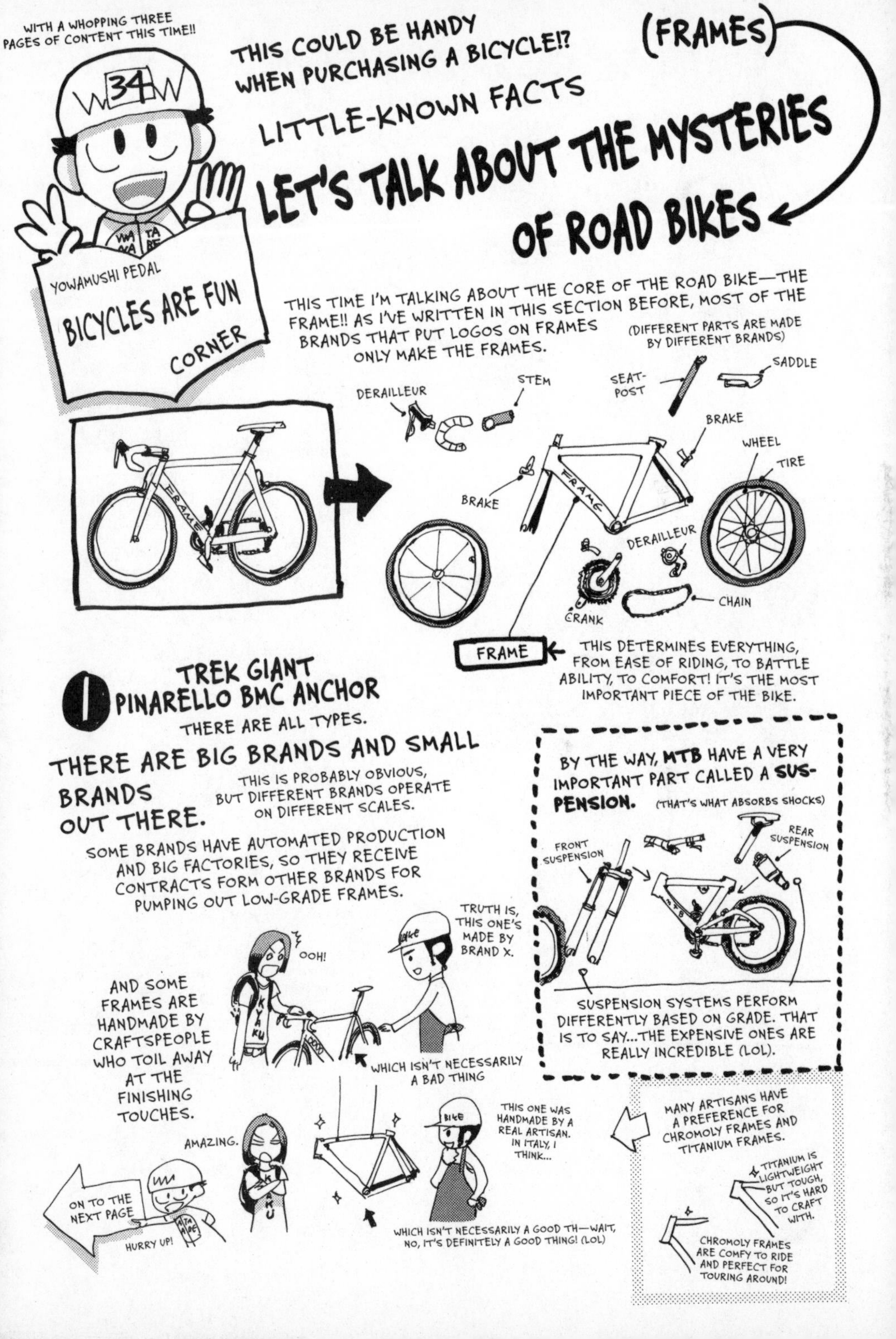
WITH A WHOPPING THREE PAGES OF CONTENT THIS TIME!!
THIS COULD BE HANDY WHEN PURCHASING A BICYCLE!?
LITTLE-KNOWN FACTS
LET'S TALK ABOUT THE MYSTERIES OF ROAD BIKES (FRAMES)
YOWAMUSHI PEDAL
BICYCLES ARE FUN CORNER
THIS TIME I'M TALKING ABOUT THE CORE OF THE ROAD BIKE—THE FRAME!! AS I'VE WRITTEN IN THIS SECTION BEFORE, MOST OF THE BRANDS THAT PUT LOGOS ON FRAMES ONLY MAKE THE FRAMES.
(DIFFERENT PARTS ARE MADE BY DIFFERENT BRANDS)
FRAME
DERAILLEUR
STEM
SEAT-POST
SADDLE
BRAKE
WHEEL
TIRE
BRAKE
FRAME
DERAILLEUR
CHAIN
CRANK
FRAME
THIS DETERMINES EVERYTHING, FROM EASE OF RIDING, TO BATTLE ABILITY, TO COMFORT! IT'S THE MOST IMPORTANT PIECE OF THE BIKE.
1
TREK GIANT PINARELLO BMC ANCHOR
THERE ARE ALL TYPES.
THERE ARE BIG BRANDS AND SMALL BRANDS OUT THERE.
THIS IS PROBABLY OBVIOUS, BUT DIFFERENT BRANDS OPERATE ON DIFFERENT SCALES.
SOME BRANDS HAVE AUTOMATED PRODUCTION AND BIG FACTORIES, SO THEY RECEIVE CONTRACTS FORM OTHER BRANDS FOR PUMPING OUT LOW-GRADE FRAMES.
TRUTH IS, THIS ONE'S MADE BY BRAND X.
OOH!
WHICH ISN'T NECESSARILY A BAD THING
AND SOME FRAMES ARE HANDMADE BY CRAFTSPEOPLE WHO TOIL AWAY AT THE FINISHING TOUCHES.
THIS ONE WAS HANDMADE BY A REAL ARTISAN. IN ITALY, I THINK...
AMAZING.
WHICH ISN'T NECESSARILY A GOOD TH—WAIT, NO, IT'S DEFINITELY A GOOD THING! (LOL)
BY THE WAY, MTB HAVE A VERY IMPORTANT PART CALLED A SUSPENSION. (THAT'S WHAT ABSORBS SHOCKS)
FRONT SUSPENSION
REAR SUSPENSION
SUSPENSION SYSTEMS PERFORM DIFFERENTLY BASED ON GRADE. THAT IS TO SAY...THE EXPENSIVE ONES ARE REALLY INCREDIBLE (LOL).
MANY ARTISANS HAVE A PREFERENCE FOR CHROMOLY FRAMES AND TITANIUM FRAMES.
TITANIUM IS LIGHTWEIGHT BUT TOUGH, SO IT'S HARD TO CRAFT WITH.
CHROMOLY FRAMES ARE COMFY TO RIDE AND PERFECT FOR TOURING AROUND!
ON TO THE NEXT PAGE
HURRY UP!

2 FULFILLMENT TIME DIFFERS DEPENDING ON THE FRAME.

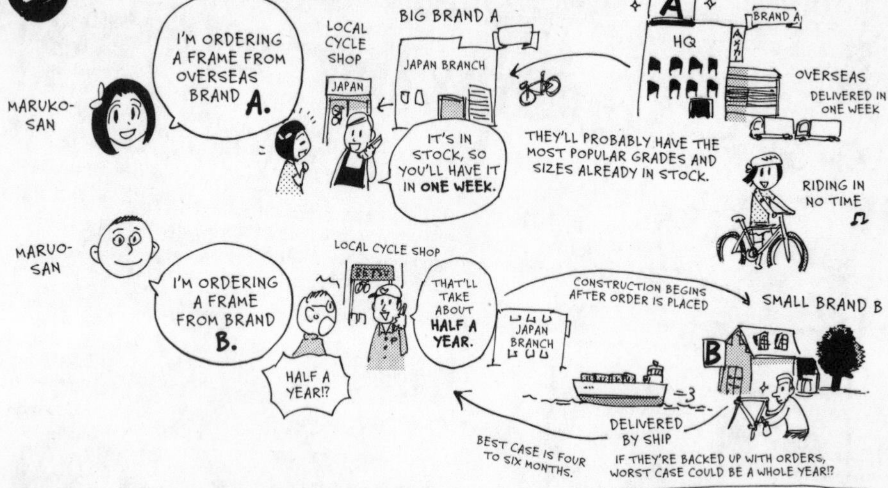

MARUKO-SAN
I'M ORDERING A FRAME FROM OVERSEAS BRAND A.
LOCAL CYCLE SHOP
JAPAN
IT'S IN STOCK, SO YOU'LL HAVE IT IN **ONE WEEK.**
BIG BRAND A
JAPAN BRANCH
A
BRAND A
HQ
OVERSEAS
DELIVERED IN ONE WEEK
THEY'LL PROBABLY HAVE THE MOST POPULAR GRADES AND SIZES ALREADY IN STOCK.
RIDING IN NO TIME ♫
MARUO-SAN
I'M ORDERING A FRAME FROM BRAND B.
LOCAL CYCLE SHOP
THAT'LL TAKE ABOUT **HALF A YEAR.**
HALF A YEAR!?
JAPAN BRANCH
CONSTRUCTION BEGINS AFTER ORDER IS PLACED
SMALL BRAND B
B
DELIVERED BY SHIP
BEST CASE IS FOUR TO SIX MONTHS.
IF THEY'RE BACKED UP WITH ORDERS, WORST CASE COULD BE A WHOLE YEAR!?

3 THE MODELS CHANGE EVERY YEAR.

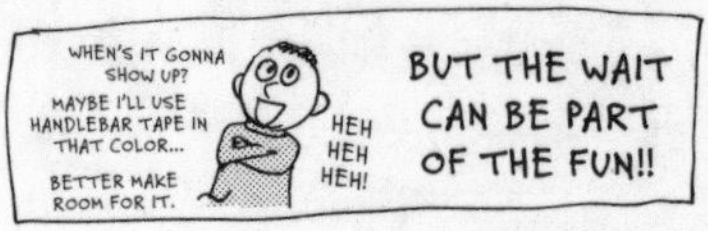

WHEN'S IT GONNA SHOW UP?
MAYBE I'LL USE HANDLEBAR TAPE IN THAT COLOR...
BETTER MAKE ROOM FOR IT.
HEH HEH HEH!
BUT THE WAIT CAN BE PART OF THE FUN!!

EVERY YEAR, THE MODELS OF SPORTS BIKES CHANGE. BIKE TECHNOLOGY IS PROGRESSING ALL THE TIME, SO THE BRANDS UPDATE THEIR DESIGNS BASED ON FEEDBACK FROM USERS. PLUS, THEY LIKE TO EXPERIMENT AND TEST OUT THEIR NEW TECH IN RACES.

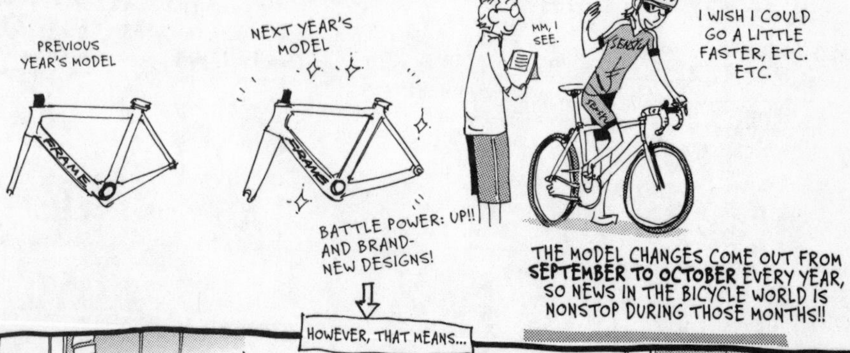

PREVIOUS YEAR'S MODEL
FRAME
NEXT YEAR'S MODEL
FRAME
BATTLE POWER: UP!! AND BRAND-NEW DESIGNS!
MM, I SEE.
I WISH I COULD GO A LITTLE FASTER, ETC. ETC.
THE MODEL CHANGES COME OUT FROM **SEPTEMBER TO OCTOBER** EVERY YEAR, SO NEWS IN THE BICYCLE WORLD IS NONSTOP DURING THOSE MONTHS!!
HOWEVER, THAT MEANS...

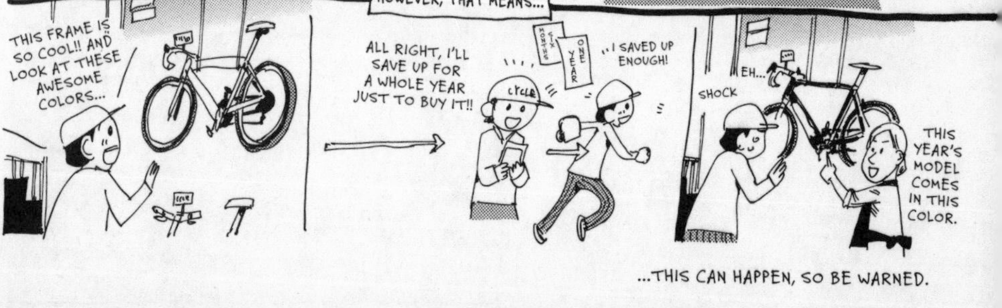

THIS FRAME IS SO COOL!! AND LOOK AT THESE AWESOME COLORS...
ALL RIGHT, I'LL SAVE UP FOR A WHOLE YEAR JUST TO BUY IT!!
SIX MONTHS
ONE YEAR
I SAVED UP ENOUGH!
CYCLE
SHOCK
EH...
THIS YEAR'S MODEL COMES IN THIS COLOR.

...THIS CAN HAPPEN, SO BE WARNED.

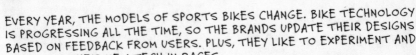

4 CATALOG SHOPPING IS THE TYPICAL WAY TO GO ABOUT IT.

IT'S NOT AS IF EVERY SHOP WILL HAVE ALL THE BIKES YOU CAN FIND IN A CATALOG, WHICH IS WHY IT'S TYPICAL TO FIND THE MODEL YOU LIKE IN A CATALOG AND ORDER IT FROM THERE. THE BICYCLE INDUSTRY HAS MUCH LOWER PRICES AND PROFIT RATIOS THAN THE CAR AND MOTORCYCLE INDUSTRIES, SO IT'S SIMPLY THE REALITY OF THE BUSINESS THAT THEY DON'T HAVE THE CAPITAL NECESSARY TO PLACE EVERY MODEL IN EVERY BRICK AND MORTAR SHOP.

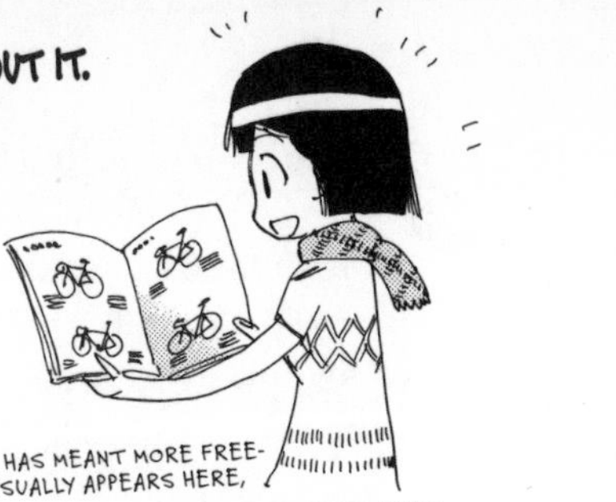

THE RECENT POPULARITY OF CARBON FRAMES HAS MEANT MORE FREEDOM IN DESIGNS, BUT BECAUSE THE LOGO USUALLY APPEARS HERE, YOU CAN'T SEE IT IN THE SIDE PROFILE IMAGES IN THE CATALOGS (LOL).

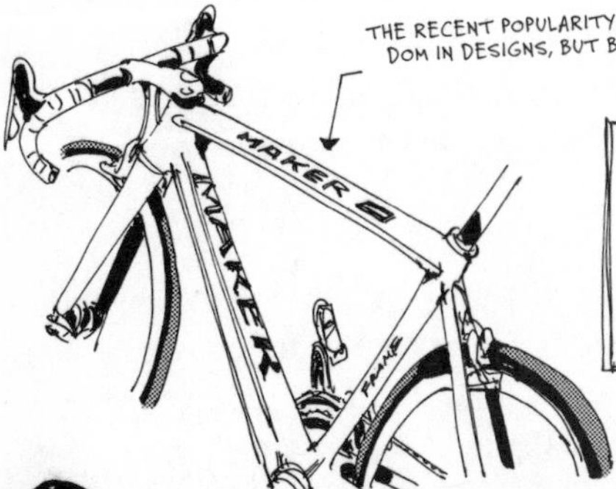
MAKER
MAKER
FRAME

BUT MOST OF THE TIME, WHEN YOUR FRAME ARRIVES...

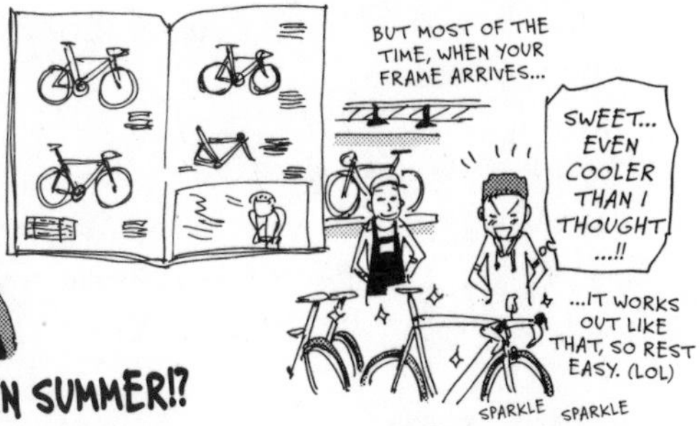
SWEET... EVEN COOLER THAN I THOUGHT...!!
SPARKLE
SPARKLE

...IT WORKS OUT LIKE THAT, SO REST EASY. (LOL)

5 FEWER FRAMES AVAILABLE IN SUMMER!?

AS I WROTE IN POINT 3, NEXT YEAR'S MODELS ARE REVEALED IN SEPTEMBER AND OCTOBER. SO SOMETIMES, IF THE PREVIOUS MODELS SOLD MORE SUCCESSFULLY THAN ANTICIPATED, SHOPS WILL BE COMPLETELY OUT OF STOCK BY SUMMER.

IF YOU TRY ORDERING IN JULY OR AUGUST, YOU MIGHT BE OUT OF LUCK...SO BE CAREFUL!

EACH BRAND PREDICTS SALES FOR THE COMING YEAR AND SO ONLY PLANS TO MAKE A LIMITED NUMBER OF FRAMES BASED ON THAT PREDICTION.

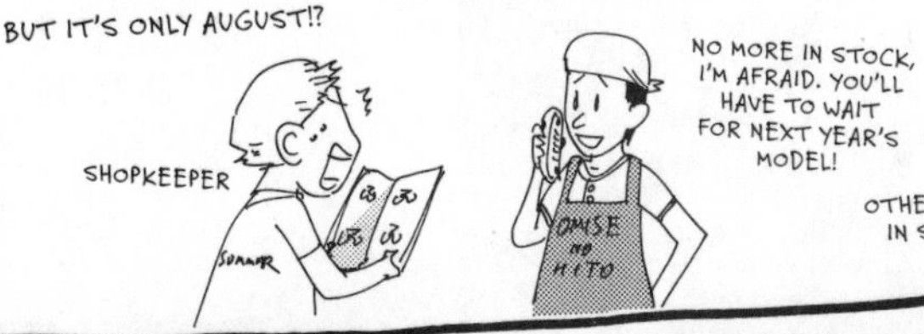
BUT IT'S ONLY AUGUST!?
NO MORE IN STOCK, I'M AFRAID. YOU'LL HAVE TO WAIT FOR NEXT YEAR'S MODEL!
SHOPKEEPER
SUMMER
OMISE NO HITO

OTHER SHOPS MAY HAVE FRAMES STILL IN STOCK, SO TRY ASKING AROUND!

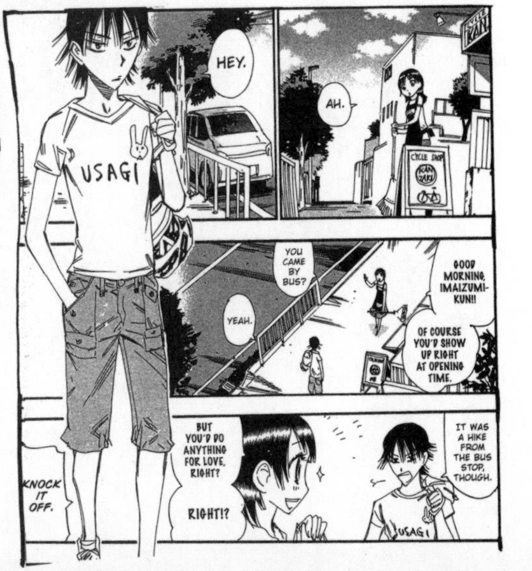
AH.
HEY.
GOOD MORNING, IMAIZUMI-KUN!!
YOU CAME BY BUS?
YEAH.
OF COURSE YOU'D SHOW UP RIGHT AT OPENING TIME.
USAGI
IT WAS A HIKE FROM THE BUS STOP, THOUGH.
BUT YOU'D DO ANYTHING FOR LOVE, RIGHT?
RIGHT!?
KNOCK IT OFF.
USAGI

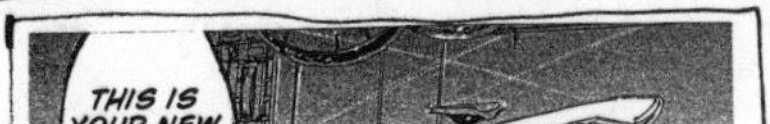
THIS IS YOUR NEW FRAME.

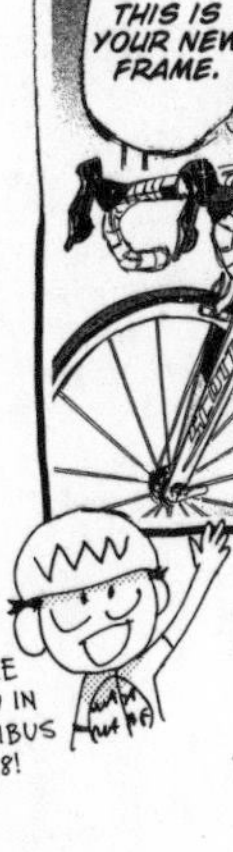

SEE YOU IN OMNIBUS 18!

IN OMNIBUS 14, IMAIZUMI SHOWED UP AT THE KANZAKI CYCLE SHOP AT OPENING TIME TO RECEIVE HIS NEW BIKE. GETTING A NEW MACHINE IS ALWAYS SO MUCH FUN! EVEN IF I FIND IT HARD TO WAIT!

It's snowing.

On a day with record snowfall in 2014, they held Cyclo Cross Tokyo in Odaiba! At the competition, three-member teams raced on an Enduro course. And the main event was a race between amazing pro cyclists!

Speaking of snowy bicycle races, the ever-popular Cyclo-cross in Europe was originally conceived as a way to train for road races during winter.

It's a struggle—getting your bike over the snow and the sand while trying to complete the required laps within the time limit. The bikes come across as the perfect middle point between road bikes and mountain bikes, don't they? It's tough, but fun!

There's something profound about cycling!

WATARU WATANABE

WATARU WATANABE

This winter, I biked from Fukuoka to my hometown in Nagasaki.

At the end of the year, I took a nice, relaxing two-day trip with the intention of arriving in Fukuoka in the afternoon. Then I planned to meet up with my family for dinner.

That day, I was going from Fukuoka Airport to Dazaifu, Tosu, Saga, Oomura, and then Nagasaki—which was 150km. I somehow made it for dinner!

On the way there, a fan of mine saw me and met up with me!

A while ago, I used to go down that long-familiar road by car. But it's fun to use a bike because I can take in the sights at my leisure.

To the left is a picture from when I rode with a local team from Nagasaki just after the New Year in 2014. It feels so good to ride near the sea!

Translation Notes

Common Honorifics

-san: The Japanese equivalent of Mr./Mrs./Miss. If a situation calls for politeness, this is the fail-safe honorific.

-kun: Used most often when referring to boys, this indicates affection or familiarity. Occasionally used by older men among their peers, but it may also be used by anyone referring to a person of lower standing.

-chan: An affectionate honorific indicating familiarity used mostly in reference to girls; also used in reference to cute persons or animals of either gender.

-senpai: A suffix used to address upperclassmen or more experienced co-workers.

-shi: A more formal version of *san* common to written Japanese, it's the default honorific used in newspapers.

no honorific: Indicates familiarity or closeness; if used without permission or reason, addressing someone in this manner would constitute an insult.

A kilometer is approximately 0.6 of a mile.

PAGE 22
Akiba: Popular nickname for Akihabara district in Tokyo.

PAGE 84
Otaku: Generally used to describe hardcore anime or manga fans, it also can be used to describe someone who is especially knowledgeable about a particular subject. In this case, calling Koga a "bicycle otaku" means that he is an expert on matters related to bicycles.

PAGE 291
300 degrees: Japan uses Celsius instead of Fahrenheit. 300 degreeås is equivalent to about 572 degrees Fahrenheit.

PAGE 297
MTB: Mountain bike.

YOWAMUSHI PEDAL VOLUME 18

Read on for a sneak
peek of Volume 18!

YOWAMUSHI PEDAL

RIDE.296 SINGLE-DIGIT TAGS

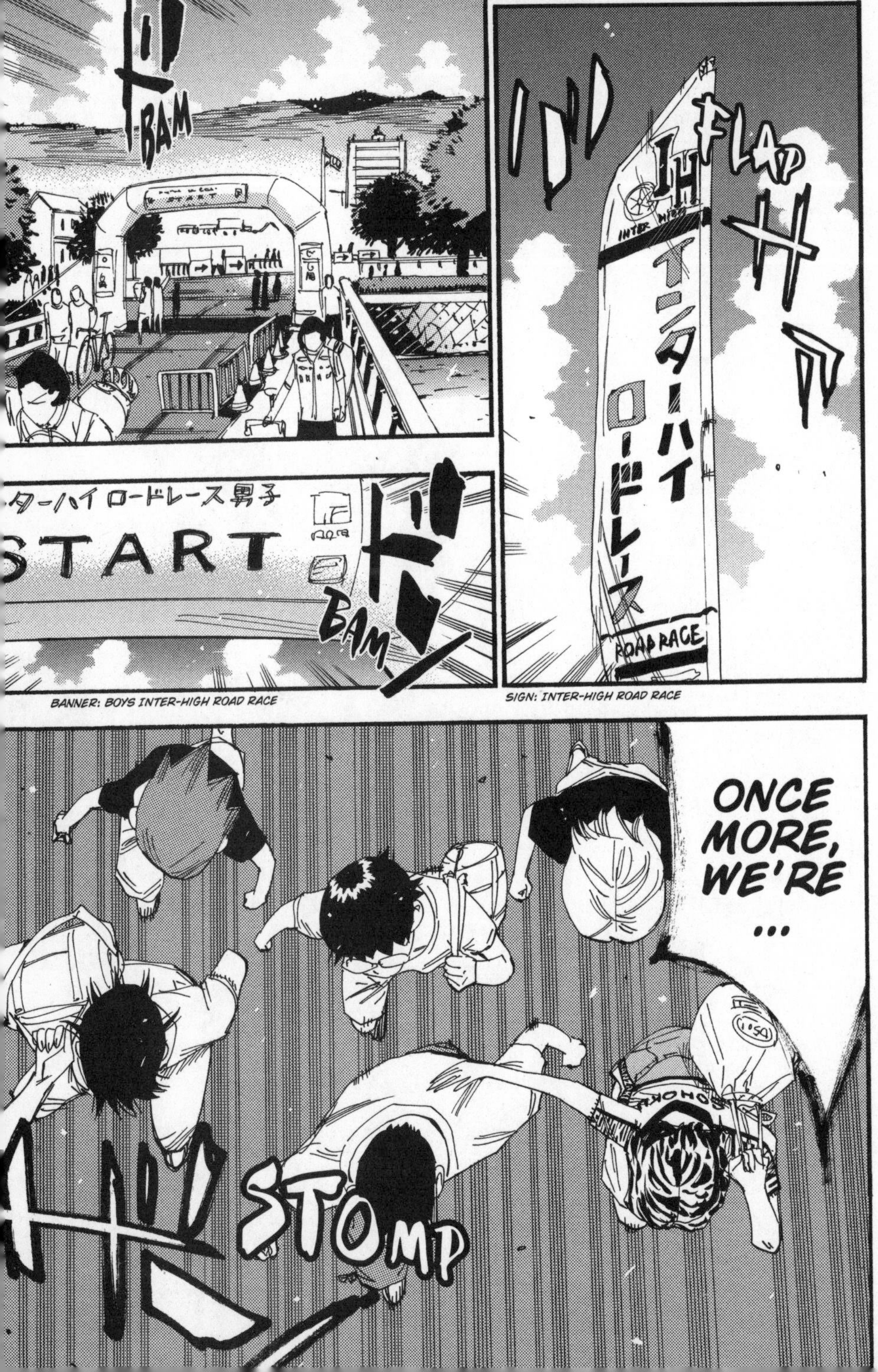
IH
INTER HIGH
FLAP
ROAD RACE
BAM
START
BAM
ONCE MORE, WE'RE ...
STOMP

SIGN: INTER-HIGH ROAD RACE

BANNER: BOYS INTER-HIGH ROAD RACE

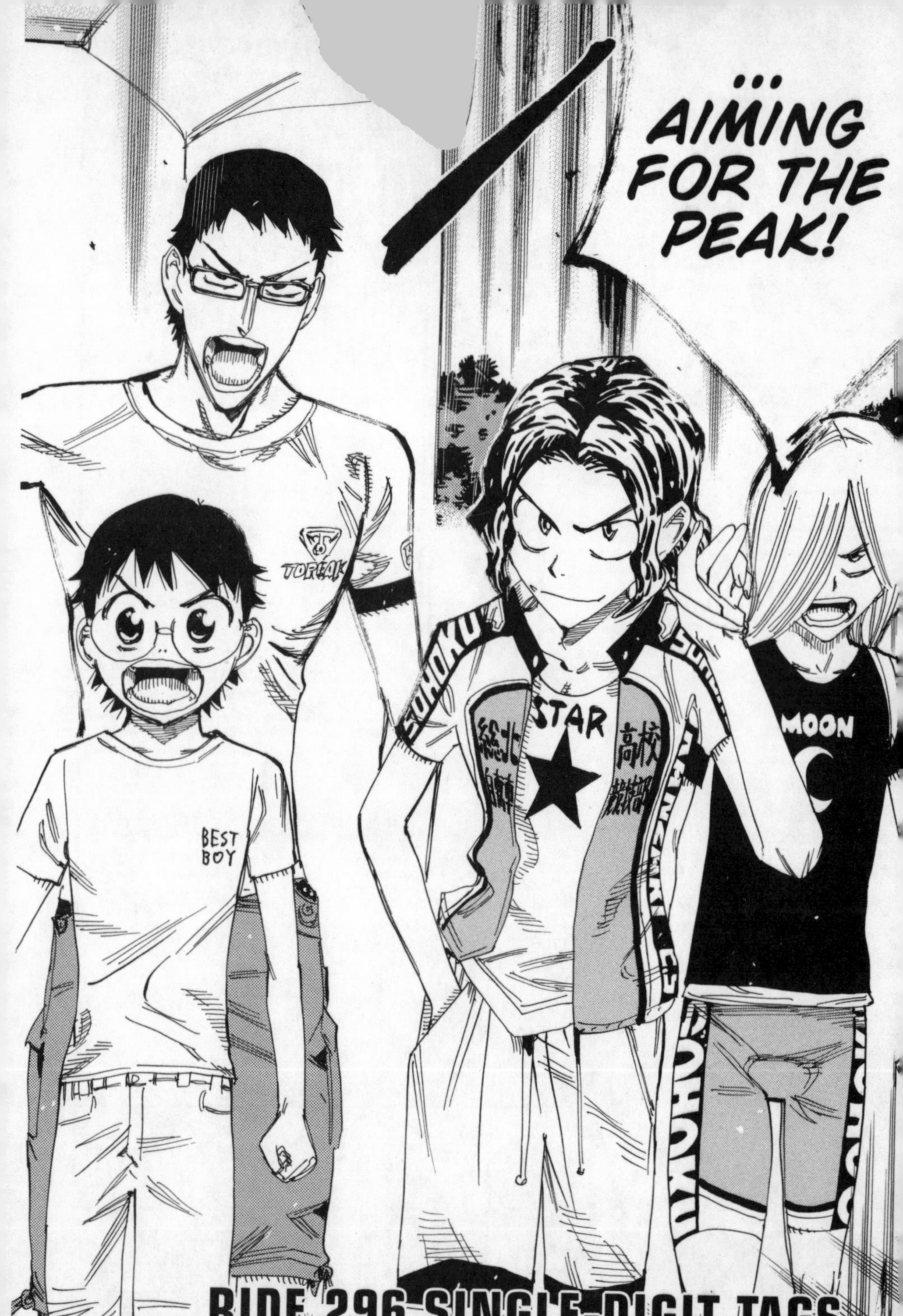
...AIMING FOR THE PEAK!
TOPEAK
BEST BOY
STAR
SOHOKU
MOON

RIDE.296 SINGLE-DIGIT TAGS

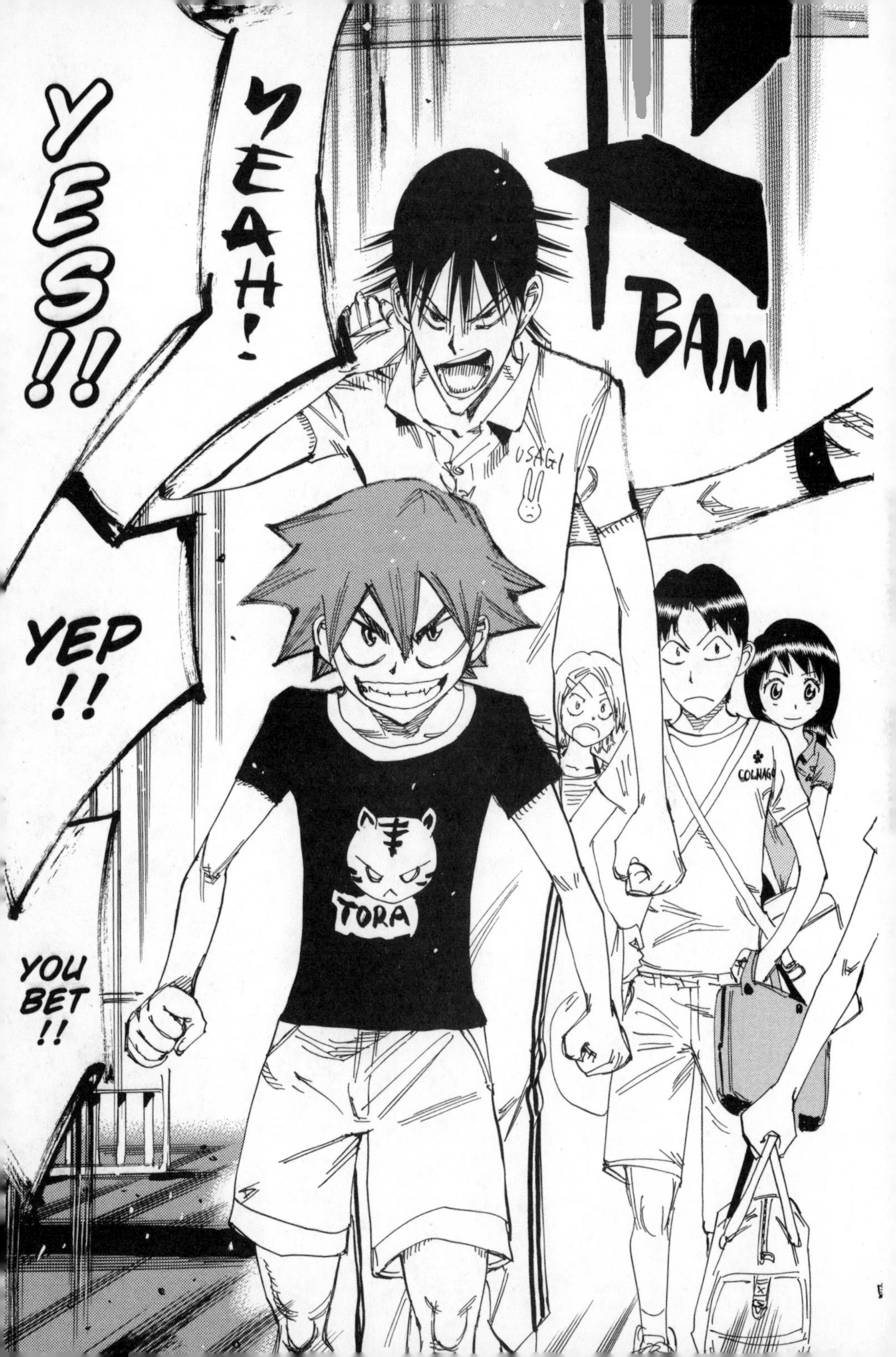
BAM
YEAH!
YES!!
YEP!!
YOU BET!!
USAGI
TORA
COLNAGO

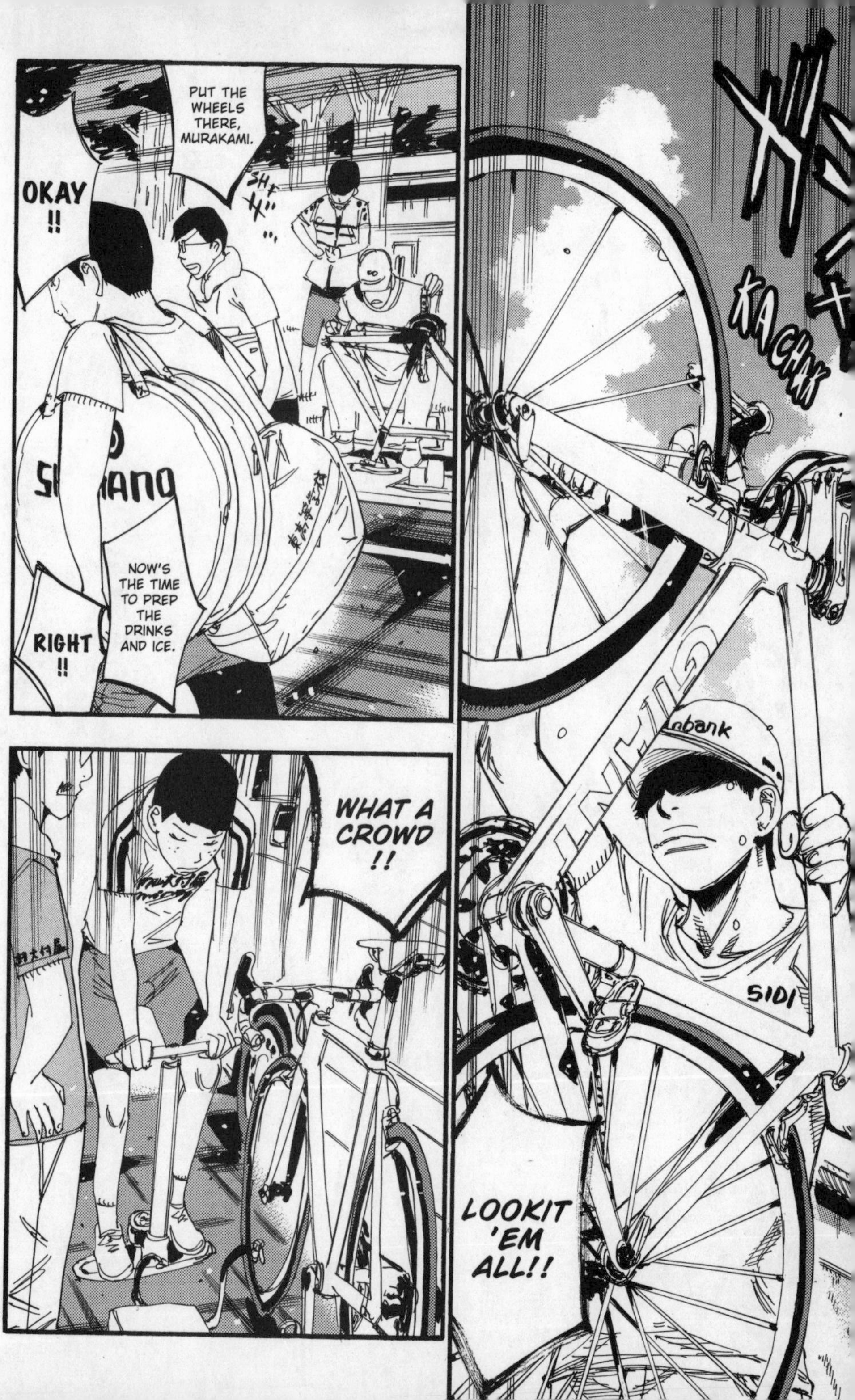
KACHAK
LOOKIT 'EM ALL!!
SIDI
PUT THE WHEELS THERE, MURAKAMI.
OKAY!!
SHIMANO
NOW'S THE TIME TO PREP THE DRINKS AND ICE.
RIGHT!!
WHAT A CROWD!!

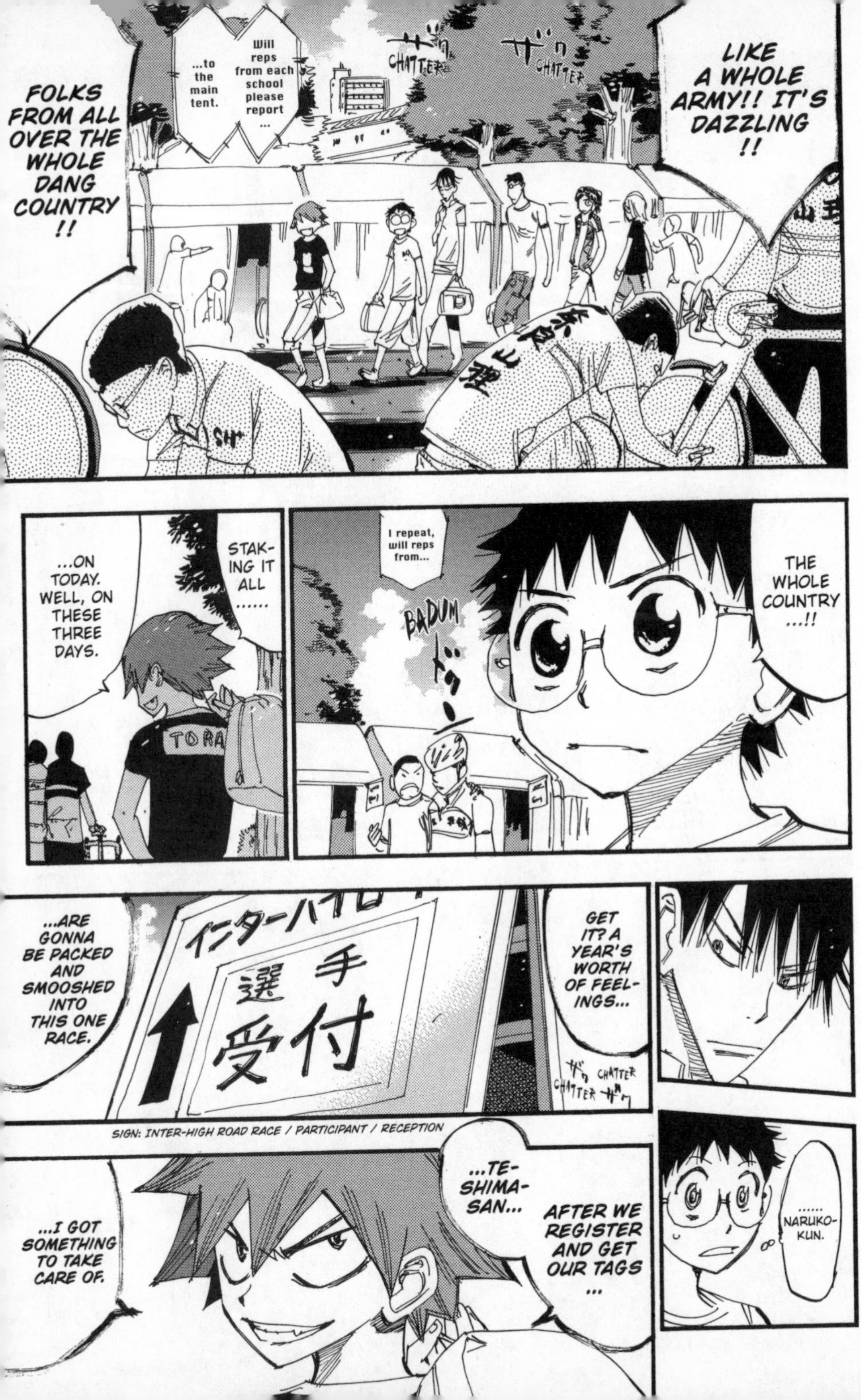
LIKE A WHOLE ARMY!! IT'S DAZZLING!!
CHATTER
CHATTER
Will reps from each school please report...
...to the main tent.
FOLKS FROM ALL OVER THE WHOLE DANG COUNTRY!!
THE WHOLE COUNTRY...!!
I repeat, will reps from...
BADUM
STAKING IT ALL......
...ON TODAY. WELL, ON THESE THREE DAYS.
GET IT? A YEAR'S WORTH OF FEELINGS...
CHATTER
CHATTER
選手
受付
...ARE GONNA BE PACKED AND SMOOSHED INTO THIS ONE RACE.
SIGN: INTER-HIGH ROAD RACE / PARTICIPANT / RECEPTION
......NARUKO-KUN.
...TESHIMA-SAN...
AFTER WE REGISTER AND GET OUR TAGS...
...I GOT SOMETHING TO TAKE CARE OF.

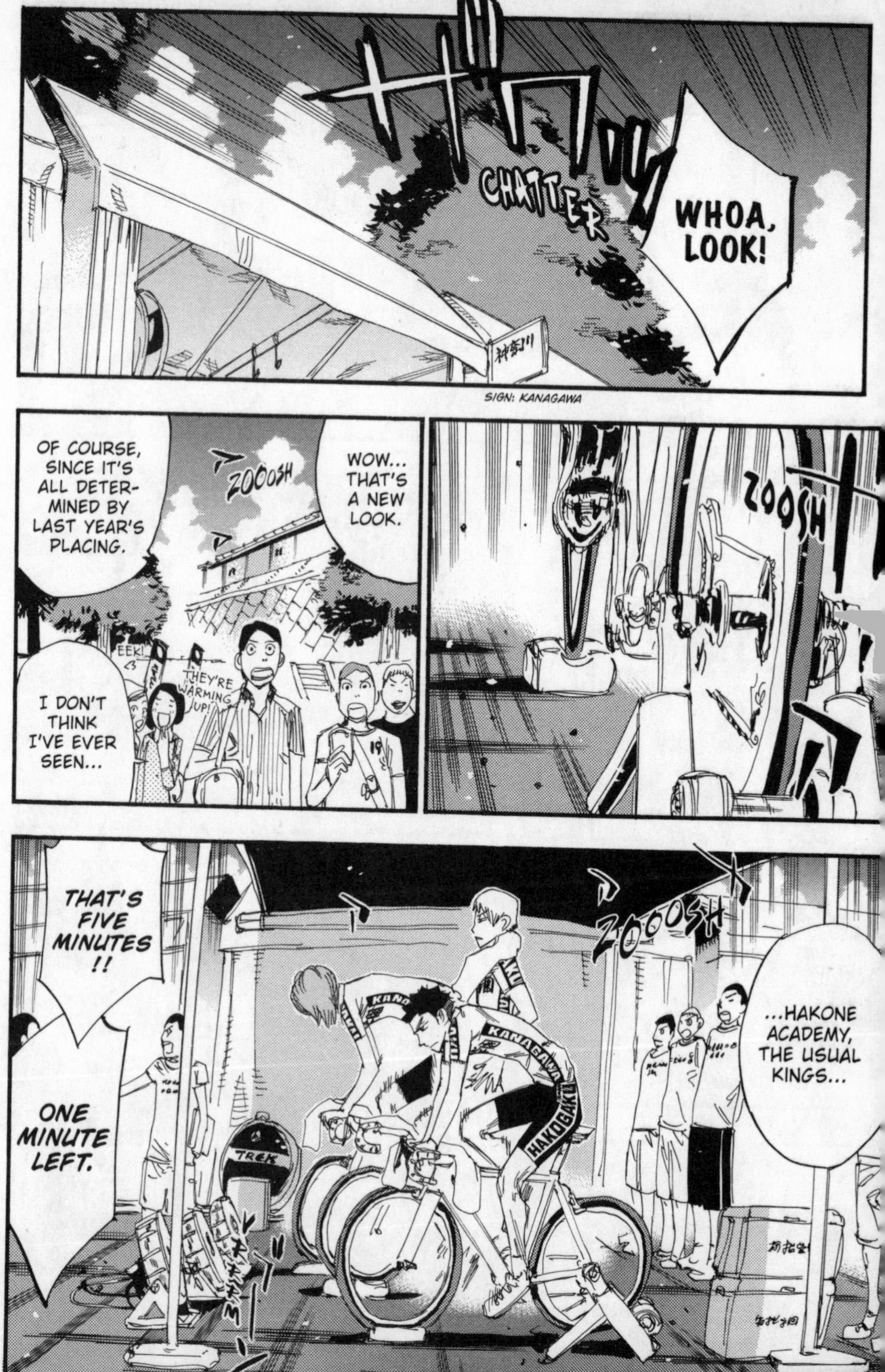
WHOA, LOOK!
CHATTER
SIGN: KANAGAWA
ZOOSH
WOW... THAT'S A NEW LOOK.
OF COURSE, SINCE IT'S ALL DETER-MINED BY LAST YEAR'S PLACING.
ZOOOSH
EEK!
THEY'RE WARMING UP!
I DON'T THINK I'VE EVER SEEN...
...HAKONE ACADEMY, THE USUAL KINGS...
ZOOOSH
KANAGAWA
HAKOGAKU
TREK
THAT'S FIVE MINUTES !!
ONE MINUTE LEFT.

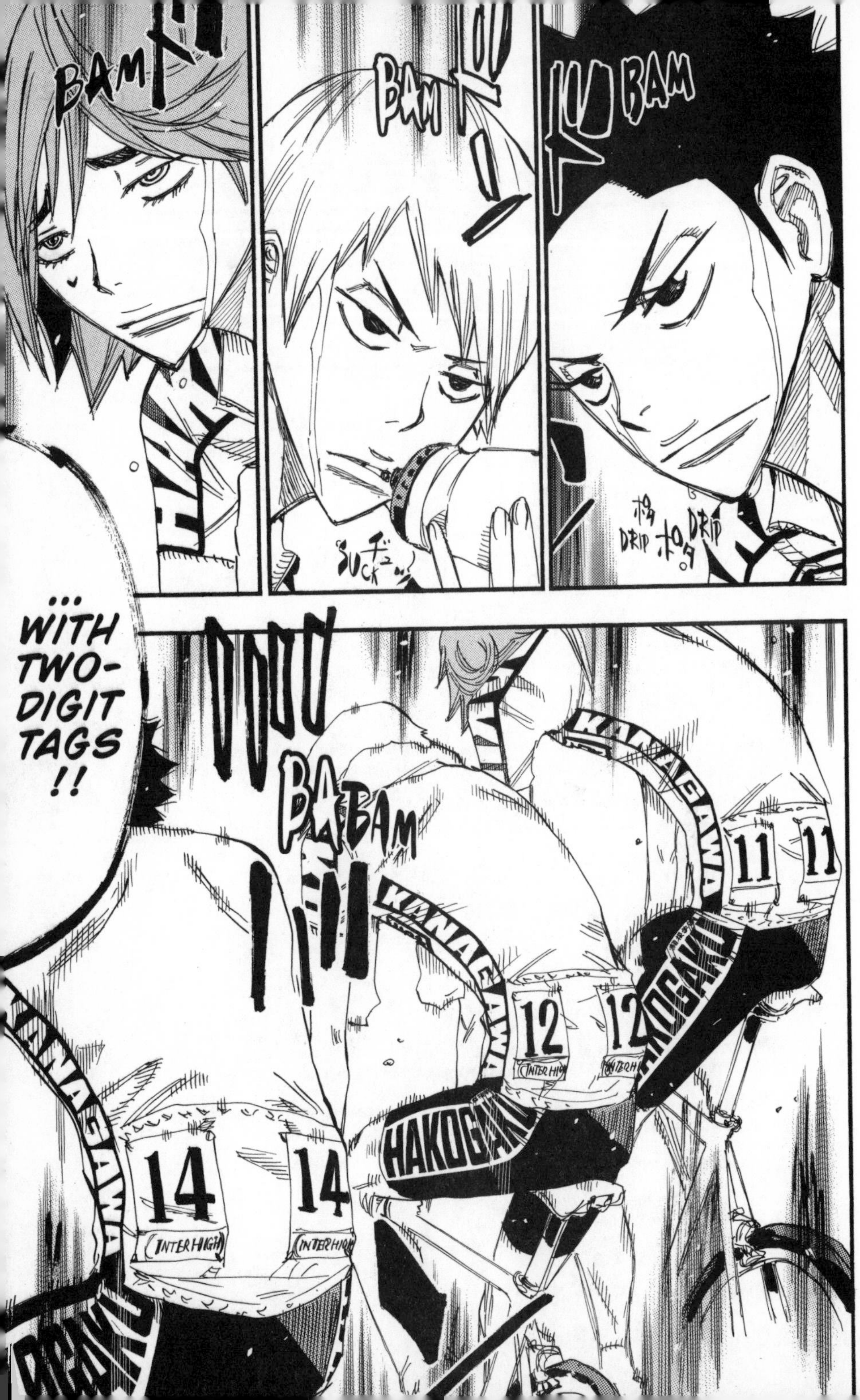
BAM
DRIP DRIP
BAM
SUCK
BAM
BABAM
...WITH TWO-DIGIT TAGS!!

mrya
05/21

YOWAMUSHI PEDAL ⑰

WATARU WATANABE

Translation: Caleb D. Cook

Lettering: Rachel J. Pierce

This book is a work of fiction. Names, characters, places, and incidents are the product of the author's imagination or are used fictitiously. Any resemblance to actual events, locales, or persons, living or dead, is coincidental.

YOWAMUSHI PEDAL Volume 33, 34
© 2014 Wataru Watanabe
All rights reserved.
First published in Japan in 2014 by Akita Publishing Co., Ltd., Tokyo.
English translation rights arranged with Akita Publishing Co., Ltd. through Tuttle-Mori Agency, Inc., Tokyo.

English translation © 2021 by Yen Press, LLC

Yen Press, LLC supports the right to free expression and the value of copyright. The purpose of copyright is to encourage writers and artists to produce the creative works that enrich our culture.

The scanning, uploading, and distribution of this book without permission is a theft of the author's intellectual property. If you would like permission to use material from the book (other than for review purposes), please contact the publisher. Thank you for your support of the author's rights.

Yen Press
150 West 30th Street, 19th Floor
New York, NY 10001

Visit us at yenpress.com
facebook.com/yenpress
twitter.com/yenpress
yenpress.tumblr.com

First Yen Press Edition: April 2021

Yen Press is an imprint of Yen Press, LLC.
The Yen Press name and logo are trademarks of Yen Press, LLC.

The publisher is not responsible for websites (or their content) that are not owned by the publisher.

Library of Congress Control Number: 2015960124

ISBNs: 978-1-9753-1063-9 (paperback)
        978-1-9753-1062-2 (ebook)

10 9 8 7 6 5 4 3 2 1

WOR

Printed in the United States of America